The H

A Practical Guide

THE HOUSING ACT 2004
A PRACTICAL GUIDE

Helen Carr
BA (Oxon)
Solicitor & Academic Leader
London Metropolitan University

Stephen Cottle
BSc, Dip Law
Barrister, Two Garden Court Chambers

Timothy Baldwin
BSc, PhD, LLB, MA
Barrister

Michael King
MA (Oxon)
Solicitor
Property and Land Law Consultant

JORDANS
2005

Published by
Jordan Publishing Limited
21 St Thomas Street
Bristol BS1 6JS

British Library Cataloguing-in-Publication Data
A catalogue record for this book is available from the British Library.

ISBN 0 85308 952 3

Typeset by MFK-Mendip, Frome, Somerset
Printed in Great Britain by Antony Rowe Limited

Foreword

There is nobody living in England and Wales who will be unaffected by the Housing Act 2004 at some time in their life. Its provisions seep into every cranny of the homes we live in, whether grand mansion, council flat, bedsit or caravan. It has implications for all – owner-occupier, tenant, traveller, student, house-guest, residential property company, and social and private landlord. The Act carries powers, duties, responsibilities, privileges and opportunities for all those involved in the supply and supervision of the homes we live in – estate agents, architects, banks, building societies, trading standards officers, building inspectors, surveyors, environmental health officers, and of course lawyers.

Lawyers and others will find in the new Act extensive new powers for local authorities to intervene in the private business of landlords and a significant number of duties that can be placed upon landlords and others. The Act brings a raft of new orders and notices, including Prohibition, Demolition and Management (Interim and Final) Orders; and Improvement, Hazard Awareness and Overcrowding Notices. It contains important new appeal opportunities and procedures, and a huge extension to the jurisdiction of the Residential Property Tribunal.

The Housing Act 2004 addresses many of the long-standing and more intransigent issues in contemporary British housing. It introduces long-awaited home information packs. It transforms the approach to housing that may damage the health of its occupiers. It introduces a licensing regime for bedsits, hostels and other houses in multiple occupation. It gives wide new powers to local authorities to intervene in the affairs of private landlords who persist in condoning unhealthy, disruptive or antisocial practices. It seeks for the first time to control the practice of some landlords of withholding damage and wear and disrepair deposits. It makes important as well as incidental adjustments to existing legislation relating to travellers, the right to buy and housing management.

Such a momentous piece of legislation requires careful and informed explanation. Parliamentary draftsmen write for those with inside knowledge, who need precision and comprehensive description. They write with half an ear for the blandishments or brickbats that may accompany subsequent judicial opinions of their effectiveness. Others have to explain their efforts and place them in a context that those affected will be able to work – or in the case of this book – also live with. The authors are very well qualified for their quest, combining the experiences of academia and the Law Commission with practical insights from the sharp end of practice.

Increasingly, simple exposition of the law in text books is insufficient to convey understanding of its implementation or challenge. The provisions of the Housing Act 2004 are illustrative of the complexity and ambition of modern housing and environment statutes. The Act combines the empowerment of the private individual, such as the prospective house purchaser, with the bolstering of local government to pursue policies that protect and promote the health and security of its local community.

The Act addresses a wide range of issues pertinent to where we live in the 21st century. Building as it does upon 150 years of government intervention in the provision, occupation and exchange of dwellings, the Housing Act 2004 needs placing in its modern context. Many of its provisions are only explicable by an appreciation of past practice. This book is careful to recognise the significance of this context and to explain the aspirations and ideas that have been expressed to lie behind its provisions. The authors remind us of the background to its passage onto the statute book, occasionally setting out at some length the chronology of its more controversial developments. They also venture prognosis on future challenges or tender occasional caution as to its efficacy or clarity. The brief context provided is invaluable to an understanding of the Act's potential.

Part 1 of the Act rolls back 150 years of legislation that was geared from its inception to deal with the structural deficiencies of Victorian housing and the health threats they posed. In its place the Act introduces a process of housing evaluation based upon prioritising and addressing inherent housing dangers that may affect its occupiers. The risk assessment approach is informed by our evolving knowledge of the relationship between the home environment and the health of occupiers. It replaces a judgment of the physical state of the building for its stability, fabric and state of repair. The ambition is considerable. It involves the re-education of the stalwarts of house condition supervision, environmental health inspectors; it also requires the co-operation of housing managers and landlords; to be fully effective it would benefit from increased attention in the public health sector. *The Housing Act 2004: A Practical Guide* in its explanation of Part 1 alone will meet the needs of all professions and individuals whose work touches on the potential hazards that lie in the home. We are a society that has long accepted the potential hazards of safety in the work place. Part 1 of the Housing Act 2004 extends this concern to the protection of occupiers from dangers at home.

The Act devotes its attention in Parts 2 to 5 with providing local government with a range of powers to address specific problems that are perceived in the privately rented sector. One of the most hazardous sectors of housing for the lack of provision of safe and adequate services, including protection from fire, has long been those dwellings which contain multiple households – bedsits, hostels and other 'houses in multi-occupation' (HMOs). The Act in Part 2 introduces the mandatory licensing of larger 'high risk' HMOs. The present volume sets out the new responsibilities in full and explains the additional powers that local authorities will have to license other HMOs at their discretion, although the authors are concerned that the complexity of the regime and the ambiguity of the HMO definition may encourage litigation.

The concept of licensing, which has already been adopted by some more progressive local authorities for a number of years for HMOs, is extended by the Act to other selective areas of the private rented sector. In doing so it provides greater opportunities for local government to exert more influence in the private rented sector in areas of low demand or where anti-social behaviour is particularly problematic. The government seeks to place some responsibility for the behaviour of tenants upon those who let them their properties. This is new ground for local authorities and the authors are cautious about its potential, whilst acknowledging the flexibility that Part 3 brings to local government to deal with significant new problems for modern housing governance.

Failing landlords face further intervention from Parts 4 and 5 of the Act on matters that are not otherwise licensable. 'Interim managements orders' and 'final management orders' can be imposed by local authorities in a variety of situations where other mechanisms may have failed or are inappropriate. New powers include 'Empty Dwelling Management Orders' which provide local authorities with power to 'step into the shoes' of landlords of the owners of unoccupied dwellings.

The universal relevance of this book is underlined by the final Parts of the Housing Act 2004 which involve something for everybody across a wide range of housing provision – home ownership, social housing, mobile home sites, protected sites for travellers, and the rented sector.

Those contemplating purchasing a home in England and Wales from 2007 will have access to Home Information Packs. Estate agents and others will find their forthcoming responsibilities explained in this book, although the precise content of these awaits explanation in future regulations. The authors nonetheless provide the essential background to the new conveyancing requirements, whilst recognising the practical and financial obstacles to implementation.

The authors of *The Housing Act 2004: A Practical Guide* emulate the magnitude of the ambition of the Act itself. They do so by patient and authoritative explanation of its many proposals. They provide the background of its parliamentary passage and contested development so that readers will better understand its implications. They do not shy from criticism where they find undue complexity or judge that initial policy analysis or future resources may be lacking. This is an impressive overview of the wide-ranging provisions of legislation that is destined to make a major difference to the housing environment. As the authors acknowledge, it is a work that will inevitably spawn further editions as regulations and central guidance add detail to the main framework. It nevertheless provides a solid and essential basis for all those charged with supplying and managing housing and performs an important role in the wider education of many more.

PROFESSOR ROGER BURRIDGE MBE
School of Law
University of Warwick
Coventry
CV4 7AL

Preface

The Housing Act 2004 is, as we point out in our introductory chapter, an epic piece of legislation both in scale and implications. The only way we have been able to respond to its challenges and to complete the task is to work as a team. Whilst team working does not come naturally to lawyers, it is fair to say that it has been very enjoyable to be a member of this particular team. We have been patient and forgiving of each other. This is all the more remarkable since Stephen became the father of Roshan during the course of writing, that Michael joined us at a very late stage and that Tim is immersed in the arduous process of pupillage. Of course the great thing about team work is that you bear collective responsibility for the inevitable mistakes, inaccuracies and confusions. Whilst we have tried hard to avoid them we apologise collectively for any mistakes that nevertheless remain, and are grateful to avoid individual responsibility.

Helen is seconded from London Metropolitan University to the Law Commission and would like to make it clear that any views expressed within the book are those of the authors and should not be attributed to the Law Commission.

HELEN CARR
London
February 2005

Contents

Table of Cases

Table of Statutes

Table of Statutory Instruments

Chapter 1

INTRODUCTION

BACKGROUND

1.1   The Housing Act 2004 ('the Act') is a significant piece of legislation. In seven parts, it has 270 sections and 16 schedules. Many of the provisions have had an unusual amount of scrutiny and debate over a number of years. They implement long-standing manifesto[1] and policy commitments.[2] Despite this, a surprising number of details remain unclear, awaiting the publication of regulations.

1.2   Moreover several changes have a certain last minute quality – in particular the tenancy deposit scheme, which was introduced into the legislation at a relatively late stage as the government overcame its initial resistance to incorporating the provisions into this particular statute.

1.3   The Act is quite different in character from recent housing statutes which have tackled high profile single issue housing problems such as homelessness and anti-social behaviour. Its focus, whilst significant, is arguably more mundane, concentrating largely on housing conditions in the private rented sector. It is also more extensive in scope. The provisions range from licensing and the implementation of the new housing health and safety rating system to restrictions on the right to buy and reforms to the regulatory regime imposed upon registered social landlords. However, the Act does build upon the local and strategic approach to housing management which has been characteristic of the government's legislative response to complex housing problems. It also continues the assault on anti-social behaviour. The licensing regimes, the changes to the right to buy and the extension of the probationary period of introductory tenancies all reflect a concern to provide local authorities with sufficient legal tools to tackle anti-social behaviour whether it occurs in the private or the social housing sector.

1.4   The most politically contentious part of the Act is the new duty on people marketing residential properties to prepare a Home Information Pack. The provisions are similar to the 'sellers' packs' which fell with the Homes Bill in 2001. The measure was resisted to the end – the Conservative and Liberal Democrat peers' amendment to the Bill was overturned on the last day of Parliament by MPs. The aim of the provisions is to improve the process of selling homes by ensuring that purchasers receive full information at the beginning of the transaction, leading to more speedy completions. Equally controversial for the social housing sector is the extension of the powers of the Housing

---

1   For instance, the licensing of houses in multiple occupation was a manifesto pledge in 1997, and the implementation of sellers' packs was a manifesto commitment in 2002.

2   The Act implements objectives first set out in the Housing Green Paper *Quality and Choice: A Decent Home for All* (ODPM, April 2000).

Corporation and the National Assembly for Wales to allow them to give grants to bodies other than registered social landlords. The hope is that this will widen the opportunities for the development of low-cost housing, but registered social landlords are concerned that they will be forced to compete with private companies who are not subject to the same regulatory regime.

1.5   Inevitably, even with such an all-embracing statute, there is some unfinished business. We await further reform to housing benefit, there is the promise of tenure reform following the Law Commission Report *Renting Homes*,[1] and there are still recommendations outstanding from the Park Homes Working Party report.[2]

1.6   The equalisation of succession rights between unmarried same-sex couples and unmarried different sex couples was originally provided for in the Bill. However, the provisions were overtaken by the Civil Partnership Act 2004 which contains a series of amendments to housing legislation, allowing the succession of civil partners and those living as if they have registered their civil partnership.

1.7   The Act applies to both England and Wales, with the exception of the introduction of the Social Housing Ombudsman for Wales.

THE PASSAGE OF THE BILL

The draft Bill

1.8   The draft Housing Bill was published for consultation in March 2003.[3] In June and July 2003, the ODPM Select Committee held an inquiry into the draft Bill. Their report was published on 22 July[4] and the Government's response was published on 10 November.[5]

The House of Commons

1.9   Table 1.1 sets out the Commons stages of the Bill.

---

1   Law Commission Report 285, November 2003 (available on the Law Commission website).
2   Report of the Park Homes Working Party available from the ODPM website at http://www.odpm. gov.uk/stellent/groups/odpm–housing/documents/page/odpm–house–603900.hcsp
3   An analysis of the responses to the draft Bill is available on the ODPM website: www.odpm.gov.uk/ stellent/groups/odpm–housing/documents/page/odpm–house–026711–01.hcsp#P19–585
4   http://www.publications.parliament.uk/pa/cm200203/cmselect/cmodpm/751/751.pdf
5   The government response to the ODPM report can be found at:
     www.odpm.gov.uk/stellent/groups/odpm–housing/documents/page/
     odpm–house–025602–01.hcsp#P27–530

Table 1.1 *Commons stages of the Housing Bill Parliamentary session 2003/04*

Stage	Date	Hansard references
First reading (HC Bill 11 Explanatory Notes Bill 11 EN)	8 December 2003	
Commons Research Paper on Bill (0402) published January 5th 2004		*http://www.parliament.uk/commons/ lib/research/rp2004/rp04–002.pdf*
Second reading	12 January 2004	House of Commons col 531
Standing Committee E 1st sitting	20 January am	Standing Committee debate Col 003
Standing Committee E 2nd sitting	20 January pm	Col 041
Standing Committee E 3rd sitting	22 January am	Col 85
Standing Committee E 4th sitting	22 January pm	Col 131
Standing Committee E 5th sitting	27 January am	Col 170
Standing Committee E 6th sitting	27 January pm	Col 202
Standing Committee E 7th sitting	29 January am	Col 243
Standing Committee E 8th sitting	29 January pm	Col 1
Standing Committee E 9th sitting	3 February am	Col 311
Standing Committee E 10th sitting	3 February pm	Col 347
Standing Committee E 11th sitting	5 February am	Col 401
Standing Committee E 12th sitting	5 February pm	Col 437
Standing Committee E 13th sitting	10 February	Col 485
Standing Committee E 14th sitting	10 February	Part 1, col 523 Part 2, col 559
Standing Committee E 15th sitting	12 February	Col 559
Standing Committee E 16th sitting	12 February	Col 597
Standing Committee E 17th sitting	24 February	Col 627
Standing Committee E 18th sitting	24 February	Col 663
8th report Joint Committee on Human Rights	15 March	HL 49/HC 427
10th report Joint Committee on Human Rights	6 April	HL 64/HC 503
Bill as amended in Committee (HC Bill 59)		
Remaining Stages	11 May	House of Commons col 169

1.10 The House of Lords stages of the Bill are set out in Table 1.2.

Table 1.2 *Lords stages of the Housing Bill Parliamentary session 2003/04*

Stage	Date	Hansard references	
First reading (HL Bill 71)	13 May		
The second reading	7 June	House of Lords	col 83
Committee sitting 1	20 July	House of Lords	col 135
Committee sitting 2	21 July	House of Lords	Part 1, col 260
			Part 2, col 309
Committee sitting 3	9 September	House of Lords	Part 1, col 695
			Part 2, col 741
Committee sitting 4	13 September	House of Lords	Part 1, col 901
			Part 2, col 945
			Part 3, col 989
Committee sitting 5	14 September	House of Lords	Part 1, col 1055
			Part 2, col 1108
Committee sitting 6	16 September	House of Lords	Part 1, col 1295
			Part 2, col 1367
Report stage 1st day	13 October	House of Lords	Part 1, col 273
			Part 2, col 372
Report stage 2nd day	19 October	House of Lords	col 655
Report stage 3rd day	20 October	House of Lords	Part 1, col 778
			Part 2, col 863
20th report Joint Committee on Human Rights	1 November	HL 182/ HC 1187	
Third Reading (HL Bill118)	3 November	House of Lords	col 311

1.11   The final stages of the Bill are set out in Table 1.3.

Table 1.3   *Final stages of the Housing Bill Parliamentary session 2003/04*

Stage	Date	Hansard reference
Consideration by Commons of Lords amendments	8 November	House of Commons col 612
Consideration of Commons amendments by Lords	16 November	House of Lords col 1365
Royal Assent	19 November	Act and Explanatory notes available on HMSO website

THE ACT: KEY FEATURES

1.12   The government press release announcing the Housing Act 2004 explained that its aim is to strengthen 'the Government's drive to reform the housing market, meet its 2010 decent homes target, whilst further enhancing local communities. Keith Hill, the housing minister said that:

> 'These measures will not only improve the lives of millions of people in private housing but also shows a Government that is determined to ensure higher standards and especially prosperous communities. From next year, better use will be made of the existing housing stock, there will be better protection for vulnerable tenants and new and innovative schemes to deliver quality social housing at an acceptable cost. As well, homebuyers and sellers will be able to look forward to long overdue reforms which will take some of the misery and frustration out of moving home.'[1]

1.13   The key features of the Act include:

- home information packs;
- housing health and safety rating;
- licensing of houses in multiple occupation;
- selective licensing;
- tenancy deposit protection;
- reforms to the right to buy;
- a social housing ombudsman for Wales;
- new provisions for gypsies and travellers; and
- new protections for the residents of Park Homes.

1.14   One extremely significant feature of the Act that has received relatively little comment is the extraordinary extension of the jurisdiction of the Residential Property Tribunal. Disputes about licensing and fitness standards will be dealt with by the tribunal rather than the county court.

---

1   ODPM news release 19 November 2004, 'Housing Act 2004 Signals Long-Awaited Reform Of The Private Sector'.

Parts of the Act

1.15   Table 1.4 sets out the parts of the Act indicating their subject matter.

Table 1.4   *The Parts of the Housing Act 2004*

Part number	Title	Comment
1	Housing Conditions	Sweeps away the housing fitness regime of the Housing Act 1985 and replaces it with the Housing Health and Safety Rating System.
2	Licensing of houses in multiple occupation	Mandatory licensing of larger high risk houses in multiple occupation and discretionary licensing of other houses in multiple occupation. Operating without a licence when one is required will attract a fine of up to £20,000.
3	Selective licensing of other residential accommodation	Local authorities will be able to introduce licensing of rented accommodation in areas of low demand or persistent anti-social behaviour. Operating without a licence when one is required will attract a fine of up to £20,000.
4	Additional control provisions in relation to residential accommodation	Includes interim and final management orders, interim and final empty dwelling management orders and overcrowding notices. Management orders are measures of last resort whereby local authorities replace the landlord or manager of rented property.
5	Home Information Packs	Vendors will have to pay for a survey of the condition of their property's structure and fittings before putting their home on the market.
6	Other provisions about housing	Includes the extension of introductory tenancies, reforms to the right to buy to tackle abuses and prevent exploitation, additional protection to the residents of mobile homes, the tenancy deposit schemes, and other miscellaneous reforms to social housing.
7	Supplementary and final provisions	Includes the extension of the powers of Residential property tribunals, powers of entry and other supplementary provisions.

INFORMATION

1.16 One result of the extended legislative process is that there has been an opportunity to prepare user friendly information about the new provisions. The 16 factsheets published by the ODPM are particularly useful. They are available on the ODPM website.[1] The eight Regulatory Impact Assessments prepared for the Bill are also very informative.[2]

IMPLEMENTATION

1.17 Section 270 of the Act provides for commencement. Some provisions of the Act came into force with Royal Assent, some came into force on 18 January 2005 and others – particularly in Part 6 – are likely to come into force relatively quickly. However, the majority of provisions are awaiting consultation and detailed regulations. Those provisions which rely for enforcement on the Residential Property Tribunal require its jurisdiction to be extended. Table 1.5 sets out general information on expected implementation – but note that it may be over-ambitious – and Table 1.6 provides more detailed information on the implementation of Part 6.

Table 1.5 *Implementation of the Housing Act 2004*

Part number	Title	Implementation
1	Housing conditions	Autumn 2005
2	Licensing of houses in multiple occupation	Autumn 2005
3	Selective licensing of other residential accommodation	Autumn 2005
4	Additional control provisions in relation to residential accommodation	Autumn 2005
5	Home Information Packs	Likely to be in 2007
6	Other provisions about housing	See Table 1.6
7	Supplementary and final provisions	

---

1 http://www.odpm.gov.uk/stellent/groups/odpm–control/documents/contentservertemplate/
odpm–index.hcst?n=5042&l=2
2 http://www.odpm.gov.uk/stellent/groups/odpm–control/documents/contentservertemplate/odpm–
index.hcst?n=4077&l=2

Table 1.6 *Implementation of Part 6 of the Housing Act 2004 in chronological order*

Section number	Subject matter	Implementation		Comment
		Date	Method	
190	Termination of rent to mortgage scheme	18 November 2004	s 270	The section is implemented on Royal Assent, but operates to terminate the scheme 8 months after Royal Assent, ie 18 July 2005.
208	Power to amend implied terms in site agreements for mobile homes	18 November 2004	s 270	Whilst this is implemented on Royal Assent the requirement for consultation and a statutory instrument means changes are unlikely to happen for some time.
216	Updating of overcrowding definitions	18 November 2004	s 270	Only implements the discretionary power so again there is no immediate change to the relevant provisions.
180	Extension of qualifying period for right to buy	18 January 2005	s 270	The extension of the qualifying period only applies to tenancies entered into on or after 18 January 2005.
182–183	Houses due to be demolished	18 January 2005	s 270	The amendment only applies where the tenant's notice claiming to exercise the right to buy was served on or after 18 January 2005.
184	Landlord's notice to complete	18 January 2005	s 270	The amendment only applies where the tenant's notice claiming to exercise the right to buy was served on or after 18 January 2005.
185–186	Repayment of right to buy discount	18 January 2005	s 270	The amendments only apply where the tenant's notice claiming to exercise the right to buy was served on or after 18 January 2005.
187	Deferred resale agreements	18 January 2005	s 270	The amendment only applies to agreements made on or after 18 January 2005.
188	Right of first refusal for landlord	18 January 2005	s 270	The amendment only applies where the tenant's notice claiming to exercise the right to buy was served on or after 18 January 2005.
189	Right to buy information	18 January 2005	s 270	Whilst the section has been implemented it requires a statutory instrument to set out the relevant matters.
195–205	Equivalent provisions applying to disposals other than under right to buy	18 January 2005	s 270	
206–207 209–211	Mobile Homes provisions other than s 208 which came into force 18 November 2004	18 January 2005	s 270	
217	Energy efficiency of residential accommodation in England	18 January 2005	s 270	The Secretary of State has until 2010 to achieve the 20 per cent increase in energy efficiency provided for.

Section number	Subject matter	Implementation		Comment
		Date	Method	
218	Implements Schedule 11 to the Act amending the operation of registered social landlords	18 January 2005	s 270	
219	Disclosure of information to RSLs for s 1 of the Crime and Disorder Act 1998 purposes	18 January 2005	s 270	
222	Rights of pre-emption in connection with assured tenancies	18 January 2005	s 270	
224	Disabled facilities grants for caravans	18 January 2005	s 270	

CONCLUSION

1.18   The Act has enormous aspirations. The housing minister in his introduction to the second reading of the Bill made this clear. The Act is designed to help in the creation of 'a fairer and better housing market and to protect the most vulnerable in housing. Together with other Government measures on housing and planning, it will make a major contribution to achieving the aims of the sustainable communities plan. The Bill is big in vision, scope and size.'[1]

1.19   It will not be clear for some time whether the changes made by the Act achieve their purpose. We will not know the details until the regulations are published. More important, however, will be the response of local authorities in particular to the new powers available to them to improve standards in the rented sector. Many of the powers appear bureaucratic and burdensome. Local authorities took some time to take on board the full range of powers available to them under the Housing Act 1996. It remains to be seen whether the government is keen to urge them to respond to poor conditions in private renting as it has been to persuade them to use their anti-social behaviour powers.

---

1   *Hansard* HC Deb, vol 416, col 531, (12 January 2004).

Chapter 2

HOUSING CONDITIONS

INTRODUCTION

2.1   Part 1 of the Housing Act 2004 ('the Act') begins by introducing a new system – which is to operate by reference to the existence of Category 1 or Category 2 hazards on residential premises – for assessing the conditions of residential premises and for that system to be used in the enforcement of housing standards.[1] The new system is called the Housing Health and Safety Rating System ('the HHSRS'), described as 'a means of identifying faults in dwellings and of evaluating the potential effect of any faults on the health and safety of the occupants or visitors'.[2]

2.2   The new system is to replace the test of fitness for human habitation contained in s 604 of the Housing Act 1985, as amended, which is now repealed.[3]

2.3   The opportunity has been taken to use the Act to introduce a new regime of enforcement measures,[4] a regime that does not include repairs notices and closing orders, which are now consigned to history.

History

2.4   In the mid-nineteenth century the Artisans and Labourers Dwelling Act marked the start of a long list of legislative provisions which required specified authorities to take action in respect of 'any premises in a condition or state dangerous to health so as to be unfit for human habitation'.[5]

2.5   In March 2001 the Government, when consulting on the replacement of the Housing Fitness Standard, stated 'there is broad consensus that the fitness standard does not reflect a modern understanding of the health and safety hazards and risks within

---

1   Housing Act 2004, s 1(1). Further statutory references are to the Housing Act 2004, unless otherwise indicated.
2   See *Housing Health and Safety Rating System Guidance* (Version 2) (ODPM, November 2004). The work involved in preparing this Guidance was commissioned by the Office of the Deputy Prime Minister and was carried out by a team from the Safe and Healthy Housing Research Unit at the Law School, University of Warwick.
3   Section 1(2)(b) and see s 258 and Sch 16.
4   Section 1(3).
5   See the discussion in *R v Cardiff CC ex parte Cross* (1981) 1 HLR 54 at 65. Thereafter the unfitness provisions were consolidated in the Housing Act 1985 and then later substituted by the Local Government and Housing Act 1989, Sch 9, para 83 which culminated in the Housing Act 1985, s 604A.

dwellings and focuses too much on conditions rather than the outcome of those conditions'.[1]

2.6 A number of faults were identified with the fitness standard.[2] The first was that the standard itself was too narrow, there being a number of conditions such as provision for fire safety or poor energy efficiency (cold homes) which plainly affected persons in occupation of a dwelling that fell outside the matters statutorily defined as relevant to fitness. Another problem was that according to the standard, a dwelling either passed or failed. This meant that being told a dwelling was unfit did not say whether it was grossly unfit or just marginally unfit. Furthermore, cases occurred where even though a dwelling might not be reasonably suitable for occupation, it could still be properly described as fit for habitation.

2.7 Despite the new Act being passed, the debate about the replacement method, the HHSRS, continues.[3]

Summary

2.8 The following table sets out a summary of the five Chapters within this part of the Act.

Table 2.1 *Quick reference guide to contents of Part 1*

Chapter	Sections	Summary
1	1–10	Enforcement of housing standards: general
2	11–19	Improvement notices
	20–27	Prohibition notices
	28–29	Hazard awareness notices
3	40–45	Emergency measures
4	46–48	Demolition orders and slum clearance declarations
5	49–53	General and miscellaneous provisions relating to enforcement action

Commentary

2.9 The Act begins by introducing the new system for assessing the conditions of residential premises which is to be used in the enforcement of housing standards.[4] Having announced how the new system is to replace the test of fitness,[5] the introductory section of the Act identifies the different types of enforcement measures which may be used. These are the improvement notice, the prohibition order, the hazard awareness notice, the taking of emergency remedial measures, the emergency prohibition order

---

1   Paragraph 1.2 of *Health and Safety in Housing – Replacement of the Housing Fitness Standard by the Housing Health and Safety Rating System*, a consultation paper published by the DETR (March 2001).
2   See D Ormandy, 'Towards Safe and Healthy Housing' [2002] JHL 50.
3   See *Project Report on Preparation of Housing Health and Safety Rating System Guidance (Version 2)* (ODPM, November 2004).
4   Section 1(1)(a), (b).
5   Section 1(2)(b).

(which are all new) and amended versions of the current powers to make a demolition order and the slum clearance declaration order.[1]

Meaning of residential premises

2.10   Residential premises are defined as including not only a dwelling and a house in multiple occupation (HMO) but also 'unoccupied HMO accommodation' and any common parts of a building containing one or more flats.[2]

2.11   The definitions of HMO and of 'unoccupied HMO accommodation' are also dealt with in the introductory section, but not without sending the reader off to the meaning of house in multiple occupation covered in numerous sections devoted to just this the subject.[3] The definition of an HMO in the rest of the Act is subject to a number of exclusions which do not apply for the purposes of deciding if a building is an HMO for the purposes of Part 1.[4] The Act includes a list of buildings which are not to be treated as an HMO for the purposes of any other part of the Act.[5] The list includes buildings occupied by students,[6] buildings occupied by religious communities[7] and any building which is occupied by two persons who form two households.[8] These are all potentially HMOs for the purposes of Part 1.[9]

The HHSRS

2.12   The new system is premised on the principle that 'Any residential premises should provide a safe and healthy environment for any potential occupier or visitor'.[10] The HHSRS is a method of risk assessment.

2.13   Risks are assessed on the basis of the likelihood of an occurrence that could cause harm and the probable severity of the outcome, if it did happen.

2.14   Government guidance explains the theory behind the HHSRS:

> 'By focusing on potential hazards, it places the emphasis directly on the risk to health and safety . . . the HHSRS provides a means of assessing dwellings which reflects the risk from any hazard and allows a judgment to be made as to whether that risk, in the particular circumstances, is acceptable or not.'[11]

---

1   Section 1(3).
2   Section 1(4).
3   Sections 254–259.
4   Sections 1(5) 255 and Sch 14, para 1(1).
5   Schedule 14.
6   Schedule 14, para 4.
7   Schedule 14, para 5.
8   Schedule 14, para 7.
9   This means that the potential for the sort of arguments that occurred (1) in *Barnes v Sheffield CC* (1995) 27 HLR 719 which related to students, and (2) in *Living Waters Christian Centres v Conwy CBC* (1998) 30 HLR 371 which related to a house for religious groups on retreat still remains for the purposes of Part 1 but is restricted by the exclusions for the purposes of Parts 2, 3 and 4 of the Act. The usefulness of the guidance in the *Barnes* case and subsequent case law for distinguishing single households will have to be reconsidered in the light of the new definition in ss 254–259.
10   *Housing Health and Safety Rating System Guidance (Version 2)* (above), para 1.12.
11   *Housing Health and Safety Rating System Guidance (Version 2)* (above), paras 1.07, 1.17.

2.15   The probable severity of the outcome is first of all subject to a weighting formula, as shown below.[1]

Table 2.2   *The classes of harm*

	Class of harm	Weighting
I	Extreme – includes death, permanent paralysis below the neck, 80% burns	10,000
II	Severe – includes asthma; legionnaires' disease, loss of hand or foot, serious fractures	1,000
III	Serious — includes eye disorders, chronic severe stress, diarrhoea, sleep disturbance, puncture wounds, serious strain or sprains.	300
IV	Moderate – includes occasional severe discomfort, severe bruising, regular colds	10

2.16   The hazard score comprises the results from first deciding on the appropriate weighting, then deciding on the likelihood of an occurrence which is subjected to a percentage figure. This may be explained by taking a simple example[2] of a window with a defective catch. The window is on the ground floor with grass below. A small child could climb out of the window. The outcome is likely to be relatively minor, say a 99% chance of bruising and perhaps a small percentage chance of a serious strain or sprain. The classes of harm would be IV for the bruising and III for the strain or sprain. Put the scenario four floors up and the potential outcome is dramatically different. The likely class of harm and the percentage chance of the type of harm both alter accordingly.

2.17   HHSRS has been advanced on the basis of 29 categories of hazard, categories which are not closed, because the whole beauty of the system is that since it is not enshrined in the primary legislation, updating is made easier. This brings with it the disadvantage of explaining the system on the shifting sands of draft guidance.

Hazards

2.18   The hazards are arranged in four main groups and are set out below.[3] The first comprise the physiological requirements of a resident, eg cold, carbon monoxide, asbestos etc. The second group which concern space, security light and noise are clubbed together as psychological requirements. The third category comprises protection from infection concerning hazards arising from problems of hygiene, sanitation, and water supply. Finally there is a group of hazards associated with accidents, eg falls associated with stairs or between levels, structural collapse etc.

A   PHYSIOLOGICAL REQUIREMENTS
   Hygrothermal conditions
   1   Damp and mould growth
   2   Excess cold
   3   Excess heat

1   *Housing Health and Safety Rating System Guidance (Version 2)* (above), para 3.06, Annex C.
2   *Housing Health and Safety Rating System Guidance (Version 2)* (above), para 3.03.
3   *Housing Health and Safety Rating System Guidance (Version 2)* (above), Annex D.

Pollutants (non-microbial)
4   Asbestos (and MMF)
5   Biocides
6   Carbon monoxide and fuel combustion products
7   Lead
8   Radiation
9   Uncombusted fuel gas
10   Volatile organic compounds

B   **PSYCHOLOGICAL REQUIREMENTS**
Space, security, light and noise
11   Crowding and space
12   Entry by intruders
13   Lighting
14   Noise

C   **PROTECTION AGAINST INFECTION**
Hygiene, sanitation and water supply
15   Domestic hygiene, Pests and Refuse
16   Food safety
17   Personal hygiene, Sanitation and Drainage
18   Water supply for Domestic Purpose

D   **PROTECTION AGAINST ACCIDENTS**
Falls
19   Falls associated with baths etc
20   Falls on the level
21   Falls associated with stairs and steps
22   Falls between levels
Electric shocks, fires, burns and scalds
23   Electrical hazards
24   Fire
25   Hot surfaces and materials
Collisions, cuts and strains
26   Collision and entrapment
27   Explosions
28   Ergonomics
29   Structural collapse and failing elements

2.19   A huge body of supporting materials has been built up which defines each of the hazards, describes the potential for harm, discusses potential sources of the hazard, gives an indication of measures and optimum standards intended to avoid or minimise the hazard and discusses a checklist of dwelling features which may have a bearing on the likelihood and severity of outcome.[1]

2.20   The calculation of a hazard score also includes appraisal of the likelihood of the feared potential occurrence occurring over the next 12 months. Once the score has been decided it is given a banding. With this in mind it becomes clearer how the Act is

---

1   *Housing Health and Safety Rating System Guidance (Version 2)* (above), Annex D.

intended to enable local housing authorities to decide on the appropriate action to take in the light of both the band into which a hazard falls and the current occupation of a given dwelling.

2.21   See the table below which shows the HHSRS Bands.[1]

Table 2.3   *How the HHSRS scores will be banded*

Band	Hazard Score Range
A	5,000 or more
B	2,000 to 4,999
C	1,000 to 1,999
D	500 to 999
E	200 to 499
F	100 to 199
G	50 to 99
H	20 to 49
I	10 to 19
J	9 or less

2.22   Although the precise way a hazard score is generated goes beyond the remit of this book (readers are referred to the extract from the current Guidance which appears at Annex A) it is necessary to have some understanding of what scoring is envisaged in order to comprehend the meaning of a Category 1 as opposed to a Category 2 hazard.

2.23   This is the case because the different categories of hazard are defined by their score – both types of hazard mean:[2]

- a hazard of a prescribed description;
- which falls within a prescribed band;
- as a result of achieving;
- under a prescribed method for calculating the seriousness of hazards of that description;
- a numerical score *above* – if is Category 1 – or *below* – if it is a Category 2 hazard – the minimum amount prescribed for a Category 1 hazard of that description.

2.24   The prescribed amount looks as if it is going to be 1,000, so that Category 1 hazards are those rated in Bands A to C and hazards rated in Bands D and lower will fall in to the residual category, Category 2.[3]

---

1   *Housing Health and Safety Rating System Guidance (Version 2)* (above), para 3.26.
2   Section 2(1).
3   *Housing Health and Safety Rating System Consultation on Enforcement Guidance* (above), Annex 4, Part 2, para 2.4.

2.25 A hazard means 'any risk of harm to the health of an actual or potential occupier of a dwelling or HMO which arises from a deficiency in the dwelling or HMO or in any building or land in the vicinity (whether the deficiency arises as a result of construction of any building, an absence of maintenance or repair or otherwise)'.[1] There are therefore five component parts to a hazard, common to both Category 1 and Category 2 hazards:

- any risk of harm to the health;
- of an actual or potential occupier;
- of a dwelling or HMO;
- which arises from a deficiency;
- in the dwelling or HMO or in any building or land in the vicinity.

2.26 Health includes mental health.[2] Harm is an adverse physical or mental effect on the health of a person and includes temporary harm.[3]

2.27 The wide terminology of 'any risk of harm to the health' in the definition makes plain that it goes much further than the previous criteria for assessing unfit housing (repair, stability, freedom from damp, internal arrangement, lighting, ventilation, water supply, drainage and facilities in relation to food and disposal of waste water). The new regime is also marked by the fact that the 'HHSRS assessment is based on the risk to the potential occupant who is most vulnerable to that risk'.[4]

2.28 Version 2 of the HHSRS Guidance treats any form of accommodation used for human habitation as a dwelling. The Act, however, ties the definition of a dwelling to a building or part of a building occupied or intended to be occupied as a separate dwelling.[5] HMO is dealt with at **2.11** above.

2.29 Version 2 of the HHSRS Guidance states that hazards in dwellings cannot only result from (i) deficiencies attributable to the design construction and maintenance of a building but also can result from (ii) deficiencies attributable to the behaviour of the occupants or neighbours, or from (iii) deficiencies attributable to both the dwelling and the occupants or neighbours.[6] This approach is consistent with the wording 'or otherwise' that comes at the end of the definition of a hazard in the Act.[7]

2.30 The final limb concerns the location of the deficiency giving rise to the hazard. The definition contemplates that enforcement action can be taken in respect of a deficiency on land in the vicinity of the building; presumably this could bring into play a choice of legislation that could be used especially if the vicinity can include a matter some distance away. The Act allows the appropriate authority to give guidance to authorities about exercising their functions under this chapter of the Act in relation to the inspection of premises and the assessment of hazards.[8] Guidance where a deficiency is on land in the

---

1   Section 2(1).
2   Section 2(5).
3   Section 2(4); and *Housing Health and Safety Rating System Guidance (Version 2)* (above), para 2.09.
4   Draft guidance, *Housing Health and Safety Rating System Consultation on Enforcement Guidance* (above), Annex 4, para 2.5.
5   Section 1(5).
6   *Housing Health and Safety Rating System Guidance (Version 2)* (above), para 2.32.
7   Section 2(1).
8   Section 9.

vicinity of a building, particularly dealing with the meaning of vicinity and the availability of other powers[1] that might apply, would also be welcome.

2.31   Before the Act was passed the Government published not only consultation on draft guidance together with draft enforcement guidance but also a project report on preparation of the HHSRS Guidance (Version 2). The project report details a large number of fairly wide ranging recommendations aimed not only at fine tuning the use of the Palm OS hand-held computers especially developed to provide an electronic survey programme but also raising formidable issues concerning the role of readings – whether or not from the hand held programmes – in arriving at judgments and issues of training.

2.32   The Act provides that Regulations under s 2 may prescribe a method for calculating the seriousness of hazards which takes into account both the likelihood of the harm occurring and the severity of the harm if it were to occur. The Regulations have not yet been published. Appraisal of Regulations based on the *HHSRS Guidance (Version 2)* will have to await a further edition of this work.

Inspections

2.33   The Act requires local housing Authorities to consider, at least once every year, the housing conditions in their district.[2] This replaces ss 605 and 606 of the Housing Act 1985 with modifications.[3]

2.34   This requirement to carry out inspections is imposed in order for the authority to determine what action to take not only under Parts 1–4 of the Act but also in relation to Part 7 of the Local Government and Housing Act 1989 (renewal areas) and under art 3 of the Regulatory Reform Order on Housing Renewal ('RRO').[4] Article 3 of the RRO contains a general power to provide assistance for housing renewal.[5] The appearance of this reference to the RRO means s 4 of the Act has to be seen in a wider context than mere repeal of the duty to inspect contained in the Housing Act 1985.

Relationship with the commitment to decent homes

2.35   The decent homes standard was first suggested in the 2000.[6] The Government intends to achieve its target that not only every tenant of a social landlord but also ever

---

1   Under the Environmental Protection Act 1990, for example.
2   Section 3(1).
3   See further discussion in the House of Commons Research Paper 04/02, pp 26–27.
4   Section 3(2)(c), (d). The full name of the RRO is the Regulatory Reform (Housing Assistance) (England and Wales) Order 2002 (SI 2002/1860).
5   Local Government and Housing Act 1989, s 93(5)(b) gives an authority power to assist others in carrying out works to land which is not owned by the authority and since June 2003 the use of that power has to be in accordance with art 3 of the RRO.
6   See Housing Green Paper, April 2000.

vulnerable private sector tenant should have a decent home by 2010[1]. Decent housing is described in para 2.18 of ODPM Circular 5/2003 as a home which:

- meets the current minimum standard for housing;
- is in a reasonable state of repair;
- has reasonably modern facilities and services; and
- provides a reasonable degree of thermal comfort.

2.36 The ODPM has set up a unit to ensure that local authorities and housing associations quantify the level of non-decent housing in their stock and develop an investment strategy towards eliminating the problem.

2.37 Circular 5/2003 continues:

> 'The need to make private sector homes decent rather than strict adherence to the traditional fitness standard will represent a significant change in practice for many local authorities. It will have major implications for the conduct of house condition surveys, as well as for the programmes of assistance which should be offered.'[2]

2.38 The first criterion for the decent home is current minimum standards. Since the use of the HHSRS will result in hazards being banded right down to Band J, the phrase minimum standard would most easily translate to there being no Category 1 hazards. However, that leaves a problem because Category 2 hazards might be considered by many to be sufficiently serious to prevent a home being 'decent'. This leans towards specifying a Band lower than C which is presently envisaged as the dividing line between the two types of category of hazard.

2.39 The new system for assessing housing conditions is borne out of primary legislation and the decent home standard is not. There is also an obvious difference in the application of the HHSRS and the decent home standard. Whereas the decent home target is to apply to housing in the social sector and vulnerable[3] households in the private sector, Part 1 of the Act applies to any dwelling.[4] Further, if a property falls below the decent home standard this does not trigger a general duty as is the case if a Category 1 hazard affects the dwelling.

Circumstances giving rise to the duty to inspect

2.40 Once the authority receives a complaint in writing made by a Justice of the Peace or by a Parish Council or from a Community Council about the condition of any residential premises in its district, the proper officer of the authority must carry out an Inspection.[5]

---

1   See ODPM Circular No 5/2003 on Housing Renewal. Achieving the decent home standard can be achieved by local housing authorities in a number of different ways, one of which is for large scale voluntary transfers; another is by means of a private finance initiative. A third method available to local housing authorities wishing to raise sufficient funds to comply with the expectation that all its tenants will have decent homes by 2010 is to transfer the management of its housing stock to an arm's length management organisation. Such a step has to be approved pursuant to s 27 of the Housing Act 1985.

2   Circular 5/2003, para 2.25.

3   Meaning those on certain benefits; see Circular 5/2003, para 2.17, footnote.

4   Defined in s 1(5).

5   Section 4(2).

2.41   There does not appear to be any demarcation which will prevent the obligation to inspect because the complaint concerns the Council's own housing stock; on the contrary, the language is in terms of 'any' residential premises. Arguably this would mean a disgruntled council tenant fed up of complaining to no avail about a hazard could present to a Justice of the Peace or to one or other or both of the two councils a copy of an independent experts' report – less might do, for example a photograph – which identified that a hazard existed on the tenant's premises which was believed to be either a Category 1 or a Category 2 hazard. If the Justice of the Peace, who has to have jurisdiction in any part of the district, or the Parish or Community Council consulted by the tenant then wrote pursuant to s 4(2)(a) of the Act, the authority's proper officer must inspect. There would then arise the thorny issue of whether or not the authority would be discriminating against its own tenants if it concluded it could not do anything about it being unable, as a result of previous case-law, to serve a notice or order on itself.[1]

2.42   The obligation to inspect also can arise by two other routes. The first is as a result of the yearly review contemplated under s 3 of the Act. If as a result of carrying out the review[2] an officer considers it would be appropriate to inspect to see if there is a hazard, in the case of any premises, the authority must arrange for such an inspection to be carried out. Secondly, even where there is no official complaint and even when it is not a product of the yearly review, if the authority 'for any other reason'[3] considers it would be appropriate to inspect to see if there is a hazard on the premises, the authority must arrange for such an inspection to be carried out.

2.43   A written representation from a Citizens Advice Bureau, Law Centre or solicitors' office or even a telephone call to the council from an upset occupier or concerned relative or neighbour, provided the call was properly recorded, would no doubt fall into this residual category.

2.44   This duty to inspect has to be read subject to s 4(5) of the Act which enables regulations to be made to make provision about the manner and extent to which premises are to be inspected.

2.45   Once the mandatory inspection, whether requested or not, has taken place, if the officer finds a Category 1 hazard, a report must be made, which has to be considered as soon as possible.[4] No such report is required if merely a Category 2 hazard is discovered, although if that is the case it will trigger the power to take action pursuant to s 7 of the Act.

Enforcement of housing standards

Duty where there is a Category 1 hazard

2.46   The Act imposes on local housing authorities a mandatory statutory duty to take the appropriate enforcement action where it considers that a Category 1 hazard exists on

---

1   See *R v Cardiff County Council ex parte Cross* [1982] 6 HLR 1 and *R (On The Application of Neckeesha Erskine) v London Borough of Lambeth and Office of the Deputy Prime Minister* [2003] EWHC 2479 (Admin).
2   Section 4(3)(b).
3   Section 4(3)(b).
4   Section 4(6) and s 4(7).

any premises[1] (one might add, in its district, although that is not spelt out). Where such a general duty arises the authority must take the most appropriate enforcement action. The action must be one of a list which is set out under s 5(2). If only one course of action is available then that is the appropriate enforcement action, otherwise if two or more courses of action identified on the list are available, the authority must take the course of action which they consider to be the most appropriate.[2] More than one course of action may be taken[3] if one course is tried and does not prove satisfactory.

2.47 The list of possible enforcement action[4] comprises:

- serving an improvement notice;
- making a prohibition order;
- serving a hazard awareness notice;
- taking emergency remedial action;
- making an emergency prohibition order;
- an amended version of the existing powers to make a demolition order;
- an amended version of the existing power to make slum clearance declaration.

A further option is:

- making a determination under s 300(1) or (2) of the Housing Act 1985 (power to purchase for temporary housing use) where the authority consider the latter course 'to be the better alternative in the circumstances'.[5]

2.48 Use of more than one of the possible enforcement measures is deemed – in certain circumstances, eg making an emergency prohibition order then making a prohibition order – a single course of action.[6]

Power where there is a Category 2 hazard

2.49 Where a Category 2 hazard exists, there is no such similar duty to take action as appears in s 5 of the Act in respect of the more serious category of hazard. Instead the section confers a power to take action.[7]

2.50 The action the authority can take if there is a Category 2 hazard does not include taking the emergency measures which are available if a Category 1 hazard exists. Otherwise the available list of possible enforcement action remains the same including serving an improvement notice, making a prohibition order, serving a hazard awareness notice, an amended version of the existing powers to make a demolition order and an amended version of the existing power to make a slum clearance declaration.

2.51 As with Category 1 hazards if there is a Category 2 hazard the Act permits more than one course of action to be taken,[8] or the same action to be taken again where the authority consider that the action taken by them so far has not proved satisfactory.

---

1   Section 5(1).
2   Section 5(3).
3   Section 5(5)(a).
4   Section 5(2).
5   Section 6(2).
6   Section 6(3), (4).
7   Section 7(1).
8   Section 7(3)(a) and (b).

Reasons

2.52   Whatever the enforcement action the authority chooses to take, it must prepare a statement of reasons for the decision to take the relevant action including reasons for that action as against any other which is available to them.[1]

The need to consider guidance

2.53   Part 1 requires a local housing authority to have regard to government guidance[2] including different guidance to different descriptions of local authorities or to local authorities in different areas about inspections and enforcement action.[3]

Consultation with fire authorities

2.54   The Act repeals all of Part XI of the Housing Act 1985 including the general provisions governing the means of escape from fire which was previously contained in s 365 of the 1985 Act.[4]

2.55   Where the local housing authority is satisfied that a prescribed fire hazard[5] exists in an HMO or in common parts of a building containing one or more flats and intend to take action under s 5(2) or s 7(2) then, before taking the action, the authority must[6] first consult the fire authority.

2.56   In the event of emergency measures being taken, the duty is subject to the rider that the duty to first consult is instead a duty to consult so far as is practicable to do so before taking those measures.[7]

ACTION TO DEAL WITH PREMISES AFFECTED BY CATEGORY 1 AND CATEGORY 2 HAZARDS

Improvement notices

History

2.57   The Housing Act 1985 contained a number of options for action to deal with poor standards of housing, whether arising out of the now defunct concept of being unfit for human habitation or because the house was in substantial disrepair, was lacking standard amenities, and/or because the house was overcrowded.

2.58   The options included serving a repairs notice governed by ss 189–208 of the Housing Act 1985 which are now repealed.[8] The repeal was contentious because it was argued disrepair might not warrant enforcement action even though it affected a

---

1   Section 8(1).
2   Consultation on a draft enforcement guidance ended in March 2004 but at date of publication is not yet available.
3   Section 9(2), (3).
4   Section 258 and Sch 16.
5   Prescribed by regulations pursuant to s 2.
6   Section 10(2).
7   Section 10(3).
8   Section 258, Sch 16.

residential occupier. The Government took the view that since an improvement notice could require action in respect of faults that could contribute to a hazard if not addressed within 12 months, the s 190 repairs notice need not be retained.[1] The draft enforcement guidance contains a brief section dealing with how authorities may approach issues of minor disrepair and conditions giving rise to discomfort which were not in themselves health hazards. The first consideration is that disrepair contributing to hazards can be assessed under the HHSRS. Other than that the advice is that authorities can consider financial assistance and other non-enforcement tools to encourage owners to remedy minor disrepair.[2]

2.59 Section 216 of the Housing Act 1985 did once cater for service of an improvement notice. This was dependent on the unfit housing being in an improvement area. This provision and others in Part 7 of the Housing Act 1985 dealing with improvement notices was repealed by the Local Government and Housing Act 1989.

2.60 The options available under the Housing Act 1985 and ancillary provisions in respect of unfit housing were re-stated four years later with an additional measure, the deferred action notice.[3] These are also now repealed.[4]

2.61 Now the improvement notice returns, bearing similarities in its operation to the old Repairs Notice.

2.62 The Act permits[5] a local housing authority which is satisfied that either a Category 1 or a Category 2 hazard exists on any residential premises to serve an improvement notice. The improvement notice enables an authority to require the person served to take such remedial action in respect of a Category 1, or as the case may be a Category 2, hazard as is specified in the notice.

2.63 Service of improvement notices and the procedure for appeals is dealt with in Schedule 1.[6] The requirements of an improvement notice are set out in the following table.

2.64

Table 2.4 *Requirements for a valid improvement notice*

The premises in relation to which an improvement notice may be served	The notice may require action to be taken in relation to the dwelling or HMO containing the residential premises on which the hazard (irrespective of which category the hazard is) exists.[7]
	If the residential premises on which the hazard exists are one or more flats or on the common parts of a building containing one or more flats then the notice can require action to be taken in relation to any part of the building.[8]

---

1   House of Commons Research Paper 04/02, pp 22–23.
2   Draft Enforcement Guidance, para 22.
3   Housing Grants Construction and Regeneration Act 1996, ss 81–91.
4   Section 258, Sch 16.
5   Sections 11, 12.
6   Section 18. See Table 2.6 at **2.97**; see also **2.98** to **2.109** below.
7   Section 11(3)(a) and s 12(3).
8   Sections 11(3)(b), 12(3).

	If the deficiency from which the hazard arises is situated in any part of a building, containing one or more flats, or its common parts, that is not included in any residential premises, then the improvement notice may only require remedial action to be taken in relation to those non residential parts if it is necessary for the action to be taken in order to protect the health and safety of any actual or potential occupiers of one or more of the flats.[1]
Circumstances for service of an improvement notice	Where the authority are satisfied that a Category 1 hazard exists;[2] or
	where the authority are satisfied a Category 2 hazard exists;[3] and
	where there is no interim or final management order in existence;[4] and
	where the notice is not in respect of land which has been approved by the authority for re-development by the owner and the re-development is being proceeded with, within any specified time limit;[5] and
	where such relevant guidance as may be issued pursuant to s 9 has been expressly considered by the authority.[6]
Where there is more than one hazard or more than one type of hazard	The notice may relate to more than one Category 1 or Category 2 hazard on the same premises or in the same building containing one or more flats.[7]
	An improvement notice in respect of a Category 2 hazard may be combined in one document with a Notice under s 11 where they require remedial action in respect of the same premises.[8]
Contents of a valid notice	1. The notice must be accompanied by a statement of reasons which explain why the authority decided to use an improvement notice rather than use any other kind of enforcement measure available to them.[9]

---

1   Sections 11(3)(c), (4), 12(3).
2   Section 11(1)(a).
3   Section 12(1)(a).
4   Sections 11(1)(b), 12(1)(b). If an improvement notice has been served and a management order comes into force the improvement notice is treated as not served, if the notice is operative when a management order comes into force then the notice ceases to have effect: see s 39. For the time when an improvement notice becomes operative see s 15 which provides that the notice is operative – subject to it being suspended and subject to whether or not the notice is subject of an appeal – 21 days after service.
5   Section 39(5).
6   Section 9(2).
7   Sections 11(6), 12(4).
8   Section 12(5).
9   Section 8(3), (4).

2. The notice must specify in relation to the hazard or to each of the hazards to which it relates:

- whether the notice is served under s 11 or 12;[1]
- the nature of the hazard and the residential premises on which it exists;[2]
- the deficiency giving rise to the hazard;[3]
- the premises in relation to which the remedial action is to be taken and the nature of that remedial action;[4]
- the date when the remedial action is to be started – which cannot be earlier than the 28th day after that on which the notice is served;[5]
- the period within which the remedial action is to be completed;[6]
- information about the right to appeal under Pt 3 of Sch 1;[7] and
- the period within which an appeal may be made.[8]

Flexibility

2.65   The flexibility of the legislation is demonstrated by five striking features.

- Firstly, improvement notices like other courses of action available to a local housing authority, do not have to be served. Parliament has merely made the option available should the local authority so choose. The courts can be expected to conclude that a refusal to serve a notice is unchallengeable, unless based on an error of law.[9]
- Secondly, if served, the authority can suspend the operation of the notice.[10]
- Thirdly, the authority has the power to vary or revoke an improvement notice either on application made by the person on whom the notice was served or of its own initiative.[11]
- Fourthly, where a decision is made to vary or to refuse to revoke there is a right of appeal to the residential property tribunal, who can confirm vary or reverse the decision.[12]
- Fifthly, where there is change in person liable to comply with the improvement notice, the new person is deemed to be in the same position as if the improvement notice was originally served on him and is deemed to have taken all relevant steps which the original recipient had taken.[13]

---

1   Section 13(2)(a).
2   Section 13(2)(b).
3   Section 13(2)(c).
4   Section 13(2)(d).
5   Section 13(2)(e), (3).
6   Section 13(2)(f).
7   Section 13(4)(a).
8   Section 13(4)(b) (21 days: see Sch 1, para 14(1)).
9   There may be scope for borrowing principles derived from case law dealing with an authority's discretion to enforce under the Town and Country Planning Act 1990, s 172.
10   Sections 11(7), 12(6) and 14.
11   Section 16(8).
12   Schedule 1, Pt 3, paras 13, 18(1), (4).
13   Section 19.

2.66   The same flexible scheme of the legislation is carried through to the provisions governing Prohibition Orders contained in ss 20–27 of the Act.

Suspension of an improvement notice

2.67   Use of suspended notices must be read subject to such guidance as is issued under s 9.

2.68   The Act allows for situations when a notice may be suspended.[1] The first situation envisaged by the Act is for the notice to be suspended until a specified time; the second is until the occurrence of an event specified in the notice. Once served the local housing authority has the power to review a suspended improvement notice at any time.[2] Should the notice be suspended generally then it would fail to comply with the requirement that it only be suspended until a time or until the occurrence of an event.[3]

2.69   There is no attempt to exhaustively list the circumstances where a suspended notice could be suspended until a certain time or try to list exhaustively list the type of events that may be specified; instead the Act gives examples.[4] The example of a specified time for suspension is the date persons of a certain description begin to use or cease to occupy any premises. The example of a specified event is when the authority notifies a person who has previously given the authority an undertaking that he has failed to comply with the terms of the undertaking. The offer of an undertaking to carry out steps which would otherwise be required by an improvement notice can only be properly accepted 'for the purposes of this section', if the terms of the undertaking not only govern the procedure for notification in case of breach but also specify that the notice will cease to be suspended if there is an act or omission which the authority considers to be a breach and which is notified to the person on whom the notice is served.[5]

2.70   How long a notice may be suspended for is hinted by the provision which requires that an authority must review the suspension of an improvement notice one year after the date of service and at subsequent intervals of not more than one year.[6]

2.71   Once a notice is suspended, the suspended improvement notice can then be varied[7] to alter the time or the events by reference to which the suspension is to come to an end.

2.72   On a review of a suspended improvement notice, there is a notification requirement with which the authority must comply.[8] Copies of the authority's decision on such a review must be served on the person on whom the notice was served and on every person on whom a copy of the notice was required to be served. These recipients are defined in Sch 1, para 5 to the Act, the contents of which are contained in the second row down in Table 2.6 at **2.97**.

---

1   Section 14(2), (3).
2   Section 17(1).
3   Section 14(1).
4   See footnote 95 and s 14(4).
5   Section 14(3), (4)(a), (b).
6   Section 17(2).
7   Section 16(4)(b).
8   Section 17(3).

Revocation and variation

2.73   The local housing authority has the power to vary or revoke on an improvement notice either on application made by the person on whom the notice was served or of its own initiative.[1] Revocation does have to be of the whole notice if the subject notice related to a number of hazards.[2] A notice can only be revoked if (i) the notice has been complied with,[3] or (ii) where the notice was served in respect of a Category 1 hazard under s 11 of the Act, if the authority considers that there are special circumstances making it appropriate to revoke the notice.[4]

2.74   Special circumstances are not required to revoke a notice in respect of a Category 2 hazard. How special, special circumstances have to be, is not dealt with by the Act. However, Guidance issued pursuant to s 9 gives the appropriate national authority[5] an opportunity to throw light on achieving some consistency of approach. Presumably if there is one circumstance it will be have to be special, but if there are a number of relevant considerations pointing in favour of revocation, they need not each be special, so long as on a composite assessment they are considered to be special.

2.75   Where the requirements of the notice are still to be met, the need to demonstrate special circumstances before a notice can be revoked is confined to revocation of a notice served in respect of a Category 1 hazard. A notice can be revoked where the notice was served in respect of a Category 2 hazard merely if the authority considers that it is appropriate to revoke the notice.[6]

Variation

2.76   The Act permits variation of an operative improvement notice by consent of the person on whom the notice was served.[7] But a suspended improvement notice can also be varied by the local housing authority unilaterally. The scope of the variation would be to alter the time or events by reference to which the suspension is to come to an end.[8] Guidance might suggest that before the varied notice is issued, some prior discussion takes place with those likely to be affected by the intended variation in order to avert appeals under para 13(1)(b) of Sch 1. Consequences for the individuals concerned would be relevant to a decision to vary as a matter of good practice, even if the Guidance, when it is published, fails to address the matter. In the absence of an appeal, the variation takes effect – when the time for appealing expires or if there is an appeal the date the decision to vary is confirmed, if it is confirmed, on appeal.[9]

---

1   Section 16(8).
2   Section 16(3)(b).
3   Section 16(1).
4   Section 16(2)(a).
5   'Appropriate national authority' is defined in s 261(1) in England as the Secretary of State and in Wales as the National Assembly of Wales.
6   Section 16(2)(b).
7   Section 16(4)(a).
8   Section 16(4)(b).
9   Section 16(7).

Change in person liable to comply with improvement notice

2.77   The Act caters for the not uncommon situation of a person subject of enforcement action, and here specifically served with an improvement notice, transferring their interest to a third party – referred to as a changeover – whilst the notice is still extant.[1] The new liable person is deemed to be in the shoes of the original recipient,[2] subject to one rider: the new liable person is not subject to any liability incurred by the original recipient.[3] To understand who the changeover provisions affect, one needs to have in mind who has to be served before an improvement notice is valid; these provisions are found in Sch 1. The person to be served depends on the type of premises involved. See Table 2.6 at **2.97** below. Perhaps the most important point is that any period for compliance or time for appeal remains unaffected.[4]

PROHIBITION ORDERS

History

2.78   The Act creates a new measure for enforcing housing standards, the prohibition order.

2.79   Prohibition notices (as opposed to prohibition orders) were once used to deal with a situation where, although not presently existing, conditions affecting the health of the community – termed a statutory nuisance – were likely to recur. The notices were also a weapon under the Control of Pollution Act 1974. Schedule 16 of the Environmental Protection Act 1990 swept away these provisions. The 1990 Act made it possible to serve a valid abatement notice even if no nuisance existed at the time of service, thus making a prohibition notice redundant.

2.80   The new prohibition order, instead of being derived from the old public health legislation, in effect replaces the old closing order which under Part 9 of the Housing Act 1985 enabled a local authority to serve a notice prohibiting use of premises for any purpose not approved by the local authority. The enabling provisions in the Housing Act 1985 for the making of a closing order have been repealed, the various provisions which referred to them amended to delete all reference to them, and so now closing orders have gone.[5] Instead there is now the prohibition order, and the emergency prohibition order.[6]

Requirements for a valid prohibition order

2.81   The Act permits a local housing authority[7] which is satisfied that either a Category 1 or a Category 2 hazard exists on any residential premises to serve a prohibition

---

1   Section 19.
2   Section 19(3), (8), (9).
3   Section 19(5).
4   Section 19(4).
5   For the amendments see s 257, Sch 15; for the repeals see s 258 and Sch 16.
6   The power to make an emergency prohibition order is contained in s 43.
7   Local housing authority is defined in s 261(2).

order.[1] The prohibition order is an order imposing such prohibition or prohibitions on the use of any premises as is or are specified.[2]

2.82   Service of prohibition orders and the procedure for appeals is dealt with in Sch 1.[3] The requirements of a prohibition order are set out in the following table.

Table 2.5   *Requirements for a valid prohibition order*

The premises which a prohibition order may prohibit use of	1. If the residential premises on which the hazard exists are a dwelling or HMO, the order may prohibit use of the dwelling or HMO.[4]
	2. If those premises on which the hazard exists are one or more flats it can prohibit use of the building containing the flats or any part of the building or any external parts.[5]
	3. If those premises are the common parts of a building containing one or more flats it can prohibit use of the building containing the flats or any part of the building or any external parts.[6]
	4. However, use of parts of a building (which comprise flats) or its external parts which are not included in any residential premises, cannot be subject of prohibition in the order unless the authority are satisfied that it is necessary for the action to be taken in order to protect the health and safety of any actual or potential occupiers of one or more of the flats.[7]
Circumstances for service of a valid prohibition order	Where a Category 1 hazard exists;[8] or
	where a Category 2 hazard exists;[9] and
	where there is no interim or final management order in existence.[10]
	Where the order is not in respect of land which has been approved by the authority for re-development by the owner and the re-development is being proceeded with;[11] and

---

1   Sections 20(1), 21(1).
2   Section 20(2).
3   Section 27. See Table 2.6 at **2.97**; and see **2.110** to **2.116** below.
4   Sections 20(3)(a), 21(3).
5   Sections 20(3)(b), 21(3).
6   Sections 20(3)(c), 21(3).
7   Sections 20(4)(b), 21(3).
8   Section 20(1)(a).
9   Section 21(1)(a).
10 Sections 20(1)(b), s 21(1)(b). If a prohibition order has been served and a management order comes into force the order is treated as not served, see s 39(2)(b); if the order is already operative when a management order comes into force then the notice ceases to have effect; see s 39(2)(a). For the time when a prohibition order becomes operative see s 24 which provides that the order is operative – subject to it being suspended and subject to whether or not the order is subject of an appeal – 28 days after service.
11 Section 39(5).

where such relevant guidance as may be issued pursuant to s 9 has been expressly considered by the authority.[1] The current draft guidance points to a number of matters which should be addressed including the availability of local accommodation for re-housing of any displaced occupants.

Where there is more than one hazard or more than one type of hazard	The order may relate to more than one Category 1 or Category 2 hazard on the same premises or in the same building containing one or more flats.[2]
	A prohibition order in respect of a Category 2 hazard may be combined in one document with an order under s 20 where they impose prohibitions in respect of the same premises or in respect of the same building containing one or more flats.[3]
Contents of a valid order	1. The notice must be accompanied by a statement of reasons which explain why the authority decided to serve a prohibition order rather than use any other kind of enforcement measure available to them.[4]

2. The order must specify in relation to the hazard or to each of the hazards to which it relates:

(a)   whether the order is served under s 20 or 21;[5]

(b)   the nature of the hazard and the residential premises on which it exists;[6]

(c)   the deficiency giving rise to the hazard;[7]

(d)   the premises in relation to which prohibitions are imposed;[8] and

(e)   any remedial action, which the authority consider would, if taken in relation to the hazard, result in their revoking the order;[9]

(f)   information about the right to appeal under Pt 3 of Sch 2;[10] and

(g)   the period within which an appeal may be made;[11] and

(h)   specify the date on which the order is made.[12]

Nature of the prohibitions that may be employed in a valid prohibition order	Such prohibitions as the authority considers appropriate in view of the hazard or hazards in respect of which the order is made.[13]

---

1   Section 9(2).
2   Sections 20(5), 21(4).
3   Section 21(5).
4   Section 8(3), (4).
5   Section 22(2)(a).
6   Section 22(2)(b).
7   Section 22(2)(c).
8   Section 22(2)(d).
9   Section 22(2)(e).
10   Section 22(6).
11   Section 22(6)(a) (specified in Sch 2, para 10 as 28 days).
12   Section 22(6)(b).
13   Section 22(3)(b).

Prohibitions may prohibit use of any specified premises or any part of those premises either for all purposes or for any particular purpose except to the extent to which any use of the premises or part is approved by the authority.[1]

Prohibitions may relate to occupation of the premises or part by (a) more than a particular number of households or persons; or (b) particular descriptions of persons.[2]

Approvals

2.83   The broad power that enables prohibitions to be imposed where the authority considers it appropriate is subject to two riders. The first is that approval for the previously prohibited use may be sought and given.[3] Secondly, if that approval is refused the person who sought the approval may appeal, within 28 days.[4] The Act sets out what might have been taken for granted: that once an approval is sought the local housing authority must act reasonably in deciding whether or not to grant the approval. The Act nevertheless spells it out: the authority cannot unreasonably withhold its approval.[5]

2.84   Furthermore, in order to facilitate a decision on whether or not to appeal, the Act imposes[6] an obligation on the authority to notify the person applying for the approval, not only of their decision to maintain the prohibition and the reasons for it,[7] but also of the right to appeal against the decision and of the time for doing so.[8]

Suspension of a prohibition order

2.85   The provisions follow the same pattern as already seen in relation to suspension of the operation of improvement notices.[9]

2.86   If served, the authority can suspend the operation of the Order.[10]

2.87   A prohibition order can be suspended until the occurrence of an event specified in the order,[11] or it may be suspended until a certain time.[12]

2.88   The Act requires that an authority must review the suspension of a prohibition order not less than one year after the order was made and at subsequent intervals of not more than one year,[13] although in any event the authority has the power to review a

---

1   Section 22(4)(a), (b).
2   Section 22(5)(a), (b).
3   Section 22(4).
4   Section 22(9).
5   Section 22(7).
6   Section 22(8). This must be done within seven days after the date of the decision to refuse the approval.
7   Section 22(8)(b).
8   Section 22(9).
9   See **2.68** to **2.72** above.
10   Section 23.
11   Section 23(1), (3).
12   Section 23(1), (2).
13   Section 26(2).

suspended prohibition order at any time.[1] The outcome of the review has to be notified. Copies of the authority's decision must be served on the person on whom the order was served. These persons are defined in Sch 2, para 1(2)(a) to the Act, the content of which is summarised in Table 2.6 at **2.97** below.

Revocation and variation

2.89   A local housing authority has the power to vary or revoke a prohibition order either on application made by the person on whom the order was served or of its own initiative.[2] Paragraphs 30 and 31 of Sch 15 insert new ss 584A and 584B into the Housing Act 1985 which govern payment and re-payment of compensation if a prohibition order is, respectively, made or revoked. The compensation is calculated by reference to diminution of the compulsory purchase value of the owner's interest in the premises caused by the making of the prohibition order. Since it is possible that a prohibition order may relate to a number of hazards, it follows that revocation need not be of the whole order.[3] This could lead to some complicated sums to arrive at the figure to be repaid.

2.90   A prohibition order can be revoked in three different circumstances:

(1)   where the authority is satisfied that the hazard in respect of which the order was made does not then exist on the specified premises;[4] or

(2)   where the order was served in respect of a Category 1 hazard, if the authority considers that there are special circumstances making it appropriate to revoke the order;[5] or

(3)   where the order was served in respect of a Category 2 hazard under s 20 of the Act if the authority considers that it is appropriate to revoke the order.[6]

Variation

2.91   The Act caters for variation of a prohibition order by consent.[7] The necessary consent is of every person on whom copies of the notice were required to be served.[8] If everyone agrees the variation takes effect at the time of the agreement.[9]

2.92   Again as with suspension of an improvement notice, once a prohibition order is suspended, it may be also be varied unilaterally.[10] If variation takes place without the agreement of the person on whom the prohibition order was served, the variation takes effect when the time for appealing expires or, if there is an appeal, the date the decision to vary is confirmed, if it is confirmed, on appeal.[11]

---

1   Section 26(1).
2   Section 25(8).
3   Section 25(3)(b).
4   Section 25(1).
5   Section 25(2)(a).
6   Section 25(2)(b).
7   Section 25(4)(a).
8   Schedule 2 lists the persons who have to be served, the references for which are given in footnotes 177 to 180 in Table 2.6 which appears at **2.97** below.
9   Section 25(6).
10   Section 25(4)(a).
11   Section 25(7).

PROCEDURE AND APPEALS RELATING TO IMPROVEMENT NOTICES AND PROHIBITION ORDERS

Introduction

2.93　Schedule 1 of the Act governs the procedure to be used in relation to an improvement notice. The Schedule is divided into three parts: service, revocation/variation, and appeals of improvement notices. Schedule 2 governs the procedure to be used in relation to a prohibition order, and is also divided into three comparable parts: service, revocation/variation, and appeals of prohibition orders.

2.94　Appeals are no longer to the county court; all the possible appeals now go to the Residential Property Tribunal.[1]

2.95　The most important point to note about the Residential Property Tribunal is that the tribunal will not have costs jurisdiction, save where there has been unreasonable conduct and then only to the extent of £500 or such other amount as may be specified in regulations.[2]

2.96　The issue of public funding or exceptional public funding for those otherwise financially eligible will therefore be critically important. This is so not only because a lot of the cases will obviously depend on the tribunal's appraisal of expert evidence but also because of a number of other factors. Such factors may include if a notice has been served on the wrong person, or the consequences for the individual who cannot afford to do the works, if the appeal is dismissed. In relation to prohibition notice appeals, the case for public funding may arise out of the overwhelming importance to an individual occupier of a successful appeal, particularly if the individual concerned would otherwise offend against an unchallenged prohibition order, simply by continuing to live in his or her home.[3]

2.97　Since the Schedules both share a similar format, the table below summarising the relevant provisions of both gives a quick reference guide:

1　Schedule 1, paras 10, 13, Sch 2, paras 7, 9.
2　Schedule 13, para 12(3).
3　See **2.137** below.

Table 2.6   Quick reference guide to Schs 1 and 2: procedure and appeals

	Improvement notice	Notices relating to revocation or variation and notices relating to refusal to revoke or vary an improvement notice	Prohibition order	Notice relating to revocation or variation and notices relating to refusal to revoke or vary a prohibition order
1 Who has to be served with the notice?	• In relation to licensed dwellings and licensed HMOs the notice should be served on the licence holder.[1] • If the dwelling or HMO is not licensed then the notice has to be served on the person having control or if an HMO then on the person managing the HMO.[2] • In the case of an HMO, which is a flat, the local housing authority must serve either the owner or the person managing the flat.[3]	Applies to all on whom the authority was required to serve the original notice.[4]	• Every person who the authority knows is an owner or occupier of any part of the premises;[5] • every person the authority knows is entitled or authorised to permit persons to occupy the whole or part of the premises;[6] or • every known mortgagee of the whole or part of the premises.[7] Each person falling in to any of the above three categories has to be served within 7 days of the order being made.[8]	On those the authority would be required to serve with a prohibition notice.

---

1   Schedule 1, para 1.
2   Schedule 1, para 2.
3   The owner can only be the person served if the authority believe that the owner ought to take the action specified in the notice; see the word 'and' at the end of Sch 1, para 3(3)(a).
4   Schedule 1, paras 6(2), 8(2).
5   Schedule 2, para 1(2)(a).
6   Schedule 2, para 1(2)(b).
7   Schedule 2, para 1(2)(c).
8   Schedule 2, para 1(3).

	Improvement notice	*Notices relating to revocation or variation and notices relating to refusal to revoke or vary an improvement notice*	*Prohibition order*	*Notice relating to revocation or variation and notices relating to refusal to revoke or vary a prohibition order*
2 Who else has to be served with a copy of the notice?	Every person who to the local housing authority's knowledge has a relevant interest (freehold, mortgage or lease) or is an occupier of the premises specified in the notice.[1]	Those who were served with a copy of the original notice.[2]	Not applicable because the category of persons who have to be served with copy of the prohibition order is so wide.	Not applicable
3 Who can appeal?	The person on whom the notice was served.[3]	The persons on whom the notice was served and if it is an appeal against refusal to revoke or vary, the person who applied for the revocation or variation.[4]	A relevant person[5] who comprise: (1) a person who is an owner, or occupier of any part of the premises; and (2) a person entitled or authorised to permit persons to occupy the whole or part of the premises; or (3) a mortgagee of the whole or part of the premises (including common parts).	A relevant person as defined in Sch 2, para 16 – which is the same group as those who can appeal against a prohibition order, listed in the adjacent column.
4 Time limit for appealing	Within 21 days from date of service, but there is a narrow discretion to extend that time.[6]	Within 28 days from the decision date specified in the notice, with the same discretion to extend.[7]	Within 28 days from the date specified in the prohibition order as the date the order was made, with the same discretion to extend.[8]	Within 28 days from the decision date specified in the notice, with the same discretion to extend.[9]

1   Schedule 1, para 5.
2   Schedule 1, para 8(2).
3   Schedule 1, para 10(1).
4   Schedule 1, para 13.
5   Schedule 2, para 16.
6   Schedule 1, para 14(1), (3).
7   Schedule 1, para 14(2).
8   Schedule 2, para 10(1), (3).
9   Schedule 2, para 10(2), (3).

	Improvement notice	Notices relating to revocation or variation and notices relating to refusal to revoke or vary an improvement notice	Prohibition order	Notice relating to revocation or variation and notices relating to refusal to revoke or vary a prohibition order
5 Nature of the appeal	Re-hearing having regard to matters of which the authority were unaware.[1] In its determination of an appeal the tribunal must have regard to any guidance given to the local housing authority under s 9.[2]	Re-hearing having regard to matters of which the authority were unaware.[3]	Re-hearing having regard to matters of which the authority were unaware.[4] In its determination of an appeal the Tribunal must have regard to any guidance given to the local housing authority under s 9.[5]	Re-hearing having regard to matters of which the authority were unaware.[6]
7 Grounds for appeal	• Open, but there are two specified grounds, which are not intended to limit the ability to appeal;[7] • one or more other persons, as owner or owners of the premises specified in the notice ought to take the action concerned or pay the whole or part of the cost of taking that action;[8] • serving an improvement notice is not the best course of action; either making a prohibition order, serving a hazard awareness notice or making a demolition order is the best course of action.[9]	None specified which fits with the nature of the appeal being by way of a re-hearing.	• Open but there is one specified ground, again not affecting the generality of the ability to appeal; • serving a Prohibition Order is not the best course of action.[10]	None specified which fits with the nature of the appeal being by way of a rehearing.

1   Schedule 1, para 15(2).
2   Schedule 1, para 17(2).
3   Schedule 1, paras 18(1), (2) and 15(2).
4   Schedule 2, para 11(2).
5   Schedule 2, para 12(2).
6   Schedule 2, paras 11(2), 13(2).
7   Schedule 1, para 10.
8   Schedule 1, para 11(2).
9   Schedule 1, para 12.
10   Schedule 2, para 8.

	Improvement notice	Notices relating to revocation or variation and notices relating to refusal to revoke or vary an improvement notice	Prohibition order	Notice relating to revocation or variation and notices relating to refusal to revoke or vary a prohibition order
8 Tribunal's power	To confirm quash or vary the notice.[1]	To confirm quash or vary the decision of the local housing authority.[2]	To confirm quash or vary the order.[3]	To confirm quash or vary the decision of the local housing authority.[4] If the appeal is against a refusal to revoke the tribunal may make an order revoking the prohibition order from a date specified in its order.[5]

1 Schedule 1, para 15(3).
2 Schedule 1, para 18(3).
3 Schedule 2, para 11(3).
4 Schedule 2, para 13(3).
5 Schedule 2, para 13(4).

Procedure and appeals relating to improvement notices

Service of improvement notices

2.98   The person to be served varies according to the status of the premises (licensed or unlicensed under Parts 2 and 3), and the type of premises, eg whether or not the dwelling is or is not an HMO, is or is not a flat and according to whether or not the premises specified in the notice, are common parts. See the quick reference guide Table 2.6 at **2.97** above.

Notification duty in relation to revocation and variation of improvement notices

2.99   Part 2 of Schedule 1 contains the notification duty where the recipient of a notice has sought revocation and or variation. It is divided into two parts, the first dealing with the situation where the authority has decided to revoke or vary an improvement notice and the second dealing with where the authority have decided to refuse to revoke or vary.

2.100   The Act stipulates that the authority must state its decision and the reasons for its decision to revoke or vary or refuse to revoke or vary an improvement notice.[1]

2.101   If the decision is to vary, not to revoke or not to vary, the notice will not be valid unless the local housing authority also sets out the right to appeal under Sch 1, Part 3 and the time for appealing, which is 28 days.

2.102   Unsurprisingly the notification duty applies to all on whom the authority was required to serve the original notice and applies as well, to those on whom copies had to be served.[2]

Appeals against improvement notices and appeals against notices relating to revocation or variation

2.103   Under Sch 1, para 15(2), the appeal, whether it is against an improvement notice, or against a refusal to revoke, or against a refusal to vary, or against a variation of an improvement notice, is to be by way of a rehearing, but may be determined by matters of which the authority were unaware.

2.104   Grounds of appeal against an improvement notice are deliberately left open. Since the appeal is by way of a re-hearing the tribunal's jurisdiction does not exclude a challenge to the primary facts. An extreme example of this would be that the notice specifies the wrong property, but a more likely challenge might be to call into question the very existence of the hazard on which the notice is (allegedly) based.

2.105   The first specified ground of appeal is that one or more other persons (who also have to be served with copies of the notice of appeal),[3] as owner or owners of the premises specified in the notice, ought to take the action concerned or pay the whole or part of the cost of taking that action. Where this ground is relied on there are a number of

---

1   Schedule 1, paras 7(a), (b), 9(a), (b).
2   Schedule 1, paras 6(2), 8(2).
3   Schedule 1, para 11(2).

considerations which the tribunal must[1] take into account when dealing with the appeal; these are the relative interests, responsibilities and degree of benefit to be gained on the one hand by the appellant and to be gained on the other hand by those the appellant seeks to argue should do or pay for taking the action required under the notice.

2.106 The second of the specified grounds for an appeal is that serving an improvement notice is not the best course of action, which instead would be either (a) making a prohibition order, (b) serving a hazard awareness notice or (c) making a demolition order. In its deliberations on any such ground of appeal the tribunal is required to have regard to the Secretary of State's Guidance.[2] Further, if requested to do so the tribunal shall identify which of the options it considers is the best course of action.[3]

2.107 The appeal against the notice itself must be made within 21 days whereas an appeal against a decision in relation to revocation or variation has to be made within 28 days. See the fourth row in the quick reference guide, Table 2.6 at **2.97** above.

2.108 There is a discretion to extend that time if the tribunal is satisfied (i) that there is good reason for the failure to appeal before the end of that period; and (ii) is satisfied there is good reason for any delay since then in applying for permission to appeal out of time.[4] If an application is made for permission to appeal, the fact that the appeal might be unanswerable if the application was granted may or may not be relevant; it depends first whether there is sufficient explanation for the delay.[5] In the absence of good reason for being out of time the only option would be to look to see if there were relevant considerations which the authority were bound to consider before serving the notice/taking the decision which had not been taken into account and then on that basis inviting the local housing authority to reconsider.

2.109 In relation to decisions to vary, to refuse to revoke or refuse to vary, the only person who can appeal is the person on whom the notice was served. This means where there has been a revocation, others such as occupying tenants also served with a copy of the improvement notice, who might disagree with the revocation, cannot appeal. The alternative remedies, perhaps, if the decision-making process was flawed and they were sufficiently affected by the decision, might include a judicial review.

Procedure and appeals relating to prohibition orders

Service of prohibition orders

2.110 Service, which must take place within seven days of the making of the prohibition order, has to be on every person who the authority knows is an owner, or occupier of any part of the premises, on every person the authority knows is entitled or authorised to permit persons to occupy the whole or part of the premises, and on every

---

1   Schedule 1, para 16(3).
2   Schedule 1, para 17(2).
3   Schedule 1, para 17(4).
4   Schedule 1, para 14(3).
5   See *Short v Birmingham CC* [2004] EWHC 2112 concerning a statutory provision that allowed for an extension of time 'only' if the court is satisfied there is good reason for the delay. The fact the word 'only' is not used here may be taken as a ground for not excluding the merits.

known mortgagee of the whole or part of the premises. If the premises specified in the order consist of or include any external common parts the authority must also serve every person who to their knowledge is an owner or mortgagee of the premises in which the common parts are comprised.[1]

Fixing a notice to some conspicuous part of the building

2.111   If a notice is fixed on some conspicuous part of the premises that will suffice as sufficient service, save in relation to persons entitled or authorised to permit persons to occupy the whole or part of the premises; fixing a copy to the building will not suffice for those falling into this category.[2]

Notification duty in relation to revocation and variation of prohibition orders

2.112   Part 2 of Schedule 2 contains the notification duty where the local housing authority has decided to revoke or vary a prohibition order. The serving of notices relating to revocation or variation of a prohibition order must be within seven days beginning with the day on which the decision is made and service and has to be on those the authority would be required to serve with a prohibition order.[3] The authority must state its decision – and the reasons for its decision – to revoke or vary or refuse to revoke or vary a prohibition order.[4] If the decision in question is to vary, not to revoke or not to vary then the notice will not be valid[5] unless the local housing authority also sets out the right to appeal under Part 3 of this Schedule and the time for appealing.[6]

Appeals against prohibition orders and against decisions relating to revocation and variation of a prohibition order

2.113   The person on whom a prohibition order is served may appeal to a residential property tribunal. The appeal (whether the appeal is against a prohibition order or instead against a refusal to revoke, refusal to vary or a variation of Prohibition Order), is to be by way of a rehearing, but may be determined by matters of which the authority were unaware.

2.114   Any appeal has to be made within 28 days but there is a narrow discretion to extend that time.[7]

Grounds of appeal against prohibition orders and against decisions relating to revocation and variation of a prohibition order

2.115   Grounds of appeal against a prohibition order are deliberately left open, which is consistent with a re-hearing. But as with appeals against improvement notices, the statute contains a specified ground. This does not preclude other grounds. The specified ground

---

1   Schedule 2, para 2(3).
2   Schedule 2, para 2(5).
3   Schedule 2, para 3(2), (3).
4   Schedule 2, paras 4(a), (b), 6(a), (b).
5   Schedule 2, paras 4(c)(i), 6(c).
6   Which is 28 days; see Sch 2, para 10(2).
7   See the comments at **2.108** and footnote 5, p 39 above.

is that serving a prohibition order is not the best course of action, which instead would be either (a) making an improvement notice, (b) serving a hazard awareness notice, or (c) making a demolition order.[1]

2.116   The time limit to appeal decisions to vary, to refuse to revoke or refuse to vary a prohibition order is within 28 days of the date specified in the notice as the date the decision was made. See again, the fourth row in the quick reference guide, Table 2.6 at **2.97** above.

HAZARD AWARENESS NOTICES

History

2.117   Unlike the improvement notice and the prohibition orders, both of which can be traced back to previous incarnations, there is no precursor to the hazard awareness notice.

2.118   The 'minded to take action notice' required under para 3 of the Housing (Fitness Enforcement Procedures) Order[2] is perhaps the closest equivalent – but the power to make such notices (as well as all of ss 81 to 91 of the 1996 Act which dealt with deferred action notices)[3] has now been abolished. It is worth bearing in mind that the taking by a local housing authority of one course of action does not prevent them from taking other action in relation to the same hazard.[4] Therefore use of a hazard awareness notice, which allows for a warning to be heeded and voluntary action taken or representations to be made, is like a pre-improvement notice or pre-prohibition order procedure.

Commentary

2.119   A hazard awareness notice is a notice advising the person on whom it is served of the existence of a Category 1 hazard on the residential premises concerned;[5] the same wording is used in relation to a Category 2 hazard.[6]

2.120   The contents of a hazard awareness notice convey to the person served the same information as an improvement notice or a prohibition order but having advised the person served that a hazard exists on the premises concerned, the person served does not have to do anything. Therefore unlike the other notices, a hazard awareness notice does not have to specify the time within which action is to be taken, neither does it have to contain details of the right to appeal and the period within which an appeal may be made, as there is no right of appeal against the notice.

---

1   Paragraphs 7 & 8 of Sch 2, called an appeal under para 7.
2   SI 1996/2885, made in exercise of powers under s 86 of the Housing Grants Construction and Regeneration Act 1996.
3   See Sch 13.
4   Section 5(5); a formulation which means the hazard awareness notice is without prejudice to recourse to other enforcement action.
5   Section 28(2).
6   Section 29(2).

Proportionality

2.121   It is a little odd that a notice that advises the person served about the existence of a hazard can appear in a list of possible enforcement action, but it does. However, there is good reason to believe that the hazard awareness notice may be the course of action that local housing authorities most frequently use. With obviating the need for litigation and proportionality[1] in mind, the intention may be that use of the hazard awareness notice may be all that is required. The notice does represent the high water mark of a 'softly, softly' approach and may meet the same incredulity which met the introduction of the deferred action notice which some saw as an excuse to do nothing. One must recall that pursuant to s 5 of the Act a local housing authority has to take what it considers to be the appropriate action if a Category 1 hazard exists.

2.122   Since copies of the notice served must also be served[2] on every person who to the local housing authority's knowledge has a relevant interest (freehold, mortgage or lease) or is an occupier of the premises specified in the notice, one can imagine that authorities may want to wait and see what happens after such a notice is served: if the person served is cajoled into action, the need for other measures may be averted.

Requirements for a valid hazard awareness notice

2.123   Service of hazard awareness notices and the procedure for appeals is dealt with in Sch 1.[3] The requirements for a valid hazard awareness notice are set out in the following table.

Table 2.7   *Requirements for a valid hazard awareness notice*

The premises in respect of which a hazard awareness notice may be served	If the residential premises on which the hazard exists are a dwelling or HMO which is not a flat, it may be served in respect of the dwelling or the HMO.[4]
	If those premises are one or more flats it may be served in respect of the building containing the flat or flats or any part of the building or any external parts.[5]
	If those premises are the common parts of a building containing one or more flats it may be served in respect of the building or any part of the building or any external parts.[6]

---

1   If an authority has to ensure that the means used to attain a given end (the objective here is the removal or repair of a deficiency giving rise to an assessed hazard) should be no more than is appropriate and necessary for attaining that end, the authority which is not careful and jumps straight to stricter measures may be vulnerable to an accusation of acting disproportionately if there is no or insufficient justification for not having first tried such a notice.

2   See note 244 below. There is one disadvantage to a Hazard Awareness Notice which is that the person served, instead of doing the works as described in the Notice, deals with the hazard in a different and less satisfactory fashion, a process over which the authority would not necessarily have control.

3   Section 28(7).

4   Section 28(3)(a).

5   Section 28(3)(b).

6   Section 28(3)(c).

However, the notice may not be served in respect of any part of a building (which comprise flats) or its external parts which are not included in any residential premises on which the hazard exists, unless the authority are satisfied (a) that the deficiency from which the hazard arises is situated there, and (b) that it is desirable for the notice to be served in the interests of the health and safety of any actual or potential occupiers of one or more of the flats.[1]

Circumstances for service of a valid hazard awareness Order	(1) Where Category 1 hazard exists;[2] or
	(2) where Category 2 hazard exists;[3] and
	(3) where there is no interim or final management order in existence;[4] and
	(4) where such relevant guidance as may be issued pursuant to s 9 has been expressly considered by the authority.[5]
Where there is more than one hazard or more than one type of hazard	(1) The notice may relate to more than one Category 1 or Category 2 hazard on the same premises or in the same building containing one or more flats.[6]
	(2) A hazard awareness notice in respect of a Category 2 hazard may be combined in one document with a notice in respect of a Category 1 hazard where they are served in respect of the same premises.[7]
Contents of a valid notice	(1) The notice must be accompanied by a statement of reasons which explain why the authority decided to serve a prohibition order rather than use any other kind of enforcement measure available to them.[8]
	(2) The notice must[9] specify in relation to the hazard or to each of the hazards to which it relates:

- the nature of the hazard and the residential premises on which it exists;
- the deficiency giving rise to the hazard;
- the premises on which the deficiency exists;
- the authority's reasons for deciding to serve the notice including their reasons for deciding that serving the notice is the most appropriate course of action; and
- details of the remedial action (if any) which the authority consider it would be practicable and appropriate to take in relation to the hazard.

1   Section 28(4).
2   Section 28(1).
3   Section 29(1).
4   Sections 28(1)(b), 29(1)(b).
5   Section 9(2).
6   Sections 28(5), 29(4).
7   Section 29(6).
8   Section 8(3), (4).
9   Sections 28(6), 29(5).

Who has to be served with the notice	(1) In relation to licensed dwellings and licensed HMOs the notice should be served on the licence holder.[1]
	(2) If the dwelling or HMO is not licensed then the notice has to be served on the person having control or if an HMO then on the person having control or the person managing the HMO.[2]
	(3) In the case of a dwelling which is unlicensed or an HMO, which is also unlicensed, and is a flat; the local housing authority has a choice of who to serve, either the owner, the person managing the flat or the person who in the authority's opinion ought to take the action specified.[3]
To whom copies must also be sent	(1) Every person who to the local housing authority's knowledge has a relevant interest (freehold, mortgage or lease) or is an occupier of the premises specified in the notice.[4]
	(2) These 'copy' notices must be served within seven days of the service of the actual notice.[5]

ENFORCEMENT: IMPROVEMENT NOTICES

2.124   There are a number of ways an authority can enforce non-compliance with an improvement notice. Firstly, failing to comply is an offence, so the person on whom the notice was served can be prosecuted. Secondly, the authority can do the required works by its servants or agents with or without the consent of the owner.[6]

2.125   On conviction for failing to comply with an improvement notice the defendant can be fined up to £20,000.[7] The only statutory defence is reasonable excuse. This has to be read in conjunction with the ouster clause[8] to the effect that if no appeal is made against an improvement notice the notice is final and conclusive as to the matters which could have been raised on an appeal. Therefore, any attempt to argue in the magistrates' court that somebody else should take the action concerned or a different enforcement measure should have been used, will come up against the argument that the magistrates' court is not the correct forum, the points should have been taken in an appeal to the Residential Property Tribunal.

2.126   To assist it in exercise of its default powers the authority can ask the court to order that the occupier or owner allows action to be taken.[9] Once such an order is made against a person then he or she is liable to be fined up to £20 per day, for as long as the failure to permit access continues.[10]

---

1   Sections 28(7), 29(7) and Sch 1, para 1.
2   Sections 28(7), 29(7) and Sch 1, para 2.
3   Sections 28(7), 29(7) and Sch 1, para 3.
4   Sections 28(7), 29(7) and Sch 1, para 5.
5   Schedule 1, para 5(4).
6   Schedule 3, Pt 2, para 3.
7   Section 30(1), (4).
8   Contained in s 15(6).
9   Section 35 and Sch 3.
10   Section 35(4), (6).

Taking of action by agreement and default powers

2.127   The Act permits a local housing authority to take any action required to be taken by the person served with an improvement notice, if the person served agrees for the work to be done, understanding that the cost of such work as the authority carry out is at his or her expense.[1]

2.128   Where the authority believes that the person served is not making reasonable progress the default powers can be relied on even before the end of the period set in the notice for completion of the action.[2]

2.129   Before any default action is taken the local housing authority must first serve a notice.[3] The notice has to contain certain information. The notice must[4] identify the premises and the hazard concerned, the notice has to state that the authority intends to enter the premises, it has to specify the action the authority intends to take and finally it must set out the power – contained in Sch 3, para 3(4) – on which it relies to enter the premises, and enables it to take the default action.

2.130   Once seven days after this notice have elapsed and once the authority has begun the default works, it becomes[5] an offence, punishable by fine up to level 4 on the standard scale, for the person served with the improvement notice, or for any workman or contractor of such person, to just be on the premises for the purpose of carrying out any works. There is a statutory defence that the person was there to do works in order to prevent danger to persons occupying the premises.[6]

Recovery of expenses for taking action in respect of an improvement notice without agreement

2.131   Part 3 of Sch 3 concern the authority's ability to recover its expenses, which are a charge on the premises giving the authority the same powers and remedies under the Law of Property Act 1925 as if they were mortgagees by deed and including the power to seek appointment of a receiver.[7]

2.132   If the authority finds itself in the situation that expenses are unlikely to be recovered and a person is profiting as a result of the default action, eg obtaining rents which would not otherwise have been obtainable if the number of people were limited to that appropriate for the premises before the action was taken – in plain English letting rooms previously uninhabitable due to defects – then the authority can[8] seek an order from the Residential Property Tribunal that that person pays to the authority such amount as the tribunal considers to be just.

---

1   Schedule 3, Pt 1.
2   Schedule 3, para 3(3).
3   Schedule 3, para 4.
4   Schedule 3, para 4(2).
5   Schedule 3, para 5.
6   Schedule 3, para 5(2).
7   Schedule 3, para 13; see also s 50(11) which carries the same wording.
8   Schedule 3, para 14.

Appealing a demand for recovery of expenses

2.133   An appeal must be made within 21 days[1] of service of a demand for the payment of expenses. The appeal is to be made to the Residential Property Tribunal who can confirm, vary or quash the demand as it considers appropriate.[2] The scope of the appeal jurisdiction would therefore be like an assessment of costs, encompassing a dispute relating to the amount of costs as well as whether or not the sums were reasonably incurred, provided such argument does not require challenge to the works specified in the improvement notice, because that would be foreclosed, only arguable on appeal against the notice itself.[3]

2.134   If reasonable progress was not being made and a person authorised by the authority carried out the work and expenses are demanded, there is an additional specified ground for appeal. The recipient of the demand may defeat the demand by persuading the tribunal on appeal, that reasonable progress was being made towards compliance with the improvement notice.[4]

The effect of an operative demand for expenses incurred in carrying out works required by an improvement notice

2.135   Once the Residential Property Tribunal confirms a demand, and provided there is no further appeal or if there was no appeal in the first place, then the demand becomes operative.[5]

2.136   At this stage the demand is final and conclusive as to matters which could have been raised on an appeal.[6] Once the demand is operative the authority can require all future payments by tenants or licensees to be made to them instead of being paid to the landlord.[7] This power is hedged about by the need to serve a recovery notice which has the effect of transferring to the authority the right to recover, receive and give a discharge for rent or sums paid in the nature of rent.[8]

ENFORCEMENT: PROHIBITION ORDERS

2.137   Using premises or permitting premises to be used, knowing that a prohibition order has become operative is an offence punishable by a fine not exceeding level 5 on the standard scale.[9] The defendant to such a charge, who is convicted, is also liable to be

---

1   Schedule 3, para 11(2).
2   Schedule 3, para 11(5).
3   Section 15(6).
4   Schedule 3, para 11(4).
5   When an improvement notice becomes operative is dealt with under s 15; it is generally 21 days after service of the notice subject to the notice being suspended and subject to an appeal being made within those 21 days. The effect of an unsuccessful appeal is that the operative time is (see Sch 1, para 19(2)(b)) when the decision is given, save where the notice was already suspended in which case the operative time will be, if later than the time the decision is given, the time when the suspension ends. Once operative, the notice is a local land charge; see s 37.
6   Schedule 3, para 9(2).
7   Schedule 3, para 12(2).
8   Schedule 3, para 12(4).
9   Section 32(1), (2)(a); level 5 is £20,000.

fined up to £20 per day thereafter, for as long as breach of the prohibition order continues.[1] Again the only statutory defence is that the defendant had a reasonable excuse for using or for permitting use of the premises.[2]

2.138   Once a prohibition order has been made and becomes operative[3] possession can be recovered against protected tenants and assured tenants simply by serving a notice to quit, but only if possession is necessary for the purpose of complying with the order.[4] Similarly, nothing in the Rent (Agriculture) Act 1976 prevents the owner recovering possession.

2.139   In the circumstances of a contractual tenancy to which the Rent (Agriculture) Act 1976 or s 1 of the Rent Act 1977 applied there is a further defence to the offence of permitting use of premises in relation to which a prohibition order has become operative. A landlord would not be guilty of this offence whilst waiting for a notice to quit to expire, provided it was served on receipt of the prohibition order, because during that period he would not be permitting the tenant to use the premises. He has no power to evict without an order of the court and the court has no power to make such an order whilst the contractual tenancy still subsists.[5]

2.140   Once a prohibition order has become operative,[6] and where the whole or part of the premises specified in the order are the subject of a lease, either the lessor or lessee may seek an order from the Residential Property Tribunal determining or varying the lease.[7] All the circumstances of the case will be relevant[8] and the Act requires that before the order sought is made, that the tribunal gives any sub-lessee the opportunity of being heard.[9]

2.141   This provision in the Act follows the wording of the Housing Act 1985, s 317 which survives in an amended form, applicable to lessors or lessees of premises in respect of which a demolition order has become operative.

2.142   The fact that there is such duplication of provisions, where the Act repeats provisions already contained in the H A 1985, is consistent with all the provisions relating

---

1   Section 32(2)(b).
2   Section 32(3).
3   This is usually 28 days after the order was made subject to any appeal and subject to whether or not the order was suspended see s 24(2)–(6).
4   Section 33 which replaces HA 1985, s 276. The requirement for a notice to quit was confirmed by the Court of Appeal in *Aslan v Murphy* (1989) 21 HLR 532. The displaced tenant would be entitled to compensation under the Land Compensation Act 1973, s 29(7)(a) as amended by s 257 and Sch 15 of HA 2004; as well as re-housing: Land Compensation Act 1973, s 39 as amended.
5   *Aslan v Murphy* (1989) 21 HLR 532 at 542.
6   When a prohibition order becomes operative is dealt with under s 24; it is generally 28 days beginning with the date specified in the order (wrongly referred to in s 24(2) as the notice) as the date on which it is made. This is subject to the order being suspended and subject to an appeal being made within the 28 days. The effect of an unsuccessful appeal under Sch 2, para 7 is that the operative time is (see Sch 2, para 14(2)(b)) when the decision is given. If the order was suspended at the time of the appeal, the operative time will be, if later than the time the decision dismissing the appeal is given, the time when the suspension ends. Once operative as just described, the prohibition order is a local land charge: see s 37.
7   Section 34(2).
8   Section 34(7).
9   Section 34(4).

to the new kinds of enforcement action[1] all being in one statute. There is another example of this where the Act repeats an already existing provision relevant to demolition orders. This is the provision[2] dealing with savings for rights arising from breach of covenant. The Act does go one step further than the still existing, although slightly amended, equivalent provision in the 1985 Act,[3] which is that it includes that no action taken pursuant to an improvement notice or prohibition order affects any remedy available to the tenant against his landlord (whether at common law or otherwise).[4]

Power of court to authorise action by one owner on behalf of another

2.143   The Act enables a magistrates' court, if satisfied that the interests of the applicant will be prejudiced as a result of a failure by another person to take either (i) any remedial action required by an improvement notice; or (ii) any action necessary to comply with a prohibition order, to make an order enabling the applicant to immediately enter on the premises specified in the notice or order and take the required action.[5]

2.144   The order must fix the period in which the action can be taken,[6] and no order can be made unless notice of the application has been given to the local housing authority.[7]

EMERGENCY REMEDIAL ACTION

2.145   The Act enables the authority to take such action as the authority considers immediately necessary in order to remove the risk of serious harm to the occupiers of premises or to the occupiers of any other residential premises caused by a Category 1 hazard.[8]

2.146   The authority may[9] obtain a warrant from a magistrate and enter, at any time[10] (by force if necessary)[11] in order to carry out the emergency remedial action.[12] The

---

1   New kinds of enforcement action are referred to in s 1(3)(a).
2   Section 38.
3   HA 1985, s 307 as now amended.
4   Section 38(3).
5   Section 36 which follows a similar format to the equivalent provision in the HA 1985, s 318, which is amended rather than repealed.
6   Section 36(2)(b).
7   Section 36(5); local housing authority is defined in s 261(2).
8   Section 40. The term immediately was described by the Government spokesman in the House or Lords as connoting 'a crisis or emergency situation' *Hansard*, HL Deb, vol 664, col 283 (21 July 2004).
9   Section 40(8).
10 Section 40(6)(a).
11 Section 240(5).
12 Under Sch 3, para 3(5) the right of entry can be exercised at any reasonable time whereas, by contrast, under s 40(6)(a) the need to desist from entering unless at a reasonable time, is dropped. People living in premises subject to an imminent serious risk to their health and safety presumably would not object to disturbance from works that would otherwise only be permissible at reasonable times. Yet the fact that entry can be at any time, and not just at any reasonable time, throws added emphasis not only on the prior notice requirements but also on the authority being able to objectively justify their assessment of the seriousness of the risk.

magistrate has to be satisfied that there are reasonable grounds for believing that the authority would not be able to gain admission to the premises without a warrant.[1] The authority may meet this criteria if it is possible to demonstrate that access having been requested and refused, is not likely to be given or that waiting for it to be given (say because the occupier was temporarily absent)[2] would defeat the purpose of entry.

2.147 There are a number of requirements before emergency action can be taken. First is the existence in residential premises of a Category 1 hazard.[3] Second, the hazard must involve an imminent risk of serious harm to residential occupiers.[4] Third, no interim or final management order is in force in respect of the premises where the hazard exists.[5] Fourth, different notice requirements must have been complied with when the authority start taking the action.[6]

Notice requirements for valid emergency remedial action

2.148 Before entering any premises,[7] a notice must be served on every person, who to the authority's knowledge is an occupier of the premises concerned and if the emergency remedial action is going ahead in common parts of a building, on every occupier of the building.[8] This notice is to be regarded as served on these persons if it is fixed to some conspicuous part of the premises or building.[9] The notice so attached must[10] state:

- the premises and the hazard concerned;
- that the authority intend to enter the premises;
- the action which the authority intends to take; and
- the power[11] under which the authority intends to enter the premises and take the action.

2.149 Additionally within seven days the authority must serve a notice, and copies of the notice, on the persons on whom the authority would be required to serve an improvement notice.[12]

2.150 These persons are, in relation to licensed dwellings and licensed HMOs:

- the licence holder; or
- if the dwelling or HMO is not licensed, the person having control; or
- if an HMO, the person having control or the person managing the HMO.

---

1   Section 40(8)(b) which amends s 240 (Warrant to authorise entry) for the purposes of enabling an authority to enter to take emergency remedial action.
2   Which is one of the criteria in s 240(4).
3   Section 40(1)(a).
4   Section 40(1)(b).
5   Section 40(1)(c).
6   Section 40(7).
7   Section 40(5) and Sch 3, para 4(4).
8   Section 40(6)(b), which amends Sch 3, para 4(3) to the Act.
9   Section 40(6)(c).
10 Schedule 3, para 4(4) as amended by s 40(6).
11 Which would be s 40, s 240 and Sch 3, Pt 2, including the power conferred in s 240(5) to enter by force if necessary.
12 Section 40(7).

In the case of an HMO which is a flat, the local housing authority has a choice of who to serve: either the owner or the person managing the flat.

2.151   Copies must also be served on every person who, to the local housing authority's knowledge, has a relevant interest (freehold, mortgage or lease), or is an occupier of the premises in relation to which the authority have begun the emergency remedial action. If the premises are the common parts to a building containing one or more flats, the notice of the emergency remedial action must also be served on occupiers of any part of the building.[1]

2.152   The notice must specify:

- the nature of the Category 1 hazard and the residential premises on which it exists;
- the deficiency giving rise to the hazard;
- the premises in relation to which emergency remedial action has been (or is to be) taken, and the nature of that action;
- the power under which that action has been (or is to be) taken (ie s 40, s 240 and Sch 3, Pt 2, including the power conferred in s 240(5) to enter by force if necessary);
- the date when that remedial action was (or is to be) started;
- that there is a right to appeal under s 45;
- the period for making an appeal.[2]

2.153   The authority needs to have reasonable grounds for believing (a) the existence of the Category 1 hazard, (b) the existence of the risk of serious harm, (c) the fact the risk is imminent, and (d) that the imminent serious risk of harm is to the health and safety of occupiers of the premises or of any other residential premises. The third matter to be specified must give the recipient sufficient information to identify the premises and the works that are going to be carried out. The remaining matters to be specified include the time for appealing, which is 28 days.[3]

Recovery of expenses in relation to emergency remedial action

2.154   The Act imports[4] the provisions[5] from Sch 3 that govern the recovery of expenses where the authority has taken default action. These include that recoverable expenses of emergency action constitute a charge on the premises.[6] The result of taking the action could then mean that if the expenses were not met, the authority could apply for an order for sale in order to realise the moneys secured by the charge.[7]

Operative time for the purposes of recovering expenses incurred in relation to emergency remedial action

2.155   No amount is recoverable until the operative time. Provisions governing the operative time have to be understood in the context of the right of appeal to the

1   Section 40(6)(b)(i) and (ii).
2   Section 41(2), (3).
3   Section 45(3).
4   Section 42(3)(a) deems any reference in Sch 3, paras 6–14 to an improvement notice to be read as a reference to the notice served under s 41.
5   Part 3 of Sch 3: see **2.131** above.
6   Schedule 3, para 13.
7   See Trusts of Land and Appointment of Trustees Act 1996, ss 14, 15.

Residential Property Tribunal. The operative time is after the time for appealing has expired.[1] If there is an unsuccessful appeal the operative time will not be until the time for appealing to the Lands Tribunal has expired or if there is such a second appeal, the date the decision is given by the Lands Tribunal confirming the authority's decision.[2]

Emergency prohibition orders

2.156 The emergency prohibition order is an order imposing with immediate effect such prohibition or prohibitions as are specified on the use of any premises.[3] The authority can only use such an order if there is a Category 1 hazard, the hazard involves imminent risk of serious harm to the health and safety of any occupiers of those or other residential premises, and no management order is in force.[4]

2.157 The order may prohibit use of a dwelling; it may prohibit use of an HMO, it may prohibit use of a building which contains one or more flats or, if the prohibition relates to common parts of a building containing one or more flats, it may prohibit use of the building or any external common parts. External common parts can only be made the subject of a prohibition order if the deficiency from which the hazard arises is situated there, and it is necessary for such use to be prohibited in order to protect the health or safety of any actual or potential occupiers of one or more of the flats.[5]

2.158 Although the criteria for the making of such an order are the same as must be demonstrated before taking emergency remedial measures, the notice requirements differ.

2.159 The notice requirements are that copies of the notice must be served on the day the order is made[6] on every person who the authority knows is an owner or occupier of any part of the premises, every person the authority knows is entitled or authorised to permit persons to occupy the whole or part of the premises, and every known mortgagee of the whole or part of the premises.[7]

2.160 Valid service occurs if a copy of the notice is fixed to a conspicuous part of the premises in relation to which the emergency prohibition or prohibitions are imposed.[8]

2.161 The emergency prohibition order so served must[9] specify in relation to the hazard or each of the hazards to which it relates:

(a) the nature of the hazard and the residential premises to which it relates;
(b) the deficiency giving rise to the hazard;
(c) the premises in relation to which prohibitions are imposed;
(d) any remedial action which the authority consider would, if taken, result in revocation of the order;

---

1 Which is 28 days: s 45(3).
2 Section 42(4)(b)(ii).
3 Section 43(2).
4 Section 43(1).
5 Sections 43(3) and 20(3)–(5). Also see point 4 in the second column of the first row in Table 2.5 at **2.82** above.
6 Or if that is not possible – see s 43(4) – as soon after that day as is possible.
7 Section 43(4) and Sch 2, paras 1 and 2.
8 Schedule 2, paras 1(4), 2(5).
9 Section 44(2).

(e)   details of the right to appeal; and

(f)   the period within which an appeal may be made.[1]

2.162   Although some of the characteristics are similar, the contents of the emergency prohibition order vary in obvious respects from the contents of the emergency remedial action notice. An obvious difference is that an emergency prohibition order has to include a description of the remedial action which the authority considers would result in their revoking the order.[2]

2.163   Once served with an emergency prohibition order the recipient may apply for the order to be revoked or varied.[3] Further notice requirements arise in relation to the authority's decision to revoke or vary or their refusal to do so, against which there is also a right of appeal.[4] Section 43(3)(b) also carries across into the provisions dealing with emergency prohibition orders the contents of s 20(3)–(5) and s 22(3)–(5) which govern the contents of a prohibition order.[5] There is a further carrying across of the contents of s 22(7)–(9) allowing for approval by the authority of any particular purpose in premises subject to a prohibition order which have been explained at **2.83** and **2.84** above.

2.164   All the enforcement provisions relating to prohibition orders, eg making it an offence to knowingly contravene the order, that are set out in ss 32 to 36, also apply to emergency prohibition orders.[6] Similarly the supplementary provisions that apply to prohibition orders also apply. This means that an emergency prohibition order is deemed not to have been served if an interim or final management order is subsequently made in respect of the same premises.[7]

Appeals against an emergency remedial action notice or an emergency prohibition order

2.165   The ability to appeal is contained in s 45 which follows a similar format to that contained in Parts 3 to both Schs 1 and 2 which govern appeals against improvement and prohibition notices and appeals against decisions relating to variation or revocation of either of those notices. The appeal is to be by way of a rehearing, but may be determined by matters of which the authority were unaware.[8]

2.166   Persons served with a notice in connection with emergency remedial action can appeal against the action being taken.[9] A relevant person can appeal against the making of an emergency prohibition order. A relevant person includes every person who is an owner or occupier of any part of the premises in relation to which the prohibitions are imposed, every person entitled or authorised to permit persons to occupy the whole or

---

1   Required by s 44(3). The time for appealing is 28 days (see s 45(3)), with a jurisdiction to extend time if the tribunal is satisfied that there is good reason for not applying in time: s 45(4).

2   Section 44(2)(d).

3   Sections 43(5)(a) and 25(8).

4   Section 43(5)(e) and Sch 2, Pt 3.

5   See the fourth row of Table 2.5 at **2.82** above.

6   Section 43(5)(b).

7   Sections 43(5)(c) and 39(2).

8   Section 45(5).

9   Sections 45(1), 40(7) and Sch 1, paras 1–4.

part of the specified premises, and every mortgagee of the whole or part of such premises (including common parts).[1]

2.167 It should be recalled that once served with an emergency prohibition order the recipient may apply for the order to be revoked or varied.[2] A decision refusing to revoke or vary can also be the subject of an appeal.[3] If an emergency prohibition order is revoked compensation can be sought.[4]

2.168 The destination of all appeals is to the Residential Property Tribunal who can confirm reverse or vary the emergency remedial action notice or confirm or vary the emergency prohibition order or revoke an emergency prohibition order from a date specified in the order. Any appeal has to be made within 28 days (in the case of an emergency remedial action notice) of the date specified in the s 41 notice and within 28 days of the date specified in the emergency prohibition order as the date on which the order was made; but there is a discretion to extend that time.[5]

DEMOLITION ORDERS AND SLUM CLEARANCE DECLARATIONS

2.169 These provisions amend existing legislation to align it with the new hazard assessment and enforcement provisions in Part 1 of the Act.

Demolition orders

The old law

2.170 A demolition order – see the HA 1985, s 267 – is an order that requires that within a specified period a dwelling house (that is not a flat or, if an HMO, that the HMO is not a flat), be vacated and thereafter demolished. In s 265 of the HA 1985 the circumstances giving rise to making of a demolition order were:

(a)   that premises were unfit for human habitation;
(b)   the owner or mortgagee had failed to offer an undertaking to make the house fit or not to use the house, or such undertaking that had been offered was unacceptable; or where an undertaking had been accepted, the party giving the undertaking failed to comply with the terms of their undertaking;
(c)   demolition would not be inappropriate because of its effect on another building.

In 1989 the circumstances giving rise to the making of such an order were changed to where the authority were satisfied it was the most satisfactory course of action. The Act now re-amends the HA 1985, s 265.[6]

---

1   Section 45(7) and Sch 2, para 16.
2   Sections 43(5)(a) and 25(8).
3   Section 43(5)(e).
4   The Act inserts new ss 584A and 584B into the HA 1985 (by Sch 15, paras 30 and 31), which govern compensation (see s 43(5)(f)) calculated by reference to diminution of the compulsory purchase value of the owner's interest in the premises caused by the making of the emergency prohibition order. The compensation is repayable if the emergency prohibition order is revoked.
5   See the discussion at **2.108** above.
6   Section 46.

The new s 265 of the Housing Act 1985

2.171   The new HA 1985, s 265 is three times the size of the one it replaces. Given that one requirement for a demolition order was that premises were unfit under s 604 of the 1985 Act and given that the entire scheme of the new system for assessing the conditions of residential dwellings is built on replacement of s 604, amendments had to be made. The new s 265(1) inserts[1] the making of a demolition order into the list of options open to a local housing authority where it is of the view that a Category 1 hazard exists on any residential premises. Where a Category 2 hazard exists in respect of a dwelling or in respect of an HMO which is not a flat, s 265(3) includes the making of a demolition order into the list of options open to a local housing authority when considering the most appropriate enforcement action, but no order can be made unless the circumstances match those specified or described in regulations made by the appropriate national authority.[2] The current draft Guidance, apart from stating the obvious to the effect that the authority should consider the impact of the cleared site on the appearance and character of the neighbourhood and should consider whether or not the accommodation would be sustainable if the hazard was remedied, does not indicate what the prescribed circumstances for knocking down a building subject to a Category 2 hazard might be. Elucidation of the type of the prescribed circumstances the Secretary of State or the National Assembly of Wales envisage before demolition of a building subject to a Category 2 hazard takes place will have to await a further edition of this book.

Clearance areas

The old law

2.172   If a local housing authority declared an area to be a clearance area, all buildings in the area had to be cleared. A clearance area could be declared where an authority was satisfied of a number of matters, including that houses in the area were unfit for human habitation, that the most satisfactory method of dealing with conditions was demolition of all buildings and that the displaced residents could be re-housed. Once declared, the authority has then to set about purchasing the area and clearing it.

The new s 289 of the Housing Act 1985

2.173   The Act makes a number of changes[3] to an already much amended piece of legislation. Section 289(2) of the HA 1985 sets out the circumstances in which a local housing authority may include Declaration of a Clearance Area within the options available to it when considering the most appropriate enforcement action to deal with a Category 1 hazard.

---

1   An authority cannot (see s 46(5), (6)) decide that demolition is the most appropriate enforcement action if an interim or final management order is in force in relation to the premises concerned or if the premises are a listed building.

2   'Appropriate national authority' is defined in s 261(1). The Act refers to the Secretary of State, but there is no identified provision which exempts s 265 of the 1985 Act from applying in Wales. If in Wales, the Act should therefore be read as meaning a demolition order cannot be made for a dwelling or HMO which is not a flat or, in respect of a building containing one or more flats, if the hazard is merely a Category 2 hazard without the circumstances of the case matching those specified in an order made by the National Assembly for Wales.

3   Section 47 introduces new s 289(2), (2A) to the Housing Act 1985.

2.174 The circumstances are that:

(a) each of the residential buildings (defined by s 289(2ZC) as a building which is a dwelling or an HMO or is a building which contains one or more flats) contains a Category 1 hazard; and

(b) that the other buildings in the area are dangerous or harmful to the health and safety of the inhabitants of the area.

2.175 Section 289(2ZB) contains a similar provision where instead of each of the buildings containing a Category 1 hazard, each contains a Category 2 hazard.

2.176 In considering making a declaration of a clearance area, the draft enforcement guidance states at paragraph 4.20 that an authority should consider:

- 'the likely long-term demand for residential accommodation;
- the degree of concentration of dwellings containing serious and intractable hazards within the area;
- the density of the buildings and street pattern around which they are arranged;
- the overall availability of housing accommodation in the wider neighbourhood in relation to housing needs and demands;
- the proportion of dwellings free of hazards and other, non-residential, premises in sound condition which would also need to be cleared to arrive at a suitable site;
- whether it would be necessary to acquire land surrounding or adjoining the proposed clearance area; and whether added land can be acquired by agreement with the owners;
- the existence of any listed buildings protected by notice pending listing – listed and protected buildings should only be included in a clearance area in exceptional circumstances and only when building consent has been given;
- the results of statutory consultations;
- the arrangements necessary for rehousing the displaced occupants and the extent to which occupants are satisfied with those arrangements;
- the impact of clearance on, and the scope for relocating, commercial premises;
- the suitability of the proposed after-use(s) of the site having regard to its shape and size, the needs of the wider neighbourhood and the socio-economic benefits which the after-use(s) would bring, the degree of support by the local residents and the extent to which such use would attract private investment into the area.'

2.177 No declaration can be made if each of the buildings contains merely a Category 2 hazard unless the circumstances of the case are prescribed by regulations.[1]

2.178 Should the residential buildings in the area being considered for the subject of a Clearance Area Declaration on the above grounds comprise buildings containing flats, then the building can only be treated as containing a Category 1 or 2 hazard if two or more flats within the building contain such a hazard.[2]

2.179 Section 289(2ZD)(a) which further defines residential buildings excludes a building which contains only one flat (rather than one or more); in these circumstances there must be two or more flats. Therefore a building only containing one flat is not deemed to be a residential building and would therefore fall under the category of 'other building' for the purposes of s 289(2)(b) and s 289(2ZB)(b).

---

1   Section 289(2ZB)(c).
2   Section 289(2ZD)(b).

Clearance area based on bad arrangement or the narrowness or bad arrangement of streets

2.180   Section 289(2ZA) repeats the original s 289(2) in the 1985 Act. This is an additional power to declare an area to be a clearance area unrelated to the existence of a Category 1 or a Category 2 hazard. The authority can go ahead and make the declaration without the circumstances of the case being specified or described by an order made by the Secretary of State. Declaring an area to be a clearance area, under this provision, depends on the authority being satisfied that as a result of their bad arrangement or the narrowness or bad arrangement of their streets, the residential buildings in an area are dangerous or harmful and that the other buildings (if any) are dangerous or harmful to the health and safety of the inhabitants of the area.

Transfer of jurisdiction in respect of appeals relating to demolition orders

2.181   Appeals against demolition orders under the HA 1985, s 269 used to be to the county court. As a result of the amendments made by the Act,[1] s 269 is changed so that the destination of the appeals will be to the Residential Property Tribunal, with an appeal from there to the Lands Tribunal. Similarly the HA 1985, ss 317 and 318 dealing with matters related to the making of a demolition order and determination of leases, are changed, removing the jurisdiction of the county court and giving it to the Residential Property Tribunal. This is also true in respect of disputes in relation to the recovery of expenses in execution of the demolition order, achieved by introducing changes to the HA 1985, s 272.

MISCELLANEOUS PROVISIONS RELATING TO ENFORCEMENT

Recovery of expenses in relation to enforcement powers

2.182   The Act re-enacts[2] ss 87 and 88 of the Housing Grants Construction and Regeneration Act 1996[3] governing the different type of administrative work an authority can charge for in discharge of its enforcement functions under Part 1 of the Act. The chargeable items include the expense of determining whether to serve an improvement notice or make a prohibition order, and the costs of carrying out a review in relation to a suspended enforcement measure.[4] The provision also sets out who can be charged[5] and permits the national authority to require the service of the demand for payment to be in a prescribed form.[6]

2.183   Section 50(9) re-enacts s 88(5) from the HA 1996 and is in similar terms to Sch 3, para 13 of the new Act. The expenses incurred in deciding to take the enforcement action and serve the notice or order, whichever it is, are a charge on the premises giving the authority the same powers and remedies under the Law of Property Act 1925, as if

---

1   Section 48.
2   Sections 49, 50.
3   Which are repealed; see s 258 and Sch 16.
4   Section 49(5).
5   Section 50(1)–(3).
6   Section 50(13).

they were mortgagees by deed and including the power to seek appointment of a receiver. The Act permits a Residential Property Tribunal which allows an appeal against the underlying notice to require the authority to repay any amounts already extracted under the power to charge.[1]

---

1   Section 49(7).

Chapter 3

LICENSING OF HOUSES IN MULTIPLE OCCUPATION

INTRODUCTION

3.1 Part 2 and certain provisions in Part 7 of the Housing Act 2004 are aimed at fulfilling the Labour Party's manifesto commitments of 1997 and 2001 to introduce a mandatory licensing scheme for houses in multiple occupation (HMOs). The aim of this new regime is to provide greater protection for the health, safety and welfare of the occupants of HMOs. The provisions concerning information sharing and other technical issues relating to HMOs and other parts of the Act in Part 7 are dealt with in Chapter 11 of this book.

3.2 These parts of the Act and their associated schedules are designed to introduce mandatory licensing of larger, 'high risk' HMOs. These parts of the Act will also provide for a discretionary licensing scheme if local housing authorities consider extending the licensing system regime to other HMOs. The Act also amends the definition of an HMO. Part 7 of the Act contains the new definition of the HMO and a duty to maintain a register of all licenses granted under Part 2 of the Act.

3.3 The Act's licensing provisions are aimed at improving housing conditions in the private sector. The general view is that this sector contains some of the worst physical housing conditions and practices of housing management. In general housing bodies have welcomed the licensing provisions with many, including the committee of the Office of the Deputy Prime Minister, calling for the Government to extend the mandatory licensing scheme to all HMOs and for local authorities to have discretionary powers to license all private sector landlords. Private landlords, in general, do not accept that poor standards in this sector can be addressed satisfactorily by licensing. They draw on the experience in Scotland of mandatory licensing.

3.4 The House of Commons research paper[1] concluded that in spite of these drawbacks HMOs are viewed as providing an affordable option for housing, which is in many circumstances the only option for people on low incomes such as students, benefit claimants and persons seeking political asylum.[2] In the future it may be the case that local authorities make greater use of this housing sector as a means of discharging its statutory duties. Nevertheless, despite the size of this housing sector, a considerable amount of

---

1   Research Paper 04/02, 5 January 2004.
2   Regulatory Impact Assessment, Housing Bill Part 2 – Licensing Houses in Multiple Occupation, December 2003. http://www.odpm.gov.uk/stellent/groups/odpm–housing/documents/pdf/odpm–house–pdf–026058.pdf

research has demonstrated that some of the very worst standards of accommodation are found in HMOs.

3.5   The 1999 consultation paper[1] and the ODPM's risk assessment report identified the following risks associated with HMOs.

3.6   The English House Condition Survey found that there were almost 640,000 private rented HMOs in England (including buildings converted to self-contained flats). While standards are poorest in the private rented sector generally, the very worst standards can be found in HMOs. The most common problems associated with multiple occupancy relate to poor fire safety standards, overcrowding, inadequate facilities and poor or unscrupulous management.

3.7   Research indicated that certain types of HMOs present significantly greater health and safety risks to tenants than comparable single occupancy dwellings. Risk assessment carried out by ENTEC for the Department of the Environment, Transport and the Regions on fire safety in HMOs concluded that in all houses converted into bedsits, the annual risk of death per person is 1 in 50,000 (six times higher than in comparable single occupancy houses). In the case of bedsit houses comprising three or more storeys the risk is 1 in 18,600 (sixteen times higher). The ENTEC report represents the only formal risk assessment available on HMOs.

3.8   Poor management and the presence of unscrupulous landlords can also increase health and safety risks for tenants even when the HMO is in an acceptable state of repair. Responsible landlords are less likely to exploit vulnerable or disadvantaged tenants and good management practice such as regular inspections can also reduce risks. Health and safety issues can also arise because of the occupancy profiles associated with HMO use. The behaviour of tenants with alcohol or drug dependencies or mental health problems can increase the risk of death or injury to both themselves and other tenants, accentuating the need for responsible and responsive management.

3.9   In parallel with HMO reforms, legislative proposals are also under way to re-cast local authorities' powers and duties with respect to house condition generally (see Chapter 2). The Housing Health and Safety Rating System (HHSRS) will apply to any unit of residential accommodation and to all landlords, and will be the principal tool in assessing physical conditions in HMOs under the licensing system.

3.10   A licensing scheme is viewed to provide proper enforcement of the HHSRS in the highest risk HMOs. Aside from physical standards in HMOs, the other main elements the reform focuses on are management competency and the 'fitness' of those managing or providing HMO accommodation. Licensing is aimed to ensure that those HMOs which present the most significant health and safety risks come to the attention of the local authority, placing a more direct obligation on landlords to provide acceptable standards.

The legal problem

3.11   The term HMO applies to a wide range of forms of housing normally in the private rental sector, for example, hostels, 'bed and breakfast' accommodation, halls of residence and supported housing regimes. Often HMOs are occupied by people living on

---

1   DETR *Licensing Houses in Multiple Occupation* (April 1999).

low income who are often part of vulnerable or disadvantaged groups. Housing conditions in HMOs may be poor with low standards of management and repair. Traditionally, these properties are viewed as the worst in the rented sector for safety, facilities, repairs and harassment of occupiers. Previous attempts at regulation have led to a confusing mish-mash of statutory controls that have evolved over several decades. As a result this Act will repeal Part 11 of the HA 1985. The Act will introduce a new regime that provides for a new definition of HMOs.

3.12   Section 345 of the HA 1985 defines an HMO as a house occupied by persons who do not form a single household. Attempts at improvements were made in the Local Government and Housing Act 1989. The government of the time expressed a desire to include parts of a building, namely flats in multiple occupation.

3.13   The problem in deciding whether a property comprises an HMO usually concerns whether or not the occupants form a single household and there are no definitive criteria for this assessment. This determination is a matter of fact and degree that depends on the circumstances of the individual case. The Department of the Environment has provided guidance on what factors should be taken into account by a local authority when considering whether a household forms a single household.[1] The vagueness of the definition has led to a number of legal challenges in the past.[2]

3.14   The Department of the Environment, Transport and Regions issued a consultation paper in 1999 in which it was noted that the existing definition of an HMO is unsatisfactory.[3] The paper noted that, on one hand, the definition is too wide in that it applies to types of buildings that do not require the same form of regulation as peoples' homes, for example accommodation for holidaymakers. However, on the other hand, the definition can be construed to be too narrow as, in some circumstances, it might not be applied to shared student accommodation.

3.15

Table 3.1   *Summary of Part 2 of the Act*

Section number	Summary	Comment
55	Application of Part 2 of the Act	Sets out the scope of licensing provisions under Part 2 and the general duties of LHAs concerning their licensing functions.
56	Designation of areas subject to additional licensing	Permits LHAs to extend licensing beyond the scope of mandatory licensing in s 55.
57	Further considerations in respect of section 56	Sets out further requirements that LHAs must consider before extending licensing.

1   Circular 12/93.
2   Cases. Section A of Library Standard note SN/SP/708.
3   DETR *Licensing Houses in Multiple Occupation* (April 1999).

Section number	Summary	Comment
58	Conditions of effective designation	Provides that designations for additional licensing schemes need to be confirmed unless covered by a general approval by the appropriate national authority.
59	Notification requirements concerning designations	Requires an LHA to publicise additional licensing designations according to provisions in regulations.
60	Duration, review and revocation of designations	Designation must from time to time be reviewed and can be revoked after a review.
61	Legal requirement for HMOs to be licensed	Every HMO to which this part applies must be licensed unless temporary exemption notice is in force or IMO or FMO in force.
62	Temporary exemptions from licensing requirements	Empowers LHAs to grant temporary exemption to licensing which would otherwise be required: Managers/owners taking steps to ensure HMO no longer needs a licence.
63	Procedure for applications for licences	Procedural requirements and fees.
64	Process of grant and refusal of a licence	Describes the grounds on which an LHA must decide whether or not to grant a licence.
65	Tests of suitability for a house for multiple occupation	Sets out what needs to be considered for a house to be suitable for occupation.
66	Tests of fitness and satisfactory management arrangements for a HMO	Sets out evidence that must be considered in determining fitness of licence holder.
67	Conditions in licences	Empowers LHA to include conditions in a licence relating to its management, use and occupation, and its content and condition.
68	General requirements and duration of licences	That a person controlling or managing an HMO must have a separate licence for each property.
69	Variation of licences	Powers to vary licences.
70	Revocation of licences	Provides for the circumstances in which a LHA may revoke a licence.
71	Procedural requirements and appeals against licensing decisions	Gives effect to procedural requirements and appeals procedures set out in Sch 5.
72	Offences: Licensing of HMOs	Creates an offence for managing an HMO without a licence: fine up to £20,000.
73	Other sanctions: unlicensed HMOs	Concerns rent repayment orders.

Section number	Summary	Comment
74	Further consequences: rent repayment orders	Rent repayment orders following conviction under s 72(1).
75	Other consequences: restrictions on terminating tenancies	Concerns loss of right of landlord to automatic possession under HA 1988, s 21, assured shortholds where HMO not licensed.
76	Transitional arrangements	Transitional arrangements for when HMO becomes licensed for the first time.
77	Meaning of HMO	Refers to ss 254–260 for definitions.
78	Index of defined expressions	Provides for definitions used in this Part of the Act.

3.16

Table 3.2　*Summary of Part 7 (HMOs) of the Act*

Section number	Summary	Comment
232	Register	Requires LHAs to keep an up-to-date register of all the licences.
233	Codes of practice	Empowers national authority to approve or modify codes of practice in relation to HMOs and non HMOs per Sch 14.
234	Management	Regulations for securing satisfactory standards of management.
254	Meaning of HMO	Definition of an HMO.
255	HMO Declarations	Circumstances where a LHA may declare a building an HMO.
256	Revocation of HMO declarations	Where HMO in force and LHA no longer satisfied of the declaration test: power to revoke declaration.
257	HMOs: certain converted blocks of flats	Defines 'certain blocks of flats' that are classified as an HMO.
258	HMOs: persons not forming a single household	Provides a definition for not a single household.
259	HMOs: persons treated as occupying premises as only or main residence	Criteria for test of occupancy as only or main residence.
260–270	Definitions associated with these provisions in Part 7	Index of definitions: see Chapter 11 for details.

3.17

Table 3.3 *Summary of Schedules concerning HMOs*

Schedule number	Summary	Comment
Schedule 4	Licences: mandatory conditions	Sets out mandatory conditions that are to be attached to licences granted under Part 2.
Schedule 5	Licences: procedures and appeals	Details of procedure for appeals.
Schedule 14	Exemption of certain buildings from definition of HMO	Describes buildings that are not HMOs for the purposes of this Act except for Part 1.

THE PROVISIONS IN DETAIL

Introductory provisions

3.18   Section 55 concerns the general provisions of licensing to which this part of the Act applies. The section imposes a duty on all local housing authorities to operate a licensing scheme for HMOs that are specified by the appropriate national authority. The HMOs which are to be licensed under Part 2 fall into two groups:

(1)   the scope of mandatory licensing as defined by regulations. It is intended that this should cover HMOs of three storeys and above in which at least five people live;
(2)   specified in additional licensing schemes made by the local housing authority under s 56.

3.19   Section 55(5) requires local housing authorities to make arrangements for implementing the licensing regime and to ensure that the applications for licences are dealt with within a reasonable time frame. Moreover, local housing authorities are required to satisfy themselves that within five years Part 1 functions need not be exercised in respect of the HMOs where licence applications have been made. It is the intention of the legislation that no HMO which is licensable requires action to be taken concerning a Category 1 or 2 hazard.

3.20   Section 56 permits local housing authorities to extend the licensing of HMOs beyond the requirements of mandatory licensing provided for by s 55. The local housing authority may designate part or all of its area as subject to its additional licensing regime for specified types of HMOs. The local authority has an obligation to consult on any additional licensing scheme with those who are likely to be affected by it.

3.21   Local housing authorities are obliged to make a determination that the management of the specified HMOs is causing problems before the local housing authority can make a designation to license them. A local housing authority when considering the quality of the management of an HMO ought to take into account the level of adherence to relevant codes of practice (s 233).

3.22   Section 57 provides for further requirements that the local housing authority must consider before extending licensing to HMOs beyond the mandatory scheme:

(1) ensuring that the extension of licensing accords with the local housing authority's housing strategy and is part of a co-ordinated approach to deal with wider issues such as management of anti-social behaviour;

(2) examining whether there are other courses of action, other than licensing, that may be used to deal with the identified problem, for example a voluntary accreditation scheme, and to conclude that extra licensing, either on its own or in conjunction with other approaches, will make a significant difference when dealing with the problems.

3.23 Section 57(5) provides the definition of anti-social behaviour for the purposes of the Act. Anti-social behaviour is defined as:

'Conduct on the part of occupiers of, or visitors to, residential premises which causes or is likely to cause a nuisance or annoyance to persons residing, visiting or otherwise engaged in lawful activities in the vicinity of such premises; or which involves or is likely to involve the use of such premises for illegal purposes.'

Designation of additional licensing areas

3.24 Sections 58, 59 and 60 concern the introduction and operation of additional licensing schemes. Section 58 provides that additional licensing schemes must either:

(1) be specifically approved by the appropriate national authority; or
(2) must meet the description of a generally approved class of designation.

In either case the scheme cannot start before three months after the designation has been made.

3.25 Section 59 provides that when a designation is made or confirmed by the local housing authority the authority should publish a notice providing prescribed information about the designation and or its confirmation. Section 59 requires the local housing authority to make this information available to the public.

3.26 Section 60 requires a designation to last no longer than five years. A local housing authority must, from time to time, review a designation. Section 60 provides the local housing authority with the power to revoke designations if they are not securing the aims. These revocations will take effect when specified. On revocation of the designation the local housing authority must publish a notice of the revocation in a manner prescribed by regulations.

Mandatory licensing

3.27 Section 61 provides that every HMO under this Part must be licensed other than an HMO covered by a temporary exemption notice or which is subject to an IMO or FMO. Section 61 provides an explanation of the licence. It explains that a licence authorises occupation of the HMO by no more than the maximum number of persons specified in the licence. Section 61 also provides an appropriate national authority with a discretionary power to make regulations to determine when licensing provisions apply in the case of certain converted blocks of flats (see s 257).

3.28   Section 61 places a duty on local housing authorities to take reasonable steps to ensure that applications for licences are made to them in respect of the HMOs that are required to be licensed in their area.

3.29   Section 62 provides for temporary exemptions from the licensing requirements. Under this section, a local housing authority has a discretionary power to serve a temporary exemption notice on managers or owners of HMOs which are capable of being licensed, who notify the local housing authority of their intention to take particularised steps to ensure that their HMO no longer requires a licence.

3.30   Under s 62 a temporary exemption notice lasts for three months but is renewable for another three months in exceptional circumstances. If an exemption is not granted, the local housing authority must notify the applicant for de-registration of the decision, the reasons behind the decision, and the right of appeal against the decision with the time limits for making the appeal.

Debate on licensing

3.31   As described in the House of Commons Research Paper there was general support for this scheme of mandatory licensing from local authorities, the Chartered Institute of Environmental Health, Shelter, the HMO Network and the Campaign for Bedsit Rights. The thrust of this support was based on a need to drive up standards in multi-occupied houses. However, landlords and letting agents are not persuaded about the need to extend local authority powers of registration over HMOs.

3.32   The National Federation of Landlords (NFLR) pointed towards the problems with mandatory licensing in Scotland. In Scotland mandatory licensing of HMOs was introduced on 1 October 2000.[1] The aims and thresholds of the Scottish scheme were similar to those of the new scheme. Initially the threshold of the Scottish scheme was properties with more than five occupants but this was reduced in 2003 to cover all properties occupied by three or more people who comprise members of two or more families.[2] The Scottish scheme also covers communal accommodation such as student residences and RSL owned properties but since March 2003 public bodies have been able to 'self certificate' their HMOs.[3]

3.33   The NFLR's publication stated that the new licensing scheme in Scotland had been met with 'massive non-compliance'.[4] Hector Currie's review also found 'wilful evasion of the licensing scheme by too many HMOs'.[5] *The Scotsman* reported on 7 December 2002 that more than 50% of landlords in Edinburgh had yet to register under the Scottish HMO legislation. The NFLR argued that low rental income, which was exacerbated by delays in housing benefits, was a crucial factor behind poor conditions and the standards of management of HMOs.

> 'The conclusion of landlords is that the proposed licensing solution is misconceived and is likely to backfire in practice. Moreover, the problems in HMOs are largely a function of the

---

1   Order made under the Civic Government (Scotland) Act 1982.
2   Scottish Executive Press Notice, 1 October 2003, *Tenants to get greater protection*.
3   Scottish Executive Press Notice, 19 March 2003, *New rules for multiple occupancy*.
4   Residential Renting, Issue 18, November 2001, pp 30–31.
5   *Review of the First Year of Mandatory Licensing of HMOs in Scotland*, Scottish Executive Research, 2002.

lowish levels of rental income, the age of the dwellings and the nature, attitude and behaviour of some of the tenants. Overall, however, 78% of all private tenants are very or fairly satisfied with their landlord, against 73% of housing association tenants and 67% of council tenants.'[1]

3.34 The NFLR favoured the approach to tackling fire problems in HMOs by improvements in technology through installing safety equipment and taking other safety measures and the education of both tenants and landlords about bad practice and how to deal with fires.[2] The NFLR argued for a reappraisal of the need for a mandatory licensing system as 'there have been fundamental developments which question the whole strategy of licensing' since the ENTEC research on fire fatalities was concluded.[3]

Grant or refusal of licences

3.35 Section 63 concerns the process of application for a licence. An application for a licence must be made to a local housing authority in accordance with its requirements that may include the payment of a fee that the local housing authority may determine. An appropriate national authority has the power to make regulations concerning applications. This may include the contents and form of the application forms, the procedure for making applications and setting the maximum fee a local housing authority may charge. Section 52 also provides that, subject to any regulations, a local housing authority may take account of its costs in running a licensing scheme when setting the fee charged.

3.36 Section 64 provides for the conditions for the grant or refusal of a licence. Under this section a local housing authority has the discretionary power to grant a licence to an applicant or some other agreed person, or refuse to grant a licence. Section 53 provides that a licence may be granted if:

(a) the house is reasonably suitable for occupation by the number of persons or households specified in the application or determined by the local housing authority; or can be rendered suitable for that number of person by conditions in the licence;

(b) the proposed licence holder is a fit and proper person who is the most appropriate person to be granted the licence;

(c) the proposed manager of the HMO is a person having control of the house (or their agent or employee) and is also a fit and proper person; and

(d) the proposed management arrangements are satisfactory.

3.37 Section 65 provides for the tests of suitability for multiple occupation of a house. This section sets out the evidence and matters that must be considered for a house to be considered to be suitable for occupancy by a set maximum number of people or households. This section provides for a power to make regulations that sets minimum standards, for example as to the number, type and quality of washing facilities and food preparation facilities and other standards regarding equipment or facilities provided. It is open for the local housing authority to prefer higher standards than those prescribed in the legislation when determining the suitability of an HMO.

---

1   Residential Renting, Issue 18, November 2001, pp 30–31.
2   Ibid.
3   Residential Renting, Issue 23, August 2003, pp 14–15.

3.38 Section 66 provides for the tests of fitness and management arrangements. This section sets out the evidence and issues that must be considered by a local housing authority when determining whether a person is or is not fit and proper to hold a licence or be a manager of an HMO. The matters to consider include whether that person, or a relevant associate has been involved in:

(1) offences of fraud;
(2) offences of dishonesty;
(3) offences of violence;
(4) drug offences;
(5) unlawful discrimination in business;
(6) contravention of housing law;
(7) breach of applicable codes of housing practice approved under s 233.

A person will not be required to disclose a spent conviction.

3.39 Section 67 provides for licence conditions which can be imposed. This section empowers a local housing authority to impose conditions in the licence that it grants. Section 67 provides that these conditions could include restrictions or prohibitions on the use of parts of the HMO by occupants, or requirements to take steps to deal with the behaviour of occupants or visitors, or to ensure that facilities are in good working order to meet the fitness standards specified in s 65, or to carry out specified works or repairs within a particular time frame. Schedule 4 conditions are mandatory in all licences. A local housing authority is required to address general health and safety issues via its functions specified in Part 1 of the Act and not via the licence condition powers specified in s 56. However, s 67 allows a local housing authority to impose conditions that relate to installation or maintenance of equipment or facilities.

3.40 Section 68 provides for the general requirements and duration of licences. The section provides that a licence must not relate to more than one HMO. The licence is valid for a period that is specified in the licence, which can be no more than five years. However, a licence may be brought to an end earlier if there is non-compliance with a provision of the licence. A licence is non-transferable and upon the death of a licence holder, a three-month temporary exemption would automatically be granted. Section 68 allows for a renewal of the exemption for another three months.

Variation or revocation of licences

3.41 Section 69 empowers the local housing authority to vary the terms of the licence with the agreement of the licence holder or without their agreement of it appears to the local housing authority that circumstances have changed concerning the relevant HMO. The change in circumstances that a local housing authority may consider relate, in particular, to the number of persons or households that are permitted to occupy the HMO; or the standards of the accommodation required for a particular number of occupants.

3.42 Under s 69 a variation of the licence made with the agreement of the licence holder takes effect immediately. If the variation is made without an agreement it does not come into effect until the time limit for appealing the decision has expired, or any appeal against the decision has been disposed of in favour of the local housing authority or the appeal has been withdrawn.

3.43 Section 70 provides the circumstances in which a local housing authority may revoke a licence. The grounds for revoking a licence include:

(1) by agreement with the licence holder;
(2) where the local housing authority believes that the licence holder is no longer a fit and proper person;
(3) where because of the number of occupants or other current standards that apply the HMO would not have been licensable under its current conditions.

3.44 Section 70 provides for a power for the appropriate national body to make regulations setting down the circumstances in which a licence may be revoked.

3.45 Except when revocation has been agreed it does not take effect until the time limit for making the appeal has expired, or any appeal has been disposed of or withdrawn by the applicant.

Procedures and appeals

3.46 Section 71 gives effect to the procedural requirements and appeals procedures set out in Sch 5 to the Act.

Enforcement

3.47 Section 72 provides for criminal offences in relation to licensing of HMOs. Section 72 makes it a criminal offence if a person controlling or managing an HMO does not have the required licence. A person found guilty of such an offence will be subject to a fine up to a maximum of £20,000.

3.48 However, under s 72 a person does not commit an offence if they have an outstanding application for a licence or for a temporary exemption.

3.49 An offence is committed by permitting the HMO to be occupied by more persons than the licence permits to occupy it. This is punishable by a fine up to a maximum of £20,000.

3.50 Breaching any condition of a licence is an offence. Such a breach is punishable by a fine not exceeding level 5 on the present scale (currently £5,000).

3.51 It is a defence to any of the above if the accused person can demonstrate that they have a reasonable excuse.

3.52 Section 73 provides for further sanctions relating to unlicensed HMOs in addition to the above offences under s 72. Section 73 provides that during any period when a person is guilty of an offence of controlling or managing an HMO which is not licensed but which should be licensed, no rent is payable by the occupiers nor can a charge be made instead of the rent. An occupier's security of tenure is not affected by s 73 and nothing in it affects the terms of occupancy except for the payment of rent.

Further consequences

3.53 Where a landlord is actually convicted of an offence[1] and the local housing authority makes an application then the Residential Property Tribunal is required to make a rent repayment in respect of all housing benefit received by the landlord except in exceptional circumstances.[2] Under s 74 in all other circumstances the tribunal has a discretion to make a rent repayment order for an amount that is considered reasonable in all the circumstances.

3.54 A landlord who is required to have a licence for an HMO but, in fact, does not have one, loses the right to automatic possession of the rented property under an assured shorthold lease under HA 1988, s 21 (as amended).[3] The restriction on the use of s 21 ceases when a landlord makes an application for a licence or for a temporary exemption notice.

Supplementary provisions

3.55 Section 76 provides for the transitional arrangements for dealing with an HMO when it becomes licensed for the first time if more persons occupy it than the licence permits. It is a defence[4] that the licence holder is taking reasonable steps to reduce the number of occupants in order to comply with the terms of the licence. Section 76 also provides that an order made under s 270 may make provision in relation to HMOs that are registered under Part 11 of the Housing Act 1985 immediately before a requirement to obtain a licence applies.

Definition of an HMO

3.56 Sections 77, 254–260 of and Sch 14 to the Act provide the definition of an HMO. Section 77 defines an HMO in accordance with ss 254–260 and includes any yard, garden, outhouses and appurtenances linked to the HMO. Section 78 provides for the general definition of terms used in this Part of the Act.

3.57 The 1999 consultation paper proposed a definition of an HMO based on that adopted in Scotland:

> 'Houses which are occupied by persons who are not all members of the same family or of one or other of two families.'[5]

3.58 Respondents to the consultation expressed strong support for this definition.[6]

3.59 The Government has moved away from the initial proposal to adopt a broad definition with specific exemptions, and has instead drawn up a detailed and complex definition spanning ss 254–260 and Sch 14. The definition provided in s 254 means, in essence, that HMOs will comprise houses, hostels, self contained flats or other relevant buildings that are occupied by persons who do not form a single household, where there is a degree of sharing of facilities, for example for cooking, or where the housing lacks such

---

1   Section 72(1).
2   Section 74.
3   Section 75.
4   Section 76(4).
5   DETR *Licensing Houses in Multiple Occupation – England* (April 1999), p 18.
6   House of Commons Research Paper 04/02, p 34.

facilities or is not self-contained. Sections 255–259 refine this initial definition and Sch 14 provides for the exception of certain buildings from the basic definition.

3.60   Section 77 provides the definition of an HMO for Part 2 of the Act. It refers to the definition contained within ss 254–259 in Part 7 of the Act.[1] It also provides that the definition of an HMO includes, in the appropriate context, any yard, garden, outhouse or appurtenance belonging to or usually enjoyed in relation to the HMO or any part of it.[2]

3.61   Section 254 provides that a building or part of it (including attachments) is an HMO[3] if it meets the conditions set for the following tests:

- the standard test;[4]
- the self-contained flat test;[5]
- the converted building test;[6]
- a declaration notice is in force in respect of the property under s 255;[7] or
- it is a converted block of flats to which s 257 applies.[8]

The standard test

3.62   A building or part of it meets the standard test if the following applies:

- it consists of one or more units of living accommodation that do not consist of flats or self-contained flats;[9]
- the living accommodation is occupied by people who do not form a single household (see s 258);[10]
- the living accommodation is occupied by people as their 'only or main residence' or they are to be treated as occupying the building in such a manner (see s 259);[11]
- the occupation of the building by the people is the only use that building is put to;[12]
- rent or some other form of payment ('consideration') is provided by at least one of the people for the occupation of the living accommodation;[13] and
- two or more of the households that occupy the living accommodation share one or more of the basic amenities, eg kitchen or bathroom,[14] or the living accommodation is lacking in one or more of the basic amenities.[15]

---

1   Section 77(a).
2   Section 77(b).
3   Ibid.
4   Section 254(1)(a).
5   Section 254(1)(b).
6   Section 254(1)(c).
7   Section 254(1)(d).
8   Section 254(1)(e).
9   Section 254(2)(a).
10   Section 254(2)(b).
11   Section 254(2)(c).
12   Section 254(2)(d).
13   Section 254(2)(e).
14   See s 254(8) where basic amenities are defined for the purposes of this section to mean (a) a toilet, (b) personal washing facilities (eg sink or bath or shower), or (c) cooking facilities.
15   Section 254(2)(f).

Self-contained flat test

3.63   A part of a building meets the self-contained flat test if it consists of a self-contained flat and s 254(2)(b) to (f) apply.[1]

Converted building test

3.64   A building or part of a building meets the converted building test if the following apply:

- it is a converted building;[2]
- it consists of one or more units of living accommodation that do not consist of a self-contained flat or flats;[3]
- the living accommodation is occupied by persons who do not form a single household;[4]
- the living accommodation is occupied by those persons as their only or main residence or they are to be treated as occupying it in that manner;[5]
- their occupation of that living accommodation constitutes the only form of accommodation;[6] and
- the rent that is payable is provided by at least one of the people in respect of their occupation of the living accommodation.[7]

Exemption

3.65   Section 254(5) provides that for any purposes of this Act, other than Part 1, a building or part of a building within s 254(1) is not an HMO if it is listed in Sch 14.

3.66   Schedule 14 describes buildings that are not HMOs for the purposes of this Act apart from Part 1. The exempt buildings include:

- those managed or controlled by RSLs and other public sector bodies;
- buildings that are regulated under other legislation and prescribed as exempt;
- certain buildings occupied by religious communities;
- buildings occupied by freeholders and long leaseholders, with less than the number of prescribed licensees or tenants that are not converted blocks within the meaning of s 257; and
- buildings occupied by no more than two people.

3.67   Buildings that are managed by universities for the occupation by students are also exempt if the university is so specified as exempt in the regulations.

---

1   Section 254(3)(a), (b).
2   Section 254(4)(a).
3   Section 254(4)(b).
4   Section 254(4)(c).
5   Section 254(4)(d).
6   Section 254(4)(e).
7   Section 254(4)(f).

Regulations

3.68   Section 254(6) provides that the appropriate national authority[1] may make regulations to make amendments of s 254 and ss 254 to 259 as the authority considers appropriate with a view to secure that any building or part of a building of a description specified in regulations is or is not to be a HMO for any purposes specified in the Act. Also the appropriate authority may by regulations make consequential arrangements of any provision of this Act, or any enactment, as the authority considers appropriate.[2]

3.69   The regulations made under s 254(6) may frame any description by reference to any matters or circumstances whatsoever.

Debate

3.70   The House of Commons research paper reports that witnesses to the ODPM: Housing, Planning, Local Government and the Regions Committee's scrutiny of the draft Housing Bill identified problems with the new definition and the intention to exclude properties owned by certain landlords. A witness said that the definition was 'extremely complex and easy to misinterpret'.[3] Other witnesses argued that it was naïve to assume that all HMOs managed by RSLs are low risk and that the exemption of HMOs managed by educational establishments 'failed to recognise the risks facing students'.[4]

3.71   In 1999 the Independent Housing Ombudsman stated that Housing Corporation regulation alone cannot ensure RSL and Housing Association Homes are properly managed.[5]

3.72   On the other hand the Chartered Institute of Housing (CIH) supports the exclusion of RSLs as does the National Housing Federation (NHF) from the scheme. However CIH recommends a review of the existing regulatory mechanisms over HMOs owned by RSLs to ensure that they are of adequate standard.[6] The British Property Federation argued that the same regulatory regime should apply to all HMOs irrespective of the sector in which they are based.[7]

3.73   The ODPM Committee recommended a return to the original definition proposed in the 1999 consultation paper and the inclusion of RSLs into the definition of HMOs and properties owned by educational establishments.[8]

---

1   Section 261 provides that an 'appropriate national authority' means in relation to England the Secretary of State (s 261(b)), and for Wales the National Assembly of Wales (s 261(b)).
2   Section 254(6)(b).
3   The National HMO Network's written submission to the Committee (DHB 10).
4   The National HMO Network, NUS, Brent Private Tenants Group – evidence to the Committee.
5   'RSLs must be licensed' *Housing Today*, 8 July 1999.
6   Licensing HMOs; Response by the CIH, July 1999.
7   BPF response, 16 July 1999.
8   ODPM Committee. Tenth Report of Session 2002–03, The Draft Housing Bill, HC 751-I, para 51. http://www.parliament.the-stationery-office.co.uk/pa/cm2003/cmselect/cmodpm/751/751.pdf

3.74 The Government accepted that the definition of HMOs may require further work but rejected the inclusion of RSL properties and properties owned by educational establishments.[1]

Parliamentary scrutiny: 2003/04

3.75 The Joint Human Rights Select Committee[2] welcomed the Bill as a whole as a means of affording protection and enhancement of people's Art 3 and Art 8 rights under the European Convention on Human Rights. Moreover the JCHR considered that it provided a means of enforcing Art 11 (right to an adequate standard of living) and Art 12 (right to the highest attainable standard of health) of the International Convention on Economic and Social Rights (ICESR). However, they did express some concerns regarding HMOs.

> '**Licensing of houses in multiple occupation**
> 4.17 Part 2 of the Bill allows (clause 54), for the licensing of "Houses of Multiple Occupation" (HMOs). This generally applicable licensing regime is intended to apply to the "larger, higher-risk HMOs" (paragraph 15 of the explanatory notes). A LHA may also designate an "additional licensing area" where a wider range of HMOs are required to be licensed (clause 55). Part 3 allows for additional licensing requirements to be imposed on rented residential accommodation in areas designated as selective licensing areas (clause 76).
>
> 4.18 Clauses 63(3)(b), and 85(3)(a) make it a requirement for the grant of a licence under Parts 2 and 3 of the Bill respectively, that that the licence holder should be a "fit and proper person" to hold a licence in respect of residential accommodation.
>
> 4.19 In deciding whether someone is a fit and proper person the LHA is to "have regard" amongst other things to any evidence which shows that the person has:
>
> a) committed any offence involving fraud or other dishonesty, violence or drugs;
> b) practiced unlawful discrimination in relation to any business;
> c) contravened any provisions of housing or of landlord and tenant law; or
> d) acted contrary to the Code of Practice under the Bill.
>
> 4.20 The LHA may also consider evidence showing that a person associated with the prospective licensee has done any of these things, where such evidence appears relevant to the prospective licensee's own fitness to hold a licence (clauses 65 and 86).
>
> 4.21 Although such evidence is not determinative in relation to the grant of a licence, reliance on it raises issues of fair procedures under Article 6, since there is nothing on the face of the Bill which would allow the person applying for a licence to refute any allegations made. This is a particular concern since it does not appear that the evidence that may be considered relates solely to convictions or other authoritative findings of unlawful behaviour. Although we note that a full appeal is available from decisions on the grant of a licence, the potential for breach of Article 6.1 at first instance is a cause for concern. We recommend that Parts 2 and 3 of the Bill should be amended to allow a person applying for a licence under those parts the opportunity to refute any allegations made against him or her under clauses 65 and 86. We draw this recommendation to the attention of each House.'

3.76 In further scrutiny the JCHR noted:[3]

---

1   *The Draft Housing Bill – Government Response Paper*, Cm 6000, November 2003 para 25. http;// www.odpm.gov.uk/stellent/groups/odpm.housing/documents/pdf/odpm–house–pdf–025602.pdf
2   8th Report 2003–2004; HL Paper 49, HC 427; 8 March 2004.
3   10th Report 2003–2004; HL Paper 64, HC 503; 29 March 2004.

'**Licensing of houses in multiple occupation**

2.10 Parts 2 and 3 of the Bill provide for licensing regimes in respect of Houses in Multiple Occupation or other residential property. In our Eighth Report, we raised a concern about the potential for a licence under part 2 or part 3 of the Bill to be refused on the basis of representations that the applicant for the licence was not a "fit and proper person" to hold a licence, without the applicant having the opportunity to refute these allegations. We were concerned that, although such evidence is not determinative in relation to the grant of a licence, reliance on it may raise issues of fair procedures under Article 6.1 (the right to a fair hearing), in the absence of an opportunity to refute any allegations made.

2.11 In response, the department points out that under para. 5 of Schedule 5, if a local housing authority proposes to refuse a licence, it must serve a notice stating the reasons for refusal, and that it must then consider any representations made within 14 days (para. 12, Schedule 5). It points out that where a local housing authority refused a licence on the basis of allegations made against an applicant, it would have to specify these allegations in a notice served under these provisions and take account of any representations made to refute the allegations. We accept that this provision allows for sufficient protection for Article 6 rights.'

CONCLUSIONS

3.78 In conclusion we are of the view that the legislation here is incredibly complex and may be the subject of intensive litigation particularly in relation to the complexity of the definition of an HMO. Although it is our view that an effective licensing or management regime of HMOs is a welcome reform it remains to be seen, because of the complexity of the provisions and exemptions, how effective in practice this reform will be. It is our view that there may be some potential problems with enforcement of the provisions as there will be an immense administrative burden placed on LHA to produce consistent compliance and enforcement. It is also our view that an effective scheme of licensing and enforcement ought to extent to RSLs and other social landlords in order to be consistent and worthwhile. It is our view that the problems that have bedevilled the Scottish system of licensing HMOs may be replicated in England and Wales under the scheme presented in the Housing Act 2004. Although the statutory duties related to enforcement and compliance lie with local authorities, it is our view that, in order to produce effective and consistent compliance and enforcement, a great deal of oversight, monitoring and review by central government departments will be required. The latter form of oversight and regulation will require significant political will and resources.

Chapter 4

SELECTIVE LICENSING

INTRODUCTION

4.1   Part 3 of the Act supplements the HMO licensing provisions of Part 2 of the Act with innovative provisions for the discretionary selective licensing by local housing authorities[1] of all privately rented housing,[2] other than exempt housing, in a particular area. Selective licensing is needed in addition to the mandatory licensing of HMOs because HMOs tend to be concentrated in areas of non-low demand and the Government is concerned to address housing problems arising as a result of low demand for housing.

4.2   Selective licensing is potentially a powerful tool for local housing authorities to control the behaviour of private landlords. However, the statutory provisions are considerably constrained. Selective licensing is only available where certain conditions are met and where the local housing authority believes that it would reduce or eliminate specific housing problems.

4.3   The targeted housing problems include:

- low housing demand;
- anti-social behaviour;
- other (as yet unspecified) challenges in the private rented sector.

4.4   Selective licensing is designed to raise standards in private renting and/or to drive out criminal or unscrupulous landlords in particular areas where private renting is problematic for the wider community.

BACKGROUND

4.5   Selective licensing was first proposed in the Housing Green Paper *Quality and Choice: A decent home for all.*[3] Paragraph 5.34 suggested giving:

> 'local authorities discretionary powers to impose licensing of privately rented dwellings or of landlords on particularly problematic types of property, or neighbourhoods. In these situations, where some of the problems arise from a surplus of housing rather than a shortage, licensing would be unlikely to have the same damaging side-effects as elsewhere, though the

---

1   Local housing authorities are defined in s 261(2)–(5).
2   That is, landlords who are not local authorities or registered social landlords.
3   DETR (April 2000).

powers would need to be used highly selectively, following careful analysis of local conditions.'

4.6 The government housing policy statement, *The way forward for housing*, published December 2000, following analysis of the consultation responses to the Green Paper, indicated an intention to consult further on options to tackle the minority of bad landlords. The subsequent consultation paper[1] on selective licensing of private landlords set out the government's concerns:

> 'Areas of low housing demand face severe and complex problems of which the visible signs (abandoned houses, boarded windows and doors, vandalism and litter) are only symptoms. Economic change, greater mobility, and obsolete housing have contributed to falling property prices and an increase in private renting. This often attracts unscrupulous, even criminal landlords and anti-social tenants, who may have been excluded from social housing. Together they may force out law-abiding tenants and owner-occupiers. Tackling the spiral of decline represents a huge challenge, even if all the key players support plans for housing renewal, regeneration and crime reduction. The need to involve the private rented sector is widely recognised and in some areas private landlords and local authorities have worked together successfully. But the activities of a minority of landlords and tenants can still undermine the best efforts of local authorities, responsible landlords, the police and others.'[2]

4.7 The consultation paper rejected licensing of the whole of the private rented sector explaining that:

> 'licensing such a large highly fragmented and highly mobile market would be a massive undertaking. To require all private rented sector landlords to be licensed would be a major intervention in the market which could carry unacceptable risks to supply in high demand areas.'[3]

4.8 Government was, however, interested in selective licensing as part of its broader strategy to combat urban decline in areas of low demand. Other approaches to arrest decline in areas of private renting could include use of local authority private landlord forums, the accreditation of landlords, and crime and disorder strategies.

4.9 The House of Commons Research Paper[4] provides some evidence of the extent of areas of low demand and the expected impact of selective licensing:

> 'The Government estimates that there are around one million dwellings in low demand in parts of five regions in the north and midlands in England. Of these, approximately 640,000 are thought to be in the private sector. One in five of these are viewed as likely to be privately rented giving a total of 128,000 privately rented dwellings subject to low demand. In Wales there are an estimated 72,000 properties in the private rented sector as a whole. On the assumption that selective licensing will be taken up by a majority of authorities that have low demand areas, the Government expects that 75% of low demand dwellings will be required to obtain a licence in England. Work by the National Assembly for Wales has indicated that a further 32,000–40,000 properties will be subject to licensing in the Principality.'

4.10 Selective licensing will also provide local housing authorities with extensive information about private renting in the licensing area and allow them to target effectively information and guidance about the management of tenancies.

---

1 October 2001.
2 Selective licensing of private landlords: consultation paper, Chapter 1, para 3.
3 Selective licensing of private landlords: consultation paper, Chapter 2, para 17.
4 Research Paper 04/02, p 45.

4.11   The greatest concern about selective licensing is its extent. Private landlords worry about the implications of the costs of licensing for their business and whether it is appropriate that they should be made to control the behaviour of their tenants.[1] Equally, however, other professionals think the provisions are not extensive enough. The House of Commons Research paper reports that:

> 'The ODPM Committee took evidence from witnesses who thought that selective licensing as set out in the draft Bill would miss out some areas that suffer from significant problems. Mr Newey of the Royal Institute of Chartered Surveyors said: "Actually, in areas of low housing demand tenants can vote with their feet because there will be alternative accommodation, and therefore we feel that this should be amended to cover areas with high demand and a high percentage of tenants in receipt of housing benefit, and then we would support selective licensing."'[2]

4.12   The availability of special interim management orders for houses (see the discussion of the relationship between Part 3 and Part 4 at **4.15–4.18** below) which fall outside of Part 2 and Part 3 of the Act may go some way to addressing such concerns.

RELATIONSHIP BETWEEN SELECTIVE LICENSING AND OTHER REQUIREMENTS OF THE ACT

Part 2 provisions

4.13   HMO and selective licensing are designed to complement each other and will run in parallel. HMO licensing:

> 'will cover the types of accommodation that consistently pose the highest risks across the country as a whole allowing selective licensing to focus on the much more localised problems of low demand. Limited licensing would ensure that HMO licensing can also be properly targeted and does not come under pressure to tackle problems other than those caused by multiple occupation.'[3]

4.14   The extent of the similarities between the two schemes of licensing can be seen in the shared provisions of Sch 4 (Mandatory conditions for licences) and Sch 5 (Procedures and appeals) to the Act and the shared enforcement provisions.

Part 4 provisions

4.15   Part 4 of the Act contains long-stop mechanisms to be used when licensing fails. It provides for interim and final management orders which allow the local housing authority in particular circumstances to step into the shoes of a failing landlord and manage the rented house when there is no fit and proper person available to hold the licence under Part 2 or Part 3 of the Act. These enforcement measures are designed as measures of last resort to ensure that the property is managed responsibly and safely for

1   See, for instance, Stimpson 'The Housing Bill hijacked by the anti-social behaviour lobby' *Successful Renting* November 2004, p 3.

2   House of Commons Research Paper 04/02, p 47.

3   Selective licensing of private landlords: a consultation paper, ODPM 2001, para 52 available on www.odpm.gov.uk/stellent/groups/ odpm–housing/documents/

the benefit of occupiers or potential occupiers and others living or owning property in the vicinity.

4.16   Management orders are also available to the local housing authority in other circumstances. Part 4 of the Act enables a local housing authority to apply to the residential property tribunal for an interim management order on properties not subject to the licensing requirements of Part 2 or Part 3. The power is available if the property concerned is an HMO which does not require licensing under Part 2 of the Act[1] or if the property is one to which special interim management orders apply.

4.17   Special interim management orders apply to houses which would not be exempt from Part 3 of the Act[2] if they were in an area of selective licensing and are not in multiple occupation and there are particular problems of anti-social behaviour in relation to the house.

4.18   For instance, when the tenants of a privately rented house which is not subject to either mandatory or selective licensing behave anti-socially, the landlord fails to take action and the impact upon the neighbourhood is serious, then a special interim management order can be made to protect the health, safety or welfare of people occupying, visiting or engaged in lawful activities in the locality of the house.

RELATIONSHIP BETWEEN SELECTIVE LICENSING AND THE HEALTH AND SAFETY RATING SYSTEM

4.19   In general local housing authorities should deal with the need to identify, remove or reduce Category 1 or Category 2 hazards by the exercise of Part 1 functions and not by means of licence conditions. However, the government recognises that there is a duplication of potential remedies for poor conditions in Part 3 houses and local authorities have a choice over which avenue to pursue.

SUMMARY OF PROVISIONS

4.20   Table 4.1 sets out a summary of the provisions of this part of the Act.

Table 4.1   *Summary of the provisions*

Section	Summary	Comment
79	Described as an introductory section it sets out the scope of Part 3 of the Act including the exemptions from selective licensing and the general duties which are imposed on local housing authorities	The limited nature of the scheme is apparent from s 79. The scheme requires partnership between the local housing authority and the community and control from the relevant national authority.

---

1   Section 102(4).
2   See s 79(3).

Section	Summary	Comment
80	Describes the power of local housing authorities to designate areas for selective licensing	Designed to limit the operation of selective licensing to specific problems but allows sufficient flexibility to respond to as yet unrecognised problems.
81	Sets out the strategic considerations necessary before a local housing authority designates a particular area	Consistent with the Government's general strategic approach to housing problems: see for example the Homelessness Act 2002 and the Local Government Act 2003, s 87.
82	Requires that designation must be confirmed or approved by the appropriate national authority	A form of national control on local initiatives.
83	Provides for the publication of the making or confirmation of the designation	The consequences of the designation are extremely significant for private landlords and private tenants and therefore the information about designation must be disseminated as widely as possible.
84	Provides for the duration, review and revocation of designations	Designations last for a maximum of five years, must be periodically reviewed and may be revoked if the review indicates it is appropriate to do so – again statutory limits on the local operation of designations.
85	Contains the requirement that houses in designated areas are licensed, sets out the exemptions from the requirement and defines the meaning of licence for the purposes of this Part	Exemptions are: ● HMOs to which Part 2 applies; ● houses to which a temporary exemption notice applies; ● houses in respect of which a management order is in force.
86	Temporary exemptions from licensing requirements	Available where the house is required to be licensed, is not licensed and the landlord notifies the local housing authority of his intention to take steps to remove the house from the scope of selective licensing.
87	Sets out the process of application for licence including fee	Regulations will provide the details of the process.
88	Provides the basis for the grant or refusal of licences, in particular the 'fit and proper person' test and the need for satisfactory management arrangements	Fit and proper person test applies to: ● proposed licence holder; ● proposed manager.

Section	Summary	Comment
89	Sets out the evidence basis for judgement about whether the relevant person is a fit and proper person and whether the proposed management arrangements are satisfactory. In particular it provides that certain things must be taken into account by the local housing authority	The local housing authority must take into account: • particular offences including fraud, dishonesty and certain sexual offences; • unlawful discrimination; • breaches of housing law or landlord and tenant law.
90	Sets out the conditions which must be imposed, the range of conditions upon which the licence may be granted and the conditions which cannot be imposed	Sch 4 to the Act contains the mandatory conditions which mirror those required in Part 2 of the Act other than the requirement for references for intending occupiers.
91–93	Sets out the general requirements of selective licensing, including duration, variation and revocation	Maximum duration of five years. Can be varied or revoked within that time.
94	Provides that appeals and procedural requirements are set out in Sch 5 to the Act	Sch 5 contains extensive notification and consultation requirements.
95–98	Provides for (i) offences arising from failure to be licensed where required and operating in breach of licence conditions (ii) rent repayment orders (iii) restrictions on using notice only procedures set out in the HA 1988, s 21	• Serious criminal penalties – failure to be licensed maximum fine of £20,000; • operating in breach liable on summary conviction to a fine not exceeding level 5 on the standard scale; • complex civil remedies.

COMMENTARY

4.21   Part 3 of the Act sets out the selective licensing regime, the limits upon selective licensing, and the operation of the scheme. It also imposes a number of duties on local housing authorities[1] that introduce selective licensing. The legislative provisions reflect the tensions inherent in introducing an innovative scheme which has the potential to be used inappropriately by local housing authorities. On one hand it may be used too extensively; on the other hand it may prove insufficiently flexible to achieve its purpose. A series of checks and balances are inserted into the provisions to ensure that local implementation is controlled by national approval and given local legitimacy through consultation and information provisions. It is possible that these requirements will be too cumbersome for the provisions to be attractive to many local authorities.

The scope of the selective licensing system

4.22   The Act provides for certain limits on selective licensing. These are that:

- selective licensing can only operate in designated areas;[2]

---

1   Local housing authorities are defined in s 261(2)–(5) of the Act.
2   Section 79(2)(a).

- even within designated areas certain tenancies and licences are exempt from selective licensing;[1]
- the appropriate national authority[2] must approve the designation either generally or specifically.[3]

The limits are designed to prevent selective licensing turning into a national system of licensing of private renting – something the government has been determined to avoid.[4]

Designation

4.23 Local housing authorities can designate either their whole area as a selective licensing area or a particular area or areas within their district.[5] Before making any decision to designate the local housing authority must consult with people likely to be affected by the designation and consider their representations.[6] An area can be designated for selective licensing only in response to three sets of housing problems:

- problematic low housing demand;
- persistent anti-social behaviour; or
- other challenging housing problems.

Low housing demand

4.24 Before implementing selective licensing of an area of low housing demand the first decision that the local housing authority must make concerns whether the area is or is likely to become an area of low housing demand.[7] The ability to anticipate future low housing demand provides valuable flexibility to local housing authorities. In making their decision about the level of housing demand the local housing authority must consider:

- the comparative value of residential premises;
- the turnover of occupiers;
- the number of properties available to buy or to rent; and
- the length of time they remain unoccupied.[8]

The appropriate national authority has the power to vary these conditions by regulation.[9]

4.25 Having decided that an area is or is likely to become an area of low housing demand then the local housing authority must consider that the designation will, in combination with other measures taken in the area, contribute to the improvement of the

---

1 Section 79(2)(b).
2 The appropriate national authority – a definition which is necessary because of the devolution settlement with Wales – is defined in s 261(1) of the Act.
3 Section 82(1).
4 Lord Rooker made this clear in the Lords: 'The Bill will provide local authorities with new powers to license private landlords in areas of low housing demand and in areas suffering from anti-social behaviour, but they will not be able to go out on a spree, licensing willy-nilly for ideological or other reasons'. *Hansard*, HL 7, vol 662, col 84, June 2004.
5 Section 80(1).
6 Section 80(9).
7 Section 80(3)(a).
8 Section 80(4).
9 Section 80(5).

social or economic conditions in the area, before it can designate the area for selective licensing.[1]

Anti-social behaviour

4.26   In order to introduce selective licensing of an area because it is experiencing problems caused by anti-social behaviour the local housing authority must consider that:

- the anti-social behaviour is causing a significant and persistent problem;[2]
- some or all of the private sector landlords who have let premises in the area are failing to take appropriate action to combat the problem;[3] and that
- the designation will, in combination with other measures taken in the area lead to a reduction in, or the elimination of the problem.[4]

4.27   It is therefore not sufficient that there is a serious problem of anti-social behaviour in the area. There must also have been a failure of private sector landlords to respond appropriately to the problem.

4.28   The provisions also make it clear that government expects selective licensing to be one part of a strategic approach to the problem of anti-social behaviour. It could for instance complement the use of ASBOs or other work with the police or other agencies in the local area.

Other challenges

4.29   The Act leaves open the possibility that selective licensing could in future be used to deal with other problems associated with private renting. The scheme can be augmented by regulations made by the appropriate national authority[5] for example to deal with strategic regeneration, high housing benefit levels, or high levels of complaints and enforcement actions. The Government explained this flexibility:

> 'At this stage, we do not intend to use that subsection, but it allows us the flexibility to reconsider the conditions if the sets of requirements under subsections (3) and (6) turn out to be too restrictive and do not enable local authorities correctly to anticipate the sort of problems that will arise and deal with them at an appropriate time.'[6]

Strategic considerations

4.30   Decisions to designate areas for selective licensing must be consistent with the local housing authority's housing strategy and in particular it must co-ordinate its approach to the operation of selective licensing with its approach to the problems of homelessness, empty properties and anti-social behaviour.[7]

4.31   Selective licensing cannot go ahead unless the local housing authority has considered (i) whether there are other courses of action available to them to achieve the

---

1   Section 80(3)(b).
2   Section 80(6)(b).
3   Section 80(6)(b).
4   Section 80(6)(c).
5   Section 80(2)(b).
6   *Hansard*, House of Commons Committee, vol 417, col 252 (29 January 2004).
7   Section 81.

same objective,[1] and that (ii) making the designation will significantly assist them in achieving that objective.[2] The use of 'significantly' is notable. In effect local housing authorities will have to be clear that selective licensing will have positive benefits, will enable them to go a long way in achieving their strategic objectives and that it will continue to be necessary once other options have been taken into account.

The role of the national authority

4.32   Whilst the designation of an area as subject to selective licensing is essentially a local decision it requires confirmation by the relevant national authority.[3] Considerable concern has been expressed that the requirement would slow down implementation of selective licensing. The ODPM Committee on the Draft Bill[4] received evidence from authorities that the requirement to get Secretary of State (or National Assembly for Wales) approval prior to establishing a selective licensing scheme 'will unnecessarily delay implementation'. There was emphasis on the need to respond rapidly to changing conditions in their areas. The Committee recommended the removal of the requirement to obtain approval.

4.33   The Government rejected that recommendation. The need for confirmation was explained during debate on the Bill in Parliament as exercising an appropriate check on the actions of the local authority: 'It makes sense for the national authority to make the confirmation, because there should be some independent confirmation of a designation by the local authority.'[5]

4.34   There are two ways in which the relevant national authority can approve the action of a local housing authority. There can be:

- a confirmation of a specific designation. Following the confirmation there must be a period of at least three months before the designation will come into force;[6] or
- general approval for certain types of designation. Where general approval has been given the designation will not come into force until at least three months after the date of designation.[7]

4.35   General approvals can be given in relation to:

- designations by a specified local authority;
- designations by local housing authorities falling within specified descriptions of such local authorities, for instance beacon councils or councils rated as excellent by the Audit Commission could in future have their designations automatically approved under a general approval.[8]

4.36   The Government has indicated that they initially expect specific approvals to be required for designations but that as the national authorities gain confidence in the

---

1   Section 81(4)(a).
2   Section 81(4)(b).
3   Section 82(1).
4   ODPM Select Committee 10th Report, 2003, para 63.
5   *Hansard*, Commons Committee, vol 417, col 249 (29 January 2004).
6   Section 82(3), (4).
7   Section 82(5), (8).
8   Section 82(6).

activities of local housing authorities there is likely to be a move to granting general approvals. Their uncertainty and their concern that the scheme gains legitimacy are evident.

> 'Once the system is up and running, perhaps a lot more could be done through general approval than through individual confirmations. This is a new approach for everyone, so it is right to start off with a process of specific confirmations, and we should be slightly cautious at the beginning about how long things will take. The system is new, and when it is first implemented, we will have to be confident that a lot of factors are taken into account. Once the system has bedded down, it should be able to work swiftly and smoothly.'[1]

The duration of designations

4.37 An area will be designated an area of selective licensing for the period specified within the designation[2] which can be no longer than five years.[3] Local housing authorities must review the operation of designations[4] and have the power to revoke a designation following a review of its operation before it expires.[5]

Exemptions and exclusions from selective licensing

4.38 Once an area is designated, landlords or their managing agents will be required to obtain a licence in order to let or manage residential property unless:

- the properties are exempt; or
- excluded from the requirements of this Part of the Act because they are covered by licensing requirements of other Parts of the Act; or
- they have the benefit of temporary exemption notices.

4.39 Exempt tenancies and licences are:
- tenancies or licences granted by registered social landlords;[6]
- tenancies or licences categorised as exempt by the Secretary of State (in England) or the National Assembly (in Wales).[7]

4.40 This second exemption provides some necessary flexibility in selective licensing; for instance, properties subject to a demolition order may be excluded from the requirement to be licensed. The Government has indicated that local authority housing and housing currently excluded from statutory protection under the HA 1988, such as business tenancies and holiday lets will also be exempt.[8]

4.41 Certain houses are excluded from the requirements of Part 3 because they are subject to other regulatory mechanisms under the Act or the landlord is intending to give up renting out the property. These are:

- HMOs covered by Part 2 of the Act (see Chapter 3);

---

1   *Hansard*, Commons Committee, vol 417, col 251 (29 January 2004).
2   Section 84(1).
3   Section 84(2).
4   Section 84(3).
5   Section 84(4).
6   Section 79(3). For the definition of 'registered social landlord' see HA 1996.
7   Section 79(4).
8   *Hansard*, HL, vol 664, col 772 (9 September 2004).

- properties with the benefit of temporary exemption notices;
- properties subject to management orders under Part 4 of the Act (see Chapter 5).[1]

Temporary exemption notices

4.42 Local housing authorities can serve a temporary exemption notice when a landlord or a manager of a house which is required to be licensed but is not informs the authority that he intends to cease renting out the property.[2]

4.43 In such circumstances the authority has the power to serve a temporary exemption notice on the landlord or manager.[3] The notice exempts the house from the licence requirement for three months from the date of service.[4]

4.44 The local housing authority can serve a second temporary exemption notice providing a further period of three months exemption running from the expiry date of the first notice if the landlord/manager notifies it that it is required. The authority has to consider that there are exceptional circumstances that justify a second notice.[5]

4.45 If the authority decide against serving a temporary exemption notice it must serve a notice on the landlord/manager informing him of the decision, the reasons for it and the date of the decision. The notice must also inform him of his right to appeal to a residential property tribunal within 28 days of the decision.[6]

4.46 The appeal operates as a rehearing but the tribunal can take into account information which was not available to the authority.[7] The tribunal may confirm or reverse the decision.[8] If it reverses the decision it must direct the authority to issue the temporary exemption notice for a three-month period commencing from a date decided upon by the tribunal.[9]

Applications

4.47 Prospective licence holders must apply to the local housing authority for licences.[10] There is a fee payable which can be set at a level which takes into acount the cost of running the selective licencing scheme. The Regulatory Impact Assessment on this Part of the Act gives some indication of probable fee levels:

> 'Work carried out with the LGA on the costs associated with HMO licensing indicated that the average cost of a license would be approximately £100. We are seeking confirmation as to likely fee levels with the Local Government Association for selective licensing, but a significantly lower figure should be achievable. As property condition would not be of

---

1 Section 85(1).
2 Section 86(1).
3 Section 86(2).
4 Section 86(4).
5 Section 86(5).
6 Section 86(6), (7).
7 Section 86(8).
8 Section 86(9)(a).
9 Section 86(9)(b).
10 Section 87(1).

primary importance under this option licence fees should be significantly below this figure, therefore, an estimate of £45 per initial licence does not seem unreasonable.'[1]

The authority can determine the application process but the process will also be subject to regulation by the appropriate national authority.[2]

4.48   The regulations will prescribe in particular the maximum fees which may be charged by the local housing authorities and specify cases where no fees are to be charged or fees are to be refunded. The scope of a local housing authority to, for instance, charge differential rates for landlords accredited by them under voluntary accreditation schemes will depend on the regulations.[3]

4.49   The applicant may apply for the licence to be granted to himself or for it to be granted to somebody else, provided that he has that person's agreement to becoming the licence holder.[4]

The grant or refusal of licences

4.50   As the vast majority of private landlords operating in the designated area will require a licence to continue their business the grounds for the grant or refusal of a licence are of critical importance. Refusals to grant licences will in effect drive undesirable landlords out of business in that area. The Regulatory Impact Assessment acknowledges that there may be potential 'negative impacts' on areas not subject to licensing if 'problem' landlords and tenants are displaced to nearby areas. Avoiding these problems 'will entail looking at how the boundaries of schemes are defined to prevent displacement into neighbouring streets and the use of the scheme beyond currently low-demand areas where there is significant evidence that there is the potential for similar decline'.[5]

4.51   When deciding whether to grant a licence or not the local housing authority is required to look at three aspects of the management of the property and if these are satisfactory then it must grant a licence. It considers:

* the proposed licence holder;
* the proposed manager (if a different person from the licence holder);
* the proposed management arrangements.

4.52   The proposed licence holder is required to be:

* a fit and proper person to be the licence holder; and
* the most appropriate person to be the licence holder.[6]

In general the person having control of the house is the most appropriate person to be the licence holder unless the contrary is shown.[7]

---

1   Regulatory Impact Assessment, Housing Bill, Part 3 Selective Licensing, p 9, available at http://
     www.odpm.gov.uk/stellent/groups/odpm–housing/documents/page/odpm–house–029704–01.hcsp
2   Section 87.
3   Section 87(6).
4   Section 88(2).
5   Regulatory Impact Assessment, Housing Bill, Part 3 Selective Licensing, p 12, available at http://
     www.odpm.gov.uk/stellent/groups/odpm–housing/documents/page/odpm–house–029704–01.hcsp
6   Section 88(3)(a).
7   Section 89(4).

4.53 The proposed manager of the house, who can be either the person having control of the house or an agent or employee of the person having control of the house,[1] is required to be a fit and proper person to be the manager.[2]

4.54 The proposed management arrangements are required to be otherwise satisfactory.[3]

Fit and proper persons

4.55 In deciding whether someone is a fit and proper person to be a licence holder or a manager the local housing authority must consider evidence that the person has been involved in certain illegal activities which would make him unfit to be a landlord or manager.[4] These activities are:

- offences involving fraud or dishonesty, violence, drugs or any offence within Sch 3 of the Sexual Offences Act 2003 which are offences requiring notification;[5]
- unlawful discrimination on grounds of sex, colour, race, ethnic or national origins or disability in or in connection with the carrying on of a business;[6]
- contraventions of housing or landlord and tenant law.[7]

4.56 Evidence of these activities is relevant if either the person who is being considered as a licence holder or a manager was involved in them himself or if someone associated or formerly associated with the person carried out the activities and it appears to the authority that such evidence is relevant.[8] The association with the perpetrator of the activities may be a personal one, work related or on any other basis.[9]

4.57 Whilst the local authority must have regard to these matters it cannot assume their relevance but must determine this in deciding whether or not the person is fit and proper. Clearly it may be appropriate to overlook minor infringements of housing law or remote associations with rogue landlords.

Satisfactory management arrangements

4.58 Decisions about satisfactory management arrangements must take into account:

- the level of competence and the fit and proper character of anyone proposed to be involved in the management of the house;[10] and
- the suitability of the proposed management structures and funding arrangements.[11]

---

1   Section 88(3)(b).
2   Section 88(3)(c).
3   Section 88(3)(d).
4   Section 89.
5   Section 89(2)(a).
6   Section 89(2)(b).
7   Section 89(2)(c).
8   Section 89(3)(b).
9   Section 89(3).
10   Section 89(6)(a), (b).
11   Section 89(6)(c).

Licence conditions

4.59 Whilst the refusal of licences is concerned with driving out bad landlords, grants of licences are focused on improving management standards. The Regulatory Impact Assessment makes particular mention of this. 'Not all landlords who currently underperform do so deliberately – many are simply lacking in competence. Central to the idea of selective licensing is that landlords are helped to manage their property effectively.'[1]

4.60 Requirements for ensuring the protection of the safety and security of the occupants are particularly important. Standards are achieved by imposing conditions on the grant of a licence. Some conditions are to be imposed in all licences.

4.61 Schedule 4 to the Act sets out the mandatory conditions for the grant of a licence. The first four requirements[2] are identical to the requirements for licences granted under Part 2 of the Act. They are conditions relating to:

- the annual inspection by the local housing authority of the up-to-date gas safety certificate for the property (if relevant);
- the safe condition of the electrical appliances and furniture which must be declared safe to the authority on demand;
- the installation and maintenance in proper working order of smoke alarms which again must be declared to the authority on demand;
- the provision to the occupiers of the house of a written statement of the terms upon which they occupy.

4.62 There is an additional mandatory requirement for Part 3 licences. The licence holder is required to obtain references for people wishing to occupy the house.[3]

4.63 These mandatory conditions are interesting as they reflect current government concerns about the private rented sector. The first three relate to the physical safety of the occupiers. Their physical safety must be ensured and demonstrated to have been ensured. The fourth condition foreshadows the Law Commission's[4] proposals on compulsory written rental agreements and the final condition reflects concerns that landlords take insufficient responsibility for the character of their occupiers and the elimination of anti-social behaviour. The House of Commons Research Paper on the Bill[5] explained that:

> 'As part of the licensing regime landlords will be required to play their part in addressing the impact that their tenants have on the wider community. Landlords will not be held responsible for everything their tenants do, but they will be expected to respond to complaints about behaviour that impacts on others and explain that such behaviour is unacceptable. Landlords will be expected to take greater care over whom they let to by asking for references from prospective tenants. As part of this the Government expects that many local authorities will want to offer some kind of reference checking service for landlords as part of the licensing regime. This will not determine whether a landlord can let to a particular

---

1   Regulatory Impact Assessment, Housing Bill Part 3, Selective Licensing, p 7, available at http://
     www.odpm.gov.uk/stellent/groups/odpm–housing/documents/page/odpm–house–029704–01.hcsp
2   Set out in Sch 4, para 1.
3   Schedule 4, para 2.
4   See Law Commission Report *Renting Homes* (November 2003).
5   House of Commons Research Paper 04/02, p 46.

person, but it will provide the landlord with more information so as to be able to make an informed decision.'

4.64 Note that this final condition applies whatever the reason for the designation of the area. The appropriate national authority has the power to alter the mandatory conditions which must be included in licences.[1]

4.65 The local housing authority has the power to impose further conditions to regulate the management, use or occupation of the house.[2] In particular it may impose restrictions on the occupation of particular parts of the house or require the landlord to take reasonable and practicable steps to prevent or reduce anti-social behaviour not only by the occupiers but also by visitors to the house.[3]

4.66 Further conditions may be imposed to improve the standards of the facilities and equipment within the house and to ensure that they are kept in proper working order.[4] It is at this point that there is a potential overlap between the working of licences under this Part of the Act and the local housing authorities' responsibilities under Part 1 of the Act. However, the Act makes it clear that whilst in general the authority should use Part 1 functions where it is appropriate and not substitute licence conditions for the use of Part 1 functions, it is not prevented from imposing conditions in licences which are designed to achieve the same outcomes as would have been achieved by the operation of Part 1 functions.[5]

4.67 Certain protections are built in for people other than the licence holder. The authority cannot include conditions which restrict or oblige someone other than the licence holder to do something unless he or she consents to the condition, and licence conditions cannot alter the terms of the tenancy or licence of the occupiers.[6] This suggests that the conditions on the use or occupation of the house by occupiers discussed earlier are concerned with whether or not particular parts can be rented out at all or the conditions upon which they can be rented out, rather than requiring the person occupying them to do so in a particular restricted way.

The operation of licences

4.68 Licences granted to properties subject to selective licensing are valid for a maximum of five years[7] and can relate to only one property.[8] Licences are also non-transferable.[9] They end on the death of a licence holder[10] but for a three-month period following the death the property is treated as if a temporary exemption notice has been served.[11] This period can be extended for a further three months where the local housing authority serves a temporary exemption notice following a request by the

---

1   Schedule 4, para 3.
2   Section 90(1).
3   Section 90(2).
4   Section 90(3).
5   Section 90(5).
6   Section 90(6), (7).
7   Section 91(4).
8   Section 91(1).
9   Section 91(6).
10   Section 91(7).
11   Section 91(8).

personal representatives of the licence holder.[1] The normal appeals procedure for temporary exemption notices applies.[2]

4.69   Licences can be varied by the local housing authority either on its own initiative or following an application by the licence holder or a relevant person.[3]

4.70   A relevant person is defined as someone other than a licence holder:

- who has an estate or interest in the house other than a short term tenant;[4] or
- someone who manages or has control of the house;[5] or
- someone on whom the licence imposes conditions.[6]

4.71   Licenses can only be terminated under the Act in one of three ways:

- expiry of the time period;
- on the death of the licence holder;
- by revocation.

Revocation of licences

4.72   A licence holder will lose his licence in two main sets of circumstances. The first set of circumstances relate to the personal characteristics of the licence holder or other people.[7] The second set of circumstances relate to the condition of the house.[8]

4.73   Revocation as a result of the personal characteristics or behaviour of the licence holder or somebody else may occur if the local housing authority consider that:

- the licence holder or somebody else has committed a serious breach of a condition of the licence or repeated breaches of conditions;[9]
- the licence holder is no longer a fit and proper person;[10]
- the house is being managed by people who are not fit and proper persons.[11]

4.74   The licence may be revoked because of conditions relating to the property where the house:

- ceases to be a house covered by this part of the Act;[12]
- becomes the subject of a licence granted under Part 2 of the Act (ie an HMO – see Chapter 3);[13]
- becomes structurally defective to the extent that the authority would deny a licence if a new application were made.[14]

---

1   Section 91(9).
2   Section 91(10).
3   Section 92.
4   This is defined as a tenant with an unexpired term of three years or less: s 92(5)(a).
5   Section 92(5)(b).
6   Section 92(5)(c).
7   Section 93(1)(b).
8   Section 93(1)(c).
9   Section 93(2)(a).
10   Section 93(2)(b).
11   Section 93(2)(c).
12   Section 93(3)(a).
13   Section 93(3)(b).
14   Section 93(3)(c).

4.75 A decision not to revoke a licence where there is a serious breach of conditions would be subject to judicial review.

4.76 In addition licences can be revoked in agreement with the licence holder[1] or in circumstances prescribed by regulation.[2] An authority can revoke a licence either on its own initiative or following an application by a licence holder or a relevant person.[3] Relevant person is defined[4] to include the people set out at **4.70** above.

4.77 The date when the revocation comes into effect is either when it is made, if the revocation was agreed with the licence holder[5] or when rights to appeal against revocation expire or are exhausted.[6]

Procedure and appeals

4.78 Schedule 5 to the Act sets out the procedural requirements and the rights of appeal. These requirements apply to licensing under both Part 2 and Part 3 of the Act.

4.79 Decisions about selective licensing made by local housing authorities are subject to extensive notice and consultation requirements which are set out in Table 4.2. These are designed to ensure that all relevant people are fully aware of the decision making process.

Table 4.2 *Schedule 5 Notice and consultation requirements*

Para	When	Served on	Information	Together with	Consultation requirements
1–2	Before grant of a licence	Applicant and each relevant person	Reasons for granting the licence. Main terms of licence. End of the consultation period.	Copy of proposed licence.	Must consider representations made in accordance with the notice and not withdrawn.
3–4	After considering representations and when proposing to grant a modified licence (unless the modifications or further modifications are not material see Sch 5, paras 9, 10)	Applicant and each relevant person	The proposed modifications. The reasons for them. The end of the consultation period.		Must consider representations made in accordance with the notice and not withdrawn.
5–6	Before refusing to grant a licence	Applicant and each relevant person	The reasons for refusing to grant the licence. The end of the consultation period.		Must consider representations made in accordance with the notice and not withdrawn.

1   Section 93(1)(a).
2   Section 93(1)(d).
3   Section 93(7).
4   Section 93(8).
5   Section 93(4).
6   Section 93(5).

Para	When	Served on	Information	Together with	Consultation requirements
7	Following grant of a licence **and within 7 days of the decision**	Applicant and the licence holder (if different from the applicant) and each relevant person	The reasons for deciding to grant the licence. The date the decision was made. The right of appeal. The period within which an appeal may be made.	A copy of the licence.	
8	Following the refusal of a licence **and within 7 days of the decision**	Applicant and each relevant person	The decision not to grant the licence. The reasons for the decision. The date when the decision was made. The right of appeal. The period within which an appeal may be made.		
14–15	Before varying the licence (Unless the local authority consider that the variation or further variation is not material or – where the licence holder agrees the variation – the authority consider it unnecessary to comply with para 14 – see para 17 & 18)	The licence holder and each relevant person	Statement that the authority is proposing a variation. The effect of the variation. The reasons for the variation. The end of the consultation period.		Must consider representations made in accordance with the notice and not withdrawn.
16	Following a decision to vary a licence **and within 7 days of the decision**	The licence holder and each relevant person	The reasons for the decision. The date on which it was made. The right of appeal. The period within which an appeal may be made.	A copy of the decision to vary the licence.	
19–20	Before refusing to vary a licence	The licence holder and each relevant person	Statement that the authority are proposing to refuse to vary the licence. The reasons for the refusal. The end of the consultation period.		Must consider representations made in accordance with the notice and not withdrawn.

Para	When	Served on	Information	Together with	Consultation requirements
21	Following refusal to vary a licence **and within 7 days of the decision**	The licence holder and each relevant person	The authority's decision not to vary the licence. The reasons for the decision. The date upon which it was made. The right of appeal. The period within which an appeal may be made.		
22–23	Before revoking a licence (unless – where the licence holder agrees the variation – the authority consider it unnecessary to comply with para 22; see para 25)	The licence holder and each relevant person	Statement that the authority are proposing to revoke the licence. The reasons for the revocation. The end of the consultation period.		Must consider representations made in accordance with the notice and not withdrawn.
24	Following the decision to revoke a licence **and within 7 days of the decision**	The licence holder and each relevant person	The reasons for the decision. The date on which it was made. The right of appeal against the decision. The period within which an appeal may be made.	Copy of the decision to revoke the licence.	
26–27	Before refusing to revoke a licence	The licence holder and each relevant person	Statement that the authority are proposing to refuse to revoke the licence. The reasons for refusal. The end of the consultation period.		Must consider representations made in accordance with the notice and not withdrawn.
28	Following refusal to revoke a licence **and within 7 days of the decision**	The licence holder and each relevant person	The reasons for the decision. The date on which it was made. The right of appeal against the decision. The period within which an appeal may be made.	Copy of the decision not to revoke the licence.	

4.80 There must be at least 14 days from the service of the notice to the end of the consultation period. If more than one notice is served then the 14 days runs from the latest notice served.

4.81 Relevant persons are defined as previously explained – see **4.70** and Sch 5, para 13.

Appeals

4.82   The provisions on appeals are set out in Sch 5, Part 3 to the Act. Appeals against decisions made by local housing authorities are to the Residential Property Tribunal.

4.83   Appeals can be made against decisions to:

- grant a licence;
- the terms of the licence;
- refuse to grant a licence;
- to vary or revoke a licence;
- to refuse to vary or revoke a licence.

4.84   Appeals can be made by an applicant or licence holder as appropriate or any relevant person. Relevant person is defined as previously at **4.70** above.

4.85   Appeals must be made within 28 days of the date set out in the notice of relevant decision. An appeal may be made out of time if the residential property tribunal is satisfied that there is a good reason for the failure to appeal within the time limit. There must also be good reason for delay, if there is delay, in applying for permission to appeal out of time.

4.86   The Residential Property Tribunal hears the case as a rehearing of the decision-making but is able to take into account information not available to the local housing authority at the time of its decision.

4.87   The tribunal may confirm, reverse or vary the decision of the local housing authority and where appropriate may direct the authority to grant a licence to the applicant on the terms it directs.

Enforcement

4.88   The Act provides three different enforcement measures which are summarised in Table 4.3 below.

Table 4.3   *Enforcement measures for selective licensing*

Section	Mechanism	Sanction	Comment
95(1)	Criminal offence of having control of or managing a house without a licence which requires a licence	Maximum fine of £20,000	Very serious consequences for non-compliance – designed as an effective deterrent.
95(2)	Criminal offence of breach of conditions of licence	Liable on summary conviction to a maximum fine not exceeding level 5 on the standard scale	Less serious offence.

Section	Mechanism	Sanction	Comment
96(5), (6)	Local housing authority applies to residential property tribunal following the commission of the offence in s 95(1)	Rent repayment order which is a rent penalty may be made – repayment of the housing benefit to the extent that the tribunal considers reasonable	No requirement for conviction – so the local housing authority is not forced to proceed with potentially time consuming and costly criminal procedures.
97(2)	Local housing authority applies to residential property tribunal following conviction for offence under s 95(1)	Rent repayment order must be made – repayment of all the housing benefit paid to the landlord unless there are exceptional circumstances	Conviction of the offence makes obtaining a rent repayment order easier.
96(5), (8)	Occupier applies to Residential Property Tribunal following either the conviction of the landlord under s 95(1) or the local housing authority obtaining a rent repayment order	Rent repayment order of the rent paid by the occupier minus any housing benefit received to the extent that the tribunal considers reasonable	The occupier's rights are dependent upon action by the local housing authority.
98	The landlord cannot serve a s 21 notice whilst the house is unlicensed	The landlord is deprived of the notice only ground for possession	Mirrors the sanction for failing to comply with tenancy deposit scheme.

Offences

4.89　It is an offence for a person who has control of or manages a house not to have a licence if it is required.[1] The maximum fine payable following summary conviction is £20,000. There are three defences available to someone who does not have the requisite licence:

- he has a reasonable excuse for his failure;[2] or
- at the relevant time he has notified the local housing authority of his intention to cease renting out the property or otherwise no longer be subject to selective licensing and his notification remains effective;[3] or
- at the relevant time he has applied for a licence and the application remains effective.[4]

4.90　The notification or application remains effective if it has not been withdrawn and:

- the authority has not made its decision about the temporary exemption notice or the grant of a licence; or

---

1　Section 95(1).
2　Section 95(4).
3　Section 95(3)(a).
4　Section 95(3)(b).

- it has decided not to grant the temporary exemption notice or the licence and
- the period for appealing against the decision of the local housing authority or the decision of the residential property tribunal has not yet expired; or
- there is an outstanding appeal against the decision (including an appeal against the decision of the residential property tribunal).[1]

4.91　Note that the commission of this offence provides the factual basis for rent repayment orders – a civil sanction for operating a house which requires licensing without a licence. See below.

4.92　It is also an offence for a licence holder or someone on whom the licence imposes a condition or conditions to breach the condition(s). This is clearly a less serious offence and the fine imposed on summary conviction must not exceed level 5 on the standard scale.[2] The person in breach of the condition(s) is not guilty of the offence if he has a reasonable excuse for failing to comply with the condition(s).[3]

Rent repayment orders

4.93　The Government introduced amendments at the very late stage of the Third Reading of the Bill in the Lords to provide for rent repayment orders to replace the rent sanction which was to have been available against landlords. A civil sanction was believed to be necessary both as a disincentive to operating without a licence and to ensure that a landlord did not profit from illegal activity. The Government were particularly concerned to ensure that housing benefit paid in these circumstances could be recouped by the local housing authority. However, the Minister explained[4] that the amendments were necessary to 'recognise the widespread concern expressed about the practical application of the provisions, in particular, the absence of clear decision-making procedures and responsibilities, as well as the potential retaliatory action by landlords for occupants withholding rent'.[5]

4.94　Rent repayment orders are only available where a house is 'unlicensed'.[6] An unlicensed house is one which is required to be licensed under the Act but is not, and where either:

- no notification has been given that the house is no longer going to be rented;[7] or

---

1　Section 95(7), (8).
2　Section 37(2) of the Criminal Justice Act 1982 provides for a standard scale, giving maximum fines for an adult on conviction for summary offences, which are currently Level 1 £200, Level 2 £500, Level 3 £1,000, Level 4 £2,500, Level 5 £5,000.
3　Section 95(4).
4　*Hansard*, House of Lords, vol 666, col 329 (3 November 2004).
5　See, for instance, the House of Commons research paper which points out that 'the provision that no rent will be payable by the residents of an unlicensed licensable HMO is controversial. The ODPM Committee received evidence from witnesses who argued that the most likely result of this would be tenants losing their homes. For example, the Local Government Association said: "We can understand why the link between non-licensing and rent has been made but we do feel that puts the tenants in a very difficult position. Most tenants now have very little security of tenure and to put them in a position where they are not paying rent may lead some rogue landlords to evict them and find somebody else to come into the property."'
6　Section 96.
7　Section 96(2)(a).

- no application for a licence has been made which continues to be effective.[1]

4.95 Note that the complex rules about the effect of illegality of contracts do not affect the enforceability of the terms of a tenancy or a licence where the illegality is as a result of the landlord failing to obtain a licence for a house which requires licensing.[2]

4.96 Rent repayment orders can be made by a residential property tribunal following applications by either the local housing authority or by the occupier of the house. There are two sets of circumstances in which a local housing authority may apply for an order which are detailed below. Applications by occupiers are therefore dependent upon the success of an authority's application.

Applications by the local housing authority

4.97 First, local housing authorities can apply to the tribunal for a rent repayment order when they can satisfy the tribunal that a house which requires licensing is not licensed and none of the statutory defences are available.[3] There does not have to have been a criminal charge or a conviction for the offence for the application to be made.[4] This avoids local housing authorities becoming embroiled in resource intensive court work simply to recoup housing benefit. Where there has not been a conviction the tribunal has a discretion to make the rent repayment order but that discretion is constrained by a number of factors.[5]

4.98 What is required before the Residential Property Tribunal can exercise its discretion to make the order is that it is satisfied that:

- at any time in the preceding 12 months the appropriate person who has control of or manages a house which requires licensing did so without a licence;[6] and that
- housing benefit has been paid to anyone in connection with the occupation of that particular unlicensed house during the unlicensed period;[7] and that
- the authority has served on the appropriate person a notice of intended proceedings which conforms with the statutory requirements[8] and the period for representations by that person set out in the notice has expired;[9] and that
- those representations have been considered.[10]

So the local housing authority has 12 months within which to reclaim housing benefit paid out on an unlicensed house.

4.99 The notice of intended proceedings must:

- inform the appropriate person that the authority are going to apply for a rent repayment order;[11]

---

1   Section 96(2)(b).
2   Section 96(3).
3   Section 96(5), (6).
4   Section 96(6)(a).
5   Section 96(5).
6   Section 96(6)(a).
7   Section 96(6)(b).
8   Section 96(6)(c).
9   Section 96(7)(b).
10   Section 96(7)(c).
11   Section 96(7)(a)(i).

- set out the reasons for doing so;[1]
- state the amount being reclaimed;[2]
- explain the calculation of the amount;[3]
- invite the appropriate person to make representations to them within a period of not less than 28 days specified in the notice.[4]

4.100   The local housing authority must also ensure that the notice of intended proceedings is received by the relevant housing benefit department and that it is kept informed of the progress of the application.[5]

4.101   The appropriate person is the person who is entitled to the rent payable in connection with the occupation of the house – normally the landlord.[6]

4.102   The rent repayment order is for an amount which is reasonable in the circumstances[7] but cannot be for payment of housing benefit paid more than 12 months before the application to the tribunal.[8] In deciding what is a reasonable amount the tribunal must take into account:

- the total amount of housing benefit and rent paid during the period of the offence;[9]
- the extent to which that amount derived from housing benefit;[10]
- the amount which was actually received by the appropriate person;[11]
- whether the appropriate person has previously been convicted of an offence of managing or controlling a house which requires a licence without a licence;[12]
- the conduct and financial circumstances of the appropriate person.[13]

4.103   Secondly the local housing authority can apply for a rent repayment order following a conviction for controlling or managing without a licence a house which requires licensing.[14] If the tribunal is satisfied that housing benefit was paid to anybody in connection with the occupation of that house whilst the offence was being committed then it must make the order.[15]

4.104   In these circumstances the rent repayment order will require the appropriate person to repay the housing benefit he or she has received to the authority unless there are exceptional circumstances when the tribunal can only order repayment of an amount it is reasonable to expect to be repaid.[16]

---

1   Section 96(7)(a)(ii).
2   Section 96(7)(a)(iii).
3   Section 96(7)(a)(iii).
4   Section 96(7)(a)(iv).
5   Section 96(9).
6   Section 96(10).
7   Section 97(5).
8   Section 97(8)(a).
9   Section 97(6)(a).
10   Section 97(6)(b)(i).
11   Section 97(6)(b)(ii).
12   Section 97(6)(c).
13   Section 97(6)(d).
14   Section 97(2)(a).
15   Section 97(2)(b).
16   Section 97(4).

4.105 A rent repayment order can be enforced by a local housing authority as a legal charge on the house registerable as a local land charge.[1] If the authority subsequently grant a licence to the appropriate person or someone acting on his or her behalf it can include a condition in the licence requiring the appropriate person to discharge the rent repayment order.[2] If it subsequently makes a management order it can make the discharge of the rent repayment order part of the management scheme.[3]

Applications by occupiers

4.106 Occupiers can only apply for a rent repayment order to cover rent that they have paid during the commission of the offence which was not covered by housing benefit and when the appropriate person has either:

- been convicted of the offence of controlling or managing without a licence a house which requires licencing;[4] or
- had a rent repayment order made against them in respect of housing benefit.[5]

4.107 The occupier therefore is prevented from initiating action against the landlord when the local housing authority has not previously taken action.

4.108 The occupier's application must be made within 12 months of the date of the conviction or the rent repayment order whichever was later.[6]

4.109 The rent repayment order is for an amount which is reasonable in the circumstances[7] but limited to the amount paid by the occupier in the 12 months preceeding the application.[8] In deciding what is a reasonable amount the tribunal must take into account:

- the total amount of rent paid less any housing benefit received by the occupier during the period of the offence;[9]
- the amount which was actually received by the appropriate person;[10]
- whether the appropriate person has previously been convicted of an offence of managing or controlling a house which requires a licence without a licence;[11]
- the conduct and financial circumstances of the appropriate person;[12]
- the conduct of the occupier.[13]

The conduct of the occupier therefore becomes relevant when s/he is attempting to reclaim rent paid. This criterion may prevent or limit the extent to which anti-social tenants can benefit from the landlord's failures.

---

1   Section 97(9).
2   Section 97(12).
3   Section 97(13).
4   Section 96(8).
5   Section 96(8).
6   Section 96(8)(c).
7   Section 97(5).
8   Section 97(8).
9   Section 97(8)(b).
10   Section 97(6).
11   Section 97(6)(c).
12   Section 97(6)(d).
13   Section 97(6)(e).

4.110   The occupier can enforce the rent repayment order as a civil debt.[1]

Restrictions on terminating tenancies

4.111   The final enforcement measure is the removal of the landlord's right to automatic possession of the house following service of a notice under s 21 of the HA 1988. Section 21 allows the landlord of an assured shorthold tenancy to regain possession simply by waiting for a two-month period. This will not be available to a landlord where the house is unlicensed. The landlord will be forced to go through the expense and delay of a full court hearing. This is a simple enforcement measure which can be easily policed by the county court and is likely to act as a substantial deterrent to operating without a licence. It also mirors the sanction provided in licensing in Part 6 of the Act in respect of the tenancy deposit scheme.

Duties on housing authorities

4.112   There is a clear tension between the desire to have control of the worst landlords and the desire for there to be limits on the action of local housing authorities in connection with selective licensing. These are most evident in the range of duties imposed by the Act upon on local housing authorities. We have described many of these in the commentary to the sections. However, it is useful to bring the duties together in one place both as a checklist and set these out in Table 4.4. Note that this Table does not include the notification and consultation duties set out in Sch 5 to the Act which we have detailed in Table 4.3.

Table 4.4   *Duties on local housing authorities under Part 3*

Section	Local housing authorities must	Comment
79(5)(a)	ensure effective implemention of selective licensing	General duty enforceable by judicial review.
79(5)(b)	ensure that all applications for licences and other issues are determined in a reasonable time	General duty enforceable by judicial review. The government gave an indication in Committee[2] that six weeks would in most cases be an appropriate time scale for decision making.
80(2)	consider that the first or second set of general conditions or any additional set of conditions prescribed by the relevant national authority are satisfied in relation to the area	The general conditions are described at **4.24–4.29** above.
80(4)	take into account a particular set of factors when making a decision that an area is an area of low housing demand	These factors are described at **4.24** above.

---

1   Section 97(14).
2   *Hansard*, House of Commons, Committee, vol 417, col 253 (29 January 2004).

Section	Local housing authorities must	Comment
80(9)	before making a designation take reasonable steps to consult persons likely to be affected by the designation and consider any representations made	The people likely to be affected in an area proposed for designation must be consulted. This is in addition to the specific consultation requirements set out in the Schedule. The actual mechanics of the consultation process are for the authority to decide.
81(2)	ensure that any exercise of the power to designate is consistent with its overall housing strategy	The problems which give rise to the need for selective licensing are complex and the Government is trying to ensure that selective licensing is part of a strategic and co-ordinated response to problem housing.
81(3)	seek to adopt a co-ordinated approach in connection with dealing with homelessness, empty properties and anti-social behaviour	
81(4)	not make a designation unless it has considered whether there are other courses of action available to it to achieve its objective(s) and that making the designation will significantly assist in the achievement of its objective(s)	
83(2)	publish a notice of the details of the designation	The notice must: • state that the designation has been made and when it comes into force; • give details of the confirmation/approval process; • further requirements as prescribed by regulation.
83(3)	make copies of the designation and prescribed information available to the public	General information requirement.
84(3)	from time to time review the operation of designations	No time interval is prescribed for this review.
84(6)	publish a notice of revocation of a designation as prescribed by regulations	General information requirement.
85(4)	take all reasonable steps to secure that applications for licences are made by those who require them	It is going to be extremely important for the credibility of licensing that landlords are fully aware of the requirements imposed upon them.

CONCLUSION

4.113　Selective licensing provides an innovative and interesting approach to problematic housing which should complement the licensing requirements in Part 2 of the Act. In particular it responds to two relatively new phenomena, low demand areas and anti-social behaviour. The scheme has been written flexibly enough so that it can respond to any problems which emerge in the future. However, the statutory provisions also reflect the inherent tensions between the need for local responsiveness and the fear of overly interventionist activities by local housing authorities into private renting. It may be that the constraints on action that the statute imposes, the need for national authority approval and the extensive duties placed upon local housing authorities in the end make it an unattractive solution.

Chapter 5

ADDITIONAL CONTROL PROVISIONS IN RELATION TO RESIDENTIAL ACCOMMODATION

INTRODUCTION

5.1 Part 4 of the Act contains mechanisms which allow the local housing authority in particular circumstances to step into the shoes of a failing landlord and manage the rented house. These enforcement measures are not designed primarily to punish the landlord but to ensure that the property is managed responsibly and safely for the benefit of occupiers or potential occupiers and others living or owning property in the vicinity.

5.2 The enforcement mechanisms in this Part of the Act are set out in Table 5.1.

Table 5.1 *Enforcement mechanisms in Part 4*

Mechanism	*Section*		*Comment*
Interim management orders	101–112	Short term	General provisions relating to operation of both interim and final management orders contained in ss 123–131 and Sch 6.
Final management orders	113–122	Longer term (maximum 5 years)	
Interim and final empty dwelling management orders	132–138		These are similar to provisions for interim and final management orders However, there are some important distinctions reflecting the different problems posed by empty homes.
Overcrowding notices	139–144		Designed to prevent overcrowding in HMOs which are not required to be licensed under Part 2 of the Act.

5.3 Interim and final management orders act as additional provisions for the enforcement of licensing under Part 2 and Part 3 of the Act. In addition, in a really quite remarkable extension to the powers of local housing authorities to intervene in the business of private landlords, in limited circumstances they provide a mechanism for ensuring appropriate management of properties which are not licensable.

5.4 Empty dwelling management orders were inserted into the Bill at Lords Committee.[1] Their role is to unlock 'the potential of empty homes' and 'to get them

---

1 Lord Rooker moved the amendments in the Committee stage in the Lords: *Hansard*, HL, vol 664, col 903 (13 September 2004); *Hansard*, HL, vol 664, col 1303 (16 September 2004) (Schedule). See Housing Bill HL 114 (17 September 2004).

back into use as homes as quickly as possible'.[1] The empty dwelling management order is designed as a back up to voluntary leasing arrangements operated by many local housing authorities and RSLs and an alternative to enforcement action under other legislation (for example via compulsory purchase).

5.5   Overcrowding notices apply to houses in multiple occupation ('HMO') that are not required to be licensed under Part 2 of the Act. Overcrowding in larger HMOs is covered in that Part since a licence only permits a house to be licensed for a specified number of occupants. For convenience we explain the provision in the Act which enables the overcrowding provisions of the HA 1985 to be reformed alongside the provisions on overcrowding notices.[2]

5.6   These provisions are in addition to provisions contained in Part 2 and Part 3 of the Act which focus on individual compliance or failure by the landlord. Table 5.2 sets out the more punitive consequences of failing to comply with the licensing requirements of Part 2 and Part 3.

Table 5.2   *Consequences for the landlord/manager of non-compliance with licensing provisions*

Sanction	Sections of Act		Comment
	Part 2	Part 3	
Refusal of licence	s 64	s 80	'Fit and proper person' test, and 'otherwise satisfactory management arrangements'.
Revocation of licence	s 70	s 93	Where there is serious breach of conditions or repeated breaches of a condition or where the authority no longer consider that the licence holder is a fit and proper person to be the licence holder and where the authority no longer consider that the management of the house is being carried on by persons who are in each case fit and proper persons.
Rent repayment order	ss 73–74	ss 96–97	A tribunal order for the repayment of housing benefit to local authority and/or rent to the occupier.
No access to s 21 of the Housing Act 1988	s 75	s 98	Paper based court application for termination of assured shorthold tenancies will not be available to landlords who do not have the necessary licence.
Criminal offence of having control of or managing a house without a licence which requires a licence	s 72(1)	s 95(1)	Maximum fine of £20,000. Very serious consequences for non-compliance – designed as an effective deterrent.

---

1   HL Committee, vol 664, col 907 (13 September 2004).
2   Section 216.

Sanction	Sections of Act		Comment
	Part 2	*Part 3*	
Criminal offence of breach of conditions of licence	s 72(2)	s 95(2)	Liable on summary conviction to a maximum fine not exceeding level 5 on the standard scale.

INTERIM MANAGEMENT ORDERS

5.7   Table 5.3 summarises the provisions on interim management orders.

Table 5.3   *Interim management orders*

Section	Provision	Comment
101(1)–(3), (5)–(7)	Introduces and describes interim management orders	Lasts a maximum of 12 months. Designed to ensure immediate steps are taken to protect the health, safety or welfare of occupiers or neighbours, and other interim measures are taken appropriate for proper management pending a longer-term solution.
102	Describes the duties and powers of local housing authorities to make interim management orders	Duties relate to unlicensed Part 2 and Part 3 houses or in certain circumstances Part 2 and Part 3 houses where the licence is to be revoked. Powers relate to HMOs which fall outside the mandatory licensing scheme in Part 2 and to properties to which s 99 (special interim management orders) apply. Housing authorities use of discretion overseen by Residential Property Tribunal.
103	Special interim management orders	Applies to a particular category of tenancies which are not exempt[1] from Part 3 of the Act.
104	The health and safety condition	Covers occupiers and others occupying or having an estate or interest in any premises in the vicinity and justifies interference with property rights of the landlord.
105	Operation of interim management orders	This deals with the appropriate dates for the commencement and cessation of the interim management order.

---

1   Exempt tenancies are defined in s 79(3), (4) of the Act and include tenancies where the landlord is a registered social landlord and other tenancies prescribed by the relevant national authorities. See Chapter 4 at **4.38–4.46**.

Section	Provision	Comment
106	Local housing authority's duties during interim management orders	Sets out specific duties on local housing authorities, firstly to protect the health safety or welfare of the occupiers and then to organise the proper management of the house.
107–110	General effect of interim management orders	Sets out the balancing exercise between the need to ensure the effective management of the house by the local housing authority and the appropriate respect for landlord's ownership of the house.
111–112	Variation and revocation of interim management orders	Provides a procedure for the variation and revocation of interim management orders by both the local housing authority and the landlord. The procedure is subject to appeal to the Residential Property Tribunal.

Commentary

5.8   Local housing authorities can make interim management orders to ensure that:

- immediate steps are taken to protect the health, safety or welfare of the occupiers of a house; or
- immediate steps are taken to protect the health, safety or welfare of the other occupiers or landowners in the neighbourhood; and
- any other appropriate steps are taken to ensure the proper management of the house pending further action.[1]

5.9   Further action means the

- grant of a licence under Part 2 or Part 3 of the Act; or
- the making of a final management order; or
- the revocation of the interim management order.[2]

5.10   Note that the interim management order can respond to the need for protection over and beyond the needs of occupiers of the house. The local authority can consider the needs of others in the vicinity whether neighbouring occupiers or people 'with an estate or interest in any premises'. Thus landlords, mortgagees, and others living nearby are covered.

5.11   Interim management orders are therefore temporary measures – designed to last a maximum of 12 months – to protect occupiers and others from risks to their health, safety or welfare and to give the local housing authority a breathing space to work on a more permanent solution to the property management problems whilst ensuring proper management of the house in the meantime.

5.12   There are limits built into interim management orders to reflect their temporary nature. As the government minister explained:

---

1   Section 101(3).
2   Section 101(3)(b).

'It is important that local authorities do not see the making of an interim management order as giving them a green light to act as if they owned the property for all time. I believe that there are already adequate safeguards to protect against this. First, the authority is under a duty to sort out the long-term management of the house as soon as practicable. It will hardly fulfil this obligation if it is embarking on an extensive programme of unnecessary works. Secondly, and most importantly, the landlord can appeal to the Residential Property Tribunal against any unreasonable expenditure incurred. If the local authority were to attempt to take unreasonable actions under the interim management order, it would find itself landed with the bill for doing so.'[1]

The duty

5.13   Local housing authorities have a duty to make interim management orders in the following two sets of circumstances.

5.14   The first set of circumstances is where an HMO which is subject to mandatory licensing or a Part 3 house:

- does not have the requisite licence under Part 2 or Part 3 of the Act; and
- either there is no prospect of it being licensed in the near future; or
- the health and safety condition is satisfied.[2]

5.15   The second set of circumstances is where either an HMO which is subject to mandatory licensing or a Part 3 house:

- does have the requisite licence under Part 2 or Part 3 of the Act; and
- the local housing authority has revoked the licence but the revocation has not yet come into force; and
- either once the revocation comes into force there is no prosect of the house being licensed in the near future; or
- when the revocation comes into force the health and safety condition will be satisfied.[3]

5.16   In other words, if a property must be licensed as a result of the provisions in Parts 2 or 3 of the Act, it must either have a licence or be subject to a management order (either interim or final) unless it has been temporarily exempted. The government explained that in general it:

'would rather that properties were licensed than subject to an interim management order. However, that will not always be possible; for instance, if no fit and proper person can be found to manage a property. Because the welfare of the tenant is paramount the Bill obliges local housing authorities to take over the management of such properties using interim management orders.'[4]

5.17   The health and safety condition is satisfied if the making of an interim management order is required to protect the health, safety or welfare of the occupiers, or people occupying neighbouring properties or with an estate or interest in neighbouring properties.[5]

---

1   *Hansard*, HL Committee, vol 664, col 804, (9 September 2004).
2   Section 102(2).
3   Section 102(3).
4   *Hansard*, HL Committee, vol 664, col 796 (7 September 2004).
5   Section 104.

5.18   The local housing authority has the discretion (but not the duty) to treat a threat to evict the occupiers in order to avoid the licensing requirements of Part 2 of the Act as a threat to the welfare of the occupiers.[1] This is potentially an important protection for occupiers of HMOs whose occupation may well be at risk as a result of licensing requirements. The power is limited to Part 2 licensing because of the more severe potential impact of evicting a number of tenants from an HMO.

5.19   Note that where the local housing authority are required to take enforcement action in respect of Category 1 hazards in relation to the house, or would be so required if they revoked the licence, and such action would protect the health, safety or welfare of the occupiers, then the health and safety condition is not satisfied.[2]

Discretionary and special interim management orders

5.20   The local housing authority also has a discretion to apply to the Residential Property Tribunal for an interim management order in other circumstances. The power is available if the property concerned is an HMO which does not require licensing under Part 2 of the Act[3] or if the property is one to which special interim management orders apply.[4]

5.21   Special interim management orders apply to houses which would not be exempt from Part 3 of the Act[5] if they were in an area of selective licensing and are not in multiple occupation.

5.22   A Residential Property Tribunal can only approve the making of an interim management order if:

●   it complies with 'categories of circumstances' prescribed by the appropriate national authority;[6] and

●   the making of an order is necessary for the protection of the health, safety or welfare of the occupiers or visitors or others engaged in lawful activities in the vicinity of the house.[7]

5.23   If the property is an HMO which does not require licensing the Residential Property Tribunal must take into account, in any decision to authorise the interim management order, the extent to which the landlord or manager has in the past complied with a code of conduct approved under the Act.[8]

5.24   The categories of circumstances must reflect (with any appropriate modifications) one or other of the sets of general conditions for selective licensing discussed in Chapter 4 at **4.24–4.30** or any additional sets of conditions that are prescribed.[9]

---

1   Section 104(3).
2   Section 104(5), (6).
3   Section 102(4).
4   Section 103.
5   See s 79(3).
6   Section 103(3).
7   Section 103(4).
8   Section 102(6).
9   See s 80.

5.25   What this means in practice is that local authorities are provided with additional tools to respond to particular problems arising from specific properties that fall outside of the problem housing that the Act concentrates on.

5.26   In particular special interim management orders enable local housing authorities to respond to anti-social behaviour in the private rented sector in areas not covered by selective licensing. Where a privately rented house is the source of anti-social behaviour, the landlord fails to take appropriate action to deal with it and the consequences are serious enough, then an order can be made to protect the health, safety or welfare of people occupying, visiting or engaged in lawful activities in the locality of the house. This is a significant extension of the power of local housing authorities over properties in their area.

5.27   The need for a tribunal to approve discretionary interim management orders is a recognition that an interim management order 'is a significant imposition on a landlord's rights. The requirement for approval by a tribunal is an appropriate safeguard where an authority is exercising its discretion to make an IMO'.[1]

5.28   The situation is quite distinct from the operation of interim management orders where properties are licensable. In such circumstances the local housing authority is under a duty to make an interim mangement order and there is no need to apply to the Residential Property Tribunal. The government explained that in those circumstances, 'A decision will already have been taken at the time the licensing requirement was introduced that that particular type of property must be subject to some form of management control.'[2] The extensive rights of appeal granted to a landlord if he or she disagrees with the decision to make an interim management order provide sufficient protection for the landlord. For those reasons it is unnecessary for the legislation to require the local housing authority to apply to the Residential Property Tribunal service for all interim management orders.

5.29   Moreover extending the requirement for an application to the Residential Property Tribunal to mandatory interim management orders would defeat the purpose of the mechanism. As the government pointed out:

> 'Management orders need to be a genuine option for local authorities and therefore as unbureaucratic as possible, unlike the current control orders which some authorities find too cumbersome. In some cases it might be essential to the health and safety of the occupiers of licensable properties, or to people living nearby that effective management controls should be put in place rapidly, not some weeks or months or even further down the line after a tribunal has considered the issue.'[3]

Commencement and expiry of interim management orders

5.30   An interim management order comes into force on the date it is made unless it is made when a licence has been revoked but the revocation has not yet come into effect. In those circumstances the interim management order comes into effect when the revocation of the licence becomes effective.[4]

---

1   *Hansard*, HL Committee, vol 664, col 795 (9 September 2004).
2   *Hansard*, HL Committee, vol 664, col 795 (9 September 2004).
3   *Hansard*, HL Committee, vol 664, col 795 (9 September 2004).
4   Section 105.

5.31   An interim management order lasts a maximum of 12 months.[1] If the order does not provide an earlier expiry date then it will cease to have effect after 12 months. Orders made when a licence has been revoked but the revocation has not yet come into effect.must contain a provision for an expiry date which is no more than 12 months after the coming into force of the order.[2]

5.32   The Act provides for certain circumstances when an interim management order can be extended. These circumstances are limited to appeals against the imposition of final management orders and enable the interim management order to continue as an elastoplast type measure until the appeal process is complete.

5.33   What is required in the case of mandatory interim management orders is that:

- the local housing authority has made a final management order but the order has not come into force because of an appeal to a Residential Property Tribunal; and
- the house is one which would be required to be licensed under Part 2 or Part 3 of the Act if it were not for the existence of the interim management order; and
- the date on which the final management order, any licence under Part 2 or 3 of the Act or another interim management order comes into force in relation to the house following the appeal is later than the expiry date of the interim management order.[3]

5.34   Where the appeal is against the imposition of a final management order and the interim management order was discretionary the local housing authority has to apply to the Residential Property Tribunal for the interim management order to continue in force beyond its expiry date pending the disposal of the appeal. The tribunal is able to make the order to extend the life of the interim management order.[4]

Duties on local housing authorities

5.35   Local housing authorities have a number of duties imposed upon them once an interim management order is in force. These are set out in Table 5.4.

Table 5.4   *Local housing authority duties during an interim management order*

Section 106 subsection	The local housing authority must	Comment
(2)	First take any immediate steps necessary for the purpose of protecting the health, safety or welfare of occupiers or of occupiers or owners of property in the vicinity.	This requirement emphasies that the prime purpose of interim management orders is the occupiers' or neighbours' health, safety or welfare.
(3)	Take steps to ensure the proper management of the house pending the grant of a licence or the making of a final management order or the revocation of the interim management order.	The duty includes ensuring that the house has fire insurance in place.

---

1   Section 105(4).
2   Section 105(6).
3   Section 105(9).
4   Section 105(10).

Section 106 subsection	The local housing authority must	Comment
(4)	If the house would require a licence under Part 2 or Part 3 but for the existence of the interim mangement order then the local housing authority must decide either to grant a licence or to make a final management order.	The grant of a licence includes the serving of a temporary exemption notice. The normal course of events would be to organise the licensing of the property. A final management order is a last resort.
(5)	If the house does not require a licence under Part 2 or Part 3 then the authority must decide either: • to make a final management order; or • to revoke the order without taking any further action.	The only long term solution for such properties is the final management order.

The effect of interim management orders

5.36   The provisions of the Act attempt to balance the needs of the authority to manage the property appropriately with the fact that the order is short term, does not equate with ownership of the property and is not meant to disturb the status quo of property ownership, particularly in relation to other parties' interests, such as mortgagees and superior landlords. As the minister explained in committee, 'We are seeking to provide a power that will allow the local authority to manage the property effectively. That is not dispossessing the owner of all of his rights'.[1]

5.37   This balancing act leads to some complexity in the provisions.

5.38   The authority has the power:

* to manage the house (subject to the rights of existing occupiers);[2]
* to authorise a manager to do so on its behalf;[3]
* to permit others to take up occupation of the premises, but only with the written consent of the legal owners.[4]

5.39   The local authority:
* does not acquire the legal estate;[5]
* is not to be treated as managing or providing the housing for the purpose of any other statutory provisions.[6]

5.40   Therefore the occupiers cannot acquire the status of secure tenants of the local authority. Nor have they got the status of legal tenancies or licences, because the authority would require the legal estate in order to create such a status.

---

1   *Hansard*, Commons Committee, vol 417 col 362 (3 February 2004).
2   Section 107(3).
3   Ibid.
4   Section 107(4).
5   Section 107(5).
6   Section 107(8).

5.41   However, if an authority does create what appear to be tenancies and licences using its powers in a management order, those agreements are to be regarded as legal leases, binding on any future owner of the property[1] and, in appropriate circumstances, registerable at the local Land Registry.[2] This will not give powers to local housing authorities to create legal leases, but any lease they do create must be treated as if it were such a lease. The reason for the provisions was explained in Parliament as follows:

> 'Leases and licences granted by a local housing authority are better thought of as being quasi-leases. This might give rise to some problems if the Land Registry ever becomes involved – if, for instance, a person attempts to register a quasi-lease or purchases a property and claims that the Land Register is defective because it fails to include a quasi-lease on its register.'[3]

5.42   The immediate landlord[4] cannot:

- receive any rent;
- manage the house; and
- create any lease or licence or other right to occupy it.[5]

5.43   The order does not affect the validity of a mortgage on the house, or of a superior lease on the house. The rights and remedies available to the mortgagee or the superior landlord continue to be available limited only in so far as such rights would prevent the local authority creating any occupancy agreements for the house.[6] If a dispute about these rights and remedies reaches the court, it may make any order in connection with the interim management order that it thinks appropriate, which includes an order quashing the interim management order.[7]

5.44   The landlord can, however, sell or otherwise dispose of the house.[8] The local housing authority cannot.

Financial arrangements

5.45   The effect of the interim management order is to place the local housing authority into the shoes of the landlord.[9] The occupiers therefore pay their rent to the local housing authority. When a local housing authority incurs reasonable expenditure in the management of the house under the interim management order then it can use the rent it collects to cover that expenditure.[10] This would include, for example, expenditure on routine repairs, capital expenditure, administrative costs and building insurance.

5.46   The rent can also cover the payment of any compensation payable to a third party in connection with the interim management order.[11]

---

1   Section 108(2).
2   Section 107(10).
3   *Hansard*, HL Committee, vol 664, col 805 (9 September 2004).
4   The immediate landlord is defined in s 109(6) as the owner or lessee of the house and someone who would be entitled to receive rent from the occupiers of the house if the order was not in existence.
5   Section 109(2).
6   Section 109(4).
7   Section 109(4).
8   Section 109(3).
9   Section 124(4).
10   Section 110(3).
11   See s 128 and **5.101–5.102** below.

5.47   The local authority is required, having deducted the relevant expenditure, to pay the relevant landlord the balance of any rents received at such intervals as it considers appropriate.[1] If there is more than one landlord the local authority can allocate the payment of the balance of rent in the proportions it considers appropriate.[2] In addition, when appropriate, it must pay interest at a reasonable rate that it has determined on such sums.[3] If the interim management order does not set out the rate of interest payable and the frequency of payment of interest the landlord can appeal to the residential tribunal.[4] Finally, it must keep proper accounts of its income and expenditure and must make them available for inspection or verification by the relevant landlord.[5]

5.48   The landlord has the right to apply to the Residential Property Tribunal for an order declaring that the relevant expenditure has not been reasonably incurred, and to ask the tribunal to require the authority to make financial adjustments reflecting the tribunal's declaration.[6]

5.49   A problem may arise when money is owed by the landlord to the local housing authority at the end of the interim management order. The minister explained in committee that:

> 'a series of possibilities might apply. If the conclusion at the end of the interim management order is that a final management order is needed, the debt would carry through and become part of the accounting machine under the final management order. It would continue to be a carried-over debt against which the ongoing rent under the final management order could be charged to repay it before any surplus income appeared down the line. Alternatively, there could be a charge on the property – or, if a licence were granted, there could be a condition attached saying that the money should be repaid within a certain period, because it would have been used for work to make a property fit for human habitation, and to make it a safe, licensable property on which a landlord could earn rent.'[7]

Local authorities therefore have sufficient flexibility to recoup their money in the most effective manner.

5.50   A further potential problem is where the landlord resides in part of the house that is subject to the interim management order. Again the local housing authority has flexibility whether to extend the scope of the interim management order to the part of the house occupied by the landlord,[8] although that flexibility is constrained by the landlord's right to appeal to the Residential Property Tribunal.

5.51   This was explained in Parliament as follows:

> 'Where an interim management order is made, the local authority can incur expenditure on such things as repairs to the house which will be reimbursed from rental income. It may not be necessary or appropriate for this to extend to the landlord's own accommodation. For example, a landlord may occupy a self-contained basement flat. It may be reasonable for the authority to exclude that flat from the interim management order so that it does not have to

---

1   Section 110(4).
2   Section 110(4).
3   Ibid.
4   Section 110(5) and Sch 6, para 24(3).
5   Section 110(6).
6   Section 110(7).
7   *Hansard*, Commons Committee, vol 417, col 373 (3 February 2004).
8   Section 102(8).

carry out repairs or do other things at the landlord's expense. The landlord would have the discretion to determine how money which would otherwise be deducted from his rental income is spent on the repair of the area in which he privately resides.

In other circumstances it might be necessary to include the landlord's accommodation in the order, where, for example, he shares facilities with the tenants such as a bathroom or kitchen, or if he was behaving in an anti-social manner, or was harassing the tenants. Inclusion in the order in those circumstances would make it far more practical for the local authority to be able to take effective legal action against him, which might include, for example, seeking authority from a court to exclude him from the property.'[1]

Variation and revocation

5.52   Interim management orders can be varied or revoked either on the initiative of the local authority[2] or following an application by a 'relevant' person – an owner or manager of a house.[3] 'Relevant' person expressly excludes tenants with a remaining interest in the property of less than three years. So short-term fixed term tenants are excluded, as are periodic tenants.

5.53   The local housing authority has to consider that it is appropriate to vary or revoke the order.[4] The local housing authority is specifically given the power to revoke interim management orders where:

- the house ceases to be an HMO to which Part 2 of the Act applies, or ceases to be subject to Part 3 of the Act (selective licensing);
- a licence is going to come into force on the house under either Part 2 or Part 3 of the Act;
- a final management order is made to replace the interim management order.[5]

5.54   A variation or revocation will not come into effect until the period for appealing against it has expired or the process of appeal has been concluded.[6] Appeals are discussed below at **5.112** et seq.

FINAL MANAGEMENT ORDERS

5.55   Table 5.5 summarises the provisions on final management orders.

Table 5.5   *Final management orders*

Section	Provison	Comment
101(4)	Definition of final management order	Makes clear that the purpose is to secure the proper management of the house on a long term basis in accordance with a management scheme.

---

1   *Hansard*, HL Committee, vol 664, col 798 (9 September 2004).
2   Section 111(3).
3   Section 111(3), (4).
4   Sections 111(1), 112(1)(d).
5   Section 112(1).
6   Section 112(2).

Section	Provison	Comment
113	Describes the duty and the power to create final management orders and sets out their relationship with interim management orders	The duty relates to circumstances where: • there is an interim management order; • the property must be licensed under the Act; but • the authority are unable to grant a licence to replace the interim management order.
114	Describes effective dates of commencement and cessation of final management orders	Final management orders last a maximum of five years.
115	Describes the duties on a local housing authority when a final management order is in force	The duties reflect the role of local housing authority as a manager of the property and require the local housing authority to review the operation of the order from time to time.
116–118	Sets out the general effects of a final management order	These effects are similar to the effects of the interim management order.
119–120	Sets out the requirement for a management scheme and accounts and provides a mechanism for the enforcement of the management scheme by the landlord	The management scheme is embedded into the order. This requires the local housing authority to be explicit about the management plan for the house and the financial arrangements. If the local housing authority deviate from the scheme then the landlord can apply to the Residential Property Tribunal either for an order requiring compliance with the scheme or for the final management order to be revoked.
121–122	Variation and revocation of final management orders	Provides a system for variation and revocation of final management orders similar to that provided for local housing authorities and landlords under interim management orders. The procedures are subject to appeal.

Commentary

5.56   Final management orders are designed to secure the proper management of a house in the longer term[1] and as a replacement for the short term interim management orders. They cannot be created except to replace an interim mangement order from its expiry date.[2]

5.57   The local housing authority must make a final management order if:

•   the house requires licensing under Part 2 or Part 3 of the Act; and
•   the authority considers that it is unable to grant a licence under Part 2 or Part 3 to replace the interim management order.[3]

5.58   The local housing authority must also make a final management order where it is necessary to replace an existing final management order when it expires if the house is one

---

1   Section 101(4).
2   Section 113(1).
3   Section 113(2).

which requires licensing under Part 2 or Part 3 of the Act and it is still unable to grant a licence.

5.59   The local housing authority has the power to create a final management order to replace an interim management order when it expires or an existing final mangement order if:

- the house does not require licensing under Part 2 or Part 3 of the Act; and
- the authority considers that making the final management order is necessary for the purpose of protecting the health, safety or welfare of the occupiers or neighbouring occupiers or property owners on a long-term basis.[1]

5.60   Final management orders come into effect only after periods for appeals have expired or the process of appeal is completed.[2] In general their duration is five years,[3] but can be for a shorter period if the order provides for a different expiry date.[4] There are provisions for lengthening the period where a replacement order is being appealed. If the house requires a licence under either Part 2 or Part 3 of the Act and without an extension of the duration of the final management order the continuation of the appeals process would result in the house being unlicensed and not subject to a management order, then the order continues in force until the appeals process is complete.[5] Otherwise the authority must apply to the tribunal for an extension of the existing order.[6]

5.61   The local housing authority's duties under the final management order are set out in Table 5.6.

Table 5.6   *Local housing authority duties during a final management order*

Section 115 subsection	The local authority must	Comment
(2)	Take such steps as it considers appropriate to ensure the proper management of the house in accordance with the management scheme.	This includes ensuring provision for fire and other insurance. Management schemes are discussed below.
(3)	From time to time review: • the operation of the order and the management scheme; • whether keeping the order in place is the best alternative.	The order should only remain if it provides the best means of dealing with the problem. No time interval specified for the review.
(4)	Vary the order if on review it considers that variations should be made.	If on the review action is considered to be necessary then that action must be taken.

---

1   Section 113(3), (6).
2   Section 114(2).
3   Section 114(3).
4   Section 114(4).
5   Section 114(6).
6   Section 114(7).

Section 115 *The local authority must subsection*	*Comment*
(5)	Grant a licence under Part 2 or Part 3 of the Act if on review it considers that is the best available alternative. Revoke the order if on review it considers that is the best available alternative.	

5.62   The effect of a final management order is similar to the effect of an interim management order. However, the local housing authority has the power to create more extensive rights to occupy the property reflecting the longer term nature of the final management order. The provisions are written in such a way that registered social landlords or other appropriate bodies will be able to carry out the management of the properties on behalf of the local authority.

5.63   The authority has the right:

- to possession of the house (subject to the rights of existing and future occupiers);[1]
- to manage the house;[2]
- to authorise a manager to do so on its behalf;[3]
- to create occupation rights similar to leases or licences.[4]

5.64   There are limits on the occupation rights which can be created by the authority.[5] It cannot create occupation rights without the consent of the landlord:

- for fixed terms which will expire after the date of expiry of the final management order; or
- which require more than four weeks notice to terminate.

5.65   It can, however, create assured shorthold tenancies without the landlord's consent as long as the mandatory six-month period, during which time there are only limited grounds for eviction and in particular the notice only ground is not available, will expire before the end of the final management order.[6]

5.66   So local housing authorities can create, without consent, rights similar to leases and licences which are excluded from the requirements of the Protection from Eviction Act 1977, and assured shorthold tenancies for occupiers of the house. What they cannot do is to create occupancy rights which will bind the landlord after the expiry of the final management order without the landlord's consent.

5.67   The local authority:

- does not acquire the legal estate and therefore cannot sell the property;[7]

---

1   Section 116(3)(a).
2   Section 116(3)(b).
3   Ibid.
4   Section 116(3)(c).
5   Section 116(4).
6   Section 116(4)(b).
7   Section 116(5).

- is not to be treated as managing or providing the housing accommodation for the purpose of any other statutory provisions.[1]

5.68   Therefore the occupiers cannot acquire the status of secure tenants of the local authority. Nor have they got the status of legal tenants or licencees, because the authority would require the legal estate in order to create such a status.

5.69   However, if an authority does create what appear to be tenancies and licences using its powers in a management order, those agreements are to be regarded as legal leases, binding on any future owner of the property and, in appropriate circumstances, registerable at the local Land Registry. This will not give powers to local housing authorities to create legal leases, but any lease they do create must be treated as if it were such a lease.[2]

5.70   A final management order is a local land charge and the local authority can enter a restriction in the Land Register in respect of it. This is designed to prevent the landlord creating new interests in the property.[3]

5.71   During a final management order the immediate landlord[4] cannot:

- receive any rent;
- manage the house; and
- create any lease or licence or other right to occupy it.[5]

5.72   The order does not affect the validity of a mortgage on the house, or of a superior lease on the house. The rights and remedies available to the mortgagee or the superior landlord continue to be available, limited only in so far as such rights would prevent the local authority creating any occupancy agreements for the house. If a mortgagee or a superior landlord take proceedings for enforcing their rights the court may make orders which vary or quash the final management order.[6]

5.73   The landlord can, however, sell or otherwise dispose of the house.[7]

MANAGEMENT SCHEMES

5.74   A key difference between an interim management order and a final management order is that a final management order must contain a management scheme.[8]

5.75   A management scheme is a scheme setting out the details of the intentions of the local housing authority in managing the house.[9] It provides an opportunity for the landlord to see what the local housing authority's intentions are for the house, and enables him or her to enforce those intentions.

---

1   Section 116(8).
2   Section 117(2).
3   Section 116(9), (10).
4   The immediate landlord is defined in s 118(6) as the owner or lessee of the house and someone who would be entitled to receive rent from the occupiers of the house if the order was not in existence.
5   Section 118(2).
6   Section 118(4).
7   Section 118(3).
8   Section 119(1).
9   Section 119(2).

5.76   Management schemes are divided into two parts. Part 1 of the scheme provides the financial details of the management plan. Table 5.7 sets out the mandatory information requirements for the plan. Table 5.8 sets out the discretionary requirements. Basically the provisions ensure that the landlord is given sufficient information to understand the financial implications of the local housing authority's intentions.

Table 5.7   *Management scheme Part 1 mandatory requirements under s 119(4)*

Section 119(4) The scheme must include	
(a)	Details of any works that the authority intend to carry out.
(b)	An estimate of the capital and other expenditure to be incurred by the authority.
(c)	The amount of rent or other payments that the authority will be seeking, taking into account the condition of the house.
(d), (e)	The amount of and provision for the payment of compensation payable to a third party whose rights are interfered with in connection with the final management order.[1]
(f)	Provision for payments to the landlord of rent etc that remain after the deduction of: • relevant expenditure; • amounts of compensation.
(g)	Explanation of how the authority will pay the landlord outstanding rent etc due following the termination of the final management order following deduction of: • relevant expenditure; • amounts of compensation.
(h)	Explanation of how the authority will pay a third party any outstanding compensation due following the termination of the final management order.

Table 5.8   *Management scheme Part 1 discretionary provisions under s 119(5)*

Section 119(4) The scheme may include	Comment
(a)	Information about how the authority intends to use the rent to meet relevant expenditure.	These provisions amplify the mandatory requirements.
(b)	Information about how the authority intend to deal with interest which accrues on the rent etc.	

---

1   The payment of compensation is dealt with in s 128.

Section 119(4) The scheme may include		Comment
(c), (d)	Information about the authority's intentions to disapply s 129 (2)–(5), ie the authority's intention to 'roll over' into the new order any excess of rent over expenditure and compensation, any deficit of compensation to a third party, any deficit owed by a landlord to the authority or any overpayment of compensation by the authority to a third party following the termination of a previous management order.	The standard provisions are in s 129 (2)–(5) which provide either: • that the landlord or a third party must be paid the amounts due following the termination of a management order; or alternatively • that the authority has the right to recover any deficit due from the landlord or a third party. Where, however, a management order is replacing a previous management order, the authority may disapply those sections[1] and 'roll over' the excess of income over expenditure or the deficit.
(e)	Information about how the authority intends to recoup from a landlord expenditure over and above what can be recovered from the rent etc.	

5.77 Part 2 of the management scheme is designed to address the reasons for the imposition of the final management order. The local authority must give an explanation as to how it intends to respond to the particular problems of the house.[2] The response may include:

- the steps it intends to make to ensure that the occupiers comply with their tenancy obligations[3] (another reference to anti-social behaviour);
- a description and explanation of the necessary repairs.[4]

5.78 In addition the authority must keep full accounts in respect of the house and allow the landlord and any other owner of the house reasonable opportunity to inspect, copy and verify the accounts.[5]

5.79 The management scheme is extremely important. It justifies the intervention by the local housing authority and limits the scope of that intervention. Its significance is underpinned by the right of the landlord[6] (or a third party[7] whose rights have been affected by the final management order) to apply to the Residential Property Tribunal for an order requiring the local housing authority to manage the house in accordance with the management scheme.[8] Following an application, the tribunal has extensive powers to ensure that the house is managed in accordance with the scheme. It can set out the steps which the authority must take to fulfil the requirements of the scheme,[9] it can vary the

---

1   Under s 129(6).
2   Section 119(6).
3   Section 119(6)(a).
4   Section 119(6)(b).
5   Section 119(7).
6   That is, an immediate landlord as defined in s 119(8).
7   Section 120(4)(b).
8   Section 120(1).
9   Section 120(3)(a).

final management order[1] and it can order the payment of damages to the applicant. Alternatively it can revoke the final management order.[2] Ultimately then the Residential Property Tribunal can provide very detailed supervision of the local housing authority's management of the house.

Variation and revocation

5.80   Final management orders can be varied[3] or revoked[4] either on the initiative of the local authority or following an application by a 'relevant' person – an owner or manager of a house.[5] 'Relevant' person expressly excludes tenants with a remaining interest in the property of less than three years.[6] So short-term fixed-term tenants are excluded as are periodic tenants. At first sight this may appear counter-intuitive but it is consistent with the concept of the local housing authority stepping into the shoes of the landlord. The provisions are not about providing extra rights to tenants to manage their property.

5.81   The local housing authority has to consider that it is appropriate to vary or revoke the order.[7] Examples of when the local housing authority would have the power to revoke are:

- if the house ceases to be an HMO to which Part 2 of the Act applies, or ceases to be subject to Part 3 of the Act (selective licensing);[8]
- if a licence is going to come into force on the house under either Part 2 or Part 3 of the Act;[9]
- if a further final management order is made to replace the existing final management order.[10]

5.82   A variation or revocation will not come into effect until the period for appealing against it has expired or the process of appeal has been concluded. Appeals are discussed below at **5.112** et seq.

GENERAL PROVISIONS – INTERIM AND FINAL MANAGEMENT ORDERS

5.83   The Act sets out some general provisions relating to the practical implications of both interim and final management orders. These relate to the impact of the orders upon occupiers, agreements and legal proceedings arising from the agreements or from the statutory provisions, furnishings and third parties. The provisions also provide a power of entry to carry out work and set out the financial and legal consequences of the termination of the orders.

---

1   Section 120(3)(b).
2   Section 120(2)(b).
3   Section 121.
4   Section 122.
5   Sections 121(3), 122(3).
6   Sections 121(4), 122(4).
7   Sections 121(1), 122(1)(d).
8   Section 122(a).
9   Section 122(b).
10   Section 122(c).

Occupiers

5.84   The rights of existing occupiers – occupiers whose occupation of the house was created prior to or at the time of the interim or final management order coming into force and who are not resident landlords[1] – are not affected by the imposition of an order on the house.[2] Whilst the order is in force the local housing authority is substituted for any non-residential lessor or licensor.[3]

5.85   The rights of new occupiers – occupiers whose occupation rights are created during the course of an interim or final management order[4] – are not affected by the creation of a final management order.

5.86   The exclusions of local authority landlords from the statutory protections offered by the Rent Act 1977, the Rent (Agriculture) Act 1976 and the HA 1988 do not apply to occupation rights under interim and final management orders.[5]

5.87   If an existing occupier has the benefit of a protected or statutory tenancy under the Rent Act 1977, the Rent (Agriculture) Act 1976 or an assured tenancy (which includes an assured shorthold tenancy) or assured agricultural occupancy under the HA 1988 then those benefits continue unaffected by the operation of the management orders.[6]

5.88   The occupiers do not become secure or introductory tenants under the HA 1985.[7]

Agreements and legal proceedings

5.89   Certain agreements between the landlord and another party which are in existence during the interim or final management order will operate as if the rights and liabilities of the landlord under the agreement are the rights and liabilities of the local housing authority. This only applies to agreements which:

- are effective at the commencement of the order;[8]
- relate to the house, either in connection with its management[9] or the provision of services or otherwise;[10]
- are specified within the order, either specifically or generally;[11] and
- the local housing authority have notified the parties in writing that it is in effect adopting the agreement.[12]

5.90   The local housing authority therefore only becomes burdened with agreements that are relevant, that it knows about and that it chooses to adopt. This provision does not include superior leases of the house to which the landlord is a party,[13] or any permitted

---

1   Section 124(2).
2   Section 124(3).
3   Section 124(4).
4   Section 124(2).
5   Section 124(7).
6   Section 124(10).
7   Section 124(9).
8   Section 125(2)(a).
9   Management includes repair, maintenance, improvement and insurance – s 125(7).
10   Section 125(2)(c).
11   Section 125(d).
12   Section 125(e).
13   Section 125(3)(a).

disposition of the house by the landlord.[1] Nor does it include any lease or licence granting occupation rights to an occupier of the house.[2] The local authority has no choice but to step into the shoes of the landlord in that situation.[3]

5.91   Legal proceedings in connection with such an agreement may be instituted by or against the local housing authority instead of by or against the landlord if the proceedings:

- originated prior to the imposition of the order;
- relate to the house;
- are specifically or generally described within the order; and
- a notice has been served on all parties stating that this applies.[4]

5.92   When the interim or final management order is terminated and is not replaced by a further order then the status quo before the imposition of the management order is restored, ie the original landlord of the house or his successor in title is substituted for the local housing authority.[5]

5.93   If the local housing authority has created agreements to occupy the house which are in effect leases or licences during the course of the interim or final management order, the landlord is substituted for the local housing authority in those agreements.[6]

5.94   The local housing authority is liable for any liability to a superior landlord that a landlord who is a lessee may have for anything done during the interim or final management order.[7]

5.95   Where other agreements have been entered into by the local housing authority in performance of its duties under the interim or final management order, the landlord will be substituted for the housing authority.[8] However, this will only apply if the authority serves a notice on the other party or parties to the agreement that the provision is to apply.[9]

5.96   The local authority may also serve a notice on all interested parties[10] that:

- the rights or liabilities arising either as a result of the operation of interim or final management orders or under any agreement where the landlord has been substituted for the local housing authority are to be treated as the rights and liabilities of the substituted landlord;[11] and
- any proceedings arising from the statutory provisions or from any agreement commenced or continued by or against the local authority may be commenced or continued by the substituted landlord instead.[12]

---

1   Section 125(3)(b).
2   Section 125(c).
3   Section 124(4).
4   Section 124(4), (5).
5   Section 130(1), (2).
6   Section 130(2).
7   Section 130(3).
8   Section 130(4).
9   Section 130(5).
10   Section 130(7).
11   Section 130(6)(a).
12   Section 130(6)(b).

5.97   If the result of this transfer of rights or liabilities to the landlord is that the landlord is required to pay damages in respect of anything done or omitted to be done by the local housing authority, then the authority must reimburse the landlord.[1]

Furniture

5.98   Any furniture, fittings or other articles which are included in the tenancy agreement become the responsibility of the local housing authority for the duration of the interim or final management order.[2] This is important because the state of repair of furniture can be crucial to the health, safety or welfare of the occupiers.

5.99   The owner of the furniture can apply in writing to the authority to reclaim the furniture and the authority can accept that application in writing with two weeks' notice.[3] If there is a dispute between two or more owners of the furniture about their respective rights and liabilities then one of the furniture owners can apply to the Residential Property Tribunal to adjust those rights and liabilities. Any order the tribunal makes can include awards of compensation or damages.[4]

5.100   The local housing authority can supply the house with the necessary furniture and the expenses incurred in doing so can be recouped since they are a necessary part of properly managing the house.[5]

Compensation to third parties

5.101   Any third party who considers that his or her rights have been affected as a result of the interim or final management order has the right to apply to the local housing authority requesting it to consider payment of compensation.[6]

5.102   The local housing authority must then:

- notify the third party of its decision as soon as possible; and
- if it decides to pay compensation then it must vary the management scheme both to specify the amount of compensation and set out how it is to be paid.[7]

Financial arrangements following the termination of the management order

5.103   At the termination of the management order the local housing authority may be owed money or may owe money. The Act provides for different methods of balancing the financial position and the local housing authority is given enforcement powers to recover any money owed to it. These provisions are summarised in Table 5.9.

---

1   Section 130(8).
2   Section 126(1), (2).
3   Section 126(3).
4   Section 126(5), (6).
5   Section 127.
6   Section 128(1).
7   Section 128(2), (3).

Table 5.9   *Financial arrangements following the termination of management orders – s 129*

Financial position	Interim management order	Final management order	Comment
129(2) The total amount of rent collected exceeds the total amount of expenditure by the local housing authority including the payment of compensation payable.	The local housing authority must as soon as possible pay the balance to the relevant landlord.		
129(3) The total amount of rent collected is less than the total amount of expenditure by the local housing authority including the payment of compensation payable.	The difference is recoverable by the local housing authority. The recoverable sum is a local land charge on the house which takes effect on the termination of the order.[1] The authority has the powers and remedies available to it as if it were a mortgagee by deed having powers of sale and lease, or accepting surrenders of leases and appointing a receiver.[2]	Not applicable.	Where the interim management order is followed by a final management order then the local authority can disapply the provision as long as the management scheme so provides and roll over the debt.[3] If the order is followed by a licence then the licence conditions can include conditions on repayment of the debt.[4]
129(5) Money is owed to the local authority in accordance with the management scheme.		The money is recoverable by the local housing authority in accordance with the scheme as a local land charge on the house which takes effect on the termination of the order.[5] The authority has the powers and remedies available to it as if it were a mortgagee by deed having powers of sale and lease, or accepting surrenders of leases and appointing a receiver.[6]	Where the final management order is followed by another final management order then the local authority can disapply the provision as long as the management scheme so provides and roll over the debt.[7] If the order is followed by a licence then the licence conditions can include conditions on repayment of the debt.[8]

---

1   Section 129(7), (8).
2   Section 125(9).
3   Section 129(6).
4   Section 129(11).
5   Section 129(7), (8).
6   Section 129(9).
7   Section 129(6).
8   Section 129(11).

Financial position	Interim management order	Final management order	Comment
129(5) Money is owed to a third party or to a landlord in accordance with the management scheme.	The section does not provide for the payment of compensation awards made as a result of the imposition of an interim management order. However, s 110 (3) enables the authority to pay the compensation out of the rent paid.	The money must be paid in accordance with the management scheme.	Where the final management order is followed by another final management order then the local authority can disapply the provision as long as the management scheme so provides and roll over excess.[1]

Power of entry to carry out work

5.104   The statute provides the local housing authority with a power of entry to the house for the purpose of carrying out works.[2] The right is exercisable at all reasonable times and against tenants or licensees. If part of the house is excluded from the scope of the interim or final management order because of the occupation of a resident landlord the right of entry is limited in that part of the house to a right to enter to carry out work in the part of the house subject to the order.[3] The Government suggested some examples where an enforceable right of entry may be required against a resident landlord:

> 'the resident landlord may resent the local authority having taken away his management of the property and may just want to make things difficult and be a member of the awkward squad; or the landlord may not care and make life difficult – for example, if certain communal features were in his flat and in disrepair.'[4]

5.105   If someone refuses entry after receiving reasonable notice then the authority may obtain an access order from the magistrates' court enforcing the power.[5] Failure to comply with the court order is an offence[6] and on summary conviction the person who refused entry is liable to a fine not exceeding level 5 on the standard scale.[7]

PROCEDURAL REQUIREMENTS FOR INTERIM AND FINAL MANAGEMENT ORDERS

5.106   There are extensive requirements set out in Sch 6 to the Act to ensure that the landlord has sufficient opportunity to express his or her views about the imposition of management orders. These requirements parallel the notification requirements for selective licensing under Part 3 of the Act.

5.107   Table 5.10 sets out the requirements before the making of a final management order which are detailed in paragraphs 1–6 of Part 1 of Sch 6. The requirements only apply to final management orders because interim management orders require speedy imposition.

---

1   Section 129(6).
2   Section 131(2).
3   Section 131(3).
4   *Hansard*, HL Committee, vol 664, col 903 (13 September 2004).
5   Section 131(4).
6   Section 131(5).
7   Section 131(6).

Table 5.10   *Sch 6, Part 1, paras 1–6: notification requirements prior to making final management orders*

When	Served on	Information	Together with	Consultation requirements
Before making a final management order	Each relevant person	Reasons for making the order. Main terms of proposed order. End of the consultation period.	Copy of proposed order	Must consider representations made in accordance with the notice and not withdrawn. The consultation period must be at least 14 days.
After considering representations and when proposing to make a modified order	Each relevant person	The proposed modifications. The reasons for them. The end of the consultation period.		Must consider representations made in accordance with the notice and not withdrawn The consultation period must be at least seven days

5.108   The requirement to re-notify relevant people of modifications to the proposed final management order does not apply if the local housing authority consider that the proposed modifications are not material in any respect.

5.109   Table 5.11 sets out the notification requirements following the making of interim or final management orders which are set out in para 7 of Part 1 of Sch 6.

Table 5.11   *Sch 6, Part 1, para 7: notification requirements following making interim or final management orders*

When	Served on	Information	Together with
As soon as practicable after making an interim or a final management order	The occupiers of the house	Reasons for making the order. The date it was made. The general effect of the order. Date it will cease to have effect. For final management orders – a general description of the way the house is to be managed by the authority in accordance with the management scheme.	Copy of the order (which in the case of final management orders will contain the management scheme).
Within seven days of the making of the order	Relevant persons	As above plus: • the decision of the authority whether to pay compensation to a third party; • the amount of the compensation if any; • rights of appeal; • the period within which the appeal must be made.	Copy of the order (which in the case of final management orders will contain the management scheme).

5.110   People are 'relevant persons' if they are owners or managers of the property. Owners are defined as people who have an estate or interest in the property but excludes those who have a lease with an unexpired term of three years or less.

5.111   Similar procedural requirements apply to the variation or revocation of interim and final management orders. The provisions are set out in Part 2 of Sch 1 to the Act – paras 9–23. They are summarised in Table 5.12.

Table 5.12   *Sch 6, Part 2: procedural requirements for the variation or revocation of management orders*

When	Served on	Information	Together with	Consultation requirements
Before varying the interim or final management order	Each relevant person	Statement that the authority is proposing a variation. The effect of the variation. The reasons for the variation. The end of the consultation period.		Must consider representations made in accordance with the notice and not withdrawn.
Following a decision to vary the interim or final management order and within seven days of the decision	Each relevant person	The reasons for the decision. The date on which it was made. The right of appeal. The period within which an appeal may be made.	A copy of the decision to vary the interim or final management order.	
Before refusing to vary the interim or final management order	Each relevant person	Statement that the authority are proposing to refuse to vary the interim or final management order. The reasons for the refusal. The end of the consultation period.		Must consider representations made in accordance with the notice and not withdrawn.
Following refusal to vary the interim or final management order and within seven days of the decision	The licence holder and each relevant person	The authority's decision not to vary the interim or final management order. The reasons for the decision. The date upon which it was made. The right of appeal. The period within which an appeal may be made.		

When	Served on	Information	Together with	Consultation requirements
Before revoking the interim or final management order	Each relevant person	Statement that the authority are proposing to revoke the interim or final management order. The reasons for the revocation. The end of the consultation period.		Must consider representations made in accordance with the notice and not withdrawn.
Following the decision to revoke the interim or final management order and within seven days of the decision	Each relevant person	The reasons for the decision. The date on which it was made. The right of appeal against the decision. The period within which an appeal may be made.	Copy of the decision to revoke the interim or final management order.	
Before refusing to revoke the interim or final management order	Each relevant person	Statement that the authority is refusing to revoke the interim or final management order. The reasons for refusal. The end of the consultation period.		Must consider representations made in accordance with the notice and not withdrawn.
Following refusal and within seven days of the decision	Each relevant person	The reasons for the decision and the date on which it was made. The right of appeal against the decision. The period within which an appeal may be made.	Copy of the decision not to revoke the interim or final management order.	

APPEALS

5.112   If a landlord disagrees with the local authority's decision to make an interim or final management order or with the terms of a management scheme, he or she can appeal against the decision to the Residential Property Tribunal. The tribunal has wide powers and considerable discretion in such circumstances and can confirm the order with or without amendments to the terms (including where relevant the terms of the management scheme) or revoke it and order that a licence should be granted or a temporary exemption notice issued.

5.113   There are three rights of appeal. These are the right to appeal against:

- the making of the order which can be appealed by a relevant person;
- the variation or revocation of an order or the refusal to vary or revoke and order which can be appealed by a relevant person;
- decisions in respect of compensation payable to third parties – appealable by the third party.

There is also an extemely limited right of appeal against the failure of an interim management order to provide for the payment of interest on any surpluses of income over expenditure when the interim management order has been made by the tribunal.

5.114   A relevant person is an owner or a manager of the house or part of the house. Tenants with unexpired terms of three years or less are specifically excluded from the definition of relevant person.[1] Providing tenants with rights of appeal was specifically rejected by the Government as both inappropriately time consuming and opening those tenants to the risk of retaliatory action by the landlord.[2]

5.115   The details are set out in Part 3 of Sch 6 to the Act and summarised in Table 5.13.

---

1   Paragraph 35 of Part 3 of Sch 6.
2   See *Hansard*, HL, vol 664, col 763 (9 September 2004).

Table 5.13 *Sch 6, Part 3: appeals against decisions relating to management orders*

Paragraph	The right to appeal against	The appellant	Time limits	Powers of the RPT	Additional comments
1(a)	The decision of the housing authority to make an interim or final management order. This right of appeal does not include a right of appeal against a discretionary interim management order[1] or an interim management order made by the tribunal in accordance with Sch 6, para 26(5).[2]	A relevant person.	28 days (or longer if RPT is satisfied of good reason for the failure to appeal before the end of the period (and for any delay in applying for permission to appeal out of time).	The RPT may confirm or vary or revoke the order. If the RPT revokes an interim or final management order and the house requires licensing under Part 2 or Part 3 then RPT must either direct the local housing authority to grant a licence on terms it directs or make an interim management order on terms it directs[3] or direct the local housign authority to serve a temproary exemption notice in respect of the house. There is a limited right of appeal against the terms of such an interim management order dealt with in para 24(2).	Operates as a rehearing but can take into account matters of which the authority was unaware. The effective date of the confirmation, variation or revocation is the date specified in the tribunal order or (in the case of a final management order) as from the tribunal's order. If no appeal is brought within the time limit the order is final and conclusive as to the matters which could have been raised on appeal.
24(1)(b)	The terms of the interim or final management order (including for final orders the terms of the management scheme).	A relevant person.	At any time the order is in force.	The RPT is limited to determining whether the order should be varied by the tribunal so as to include a term providing for the matter in question and(if so) what provision should be made by the term.	Operates as a rehearing but can take into account matters of which the authority was unaware.

1   That is, one made under s 102(4) or (7).
2   That is, one made by the tribunal on the revocation of a final management order.
3   The tribunal can do this despite s 102(9) which provides that nothing in s 102 'requires or authorises the making of an interim management order in respect of a house if (a) an interim management order has been previously made in respect of it and (b) the authority have not exercised any relevant function in respect of the house at any time after the making of the order'.

Paragraph	The right to appeal against	The appellant	Time limits	Powers of the RPT	Additional comments
24(2)	The decision of the tribunal to make an interim management (either on revocation of a management order or as a result of an application by the local housing authority) the right of appeal is limited to the failure of the order to provide for the rate of interest and the intervals at which payment of interest on the surplus of rent over expenditure is paid to the landlord.[1]	A relevant person.			
28	The decision or refusal to vary or revoke an interim management order or a final management order.	A relevant person.	28 days (or longer if RPT is satisfied of good reason for the failure to appeal before the end of the period (and for any delay in applying for permission to appeal out of time).	The tribunal may confirm, reverse or vary the decision of the local housing authority. If the appeal is against a decision of the authority to refuse to revoke the order, the tribunal may make an order revoking the order as from a date specified in its order.	Operates as a rehearing but can take into account matters of which the authority was unaware.
32	A local housing authority decision not to pay compensation to a third party in respect of any interference with his rights as a result of the interim or final management order or the decision as to the amount of compensation.	The third party.	28 days from the date when the authority notifies the third party of its decision in relation to compensation.[2]	The tribunal may confirm, reverse or vary the decision of the local housing authority. Where the tribunal reverses or varies the decision in respect of a final management order it must vary the management scheme accordingly.	Operates as a rehearing but can take into account matters of which the authority was unaware

1   This appeal right is specifically mentioned in s 110(5)(a) and (b).
2   Under s 128(2).

5.116 The availability of a right to appeal has additional significance because it determines the operative periods of orders under the Act. The time period during which an appeal right remains outstanding and an order not operative under the Act is set out in Table 5.14.

Table 5.14 *Sch 6, Part 3: the operative time of orders*

For the purposes of	*If . . .*	*The operative time is*
The coming into force of final management orders[1]	No appeal is made under para 24 before the end of 28 days	28 days after the date of the order.
	An appeal is made under para 24 and a decision of the RPT is made which confirms the order[2]	The expiry of the period within which an appeal may be made to the Lands Tribunal if an appeal is not made within that period; or if an appeal to the Lands Tribunal is made the time when a decision is made by the Lands Tribunal to confirm the order.
	The appeal is withdrawn – this operates as a decision to confirm the order.	
The variation or revocation of interim or final management orders[3]	No appeal is made under para 28 before the end of 28 days	28 days after the decision to vary or revoke or to refuse to vary or revoke the interim or final management order.
	An appeal is made under para 28 and a decision of the RPT is made which confirms the variation or revocation	The expiry of the period within which an appeal may be made to the Lands Tribunal if an appeal is not made within that period; or if an appeal to the Lands Tribunal is made the time when a decision is made by the Lands Tribunal to vary or revoke the order.
	The appeal is withdrawn – this operates as a decision to vary or revoke the order appealed against.	

---

1   Under s 114(2) The operative period is set out in Sch 6, Pt 3, para 27.
2   A decision which confirms the order includes a decision which confirms it with variation.
3   Under ss 111(2), 112(2), 121(2) or 122(2). The operative period is set out in Sch 6, Pt 3, para 31.

CONCLUSION

5.117   Interim and final management orders provide local housing authorities with mechanisms to ensure necessary improvements in the physical conditions, the management of the rented accommodation and the behaviour of the occupiers where there is no available 'fit and proper' person to take on the responsibilities of a licence in areas where licensing is required under Part 2 or Part 3 of the Act. They also provide local housing authorities with the power to impose measures in response to the needs of the occupiers or the neighbours of 'problem' housing which falls outside of the requirements of Part 2 and Part 3 in certain limited circumstances.

5.118   The impact of the provisions is debatable. Either they are over-bureaucratic because of the need to constrain the local housing authority in dealing with someone else's property and will be used very little or they represent a major step towards a national system of licensing for all private rented housing. It will be interesting to see how the use of the provisions develops.

EMPTY DWELLING MANAGEMENT ORDERS

5.119   Table 5.15 summarises the provisions on empty dwelling management orders ('EDMOs').

Table 5.15   *Empty Dwelling Management Orders*

Section Number	Summary	Comment
132	EDMOs: introductory	This provides the definitions contained in this chapter and cross refers to Sch 7.
133	Making interim EDMOs	Detailed provisions for local housing authority for making interim EDMOs.
134	Authorisation of the making of interim EDMOs	Role of the RTP and conditions to be applied in authorising an interim EDMO.
135	Local authority's duties once interim EDMOs in force	Describes continuing duties on local housing authority for interim EDMOs.
136	Making final EDMOs	Local housing authority final EDMOs.
137	Local authority's duties once final EDMOs in force	Local housing authority duties concerning final EDMOs.
138	Compensation – third parties	Compensation provisions for third parties.

Background

5.120   The consultation paper *Empty Homes: temporary management, lasting solutions*[1] set out measures to bring more unoccupied privately owned homes back into use. The consultation paper gave two specific objectives:

- to provide a mechanism for bringing empty homes back into use that complements voluntary leasing arrangements and is not as protracted and over-prescriptive as existing enforcement powers;
- to provide a mechanism for bringing dilapidated empty homes back into use that does not require owners to fund renovation from their own resources.'

5.121   The consultation and the ODPM's risk assessment[2] of the proposals for reform considered that an empty home was a wasted resource both for the owner who could otherwise make financial gains by letting or selling the property, and for those who are in need of housing. In addition, it was considered that empty homes may have negative impacts particularly with regard to anti-social behaviour both on neighbouring residents and the wider community.

5.122   According to Government statistics the number of privately owned empty homes has been decreasing since the early 1990s. Nonetheless numbers still remain significant. It was estimated that in 2003 there were 308,000 long-term[3] empty dwellings in the private sector across England.[4] The private sector, which accounts for 80% of the dwelling stock in England, accounted for nearly 84% of empty homes.

5.123   The proposals for EDMOs were introduced late in the Parliamentary process. The hint that the government were planning to introduce such provisions in the Lords during the second reading of the Bill prior to any introduction of an amendment where Lord Rooker stated:

> 'The other issue is empty homes. There has been a lot of support to allow local authorities to make empty homes management orders on long-term empty homes. There was a limited debate on the matter in the other place; we will have a much wider debate in this House. We consulted on the issue last year, so it is not new; we received a positive response. Now is the right time to legislate to deal with the hard core of long-term empty homes.'[5]

Lord Rooker formally introduced the government amendments on 13 September 2004.[6]

---

1   ODPM (May 2003).
2   www.odpm.gov.uk./stellent/groups/odpm–housing/documents/source/odpm–housing–source–03104.doc
3   A long-term empty dwelling refers to a dwelling that has remained vacant for more than six months.
4   Local Authority Housing Investment Programme returns, April 2003.
5   *Hansard*, HL, vol 662, col 87 (7 June 2004).
6   *Hansard*, HL, vol 664, col 903 et seq (13 September 2004).

The provisions in detail

EDMOs

5.124   An EDMO allows a local housing authority to effectively 'step into the shoes' of the owner of an unoccupied dwelling.

5.125   There are two types of order – interim EDMO and final EDMO.[1] EDMOs allow a local housing authority to secure the occupation and proper management of privately owned houses and flats that have been unoccupied for a specified period of time and where certain other conditions are met.[2]

5.126   An EDMO is made against the person with the most relevant interest in the dwelling – known as the 'relevant proprietor'.[3] Where the dwelling is held on a freehold this would be the freeholder. Where the dwelling is subject to a lease, the relevant proprietor would be the leaseholder with the shortest unexpired term, provided it still has more than seven years to run. Where the dwelling is subject to a lease that has less than seven years left to run, the relevant proprietor would be the next person up in the chain of ownership with a lease of more than seven years or, if there is no such superior lease, the freeholder.[4] Any other person with an interest in the dwelling is treated as a third party to an EDMO.[5]

Effect on ownership rights

5.127   When an EDMO is in force, the local housing authority takes over most of the rights and responsibilities of the relevant proprietor and may exercise them as if it were the relevant proprietor. For example, it has the right to possession of the dwelling whilst the order is in force. However, the local housing authority does not become the legal owner of the property and cannot sell the property or mortgage it.

5.128   A relevant proprietor is not entitled to receive any rent or other payments from anyone occupying the dwelling and may not exercise any rights to manage the dwelling whilst an EDMO is in force. Nevertheless, the relevant proprietor retains their right to dispose of their interest in the property.

5.129   The validity of a mortgage or superior lease of the property and any rights or remedies available to the mortgage lender or lessor are unaffected by the EDMO, except where they would prevent the local housing authority exercising its power to grant a tenancy or some other right to occupy the dwelling.

5.130   An EDMO is classified as a local land charge and the local housing authority may apply to have details of it entered on the Land Registry. Any sum of money recoverable from the relevant proprietor under an EDMO is, until recovered, a charge on the dwelling.

---

1   Section 132(1)(a), (b), (2), (3).
2   Section 132(4)(a), (b).
3   Section 132(4)(c).
4   Ibid.
5   Section 132(4)(d).

Arrangements for compensation

5.131 A third party may apply to a Residential Property Tribunal ('RPT') for an order requiring a local housing authority to pay them compensation for any interference with their rights in respect of a property on which an application for authorisation of an interim EDMO is made.

5.132 A third party may also request a local housing authority to pay compensation for interference with their rights in respect of a dwelling on which a final EDMO is made and they may appeal to a RPT if the local housing authority refuses to pay compensation or they consider the amount is inadequate.

Termination of leases

5.133 When applying for authorisation to make an interim EDMO, or in making a final EDMO, a local housing authority may apply to a RPT for an order to terminate an existing lease or licence of the property. This allows for the termination of a lease or licence where the property is not being occupied.

5.134 If the local housing authority is unable to terminate an occupation arrangement by serving notice to quit, the RPT may make an order of termination provided it is satisfied the dwelling is not being occupied under a lease or licence and the local housing authority requires possession of it to secure occupation.

5.135 In making an order terminating a lease or licence, a RPT may require the local housing authority to pay compensation to the dispossessed person.[1] Compensation paid out by the local housing authority can be recovered out of any surplus rent obtained under the EDMO.[2]

Interim EDMOs

5.136 In order to make an interim EDMO, a local housing authority must apply for authorisation from a RPT.[3] For this application to be effective there must be no one in occupation of the property, whether or not the occupation is lawful or unlawful.[4] The local housing authority must consider that making an interim EDMO is the most appropriate course of action taking account of the rights of the owner and the wider community in which the dwelling is located.

Authorisation of interim EDMOs

5.137 Before a Residential Property Tribunal can authorise the making of an interim EDMO it must be satisfied that:

- the property has been wholly unoccupied for at least the prescribed period of time (the minimum period will be six months);[5]

---

1   Schedule 7, para 22(6).
2   Schedule 7, para 23.
3   Section 133(1) subject to s 134.
4   Section 133(2).
5   Section 134(1), (2)(a).

- the owner does not intend to take immediate steps to secure occupation of the property;[1]
- there is a reasonable prospect that the property will become occupied if an interim EDMO is made;[2] and
- the local housing authority has complied with its duties in seeking to make an interim EDMO, including any matters that may be set out in regulations.[3]

5.138 In authorising an interim EDMO the RPT must take account of the interests of the wider community and the effect on third parties.[4] The RPT must also be satisfied that the case does not come within any exempt category that may be provided by the appropriate national authority (the Secretary of State in England or the National Assembly in Wales).[5]

5.139 The provisions provide that the appropriate national authority may, in particular, prescribe exemptions to cover the following circumstances:

- the principal homes of absent owners;
- second homes and holiday homes;
- homes undergoing repairs of renovation or awaiting planning or building regulations approval;
- homes on the market for sale or letting; and
- homes where the relevant proprietor died less than a specified period of time before the application for an order was made.[6]

5.140 An interim EDMO comes into force as soon as it has been authorised and can last for a maximum of 12 months.[7] Once an interim EDMO is in force, a local housing authority must take steps to secure occupation and proper management of the property.[8] Nevertheless, the local housing authority may only grant a tenancy (or some other right of occupation) to someone with the consent of the relevant proprietor.[9]

Final EDMOs

5.141 A local housing authority may make a final EDMO either to replace an interim EDMO or a previous final EDMO if the local housing authority considers the property would otherwise become or remain unoccupied.[10] (For example, if the relevant proprietor refused to allow a tenancy to be granted under an interim EDMO and the local housing authority considered that once the order ceased to have effect the property would be likely to remain unoccupied, that would be grounds to revoke the interim EDMO early and make a final EDMO to replace it.)

5.142 If a property that is subject to a final EDMO is unoccupied, a local housing authority may make a new final EDMO to replace it provided that the local housing

---

1   Section 134(2)(c).
2   Section 134(2)(b).
3   Section 134(2)(c), (d).
4   Section 134(3)(a), (b), (4).
5   Section 134(5).
6   Section 134(6).
7   Section 135(1), Sch 7, Part 1, para 1.
8   Section 135(2)–(4).
9   Section 135, Sch 7, para 7.
10 Section 136(1)(a), (b).

authority is satisfied it has taken all steps it was appropriate for it to take to secure occupation of the property.[1]

5.143 In this process the local housing authority must consider that making a final EDMO is the most appropriate course of action when taking account of the interests of the community and the effect the final EDMO will have on the rights of the relevant proprietor and any third parties to the EDMO.[2]

5.144 A local housing authority does not need to obtain authorisation from a RPT to make a final EDMO.

5.145 Once a final EDMO is in force the local housing authority has a number of duties.[3] A local housing authority is under a duty to review the operation of a final EDMO from time to time.[4] If the property is unoccupied, the local housing authority must consider whether there are any steps it could take to secure occupation or whether it is necessary to keep the EDMO in force. If the local housing authority concludes that there are no steps it could take to secure occupation, or that keeping the order in force is not necessary, the local housing authority must revoke the EDMO.[5]

5.146 A final management order can only be made if an interim management order comes to an end or is otherwise revoked or it is made to immediately follow a previous final management order (which has ended or been revoked).

5.147 Subject to any appeal, a final EDMO comes into force no earlier than the day after the period for appealing has expired and lasts for the period specified in the order, which can be up to seven years.

Management scheme

5.148 A final EDMO must contain a management scheme setting out how the local housing authority intends to carry out its duties and how it will account for moneys expended and collected whilst it is operative. The local housing authority must keep full accounts of income and expenditure and provide anyone with a relevant interest in the dwelling reasonable access to inspect them.[6]

5.149 The management scheme must include details of the following:[7]

- work the local housing authority intends to carry out to the dwelling and an estimate of expenditure;
- the rent the dwelling might be expected to fetch on the open market and the rent the local housing authority will seek to obtain;
- any compensation payable to third parties;
- where the amount of rent payable is less than the open market rent, the management scheme must account for the difference. For example, the local housing authority is permitted to charge a sub-market rent, but it must make up any shortfall out of its own resources.

---

1 Section 136(2).
2 Section 136(3)–(5).
3 Section 137(1).
4 Section 137(4).
5 Section 137(6)(a).
6 Schedule 7, Pt 3, para 13.
7 Ibid.

5.150   The management scheme must also include details of how the local housing authority intends to pay the relevant proprietor, any surplus remaining after deduction of its relevant expenditure and any compensation payable.[1]

5.151   The management scheme may also state if the local housing authority intends to carry over any surplus to a subsequent final EDMO or, where there is a deficit, how it intends to recover the deficit under a subsequent final EDMO.[2]

5.152   Anyone affected by a management scheme who considers the local housing authority is not managing the dwelling in accordance with the management scheme may apply to a Residential Property Tribunal for an order requiring the local housing authority to do so.[3]

Notification procedures

5.153   Before applying to a RPT for authorisation to make an interim EDMO, a local housing authority must make reasonable efforts to contact the owner and find out if he has any intentions to bring the dwelling back into occupation.[4]

5.154   Before making a final EDMO, a local housing authority must serve a copy of the proposed order on all relevant persons and a notice stating the reason for making the order and the main terms of it. The notice must also invite representations about the proposal (which the local housing authority must consider).[5]

5.155   When an interim or final EDMO is made the local housing authority must, within seven days, serve a copy of the order and a notice on the relevant proprietor and other persons with an interest in the dwelling.[6]

5.156   The notice must state:[7]

- the reason for making the order and the date on which it is made;
- the general effect of the order;
- the date on which it is proposed the order will cease to have effect.

In addition, the notice must advise of any right to appeal against the order.[8]

Variation and revocation of EDMOs

5.157   A relevant proprietor or someone else with an interest in the dwelling is entitled to ask the local housing authority to vary or revoke an interim or final EDMO at any time.[9]

5.158   The terms of an interim or final EDMO (including the terms of a management scheme) may be varied if the local housing authority considers it appropriate to do so. A person with an interest in the dwelling may request a variation and may appeal to a RPT

---

1   Schedule 7, Pt 3, para 13.
2   Ibid.
3   Schedule 7, Pt 3, para 14.
4   Ibid.
5   Ibid.
6   Ibid.
7   Ibid.
8   Ibid.
9   Schedule 7, Pt 3, para 15 et seq.

against a decision of the local housing authority to vary or, as the case may be, refusal to vary the order.[1]

5.159   A local housing authority may revoke an EDMO if:[2]

- it concludes that there are no steps it can take to secure occupation of the dwelling;
- it is satisfied that the dwelling will become or continue to be occupied following revocation;
- it is satisfied that the dwelling is to be sold;
- a final EDMO (or subsequent final EDMO) has been made to replace the order;
- it concludes that it should revoke the order so it does not interfere with the rights of a third party;
- in any other circumstance it considers it appropriate to do so.

5.160   However, if the dwelling is occupied at the time the revocation is proposed, the local housing authority may only revoke with the consent of the relevant proprietor (unless the revocation is necessary so that a final EDMO may be made). This restriction is provided so that the relevant proprietor is not left to manage tenancies he did not enter into. Therefore, if the local housing authority decides to revoke the order and hand back responsibility for the dwelling to the relevant proprietor, it must first bring to an end any occupation, unless the relevant proprietor is willing for the occupation to continue.[3]

5.161   The local housing authority may make revocation subject to payment of any expenditure incurred by it that has not already been recouped from rental income. It might also refuse to revoke the order on the grounds that the property would be likely to be left vacant.

5.162   Where revocation is refused, a right of appeal to a Residential Property Tribunal is provided.

Money matters

5.163   A local housing authority may use any rent collected from a person occupying the dwelling to meet its expenditure and to pay any compensation it is required to pay to a third party. When an EDMO ceases to have effect, the local housing authority must pay the relevant proprietor any surplus after deduction of such relevant sums (and if appropriate interest on the balance). However, in the case of an interim EDMO, a local housing authority is not required to pay any surplus to the relevant proprietor if the order is followed by a final EDMO.

5.164   If, when an EDMO ceases to have effect, there is a deficit rather than a surplus after deduction of relevant sums, the local housing authority cannot recover the amount from the relevant proprietor unless:

- he has agreed to pay it, for example, as a condition for revoking the order early; or
- it is an amount equivalent to a service charge paid by the local housing authority;
- in the case of an interim EDMO, the local housing authority considers the relevant proprietor unreasonably refused consent to allow it to grant a tenancy.

---

1   Schedule 7, Pt 3, para 15 et seq.
2   Ibid.
3   Ibid.

5.165   If a final EDMO is made to replace either an interim EDMO or a previous final EDMO, any deficit may be carried over and recovered from income under the subsequent order.

Appeals

5.166   A person who is affected may appeal to a RPT against:[1]

- a decision of a local housing authority to make a final EDMO;
- the terms of a final EDMO (including the terms of a management scheme); or
- the terms of an interim EDMO (relating to payment of any balance of rent left after deduction of relevant expenditure and any compensation payable to a third party or a dispossessed landlord or tenant);
- a decision of the local authority to vary or revoke an interim or final EDMO or its refusal to vary or revoke an interim or final EDMO;

5.167   A third party may appeal to a RPT against a decision of a local housing authority not to pay compensation to him, or a decision relating to the amount of compensation payable.[2]

Other matters

Repairs and renovation works

5.168   There are no restrictions on the works of repair or renovation a local housing authority may undertake under an EDMO.[3] However, the work must be commensurate with the income it is likely to receive during the lifetime of the order. As an interim EDMO can only last for 12 months, it is unlikely that a local housing authority would expend larger sums of money to renovate a dwelling without obtaining the relevant proprietor's consent to the grant of a tenancy.

5.169   A local housing authority is more likely to consider undertaking significant work under a final EDMO as it would have up to seven years to recoup the cost from rental income. Details of any work the local housing authority intends to carry out must be contained in the management scheme. Someone with an estate or interest in the dwelling may object to such provision in the management scheme and appeal against the terms of it to a Residential Property Tribunal.

Furniture

5.170   A local housing authority has the right to possession of furniture or other articles in a dwelling that is owned by the relevant proprietor whilst the order is in force. But the relevant proprietor may request possession of the furniture. A local authority may renounce the right to possession of such furniture by notifying the relevant proprietor. If so, the authority must store the furniture at its own cost.[4]

---

1   See Sch 7, Part 4.
2   Ibid and s 138.
3   See Sch 7.
4   Schedule 7, paras 20 and 21.

5.171 A local authority may supply furniture to a dwelling subject to an interim or final EDMO and can recover the cost of it as relevant expenditure.[1]

Powers of entry

5.172 A local housing authority has the right to enter a dwelling subject to an EDMO to survey its condition or to carry out works. Any occupier who prevents an officer, employee, agent or contractor of a local housing authority from carrying out their duties may be ordered to stop by a magistrate's court. Failure to comply with an order of the court is an offence.[2]

5.173 A local housing authority may apply to a court for a warrant to authorise entry to a dwelling subject to an EDMO.[3]

OVERCROWDING AND OVERCROWDING NOTICES

Introduction

5.174 Overcrowding provisions are now to be found in two statutes. The first place where the overcrowding provisions appear is in Part 10 of the HA 1985.[4] The Act does not repeal them, although it lays the ground for doing so. So for the time being Part 10 stays.

5.175 The Act[5] enables the appropriate national authority[6] to make such provision as it considers appropriate for determining whether a dwelling is overcrowded for the purposes of Part 10 of the HA 1985 and provides[7] that an order under this section may modify any enactment when making provision for:

- regulating decisions by local housing authorities as to whether premises are overcrowded; and prescribing:[8]
- the factors that must be taken into account when arriving at such decisions;[9] and
- the procedures that local authorities should follow when making such decisions.[10]

---

1   Schedule 7, paras 20 and 21.
2   Schedule 7, para 25.
3   Schedule 7, para 25(3).
4   The provisions in the HA 1985, ss 324–338 are based on it being an offence to cause or permit overcrowding measured by the room standard or the space standard. The former prohibits persons over ten of the opposite sex (apart from adults living together) sharing the same room and the latter being contravened when the number of persons sleeping in a dwelling is in excess of the permitted number. The space standard is defined in the legislation by reference to tables detailing the aggregate floor areas for all rooms in a dwelling and the respective permitted number. Regulations provide guidance on the method of measurement. In respect of the space standard children under one year of age do not count, and children over one and under 10 count as half a person.
5   Section 216.
6   Appropriate national authority is defined in s 261(1).
7   Section 216(3).
8   Section 216(2).
9   Section 216(2)(a).
10   Section 216(2)(b).

5.176   The above provisions are to be kept separate from the provisions concerning overcrowding in HMOs,[1] which used to be in Part 11 of the Housing Act 1985[2] and which have now been repealed[3] with new provisions being put in their place.[4]

Overcrowding notices

5.177   The effect of an overcrowding notice is that the person served must comply with the terms of the notice and if they fail to do so they commit an offence for which they are liable to be fined up to level 4. The notice must do either of two things. Either it must contain a requirement prohibiting the person served from permitting new residents[5] which could be done if the authority believe an excessive number of persons is likely to be accommodated.[6] Alternatively, the notice may be served which requires the person served to refrain from permitting a room to be occupied otherwise than in accordance with the notice or refrain from permitting a situation where it is not possible to avoid persons (who are not living together as man and wife) of opposite sexes sleeping in the same room.[7]

5.178   Whether or not the notice imposes a requirement as to new residents, children under 10 are to be disregarded.[8]

5.179   The important point to note is that the provisions will not apply to licensed HMOs because they can be dealt with under the licensing procedure under Part 2 of the Act. The Government's spokesman in the House of Lords considered that it would be tantamount to introducing a shadow licensing regime to require local housing authorities when deciding whether or not to serve an overcrowding notice to have regard to the prescribed standards for application to HMOs under Part 2.[9] This means there is scope for different authorities to apply different standards for room sizes.

---

1   Section 146(1) provides that an HMO means a house in multiple occupation for the purposes of Part 6 as defined in ss 254 to 259.
2   HA 1985, ss 358–364.
3   Section 258 and Sch 16.
4   Sections 139–144.
5   Section 142.
6   Section 139(2).
7   Section 141.
8   Sections 141(2)(a), 142(3)(a).
9   *Hansard*, HL, vol 664, col 946 (13 September 2004).

5.180

Table 5.16 *Summary of the provisions relating to overcrowding notices*

	Overcrowding notice
The premises in relation to which an overcrowding notice may be served	HMOs[1] in relation to which no interim or final management order is in force and which is not required to be licensed under Part 2.[2]
Circumstances for service of an overcrowding notice	Where the local housing authority considers that an excessive number of persons is being, or is likely to be, accommodated in the HMO concerned;[3] and where: ● at least seven days before the local housing authority has (a) informed in writing every relevant person[4] of their intention to serve the notice; and (b) ensured that, so far as is reasonably possible, every occupier of the HMO concerned is informed of the authority's intention;[5] ● the local housing authority has given the relevant persons an opportunity of making representations about the intention to serve the notice.[6]
Contents of a valid notice	The notice must state in relation to each room in the HMO concerned: ● what the local housing authority consider to be the maximum number of persons by whom the room is suitable to be occupied as sleeping accommodation at any one time; or that the local housing authority consider that the room is unsuitable to be occupied as sleeping accommodation;[7] ● the requirement not to permit excessive numbers to sleep in the HMO or the requirement not to admit new residents.[8]
Who has to be served with the notice	A person who is to the knowledge of the local authority a person having an estate or interest in the HMO or a person managing or having control of it.
To whom copies must also be sent	Not applicable but as far as is reasonably possible the local housing authority must ensure that every occupier of the HMO concerned is informed, at least seven days in advance of the authority's intention to serve an overcrowding notice.[9]
Who can appeal	A person aggrieved by the notice.[10]
Grounds	Unlimited.

---

1   Defined in ss 254–259.
2   Section 139(1)(a), (b) and see s 61 for requirements for an HMO to be licensed.
3   Section 139(2).
4   Section 139(9) defines relevant person as a person who is to the knowledge of the local authority a person having an estate or interest in the HMO or a person managing or having control of it.
5   Section 139(3).
6   Section 139(4); consultation involves not only providing sufficient information to the consultees to permit them to make an intelligible response but also conscientiously considering the various responses that may be received; it must go without saying that in addition to telling the relevant persons that their views are sought, as the statute requires, this would also be done.
7   Section 140(1).
8   Section 140(3).
9   Section 139(3)(b).
10   Section 143(1).

	Overcrowding notice
Destination of appeal	The Residential Property Tribunal.[1]
Time limit for appealing	21 days[2] with a limited discretion to extend.[3]
Nature of the appeal	By way of rehearing but the appeal may be determined having regard to matters of which the authority were unaware.[4]
Power of the tribunal	The tribunal can confirm, quash or vary the notice.

5.181   The result of an overcrowding notice served with the requirement that the person served must stop permitting a room to be occupied as sleeping accommodation[5] would mean those using the room concerned would be aggrieved and have the necessary standing to appeal. If a person had an agreement to enter a tenancy for a room and it was agreed a number of other members of the family would be permitted occupiers then this would be an assured tenancy.[6] In those circumstances even though not yet in occupation, the tenant having a legal estate might qualify as an aggrieved person if the overcrowding notice prevented occupation of the premises demised.

1   Section 143(1).
2   Section 139(5); after which time, if no appeal is brought the notice becomes operative; the notice is then treated as final and conclusive and a person who contravenes the notice commits an offence; see s 139(6) and s 139(7). If an appeal is brought the notice will then not become operative until after the time for appealing to the Lands Tribunal against the tribunal's decision has expired. If such a second appeal is mounted the notice will not become operative unless and until the Lands Tribunal confirms the notice: see s 143(4).
3   Section 143(6).
4   Section 143(2). It is arguable that given that the ability to appeal under the HA 1985 was also given to persons aggrieved that the scope of the appeal may also encompass an allegation that the building is not an HMO or that the authority did not have the power to serve the notice; as was found to be the case in relation to the previous legislation; see *Nolan v Leeds CC* (1990) 23 HLR 136.
5   Section 141(1)(a).
6   HA 1988, s 45(1).

Chapter 6

HOME INFORMATION PACKS

INTRODUCTION

6.1 Part 5 of the Housing Act 2004 introduces a new legal duty on a seller or, more usually, the agent, of residential properties in England and Wales to have, before marketing and at the very start of the process, a home information pack of standard documents available for prospective buyers.

6.2 The Act does not prescribe definitively what documents or information shall be required in the home information pack. It is anticipated that the pack will contain documents and information which are currently available only after terms of the sale are agreed and before exchange of contracts including a report on the condition of the property.

Background

6.3 These provisions were contained in the seller's pack proposals in the Homes Bill 2000 introduced in Parliament in December of that year. That Bill completed its passage through the House of Commons ('the Commons') but then fell through lack of time and opposition in the House of Lords ('the Lords') when Parliament was dissolved for the general election in 2001.

6.4 The Government claims a manifesto commitment to introduce these provisions. The manifesto prior to the 2001 election contains the following statement:

> 'Labour will make it easier for people buying and selling homes through a new seller's pack.'

It is to be noted that there is no provision in that manifesto for the furnishing of the pack to be compulsory or for it to contain any particular document such as a home condition report.

6.5 The Housing Bill was introduced in Parliament in December 2003, three years almost to the day after the Homes Bill 2000. The provisions were broadly similar to those of the earlier Bill although the name of the pack was changed from 'seller's pack' to 'home information pack' and the sanctions from criminal to civil, in response to considerable criticism.

6.6 The passage of Part 5 of the Bill was hard fought, as were the equivalent provisions in the Homes Bill, in the face of widespread opposition from the main participants in the house transfer process, who doubted the relevance and efficacy of the proposals in the agreed quest for improvement to the process.

6.7   As a result, the Bill took nearly a year to pass through Parliament and received the Royal Assent on 19 November 2004 only after a Lords' amendment to make the provision of the pack voluntary was overturned by the Commons at the very end of the Parliamentary Session.

Implementation timetable and further measures

6.8   The Minister, Lord Rooker, explained that:

> 'We have a clear timetable of work and intend to publish final details of the contents of the pack and their application as early as spring next year, with the regulations to follow shortly afterwards . . . We announced . . . at an earlier stage our intention to have a dry run at the pack on a voluntary basis in the six-month period before the launch of the compulsory scheme in 2007. During that period, we will test out all the components of the statutory schemes . . . I can give an assurance that, unless there are unforeseen practical problems that we subsequently identify with the industry, we will undertake a full exercise in a designated area to run alongside the voluntary dry run in the rest of England and Wales . . . The region must be big enough to allow us to know that the thing will work.'[1]

6.9   In the same debate Baroness Hanham pointed out why this was unsatisfactory:

> 'I am bound to observe, at this stage of the Bill, that not one regulation or code of guidance to govern the dry run has been seen by the House . . . We do not know who will report on it or when they will report on it. The only thing we know is that it will start in 2007. What is going to start? We have not the faintest idea. That has been the situation all the way through the progress of the Bill. It is extraordinary that we still have no clear idea how something as important as a pilot for this part of the Bill will be operated . . . Apart from that, as things stand, Parliament will not know the outcome of the pilot. It will not have an opportunity to consider the results before they are implemented throughout the country . . . Throughout the passage of the Bill it [the pilot scheme] has been held up as the Government's answer to how the home information packs will be tested. Yet, unless the Minister changes his mind today, Parliament is not to have any look at the scheme. It is to have no further role in it whatever.'[2]

6.10   Later in the debate the Minister said:

> 'It [the House] certainly will discuss it [the matter]. Although I cannot say whether that would be by means of secondary legislation, I am sure that it would be tabled . . . Equally the other place will discuss it.'[3]

6.11   Baroness Hanham failed in her attempt to persuade the Lords to adopt an amendment which would have obliged the Minister to report to Parliament on the outcome of the pilot scheme and for an order to be obtained for the continuation of the scheme by statutory instrument subject to the approval of both Houses of Parliament.

6.12   The Minister made it clear that there is no fixed date for implementation in 2007:

> 'I do not say that it will be fixed to the last month or even to the quarter of the year.'[4]

In the Committee debate in the Lords the Minister said:

---

1   *Hansard*, HL Deb, 16 November 2004, col 1369/1370.
2   *Hansard*, HL Deb, 16 November 2004, col 1372.
3   *Hansard*, HL Deb, 16 November 2004, col 1377.
4   *Hansard*, HL Deb, 16 November 2004, col 1377.

'We have no intention of introducing the home information pack requirement until we are satisfied all the pieces of the jigsaw – and it is a jigsaw – are in place. We will not, for example, introduce the home information report until we are satisfied that adequate numbers of appropriately qualified and insured home inspectors are available ... The research to date suggests the beginning of 2007 is an achievable target for implementing home information packs. It is challenging but nevertheless achievable. If the blueprint shows that is not the case, we will think again ... Unless we are ready and convinced, we will not do it ... There is no question of us implementing this proposal until everything is in place for a successful introduction.'[1]

THE PROVISIONS IN DETAIL

Meaning of 'residential property' and 'home information pack'

Residential property

6.13   Residential property is defined as premises in England and Wales consisting of a single dwelling-house, comprising a building or part of a building occupied or intended to be occupied as a separate dwelling, including one that is being or is to be constructed.[2] There was some debate as to whether 'or intended to be occupied' should be deleted. The Government opposed this on the basis that there was no justification for excluding unoccupied properties from the scheme. There was also debate concerning the possible deletion of 'and includes one that is being or is to be constructed' and it became clear that the Government would in all probability exercise its powers under s 163(9) to exclude home condition reports from packs for first sales of newly built properties where there was a satisfactory warranty but not for second and subsequent sales.

Home information pack

6.14   A home information pack is defined as 'a collection of documents relating to the property or the terms on which it is or may become available for sale.'[3] There was debate on whether 'or may become' should be deleted. The Government opposed this on the basis that this would create a loophole since it would permit pre-marketing that would amount to marketing in all but name but without triggering the home information pack duties, it being the intention to stipulate that the pack should in all cases be available on day one of marketing.

6.15   There was a proposed amendment which would have added a further sub-section (3) to s 148 which, whilst not germane to this section, made an important point on the Bill as a whole. This would have allowed the Minister 'by regulations to prescribe the operational date of all or part of the introduction of this Part with regard to the capacity effectively to implement' and that no regulations could be made under this section 'unless a draft of the regulations had been laid before, and approved by a resolution of, each House of Parliament.' The first part of the amendment was aimed at the concern that there would not be enough inspectors to deal with the anticipated level of home condition reports. This elicited a response from the Minister that the home condition

---

1   *Hansard*, HL Deb, 13 September 2004, col 972/973.
2   Section s 148(1).
3   Section 148(2).

report proposal would not be implemented were this to be the case. The second part highlighted an increasing trend to relegate important matters to regulations which are not on the face of the Bill and therefore not subject to the same if any level of Parliamentary scrutiny. This is particularly true if the negative procedure is used rather than the positive, as is almost always the case. The amendment was not accepted.

Meaning of 'on the market' and related expressions

6.16 'On the market' is defined as 'when the fact that it is or may become available for sale is, with the intention of marketing the property, first made public in England and Wales by or on behalf of the seller.'[1] There was much debate on what was meant by 'may become available for sale' in s 149(2). It was argued that this would take away the right of pre-marketing as soon as possible – day one marketing. This was presented as an erosion of freedom and would also result in a distortion of the market. The Government declined to accept the argument and said that 'it would open a loophole' – a phrase it continually used – 'by enabling a marketing process to begin before that information had been properly assembled.'[2]

6.17 A fact (that the property is or may become available for sale) is 'made public' when it is advertised or otherwise communicated to the public or a section of the public.[3] The expression 'a section of the public' caused concern since it is not defined in the Bill. It is not helped by the argument that 'the phrase has been used in other Acts of Parliament where some flexibility is desirable.'[4] If, as in this Act, sanctions follow breaches, it would seem important that clear definitions are included so that there can be no doubt. Lord Bassam on behalf of the Government said in the Lords:

> 'Family members, individuals or small groups of people – one's immediate colleagues at work, for example – would not be considered as a section of the public for these purposes. Marketing to such people will therefore not be affected by the duties described elsewhere in this part of the Bill. Generally speaking, the seller would know such people in a private capacity and the property would therefore not be available for sale on the open market.'[5]

6.18 The use of the word 'generally' is unhelpful, as was the further statement by Lord Bassam that:

> 'his (Lord Phillips') example depends very much on the exact form of words used. Of course there will always be difficulties in those sets of circumstances. In the end, this legislation will work well if we use our common sense and have goodwill.'[6]

Acting as estate agent and marketing the property

6.19 Section 150 sets out the circumstances in which a person is regarded as acting as an estate agent although not necessarily calling himself one (eg a solicitor agent). This section was used as an opportunity to argue for regulation of estate agents in view of their enhanced role in the process as a result of this legislation. An amendment was proposed

---

1   Section 149(2).
2   *Hansard*, HL Deb, 13 September 2004, col 995.
3   Section 149(4).
4   *Hansard*, HL Deb, 13 September 2004, col 996.
5   *Hansard*, HL Deb, 13 September 2004, col 996.
6   *Hansard*, HL Deb, 13 September 2004, col 997.

which would have had that effect. Whilst saying, 'We do not say that we do not agree with the amendment'[1] the Government countered this by bringing into the Bill 'a requirement for estate agents to belong to a redress scheme approved by the Secretary of State' (ss 172–174).

6.20 More than one person can be considered responsible for marketing of a property.[2]

6.21 Section 152 sets out the circumstances in which an estate agent will be considered responsible for marketing a property and when that responsibility ceases. The Government made it clear that responsibility will only cease 'when *all* the following three conditions are met: his contract with the seller is terminated; he has ceased to take any action to make public the fact that the property is on the market; and any such action taken on his behalf has ceased.'[3]

Responsibility of the seller

6.22 Responsibility of the seller is contained in s 153 and is a parallel section to s 152. A seller will be considered responsible for marketing if (a) he personally takes the action which makes it known that the property is for sale or (b) a person who is not acting as an estate agent (eg a friend or relative) takes the step which puts the property on the market on the seller's behalf. In addition to the conditions set out in s 152 for responsibility to cease is the further one of the seller instructing someone to act as an estate agent to carry out the marketing and the seller ceasing to carry out any marketing activity.

6.23 In s 152 and s 153 responsibility is said to cease when the property is taken off the market or sold.[4] There is no definition of 'sold', but it is likely to be when contracts are exchanged. Likewise 'taken off the market' is not defined, but the Explanatory Notes say that 'this is an ordinary expression that should be given its usual meaning'.

Duty to have a home information pack

6.24 Section 155 imposes a duty on the responsible person to have in his possession or under his control a home information pack. It also refers to s 163 and the regulations thereunder and states that the pack must comply with the requirements of those regulations. The section sets out certain exceptions which apply where the seller is the responsible person or might appear to be so. This section was the forum for a concerted attempt in the Lords by opposition and some cross-bench peers to make the provision of the pack voluntary. This resulted in the Government being defeated on this on Third Reading by 179 to 132 and the Bill being sent back by the Government to the Lords, who for no very clear reason reversed its vote, the result being that the compulsory element was reinstated. In Committee in the Lords the Minister said:

> 'If we are not confident that it will work, if we are not geared up and the industry is not geared up and we have not got the staff trained, it will not be brought in.[5]

---

1   *Hansard*, HL Deb, 13 September 2004, col 1006.
2   Section 151(2)(a).
3   *Hansard*, HL Deb, 13 September 2004, col 1009.
4   Sections 152(3) and 153(4).
5   *Hansard*, HL Deb, 13 September 2004, col 1013.

...

A case can be made for a voluntary basis, but it would not improve the buying and selling of homes. We cannot make such a case at the same time as saying that we are going to improve the system.'[1]

6.25 There was also an unsuccessful attempt under this section to allow day one marketing without a pack, that to follow within 14 days of marketing. The Minister said:

'I fully admit that this is an area which probably causes the most concern.'[2]

Referring to s 163(9) the Minister added:

'There is no question of the Government introducing home information packs in a way that will cause unnecessary delay in getting homes on to the market. That is not our purpose.'[3]

6.26 There was also an unsuccessful attempt to relieve an individual who markets a property himself from having a home information pack on the basis that otherwise DIY sellers would be discouraged.

Duty to provide copy of home information pack on request

6.27 Section 156(1) imposes the duty to supply the pack (or any part of it) within the 'permitted period', defined as 14 days from the date of the request but subject to s 157(5).[4]

6.28 The documentation that must be supplied by the seller is detailed in s 156(2). This has to comply with the requirements of any regulations under s 163 at the time when the document is provided.

6.29 Section 156(4) contains exceptions to the duty referred to above where the responsible person believes on reasonable grounds that the person requesting could not afford, is not genuinely interested, or is not a person to whom the seller is likely to be prepared to sell the property! It is considered by many to be one of the more bizarre – or, in the words of Lord Hanningfield in the Lords on Third Reading, 'curious'[5] – sub-sections in the Act. Lord Hanningfield added:

'Subsection 4 places an onus on the agent to possess such extraordinary powers of wit and intelligence that, frankly, such people should not be estate agents but secret agents working for MI6 ...This subsection calls for an estate agent who can estimate another person's wealth from the moment that they step into the shop, who can tell a con man from any other member of the public, and – most bizarrely – can tell whether a potential buyer will not be approved by the seller ... This is silly legislation and let us please get rid of it.'[6]

As Baroness Hanham later said: 'How will it be enforced?'[7] These concerns were of no avail and the sub-section remains an unfathomable part of the Bill. At least we know from it that nothing in it authorises the doing of anything which constitutes an unlawful act of discrimination.

1   *Hansard*, HL Deb, 13 September 2004, col 1016.
2   *Hansard*, HL Deb, 14 September 2004, col 1058.
3   *Hansard*, HL Deb, 14 September 2004, col 1059.
4   Section 156(9).
5   *Hansard*, HL Deb, 14 September 2004, col 1080.
6   *Hansard*, HL Deb, 14 September 2004, col 1080/1081.
7   *Hansard*, HL Deb, 14 September 2004, col 1081.

6.30   The duty does not apply if the seller as the responsible person can show that s 155(2) applies and takes reasonable steps to inform the potential buyer that the request should be made to the other person.[1]

6.31   The responsible person may charge a sum not exceeding the reasonable cost of making and, if requested, sending a paper copy of the pack or document.[2] The permitted period is 14 days beginning with the day on which the request is made but subject to s 157(5).[3] If the responsible person ceases to be responsible, the duty to comply with the request ceases.[4] An electronic copy does not constitute compliance unless the buyer acquiesces.[5]

6.32   There were two amendments proposed in the Lords in Committee, both of which were unsuccessful, the second going to a vote. The first addressed the issue of confidentiality, the fear being that the dissemination of packs would be uncontrollable. The second sought to impose an obligation on the buyer to reimburse the cost to the seller or other responsible person who originally paid for the preparation of the pack, putting a cap on the amount.

Imposition of conditions

6.33   A potential buyer may be required to comply with either one or both of the following conditions:

(a)   the payment of the charge set out in s 156(8); and
(b)   the requirement that the buyer accept any terms specified in writing by the seller relating to the use or disclosure of the copy (or any information contained in or derived from it).[6]

6.34   A condition is only effective if it is notified to the potential buyer before the end of the period of 14 days beginning with the day on which the request is made. Where this happens the permitted period under s 156 is the period of 14 days beginning with:

(a)   making the payment demanded; and
(b)   accepting the proposed terms (or such other terms as may be agreed in substitution).

These conditions were added on Report/Third Reading in the Commons. The effect is possibly to put back the date by which the pack has to be provided for a further 14 days or more and therefore delay, even more, marketing.

Duty to ensure authenticity of documents in other situations

6.35   Where a responsible person provides a potential buyer with, or allows them to inspect, any document purporting to be a copy of the home information pack, or a document (or part thereof) included in that pack, the responsible person is under a duty to ensure that the document is authentic.[7] A document will not be authentic unless, at

---

1   Section 156(6), (7).
2   Section 156(8).
3   Section 156(9).
4   Section 156(10).
5   Section 156(11).
6   Section 157.
7   Section 158(1).

the time it is provided or inspected, it is a copy of a home information pack (or part thereof) and that pack, or document, complies with the requirements of any regulations made under s 163.[1] It is an absolute duty. The Lords declined to agree a proposal to amend by inserting 'to take all reasonable care'. However, an indication was given by the Minister in Committee in the Lords that:

> 'The trading standards officer would not serve a penalty charge notice on someone who had taken care to ensure the authenticity of the contents of the pack; it would certainly be most unreasonable to do so. We can put that on record now … We are happy to put on the record that we would regard it as most unlikely that an estate agent who relies on the authenticity of documents supplied from a reliable source will be in breach of any duty to ensure authenticity.'[2]

Application of ss 155 to 158

6.36   Section 154 provides that the person responsible for marketing is subject to the duties imposed by ss 155–158 until his responsibility ceases and that (a) each of those duties is subject to any exception which is provided for in those sections and (b) the duty under s 156(1) is also subject to any conditions imposed under s 157.

Other duties of person acting as estate agent

6.37   Section 159 provides that where an estate agent accepts instructions to market, a copy of the pack, which complies with the requirements of the regulations under s 163, must be in his possession or under his control before taking any action (with the intention of marketing) to communicate to a potential buyer information that the property is, or may become, available. As the Minister said in Committee:

> 'This (section) imposes a duty which affects only estate agents and which applies where some kind of marketing activity takes place that is too limited to trigger the duties imposed by Clauses (155, 156 and 158) … Such an action communicates the fact that a property is, or is about to become, available for sale, but does not put it on the market or make public the fact that the property is on the market … The whole purpose of Clause (159) is to capture an activity that, while amounting to it, does not meet the definition of 'marketing' set out elsewhere in the Bill.'[3]

6.38   Whether the Minister has succeeded is open to doubt. As the Earl of Caithness later said:

> 'Defining it in the way explained by the Minister creates a huge grey area over when a property is on the market … This is an area where there is a potential for conflict and potential grounds for court actions.'[4]

Residential properties not available with vacant possession

6.39   Under s 160 the duties will not apply, for example, where a property is sold subject to a tenancy, but any property marketed will be assumed to be vacant unless the marketing makes it clear that it is not being sold with vacant possession.

---

1   Section 158(2).
2   *Hansard*, HL Deb, 14 September 2004, col 1092/1093.
3   *Hansard*, HL Deb, 14 September 2004, col 1109/1110.
4   *Hansard*, HL Deb, 14 September 2004, col 1110/1111.

Power to provide for further exceptions

6.40   Section 161 allows the Secretary of State to revisit exceptions by regulations. The section was used to attempt to permit marketing with an incomplete pack. The Minister said:

> 'We share the Baroness's concern on the issue. I can assure her that regulations to be made under Clause (163(9)(a)) will achieve this effect without further amendment to the Bill.'[1]

A similar answer was given on an attempt to introduce an amendment excluding disadvantaged area properties from the duties.

Suspension of duties under ss 155 to 159

6.41   Section 162 gives the Government the power to suspend by order the home information pack duties for a specified period and subsequently to revive and further suspend those duties. The Minister described it 'as a long stop in case things go wrong'.[2] This section was added to the Bill at the very last moment on 16 November when the Lords considered the refusal of the Commons to accept the Lords' amendments on Third Reading. The Minister confirmed that there would be a voluntary 'dry run', but also a 'full exercise in a designated area to run alongside the voluntary dry run in the rest of England and Wales.'

Contents of home information packs

6.42   The content of home information packs will be prescribed by regulation at a later date and will essentially be at the discretion of the Secretary of State and therefore without effective scrutiny by Parliament.[3] The regulations can also prescribe particular information which is required or authorised to be included in, or which is to be excluded from, any such document. On the question of what has to be available in the pack before marketing the Government said:

> 'Our expectation . . . would be that marketing could commence without it (information hard to obtain). But if the information exists and despite reasonable efforts it is not available within a reasonable timescale then we propose to provide by regulation that marketing can commence and that the missing information can be added when it practically becomes available.'[4]

6.43   An unsuccessful attempt was made to require under s 163(1) that a statutory instrument under this Part was not to be made unless a draft had been laid and approved by a resolution of each House of Parliament. As Baroness Hamwee said:

> 'These are very important regulations. They are almost of the status of the primary legislation in their importance.'[5]

6.44   A prescribed document or information in it must relate to matters connected with the property (or the sale of the property) that would be of interest to potential buyers.[6]

---

1   *Hansard*, HL Deb, 14 September 2004, col 1112.
2   *Hansard*, HL Deb, 16 November 2004, col 1371.
3   Section 163.
4   *Hansard*, HL Deb, 14 September 2004, col 1121.
5   *Hansard*, HL Deb, 14 September 2004, col 1127.
6   Section 163(4).

6.45   Section 163(5) contains an indication of the information which may be considered relevant, always subject to s 163(9). Section 163(5)(a) refers to information about 'the terms on which it is proposed to sell it'. During the debate in Committee in the Lords the Minister said:

> 'We do not propose to include in the pack a contract or even a document that is capable of becoming a contract when a buyer is found. I can be quite clear about that reassurance.'[1]

Later in the debate the Minister said:

> 'We do not intend that the home information pack should change the principle of caveat emptor – that is not our intention. I did not do Latin – that means 'let the buyer beware'.'[2]

6.46   The Minister used the debate on s 163(5) as an opportunity to comment on updating the pack:

> 'It is not our intention to require the seller to update the pack . . . The information in the pack must not be more than three months old at the point that marketing commences. This does not mean it has to be updated every three months . . . I am saying . . . that no one has to update and have another survey or home condition report done every three months . . . I am making that clear.'[3]

6.47   Further information on what the regulations may require or authorise are contained within s 163(6)–(10).

Home condition reports

6.48   Regulations may require a home condition report to be made by an individual who is a member of an approved certification scheme following an inspection carried out by him in accordance with the provisions of the scheme.[4] This prompted a debate in the Lords on the level of competence required of the Inspector. It is mooted that this would be an NVQ. As was pointed out in the Lords, this is nowhere near the qualification of a chartered surveyor, the person who currently does surveys.

6.49   The Government is able to make provision for the approval of one or more certification schemes.[5]

6.50   The criteria on which the Government must assess the scheme before granting approval are listed in s 164(5). During the debate in Committee in the Lords an amendment was proposed – unsuccessfully – that there should be a requirement to ensure that members of the scheme are completely independent and have no links financial or otherwise with the responsible person. This was designed to overcome a perception that there would otherwise be a clear conflict of interest which would not be in the consumer interest and, as the Earl of Caithness said, would be 'utterly unacceptable'.[6] The Government said:

---

1   *Hansard*, HL Deb, 14 September 2004, col 1134.
2   *Hansard*, HL Deb, 14 September 2004, col 1134.
3   *Hansard*, HL Deb, 14 September 2004, col 1135/1136.
4   Section 164(3); there was an unsuccessful amendment to change the word 'may' to 'shall'.
5   Section 164(4).
6   *Hansard*, HL Deb, 14 September 2004, col 1160.

'We recognise and understand the concern that this objectivity could be compromised if there were to be any potential or actual conflict of interest.'[1]

6.51 Regulations may require or authorise an approved certification scheme to contain provision about any matter relating to the home condition reports.[2] Section 164 does not limit the Government's power under s 163 to make provision about home condition reports in the regulations.

Register of home condition reports

6.52 The Secretary of State is given power to make regulations that may make provision for and in connection with a register of the home condition reports.[3] The register can be kept by (or on behalf of) the Secretary of State or by such other person as the regulations may specify.[4] The regulations may prescribe a fee for registration.[5]

6.53 No person may disclose the register or any document (or part) contained in it or any information contained in, or derived from, the register except in accordance with any provision of the regulations which authorises or requires such a disclosure to be made.[6] Contravention of s 165(4) is made a criminal offence with a fine on summary conviction not exceeding level 5 on the standard scale.[7]

6.54 The circumstances in which a person on payment of the prescribed fee may inspect the register or any document (or part) contained in it, get copies or be given information contained in or derived from the register and disclose anything obtained is set out in s 165(5).

6.55 The purposes which may be prescribed may be public purposes or purposes of private undertakings or other persons.[8]

6.56 Nothing in s 165 is to limit the power of the Secretary of State to make regulations under s 163 to prescribe the contents of the home information pack.

Enforcement authorities

6.57 Every local weights and measures authority (through Trading Standard Officers) is an enforcement authority.[9] The Minister said in Committee in the Lords:

'They will do the job in the same way they do it now. First, they will presumably operate on the basis of complaints from the public, because that is what trading standard officers do. Secondly, they will police the system on the basis of the risk that they countenance from the areas they are asked to police . . . I refer to the amount of penalty prescribed by the Secretary of State. The Bill as amended sets a maximum of £500. We have in mind setting the charge

---

1   *Hansard*, HL Deb, 14 September 2004, col 1161.
2   Section 164(7).
3   Section 165(1).
4   Section 165(2).
5   Section 165(3).
6   Section 165(4).
7   Section 165(7).
8   Section 165(6).
9   Section 166(1).

initially at about £200. The trading standards officer's primary enforcement role will be to inform and advise. A penalty will be issued only as a last resort.'[1]

6.58   Sections 166(2) and 168(1) were amended in Committee in the Lords to include not only the duties under ss 155–159 and s 167(4) but also under s 172(1).[2] In summary, this means that in the case of s 166(2) it is the duty of each enforcement authority to enforce the duties:

(a)   to have a home information pack;[3]
(b)   to provide a copy of home information pack on request;[4]
(c)   to ensure authenticity of documents in other situations;[5]
(d)   of persons acting as estate agents;[6]
(e)   to comply within the permitted period;[7] and
(f)   requiring every estate agent to be a member of an approved redress scheme.[8]

In the case of s 168(1) the authorised officer may give a penalty notice if he believes that a person has committed a breach of the same duties.

Power to require production of home information packs

6.59   The proper enforcement authority has power to require production of the home information pack from a person who appears to it to be subject to a duty under s 155 or s 159(2) to produce for inspection a copy of, or any document included in, the home information pack.[9] A requirement under s 167 may not be imposed more than six months after the last day on which the person concerned was subject to a duty under s 155 or s 159(2) (as the case may be).[10] Subject to s 167(5), it is the duty of a person subject to such a requirement to comply with it within the period of 7 days beginning with the day after that on which it is imposed.[11] A person is not required to comply with such a requirement if he has a reasonable excuse for not complying with it.[12]

Penalty charge notices

6.60   A penalty notice may not be given after the end of the period of six months beginning with the day (or in the case of a continuing breach the last day) on which the breach of duty was committed.[13] It is an offence to obstruct or impersonate an enforcement officer.[14]

---

1   *Hansard*, HL Deb, 16 September 2004, col 1301/1302.
2   *Hansard*, HL Deb, 16 September 2004, col 1295/1302.
3   Section 155.
4   Section 156.
5   Section 158.
6   Section 159.
7   Section 167(4).
8   Section 172(1).
9   Section 167(1).
10   Section 167(3).
11   Section 167(4).
12   Section 167(5).
13   Section 168(2). Further provisions about penalty charge notices are contained within Sch 8.
14   Section 169.

Right of private action

6.61 Section 170 provides that a potential buyer may recover from a person breaching the duty in the Act any reasonable fee paid by him in order to obtain the prescribed document, on condition that (a) the property is on the market or the parties are attempting to reach an agreement for the sale and (b) no authentic copy has been provided. It makes it clear that it is immaterial that the request did not specify the prescribed document but was for a copy of the home information pack or a part of the pack which includes (or ought to have included) that document.

Application of Part 5 to sub-divided buildings

6.62 Where a sub-divided building is marketed as a single property the duties apply. An example would be where a property has been divided into flats but is marketed as a single building.[1]

Power to require estate agents to belong to a redress scheme

6.63 Section 172 gives the Secretary of State power to require every estate agent to be a member of an approved redress scheme. Section 172, s 173 and s 174 were added to the Bill on 16 September in Committee in the Lords. They are significant additions giving the Government the power to create a redress scheme and require by order every estate agent to be a member. One or more schemes can be approved and approval can be withdrawn. If implemented this would go some way towards the registering and licensing of estate agents. Some would say – and the National Association of Estate Agents is amongst them – that full regulation is long overdue for the protection of the consumer. As the Minister said:

> 'The introduction of home information packs will enhance the role for estate agents in the home buying and selling process. Agents will be marketing homes with home information packs and will also have the opportunity to be pack providers ... This will put agents in a central and highly influential position.'[2]

6.64 This being so, it is difficult to understand the reluctance to regulate rather than this halfway move. The Minister went on to say:

> 'Sellers and buyers would be able to make complaints. The process would be independent and free to complainants. Members of an approved redress scheme would be under an obligation to abide by any recommendation or sanction resulting from an adjudication on a complaint ... We envisage that redress schemes may also operate on a voluntary basis. The voluntary element could relate to activities that are not connected with agents' activities with regard to home information packs.'[3]

Approval and withdrawal of approval of redress schemes

6.65 The Government must have regard to the following matters when determining whether a scheme is satisfactory and also what must be provided for before a scheme is approved:

---

1   Section 171.
2   *Hansard*, HL Deb, 16 September 2004, col 1295.
3   *Hansard*, HL Deb, 16 September 2004, col 1295/1296.

(a)   the provisions of the scheme;

(b)   the manner in which the scheme will be operated; and

(c)   the interests of the members of the scheme and of sellers and potential buyers.[1]

6.66   Before withdrawing his approval for a redress scheme the Secretary of State must serve notice on the person administering the scheme that he proposes to withdraw his approval, the grounds for withdrawal, and the period in which representations about the proposed withdrawal may be made.[2] The person administering the scheme must give a copy of the notice to each member of the scheme.[3] Withdrawal is effective from the date specified by the Secretary of State in the notice.[4]

Office of Fair Trading

6.67   The circumstances in which a breach of the duties by a person acting as estate agent will be communicated to the OFT are set out in s 175. The ultimate sanction will be the requirement that the agent cease trading. It is likely that the same sanction could be applied to a solicitor estate agent.

Grants

6.68   The Secretary of State may make grants towards inter alia the cost of developing a certification scheme and the development of a register for the purposes of any provision made or expected to be made in regulations under s 163.[5] As an example of the large amount of taxpayers' money committed before the legislation was even passed, the Government was asked in Committee in the Lords by the Earl of Caithness the total amount of two contracts to which Lord Bassam said:

> 'My noble friend Lord Rooker (the Minister) has provided me with a copy of this. The total value of the contract is £2,114,913.'[6]

CONCLUSIONS

6.69   Part 5 has not met with universal approval – far from it. However, it is now law and it remains to be seen how it will develop when implemented in 2007. There is no doubt that the Government is committed to the concept and has already invested millions of pounds of tax payers' money in setting up an accreditation scheme for home inspectors despite the fact that Parliament had not approved the scheme. The controversial elements are the home condition report and the compulsory nature of the pack. Had the former been omitted or made voluntary and had the provision of the pack been voluntary it is clear that the proposals would have been fairly uncontroversial. The argument put forward by the opponents of the scheme was that if the proposals were that good sellers without compulsion would have favoured them. This is an argument which was not satisfactorily countered by the Government.

---

1   Section 173(2).
2   Section 174(2)
3   Section 174(5).
4   Section 174(4).
5   Section 176.
6   *Hansard*, HL Deb, 14 September 2004, col 1158.

6.70   There are a number of important questions which will require further attention. Will a buyer accept a home condition report prepared on behalf of a seller without unacceptable pressure by the seller or the agent? For this to happen there will have to be a robust defence of the interests of the consumer to avoid the clear dangers of conflict of interest and undue influence. There is already a significant body of commercial providers who have a vested interest in the preparation of packs and this must not be allowed to override consumer interests. There are associated problems of indemnity insurance and the quality of inspectors. If these concerns are not met it is difficult to see how packs will succeed, since buyers will obtain their own condition report/survey, as happens at present, and the perceived advantage of speeding up the process and upfront information will not be deliverable.

6.71   Will the added cost to the seller of the pack and in particular the home condition report and searches be acceptable? Will there be an attempt to pass this cost to the buyer and pressure therefore be brought to bear on the buyer to accept the report and searches rather than commission his own more up to date ones, bearing in mind that there is no obligation on the seller to update the pack or the constituent parts of it?

6.72   Will the supply of houses be affected by the Act? It is mooted that only the most committed sellers will market their properties, given the cost of preparing the pack. If so, what will be the inflationary effect on the property market and therefore on the economy?

6.73   On the other hand, will the Government be proved right and its critics wrong and the delays in the house buying process be improved by the compulsory upfront provision of the packs and their documents despite the inbuilt delay in marketing for up to 28 days by the provisions in the Act? Will the problem of chains, the real bugbear of the process, be overcome by the packs, or will this prove illusory?

6.74   As Baroness Hamwee said in the Lords, 'Is there a place for the state in enforcing the provisions rather than leaving it entirely to matters between citizens?'[1]

6.75   Time will tell whether this Act truly results in an improvement to the home buying and selling process.

---

1   *Hansard*, HL Deb, 16 September 2004, col 1300.

Chapter 7

RIGHT TO BUY AND OTHER CHANGES TO SOCIAL HOUSING

INTRODUCTION

7.1   Whilst the HA 2004 is primarily concerned with improving standards in the private rented sector the Government has used the opportunity provided by the legislation to enhance further local housing authorities' powers to tackle anti-social behaviour and eliminate particular abuses in social housing. The Act also modernises and tidies up certain other aspects of social housing.

7.2   This chapter provides a commentary on the provisions in Part 6 of the Act other than:

- changes to the security regime for mobile homes (discussed in Chapter 8);
- the tenancy deposit scheme (discussed in Chapter 10); and
- provisions relating to gypsies and travellers (discussed in Chapter 9).

The provision[1] enabling the appropriate national authority[2] to update the overcrowding standards set out in Part 10 of the HA 1985 is discussed alongside overcrowding notices in Chapter 5. Further details relating to the implementation of the provisions discussed in this chapter are set out in Chapter 1.

ANTI-SOCIAL BEHAVIOUR AND THE RIGHT TO BUY

Introduction

7.3   The problems for local authority landlords arise from the secure status of their tenants and the package of rights collectively described as the Tenant's Charter, in particular the right to buy. The provisions in the Act continue the trajectory of measures introduced by the HA 1996[3] and the Anti-social Behaviour Act 2003.[4] They further erode the notion of the unconditional tenancy for life which began with the introduction of introductory tenancies and demoted tenancies.

7.4   The idea of 'conditionality', that rights and responsible behaviour go hand in hand is also clear in the amendments to the right to buy that the Act introduces. The Government put it this way, 'We have to ensure that (the right to buy) works well and does not provide scope for rip-offs. No one can support that form of exploitation at the

---

1   Section 216(3).
2   Appropriate national authority is defined in s 261(1).
3   See Cowan et al *The Housing Act 1996 – a practical guide* (Jordans, 1997).
4   See Carr et al *The Anti-social Behaviour Act 2003 – special bulletin* (Jordans, 2004).

expense of the public purse'.[1] The measures work by amending the statutory provisions contained in the HA 1996 and the HA 1985.

Background

Introductory tenancies

7.5   The Act amends the introductory tenancy regime provided by the HA 1996. The 1996 Act – in ss 124 to 143 – gives local authorities the discretion to operate an introductory tenancy regime. If they do so elect, every tenancy granted subsequent to the election is an introductory tenancy for the first 12 months of its existence. At the end of the 12-months' trial period the tenancy ceases to be an introductory tenancy and becomes a secure tenancy.

7.6   The great advantage to the landlord is that it is extremely easy to terminate the introductory tenancy in contrast to the secure tenancy. Whilst the possession procedure in the 1985 Act requires notice, grounds and a court order with the court retaining a discretion as to whether to order possession or not, the procedure[2] in the 1996 Act significantly reduces the role of the court. The termination of introductory tenancies shares the requirements of notice to be served on the tenant by the landlord and a court order. There are relatively strict requirements for the notice which must set out, alongside other prescribed information, the reasons for the proceedings and inform the tenant of his or her right to request a review of the landlord's decision to seek an order for possession. However, if the landlord confirms the decision to evict and the case proceeds to court, the court has no alternative other than to grant possession. In essence therefore the decision to evict an introductory tenant is an administrative one.

7.7   The provisions within the HA 2004 enable the local authority to extend the 12-month period of the introductory tenancy by an additional six months where the landlord has continuing concerns about the behaviour of the tenant.

7.8   This measure was trailed in the White Paper, *Respect and Responsibility – Taking a Stand Against Anti-social Behaviour*[3] and the Ministerial foreword to the draft Housing Bill and consultation paper.[4] Its function is simply to allow local authority landlords a few more months to decide whether or not they have a reason to prevent a particular person not only continuing as a tenant but also being promoted to the added benefits of a secure tenancy.

7.9   What is particularly interesting is that, in contrast to the universal application of the introductory tenancy regime itself, the power to extend the trial period is an individual targeted power, more akin to the power to terminate the tenancy. It is for this reason that the power carries with it a right for the individual tenant to request a review of the decision. The question is, will local authorities see this as an alternative to eviction, a last chance, or will it be about the tenant having to prove they really deserve the privilege of the secure tenancy regime? Either way there is an increasing emphasis on the conditionality of the rights of social housing. Eviction from an introductory tenancy will

---

1   *Hansard*, HL, vol 664, col 1329 (16 September 2004).
2   Set out in HA 1996, s 128.
3   Cm 5778, 2003.
4   See www.odpm.gov.uk/stellent/groups/odpm–housing/documents/downloadable/odpm–house–
     609312.rtf

almost inevitably mean that a subsequent application for social housing will be rejected because the homelessness was intentional.

The right to buy

7.10   The majority of the provisions within chapter 1 of Part 6 are amendments to the statutory right to buy scheme set out in the HA 1985. The right to buy, which was first introduced in the HA 1980, enables secure tenants to buy the homes that they live in, at a discount, from their landlord. The right to buy extends to secure tenants of local authorities and housing action trusts and pre-1988 secure tenants of non-charitable housing associations. Former local authority tenants of housing stock which has been transferred retain a preserved right to buy.

7.11   The discount on market value can be substantial, ranging between 32–60% on a house and 44–70% on a flat. The amount of discount is dependent upon the period of time that the tenant has been a public sector tenant.[1] Discounts have to be repaid if the property is sold again within a relatively short period.

7.12   The Government has already acted to limit the discounts available under the right to buy in particular areas of housing pressure. Forty-one local authorities in London and Southern England had their maximum discount available under the right to buy limited to £16,000 by means of a statutory instrument which came into force in March 2003.[2]

7.13   Some properties have always been excluded from the right to buy. These are set out in Sch 5 to the HA 1985 and include mutual co-operatives and properties specifically designed for the elderly or the disabled.

7.14   In certain rural areas where there is little affordable housing subsequent disposals of right to buy properties have been restricted.[3] Such properties once purchased by their tenants may be sold to wealthy city dwellers looking for second or holiday homes.

7.15   The original statutory scheme contains a series of safeguards aimed at preventing local authority landlords frustrating its operation. It is those safeguards which are now, in the opinion of the Government, enabling tenants, in particular anti-social tenants, to exploit the right to buy system.

7.16   In particular under the right to buy provisions the local authority landlord becomes subject to a statutory duty to convey the freehold or to grant a lease to the purchaser.[4] The duty arises once all the necessary matters have been determined,[5] and is enforceable by injunction, notwithstanding the existence of a possession claim in respect of the same property.[6]

7.17   The right to buy has been extremely successful. Since it was introduced there have been more than 2.2 million properties sold.[7]

---

1   See SI 1992/1703.
2   SI 2003/498.
3   HA 1985, s 157.
4   The right to buy provisions are contained in Part 5 of the HA 1985 as amended.
5   See HA 1985, s 138(1).
6   But see *Bristol CC v Lovell* [1998] 30 HLR 770 where the House of Lords held that a court can regulate its jurisdiction regarding whether or not to hear a claim for such an injunction before a possession trial.
7   Housing Bill Research Paper 04/02 (5 January 2004), p 78.

Summary of provisions

7.18   Table 7.1 summarises the provisions of Part 6, Chapter 1.

Table 7.1   *Summary of the provisions*

Section	Summary	Comment
179	Provides a power for local authorities to extend the trial period of the introductory tenancy for six months and provides a right for the introductory tenant whose trial period is extended to request a review of the decision.	Amends HA 1996, s 125.
180	Extension of the qualifying period for right to buy from two to five years.	Reduces the scope of the right to buy. Amends HA 1985, s 119(1) but it does not reduce the amount of discount payable.
181	Substitution – in England – of the Residential Property Tribunal for the Secretary of State for determining some disputes in relation to the exercise of the right to buy.	Limited to disputes about the exclusion of elderly people's accommodation from the right to buy. The dispute resolution procedure is preserved but transferred to the Residential Property Tribunal. Amendment to HA 1985, Sch 5, para 11.
182–184	Landlords can serve initial or final demolition notices suspending or terminating the right to buy when houses are due to be demolished.	The exclusion of houses due to be demolished from the right to buy is to eliminate a particular problem of abuse. There are constraints built into the procedure preventing the landlord from abusing the exclusion. Inserts new HA 1985, Sch 5, para 13 and inserts HA 1985, ss 138A–138C.
185–187	The discount repayment period is extended from three to five years. Changes the calculation for repayment of discounts, clarifies the discretion to require repayment and makes discounts repayable where there are deferred sale agreements.	Limits the potential for profits arising from the right to buy and aims in particular to eliminate the ability of purchasers to avoid the provisions through deferred sales agreements. Introduces new HA 1985, ss 155A–155C and s 163A.
188	Introduces a new right of first refusal to the landlord.	Inserts a new HA 1985, s 156A.
189	Provides that local authority landlords will provide information to help tenants decide whether to exercise the right to buy.	Inserts new HA 1985, ss 121A, 121B and amends s 104 of that Act.

Section	Summary	Comment
190	Termination of rent to mortgage scheme.	Introduces new HA 1985, s 142A. The right is terminated eight months after Royal Assent.
191–193	Suspension of mutual exchange and the landlord's obligation to complete the right to buy where there is anti-social behaviour Enables the landlord to apply to court for an order suspending the right to buy.	Introduces a new Ground 2A into HA 1985, Sch 3. Inserts new HA 1985, ss 121(3), 121A, 138(2A), (2B), (2C).
194	Disclosure of information as to orders.	Enables the landlord to obtain sufficient information to enable it to exercise its discretion under HA 2004, ss 191–193. Also discussed at this point is s 219, a disclosure power given to registered social landlords for the purposes of the Crime and Disorder Act 1998.

7.19 Chapter 2 of Part 6 of the Act contains provisions designed to mirror the impact of the amendments to the right to buy scheme upon voluntary disposals by landlords. In addition there is a useful amendment[1] to the HA 1996 to ensure that the right of assured tenants to acquire a dwelling is not ended by collective enfranchisement.

Commentary

Introductory tenancies

7.20 If a local authority or Housing Action Trust landlord has reasons for wanting the tenant to continue as an introductory tenant for a period it can extend the 12-month trial period of the introductory tenancy by six months when two particular conditions are met:[2]

- the landlord must have served a notice of extension on the tenant at least eight weeks before the last day of the 12-month trial period[3] (described in the Act as the original expiry date); and
- the tenant must either not have requested a review of that decision or, if he has, the review decision confirmed the landlord's decision to extend the trial period.[4]

7.21 Notices of extension are notices that:

- state that the landlord has decided that the period for which the tenancy is to be an introductory tenancy should be extended by six months;[5] and
- set out the reasons for the landlord's decision;[6] and

---

1   Section 202 amending HA 1996, s 16.
2   HA 1996, s 125A(1).
3   HA 1996, s 125A(2).
4   HA 1996, s 125A(3).
5   HA 1996, s 125A(4).
6   HA 1996, s 125A(5).

- inform the tenant of his right to request a review of the landlord's decision and of the time within which such a request must be made.[1]

7.22   The tenant has 14 days from the date of the service of the notice of extension to request a review of the landlord's decision.[2] Following a request, the landlord must review its decision[3] and, if the review confirms the original decision, inform the tenant of the reasons for that decision[4] before the expiry of the original introductory tenancy.[5]

7.23   The procedure for review will be prescribed by regulations.[6] The regulations will include a requirement that the decision on review is made by a person of appropriate seniority who was not involved in the original decision and will set out the circumstances when the person concerned is entitled to an oral hearing and his or her rights to representation at such a hearing.[7]

7.24   The power to extend the trial period only applies to those introductory tenancies which have commenced after the implementation of this provision. If landlords want to take advantage of the procedure they are going to have to keep their introductory tenants under review during the trial period and make informed decisions at the latest around the nine-month mark of the introductory tenancy. They must also be prepared to review any decision they make extremely expeditiously.

Restricting the benefits of the right to buy

7.25   The Government has acted to further restrict the benefits of the right to buy. It has been particularly concerned by exploitation of the rules resulting in large cash gains for individual tenants and third party companies in a rising housing market.[8]

Extension of qualifying period

7.26   A tenant has to have been a secure tenant for a set period before he or she becomes eligible to exercise the right to buy. The HA 1985 set that period at three years originally and it was subsequently reduced to two years.[9] This is now changed to five years.[10] However, the discount on the market price, which increases for each year of the tenancy, remains at 35% for a house and 50% for a flat after the five year period.[11] In other words, whilst the tenant has to wait longer before exercising the right to buy, the discount he or she earns after a period of five years remains the same.

7.27   The Government explained that it believed that:

---

1   HA 1996, s 125A(5).
2   HA 1996, s 125B(1).
3   HA 1996, s 125B(2).
4   HA 1996, s 125B(5).
5   HA 1996, s 125B(6).
6   HA 1996, s 125B(3).
7   HA 1996, s 125B(4).
8   See research commissioned by the ODPM which estimates that between 1998 and 2002 the equivalent of 6% of all homes sold under the right to buy in Inner London have been acquired by companies making deals with tenants to acquire the properties for speculative purposes.
9   HA 1985, s 119(1).
10   Section 180(1).
11   Section 180(2), (3).

'The two-year period is too short. Tenants can count any period of tenancy with a wide range of public bodies, no matter how long ago, towards qualifying for right to buy. That means that many tenants who have previously spent time as public sector tenants qualify for right to buy as soon as they move into their council homes. Extending the period to five years will encourage tenants to make a longer-term commitment to the community before they can buy.'[1]

7.28 The extension of the period after which the right to buy can be exercised only applies to public sector tenancies created after the implementation of the section.[2]

The impact of a subsequent sale

7.29 Any tenant who exercises their right to buy and pays a discounted price for the property has to have a covenant inserted into the purchase document stating that if they sell the property within a set period of their purchase, they will pay back the discount if the landlord demands that they do so.[3] That period, which was three years, is extended to five years by the 2004 Act.[4]

7.30 The basis upon which the repayable amount is to be calculated has also changed. It is no longer the repayment of the flat amount of discount received but is calculated at the percentage of the value of the house that the discount represented.[5] So tenants will no longer benefit from windfall gains as a result of house price inflation.

7.31 However, increases in the value of the property as a result of improvements subsequent to the purchase of the property by the former tenant are disregarded.[6] The value of the improvements is to be agreed, or in the event of a dispute, settled by the district valuer.[7]

7.32 The landlord has always had discretion about whether or not to demand a repayment of the discount.[8] The extent of this discretion is now clarified. The landlord may require the repayment of a sum it considers appropriate, up to the maximum value that the discount represented.[9] However, for each complete year following the purchase of the property the maximum amount of discount repayment which can be demanded falls by one-fifth.[10]

7.33 There may be some circumstances, for instance where the former tenant is forced by necessity to sell, perhaps because of bereavement or harassment, where it would be appropriate for the landlord to forego repayment of some or all of the discount to which it was entitled.

7.34 The amendments do not apply to tenants who served notice of their claim to exercise the right to buy prior to the implementation of the section.[11] Any disposal of the

---

1   *Hansard*, HL, vol 664, col 1328 (16 September 2004).
2   Section 180(5).
3   HA 1985, s 155.
4   Section 185(2).
5   HA 1985, s 155A(2) inserted by HA 2004, s 185.
6   HA 1985, s 155C(1) inserted by HA 2004, s 186.
7   HA 1985, s 155C(2) inserted by HA 2004, s 186.
8   HA 1985, s 155.
9   HA 1985, s 155A inserted by HA 2004, s 185.
10   HA 1985, s 155A(3).
11   Section 185(5).

property in such a case subsequent to the section coming into force is treated as if the original words of the section continued in force.[1]

Deferred resale agreements

7.35　The repayment of discount amendments attempt to capture another type of 'inappropriate' gain from the right to buy. This occurs when a tenant or a former tenant, in order to avoid repayment of the discount, enters into a deferred resale agreement. The gains from such sales are to be treated as arising during the discount repayment period.

7.36　Agreements or arrangements[2] are caught if they are made:

- between the secure tenant or his successor in title and any other person;[3]
- expressly or impliedly in connection with the tenant exercising or having exercised the right to buy;[4]
- before the end of the discount period;[5]

and either require or may require a disposal of the property to be made to any person after the end of the discount period.[6]

7.37　There is no requirement for any agreement to specify the date of the proposed disposal of the property and it is irrelevant whether the disposal of the property is subject to any condition.[7]

7.38　Regulations will flesh out the details of the provision.[8]

7.39　The amendment only applies to agreements made subsequent to its implementation. The relevant discount period will be three years if the tenant served their notice claiming the right to exercise the right to buy prior to the implementation of the HA 2004, s 185, or five years if the notice was served subsequently.[9]

Right of first refusal for landlord

7.40　The final change which affects the resale of right to buy properties is that social landlords are given a right of first refusal for a 10-year period after the exercise of the right to buy.[10] If someone sells such a property without first offering it to the social landlord then the sale is void. It is expected that this will operate as a major disincentive to exploitation of the rules. However, the provisions will inevitably be complex because the nature of the former landlord is likely to change over a 10-year period, for instance as a result of the transfer of all of its rented properties. The details will be provided in regulations.

1　Section 185(7).
2　Agreements are defined to include arrangements: HA 1985, s 163A(7) inserted by HA 2004, s 187.
3　HA 1985, s 163A(3) inserted by HA 2004, s 187.
4　HA 1985, s 163A(3)(a).
5　HA 1985, s 163A(3)(b).
6　HA 1985, s 163A(3)(c).
7　HA 1985, s 163A(4).
8　HA 1985, s 163A(5).
9　HA 1985, s 163A(7).
10　Section 188 which inserts a new s 156A into the HA 1985.

7.41   The section works by compulsorily inserting a covenant into the purchase document for the right to buy property.[1] This provides that for a period of 10 years there can be no subsequent sale of the property unless it complies with the prescribed conditions.[2] The limitation on subsequent sales is a local land charge which must be registered on the register of title.[3]

7.42   The conditions will be set out in regulations and provide for a right of first refusal either to the landlord who conveyed the right to buy property or any other person determined by the regulations.[4]

7.43   The former tenant or his or her successor in title[5] will be required to offer to dispose of the property to a prescribed recipient.[6] The recipient will either be able to accept the offer or nominate someone else to accept the offer.[7] That other person must either be someone prescribed by regulations or someone whom the recipient considers to be a more appropriate person to accept the offer.[8] If there is such a nomination then the former tenant, the nominated person and anyone else prescribed must be informed of the nomination.[9]

7.44   The regulations will also provide procedural requirements for the operation of the right of first refusal including the manner in which any offer, acceptance or notification is to be communicated, the period of time within which the offer may be accepted and at what point the offer lapses and the former tenant is able to make a disposal on the open market.[10] The Government has indicated that the right of first refusal will only be available for eight weeks since it would be inappropriate for vendors to be uncertain about the progress of their sale.[11]

7.45   It is already possible for a landlord to insert a provision in a purchase document which restricts the resale of right to buy properties which are in National Parks, areas of outstanding beauty or areas prescribed as rural areas. In such sales the landlord has had a choice. It can either restrict sales to people who have lived or worked in the area for the previous three years or insert a right of first refusal.[12] This choice is retained but the amended generally applicable right of first refusal replaces the right of first refusal within rural sales[13] and relevant sections of the 1985 Act are amended accordingly.[14]

7.46   Despite being pressed the Government refused to ban the right to buy in rural areas. The minister argued that:

---

1   HA 1985, s 156A(1).
2   HA 1985, s 156A(2).
3   HA 1985, s 156A(11), (12).
4   HA 1985, s 156A(4).
5   HA 1985, s 156A(7).
6   HA 1985, s 156A(6)(a).
7   HA 1985, s 156A(6)(b).
8   HA 1985, s 156A(6)(c).
9   HA 1985, s 156A(6)(d).
10   HA 1985, s 156A(6)(e)–(h).
11   *The right to buy and right to acquire schemes and voluntary sales to social tenants: right of first refusal for social landlords to buy back homes offered for resale*, March 2004, ODPM.
12   HA 1985, s 157.
13   HA 1985, s 157 amended by HA 2004, s 188(2).
14   Amendments are made to HA 1985, ss 158 and 162.

'exempting rural areas from the right to buy would, I think most contributors to this debate have said, unfairly discriminate against those who wanted to become home owners in those areas. It would be too inflexible and very sweeping for all tenants who happen to live in rural areas to be denied the chance of home ownership. The existing restrictions on reselling, which recycle former right-to-buy homes to local people and are already in place in a significant part of the country, are sufficient. Tenants can choose to buy or to continue to rent, while landlords can choose to impose one or other of the two resale restrictions, or not to include any restriction.'[1]

7.47 The landlord can only insert the covenant providing for the right of first refusal where the Secretary of State consents or where the landlord is a housing association, where the Housing Corporation consents or for a housing association in Wales, the Secretary of State for Wales.[2] Such consent can either be given in relation to a particular sale under the right to buy or generally.[3]

7.48 The amendments only apply to sales of right to buy property where the tenant's notice of claim of the exercise of the right to buy is served subsequent to the implementation of the section.[4]

Exceptions to the right to buy

7.49 The Act introduces a new exception to the right to buy. Properties are excluded from the right to buy if they are due to be demolished within 24 months. This exception is designed to prevent inappropriate exploitation of the right to buy rules which have resulted in excessive profits arising from the operation of the right to buy, particularly in areas of regeneration.

7.50 A local housing authority can recover possession against a secure tenant, if suitable alternative accommodation is available and the court considers it reasonable to make an order for possession, on the ground that it intends to demolish the dwelling within a reasonable period of time.[5] Before the court can entertain such a possession claim the authority must serve a notice of intention to seek possession. Service of such a notice does not exempt a secure tenant from the right to buy, only if the claim was issued, heard and a possession order made would that be the case.[6]

7.51 The Government described the problem local authorities face in this way:

'Currently, when tenants know that demolition is likely, they are able to buy at a discount knowing that when the property has to be repurchased using compulsory powers they will be entitled to full market value plus home loss compensation. This adversely affects the financial viability of regeneration schemes.'[7]

7.52 The provisions introduce a two-stage process of excluding properties which are likely to be demolished from the right to buy. The first stage is the initial demolition

1   *Hansard*, HL, vol 664, col 1335, (16 September 2004).
2   See the definition of 'relevant authority' in HA 1985, s 6A.
3   HA 1985, s 156A(9).
4   Section 188(5).
5   HA 1985, Sch 2, Ground 10.
6   HA 1985, s 121.
7   *Hansard*, HL, vol 664, col 1337 (16 September 2004).

notice which will suspend a landlord's obligation to complete a right-to-buy purchase. Once the notice is served, the landlord is no longer under a duty to convey.[1]

7.53   The second stage is the final demolition notices which will terminate any right to buy claims and prevent new ones being made. In both cases there will be a prescribed notification procedure that landlords must follow. Notices must set out the reasons for demolition and the effect of the notice served. Landlords must also publicise them locally.

Initial demolition notices

7.54   The first stage of the process designed to prevent tenants' exploiting proposed demolition of their properties is the initial demolition notice. The operation of the right to buy is suspended by the service of the notice.[2] The Government explained:

> 'It will not prevent new right-to-buy applications being made but it will provide a breathing space in which landlords can properly develop schemes and, where necessary, follow the statutory compulsory purchase procedures. Tenants' interests are protected. Right-to-buy claims can continue to be made and will be processed as normal so that if a demolition plan fails to proceed, the application can then be completed.'[3]

7.55   A new Sch 5A is inserted into the HA 1985[4] and describes the nature and effect of initial demolition notices.

7.56   Initial demolition notices are notices which come into effect when served on secure tenants and:

- state that the landlord intends to demolish the property;
- set out the reasons for this;
- specify the period within which it intends to demolish the property. This period must be no longer than is reasonable to carry out the proposed demolition and in any case be no longer than five years after the service of the initial demolition notice;
- state that the right to buy is suspended whilst the initial demolition notice is in force.[5]

7.57   An initial demolition order must also state that the notice does not prevent:

- the tenant making a claim to exercise the right to buy;
- the taking of steps in connection with such a claim; or
- the reactivation of the right to buy once the notice ceases to be in force.[6]

7.58   The notice must explain the effect of any subsequent service of a final demolition notice in respect of the property. Therefore it must set out that:

---

1   The following facts illustrate the issue: if tenants claim the right to buy, the right is admitted and otherwise all matters are agreed, if then the local housing authority inform the tenants that their house is scheduled for demolition, in the absence of Sch 5A, the authority has to jockey for position with its possession claim against the tenants' competing claim for an injunction and lack the certainty of knowing the outcome. See *Bristol CC v Lovell* [1998] 30 HLR 770 which overruled *Dance & Dance v Welwyn Hatfield District Council* [1990] 1 WLR 1097, CA in which case the facts were as just described.
2   HA 1985, s 138A inserted by HA 2004, s 183(2).
3   *Hansard*, HL, vol 664, col 1338 (16 September 2004).
4   By Sch 9.
5   HA 1985, Sch 5A, para 1(1).
6   HA 1985, Sch 5A, para 1(2)(a).

- the right to buy will not arise in connection with that property whilst the final demolition notice is in force; and
- that any existing claim to the right to buy will cease to be effective.[1]

7.59 If there is an existing claim to exercise the right to buy when the initial demolition order is served the notice must explain the details of the right to compensation for conveyancing related expenses including the method of claiming compensation.[2]

7.60 The local authority's intention to demolish properties must be publicised for the purpose of initial demolition notices in the same way as it must be publicised for final demolition notices. A notice of intent to demolish must appear in:

- a local newspaper;
- any newspaper published by the landlord; and
- on the landlord's website if it has one.[3]

7.61 The public notice must contain, in the case of initial demolition notices:

- sufficient information to enable the properties which are to be demolished to be identified;
- the reasons why the landlord intends to demolish the properties;
- the period within which the landlord intends to demolish the properties;
- the date when the initial demolition notice will cease to be in force (unless revoked or terminated earlier);
- information that during the period of validity of the notice the landlord will not be under any obligation to complete purchases in connection with the right to buy;
- an explanation of the possibility of a right to compensation in respect of expenditure incurred in pursuing any existing claim to the right to buy.[4]

7.62 Both the landlord's and the Secretary of State's power to revoke final demolition notices applies equally to initial demolition notices.[5] If the landlord decides not to proceed with demolition it must serve a notice – a revocation notice upon the tenant. The revocation notice must inform the tenant of the landlord's decision and that the demolition notice is revoked from the date of service of the revocation notice.[6]

7.63 If it appears to the Secretary of State that the landlord has no intention of demolishing the property then he may revoke the initial demolition notice and serve a revocation notice to that effect on the tenant.[7] He must have previously served a notice upon the landlord which informs it of the Secretary of State's intention.[8] The demolition notice ceases to have effect upon the service of the revocation notice.[9]

7.64 There are two further ways in which initial demolition orders cease to have effect. Firstly, they are revoked if a compulsory purchase order which is necessary in order for

---

1   HA 1985, Sch 5A, para 1(2)(b).
2   HA 1985, Sch 5A, para 1(3).
3   HA 1985, Sch 5, para 13(7).
4   HA 1985, Sch 5A, para 2(3).
5   HA 1985, Sch 5A, para 3(1).
6   HA 1985, Sch 5, para 15(4).
7   HA 1985, Sch 5, para 15(5).
8   HA 1985, Sch 5, para 15(6).
9   HA 1985, Sch 5, para 15(7).

demolition plans to proceed is not confirmed or is quashed by the courts.[1] The Government explained:

> 'It would be unfair to bring right-to-buy claims to an end and prevent new ones being made in cases where a regeneration scheme, and hence the need for demolition, depended upon the purchase of local owner-occupied properties which may never take place.'[2]

In the event of this happening the landlord must, as soon as is reasonably practicable, serve a notice on the tenant informing him or her that the notice has ceased to be in force and the reasons for this.[3]

7.65   Secondly, if a final demolition notice comes into force in respect of the property then the initial demolition ceases to have effect from that date.[4] The final demolition notice must state that it is replacing the initial demolition notice.[5]

7.66   If an initial demolition notice ceases to be in force for any reason other than the property being demolished then no further initial or final demolition notice may be served in connection with that property for five years[6] unless:

- it is served with the consent of the Secretary of State; and
- it states that it is so served.[7]

The Secretary of State's consent may be conditional.[8]

7.67   This proviso does not apply to a final demolition notice served at a time when an initial demolition notice was served with the consent of the Secretary of State.[9] In such circumstances a final demolition order can be served.

7.68   The suspension of the right to buy as a result of the initial demolition notice only applies to a tenant's notice of claim to exercise the right to buy subsequent to the implementation of the section.[10]

Final demolition notices

7.69   Whilst initial demolition notices suspend the right to buy, final demolition notices prevent the right to buy arising whilst they are in force in relation to the property.[11] This is achieved by the insertion of new paras 13–16 into Sch 5[12] to the HA 1985.[13]

7.70   A final demolition notice is a notice which:

- states that the landlord[14] intends to demolish the property;[15]

---

1   HA 1985, Sch 5A, para 3(2).
2   *Hansard*, HL, vol 664, col 1338 (16 September 2004).
3   HA 1985, Sch 5A, para 3(7).
4   HA 1985, Sch 5A, para 3(8).
5   HA 1985, Sch 5A, para 3(9).
6   HA 1985, Sch 5A, para 4(2), (3).
7   HA 1985, Sch 5A, para 4(2), (3).
8   HA 1985, Sch 5A, para 4(5).
9   HA 1985, Sch 5A, para 4(4).
10 Section 182(2).
11 HA 1985, Sch 5, para 13(1) and s 138B.
12 Schedule 5 lists the exceptions to the right to buy.
13 Section 182(1).
14 The definition of landlord includes a superior landlord: HA 1985, Sch 5, para 13(9).
15 HA 1985, Sch 5, para 13(2)(a).

- sets out the reasons for the demolition;[1]
- specifies the date by which it intends to demolish the premises[2] – which must be within 24 months of the service of the notice on the tenant;[3]
- specifies the date when the notice will cease to be in force (unless it is subsequently extended);[4]
- states that the right to buy does not arise in respect of the property.[5]

7.71   If the final demolition notice is served at a time where there is an existing claim to exercise the right to buy in respect of the property the notice should not state that the right to buy does not arise.[6] Instead it must state that:

- the claim to exercise the right to buy ceases to be effective at the time the claim comes into force;[7] and
- there is a right to compensation for certain expenditure incurred in the claim.[8]

The notice must also give details of the right to compensation and how it is to be exercised.[9]

7.72   The notice must be served on every occupier of a property within a building[10] (although an accidental failure to serve a notice on a particular occupier can be overlooked) and can only be served if one of the conditions A–C is satisfied.[11]

7.73   Condition A is that the proposed demolition of the property does not form part of a scheme involving the demolition of other premises.[12]

7.74   Condition B is that the proposed demolition of the property does form part of a scheme involving the demolition of other premises but none of those other premises needs to be acquired by the landlord in order for the landlord to be able to demolish them.[13]

7.75   Condition C is that the proposed demolition of the property does form part of a scheme involving the demolition of other premises and one or more those premises need to be acquired by the landlord in order for the landlord to be able to demolish them, but in each case arrangements for their acquisition are in place.[14]

7.76   Arrangements for acquisition are in place if:

- an agreement under which the landlord is entitled to acquire the premises is in force; or
- a notice to treat has been given in respect of the premises under s 5 of the Compulsory Purchase Act 1965; or

---

1   HA 1985, Sch 5, para 13(2)(b).
2   HA 1985, Sch 5, para 13(2)(c).
3   HA 1985, Sch 5, para 13(4).
4   HA 1985, Sch 5, para 13(2)(c).
5   HA 1985, Sch 5, para 13(2)(e).
6   HA 1985, Sch 5, para 13(3).
7   HA 1985, Sch 5, para 13(3)(a).
8   HA 1985, Sch 5, para 13(3)(b).
9   HA 1985, Sch 5, para 13(3).
10   HA 1985, Sch 5, para 13(6).
11   HA 1985, Sch 5, para 13(2)(d).
12   HA 1985, Sch 5, para 14(2).
13   HA 1985, Sch 5, para 14(3).
14   HA 1985, Sch 5, para 14(4).

- a vesting declaration has been made in respect of the premises under s 4 of the Compulsory Purchase (Vesting Declarations) Act 1981.[1]

7.77 The landlord is also required to give general publicity to its intention to demolish premises. A notice of intent to demolish must appear in:

- a local newspaper;
- any newspaper published by the landlord; and
- on the landlord's website if it has one.[2]

7.78 Such a notice must contain:

- sufficient information to enable identification of the premises that the landlord intends to demolish;
- the reasons why the landlord intends to demolish the premises;
- the proposed demolition date;
- the date when any final demolition notice will cease to be in force (unless extended);
- that the right to buy will not arise in respect of those premises or properties within those premises;
- that there may be a right to compensation in respect of certain expenditure incurred in respect of any existing claim.[3]

7.79 If the landlord decides not to proceed with demolition it must serve a notice – a revocation notice – upon the tenant. The revocation notice must inform the tenant of the landlord's decision and that the demolition notice is revoked from the date of service of the revocation notice.[4]

7.80 The Secretary of State has certain powers in relation to final demolition notices.

7.81 Firstly, he can extend or further extend the period during which a final demolition order is in force.[5] Any decision to extend the period may impose notice requirements upon the landlord.[6] He can only extend the period of the demolition notice whilst it remains in force, although the power to extend may also operate during a period of extension of the final demolition order.[7]

7.82 Secondly, if it appears to the Secretary of State that the landlord has no intention of demolishing the property, then he may revoke the demolition notice and serve a revocation notice to that effect on the tenant.[8] He must have previously served a notice upon the landlord which informs it of the Secretary of State's intention.[9] The demolition notice ceases to have effect upon the service of the revocation notice.[10]

7.83 Finally, once a demolition notice ceases to be in force and the property has not been demolished then no further final demolition notice may be served on that property

---

1   HA 1985, Sch 5, para 14(5).
2   HA 1985, Sch 5, para 13(7).
3   HA 1985, Sch 5, para 13(8).
4   HA 1985, Sch 5, para 15(4).
5   HA 1985, Sch 5, para 15(1).
6   HA 1985, Sch 5, para 15(2).
7   HA 1985, Sch 5, para 15(3).
8   HA 1985, Sch 5, para 15(5).
9   HA 1985, Sch 5, para 15(6).
10   HA 1985, Sch 5, para 15(7).

for a period of five years, unless the Secretary of State consents to the service and the notice states that it is served with the Secretary of State's consent.[1]

7.84   The new exception only applies to a tenant's notice of claim to exercise the right to buy subsequent to the implementation of the section.[2]

Compensation once a demolition order is served

7.85   A secure tenant who reasonably incurs conveyancing expenses in connection with the exercise of his or her right to buy which is either suspended by the service of an initial demolition notice, or terminated by a final demolition notice, is entitled to compensation.[3]

7.86   To claim compensation the tenant must serve a notice on the landlord stating the amount claimed within three months of the demolition notice coming into effect. The claim must be supported with receipts.[4]

Disputes about right to buy

7.87   The only other provision in connection with exceptions to the right to buy is concerned with the replacement of the Secretary of State as the determiner of disputes in relation to para 11 of Sch 5 to the HA 1985 with, in England, the residential property tribunal.[5] The Secretary of State remains the appropriate authority to determine disputes in Wales.[6]

7.88   Paragraph 11 of Sch 5 to the HA 1985 relates to single dwelling-houses particularly suitable for elderly persons. Disputes in connection with this are currently running at around 400 per year with the tenant succeeding in about 100 of these cases.[7]

7.89   Applications made to the Secretary of State in the 28 days preceding the implementation of the section are also to be determined by the residential property tribunal.[8]

7.90   The Government explained that this measure was largely a tidying up provision which:

> 'will make no substantive difference to the determination of appeals. We do not propose to change the statutory rules in paragraph 11 that determine whether a property is particularly suitable for occupation by elderly persons. Determinations by a residential property tribunal will be subject to judicial review, as are those of the Secretary of State at present. That will have the benefit of making the process more transparent and bringing together housing and related appeals and determinations under a single jurisdiction, and will over time afford opportunities for greater efficiency. The National Assembly for Wales will assess the position there independently.'[9]

---

1   HA 1985, Sch 5, para 15(8).
2   Section 182(2).
3   HA 1985, s 138C.
4   HA 1985, s 138C(2), (4).
5   HA 1985, Sch 5, para 11(4) amended by HA 2004, s 181.
6   HA 1985, Sch 5, para 11(5) amended by HA 2004, s 181(3).
7   *Hansard*, HC, vol 421, col 237 (11 May 2004).
8   Section 181(5), (6).
9   *Hansard*, HC, vol 421, col 238 (11 May 2004).

Rebalancing the right to buy

7.91   The Act introduces three other measures, which can perhaps be described collectively as part of a rebalancing exercise of the respective rights of landlords and tenants in connection with the right to buy, with the intention of eliminating abuse. The measures are amending the landlord's notice to complete, extending the information available to secure tenants about the right to buy and the abolition of the rent to mortgage scheme.

LANDLORD'S NOTICE TO COMPLETE

7.92   The first of these measures is the landlord's notice to complete.

7.93   The right to buy measures provide a safeguard for tenants whose landlord was reluctant to proceed with the right to buy and delayed the progress of the transaction. The tenant can serve a notice on the landlord if it fails to progress the transaction for a period of a month. If the landlord does not remedy the position then it faces a financial penalty.[1]

7.94   Clearly there are difficulties for the landlord if the tenant delays completion unnecessarily. In particular, in a rising property market the landlord will be faced with selling the property at a price that is increasingly lower than its market value at the time of completion. The provisions within the HA 1985 recognise this and provide a procedure to enable the landlord to force the tenant to progress the transaction. The landlord is able to serve a notice on the tenant requiring him or her to complete the transaction or to specify the matters which remain outstanding and which prevent completion.[2] If the tenant fails to comply with this notice within a period specified in the notice (which must be at least 56 days), then the landlord can serve a second notice requiring the tenant to complete and if he or she fails to do so within a further period of at least 56 days then the tenant's claim to exercise the right to buy is deemed withdrawn.[3]

7.95   However, the landlord must wait 12 months before serving the first notice as well as suffering the inconvenience of pursuing a tenant who is delaying the transaction deliberately. This means that tenants have at least 16 months to complete their purchase, in contrast with the one month period available to landlords.

7.96   The 2004 Act reduces the period of time that the landlord must wait before serving the first notice to complete from 12 months to three months.[4] The Government explained:

> 'The new clause attempts to shift the balance so that, instead of having to wait for at least 12 months, a landlord can serve a first notice to complete after three months, if they wish. It still gives the tenant more time than the landlord, it brings the total time in line with the private sector and it addresses a loophole that people have exploited.'[5]

7.97   The amendment does not apply in any case where the tenant's notice of claim to exercise the right to buy was served prior to the implementation of the section.[6]

---

1   HA 1985, s 153A.
2   HA 1985, s 140.
3   HA 1985, s 141.
4   Section 184 amending HA 1985, s 140.
5   *Hansard*, HC, vol 421, col 238, (11 May 2004).
6   Section 184(3).

INFORMATION ABOUT THE RIGHT TO BUY

7.98   The HA 1985 requires landlords to inform their tenants about the right to buy as well as placing a duty upon them to provide information about the terms of their tenancies and the repairing obligations of the landlord.[1]

7.99   The 2004 Act replaces that requirement with a more extensive duty to prepare a document contining information about the right to buy.[2] This document, 'requires landlords also to supply information to tenants on the responsibilities and consequences of being a home owner. The aim is to help them to decide whether to exercise their right to buy.'[3] The information is to be provided free of charge and revised regularly.[4]

7.100   The details of the information to be provided are to be specified in regulations.[5]

RENT TO MORTGAGE

7.101   The original right to buy provisions in the HA 1980 contained a 'right to a mortgage'. This was abolished in 1993 and replaced with the 'rent-to-mortgage' scheme.[6] Under this:

> 'a secure tenant who wishes to exercise RTB but who cannot afford to pay the full purchase price in 'one go' may transmute the rent he/she pays to the discounted purchase price of a 'share' of his /her dwelling along with a right to purchase the remainder at some future time.'[7]

7.102   Hughes and Lowe predicted at the time the scheme was unlikely to be successful: '. . . many tenants will be excluded because they are 'on' housing benfit, while those entitled to a RIM purchase are probably likely to be able to raise the full purchase price from the ordinary mortgage market.'[8]

7.103   The HA 2004 terminates the rent to mortgage scheme.[9] It will not be available to a tenant who serves a notice claiming to exercise the right to buy later than eight months following the passage of the Act.[10] The grace period of eight months after Royal Assent is designed to allow existing tenants who are eligible to buy under the rent to mortgage scheme to do so.[11]

7.104   The provision was explained by the Government as follows:

> 'Rent-to-mortgage enables tenants to buy a share in their houses if they cannot afford to buy them outright under the right to buy . . . [It is] a scheme that has seen very little take-up since it was launched 10 years ago – and is expensive to administer – as well as thwarting the Government's policy of streamlining the number of low-cost home ownership schemes, a key recommendation of the Home Ownership Task Force.'[12]

---

1   HA 1985, s 104.
2   HA 1985, s 121A inserted by HA 2004, s 189.
3   *Hansard*, HL, vol 664, col 1346 (16 September 2004).
4   HA 1985, ss 121B(3) and 121A(4) inserted by HA 2004, s 189.
5   HA 1985, s 121A(2).
6   See HA 1985, s 143.
7   Hughes and Lowe *Social Housing Law and Policy* (Butterworths, 1995), p 76.
8   Ibid.
9   Section 190 which inserts a new s 142A into the HA 1985.
10   HA 1985, s 142A(2).
11   *Hansard*, HC, vol 417, col 6034 (12 February 2004).
12   *Hansard*, HL, vol 664, col 1348 (16 September 2004).

Anti-social behaviour and secure tenants' rights

7.105   The Act provides a number of other measures designed to restrict further the rights of anti-social secure tenants. Compared with previous measures within the HA 1996 and the Anti-social Behaviour Act 2003 the changes are relatively minor. However, the Government argues that the measures are necessary to prevent anti-social tenants gaining rights when they have failed to behave responsibly and to enable social landlords to manage the problem of anti-social behaviour more effectively.

Mutual exchange

7.106   One particular right which secure tenants have is the right to mutual exchange. This right allows two tenants of social landlords to exchange homes by legally assigning their tenancies to one another.[1] The landlords of both tenants must consent to the exchange. In the case of secure tenants, the consent may only be refused on one of the grounds set out in Sch 3 to the HA 1985. Those grounds include for instance where there is a possession order against one of the tenants involved in the exchange,[2] or where the accommodation is considered to be more extensive than is reasonably required by the proposed assignee.[3]

7.107   The Act inserts another ground for refusal of consent into Sch 3.[4] The application for mutual exchange can be refused if court orders or applications for court orders have been made as a result of anti-social behaviour by the tenant, the proposed assignee or a person residing with either of them.[5]

7.108   The relevant court orders[6] are:

- suspended possession orders on nuisance/anti-social behaviour grounds;[7]
- demotion orders[8] (clearly here only applications are relevant since a demotion order would deprive the tenant of the right to mutual exchange);
- injunctions against anti-social behaviour;[9]
- injunctions against anti-social behaviour to which a power of arrest is attached;[10]
- anti-social behaviour orders.[11]

7.109   The ground for refusal of consent only exists for as long as an application for an order is pending or an order remains in force.[12] If an application is not granted or an order ceases to be in force the tenant has the right to apply for a mutual exchange on the same basis as any other secure tenant.

7.110   The Government explained the purpose of the provision as follows:

---

1   HA 1985, s 92.
2   Ground 1.
3   Ground 3.
4   Ground 2A.
5   Section 191(1).
6   More extensive detail is available on these orders in Carr et al *Anti-social Behaviour Act 2003 A special bulletin* (Jordans, 2004).
7   These grounds are Ground 2 of Sch 2 to the HA 1985 or Ground 14 of Sch 2 to the HA 1988.
8   HA 1985, s 82A; HA 1988, s 6A.
9   Either under HA 1996, s 152, 153A, 153B or 153D.
10   Either under HA 1996, s 153 or Anti-social Behaviour Act 2003, s 91.
11   Under Crime and Disorder Act 1998, s 1.
12   Section 191.

'. . . [it] is to allow social landlords better to manage their stock by preventing concentrations of antisocial tenants in particular areas. Problems can be worsened when people who behave antisocially are permitted to move closer to their anti-social friends or relatives. In many cases, those people are already frequent visitors to the area and are known by other tenants and residents to cause problems. Landlord-tenant relationships in the area may be severely undermined when the landlord proves unable to prevent an exchange. We believe also that the measure may be useful in individual cases, for example, where a landlord wants to continue to monitor a tenant's behaviour in their existing property, thereby facilitating the rehabilitation of antisocial tenants.'[1]

As the minister pointed out, 'The concept is interesting: a social landlord might in certain circumstances wish to retain a troublesome tenant in a locality'.[2]

7.111   Note that the new provision not described as punitive. It is:

'about allowing the landlord to manage his or her stock effectively in the interests of the tenants and the surrounding community. If the tenant's behaviour improves, they can apply again; there is clear provision for that. If the landlord is satisfied that there are no longer any housing management concerns, he or she may be prepared to consent to an exchange.'[3]

The right to buy and anti-social behaviour

7.112   The Act introduces three measures in response to particular problems arising in connection with the exercise of the right to buy by anti-social secure tenants.

SUSPENSION BY THE COURT OF THE RIGHT TO BUY

7.113   The right to buy cannot be exercised by a secure tenant in particular circumstances. These circumstances include where there is a possession order in force on the property.[4] The Act provides an additional circumstance when the right to buy cannot be exercised – when, following an application by a landlord, a court makes an order suspending the right to buy because of anti-social behaviour.[5]

7.114   The court may make such an order only if it is satisfied that:

- the tenant or a person residing in or visiting the property, has engaged in or threatened to engage in anti-social behaviour;[6] and
- it is reasonable to make the order.[7]

7.115   In deciding whether it is reasonable to make the order the court must take into account:

- whether it is desirable for the property to be managed by the landlord during the suspension period; and
- the impact that any anti-social behaviour has had on other people, or would have if it was repeated.[8]

7.116   The order:

---

1   *Hansard*, HC, vol 417, col 608 (12 February 2004).
2   Ibid.
3   Ibid.
4   HA 1985, s 121(1).
5   HA 1985, s 121A inserted by HA 2004, s 192.
6   As defined in HA 1996, s 153A or 153B.
7   HA 1985, s 121A.
8   HA 1985, s 121A(4).

- suspends any existing claim to the right to buy for the period of suspension set out in the order;[1] and
- disapplies the landlord from the duty to complete the transaction.[2]

However, the order does not suspend the computation of the discount period.[3]

7.117 The court may make further orders to extend the period of suspension but can only do so if there has been anti-social behaviour since the making of the suspension order and it is reasonable to make the order.[4] In deciding whether it is reasonable to make the order the court must take into account:

- whether it is desirable for the property to be managed by the landlord during the suspension period; and
- the impact that any anti-social behaviour has had on other people, or would have if it was repeated.[5]

7.118 Regulations will provide for the continuing of the effect of a suspension order where the secure tenancy, as a result of a voluntary transfer, is replaced by an assured tenancy.

7.119 The provision was explained by the Minister as follows:

'Through the new clause, we are trying to ensure that the right to buy does not become a get-out clause that allows antisocial tenants to subvert the other measures that have been introduced to tackle anti-social behaviour. By stipulating that the decision is for the courts, not for local authorities, we have taken care to ensure that, in situations where, in effect, a tenant's property rights are at stake, a fair process is gone through in achieving our aim of dealing with antisocial behaviour.'[6]

SUSPENSION OF THE LANDLORD'S OBLIGATION TO COMPLETE THE RIGHT TO BUY

7.120 Another provision of the Act provides an alternative strategy for the landlord where it has already applied for or obtained an order against a secure tenant or someone residing with him for anti-social behaviour and the tenant commences the right to buy provisions.

7.121 Once the right of the secure tenant to exercise the right to buy has been established then the landlord is, in most circumstances, under a duty to complete the transaction.[7] The duty does not apply if the tenant owes the landlord rent.[8] However, the landlord can be put in a difficult position if it commences proceedings to evict the tenant for anti-social behaviour. As the minister explained:

'One unintended consequence of the obligation to complete a right-to-buy sale can be that it causes a race between the tenant trying to complete the sale and the landlord attempting to evict the tenant. Often, the right-to-buy purchase is completed more quickly than the possession proceedings and the tenant escapes the consequences of his errant behaviour.'[9]

---

1   HA 1985, s 121A(5)(a).
2   HA 1985, s 121A(5)(b).
3   HA 1985, s 121A(5)(c).
4   HA 1985, s 121A(6), (7).
5   HA 1985, s 121A(8).
6   *Hansard*, HC, vol 421, col 241 (11 May 2004).
7   HA 1985, s 138.
8   HA 1985, s 138(2).
9   *Hansard*, HC, vol 417, col 609, (12 February 2004).

7.122   The Act provides a further exception to the duty to complete the transaction. If there is an application before a court for a demotion order,[1] or for possession on the basis of nuisance/anti-social behaviour,[2] or for a suspension order[3] then the landlord is not under a duty to complete the transaction until the court decides the matter without making an order or the application is withdrawn.[4]

7.123   The aim of the provisions is 'to prevent antisocial tenants from escaping such consequences because they complete the purchase of their home before the landlord can take effective action against them. That is an entirely reasonable proposition'.[5]

7.124   The combined effect of the power of the court to order suspension of the right to buy and the suspension of the landlord's duty to complete is that the anti-social tenant cannot enforce the right to buy either where he or she is the subject of an application to suspend the right to buy, or where the landlord is taking or has succeeded in a wide range of court action against the tenant. The landlord is protected whether the tenant anticipates the court action and initiates the right to buy in an attempt to avoid it or where the tenant tries to exercise the right to buy in response to the landlord commencing proceedings.

Disclosure of information

7.125   The effectiveness of the provisions enabling the landlord to refuse mutual exchange or suspend the right to buy transaction depend upon the landlord having sufficient information about any anti-social behaviour committed by a tenant, or other resident in the property which has triggered court action against that person. The landlord may not itself hold this information; for instance, a resident in the premises may have been a former tenant of a registered social landlord who has been evicted for anti-social behaviour.

7.126   The Act enables someone to provide relevant information about anti-social behaviour to a landlord of a secure tenant so that it can decide whether or not to let a mutual exchange or a right to buy sale proceed.[6]

7.127   Relevant information is defined as information relating to any order or application relevant to the withholding of consent to mutual exchange or the suspension of the landlord's obligation to complete the right to buy sale, including information identifying the person in respect of whom any such order or application has been made.[7] The information disclosed must be about orders either in force or pending.

7.128   The Act also allows regulations to be made enabling information to be disclosed to a landlord of an assured tenant on the same basis in respect of applications for the preserved right to buy and the right to acquire.[8]

---

1   Under HA 1985, s 82A.
2   Under Ground 2 of Sch 2 to the HA 1985.
3   HA 1985, s 121A.
4   HA 1985, s 138(2A)–(2C) inserted by HA 2004, s 193.
5   *Hansard*, HC, vol 417, col 609 (12 February 2004).
6   Section 194.
7   Section 194(3).
8   Section 194(4).

Registered social landlords

7.129   A similar extension of information disclosure powers is made elsewhere in Part 6 for the purpose of providing social landlords with sufficient information to enable them to respond appropriately to anti-social behaviour. Registered social landlords[1] are included by the Act in the list of authorities to which information can be disclosed for the purposes of the Crime and Disorder Act 1998. Information can be disclosed where it would otherwise be confidential whenever it would be necessary or expedient for the purposes of the Crime and Disorder Act.[2] This would allow disclosure of information relating to anti-social behaviour orders, crime and disorder strategies, parenting orders or child safety orders.

7.130   The Joint Committee on Human Rights expressed concerns about this provision:

> 'Other authorities to which information may be disclosed under section 115 of the 1998 Act include chief officers of police, police authorities, local authorities, and health authorities. All of these bodies are obvious public authorities with obligations to comply with Convention rights under section 6 of the Human Rights Act. The status of Registered Social Landlords as public authorities is, by contrast, much more ambiguous. Although in certain cases Registered Social Landlords may be functional public authorities under the HRA, on the current law, many RSLs are likely to fall outside the functional public authority category.'[3]

7.131   The Government responded to the concerns by setting out their opinion that the Human Rights Act 1998 would apply to registered social landlords without further amendment:

> 'Where a function is public in nature, section 6 applies and the body concerned must carry out those functions in a way that is compatible with convention rights. In our view the power to receive information under section 115 of the Crime and Disorder Act will be a function of a public nature as it is intrinsically linked to the power in section 1 of that Act to apply for an anti social behaviour order. It therefore must be exercised compatibly with Convention rights.'[4]

Disposals attracting discounts other than under right to buy

7.132   Chapter 2 of Part 6 of the Act contains provisions designed to ensure that the changes made in respect of the right to buy in ss 185–188 of the Act apply appropriately to voluntary disposals by local authorities,[5] by registered social landlords[6] and by housing action trusts of properties at a discount under the HA 1985.

7.133   Voluntary disposals can only take place with consent. General consents have been issued by the Secretary of State in relation to disposals by local authorities and by the Housing Corporation in relation to disposals by social landlords permitting sales at a discount, but only on terms that mirror the right to buy scheme. Although there is

---

1   Section 219.
2   Crime and Disorder Act 1998, s 115.
3   Joint Committee on Human Rights, 8th Report, para 4.24.
4   Letter from Rt Hon Keith Hill MP, Minister for Housing and Planning, Office of the Deputy Prime Minister, to the Chair, re the Housing Bill: Clause 207 and the Eighth Report appended to 23rd Report of Joint Committee on Human Rights (23 November 2004).
5   Under HA 1985, s 32.
6   Under HA 1996, s 9.

provision for voluntary disposals by housing action trusts, no general consent has been issued by the Secretary of State because such voluntary disposals are very rare. Specific consent can be granted to sell properties on more generous terms, however, if necessary or desirable in particular circumstances.

7.134   The general rule of thumb is that voluntary disposals should not be on terms more favourable than the right to buy, as that might enable evasion of the right-to-buy scheme. The provisions in Part 6, Chapter 2 in general ensure that this is the case. However, the right of first refusal is not to be included automatically as part of a consent to a voluntary disposal for local authority or social landlord's voluntary disposals. Nonetheless, the Government gave assurances that, 'as a matter of practice, the right of first refusal will be included in the vast majority of voluntary disposals'.[1] The distinction is required in order to preserve the landlord's choice between a right of first refusal and a restriction requiring sales to be made only to local workers or residents in designated rural areas. There is no need for the housing action trust to have this choice as they operate only in urban areas.

Conclusion

7.135   These provisions provide for substantial changes in the law in relation to social tenants' rights which are quite surprising within an Act ostensibly focusing on the private rented sector. It is indicative of the seriousness with which the Government treats anti-social behaviour and other abuses of the security given to social tenants. The tools provided with these chapters of Part 6 close important loopholes in the existing law and will make any lack of action to eradicate anti-social behaviour on large housing estates dominated by social rented housing even less excusable.

MISCELLANEOUS PROVISIONS

7.136   Part 6 contains a number of other changes to housing law as it affects social landlords. The changes are varied, but in general are designed to iron out inadvertent anomalies in housing law, to update some of its concerns and to modernise the regulation of social landlords. This section of the chapter starts by outlining the provisions which are relevant to registered social landlords before setting out the remaining provisions.

The right to acquire

7.137   The first of the anomalies to be rectified is the accidental erosion of the right to acquire as a result of the collective right to enfranchise given to long leaseholders. The Act provides an amendment to the right to acquire provisions set out in the HA 1996. The right to acquire is a statutory scheme[2] under which some tenants of registered social landlords are given a right to purchase their rented home at a discount in a similar fashion to the right to buy scheme for secure tenants. Problems have been caused by the legal effect of the collective right to enfranchise which transferred the freehold to the long leaseholders. The right to acquire could only apply if the freehold interest in the dwelling must at all times have been held by a registered social landlord or a public sector

---

1   *Hansard*, HL, vol 664, col 1344 (16 September 2004).
2   Set out in HA 1996, s 16.

landlord.[1] Therefore the effect of the registered social landlord's long leaseholders enfranchising is that the other assured tenants in the same block who are not long leaseholders lose their statutory right to acquire. This, as the Explanatory Notes to the Act point out,[2] was an unintended consequence of leasehold legislation.

7.138 The Act extends the definition of freehold interest in the dwelling so that it still applies even where a mandatory leaseback has taken place.[3] The section thereby preserves the right to acquire for registered social landlord assured tenants in cases where a group of leaseholders in the same block buy the freehold. The right to acquire is conferred also upon those from whom it has already inadvertently been removed.

Grant giving powers

7.139 One of the most controversial sections of the Act concerns the extension of the grant-giving powers of the Housing Corporation in England and the National Assembly for Wales to companies other than registered social landlords. The grants are used for a broad range of construction, acquisition, repair and improvement programmes to provide affordable housing in a variety of ways. Prior to the implementation of the changes the grant giving powers have been limited to registered social landlords.

7.140 As the Government explained:

> 'There are around 2,000 registered social landlords in England and 100 in Wales with a variety of constitutions. Some are industrial and provident societies; some are non charitable or charitable companies; and some are charities. In England, around 300 registered social landlords currently bid for grant under s 18 of the HA 1996 to support their housing activities, in particular the construction, acquisition, improvement or conversion of housing for ownership or rent.'[4]

Registered social landlords are required to submit to a detailed regulatory code supervised by the Housing Corporation.

7.141 The changes, which were not contained in the draft Housing Bill, were trailed by the ODPM in *Sustainable Communities: building for the future*[5] and consulted upon in *Increasing the effectiveness of powers to regulated registered social landlords.*[6]

7.142 The ODPM Committee considering the draft Bill expressed concerns about the proposal,[7] quoting evidence from the Chartered Institute of Housing. 'A proposal to give SHG to profit making bodies not subject to the code is therefore a significant step, yet the consultation paper is sketchy about the arguments for this and how it will operate.' The Institute suggested that the Government's aims could be achieved differently:

---

1   HA 1996, s 16(3)(a).

2   At para 467.

3   HA 1996, s 16(3A) inserted by HA 2004, s 202.

4   ODPM Regulatory Impact Assessment *Increasing the effectiveness of powers to regulate Registered Social Landlords*, para 5.

5   ODPM (February 2003) www.odpm.gov.uk/stellant/groups/odpm–communities/documents/pdf/ odpm–comm–pdf–022184.pdf: 'We are considering whether to extend the Housing Corporation's power to fund bodies other than housing associations, with a view to widening the opportunities for encouraging new housing development.' (Paragraph 319.)

6   ODPM (March 2003).

7   This was despite the proposal not being contained in the draft Bill as the consultation exercise on the proposal was being conducted at the same time as the scrutiny of the draft Bill.

'We would share the need to build more houses for a reduced amount of money. I think there are two prongs to the dangers, if you like. One is we think there are probably a whole load of reforms that can be brought into place to make the existing arrangements with registered social landlords more effective, not least planning reforms, some of which have been dealt with elsewhere. Also, something like reducing the total number of RSLs that do development . . . If you reduce the number of housing associations who can do development they will all do more development. The other thing that private developers will say is that they produce more standard house types. Again, you could look at that for RSLs. You can achieve the same kind of savings through modernising the RSL development process rather than giving grant to developers . . . Our fundamental concern is do not give grant to unregulated organisations, let us try first at improving and modernising the RSL development sector.'[1]

7.143   The ODPM recommended that 'the Government considers way to streamline and improve the effectiveness of registered social landlords before introducing any measures to pay Social Housing Grant to private developers'. Nonetheless, the Government has enacted the measure. The Regulatory Impact Assessment drawn up in response to the consultation exercise explained the government's argument as follows:

'This proposal aims to widen the opportunities for encouraging new housing development by enabling the Relevant Authority to invite bids for grant and to give grants to organisations other than RSLs. By challenging RSLs to compete with new private developers on price, and challenging new providers to compete with RSLs in meeting development standards, we expect value for money will be maximised. The National Housing Federation, on behalf of its RSL members in England, identified in its consultation response a number of potential risks to the RSL sector resulting from this proposal. These include difficulties in enforcing conditions attached to a payment of grant, a lack of effective safeguards ensuring that subsidy is granted only where it is genuinely required, and risk of a reduction in the supply of properties for those with special needs. There was considerable agreement amongst respondents both for and against the proposal that there needs to be a "level playing field" between all bidders for grant from the Relevant Authority. This means that in the value for money assessment of bids for grant, account needs to be taken of the additional costs arising from the regulatory requirements on RSLs, that grant conditions for new providers should specify the same scheme development standards for the construction of grant-aided property that apply to RSLs, and that there should be appropriate and robust safeguards within the conditions on subsidy to non-regulated organisations. We believe that the priority need for more affordable housing is an overwhelming impetus to testing new approaches to provision, including making grants from the Relevant Authority available to a wider number of bidders. The issues raised by consultees are therefore being carefully considered and progressed with a view to minimising potential risks. We know from the consultation responses that it seems most likely that the greatest competition between RSLs and other organisations will be for grant for Low Cost Home Ownership schemes. In the meantime, and in order to increase competition for grant and so maximise the value of public subsidy, this proposal introduces a new power to the 1996 Act which will enable the Relevant Authority to pay grant to, and if necessary, clawback resources from, organisations other than RSLs.'[2]

7.144   In essence the Government's case is that the need for affordable housing is too pressing for it to reject any opportunity which not only offers value for money by increasing the competitiveness of registered social landlords but also is likely to improve delivery of homes.

---

1   ODPM: *Housing, Planning, Local Government and the Regions* 10th Report, para 208.
2   ODPM Regulatory Impact Assessment *Increasing the effectiveness of powers to regulate Registered Social Landlords* paras 6–8. www.odpm.gov.uk/stellent/groups/odpm–housing/documents/page/odpm–house–026062.hcsp

7.145   The Minister gave some indication of how the Government saw the provisions working:

'We expect the commercial sector's role to evolve and emerge over time. We think it likely that in the early days it will be most interested in the new-build Homebuy model. I shall outline the details. A non-RSL might bid for grant to provide developments where purchasers pay 75 per cent of the market value of the property and the non-RSL holds the remaining 25 per cent share. The purchaser pays no interest on that 25 per cent, but when he sells the property, 25 per cent of the sale price is paid back to the developer. The grant conditions may stipulate that the 25 per cent, or a portion of it, must in turn be refunded to the relevant authority or reinvested in a new scheme approved by the relevant authority. That is, in principle, the same as the current Homebuy option offered by some RSLs, and it has freed up social units for rent by enabling people to move into home ownership. The other products – shared ownership and homes to rent on the basis of assured tenancies or assured shorthold tenancies – will be more complex and more difficult to establish because they involve a long-term landlord relationship with tenants or shared owners. We think that those relationships might best be managed by RSLs. That might be achieved by an RSL managing or taking over the properties from the non-RSL. The relevant authority will clearly need to listen to the views of the commercial sector to test that.'[1]

7.146   The Government has also sought to allay the considerable anxieties about the provisions within the social housing sector:

'When drafting the clause we intended to create, as far as possible, a level playing field for all bidders for grants for these purposes. New providers will not be able to receive a grant unless their scheme proposals can match or exceed RSL performance both in terms of the number of homes to be delivered and in terms of quality.'[2]

Nonetheless, there are a number of outstanding questions for social housing providers which will not be fully addressed until the regulations are complete.

7.147   The Fact Sheet produced by the ODPM[3] to accompany this change states that the government expects:

'that a programme of £200 million will be approved in 2005–06, following a competition for grant for which both RSLs and non-RSLs could bid. The rest of the Approved Development Programme for 2004–06, which was announced in March 2004, would be delivered through grants to RSLs under section 18 of the HA 1996.'

7.148   The Housing Corporation published a policy paper in November 2004[4] indicating how it intends to operate its new powers and setting out a pilot programme for grants to unregistered bodies for the year 2005–06.

The grant giving power

7.149   The Act[5] therefore extends the powers of the relevant authority (the Housing Corporation in respect of England, and the National Assembly for Wales in respect of

1   *Hansard*, HC, vol 418, col 635 (24 February 2004).
2   *Hansard*, HC, vol 418, col 637 (24 February 2004).
3   Factsheet 11: *Payment of grants to bodies other than Registered Social Landlords* http://
    www.odpm.gov.uk/stellent/groups/odpm–housing/documents/page/odpm–house–030209–
    02.hcsp#P33–2359
4   *New Partnerships in Affordable Housing: a Pilot Investment Programme open to Housing Associations and
    Unregistered Bodies* (Housing Corporation, 26 November 2004).
5   Section 220, which inserts new s 27A into the HA 1996.

Wales) to enable it to award grants to companies[1] other than registered social landlords. It is expected that grants will only be awarded to registered companies or ALMOs.[2]

7.150   Grants may be given for the full range of purposes necessary to increase the supply of affordable housing.[3] This can be, for instance, by providing loans to help people acquire homes, or to sell people homes on equity percentage arrangements or shared ownership terms or to provide homes for renting. The activities which can be funded include:

- acquisition;
- repair and improvement;
- conversion;
- construction.

These purposes reflect the social housing purposes for which the social housing grant is provided to registered social landlords.

7.151   The Secretary of State has power to make any necessary provisions in connection with the making of grants[4] including in particular:

- defining equity percentage arrangements;
- specifying or describing the bodies who may grant mortgages to prospective purchasers;
- setting out the priority of such mortgages.[5]

7.152   The grant may be subject to conditions imposed either by the Secretary of State, where the grant is given by the Housing Corporation,[6] or by the Housing Corporation[7] or the National Assembly for Wales.[8] The conditions imposed by the Housing Corporation or the National Assembly for Wales can include conditions requiring a sum to be paid to it by the grant recipient in specified circumstances, with or without interest.[9] The Government indicated that it expected the conditions imposed by the Housing Corporation to replicate for non-registered social landlords the design, construction and management standards that currently apply to registered social landlords receiving grant.[10]

7.153   Where the conditions are prescribed by the Secretary of State, the Housing Corporation is under a duty to impose those conditions on any grant it makes, and is prevented from imposing conditions itself which conflict with the prescribed conditions.[11]

7.154   The Housing Corporation or the National Assembly for Wales must detail:

---

1   The section uses the word 'persons' – the Interpretation Act 1978 defines persons as including a body of persons corporate or unincorporate.
2   *Hansard*, HC, vol 418, col 638 (24 February 2004).
3   HA 1996, s 27A(2).
4   HA 1996, s 27A(3).
5   HA 1996, s 27A(4).
6   HA 1996, s 27A(5).
7   HA 1996, s 27A(8).
8   HA 1996, s 27A(8).
9   HA 1996, s 27A(9).
10   *Hansard*, HL, vol 665, col 900 (20 October 2004).
11   HA 1996, s 27A(7).

- the application procedure for grants;
- the circumstances in which they will be payable;
- the calculation method and any limitations on the amount payable; and
- how grants will be paid.[1]

Transfers

7.155   A property which has been built, converted or renovated by a body which is not a registered social landlord using a grant from the Housing Corporation or the National Assembly for Wales may be transferred[2] either to another non-registered social landlord or to a registered social landlord.

7.156   If the transfer is to another non-registered social landlord, the grant is treated as if it were payable to that other non-registered social landlord.[3] Any conditions applied to the grant are transferred to the transferee where either the whole or part of the grant has been paid.

7.157   If the transfer is to a registered social landlord, the grant is treated as if it had been given to the registered social landlord under s 18 of the HA 1996.[4] This means that it will attract the grant conditions which would usually be imposed if the grant had been given under s 18.[5]

The right to acquire

7.158   Tenants of properties funded through grants given to bodies which are not registered social landlords have the equivalent right to acquire their home to the right enjoyed by tenants of registered social landlords.[6]

7.159   Where a grant has been given to a body which is not a registered social landlord the Housing Corporation or the National Assembly for Wales must notify the grant recipient that any dwelling funded by the grant may be subject to a right to acquire.[7] This replicates the duty upon the relevant authority where grants are given to registered social landlords.[8]

7.160   In order for a property to attract the right to acquire it has to have remained within the social rented sector.[9] Properties which have benefited from grant moneys will be regarded as having remained within the social rented sector if they have been continuously used by the grant recipient, or a person treated as the grant recipient,[10] in accordance with the purposes for which the grant was made or any other purposes agreed to by the Housing Corporation or the National Assembly for Wales.[11]

---

1   HA 1996, s 27A(6).
2   A property is transferred when it vests in or is leased for a term of years to, or reverts to, the transferee: HA 1996, s 27B(1)(b), (2)(b).
3   HA 1996, s 27(B)(1).
4   HA 1996, s 27(B)(2).
5   HA 1996, s 27(B)(3).
6   HA 1996, s 16A inserted by s 221 of the HA 2004. The right to acquire is set out in HA 1996, s 16.
7   HA 1996, s 16A(3).
8   HA 1996, s 16(4).
9   HA 1996, s 16(1)(b).
10   Under HA 1996, s 27(B).
11   HA 1996, s 16A(4).

Amendments relating to registered social landlords

7.161   The Act[1] introduces 26 paragraphs of detailed amendments to various statutory provisions relating to social landlords.[2] The powers of the relevant authority (the Housing Corporation in England and the National Assembly for Wales in Wales) to register and regulate registered social landlords are also amended. The amendments are consistent with the extension of grant giving powers also introduced by the Act.[3]

7.162   There are also miscellaneous amendments to the HA 1996 covering the transfer of net assets on termination of a charity[4] plus provisions[5] exempting registered social landlords from certain audit requirements previously applicable pursuant to the Companies Act 1985.

Social Housing Ombudsman for Wales

7.163   The Act inserts three new sections and a whole new schedule in to the HA 1996[6] which:

- introduce a scheme, to be headed by a new Social Ombudsman for Wales, for investigation of complaints in relation to social landlords in Wales;
- enable the National Assembly for Wales to issue regulations concerning such investigations; and
- define the meaning of social landlord in Wales and gives the National Assembly the power to amend or add to the description of landlords to be treated as social landlords.

7.164   The Social Ombudsman is to be the existing Local Commissioner for Wales.[7] The Schedule deals with related matters concerning the appointment of the Ombudsman and his or her powers.

7.165   The provision eliminates the anomalous situation where the tenants of registered social landlords in England are able to complain to the Housing Ombudsman about the behaviour of their landlords without a parallel scheme being available in Wales.

Rights of pre-emption in connection with assured tenancies

7.166   The Act[8] enables landlords of shared ownership properties to include rights of first refusal in their shared ownership leases in order to help with the retention of affordable housing units. It achieves this by excluding rights of first refusal from the security of tenure provisions of the HA 1988.[9]

7.167   Shared ownership is a scheme designed to enable those on low incomes to purchase a share in their home and pay rent on the remaining share of the property. The purchaser is granted a long lease and becomes the sole legal owner of the property, but the

---

1   Section 218.
2   Set out in Sch 11.
3   Sections 220, 221.
4   Schedule 11, para 16.
5   Schedule 11, para 18.
6   HA 1996, ss 51A–51C and Sch 2A inserted by HA 2004, s 228.
7   HA 1996, s 51A(2).
8   Section 222.
9   HA 1988, s 5.

landlord retains a share of the equity equal to the percentage of the purchase price that was paid. The owner can increase his or her share of ownership of the property (this progress in ownership is described as 'staircasing'). The long lease is an assured tenancy protected by the HA 1988 because the rental levels are too high for it to be excluded from that Act.

7.168   The Government explained the provision as follows:

> '[I]t prevents rights of first refusal in assured tenancies from being caught by section 5 of the HA 1988, which protects the security of tenure of assured tenants. The effect will be to enable landlords of shared ownership properties to include rights of first refusal in their shared ownership leases. It will help retain affordable housing that might otherwise move into the open market. It will also allow a registered social landlord to retain a sensible management role and provide new subsidy where an owner has 'staircased up' to a significant level of ownership.'[1]

Allocation of housing accommodation by local authorities

7.169   Local housing authorities are required to have an allocation scheme to determine priorities and the procedure to be followed when allocating housing accommodation. In framing their allocation scheme, local housing authorities must ensure that 'reasonable preference' is given to certain categories of people. Section 167(2)(d) of the HA 1996 provides that reasonable preference for an allocation is given to people who need to move on 'medical or welfare grounds'. The Act[2] amends s 167(2)(d) of the HA 1996 to make clear that 'medical and welfare grounds' includes people who need to move on grounds relating to a disability.

7.170   The amendment was introduced in response to narrow interpretations of the law on allocations which enabled local authorities to exclude from reasonable preference for allocations those who needed to move because of disability rather than medical or welfare grounds.

7.171   The Government gave further commitments on the issue of housing and disability:

> 'On Report, I gave a commitment that when our statutory code of guidance on allocations was updated next year, we would focus on disability housing registers. I will further commit that when the new clause is considered in the guidance, we will make sure to explain that people who need to move on "grounds relating to a disability" include those who have access needs as a result of their disability. This issue sometimes involves a pedantic jobsmith in the local housing department: he is doing what he thinks is his job, but sometimes it is not common sense.'[3]

Disabled facilities grant

7.172   The Act enables disabled caravan dwellers to apply for a grant to adapt their caravans. Previously the grants were not available to occupiers of caravans unless it was a qualifying park home. The Act achieves this by inserting into Housing Grants, Construction and Regeneration Act 1996 a number of detailed changes.[4]

---

1   *Hansard*, HL, vol 665, col 904 (20 October 2004).
2   Section 223.
3   *Hansard*, HL, vol 666, col 307 (3 November 2004).
4   Section 224.

Annual reports by local housing authorities

7.173   Now that local housing authorities have to produce a best value performance plan the additional duty[1] to send its tenants an annual report, duplicated much of the same information relating to how the authority was functioning. Hence the Act repeals the duty to send annual reports to tenants.[2]

Energy efficiency

The context

7.174   The 'Earth Summit' in Rio in 1992 led to the establishment of the UN Framework Convention on Climate Change ('UNFCCC'). The UNFCCC has organised annual 'Conferences of the Parties' since 1995. At the Conference of the Parties in Kyoto in 1997, major countries agreed a plan (the Kyoto Protocol) including definite commitments to reduce emissions. At a subsequent Conference of the Parties in November 2001 most industrialised countries including the Government, agreed to reduce carbon dioxide emissions from a 1990 base figure by 5% by 2010. Separately, the UN established the Intergovernmental Panel on Climate Change ('IPCC') to organise work into the details of the science, impacts, and possibilities for remedial action. This Panel has issued three major 'Assessment Reports' since it was formed, the latest in early 2001. The first of these included the assertion that stabilisation of greenhouse gas concentrations in the atmosphere requires an immediate 60% reduction, at least, in emissions.

7.175   The Government published the UK's climate change programme in November 2000. The programme set out a range of policies that would deliver the UK's Kyoto target to reduce greenhouse gas emissions by 12.5% below 1990 levels by 2008–2012 and move towards its domestic goal to cut carbon dioxide emissions by 20% below 1990 levels by 2010. There have been a number of legislative provisions which attempt to achieve change in energy consumption. Most relevant to housing is the Sustainable Energy Act 2003 which placed a duty on the Secretary of State in respect of England, and the National Assembly for Wales in respect of Wales, each to designate, and take reasonable steps to achieve, at least one published energy efficiency aim for residential accommodation.

7.176   The Act imposes a duty on the Secretary of State who must take reasonable steps to ensure that by 2010 the general level of energy efficiency of residential accommodation[3] in England has increased by at least 20% compared with the general level of such energy efficiency in 2000.[4] The Act uses the definition of residential accommodation

---

1   Local Government and Housing Act 1989, s 167.
2   Section 227.
3   Residential accommodation is defined in s 1 of the Home Energy Conservation Act 1995 and includes all residential accommodation regardless of whether owner occupied or rented and mobile homes.
4   Section 217.

given in s 1 of the Home Energy Conservation 1995.[1] The Act[2] states expressly that it does not affect the duties imposed by the Sustainable Energy Act 2003.[3]

7.177 The provision was forced upon a reluctant government who resisted it until the day before the end of the parliamentary session arguing that it was unnecessary in light of their commitments under the Sustainable Energy Act 2003.

> 'We continue to take the view that its effect will be broadly in line with that of existing policies on residential energy efficiency and that there has been no retreat on the Government's part. However, we recognise the strength of feeling on the issue. We still believe that duties based on specific numerical figures are inflexible and are better avoided in primary legislation. But we have decided to accede to the principle of the amendment as providing some comfort that the Government stand by the energy efficiency aim they have declared.'[4]

7.178 The statutory duty in itself will not achieve change. The Secretary of State will need to set detailed targets which will undoubtedly need policing and it is unclear how much policing of their energy consumption people will tolerate. Politicians are inevitably reluctant to confront prevailing attitudes to energy efficiency but this means that the chances of meeting the Kyoto target are receding. Like 'a tortoise proceeding purposefully towards its chosen delicacy'[5] the Government might well argue that it has always been taking reasonable steps and so has never been in breach of its duty imposed by the Act.

7.180 The duty is best seen as aspirational, as the Government explained:

> 'the increase is to the general level here. It is not specific to new build or otherwise. It is a broader benefit that does not just apply to new houses that come on stream. It is not about bribery; it is not about coercion. As the noble Baroness, Lady Maddock, said, it is about providing for the future and ensuring that we use energy efficiency savings wisely; that we invest in energy wisely; and that we conserve energy wisely, so that future generations will have access to sources of energy.'[6]

Conclusion

7.181 This is a truly miscellaneous set of provisions most of which whilst providing useful reform are of relatively minor significance. However, the provision of a social housing ombudsman for Wales provides a very welcome equalisation of rights with the tenants of registered social landlords in England and the extension of grant giving powers of the Housing Corporation and the National Assembly has the power to transform the future provision of affordable housing.

---

1 Section 217(3).

2 Section 217(2).

3 To designate, and take reasonable steps to achieve, at least one published energy efficiency aim for residential accommodation.

4 *Hansard*, HL, vol 666, col 1397 (16 November 2004).

5 Words of Stephen Sedley, now Lord Justice Sedley, when arguing whether or not a county council which was trying to comply with the duty to provide gypsy caravan sites under the CSA 1968; s 6 was in breach of that duty, when it was shown that a number of gypsies residing and resorting to the district were not accommodated.

6 *Hansard*, HL, vol 666, col 1399 (16 November 2004).

Chapter 8

MOBILE HOMES

INTRODUCTION

8.1 In broad terms the Act changes the relevant statutory provisions which apply to Mobile Home Agreements by:

(1) requiring particulars of the agreements to be given in advance;[1]
(2) by altering the implied terms relating to termination of agreements and disposition by the occupier of their mobile home;[2] and
(3) enabling further amendment by the appropriate national authority of the terms implied in site agreements.[3]

These changes could be just the tip of the iceberg since there are far more extensive changes in the pipeline. In relation to mobile home parks and in reference to these wider changes the Government has stated:

> 'These sites provide a positive contribution to the current affordable housing shortages which is more prominent in the rural locations where most parks are situated. As has been stated elsewhere in this paper these proposals promote the protection of a vulnerable sector of society who have very few resources and few explicit rights which is a massive benefit in itself that fully justifies the proposed amendments.'[4]

Therefore, watch out for when the enabling provision for further amendment is to be used.

BACKGROUND PROVISIONS

8.2 The Mobile Homes Act 1983 ('MHA 1983') requires site owners to prepare and deliver written particulars of agreement, regulates the contractual arrangements between home occupiers and site owners and confers jurisdiction on county courts to determine other issues which may arise as between the parties.

---

1 Section 206.
2 Section 207.
3 Section 208; appropriate national authority is defined in s 261(1): for England being the Secretary of State, and for Wales being the National Assembly for Wales.
4 Paragraph 4 of the Regulatory Impact Assessment (RIA) of the intended changes to the 1983 Written Statement Regulations which would introduce new implied terms presently contained in Sch 1 of the Mobile Homes Act 1983.

Protected site

8.3   The relevant legislation[1] is limited to situations where the mobile home is stationed on a protected site. The Act makes no changes in this respect. A protected site is land in respect of which a site licence is required. Land cannot be a protected site even if a site licence is required if residential use of that land is limited to certain times of the year, ie by a requirement that the land is vacated between October and March. Such a stipulation can sometimes be a feature of planning permissions for certain caravan sites which is then reflected in the terms of the site licence itself.

Meaning of mobile home

8.4   'Mobile home' is given[2] the same meaning as 'caravan', in Part 1 of the Caravan Sites and Control of Development Act 1960 which provides:

> '"caravan" means any structure designed or adapted for human habitation which is capable of being moved from one place to another (whether by being towed, or being transported on a motor vehicle or trailer) and any motor vehicle so designed or adapted, but does not include –
>
> (a)   any railway rolling stock which is for the time being on rails forming part of a railway system, or
>
> (b)   any tent.'[3]

8.5   But this requirement of being lawfully moved when assembled was altered by subsequent legislation that provides that a structure designed or adapted for human habitation which is composed of not more than two sections 'shall not be not treated as not being (or as not having been) a caravan' only by reason that it cannot be lawfully moved on the highway when assembled.[4]

8.6   Additionally a mobile home that is in excess of any of the following limits:

- length: 60 feet;
- width: 20 feet;
- overall height: 12 feet;
- overall height of living accommodation (from the lowest level to the ceiling at the highest level): 10 feet;

cannot be a caravan for the purposes of the 1960 Act.[5]

---

1   MHA 1983.

2   MHA 1983, s 5(1).

3   Caravan Sites and Control of Development Act 1960, s 29.

4   Caravan Sites Act 1968, s 13. In *Howard v Charlton* [2002] EWCA 1086 the site owner brought a possession claim contending that because the occupier's mobile home had a porch, (of painted boarding which had a Perspex roof that was later replaced at the same time as the roof to the original home with tile roof covering both parts) the home was no longer a mobile home within the terms of the Act since it could neither be moved as a single structure nor moved lawfully on the highway since it was over 12 feet wide. Lord Justice Carnwath remarked at para 9: 'It is immediately apparent that something may be a caravan though it bears no relation to what might be regarded as a caravan in ordinary language'. The claim was dismissed on the basis that the terms of the agreement relating to termination continued to apply even if the home ceased to be a mobile home within the Act.

5   Caravan Sites Act 1968, s 13(2).

THE GOVERNMENT'S PROPOSED CHANGES NOT INCLUDED IN THE ACT[1]

8.7 Reform of the provisions relevant to mobile homes has only just been begun by the amendments now introduced by the Act. The scale of the further changes envisaged by the Government makes the amendments at present contained in the Act look limited.

8.8 It is to the Government's credit that changes to Park Home legislation, which is estimated[2] to affect between 120,000 and 250,000 people on about 2,000 sites, was not consigned to a subsequent private members bill, with all the pitfalls such bills do face, but instead forms part of this Housing Act. But given that provisions affecting Park Homes were not envisaged in the draft bill, there is still some catching up to do.

8.9 There is the odd situation of the Act becoming law whilst the Government is still in the process of formulating its response to the consultation process on many further potential changes. These may or may not become law since the Government's response to the consultation process is awaited and because any order, introducing the further changes, has to be laid before, and approved by both Houses of Parliament. The changes that are being considered are set out in the ODPM *Park Home Statutory Instruments Consultation on Implied Terms and Written Statement* published in July 2004. The proposed changes, which have been slightly paraphrased, are intended to:

(1)   Clarify that the occupation agreement permits the siting of a replacement home purchased by the occupier on the same pitch.

(2)   Permit site owners to terminate agreements because the home is no longer the occupier's only or main residence only if the court considers it reasonable to do so.

(3)   Permit site owners to terminate agreements only because the current condition of the home is having a detrimental effect on the amenity of the site without reference to five year 'relevant periods'.

(4)   Require that, if the site owner wishes to withhold approval, he must make available first a list of the criteria under which approval would be withheld.

(5)   Ensure that site owners cannot require that the assignment transaction, and the payment of funds from a prospective purchaser, be conducted through him/herself or an agent specified by them.

(6)   Stipulate that commission on sale does not apply to a gift of the mobile home.

(7)   Permit occupiers to gift their mobile home, and assign the agreement, to anyone, not just family members.

(8)   Stipulate that homes may only be moved for essential and/or emergency works or to meet health and safety requirements of the local authority and when this takes place for: the new pitch to be 'broadly comparable' to the initial pitch; all expenses of the move to be borne by the site owner; if possible the home must be returned to the original pitch upon completion of the work.

(9)   Entitle occupiers to quiet enjoyment of the pitch as an automatic right.

(10)   Ensure that the site owner be required to provide 24 hours' written notice to enter the pitch except in the case of an emergency.

---

1   See ODPM *Park Home Statutory Instruments Consultation on Implied Terms and Written Statement* (July 2004), pp 9–10.

2   Ibid, para 2.2.

(11)   Require the occupier to pay the owner a monthly pitch fee, to be agreed with the site owner 28 days before the day that the agreement begins. This fee will include the costs of maintenance and improvements, the provision of all services and the use of any amenities. The written agreement should specify: exactly for what services the sums are payable; the times at which payments are to be made; the amount payable; and the date for review.

(12)   The pitch fee shall be reviewed annually by both parties on a specified date stated in the agreement. In reviewing the pitch fee the following must be adhered to: pitch fees must rise no more than the corresponding rise in the All Items Retail Price Index issued by the Office of National Statistics over the year; all increases to the pitch fee should be negotiated between occupiers, or their authorised representatives and the site owner; the owner must, on request from any occupier, furnish documentary evidence in support of the stated costs of all expenditure; costs incurred by the owner for work on newly developed areas of the park shall not be charged to existing residents.

(13)   In reviewing the pitch fee regard shall be had to: sums expended by the owner for the benefit of occupiers of mobile homes; any costs of improvements shall be shared between owner and occupiers in agreed proportions. A return on investment of 10% of the reasonable cost of undertaking improvements which were completed during the previous 12 months will be acceptable. The term 'improvements' will exclude any work necessary to comply with the licensor's repairing obligation under the terms of the written statement.

(14)   Require the site owner to issue a notice, in writing, to all mobile home owners, 28 days before the review date giving his proposals for the amount of the following year's pitch fee and the reasons for any increase: if occupiers agree with the proposals then payment of the revised pitch fee will commence on the agreed date; if no increase is requested, then payment of the pitch fee will commence on the agreed date and the schedule will be endorsed with a 0% increase for that year.

(15)   Ensure that any occupier or group of occupiers has the right to request written documentation to show sums expended with a view to reaching an agreement. Failure to negotiate will invalidate any proposed increase and the current level of pitch fee shall remain payable and future reviews will not be able to retrospectively increase the pitch fee.

(16)   Require the occupier to pay all charges due to the owner in respect of the amount of electricity, gas or water used, in the event that any of these services are purchased from the owner. The charges mentioned are to be charged separately from the pitch fee and will not be subject to the pitch fee review clause. The owner shall not impose or demand charges or payments other than those made in accordance with the above or as required by law.

(17)   Make the occupier undertake to keep the mobile home and pitch including all fences and outbuildings in a sound state of repair and condition and to keep the exterior thereof clean and tidy.

(18)   Make the site owner undertake to keep and maintain those parts of the park which are for common use in a good state of repair and condition.

(19)   Prohibit the site owner or his agents from doing or causing to be done anything to obstruct the occupier's right to maintain or repair or refurbish the mobile home or to arrange with competent contractors to repair or refurbish the home.

(20) Ensure that before carrying out improvements on the park, the site owners must consult residents for a minimum period of 28 days.

(21) Entitle occupiers to the details of their plot size in writing with measurements from fixed points such as kerbs, structures and concrete base.

(22) Entitle occupiers to form resident associations that must be recognised by site owners for negotiations on pitch fees, if 60% of residents on a site have joined.

(23) Stipulate that the site owner's current name and address (and any address for service if different) must be contained in demands for pitch fee. Any change in details should be amended in 28 days. Failure to comply with this will result in the residents not having to pay any pitch fee increases until the information is provided.

THE AMENDMENTS NOW INTRODUCED BY THE ACT

8.10 The Act makes the following changes:[1]

- Repeal[2] of the requirement that a written statement of terms be delivered within three months of the agreement to station the mobile home on the park. This is replaced with a new requirement (that can be shortened if the proposed occupier consents in writing)[3] that the written statement must be given 28 days before any agreement for the sale of the home to the proposed occupier is made or 28 days before the agreement to which this Act applies is entered into.[4]

- A new requirement on site owners to follow the same procedure (of 28 days' prior notification of the terms of the proposed agreement) in relation to any variations of the agreement.[5]

- Giving mobile home occupiers the right to apply to the court within six months[6] of any variation to their agreement to ask the court to vary or delete any express term.[7]

- Significant amelioration of the impact of a ground on which a site owner was previously able to recover possession. In the 1983 Act if the owner persuaded the court that it could be satisfied that, having regard to its age and condition, the mobile home is having a detrimental effect on the amenity of the site; or is likely to have such an effect before the end of the next five-year anniversary of when the agreement began, then the court had no discretion but to grant a possession order. The Act knocks out the word 'age'.[8] More significantly, the court can instead adjourn the possession claim subject to the occupier complying with an order which

---

1   Changes that apply to all agreements (s 207(6)) which exist on the day the section comes into force (18 January 2005: s 270(3)(a)); save (s 207(7)(a)) that a possession claim brought before that day will not attract the court's power to adjourn introduced by s 207(2). Similarly a request for approval will not attract the new procedure and reversed burden of proof unless the request is made after 18 January 2005 (s 207(7)(b)).

2   Section 206(1).

3   MHA 1983, s 1(4) inserted by HA 2004, s 206(1).

4   MHA 1983, s 1(3) inserted by HA 2004, s 206(1).

5   MHA 1983, s 1(8) inserted by HA 2004, s 206(1).

6   The existing right to apply to court within six months of being given the written agreement is retained although in an amended form; see MHA 1983, s 2(2) as amended by HA 2004, s 206(2)(a).

7   MHA 1983, s 2(3A) inserted by HA 2004, s 206(2).

8   Section 207(2)(a).

specifies a time for completing the works.[1] If the works are carried out the possession claim cannot be further pursued.[2] Such an adjournment is dependent on the occupier demonstrating to the court that even though[3] the condition of his or her mobile home is having a detrimental effect on the amenity of the site; or is likely to have such an effect before the end of the next five-year anniversary of when the agreement began, it would be reasonably practical[4] for particular repairs to be carried out that would result in the home ceasing to have such detrimental effect, and he or she intends to do those works.[5]

- Altering the provisions governing sale of the mobile home by switching the burden of proof to the site owner to show that a withholding of consent is reasonable[6] or that any conditions attached to an approval were reasonable conditions[7] to be imposed, whilst also making the seeking of approval and the site owner's decision in respect of the request subject to a written procedure.[8]

- Altering the provisions governing the making of a gift of the mobile home so that they are subject to the same written procedure.[9]

- Creating an additional right to apply to the county court. The procedure in both cases means that if a site owner fails to notify the occupier that the proposed purchaser of the home, or assignee of the agreement or intended recipient of the home is approved or if the owner fails to set out any conditions that are being imposed in the notification or explain the reasons, if that is the case, for withholding consent,[10] the occupier can seek a court declaration that the person is approved.[11]

- Last but not least, the Act permits the appropriate national authorities to make the proposed further detailed amendments to the terms contained in Sch 1 to the 1983 Act.[12] The power cannot be exercised without the draft order being laid before and approved by a resolution of each House of Parliament.[13] The Act also requires[14] consultation in relation to any such order but allows consultation that has already taken place before the Act was passed to count as if undertaken after that date.[15] Hence the way is open for the Government to introduce its extensive proposed changes,[16] as already set out.

---

1   MHA 1983, Sch 1, para 6(4) inserted by HA 2004, s 207(2).
2   MHA 1983, Sch 1, para 6(5) inserted by HA 2004, s 207(2).
3   MHA 1983, Sch 1, para 6(3)(a) inserted by HA 2004, s 207(2).
4   MHA 1983, Sch 1, para 6(3)(b) inserted by HA 2004, s 207(2).
5   MHA 1983, Sch 1, para 6(3)(c) inserted by HA 2004, s 207(2).
6   MHA 1983, Sch 1, para 8(1F)(c) inserted by HA 2004, s 207(3).
7   MHA 1983, Sch 1, para 8(1F)(b) inserted by HA 2004, s 207(3).
8   MHA 1983, Sch 1, para 8(1A)–(1E) inserted by HA 2004, s 207(3).
9   MHA 1983, Sch 1, para 9(2) inserted by HA 2004, s 207(4).
10   In *Berkeley Leisure Group v Lee* [1996] 29 HLR 663 it was held that if a site owner unreasonably refuses to consent to the assignment of the mobile home agreement, this does not give rise to a cause of action.
11   MHA 1983, Sch 1, para 8(1E) inserted by HA 2004, s 207(3).
12   MHA 1983, s 2A(1), (3) inserted by HA 2004, s 208. The proposed further amendments are set out at **8.9** above.
13   MHA 1983, s 2A(6) inserted by HA 2004, s 208.
14   MHA 1983, s 2A(5) inserted by HA 2004, s 208.
15   Section 208(2) and MHA 1983, s 2A(6) inserted by HA 2004, s 208.
16   See ODPM *Park home statutory instruments: implied terms and written statement consultation* (July 2004), pp 9–10.

8.11   There is a supplementary provision[1] that creates an actionable statutory tort. This is a duty that is imposed on a person where although he or she has an estate or interest in the protected site, he or she is not actually the site owner. If such a person receives a request from the occupier made to the site owner to approve an intended purchaser and or assignee of the agreement or donee of the home, then the recipient of the request must take such steps as are reasonable to secure that the site owner receives the request within 28 days. The Act gives the mobile home occupier a cause of action against a recipient of the request who fails to perform this duty.[2]

8.12   Under the new s 2A of the 1983 Act provision is made for introducing the intended further changes, to be done by a new statutory instrument. When the power is exercised, the order can affect the implied terms in all existing agreements between site owners and occupiers, that is, agreements which were made before the day on which the statutory instrument comes into force. This is a crucial provision. It means all agreements in existence at the time the order containing the further amendments came into force would get the benefit of the further amendments. But after that any further amendments would only apply to mobile home agreements entered in to after any further order comes into force.[3]

---

1   A new Part 3 added to MHA 1983, Sch 1 was inserted by HA 2004, s 207(5).

2   MHA 1983, Sch 1, Pt 3, para 2.

3   MHA 1983, s 2A(4).

Chapter 9

GYPSIES AND TRAVELLERS

PROTECTED SITES TO INCLUDE SITES FOR GYPSIES AND SUSPENSION OF EVICTION ORDERS

The content of the provisions

9.1   Before putting the changes into context it is worth briefly describing their effect. As a result of the Act, gypsies facing eviction from a council-run site for not complying with the terms of their licence can resist outright eviction by going to the hearing of the possession claim to ask the Court to suspend the order for possession.[1] The Government has given an example:

> '[I]f possession is sought because of breaches of the occupation agreement, such as rent arrears, the eviction order could be suspended so long as the rent was paid in future, plus regular payments towards the arrears. In cases that deal with anti-social behaviour on sites, the eviction order could be suspended so long as the occupier's behaviour was acceptable.'[2]

9.2   Furthermore the disparity between the status of those on sites owned by district councils and those owned by county councils is removed.[3] The changes are not retrospective so any proceedings already commenced before the Act comes into force will not be affected.[4] The suspension of the possession order can be for up to 12 months,[5] but by the time such period is about to expire there might be further legislative change on the horizon. This would be a reason for an impending eviction to be reconsidered in the light of its effect on rights under the European Convention of Human Rights as considered in the case of *Connors v United Kingdom*.[6] However, at present there is no clear indication when the Government's consideration of how best to bring the management of public sites more in line with social housing might be concluded.[7] On 1 November 2004, Keith Hill (Minister for Housing and Planning) wrote:

> 'You will also be aware that we are considering the tenure of local authority Gypsy and Traveller sites as part of our aim to mainstream site provision, one of the options being to look at the comparison with social housing. You will appreciate that this area of housing law is

---

1   Section 211(1).

2   Letter dated 1 November 2004 from Minister for Housing and Planning to the Chair of Parliament's Joint Committee on Human Rights, referred to in para 3.2 of the 23rd Report of Session 2003–04 and published as an appendix to that report.

3   Section 209(2). Section 209 comes into force two months after the Act was passed (s 270(2)(a)).

4   Sections 209(3), 211(2).

5   Caravan Sites Act 1968, s 4(3).

6   (2004) 16 BHRC 639; [2004] HLR 52 at 991.

7   Lord Bassam of Brighton stated a detailed review of security of tenure (for those on gypsy sites) is continuing: *Hansard*, HL Deb, vol 664, col 1404 (16 September 2004).

highly complex, and given the timescales involved it has not been possible to include appropriate measures in the Housing Bill. The Law Commission is undertaking a review of rented tenure and is due to report early next year. It is our intention to consider the security of tenure of Gypsy and Traveller sites in the context of that review.'[1]

History

9.3   Since 1960 it has been an offence for an occupier of land to cause or permit any part of the land to be used as a caravan site unless the occupier is the holder of a site licence granted by the local authority authorising use of the land as a caravan site.[2] Part 1 of the Caravan Sites Act 1968 ('CSA 1968') introduced for the first time limited security for occupiers of residential caravans. But the caravan had to be on a protected site. This was defined as 'any land in respect of which a site licence is required under the Caravan Sites and Control of Development Act 1960'. Land cannot be a protected site even if a site licence is required if residential use of that land is limited to certain times of the year, ie by a requirement that the land is vacated between October and March. Such a stipulation can sometimes be a feature of planning permissions for certain caravan sites which is then reflected in the terms of the site licence itself.

9.4   The security introduced by the CSA 1968 was limited since beyond the contractual right not to be dispossessed during the currency of the residential contract, the only protections afforded were:

(1)   the deterrent effect of making the perpetrator of an unlawful eviction liable to prosecution;[3]
(2)   the right to four weeks notice in writing of termination of contract;[4] and
(3)   in certain circumstances, the ability to ask the court to suspend the possession order (which otherwise the landowner was entitled to) for up to 12 months.[5]

9.5   In 1975 greater protection was given to a person stationing his own caravan[6] on a licensed caravan site for occupation as his only or main residence. This was then further extended in 1983 when Parliament made the site owner's ability to recover possession of the caravan pitch dependent on proof of breach of agreement plus, even if breach was established, the court could withhold a possession order unless persuaded that it was reasonable to grant one.[7]

9.6   However, a gypsy sometimes got none of the above. This was because whilst there was a duty to provide sites for gypsies residing and resorting to an area,[8] municipal sites

---

1   See footnote 2 on previous page.
2   Caravan Sites and Control of Development Act 1960, ss 1–12.
3   CSA 1968, s 3.
4   CSA 1968, s 2.
5   CSA 1968, s 4.
6   The mobile home legislation defines a mobile home as a caravan within the meaning of Part 1 of the Caravan Sites and Control of Development Act 1960 ('CSCDA 1960') which is further defined in the CSA 1968, s 13 as including – although the provision is peppered with double negatives – a structure of not more than two sections separately constructed and designed to be assembled on site not being in excess of 60 feet long, 20 feet wide and 10 feet high – hence park homes looking like bungalows can be caravans.
7   Mobile Homes Act 1975 followed by Mobile Homes Act 1983 ('MHA 1983').
8   CSA 1968, s 6, repealed on 3 November 1994 by the Criminal Justice and Public Order Act 1994, s 80.

were often provided by county councils who were under that duty and according to an amendment introduced in 1980[1] a site licence was not required for use of land by a county council as a site providing accommodation for gypsies.[2]

9.7 This in itself was not contentious. However, s 1(2) of the 1968 Act was not amended when this change was introduced. That section counted back in land occupied by local authorities (even though they did not require a site licence). The result of not changing the 1968 Act when the 1980 amendment was introduced meant gypsies on a county council run site were worse off than if living on a district council site where the limited security applied.

9.8 Thus gypsies did not even get the benefit of the limited security on a gypsy caravan site occupied and owned by a county council.[3] The security conferred by the MHA 1983 bypassed gypsies on account of making the provisions in the Act only applicable to land forming part of a protected site[4] and defining protected site as not including land occupied by a local authority as a caravan site providing accommodation for gypsies.[5]

9.9 The provision in the Act now states 'Protected sites are to include sites for gypsies'.[6] At first blush and in the light of the above history, this sounds dramatic but in fact the only amendment is to the CSA 1968, so the Act does not reverse the difference in treatment that dates back to 1975, when non-gypsy caravan dwellers (ie those on mobile home parks) were given greater security.

9.10 The Government sought to justify the difference in treatment before the European Court and lost.[7] The Connors were gypsies living on a gypsy caravan site who took their case to Strasbourg, having been unable to contest the allegations of nuisance relied on for terminating their agreement to occupy a council run gypsy caravan site. The European Court in its judgment described the main issue in the case in the following terms:

'The central issue in this case is therefore whether, in the circumstances, the legal framework applicable to the occupation of pitches on local authority gypsy sites provided the applicant with sufficient procedural protection of his rights.'[8]

9.11 It seems the Government recognises[9] that the Act does not fully address the European Court's conclusion:

'even allowing for the margin of appreciation which is to be afforded to the State in such circumstances, the Court is not persuaded that the necessity for a statutory scheme which permitted the summary eviction of the applicant and his family has been sufficiently demonstrated by the Government. The power to evict without the burden of giving reasons liable to be examined as to their merits by an independent tribunal has not been convincingly

---

1   Local Government Planning and Land Act 1990, s 176.
2   CSCDA 1960, Sch 2, para 11A.
3   Which were the facts in *Stoke on Trent CC v Frost* [1992] 24 HLR 290.
4   MHA 1983, s 1(a).
5   MHA 1983, s 5(1).
6   Section 209.
7   *Connors v United Kingdom* (2004) 16 BHRC 639; [2004] HLR 52 at 991.
8   At para 85.
9   See footnote 2 on p 207.

shown to respond to any specific goal or to provide any specific benefit to members of the gypsy community'.[1]

9.12 The amendment sought unsuccessfully in the House of Lords[2] was aimed at the definition of protected site in s 5(1) of the MHA 1983 so that protected site included any gypsy and traveller site managed by a county council or a district council. The Government's response, made in the same debate, was more descriptive than reasoned:

> 'Amending the Mobile Homes Act in the way suggested would have wider consequences. It would confer succession rights to the occupation agreement, allow residents to assign their occupation agreements to others and allow local authorities to charge commission on the sale of caravans. This is another reason why the amendment is unsuitable.'[3]

9.13 Thus the central thrust of the Act in respect of tenure is as follows. First, it overrides the effect of the Court of Appeal's decision in *Stoke on Trent CC v Frost*[4] and corrects (24 years later) the oversight of not amending CSA 1968, s 1(2) when the 1980 amendment was made.[5] This means once a county council has determined a pitch licence, the gypsy or traveller concerned would have a rule of law on their side restricting the right of the site owner to recover possession.[6] Secondly, the Act gives the court the power to suspend any possession order which in any event it would still have no choice, but to make. Thirdly, the following provision[7] extends the scope of the offence of harassment to catch acts likely to interfere with the peace or comfort of an occupier on a protected site and strengthens the powers of the courts once an offence is proved.

9.14 There now remains a limbo situation before the Government gives gypsies the right to contest, before any possession order is made, whether or not they have been guilty of breach of their occupation agreement and makes the grant of any possession order subject to reasonableness.

EXTENSION OF PROTECTION FROM HARASSMENT

9.15 The object of the CSA 1968[8] was to confer on all permanent occupiers of caravans (a definition capable of including a mobile home) protection against harassment by making it a criminal offence.[9] The fact that this did not apply to gypsies living on a county council site has been explained above.[10] The Act, apart from removing this anomaly, now extends[11] the protection against harassment provisions in the 1968 Act in two ways. The Act amends the CSA 1968, making it similar to the existing provision for

---

1   At para 94.
2   Moved by Lord Avebury: *Hansard*, HL Deb, vol 664, col 1400 (16 September 2004).
3   Ibid.
4   [1992] 24 HLR 290; CSA 1968, s 6, repealed on 3 November 1994 by the Criminal Justice and Public Order Act 1994, s 80.
5   Section 209(2); see footnote 6 on p 208.
6   As has been the case for gypsies on local authority sites: see CSA 1968, s 3(1)(b) (now extended to gypsies on any county council sites).
7   Section 210 by inserting a new s 1(1A) into the CSA 1968.
8   CSA 1969, s 3.
9   Which can be prosecuted by the local authority: CSA 1968, s 14.
10 The combined effect of CSA 1968, s 1(2) and CSCDA 1960, Sch 2, para 11A.
11 Section 210.

conventional house dwellers.[1] The other amendment, also in line with protection for users of mainstream accommodation, is to make the offence easier to prove. Instead of needing to show an intent,[2] the successful prosecution can instead depend on demonstrating that the owner had reasonable cause to believe that his conduct was likely to cause the caravan dweller:

- to abandon occupation of the caravan; or
- remove it from the site; or
- refrain from exercising any right or pursuing any remedy in respect thereof.[3]

9.16   But there could be a problem with this: gypsy caravan sites are often municipal sites where the site owners are often one and the same as the prosecuting authority.[4] Where authorities adopt best practice the problem is non-existent; however, gypsies and travellers, whatever site they are on, when faced with a site owner who is misbehaving, are now able to enrol the assistance and get a letter from an Advice Bureau or solicitors pointing out to the owner that he or she should seek legal advice because what they are doing could result in a heavy fine or land the responsible[5] person in jail.[6]

ACCOMMODATION NEEDS OF GYPSIES

Introduction

9.17   The Chair of the Gypsy Council said in oral evidence in[7] the pre-legislative scrutiny of the Housing Bill:

> 'it is about time that we were taken as part of the whole community and part of the housing needs of this country, which is vital. If it is not, and we are continually separated off into this obscure little group that everybody thinks is a problem, that is how we are going to be viewed. If we are put into the Housing Bill and included as part of the housing needs of this country then you might start changing opinions.'

9.18   The call was apparently heeded. The notion of bringing site provision more closely within housing provision echoed a recommendation made in a study of provision

---

1   Section 210(3): by inserting a new s 3(1A) into the CSA 1968 which is in similar terms to the Protection from Eviction Act 1977, s 1(3A).
2   Section 210(2) substitutes the words 'calculated to interfere' in CSA 1968, s 3(1) with the words 'likely to interfere'.
3   CSA 1968, s 3(1)(c)(i), (ii).
4   CSA 1968, s 14(2) permits only local authorities to institute proceedings for an offence.
5   CSA 1969, s 14(1) makes both the individual and the body who employs him liable to prosecution.
6   Section 210(4) inserts a new CSA 1968, s 3(3) that doubles the period of possible imprisonment on summary conviction from six to 12 months and enables magistrates additionally to impose a fine not exceeding the statutory maximum, plus the Act enables the Crown Court to impose a two-year term of imprisonment.
7   ODPM Housing Planning Local Government and the Regions Committee 10th Report, Vol 751 III, Oral Evidence and Supplementary Written Evidence, 23 June 2003.

of sites in England.[1] The Act now requires every local housing authority[2] to carry out an assessment of the accommodation needs[3] of gypsies and travellers residing in or resorting to their district.[4] The assessment is to be carried out when undertaking a review of housing needs in their district under s 8 of the HA 1985. It remains to be seen if opinions are to be changed.

9.19   The Act hangs the duty to assess gypsies' and travellers' accommodation needs on a statutory peg, and firmly puts the responsibility on the local housing authority to do so, although arguably it was already the Government's policy that planning authorities had the responsibility for doing this. Both Technical Advice Note 2 for Wales and PPGs 12 & 3 for England exhort local planning authorities to cater in the formulation of their housing policies for the needs of all sections of the communities they serve, including those with special accommodation needs. Such special needs are discussed within the same Guidance whilst referring to travellers' needs. This also reflects Circular Guidance (1/94 and 2/94), now in the process of being replaced, to the effect that planning authorities are required to have adequate policies capable of meeting the land use requirements of gypsies whilst safeguarding amenity.[5] The problem has been that in the interests of safeguarding amenity local planning authorities sometimes have few, if any, rural locations where a gypsy caravan park would accord with policy. So unauthorised encampments become the hallmark of lack of provision for a community of which a substantial percentage has no lawful stopping place. It is this dilemma which the Government is seeking to address both by mainstreaming accommodation needs of gypsies and travellers by this Act's widening of s 8 of the Housing Act 1985 and by giving planning guidance a 'new direction'.[6]

Housing strategies

9.20   Section 8 of the HA 1985 does not require a local housing authority to fulfil such assessed need as it may identify in its review of housing needs. But the same authorities are

---

1   The *Report on the Provision and Condition of Local Authority Gypsy/Traveller Sites in England* (ODPM, October 2002) summarises the information and conclusions of research on the extent and quality of local authority gypsy sites carried out by the Centre for Urban and Regional Studies at the University of Birmingham. The Report noted that 70% of local authorities did not have any written gypsy/traveller accommodation policy and commented that this reflected the lack of a specific duty on local authorities to consider their needs.

2   Local housing authority is defined in s 261(2).

3   Accommodation needs are defined as including the need for the provision of sites on which caravans can be stationed.

4   Section 225.

5   The difference in treatment that results in development plan housing policies being geared to meet an identified assessed figure of further conventional housing, with locations identified in the development plan policies for where the proposed further housing that is needed will go, is glaring when compared to many development plan gypsy policies which are entirely blind to the amount of any existing or further land use requirements of gypsies. The difference in treatment between housing policies geared to meet the assessed needs of those the policy is designed to cater for and the many gypsy policies that are not even based on an up-to-date assessment of what the need is, more idling rather than being geared to effectively providing what is required, might be impossible to justify now the Act has introduced this statutory duty to ascertain the accommodation needs of gypsies and travellers residing in or resorting to their district.

6   Paragraph 3 of the Introduction to the ODPM consultation paper *Planning for Gypsy and Traveller Sites* (December 2004).

required to formulate and publish every five years a homelessness strategy for (amongst other things) securing that sufficient accommodation is and will be available for people in their district who are or may become homeless.[1] The Act also makes it mandatory that local housing authorities when exercising their functions should take account of any strategy required of them, under s 87 of the Local Government Act 2003.[2] This provision in the 2003 Act enables the appropriate person[3] to require a strategy in respect of such matters relating to housing[4] as the appropriate person may specify. Such a strategy might be consolidated into a combined document with the homelessness strategy required by the Homelessness Act 2002.

Methodology

9.21   A review of existing municipal sites that found, for example, a number of families overcrowded through younger family members marrying and starting their own families, would presumably count those occupying the number of caravans that exceeded the permitted number of caravans for the size of the pitch, as persons who are or may become homeless. Such a review might further identify any gypsies currently in council accommodation, reluctantly so because of the absence of any lawful site to go to, who are perhaps mostly using their caravans parked on the drive to live in. Such hidden need for an adequate place to put their caravan may be assessed in addition to the notorious need of those on unlawful encampments by the side of the road and in addition to those who might be squatting on a semi permanent basis, sites originally allocated as transit sites.

9.22   Such are the permutations of where to look in order to carry out the assessment, including of course talking to the gypsies themselves, that rather than relying on some pro forma questionnaire mailed out to the those gypsies with a fixed address, a method that might be employed for the settled population, some local authorities may find they need to consider retaining consultants or using the research capabilities of a university to carry out the assessment for them. However, authorities must await government guidance issued pursuant to the Act.[5]

---

1   Homelessness Act 2002, ss 1(1)(b), 3(1)(b).

2   Section 225(3).

3   Defined as the same as the national authorities in s 261(1); referred to in the Local Government Act 2003 as the appropriate person, either the Secretary of State or the Welsh Assembly.

4   Local Government Act 2003 s 87(4) is substituted by HA 2004, Sch 15, para 47 so that it now reads: '"housing" includes accommodation needs of gypsies and travellers within the meaning of section 217 of the Housing Act 2004'.

5   Section 226(1)(a); the methodology and guidance is now being developed: see the discussion in *Hansard*, HL Deb, vol 664, col 1390 (16 September 2004) and Lord Bassam's response at col 1398 'that local authorities will work with regional housing boards to ensure that local and regional needs are met within the system'. See also paragraph 1 of Annex D to the recent ODPM consultation paper *Planning for Gypsy and Traveller Sites* (December 2004) which states that Guidance will be issued setting out a baseline of factors to be considered as well as a recommended methodology.

Meaning of gypsies and travellers

9.23   The Act provides an opportunity to depart from the definition of gypsy.[1] One of the main issues is whether a person can be a traveller without travelling to look for work, because before the regulations are published the Government will have to address whether the Act intends the accommodation needs of sedentary gypsies to be counted.[2]

9.24   The current statutory definition of gypsy was drafted in the context[3] of case-law[4] concerning an alleged offence under s 127 of the Highways Act 1959 which provided:

> 'If without lawful authority or excuse ... (c) ... a gipsy pitches a booth stall or stand or encamps on a highway, he shall be guilty of an offence.'

9.25   The court rejected the contention that gipsy referred only to a person of Romany race, unsurprisingly observing to the effect that otherwise the prosecution was based on the defendant being of a particular racial group , which could not be correct. The need in that particular case, to avoid an ethnic element to the definition of gypsy, has had an enduring effect.

9.26   A year later Parliament introduced a definition of gypsy as persons of nomadic habit of life whatever their race or origin.[5]

9.27   The Court of Appeal recently observed that in order to decide if a person was a statutory gypsy, the definition involved addressing:

> 'Are they at that time following such a habit of life in the sense of a pattern and/or a rhythm of full-time or seasonal or other periodic travelling? The fact that they may have a permanent base from which they set out on, and to which they return from, their periodic travelling may not deprive them of nomadic status. And the fact that they are temporarily confined to their permanent base for personal reasons such as sickness and/or, possibly, in the interests of their children, may not do so either, depending on the reasons and the length of time, passed and projected, of the abeyance of their travelling life. But if they have retired permanently from

---

1   Section 225(5) states that 'gypsies and travellers' has the meaning given by regulations made by the appropriate authority; a new definition is inevitable to explain why travellers have been included in addition to gypsies and whether travellers are non-ethnic gypsies. In *O'Leary v Allied Domecq* (unreported) 29 August 2000, a case concerning a 'no travellers' sign, Judge Goldstein sitting at the Bloomsbury County Court, decided that Irish Travellers are an ethnic minority, a distinct racial group, because they have a long shared history and cultural tradition following *Commission for Racial Equality v Dutton* [1989] QB 783, CA (Civ Div) which decided gypsies were a distinct racial group.

2   The ODPM consultation paper *Planning for Gypsy and Traveller Sites* (December 2004) suggests the new test for the nomadic habit of life required by the present statute will permit a non economically active gypsy or traveller to come within the new definition, provided the reason he or she is not nomadic is for an identified reason (need for settled site whilst children attend school – which will include most extended families – and ill health, old age or caring responsibilities, or the widows or widowers of such former dependants).

3   *Greenwich LBC v Powell* [1989] 21 HLR 218 at 224 per Lord Bridge of Harwich.

4   *Mills v Cooper* [1967] 2 QB 459.

5   This definition appeared in CSA 1968, s 16 and was then moved, save for the purposes of the MHA 1983, to CSCDA 1960, s 24(8) by the Criminal Justice and Public Order Act 1994, s 80. The definition still remains in the 1960 Act.

travelling for whatever reason, ill-health, age or simply because they no longer wish to follow that way of life, they no longer have a 'nomadic habit of life.'[1]

9.28   Plainly from the point of view of a sick or elderly gypsy who cannot travel any more, who has a deep rooted aversion to bricks and mortar, whose immutable characteristic is the identification with the caravan in which he or she used to live and who has never lived in a house in all of his or her life, and where, perhaps, their extended family still travel, their accommodation need will not necessarily have altered. This is so even though the correct[2] (but unhelpful) position is that individually, on the basis of case law, he or she might be considered no longer a gypsy.

9.29   Hence the fact that the Act has reserved to subsequent regulations the meaning of gypsy and traveller is very significant, if some of the gaps left from the current definition and related case law on the meaning of gypsy can be filled. Because of the way that the Act is phrased, the National Assembly for Wales can adopt a different meaning to that which is used in England.

9.30   The regulations might avoid the need for those making the assessment to carry around in their heads the various contingencies and subtleties identified by Auld LJ. There is a basis for moving forward from the focus on nomadism, not least because a number of gypsies and travellers on municipal sites are mostly sedentary because of the lack of lawful stopping places.[3] There is also a chance to move away from the misplaced economic determinism that would only accept a person as a gypsy or traveller if their travels, for example to a horse fair, involved earning some money.[4] The alternative could result in a gypsy's accommodation needs being assessed or sometimes not assessed according to whether or not they had been looking for work when away from their site, rather than, as is so often the case, merely participating in traditional events, their main work being something they do each day by going out from their site, to which they return after work. The meaning of gypsy and traveller to be contained in the regulations also allows an escape from any possibility of pressure to go out on the road, when there is nowhere to stop, simply out of a need to prove nomadism.

---

1   Per Auld LJ in *Wrexham County Borough Council v [1] The National Assembly for Wales [2] Michael Berry & [3] Florence Berry* [2003] EWCA Civ 835. It can be argued that this dictum will be consigned to history once new guidance incorporating a new definition is issued. Such a proposition is weakened by the absence of any amendment by the Act to the statutory definition – for which see the preceding footnote.

2   Correct for the time being. If the *Berry* case is deemed admissible, it will be considered by the European Court. Quite independently of that, the Government is presently considering whether or not to define gypsies and travellers in terms that go beyond the current statutory definition to additionally include members of ethnic groups for whom living in a caravan is part of their traditional way of life, so partly dropping the need to always show nomadic habit of life. See *Hansard*, HL Deb, vol 664, col 1398 (16 September 2004).

3   In *Basildon District Council v First Secretary of State and Cooper* [2004] EWCA Civ 473, a case concerning a private rather than a council run site, it was found that the Coopers 'had only moved to the site when it became too difficult for them to live on the roadside'.

4   In *R v South Hams DC ex parte Gibb* [1995] QB 158 the court identified that there should be a connection between a gypsy's movement and his or her means of livelihood. In the *Wrexham* case [2003] EWCA Civ 835, Auld LJ observed at para 42 that now the definition was unshackled from the previous duty to provide sites (see CSA 1968, s 6) it is possible to reconsider the need to show that any nomadic habit is for the purpose of work.

Policy options

9.31 The Act is significant not only because it opens up for broader definition the meaning of gypsies and travellers and because it makes it a statutory duty for local housing authorities to find out what need there is for sites for gypsies and travellers, but also because it fails to identify the principal method which the Government envisages for meeting that need. The Act vastly improves the situation but does not grasp the nettle represented by the social costs to all involved of unauthorised encampments.

9.32 The Act indicates which of the available three options the Government prefers for responding to the results of a housing needs assessment which identifies a need for further places, including transit sites, for gypsies and travellers to lawfully reside. The first option is through the planning system, which would require land for sites to be identified in policies that enabled applications to be passed.[1] The next option is that the Homelessness Act 2003 provides the vehicle for meeting the need, so that local housing authorities specify action which it expects to be taken to meet the need.[2] The Act makes no amendment to the 2003 Act's use of the phrase 'accommodation', or clarification of that term so that it includes sites on which caravans can be stationed. Another important change that would have to be made to facilitate such an option would be to enable registered social landlords to build sites on which caravans can be stationed. This would mean that gypsies and travellers without a lawful stopping place being evicted from the side of the road could apply under Part 7 of the Housing Act 1996 and be accommodated in something other than bricks and mortar. The third and most likely option indicated by reference to the Local Government Act 2003 is that the national authorities will impose requirements[3] on housing authorities to have a strategy that addresses any unmet need for further gypsy sites. This view is re-enforced by the requirement in the Act that the authority who are the local housing authority must take the strategy into account in exercising their functions, including functions exercisable otherwise than as a local housing authority.[4] How this will done remains to be seen.

Commentary

9.33 In undertaking its periodical review[5] of housing needs in their district, the local authority must not only assess the accommodation needs of gypsies but also have regard to any guidance issued by the national authority regarding the carrying out of the assessment.[6]

---

1   Currently this option now contained in Circular Guidance – in England 1/94, in Wales 2/94 – is subject to reinvigoration – see the ODPM consultation paper *Planning for Gypsy and Traveller Sites* (December 2004). The problem from the point of view of local planning authorities might be that their efforts to adopt the required policies which specify where gypsy caravan sites would broadly be in accordance with policy will be derailed by objectors from the districts affected. This will require a tough stance from the appropriate authorities or else 'nimbyism' might continue to rule.
2   Homelessness Act 2003, s 3(3).
3   Local Government Act 2003, s 87(1)(b).
4   Section 225(3).
5   The duty to review is contained in the Housing Act 1985, s 8.
6   Section 225(1), (4)(a) and s 226(1)(a); national authority is defined in s 261(1).

9.34 Further, in preparing any strategy that they might have been required to have,[1] the local housing authority must have regard to any guidance issued by the national authority.[2]

9.35 The nature of the policy options identified above and the importance of giving the lead to authorities sometimes hedged about by opposition to further sites, is perhaps reflected by the fact that the Act contemplates that no guidance can be given which has not been laid in draft before each House of Parliament[3] and states that the Secretary of State cannot proceed with the guidance as drafted, if either House resolves that it should be withdrawn.[4]

---

1   Under the Local Government Act 2003, s 87.
2   Section 225(4)(b).
3   Section 226(2).
4   Section 226(4).

Chapter 10

TENANCY DEPOSITS

INTRODUCTION

10.1   Chapter 4 of Part 6 of the Act introduces the requirement that any landlord who takes a deposit from a tenant must secure that deposit in an approved tenancy deposit scheme. The requirement is limited to assured shorthold tenancies – the standard form of tenancy in the private rented sector.

10.2   The requirement has two statutory purposes.[1] The first is to ensure that the deposit money is appropriately protected. The second is to facilitate the resolution of disputes that may arise in connection with tenancy deposits.

10.3   However, the introduction of the protection of tenancy deposits also serves the underlying purpose of penalising bad landlord practice in the private rented sector and improving the image of private renting. It shares this purpose with much of the rest of the Act.

10.4   Private landlords frequently take deposits from tenants to protect themselves from financial loss as a result of any damage that may be caused to the property or its contents or the tenant's failure to pay rent. The tenant does not forfeit the entire deposit as a result of breach of contract, only the amount necessary to reimburse the landlord for his loss.

10.5   The law on tenancy deposits is based upon contract and prior to these provisions there has been little statutory regulation.[2] Many landlords have treated deposits as their own money during the course of the tenancy, for instance earning interest on the capital sum and the new requirements represent a significant cultural change which has led to

---

1   See the ODPM Factsheet 14: Tenancy deposit schemes at http://www.odpm.gov.uk/stellent/groups/ odpm–housing/documents/page/odpm–house–033540.hcsp

2   There is indirect statutory regulation of deposits in the Rent Act 1977, s 128 which prohibits demands for the payment of a premium in relation to a Rent Act protected tenancy. An illegal premium is 'any sum paid by way of a deposit, other than one which does not exceed one sixth of the annual rent and is reasonable in relation to the potential liability in respect of which it is paid.' It is this provision which gives rise to the widely held belief that a deposit cannot be more than two months rent. However, since no protected tenancies have been capable of creation since the 15 January 1989 when the HA 1988 came into force, the provision is now only of historic interest.

resentment from landlords who believe they are being penalised for the bad behaviour of a minority.[1]

10.6 Disputes can arise about the return of deposits in a number of circumstances. There may be disagreement about:

- the condition of the property or its contents at the commencement of the tenancy and therefore the extent to which the tenant is responsible for any deterioration;
- the extent to which deterioration is a result of fair wear and tear;
- what are reasonable costs for cleaning and repair and to what standard should work be done.

10.7 Landlords may also simply refuse to return deposits without any attempt at legitimate justification knowing that few tenants are likely to use county court procedures to reclaim their deposit. Even if tenants obtain a judgment in their favour it is still possible for a determined person to avoid enforcement of the judgment.

10.8 Private sector tenants may be vulnerable to the unlawful retention of their deposit at the end of the tenancy for a number of reasons. They tend to be poorer, younger and more mobile than the general population. They may require money to finance the deposit on their next tenancy, they may be moving out of the area to another job and face difficulties pursuing the return of their money from a distance and they may lack confidence in using the legal system to obtain redress.

10.9 Landlords are also affected by the difficulties surrounding deposits. Not only is their professional image tarnished by the bad practice of some landlords, tenants also regularly withhold the last month's rent in lieu of the deposit which means that the whole purpose of the deposit from the landlord's perspective is defeated. Moreover, small landlords are as likely to be affected by the time, expense and stress involved in small claims procedures as tenants.

10.10 The scale of the problem is indicated by figures from the Survey of English Housing 2001–02 which suggested that up to 20% of private tenants in the previous three years considered that part or all of the deposit from their most recent tenancy was unreasonably withheld. The Government tentatively estimate that the amount of money wrongfully withheld from tenants is £16.5 million.[2]

---

1   See, for instance, the journal of the National Federation of Residential Landlords, *Residential Renting*, Issue 22, May 2003, p 7: 'The whole principle of targeting and criminalising the innocents as the means of identifying the tiny minority of rogues is highly questionable, particularly when the problem itself is greatly exaggerated. Allegations that up to 48% of private tenants suffer the wrongful withholding of deposits are quite preposterous. Why introduce a huge, monolithic bureaucracy embroiling the large majority of landlords who treat their tenants fairly, when NFRL has proposed a targeted and non-bureaucratic alternative?'

2   See ODPM Regulatory Impact Assessment: Housing Bill Part 6 – Tenancy Deposit Protection, para 12 at http://www.odpm.gov.uk/stellent/groups/odpm–housing/documents/page/odpm–house–031043.hcsp

BACKGROUND

10.11 The difficulties that private sector tenants face in reclaiming their tenancy deposits was raised by the National Consumer Council and the National Association of Citizens Advice Bureaux[1] (NACAB) in the mid-1990s.

10.12 NACAB proposed an amendment to the Housing Bill in 1996 to introduce a tenancy deposit protection scheme.[2] The then Government, whilst rejecting the amendment, undertook to consult interested parties and research the experience of other jurisdictions.[3]

10.13 NACAB published a report, *Unsafe Deposits: CAB Clients' experience of rental deposits*, in June 1998. This highlighted the extensive unjustified retention of tenancy deposits – their research into the experiences of their clients suggested that 48% of those surveyed had had a deposit unreasonably withheld in the previous five years.

10.14 The Government responded by setting up a pilot voluntary Tenancy Deposit Scheme in March 2000. The scheme, administered by the Independent Housing Ombudsman, was intended to run in five areas, initially for two years, then extended for a further two years.[4] The scheme rapidly extended to the whole of the country as it was artificial to confine its operation to set local authority areas when landlords had national or regional portfolios of properties.

10.15 Sensitive to the traditional hostility between landlords and tenants, the Government attempted to create consensus by setting up a steering group which was representative of landlords, agents and tenants. This group informed the development of the voluntary scheme, in particular its two-pronged approach to the protection of deposits, either by way of a custodial scheme or by way of an insurance scheme.

10.16 Insurance schemes are attractive to landlords as they are only required to hand over the deposit to the scheme in the event of an adjudication or a dispute. From the government's perspective they allow industry bodies to develop professional expertise when establishing schemes, which is likely to lead to greater take-up by landlords and improved professional standards.

10.17 The pilot scheme also responded to the difficulties of court based dispute resolution by providing for the independent arbitration of disputes.

10.18 In the meantime the Government consulted on the scale of the tenancy deposit problem and the question of whether there was a need for compulsory statutory

---

1   Known as *Citizens Advice* since 2003.

2   See *Hansard* (HL) vol 574, col 899 (17 July 1996).

3   Particularly influential is the New South Wales scheme. All bond money paid in New South Wales must be lodged by the landlord with the Rental Bond Board (RBB) within seven days of the tenant paying the deposit. The RBB holds the bond until the tenant moves out and then it decides if the tenant gets it all back or if the landlord has sufficient grounds (eg unpaid rent or damage to the premises) for claiming some or all of the bond. For further information see www.fairtrading.nsw.gov.au/realestaterenting/tenantslandlords/rentalbonds.html

4   Although it only ran for one year of the two year extension.

protection of deposits[1] and commissioned an independent evaluation of the pilot tenancy deposit scheme.[2]

10.19   The Government reported that:

> 'An independent evaluation of the TDS concluded that a national voluntary scheme would have little impact within the PRS, as take up of the pilot had been disappointing, and a voluntary scheme would attract only operators with existing good deposit management systems. The evaluation noted that tenants tended to anticipate difficulties with deposits, particularly as many had previously experienced the non-return of a deposit. Therefore a mandatory scheme, particularly if based on a custodial model, would be popular amongst tenants. By contrast landlords and agents viewed the management of deposits as unproblematic. They feel that a mandatory scheme would impose costs that would eventually be passed on to tenants across the whole sector, would be difficult and costly to enforce and therefore incapable of tackling the most serious abuses.'[3]

10.20   The voluntary scheme was wound up in 2003 when it became apparent that it would not be self-financing because of insufficient take-up by landlords and that the Government was seriously considering legislation.

10.21   The Government decided that legislation on the compulsory protection of tenancy deposits was necessary. Originally the suggested vehicle for this was not the Housing Bill 2004 but the Bill which is to be produced as a result of the Law Commission's work on the reform of tenure.[4] Continued backbench pressure, ably assisted by adroit publicity from Shelter and Citizens Advice resulted in a ministerial statement on 19 May 2004 proposing amendments to the Housing Bill to provide for tenancy deposit protection.

> 'Our intention is to add provisions to the Housing Bill to require that tenancy deposits should be subject to safeguarding arrangements. The Government accept that it will need to sponsor a scheme to provide for the safeguarding of the deposits sought by the majority of landlords. But it also recognises that members of trade or professional bodies should be able to look to those bodies to provide their own schemes if these schemes provide sufficient protection and the Government are able to approve them.'[5]

10.22   The industry had already begun to self-regulate the holding of deposits as part of a general movement towards enhanced self-regulation. The Royal Institute of Chartered Surveyors (RICS) and the Association of Residential Letting Agents (ARLA) each required their members to hold client money in separate accounts. Following the

---

1   See Tenancy money: probity and protection: consultation paper (ODPM, 2002) available on the ODPM website at http://www.odpm.gov.uk/stellent/groups/odpm–housing/documents/page/odpm–house–609032–01.hcsp

2   Rugg and Bevan *An Evaluation of the Pilot Tenancy Deposit Scheme* (ODPM, 2002).

3   See Tenancy money: probity and protection: consultation paper (ODPM, 2002) at http://www.odpm.gov.uk/stellent/groups/odpm–housing/documents/page/odpm–house–609032–01.hcsp

4   The Government continues to see a close link between the Law Commission's work in Renting Homes and the protection of tenancy deposits. In ODPM Factsheet 14: Tenancy deposit schemes, they write 'We continue to see lining the safeguarding of tenancy deposits to standard written agreements as sensible. In February this year we asked the Law Commission to draft indicative clauses on tenancy deposits alongside their draft Bill. We will revisit provision for tenancy deposit protection in the context of these draft clauses and the rest of the Law Commission's draft Bill.' See http://www.odpm.gov.uk/stellent/groups/odpm–housing/documents/page/odpm–house–033540.hcsp

5   *Hansard*, HC, vol 421, col 52WS (19 May 2004).

winding up of the voluntary scheme and in anticipation of legislation in the medium term ARLA has developed its own voluntary insurance-based tenancy deposit scheme for regulated agents (TDSRA) which has the support of RICS and the National Association of Estate Agents (NAEA).[1]

COMMENTARY

Summary of provisions

10.23   Sections 212–215 of and Sch 10 to the Act in essence do two things. First, they impose a duty upon the appropriate national authority to make arrangements for there to be one or more tenancy deposit schemes. Second, they require all landlords who take a deposit from an assured shorthold tenant[2] to deal with that deposit in accordance with the requirements of a tenancy deposit scheme within 14 days of the receipt of that deposit.

10.24   The statutory scheme draws upon the experience of the pilot tenancy deposit scheme but is significantly different because it is compulsory and imposes serious sanctions upon landlords who fail to participate.

10.25   Allowing the provision of two types of tenancy deposit schemes, the custodial scheme and the insurance scheme, provides a useful compromise model for deposit protection. The loss of the advantages of scale and simplicity that one national scheme would have possessed, (particularly beneficial in terms of the level of income generated from interest on deposits held) is balanced against the advantages of allowing professional organisations to bid to run their own schemes. However, the process is not limited to professional landlord organisations, any private organisation can bid to run a scheme. As the regulatory impact assessment points out:

> 'By procuring a number of schemes via a competitive tendering process the Government can thoroughly examine the merits of each proposed scheme against certain set criteria. This should lead to a higher quality of scheme being procured.'[3]

10.26   Moreover, bidding is not limited to insurance schemes. The Government pointed out that:

> 'Whereas, up until now, industry organisations have considered only insurance-based schemes, under these provisions there is now potential for an industry body to set up and manage a custodial scheme. Indeed, there is nothing in the provisions to prevent one organisation managing more than one scheme. However, membership of or access to a tenancy deposit scheme should be entirely separate from membership of any other organisation.'[4]

---

1   For further details of the scheme see 'What is the Tenancy Deposit Scheme' *Successful Renting*, November 2004, p 30.

2   Note that the provisions do not apply to high rent tenancies which fall outside of the Housing Act 1988.

3   Regulatory Impact Assessment, para 63 at http://www.odpm.gov.uk/stellent/groups/odpm–housing/ documents/page/odpm–house–031043–03.hcsp#

4   *Hansard*, HL, vol 665, col 880 (20 October 2004).

Tenancy deposit schemes

10.27   The Secretary of State and the National Assembly for Wales are required to ensure that one or more tenancy deposit schemes are established.[1] The statutorily stated purposes of the schemes are to safeguard tenancy deposits and facilitate dispute resolution in relation to deposits.[2]

10.28   Deposits paid on behalf of tenants, whether by individuals or organisations, as well as all deposits paid by assured shorthold tenants, are protected by the scheme.[3] So parents who pay their student child's deposit are protected, as are local authority deposit schemes.

10.29   A deposit is a sum of money (cash or cheques)[4] paid to a landlord or an agent as security for the performance of any obligations of the tenant or the discharge of any liability of his arising from the tenancy.[5] The Act makes it unlawful to require a deposit of property[6] other than money[7] and there can be no contracting out of the provisions.[8] The provisions suggest that letters of guarantee would fall outside of the scope of the tenancy deposit scheme.

10.30   The scheme or schemes provided must conform with the requirements of Sch 10 to the Act. This provides that a scheme must be either:

- a custodial scheme; or
- an insurance scheme;[9]

and specifies the characteristics of each of these types of scheme. The Act makes it clear that the detailed operation of the scheme(s) will be set out in regulations. The Government minister pointed out:

> 'We estimate that about £700 million-worth of deposits will be safeguarded by these schemes. We intend to specify the detail of how that money should be safeguarded and how the schemes should operate in practice in our contractual arrangements. That will ensure that such monies are kept safely and dealt with in accordance with our requirements.'[10]

---

1   Section 212(1).
2   Section 212(2).
3   Section 213(10).
4   Section 218(8).
5   Section 212(8).
6   The Government explained (*Hansard*, HL, vol 665, col 883 (20 October 2004)) that:
     'assisted deposit schemes, which provide a valuable service offering an opportunity for the
     disadvantaged, such as the homeless or those on low incomes, to enter into private rented housing,
     are not undermined by these provisions. Of course, some such schemes offer a letter of guarantee to
     the landlord of an amount up to the value of the deposit. The organisation promises to pay the
     landlord at the end of the tenancy if the tenant has been found to have caused any damage to or theft
     from the property. We have altered the definition of a deposit so that it consists of "movable
     property" in order that such guarantees fall outside the scope of the provisions and the organisations
     offering them can continue to operate effectively.'
7   Section 213(11).
8   Section 213(2).
9   Schedule 10, para 1.
10   *Hansard*, HL, vol 665, col 880 (20 October 2004).

Custodial schemes[1]

10.31   Custodial schemes work by requiring a landlord who is paid a deposit by a shorthold tenant to pay that deposit into the scheme's designated account within 14 days of receipt. The deposit will be held in the scheme until the termination of the tenancy.

10.32   At that point the landlord and tenant can agree the basis of the refund of the deposit and apply to have it paid in accordance with that agreement. The scheme, if satisfied that there is a genuine agreement between the landlord and tenant, must pay out within 10 days of being notified of the agreement.

10.33   If a dispute about the refund of the deposit goes to court, the scheme is required to pay out the deposit in accordance with the final court decision on the matter within 10 days of notification by the landlord or the tenant. Note, however, that disputes should not go to court. Schemes have to provide for alternative dispute resolution[2] and although these will not be compulsory the delays involved in county court procedures are likely to make alternative dispute resolution attractive to the parties. It could also be argued that the Civil Procedure Rules would result in any application to court which had not used such procedures facing serious cost sanctions. Whilst the Court of Appeal decision in *Halsey v Milton Keynes NHS Trust*[3] indicated that courts cannot compel mediation, it also indicated that courts could penalise unreasonable refusals to mediate.

10.34   The scheme can retain the interest accruing on the deposits held in the designated account which can be used to fund the administration of the scheme.

Insurance schemes[4]

10.35   Insurance schemes allow deposits which are taken by landlords to be retained by those landlords until the termination of the tenancy. At that point the deposit is either repaid to the tenant in full or as much is repaid to the tenant as agreed between the landlord and the tenant.

10.36   If a tenant disagrees with the amount of the deposit which is refunded to him or her then the tenant must notify the scheme that he has requested the repayment of that money and that it has not been repaid to him within 10 days of his request.

10.37   At this point the landlord has to pay the disputed amount of the deposit into the scheme's designated account within 10 days of the request. This removes any perverse incentive on the landlord to hold onto the deposit and profit from any delay. The money will be held until the dispute is resolved either as a result of agreement between the landlord and the tenant, or as a result of a final court decision. The money will then be paid out within 10 days of notification of the agreement or court decision.

10.38   If the landlord fails to pay the disputed amount into the scheme's account when requested then he or she is required to reimburse the scheme for any amount paid out to the tenant. The scheme must be insured against the failure of landlords to comply with these requirements.

---

1   The requirements are set out in Sch 10, paras 3, 4.
2   Schedule 10, para 10.
3   [2004] EWCA (Civ) 576.
4   The requirements are set out in Sch 10, paras 5–7.

10.39   The scheme can charge fees for membership and require contributions to cover the cost to the insurance. It can also terminate the membership of landlords who fail to comply with its requirements. The scheme is required to provide alternative dispute procedures.[1]

Information requirements

10.40   Clearly the scheme will only be effective in protecting tenants' money if they are aware of it and its implications.

10.41   Landlords are therefore required to give tenants information about the scheme that they are using to protect the deposit and the statutory provisions relating to tenancy deposits within 14 days of receipt of the deposit.[2]

10.42   Both insurance and custodial schemes are required to inform tenants whether or not a deposit is being held in accordance with the scheme.[3]

Non-compliance

10.43   If a landlord who has been paid a deposit fails to pay it into a scheme within 14 days or fails to provide the required information, the tenant or anyone else who has paid the deposit can apply to the county court for an order either that the deposit is repaid to the applicant or that it is paid into the custodial scheme within 14 days.[4]

10.44   The court must also order the landlord to pay the tenant compensation of three times the amount of the deposit within 14 days of its decision.[5] This provision is designed to concentrate the mind of the landlord, or as the Government put it: 'We believe that this provides a greater certainty for landlords that they will face a financial penalty if they do not comply with the provisions.'[6]

10.45   Equally important for the landlord is that he or she will be unable to serve a s 21 notice[7] upon the tenant to terminate the assured shorthold tenancy whilst he or she is failing to comply with the requirements of the provisions. The loss of the s 21 notice which allows the landlord to regain possession after a two-month notice period without having to prove a ground for eviction in court, is a serious commercial loss to a private landlord.[8]

Dispute resolution

10.46   Both insurance and custodial schemes are required to provide alternative dispute resolution procedures to resolve disputes about deposits between landlords and tenants, although they cannot make the use of such procedures compulsory.[9] The provisions do

---

1   Schedule 10, para 10.
2   Section 213(5).
3   Schedule 10, para 9.
4   Section 214.
5   Section 214(4).
6   *Hansard*, HL, vol 665, col 884 (20 October 2004).
7   This refers to HA 1988, s 21, the notice only ground available to landlords to terminate assured shorthold tenancies.
8   Section 215.
9   Schedule 10, para 10.

not remove tenants' common law remedies for unlawful withholding of deposits. Tenants' representatives are concerned that landlords will refuse to use alternative dispute resolution and insist on much slower court procedures. This may place tenants at a disadvantage since they may require the money as deposit on their next rented property. They may therefore accept a smaller sum from the landlord in order to access some money quickly.

CONCLUSION

10.47   The introduction of statutory protection of tenancy deposits is a major step forward for tenants. It should also be viewed positively by responsible landlords and their professional organisations, as it allows them to participate fully in the rehabilitation of the reputation of the private rented sector. However, there are some drawbacks. An unscrupulous landlord may still be able to avoid repayment of the whole of the deposit simply by offering a percentage and saying that if the tenant fails to accept what is on offer their alternative is a time-consuming fight in the small claims court. Moreover, as a Liberal Democrat peer pointed out:

> 'The problem is that some landlords will fail to pay the deposit into the scheme as is required
> of them and as the Bill is currently drafted the only sanction the tenant has is to go to court
> about it. That is the same problem tenants have today when they are aggrieved about their
> deposit not being returned to them. Without some support for the tenant in this, I fear that
> despite the excellent intentions of this important addition to the Bill, the whole tenancy
> deposit scheme begins to look less likely to work on the ground.'[1]

This problem may not be so acute in insurance schemes since the scheme will repay the tenant the deposit and pursue the landlord for the money.

10.48   It also relies on tenants to police the system since 'tenants will need to take some responsibility themselves to ensure that they only use landlords or agents who participate in a scheme'.[2] This may be difficult in areas where rental accommodation is at a premium. On the other hand the provisions do not allow tenants the option of paying the deposit money direct into the scheme and thereby being sure that their money is safeguarded. Finally the schemes are potentially bureaucratic and perhaps not sensitive enough to the high mobility of many tenants in the private rented sector. It might have been useful to allow tenants to authorise the transfer of deposit money from tenancy to tenancy as the tenant moves, avoiding burdens on landlords and the scheme.

10.49   In addition, the scheme does not deal with problem of unreasonable administrative charges, for instance excessive charges for credit checks prior to commencement of a tenancy or charges made for the renewal of a tenancy when the only work involved is photocopying the existing tenancy. The Government's response was to suggest that this was a particularly complex problem. It recognises that many administrative charges are reasonable. Moreover:

---

1   *Hansard*, HL, vol 665, col 875 (20 October 2004).
2   See ODPM Factsheet 14: Tenancy deposit schemes, p 6 at http://www.odpm.gov.uk/stellent/groups/
     odpm–housing/documents/page/odpm–house–033540.hcsp

'The ability to curb such fees goes beyond the scope of these provisions, which are concerned only with the protection of tenancy deposits. We hope that tenants' awareness of the new deposit protection provisions would lead them not to deal with agents or landlords who took an extortionate non-refundable fee instead of a deposit. Preventing landlords from charging unjustified additional fees would not be possible by way of a simple amendment to these provisions. Careful thought would be required on what would amount to 'unjustified'. If we were to legislate for the prevention of taking other fees, one undesirable effect would be that landlords who still wish to avoid safeguarding a deposit would simply add the value on to the rent they charge.'[1]

10.50 Nonetheless the introduction of the scheme is a considerable achievement of which the Government is proud.

'We have put something in place in legislation which will not only stand the test of time but, more importantly, will match the very understandable concerns over tenancy deposits which have been expressed by tenants – and to a degree by landlords – over a considerable period of time.'[2]

1   *Hansard*, HL, vol 665, col 881 (20 October 2004).
2   *Hansard*, HL, vol 665, col 883 (20 October 2004).

Chapter 11

MISCELLANEOUS PROVISIONS

INTRODUCTION

11.1   This chapter describes the remaining provisions contained in Part 7 of the Housing Act 2004. The most significant provisions concern the extension of the jurisdiction of the Residential Property Tribunal (RPT) which becomes the normal venue for the resolution of disputes arising as a result of the Act. There are also provisions which provide for the sharing of information and provisions which set out the necessary powers of entry for the purposes of Parts 1–4 of the Act.

RESIDENTIAL PROPERTY TRIBUNALS

11.2   Section 229 provides that the jurisdiction under this Act or any other enactment given to a RPT is to be exercised by a Rent Assessment Committee constituted under the Rent Act 1977 and when exercising that jurisdiction, a committee is a RPT.[1] The section also provides that the appropriate national authority can, by order approved by both Houses of Parliament, confer additional jurisdiction on the RPT and modify the Act or any other enactment accordingly.

Powers and procedure of RPTs

11.3   Section 230 confers powers on the RPT to give directions in order to dispose of appeals and applications effectively so as to avoid the necessity for repeated appeals or applications in relation to the same matter. The section also gives effect to Sch 13, which provides for regulations to govern tribunal procedures.

Appeals from RPTs

11.4   Section 231 provides that an appeal against a decision of the RPT is to the Lands Tribunal. An appeal can only be made with the permission of the RPT or the Lands Tribunal and only within the time specified in the Lands Tribunal rules.

---

1   These reforms were introduced after the conclusion of the debates in the Commons. These provisions were not presented for consultation or publication in HC Bill 11 (8 December 2003) but were introduced as clause 190 et seq of HC Bill 59 (1 March 2004) following amendment in Commons Committee E. The Lords debated the amendments in HL Bill 71 (13 May 2004).

INFORMATION SHARING

11.5   Section 235 allows a local housing authority to require the production of documentation that the authority might need to carry out its functions under Parts 1 to 4 of the Act and to investigate whether an offence has been committed under those Parts in relation to any premises.

11.6   A notice requiring the production of documentation must specify or describe the documents, or class of documents, which must be produced and must specify a time and place at which they must be produced. The notice must explain the consequences of not complying with the notice. Once a document has been produced it may be copied by the person who receives it.

11.7   A document is defined as including information which is not in legible form. This might include, for example, documents held on computer in a zipped file.[1] Only a 'relevant person' can be required to produce documentation under this section.[2]

11.8   Section 236 provides enforcement powers relating to s 235. Anyone failing to comply with a notice to produce a document commits an offence and is liable to a fine not exceeding level 5 (currently £5,000). Anyone deliberately altering or destroying a requested document can be subject to an unlimited fine if tried in the Crown Court. The defence of reasonable excuse for failing to comply with the notice is available.[3]

11.9   Section 237 allows a local housing authority to use information that it has obtained for housing benefit or council tax purposes in order to carry out its functions under Parts 1 to 4 of this Act. This information may also help the local housing authority to decide the actual number of occupants of a dwelling, in relation to hazards under Part 1, particularly those that could be exacerbated by over-occupation, eg fire.

11.10   Section 238 makes it an offence to knowingly or recklessly supply false or misleading information under Parts 1 to 4 or Part 7 of the Act, or to another person who will then use that information under Parts 1 to 4 or Part 7 of the Act.

POWERS OF ENTRY

11.11   Section 239 gives a local housing authority powers of access to properties in pursuance of its duties under Parts 1 to 4 and Part 7 of the Act.

11.12   The power of entry is exercisable where an inspection is to take place under s 4, or the premises to be inspected are the subject of an improvement notice or prohibition order, or a management order under Part 4 of the Act is in force.

11.13   The person exercising the power of entry must be authorised in writing and this authorisation should set out the purpose for which the entry is authorised. Before exercising the power of entry the person authorised to enter must give at least 24 hours' notice to the owner or occupier of the premises that they intend to enter. However, the

---

1   Section 235(6).
2   Section 235(7).
3   Section 236(2).

power of entry may be exercised at any reasonable time, without giving prior notice if entry is required to ascertain whether an offence has been committed under s 72, s 95 or s 233(3) of the Act.

11.14 Permission under s 239 does not include a power to use force to obtain entry. This power of entry includes entry for the purpose of taking samples. This power could be used:

- to gain access to a property to ensure that a HMO is suitable for multiple occupation and reaches the prescribed standards set out in Part 2; or
- when the local housing authority wished to establish whether the provisions of an improvement notice or prohibition order have been properly complied with.

Warrant to authorise entry

11.15 Section 240 enables a magistrate to issue a warrant authorising entry to premises for the purposes of an inspection under s 4, or an inspection to determine whether any functions under Parts 1 to 4 of Part 7 should be exercised, or surveying or examining premises which are the subject of an improvement notice, a prohibition order or a management order under Part 4.

11.16 A warrant should specify the purposes for which the entry is allowed. A warrant to authorise entry may only be granted when either entry under s 239 has been refused, or the property is empty and immediate access is necessary, or prior warning of entry is likely to negate the purpose of access. A power of entry under a warrant may include the power to enter by force if necessary.

Penalty for obstruction

11.17 Section 241 makes it a criminal offence to obstruct a representative of a local housing authority in carrying out the local housing authority's functions under Parts 1 to 4 and ss 239 and 240. The maximum penalty on summary conviction is a fine not exceeding level (currently £2,500).

Additional notice requirements

11.18 Section 242 allows the owner of a property to require notice from the local housing authority of any relevant action taken under Parts 1 to 4 relating to their property. This provision is intended to ensure that any owner who is not actually managing or controlling his property is kept informed.

Authorisation for other purposes

11.19 Section 243 requires that a person exercising the powers set out in subsection (1), including the power to require the production of documents under s 235 and the power of entry under s 239, must be authorised by the appropriate officer of the local housing authority.

11.20 Section 243(3) defines the appropriate officer as a person who is a deputy chief officer within the meaning of s 2 of the Local Government and Housing Act 1989 and whose duties consist of or include duties relating to the exercise of the relevant functions, or is an officer to whom such a person reports or is accountable.

Forms of notice

11.21   Section 244 allows the appropriate national authority to prescribe the form of any notice, statement or document required under the Act.

Power to dispense with notices

11.22   Section 245 provides that the appropriate national authority may allow a local housing authority to dispense with the service of a notice if it is reasonable to do so. Before giving a dispensation, the appropriate national authority must have regard to the need to ensure as far as possible that the interests of any person are not prejudiced by the dispensation.

OTHER MISCELLANEOUS PROVISIONS

11.23   Sections 246–248 make provision for the service of documents, including the service of documents in electronic form.

11.24   Section 249 makes provision regarding proof of designations made by a local housing authority under Part 2 or 3 stating that a certified copy of the scheme is prima facie evidence that the scheme has been made.

Orders and regulations

11.25   Section 250 makes provision in relation to orders and regulations made under the Act. Any power of the Secretary of State or the National Assembly for Wales to make orders or regulations under the Act is exercisable by statutory instrument. The Secretary of State must consult the National Assembly for Wales before making any regulations under Part 5 which relate to residential properties in Wales.

11.26   The section provides for different procedures to apply in different cases. Detailed and technical orders and regulations will be subject to the negative resolution procedure. Orders and regulations listed in s 250(5) are subject to the affirmative resolution procedure in Parliament.

Offences by corporate bodies

11.27   Section 251 provides for offences by a body corporate. It provides that a representative of an organisation, namely a director, manager, secretary or other similar officer of the body corporate, is capable of being liable as well as the organisation itself.

Power to up-rate level of fines for certain offences

11.28   Section 252 empowers the Secretary of State to change the fines for certain offences in line with inflation.

Local inquiries

11.29 Section 253 empowers the appropriate national authority to require a local inquiry to be held in connection with the carrying out of its functions under the Act, if it considers that it is appropriate to do so.

Legal presumptions

11.30 Section 260 provides that in any legal proceedings it is presumed in respect of a building that the sole use condition or the significant use condition is met, unless there is evidence to the contrary.

Interpretation of terms

11.31 Section 261 provides the meaning of appropriate national authority. In relation to England, the expression means the Secretary of State. In relation to Wales, it means the National Assembly for Wales. The section also defines the expression local housing authority.

11.32 Section 262 provides the meaning, for the purpose of the Act, of 'lease', 'tenancy', 'occupier' and 'owner', and derivations of those terms. In particular s 262(4) provides that the definition of 'lessee' includes a statutory tenant. The expressions include lettings granted by the local housing authority, but the definition of 'occupier' does not apply where any different definition is provided elsewhere in the Act for specific purposes.

11.33 Section 263 defines for the purpose of the Act that the 'person having control' is the person who receives (directly or as an agency or trustee) the market rents from the tenants for a given premises or is otherwise entitled to receive the rents if the premises were let (namely an owner).

11.34 'Person managing' is someone who receives the rents directly from the occupier (but 'rent' includes ground rent). Such a person could be a managing agent.

11.35 Section 264 provides that that the appropriate national authority can prescribe rules with respect to the calculation of numbers of persons for the purposes of any provision of the Act, any provision made under the Act or any order or licence made or granted under the Act.

Minor and consequential amendments

11.36 Section 265 gives effect to Sch 15 to the Act which contains minor and consequential amendments.

11.37 Section 265(2) empowers the Secretary of State to make supplementary, incidental and consequential provisions by order for the purposes of the Act.

11.38 Section 265(3) allows such an order to modify any Act or subordinate legislation for those purposes.

11.39 Any order made under s 265(3) is subject to the affirmative resolution procedure in Parliament. The power in s 265(2) is also exercisable by the National Assembly for Wales in relation to provisions dealing with matters with respect to which the functions are exercisable by the Assembly.

REPEALS

11.40   Section 266 gives effect to Sch 16 to the Act which contains repeals.

DEVOLUTION

11.41   Functions of the Secretary of State under the Housing Acts of 1985, 1988 and 1996 are exercisable, as respects Wales, by the National Assembly for Wales, pursuant to the National Assembly for Wales (Transfer of Functions) Order 1999.[1] This section provides that the reference in that Order to those acts is to be treated as a reference to those acts as amended by the Act.

11.42   The Act applies to the Isles of Scilly, but s 268 allows the Secretary of State to make modifications as to how the Act applies, by order.

COMMENCEMENT AND EXTENT

11.43   Section 270 provides that in general the Act extends to England and Wales and makes provision for commencement. Section 270(9) enables the Secretary of State, by order, to make transitional provisions in connection with the coming into force of any provision of this Act. Section 270(10) enables the National Assembly for Wales to make such provision for matters with respect to which functions are exercisable by the Assembly.

---

1   SI 1999/672.

Appendix 1

HOUSING ACT 2004
2004 CHAPTER 34

An Act to make provision about housing conditions; to regulate houses in multiple occupation and certain other residential accommodation; to make provision for home information packs in connection with the sale of residential properties; to make provision about secure tenants and the right to buy; to make provision about mobile homes and the accommodation needs of gypsies and travellers; to make other provision about housing; and for connected purposes.

[18th November 2004]

BE IT ENACTED by the Queen's most Excellent Majesty, by and with the advice and consent of the Lords Spiritual and Temporal, and Commons, in this present Parliament assembled, and by the authority of the same, as follows: –

Part 1
Housing Conditions

Chapter 1
Enforcement of Housing Standards: General

New system for assessing housing conditions

1 New system for assessing housing conditions and enforcing housing standards

(1) This Part provides –

    (a) for a new system of assessing the condition of residential premises, and

    (b) for that system to be used in the enforcement of housing standards in relation to such premises.

(2) The new system –

    (a) operates by reference to the existence of category 1 or category 2 hazards on residential premises (see section 2), and

    (b) replaces the existing system based on the test of fitness for human habitation contained in section 604 of the Housing Act 1985 (c 68).

(3) The kinds of enforcement action which are to involve the use of the new system are –

    (a) the new kinds of enforcement action contained in Chapter 2 (improvement notices, prohibition orders and hazard awareness notices),

    (b) the new emergency measures contained in Chapter 3 (emergency remedial action and emergency prohibition orders), and

    (c) the existing kinds of enforcement action dealt with in Chapter 4 (demolition orders and slum clearance declarations).

(4) In this Part 'residential premises' means –

    (a) a dwelling;
    (b) an HMO;
    (c) unoccupied HMO accommodation;
    (d) any common parts of a building containing one or more flats.

(5) In this Part –

'building containing one or more flats' does not include an HMO;

'common parts', in relation to a building containing one or more flats, includes –

    (a) the structure and exterior of the building, and
    (b) common facilities provided (whether or not in the building) for persons who include the occupiers of one or more of the flats;

'dwelling' means a building or part of a building occupied or intended to be occupied as a separate dwelling;

'external common parts', in relation to a building containing one or more flats, means common parts of the building which are outside it;

'flat' means a separate set of premises (whether or not on the same floor) –

    (a) which forms part of a building,
    (b) which is constructed or adapted for use for the purposes of a dwelling, and
    (c) either the whole or a material part of which lies above or below some other part of the building;

'HMO' means a house in multiple occupation as defined by sections 254 to 259, as they have effect for the purposes of this Part (that is, without the exclusions contained in Schedule 14);

'unoccupied HMO accommodation' means a building or part of a building constructed or adapted for use as a house in multiple occupation but for the time being either unoccupied or only occupied by persons who form a single household.

(6) In this Part any reference to a dwelling, an HMO or a building containing one or more flats includes (where the context permits) any yard, garden, outhouses and appurtenances belonging to, or usually enjoyed with, the dwelling, HMO or building (or any part of it).

(7) The following indicates how this Part applies to flats –

    (a) references to a dwelling or an HMO include a dwelling or HMO which is a flat (as defined by subsection (5)); and
    (b) subsection (6) applies in relation to such a dwelling or HMO as it applies in relation to other dwellings or HMOs (but it is not to be taken as referring to any common parts of the building containing the flat).

(8) This Part applies to unoccupied HMO accommodation as it applies to an HMO, and references to an HMO in subsections (6) and (7) and in the following provisions of this Part are to be read accordingly.

2 Meaning of 'category 1 hazard' and 'category 2 hazard'

(1) In this Act –

'category 1 hazard' means a hazard of a prescribed description which falls within a prescribed band as a result of achieving, under a prescribed method for calculating the seriousness of hazards of that description, a numerical score of or above a prescribed amount;

'category 2 hazard' means a hazard of a prescribed description which falls within a prescribed band as a result of achieving, under a prescribed method for calculating the seriousness of hazards of that description, a numerical score below the minimum amount prescribed for a category 1 hazard of that description; and

'hazard' means any risk of harm to the health or safety of an actual or potential occupier of a dwelling or HMO which arises from a deficiency in the dwelling or HMO or in any building or land in the vicinity (whether the deficiency arises as a result of the construction of any building, an absence of maintenance or repair, or otherwise).

(2) In subsection (1) –

'prescribed' means prescribed by regulations made by the appropriate national authority (see section 261(1)); and

'prescribed band' means a band so prescribed for a category 1 hazard or a category 2 hazard, as the case may be.

(3) Regulations under this section may, in particular, prescribe a method for calculating the seriousness of hazards which takes into account both the likelihood of the harm occurring and the severity of the harm if it were to occur.

(4) In this section –

'building' includes part of a building;

'harm' includes temporary harm.

(5) In this Act 'health' includes mental health.

Procedure for assessing housing conditions

3 Local housing authorities to review housing conditions in their districts

(1) A local housing authority must keep the housing conditions in their area under review with a view to identifying any action that may need to be taken by them under any of the provisions mentioned in subsection (2).

(2) The provisions are –

(a) the following provisions of this Act –
   (i) this Part,
   (ii) Part 2 (licensing of HMOs),
   (iii) Part 3 (selective licensing of other houses), and
   (iv) Chapters 1 and 2 of Part 4 (management orders);
(b) Part 9 of the Housing Act 1985 (c 68) (demolition orders and slum clearance);
(c) Part 7 of the Local Government and Housing Act 1989 (c 42) (renewal areas); and
(d) article 3 of the Regulatory Reform (Housing Assistance) (England and Wales) Order 2002 (SI 2002/1860).

(3) For the purpose of carrying out their duty under subsection (1) a local housing authority and their officers must –

(a) comply with any directions that may be given by the appropriate national authority, and
(b) keep such records, and supply the appropriate national authority with such information, as that authority may specify.

4 Inspections by local housing authorities to see whether category 1 or 2 hazards exist

(1) If a local housing authority consider –

(a) as a result of any matters of which they have become aware in carrying out their duty under section 3, or
(b) for any other reason,

that it would be appropriate for any residential premises in their district to be inspected with a view to determining whether any category 1 or 2 hazard exists on those premises, the authority must arrange for such an inspection to be carried out.

(2) If an official complaint about the condition of any residential premises in the district of a local housing authority is made to the proper officer of the authority, and the circumstances complained of indicate –

(a) that any category 1 or category 2 hazard may exist on those premises, or
(b) that an area in the district should be dealt with as a clearance area,

the proper officer must inspect the premises or area.

(3) In this section 'an official complaint' means a complaint in writing made by –

(a) a justice of the peace having jurisdiction in any part of the district, or
(b) the parish or community council for a parish or community within the district.

(4) An inspection of any premises under subsection (1) or (2) –

(a) is to be carried out in accordance with regulations made by the appropriate national authority; and
(b) is to extend to so much of the premises as the local housing authority or proper officer (as the case may be) consider appropriate in the circumstances having regard to any applicable provisions of the regulations.

(5) Regulations under subsection (4) may in particular make provision about –

(a) the manner in which, and the extent to which, premises are to be inspected under subsection (1) or (2), and
(b) the manner in which the assessment of hazards is to be carried out.

(6) Where an inspection under subsection (2) has been carried out and the proper officer of a local housing authority is of the opinion –

(a) that a category 1 or 2 hazard exists on any residential premises in the authority's district, or
(b) that an area in their district should be dealt with as a clearance area,

the officer must, without delay, make a report in writing to the authority which sets out his opinion together with the facts of the case.

(7) The authority must consider any report made to them under subsection (6) as soon as possible.

Enforcement of housing standards

5 Category 1 hazards: general duty to take enforcement action

(1) If a local housing authority consider that a category 1 hazard exists on any residential premises, they must take the appropriate enforcement action in relation to the hazard.

(2) In subsection (1) 'the appropriate enforcement action' means whichever of the following courses of action is indicated by subsection (3) or (4) –

    (a) serving an improvement notice under section 11;
    (b) making a prohibition order under section 20;
    (c) serving a hazard awareness notice under section 28;
    (d) taking emergency remedial action under section 40;
    (e) making an emergency prohibition order under section 43;
    (f) making a demolition order under subsection (1) or (2) of section 265 of the Housing Act 1985 (c 68);
    (g) declaring the area in which the premises concerned are situated to be a clearance area by virtue of section 289(2) of that Act.

(3) If only one course of action within subsection (2) is available to the authority in relation to the hazard, they must take that course of action.

(4) If two or more courses of action within subsection (2) are available to the authority in relation to the hazard, they must take the course of action which they consider to be the most appropriate of those available to them.

(5) The taking by the authority of a course of action within subsection (2) does not prevent subsection (1) from requiring them to take in relation to the same hazard –

    (a) either the same course of action again or another such course of action, if they consider that the action taken by them so far has not proved satisfactory, or
    (b) another such course of action, where the first course of action is that mentioned in subsection (2)(g) and their eventual decision under section 289(2F) of the Housing Act 1985 means that the premises concerned are not to be included in a clearance area.

(6) To determine whether a course of action mentioned in any of paragraphs (a) to (g) of subsection (2) is 'available' to the authority in relation to the hazard, see the provision mentioned in that paragraph.

(7) Section 6 applies for the purposes of this section.

6 Category 1 hazards: how duty under section 5 operates in certain cases

(1) This section explains the effect of provisions contained in subsection (2) of section 5.

(2) In the case of paragraph (b) or (f) of that subsection, the reference to making an order such as is mentioned in that paragraph is to be read as a reference to making instead a determination under section 300(1) or (2) of the Housing Act 1985 (c 68) (power to purchase for temporary housing use) in a case where the authority consider the latter course of action to be the better alternative in the circumstances.

(3) In the case of paragraph (d) of that subsection, the authority may regard the taking of emergency remedial action under section 40 followed by the service of an improvement notice under section 11 as a single course of action.

(4) In the case of paragraph (e) of that subsection, the authority may regard the making of an emergency prohibition order under section 43 followed by the service of a prohibition order under section 20 as a single course of action.

(5) In the case of paragraph (g) of that subsection –

    (a) any duty to take the course of action mentioned in that paragraph is subject to the operation of subsections (2B) to (4) and (5B) of section 289 of the Housing Act 1985 (procedural and other restrictions relating to slum clearance declarations); and

    (b) that paragraph does not apply in a case where the authority have already declared the area in which the premises concerned are situated to be a clearance area in accordance with section 289, but the premises have been excluded by virtue of section 289(2F)(b).

7 Category 2 hazards: powers to take enforcement action

(1) The provisions mentioned in subsection (2) confer power on a local housing authority to take particular kinds of enforcement action in cases where they consider that a category 2 hazard exists on residential premises.

(2) The provisions are –

    (a) section 12 (power to serve an improvement notice),
    (b) section 21 (power to make a prohibition order),
    (c) section 29 (power to serve a hazard awareness notice),
    (d) section 265(3) and (4) of the Housing Act 1985 (power to make a demolition order), and
    (e) section 289(2ZB) of that Act (power to make a slum clearance declaration).

(3) The taking by the authority of one of those kinds of enforcement action in relation to a particular category 2 hazard does not prevent them from taking either –

    (a) the same kind of action again, or
    (b) a different kind of enforcement action,

in relation to the hazard, where they consider that the action taken by them so far has not proved satisfactory.

8 Reasons for decision to take enforcement action

(1) This section applies where a local housing authority decide to take one of the kinds of enforcement action mentioned in section 5(2) or 7(2) ('the relevant action').

(2) The authority must prepare a statement of the reasons for their decision to take the relevant action.

(3) Those reasons must include the reasons why the authority decided to take the relevant action rather than any other kind (or kinds) of enforcement action available to them under the provisions mentioned in section 5(2) or 7(2).

(4) A copy of the statement prepared under subsection (2) must accompany every notice, copy of a notice, or copy of an order which is served in accordance with –

    (a) Part 1 of Schedule 1 to this Act (service of improvement notices etc),
    (b) Part 1 of Schedule 2 to this Act (service of copies of prohibition orders etc), or
    (c) section 268 of the Housing Act 1985 (service of copies of demolition orders),

in or in connection with the taking of the relevant action.

(5) In subsection (4) –

(a) the reference to Part 1 of Schedule 1 to this Act includes a reference to that Part as applied by section 28(7) or 29(7) (hazard awareness notices) or to section 40(7) (emergency remedial action); and

(b) the reference to Part 1 of Schedule 2 to this Act includes a reference to that Part as applied by section 43(4) (emergency prohibition orders).

(6) If the relevant action consists of declaring an area to be a clearance area, the statement prepared under subsection (2) must be published –

(a) as soon as possible after the relevant resolution is passed under section 289 of the Housing Act 1985, and

(b) in such manner as the authority consider appropriate.

9 Guidance about inspections and enforcement action

(1) The appropriate national authority may give guidance to local housing authorities about exercising –

(a) their functions under this Chapter in relation to the inspection of premises and the assessment of hazards,

(b) their functions under Chapter 2 of this Part in relation to improvement notices, prohibition orders or hazard awareness notices,

(c) their functions under Chapter 3 in relation to emergency remedial action and emergency prohibition orders, or

(d) their functions under Part 9 of the Housing Act 1985 (c 68) in relation to demolition orders and slum clearance.

(2) A local housing authority must have regard to any guidance for the time being given under this section.

(3) The appropriate national authority may give different guidance for different cases or descriptions of case or different purposes (including different guidance to different descriptions of local housing authority or to local housing authorities in different areas).

(4) Before giving guidance under this section, or revising guidance already given, the Secretary of State must lay a draft of the proposed guidance or alterations before each House of Parliament.

(5) The Secretary of State must not give or revise the guidance before the end of the period of 40 days beginning with the day on which the draft is laid before each House of Parliament (or, if copies are laid before each House of Parliament on different days, the later of those days).

(6) The Secretary of State must not proceed with the proposed guidance or alterations if, within the period of 40 days mentioned in subsection (5), either House resolves that the guidance or alterations be withdrawn.

(7) Subsection (6) is without prejudice to the possibility of laying a further draft of the guidance or alterations before each House of Parliament.

(8) In calculating the period of 40 days mentioned in subsection (5), no account is to be taken of any time during which Parliament is dissolved or prorogued or during which both Houses are adjourned for more than four days.

10 Consultation with fire and rescue authorities in certain cases

(1) This section applies where a local housing authority –

(a) are satisfied that a prescribed fire hazard exists in an HMO or in any common parts of a building containing one or more flats, and

(b) intend to take in relation to the hazard one of the kinds of enforcement action mentioned in section 5(2) or section 7(2).

(2) Before taking the enforcement action in question, the authority must consult the fire and rescue authority for the area in which the HMO or building is situated.

(3) In the case of any proposed emergency measures, the authority's duty under subsection (2) is a duty to consult that fire and rescue authority so far as it is practicable to do so before taking those measures.

(4) In this section –

'emergency measures' means emergency remedial action under section 40 or an emergency prohibition order under section 43;

'fire and rescue authority' means a fire and rescue authority under the Fire and Rescue Services Act 2004 (c 21);

'prescribed fire hazard' means a category 1 or 2 hazard which is prescribed as a fire hazard for the purposes of this section by regulations under section 2.

Chapter 2
Improvement Notices, Prohibition Orders and Hazard Awareness Notices

Improvement notices

11 Improvement notices relating to category 1 hazards: duty of authority to serve notice

(1) If –

(a) the local housing authority are satisfied that a category 1 hazard exists on any residential premises, and
(b) no management order is in force in relation to the premises under Chapter 1 or 2 of Part 4,

serving an improvement notice under this section in respect of the hazard is a course of action available to the authority in relation to the hazard for the purposes of section 5 (category 1 hazards: general duty to take enforcement action).

(2) An improvement notice under this section is a notice requiring the person on whom it is served to take such remedial action in respect of the hazard concerned as is specified in the notice in accordance with subsections (3) to (5) and section 13.

(3) The notice may require remedial action to be taken in relation to the following premises –

(a) if the residential premises on which the hazard exists are a dwelling or HMO which is not a flat, it may require such action to be taken in relation to the dwelling or HMO;
(b) if those premises are one or more flats, it may require such action to be taken in relation to the building containing the flat or flats (or any part of the building) or any external common parts;
(c) if those premises are the common parts of a building containing one or more flats, it may require such action to be taken in relation to the building (or any part of the building) or any external common parts.

Paragraphs (b) and (c) are subject to subsection (4).

(4) The notice may not, by virtue of subsection (3)(b) or (c), require any remedial action to be taken in relation to any part of the building or its external common parts that is not included in any residential premises on which the hazard exists, unless the authority are satisfied –

    (a) that the deficiency from which the hazard arises is situated there, and

    (b) that it is necessary for the action to be so taken in order to protect the health or safety of any actual or potential occupiers of one or more of the flats.

(5) The remedial action required to be taken by the notice –

    (a) must, as a minimum, be such as to ensure that the hazard ceases to be a category 1 hazard; but

    (b) may extend beyond such action.

(6) An improvement notice under this section may relate to more than one category 1 hazard on the same premises or in the same building containing one or more flats.

(7) The operation of an improvement notice under this section may be suspended in accordance with section 14.

(8) In this Part 'remedial action', in relation to a hazard, means action (whether in the form of carrying out works or otherwise) which, in the opinion of the local housing authority, will remove or reduce the hazard.

12 Improvement notices relating to category 2 hazards: power of authority to serve notice

(1) If –

    (a) the local housing authority are satisfied that a category 2 hazard exists on any residential premises, and

    (b) no management order is in force in relation to the premises under Chapter 1 or 2 of Part 4,

the authority may serve an improvement notice under this section in respect of the hazard.

(2) An improvement notice under this section is a notice requiring the person on whom it is served to take such remedial action in respect of the hazard concerned as is specified in the notice in accordance with subsection (3) and section 13.

(3) Subsections (3) and (4) of section 11 apply to an improvement notice under this section as they apply to one under that section.

(4) An improvement notice under this section may relate to more than one category 2 hazard on the same premises or in the same building containing one or more flats.

(5) An improvement notice under this section may be combined in one document with a notice under section 11 where they require remedial action to be taken in relation to the same premises.

(6) The operation of an improvement notice under this section may be suspended in accordance with section 14.

13 Contents of improvement notices

(1) An improvement notice under section 11 or 12 must comply with the following provisions of this section.

(2) The notice must specify, in relation to the hazard (or each of the hazards) to which it relates –

    (a) whether the notice is served under section 11 or 12,

(b) the nature of the hazard and the residential premises on which it exists,

(c) the deficiency giving rise to the hazard,

(d) the premises in relation to which remedial action is to be taken in respect of the hazard and the nature of that remedial action,

(e) the date when the remedial action is to be started (see subsection (3)), and

(f) the period within which the remedial action is to be completed or the periods within which each part of it is to be completed.

(3) The notice may not require any remedial action to be started earlier than the 28th day after that on which the notice is served.

(4) The notice must contain information about –

(a) the right of appeal against the decision under Part 3 of Schedule 1, and

(b) the period within which an appeal may be made.

(5) In this Part of this Act 'specified premises', in relation to an improvement notice, means premises specified in the notice, in accordance with subsection (2)(d), as premises in relation to which remedial action is to be taken in respect of the hazard.

14 Suspension of improvement notices

(1) An improvement notice may provide for the operation of the notice to be suspended until a time, or the occurrence of an event, specified in the notice.

(2) The time so specified may, in particular, be the time when a person of a particular description begins, or ceases, to occupy any premises.

(3) The event so specified may, in particular, be a notified breach of an undertaking accepted by the local housing authority for the purposes of this section from the person on whom the notice is served.

(4) In subsection (3) a 'notified breach', in relation to such an undertaking, means an act or omission by the person on whom the notice is served –

(a) which the local housing authority consider to be a breach of the undertaking, and

(b) which is notified to that person in accordance with the terms of the undertaking.

(5) If an improvement notice does provide for the operation of the notice to be suspended under this section –

(a) any periods specified in the notice under section 13 are to be fixed by reference to the day when the suspension ends, and

(b) in subsection (3) of that section the reference to the 28th day after that on which the notice is served is to be read as referring to the 21st day after that on which the suspension ends.

15 Operation of improvement notices

(1) This section deals with the time when an improvement notice becomes operative.

(2) The general rule is that an improvement notice becomes operative at the end of the period of 21 days beginning with the day on which it is served under Part 1 of Schedule 1 (which is the period for appealing against the notice under Part 3 of that Schedule).

(3) The general rule is subject to subsection (4) (suspended notices) and subsection (5) (appeals).

(4) If the notice is suspended under section 14, the notice becomes operative at the time when the suspension ends.

This is subject to subsection (5).

(5) If an appeal against the notice is made under Part 3 of Schedule 1, the notice does not become operative until such time (if any) as is the operative time for the purposes of this subsection under paragraph 19 of that Schedule (time when notice is confirmed on appeal, period for further appeal expires or suspension ends).

(6) If no appeal against an improvement notice is made under that Part of that Schedule within the period for appealing against it, the notice is final and conclusive as to matters which could have been raised on an appeal.

16 Revocation and variation of improvement notices

(1) The local housing authority must revoke an improvement notice if they are satisfied that the requirements of the notice have been complied with.

(2) The local housing authority may revoke an improvement notice if –

(a) in the case of a notice served under section 11, they consider that there are any special circumstances making it appropriate to revoke the notice; or
(b) in the case of a notice served under section 12, they consider that it is appropriate to revoke the notice.

(3) Where an improvement notice relates to a number of hazards –

(a) subsection (1) is to be read as applying separately in relation to each of those hazards, and
(b) if, as a result, the authority are required to revoke only part of the notice, they may vary the remainder as they consider appropriate.

(4) The local housing authority may vary an improvement notice –

(a) with the agreement of the person on whom the notice was served, or
(b) in the case of a notice whose operation is suspended, so as to alter the time or events by reference to which the suspension is to come to an end.

(5) A revocation under this section comes into force at the time when it is made.

(6) If it is made with the agreement of the person on whom the improvement notice was served, a variation under this section comes into force at the time when it is made.

(7) Otherwise a variation under this section does not come into force until such time (if any) as is the operative time for the purposes of this subsection under paragraph 20 of Schedule 1 (time when period for appealing expires without an appeal being made or when decision to vary is confirmed on appeal).

(8) The power to revoke or vary an improvement notice under this section is exercisable by the authority either –

(a) on an application made by the person on whom the improvement notice was served, or
(b) on the authority's own initiative.

17 Review of suspended improvement notices

(1) The local housing authority may at any time review an improvement notice whose operation is suspended.

(2) The local housing authority must review an improvement notice whose operation is suspended not later than one year after the date of service of the notice and at subsequent intervals of not more than one year.

(3) Copies of the authority's decision on a review under this section must be served –

(a) on the person on whom the improvement notice was served, and
(b) on every other person on whom a copy of the notice was required to be served.

18 Service of improvement notices etc and related appeals

Schedule 1 (which deals with the service of improvement notices, and notices relating to their revocation or variation, and with related appeals) has effect.

19 Change in person liable to comply with improvement notice

(1) This section applies where –

(a) an improvement notice has been served on any person ('the original recipient') in respect of any premises, and
(b) at a later date ('the changeover date') that person ceases to be a person of the relevant category in respect of the premises.

(2) In subsection (1) the reference to a person ceasing to be a 'person of the relevant category' is a reference to his ceasing to fall within the description of person (such as, for example, the holder of a licence under Part 2 or 3 or the person managing a dwelling) by reference to which the improvement notice was served on him.

(3) As from the changeover date, the liable person in respect of the premises is to be in the same position as if –

(a) the improvement notice had originally been served on him, and
(b) he had taken all steps relevant for the purposes of this Part which the original recipient had taken.

(4) The effect of subsection (3) is that, in particular, any period for compliance with the notice or for bringing any appeal is unaffected.

(5) But where the original recipient has become subject to any liability arising by virtue of this Part before the changeover date, subsection (3) does not have the effect of –

(a) relieving him of the liability, or
(b) making the new liable person subject to it.

(6) Subsection (3) applies with any necessary modifications where a person to whom it applies (by virtue of any provision of this section) ceases to be the liable person in respect of the premises.

(7) Unless subsection (8) or (9) applies, the person who is at any time the 'liable person' in respect of any premises is the person having control of the premises.

(8) If –

(a) the original recipient was served as the person managing the premises, and
(b) there is a new person managing the premises as from the changeover date,

that new person is the 'liable person'.

(9) If the original recipient was served as an owner of the premises, the 'liable person' is the owner's successor in title on the changeover date.

Prohibition orders

20 Prohibition orders relating to category 1 hazards: duty of authority to make order

(1) If –

    (a) the local housing authority are satisfied that a category 1 hazard exists on any residential premises, and

    (b) no management order is in force in relation to the premises under Chapter 1 or 2 of Part 4,

making a prohibition order under this section in respect of the hazard is a course of action available to the authority in relation to the hazard for the purposes of section 5 (category 1 hazards: general duty to take enforcement action).

(2) A prohibition order under this section is an order imposing such prohibition or prohibitions on the use of any premises as is or are specified in the order in accordance with subsections (3) and (4) and section 22.

(3) The order may prohibit use of the following premises –

    (a) if the residential premises on which the hazard exists are a dwelling or HMO which is not a flat, it may prohibit use of the dwelling or HMO;

    (b) if those premises are one or more flats, it may prohibit use of the building containing the flat or flats (or any part of the building) or any external common parts;

    (c) if those premises are the common parts of a building containing one or more flats, it may prohibit use of the building (or any part of the building) or any external common parts.

Paragraphs (b) and (c) are subject to subsection (4).

(4) The notice may not, by virtue of subsection (3)(b) or (c), prohibit use of any part of the building or its external common parts that is not included in any residential premises on which the hazard exists, unless the authority are satisfied –

    (a) that the deficiency from which the hazard arises is situated there, and

    (b) that it is necessary for such use to be prohibited in order to protect the health or safety of any actual or potential occupiers of one or more of the flats.

(5) A prohibition order under this section may relate to more than one category 1 hazard on the same premises or in the same building containing one or more flats.

(6) The operation of a prohibition order under this section may be suspended in accordance with section 23.

21 Prohibition orders relating to category 2 hazards: power of authority to make order

(1) If –

    (a) the local housing authority are satisfied that a category 2 hazard exists on any residential premises, and

    (b) no management order is in force in relation to the premises under Chapter 1 or 2 of Part 4,

the authority may make a prohibition order under this section in respect of the hazard.

(2) A prohibition order under this section is an order imposing such prohibition or prohibitions on the use of any premises as is or are specified in the order in accordance with subsection (3) and section 22.

(3) Subsections (3) and (4) of section 20 apply to a prohibition order under this section as they apply to one under that section.

(4) A prohibition order under this section may relate to more than one category 2 hazard on the same premises or in the same building containing one or more flats.

(5) A prohibition order under this section may be combined in one document with an order under section 20 where they impose prohibitions on the use of the same premises or on the use of premises in the same building containing one or more flats.

(6) The operation of a prohibition order under this section may be suspended in accordance with section 23.

22 Contents of prohibition orders

(1) A prohibition order under section 20 or 21 must comply with the following provisions of this section.

(2) The order must specify, in relation to the hazard (or each of the hazards) to which it relates –

- (a) whether the order is made under section 20 or 21,
- (b) the nature of the hazard concerned and the residential premises on which it exists,
- (c) the deficiency giving rise to the hazard,
- (d) the premises in relation to which prohibitions are imposed by the order (see subsections (3) and (4)), and
- (e) any remedial action which the authority consider would, if taken in relation to the hazard, result in their revoking the order under section 25.

(3) The order may impose such prohibition or prohibitions on the use of any premises as –

- (a) comply with section 20(3) and (4), and
- (b) the local housing authority consider appropriate in view of the hazard or hazards in respect of which the order is made.

(4) Any such prohibition may prohibit use of any specified premises, or of any part of those premises, either –

- (a) for all purposes, or
- (b) for any particular purpose,

except (in either case) to the extent to which any use of the premises or part is approved by the authority.

(5) A prohibition imposed by virtue of subsection (4)(b) may, in particular, relate to –

- (a) occupation of the premises or part by more than a particular number of households or persons; or
- (b) occupation of the premises or part by particular descriptions of persons.

(6) The order must also contain information about –

- (a) the right under Part 3 of Schedule 2 to appeal against the order, and
- (b) the period within which an appeal may be made,

and specify the date on which the order is made.

(7) Any approval of the authority for the purposes of subsection (4) must not be unreasonably withheld.

(8) If the authority do refuse to give any such approval, they must notify the person applying for the approval of –

(a) their decision,
(b) the reasons for it and the date on which it was made,
(c) the right to appeal against the decision under subsection (9), and
(d) the period within which an appeal may be made,

within the period of seven days beginning with the day on which the decision was made.

(9) The person applying for the approval may appeal to a residential property tribunal against the decision within the period of 28 days beginning with the date specified in the notice as the date on which it was made.

(10) In this Part of this Act 'specified premises', in relation to a prohibition order, means premises specified in the order, in accordance with subsection (2)(d), as premises in relation to which prohibitions are imposed by the order.

23 Suspension of prohibition orders

(1) A prohibition order may provide for the operation of the order to be suspended until a time, or the occurrence of an event, specified in the order.

(2) The time so specified may, in particular, be the time when a person of a particular description begins, or ceases, to occupy any premises.

(3) The event so specified may, in particular, be a notified breach of an undertaking accepted by the local housing authority for the purposes of this section from a person on whom a copy of the order is served.

(4) In subsection (3) a 'notified breach', in relation to such an undertaking, means an act or omission by such a person –

(a) which the local housing authority consider to be a breach of the undertaking, and
(b) which is notified to that person in accordance with the terms of the undertaking.

24 Operation of prohibition orders

(1) This section deals with the time when a prohibition order becomes operative.

(2) The general rule is that a prohibition order becomes operative at the end of the period of 28 days beginning with the date specified in the notice as the date on which it is made.

(3) The general rule is subject to subsection (4) (suspended orders) and subsection (5) (appeals).

(4) If the order is suspended under section 23, the order becomes operative at the time when the suspension ends.

This is subject to subsection (5).

(5) If an appeal is brought against the order under Part 3 of Schedule 2, the order does not become operative until such time (if any) as is the operative time for the purposes of this subsection under paragraph 14 of that Schedule (time when order is confirmed on appeal, period for further appeal expires or suspension ends).

(6) If no appeal against a prohibition order is made under that Part of that Schedule within the period for appealing against it, the order is final and conclusive as to matters which could have been raised on an appeal.

(7) Sections 584A and 584B of the Housing Act 1985 (c 68) provide for the payment of compensation where certain prohibition orders become operative, and for the repayment of such compensation in certain circumstances.

25 Revocation and variation of prohibition orders

(1) The local housing authority must revoke a prohibition order if at any time they are satisfied that the hazard in respect of which the order was made does not then exist on the residential premises specified in the order in accordance with section 22(2)(b).

(2) The local housing authority may revoke a prohibition order if –

(a) in the case of an order made under section 20, they consider that there are any special circumstances making it appropriate to revoke the order; or

(b) in the case of an order made under section 21, they consider that it is appropriate to do so.

(3) Where a prohibition order relates to a number of hazards –

(a) subsection (1) is to be read as applying separately in relation to each of those hazards, and

(b) if, as a result, the authority are required to revoke only part of the order, they may vary the remainder as they consider appropriate.

(4) The local housing authority may vary a prohibition order –

(a) with the agreement of every person on whom copies of the notice were required to be served under Part 1 of Schedule 2, or

(b) in the case of an order whose operation is suspended, so as to alter the time or events by reference to which the suspension is to come to an end.

(5) A revocation under this section comes into force at the time when it is made.

(6) If it is made with the agreement of every person within subsection (4)(a), a variation under this section comes into force at the time when it is made.

(7) Otherwise a variation under this section does not come into force until such time (if any) as is the operative time for the purposes of this subsection under paragraph 15 of Schedule 2 (time when period for appealing expires without an appeal being made or when decision to revoke or vary is confirmed on appeal).

(8) The power to revoke or vary a prohibition order under this section is exercisable by the authority either –

(a) on an application made by a person on whom a copy of the order was required to be served under Part 1 of Schedule 2, or

(b) on the authority's own initiative.

26 Review of suspended prohibition orders

(1) The local housing authority may at any time review a prohibition order whose operation is suspended.

(2) The local housing authority must review a prohibition order whose operation is suspended not later than one year after the date on which the order was made and at subsequent intervals of not more than one year.

(3) Copies of the authority's decision on a review under this section must be served on every person on whom a copy of the order was required to be served under Part 1 of Schedule 2.

27 Service of copies of prohibition orders etc and related appeals

Schedule 2 (which deals with the service of copies of prohibition orders, and notices relating to their revocation or variation, and with related appeals) has effect.

Hazard awareness notices

28 Hazard awareness notices relating to category 1 hazards: duty of authority to serve notice

(1) If –

    (a) the local housing authority are satisfied that a category 1 hazard exists on any residential premises, and

    (b) no management order is in force in relation to the premises under Chapter 1 or 2 of Part 4,

serving a hazard awareness notice under this section in respect of the hazard is a course of action available to the authority in relation to the hazard for the purposes of section 5 (category 1 hazards: general duty to take enforcement action).

(2) A hazard awareness notice under this section is a notice advising the person on whom it is served of the existence of a category 1 hazard on the residential premises concerned which arises as a result of a deficiency on the premises in respect of which the notice is served.

(3) The notice may be served in respect of the following premises –

    (a) if the residential premises on which the hazard exists are a dwelling or HMO which is not a flat, it may be served in respect of the dwelling or HMO;

    (b) if those premises are one or more flats, it may be served in respect of the building containing the flat or flats (or any part of the building) or any external common parts;

    (c) if those premises are the common parts of a building containing one or more flats, it may be served in respect of the building (or any part of the building) or any external common parts.

Paragraphs (b) and (c) are subject to subsection (4).

(4) The notice may not, by virtue of subsection (3)(b) or (c), be served in respect of any part of the building or its external common parts that is not included in any residential premises on which the hazard exists, unless the authority are satisfied –

    (a) that the deficiency from which the hazard arises is situated there, and

    (b) that it is desirable for the notice to be so served in the interests of the health or safety of any actual or potential occupiers of one or more of the flats.

(5) A notice under this section may relate to more than one category 1 hazard on the same premises or in the same building containing one or more flats.

(6) A notice under this section must specify, in relation to the hazard (or each of the hazards) to which it relates –

    (a) the nature of the hazard and the residential premises on which it exists,

    (b) the deficiency giving rise to the hazard,

    (c) the premises on which the deficiency exists,

    (d) the authority's reasons for deciding to serve the notice, including their reasons for deciding that serving the notice is the most appropriate course of action, and

    (e) details of the remedial action (if any) which the authority consider that it would be practicable and appropriate to take in relation to the hazard.

(7) Part 1 of Schedule 1 (which relates to the service of improvement notices and copies of such notices) applies to a notice under this section as if it were an improvement notice.

(8) For that purpose, any reference in that Part of that Schedule to 'the specified premises' is, in relation to a hazard awareness notice under this section, a reference to the premises specified under subsection (6)(c).

29 Hazard awareness notices relating to category 2 hazards: power of authority to serve notice

(1) If –

(a) the local housing authority are satisfied that a category 2 hazard exists on any residential premises, and

(b) no management order is in force in relation to the premises under Chapter 1 or 2 of Part 4,

the authority may serve a hazard awareness notice under this section in respect of the hazard.

(2) A hazard awareness notice under this section is a notice advising the person on whom it is served of the existence of a category 2 hazard on the residential premises concerned which arises as a result of a deficiency on the premises in respect of which the notice is served.

(3) Subsections (3) and (4) of section 28 apply to a hazard awareness notice under this section as they apply to one under that section.

(4) A notice under this section may relate to more than one category 2 hazard on the same premises or in the same building containing one or more flats.

(5) A notice under this section must specify, in relation to the hazard (or each of the hazards) to which it relates –

(a) the nature of the hazard and the residential premises on which it exists,

(b) the deficiency giving rise to the hazard,

(c) the premises on which the deficiency exists,

(d) the authority's reasons for deciding to serve the notice, including their reasons for deciding that serving the notice is the most appropriate course of action, and

(e) details of the remedial action (if any) which the authority consider that it would be practicable and appropriate to take in relation to the hazard.

(6) A notice under this section may be combined in one document with a notice under section 28 where they are served in respect of the same premises.

(7) Part 1 of Schedule 1 (which relates to the service of improvement notices and copies of such notices) applies to a notice under this section as if it were an improvement notice.

(8) For that purpose, any reference in that Part of that Schedule to 'the specified premises' is, in relation to a hazard awareness notice under this section, a reference to the premises specified under subsection (5)(c).

Enforcement: improvement notices

30 Offence of failing to comply with improvement notice

(1) Where an improvement notice has become operative, the person on whom the notice was served commits an offence if he fails to comply with it.

(2) For the purposes of this Chapter compliance with an improvement notice means, in relation to each hazard, beginning and completing any remedial action specified in the notice –

(a) (if no appeal is brought against the notice) not later than the date specified under section 13(2)(e) and within the period specified under section 13(2)(f);

(b) (if an appeal is brought against the notice and is not withdrawn) not later than such date and within such period as may be fixed by the tribunal determining the appeal; and

(c) (if an appeal brought against the notice is withdrawn) not later than the 21st day after the date on which the notice becomes operative and within the period (beginning on that 21st day) specified in the notice under section 13(2)(f).

(3) A person who commits an offence under subsection (1) is liable on summary conviction to a fine not exceeding level 5 on the standard scale.

(4) In proceedings against a person for an offence under subsection (1) it is a defence that he had a reasonable excuse for failing to comply with the notice.

(5) The obligation to take any remedial action specified in the notice in relation to a hazard continues despite the fact that the period for completion of the action has expired.

(6) In this section any reference to any remedial action specified in a notice includes a reference to any part of any remedial action which is required to be completed within a particular period specified in the notice.

31 Enforcement action by local housing authorities

Schedule 3 (which enables enforcement action in respect of an improvement notice to be taken by local housing authorities either with or without agreement and which provides for the recovery of related expenses) has effect.

Enforcement: prohibition orders

32 Offence of failing to comply with prohibition order etc

(1) A person commits an offence if, knowing that a prohibition order has become operative in relation to any specified premises, he –

(a) uses the premises in contravention of the order, or
(b) permits the premises to be so used.

(2) A person who commits an offence under subsection (1) is liable on summary conviction –

(a) to a fine not exceeding level 5 on the standard scale, and
(b) to a further fine not exceeding £20 for every day or part of a day on which he so uses the premises, or permits them to be so used, after conviction.

(3) In proceedings against a person for an offence under subsection (1) it is a defence that he had a reasonable excuse for using the premises, or (as the case may be) permitting them to be used, in contravention of the order.

33 Recovery of possession of premises in order to comply with order

Nothing in –

(a) the Rent Act 1977 (c 42) or the Rent (Agriculture) Act 1976 (c 80), or
(b) Part 1 of the Housing Act 1988 (c 50),

prevents possession being obtained by the owner of any specified premises in relation to which a prohibition order is operative if possession of the premises is necessary for the purpose of complying with the order.

34 Power of tribunal to determine or vary lease

(1) Subsection (2) applies where –

 (a) a prohibition order has become operative, and
 (b) the whole or part of any specified premises form the whole or part of the subject matter of a lease.

(2) The lessor or the lessee may apply to a residential property tribunal for an order determining or varying the lease.

(3) On such an application the tribunal may make an order determining or varying the lease, if it considers it appropriate to do so.

(4) Before making such an order, the tribunal must give any sub-lessee an opportunity of being heard.

(5) An order under this section may be unconditional or subject to such terms and conditions as the tribunal considers appropriate.

(6) The conditions may, in particular, include conditions about the payment of money by one party to the proceedings to another by way of compensation, damages or otherwise.

(7) In deciding what is appropriate for the purposes of this section, the tribunal must have regard to the respective rights, obligations and liabilities of the parties under the lease and to all the other circumstances of the case.

(8) In this section 'lessor' and 'lessee' include a person deriving title under a lessor or lessee.

Enforcement: improvement notices and prohibition orders

35 Power of court to order occupier or owner to allow action to be taken on premises

(1) This section applies where an improvement notice or prohibition order has become operative.

(2) If the occupier of any specified premises –

 (a) has received reasonable notice of any intended action in relation to the premises, but
 (b) is preventing a relevant person, or any representative of a relevant person or of the local housing authority, from taking that action in relation to the premises,

a magistrates' court may order the occupier to permit to be done on the premises anything which the court considers is necessary or expedient for the purpose of enabling the intended action to be taken.

(3) If a relevant person –

 (a) has received reasonable notice of any intended action in relation to any specified premises, but
 (b) is preventing a representative of the local housing authority from taking that action in relation to the premises,

a magistrates' court may order the relevant person to permit to be done on the premises anything which the court considers is necessary or expedient for the purpose of enabling the intended action to be taken.

(4) A person who fails to comply with an order of the court under this section commits an offence.

(5) In proceedings for an offence under subsection (4) it is a defence that the person had a reasonable excuse for failing to comply with the order.

(6) A person who commits an offence under subsection (4) is liable on summary conviction to a fine not exceeding £20 in respect of each day or part of a day during which the failure continues.

(7) In this section 'intended action', in relation to any specified premises, means –

(a) where an improvement notice has become operative, any action which the person on whom that notice has been served is required by the notice to take in relation to the premises and which –
  (a) (in the context of subsection (2)) is proposed to be taken by or on behalf of that person or on behalf of the local housing authority in pursuance of Schedule 3, or
  (b) (in the context of subsection (3)) is proposed to be taken on behalf of the local housing authority in pursuance of Schedule 3;
(b) where a prohibition order has become operative, any action which is proposed to be taken and which either is necessary for the purpose of giving effect to the order or is remedial action specified in the order in accordance with section 22(2)(e).

(8) In this section –

'relevant person', in relation to any premises, means a person who is an owner of the premises, a person having control of or managing the premises, or the holder of any licence under Part 2 or 3 in respect of the premises;

'representative' in relation to a relevant person or a local housing authority, means any officer, employee, agent or contractor of that person or authority.

36 Power of court to authorise action by one owner on behalf of another

(1) Where an improvement notice or prohibition order has become operative, an owner of any specified premises may apply to a magistrates' court for an order under subsection (2).

(2) A magistrates' court may, on an application under subsection (1), make an order enabling the applicant –

(a) immediately to enter on the premises, and
(b) to take any required action within a period fixed by the order.

(3) In this section 'required action' means –

(a) in the case of an improvement notice, any remedial action which is required to be taken by the notice;
(b) in the case of a prohibition order, any action necessary for the purpose of complying with the order or any remedial action specified in the order in accordance with section 22(2)(e).

(4) No order may be made under subsection (2) unless the court is satisfied that the interests of the applicant will be prejudiced as a result of a failure by another person to take any required action.

(5) No order may be made under subsection (2) unless notice of the application has been given to the local housing authority.

(6) If it considers that it is appropriate to do so, the court may make an order in favour of any other owner of the premises which is similar to the order that it is making in relation to the premises under subsection (2).

Supplementary provisions

37 Effect of improvement notices and prohibition orders as local land charges

(1) An improvement notice or a prohibition order under this Chapter is a local land charge if subsection (2), (3) or (4) applies.

(2) This subsection applies if the notice or order has become operative.

(3) This subsection applies if –

(a) the notice or order is suspended under section 14 or 23, and
(b) the period for appealing against it under Part 3 of Schedule 1 or 2 has expired without an appeal having been brought.

(4) This subsection applies if –

(a) the notice or order is suspended under section 14 or 23,
(b) an appeal has been brought against it under Part 3 of Schedule 1 or 2, and
(c) were it not suspended –
   (i) the notice would have become operative under section 15(5) by virtue of paragraph 19(2) of Schedule 1 (improvement notices: confirmation on appeal or expiry of period for further appeal), or
   (ii) the order would have become operative under section 24(5) by virtue of paragraph 14(2) of Schedule 2 (prohibition orders: confirmation on appeal or expiry of period for further appeal).

38 Savings for rights arising from breach of covenant etc

(1) Nothing in this Chapter affects any remedy of an owner for breach of any covenant or contract entered into by a tenant in connection with any premises which are specified premises in relation to an improvement notice or prohibition order.

(2) If an owner is obliged to take possession of any premises in order to comply with an improvement notice or prohibition order, the taking of possession does not affect his right to take advantage of any such breach which occurred before he took possession.

(3) No action taken under this Chapter affects any remedy available to the tenant of any premises against his landlord (whether at common law or otherwise).

39 Effect of Part 4 enforcement action and redevelopment proposals

(1) Subsection (2) applies if –

(a) an improvement notice or prohibition order has been served or made under this Chapter, and
(b) a management order under Chapter 1 or 2 of Part 4 comes into force in relation to the specified premises.

(2) The improvement notice or prohibition order –

(a) if operative at the time when the management order comes into force, ceases to have effect at that time, and
(b) otherwise is to be treated as from that time as if it had not been served or made.

(3) Subsection (2)(a) does not affect any right acquired or liability (civil or criminal) incurred before the improvement notice or prohibition order ceases to have effect.

(4) Subsection (5) applies where, under section 308 of the Housing Act 1985 (c 68) (owner's re-development proposals), the local housing authority have approved proposals for the re-development of land.

(5) No action is to be taken under this Chapter in relation to the land if, and so long as, the re-development is being proceeded with (subject to any variation or extension approved by the authority) –

(a) in accordance with the proposals; and
(b) within the time limits specified by the local housing authority.

Chapter 3
Emergency Measures

Emergency remedial action

40 Emergency remedial action

(1) If –

(a) the local housing authority are satisfied that a category 1 hazard exists on any residential premises, and
(b) they are further satisfied that the hazard involves an imminent risk of serious harm to the health or safety of any of the occupiers of those or any other residential premises, and
(c) no management order is in force under Chapter 1 or 2 of Part 4 in relation to the premises mentioned in paragraph (a),

the taking by the authority of emergency remedial action under this section in respect of the hazard is a course of action available to the authority in relation to the hazard for the purposes of section 5 (category 1 hazards: general duty to take enforcement action).

(2) 'Emergency remedial action' means such remedial action in respect of the hazard concerned as the authority consider immediately necessary in order to remove the imminent risk of serious harm within subsection (1)(b).

(3) Emergency remedial action under this section may be taken by the authority in relation to any premises in relation to which remedial action could be required to be taken by an improvement notice under section 11 (see subsections (3) and (4) of that section).

(4) Emergency remedial action under this section may be taken by the authority in respect of more than one category 1 hazard on the same premises or in the same building containing one or more flats.

(5) Paragraphs 3 to 5 of Schedule 3 (improvement notices: enforcement action by local authorities) apply in connection with the taking of emergency remedial action under this section as they apply in connection with the taking of the remedial action required by an improvement notice which has become operative but has not been complied with.

But those paragraphs so apply with the modifications set out in subsection (6).

(6) The modifications are as follows –

(a) the right of entry conferred by paragraph 3(4) may be exercised at any time; and
(b) the notice required by paragraph 4 (notice before entering premises) must (instead of being served in accordance with that paragraph) be served on every person, who to the authority's knowledge –

    (i)   is an occupier of the premises in relation to which the authority propose to take emergency remedial action, or

    (ii) if those premises are common parts of a building containing one or more flats, is an occupier of any part of the building; but

  (c) that notice is to be regarded as so served if a copy of it is fixed to some conspicuous part of the premises or building.

(7) Within the period of seven days beginning with the date when the authority start taking emergency remedial action, the authority must serve –

  (a) a notice under section 41, and

  (b) copies of such a notice,

on the persons on whom the authority would be required under Part 1 of Schedule 1 to serve an improvement notice and copies of it.

(8) Section 240 (warrant to authorise entry) applies for the purpose of enabling a local housing authority to enter any premises to take emergency remedial action under this section in relation to the premises, as if –

  (a) that purpose were mentioned in subsection (2) of that section, and

  (b) the circumstances as to which the justice of the peace must be satisfied under subsection (4) were that there are reasonable grounds for believing that the authority will not be able to gain admission to the premises without a warrant.

(9) For the purposes of the operation of any provision relating to improvement notices as it applies by virtue of this section in connection with emergency remedial action or a notice under section 41, any reference in that provision to the specified premises is to be read as a reference to the premises specified, in accordance with section 41(2)(c), as those in relation to which emergency remedial action has been (or is to be) taken.

41 Notice of emergency remedial action

(1) The notice required by section 40(7) is a notice which complies with the following requirements of this section.

(2) The notice must specify, in relation to the hazard (or each of the hazards) to which it relates –

  (a) the nature of the hazard and the residential premises on which it exists,

  (b) the deficiency giving rise to the hazard,

  (c) the premises in relation to which emergency remedial action has been (or is to be) taken by the authority under section 40 and the nature of that remedial action,

  (d) the power under which that remedial action has been (or is to be) taken by the authority, and

  (e) the date when that remedial action was (or is to be) started.

(3) The notice must contain information about –

  (a) the right to appeal under section 45 against the decision of the authority to make the order, and

  (b) the period within which an appeal may be made.

42 Recovery of expenses of taking emergency remedial action

(1) This section relates to the recovery by a local housing authority of expenses reasonably incurred in taking emergency remedial action under section 40 ('emergency expenses').

(2) Paragraphs 6 to 14 of Schedule 3 (improvement notices: enforcement action by local authorities) apply for the purpose of enabling a local housing authority to recover emergency

expenses as they apply for the purpose of enabling such an authority to recover expenses incurred in taking remedial action under paragraph 3 of that Schedule.

But those paragraphs so apply with the modifications set out in subsection (3).

(3) The modifications are as follows –

(a) any reference to the improvement notice is to be read as a reference to the notice under section 41; and
(b) no amount is recoverable in respect of any emergency expenses until such time (if any) as is the operative time for the purposes of this subsection (see subsection (4)).

(4) This subsection gives the meaning of 'the operative time' for the purposes of subsection (3) –

(a) if no appeal against the authority's decision to take the emergency remedial action is made under section 45 before the end of the period of 28 days mentioned in subsection (3)(a) of that section, 'the operative time' is the end of that period;
(b) if an appeal is made under that section within that period and a decision is given on the appeal which confirms the authority's decision, 'the operative time' is as follows –
   (i) if the period within which an appeal to the Lands Tribunal may be brought expires without such an appeal having been brought, 'the operative time' is the end of that period;
   (ii) if an appeal to the Lands Tribunal is brought, 'the operative time' is the time when a decision is given on the appeal which confirms the authority's decision.

(5) For the purposes of subsection (4) –

(a) the withdrawal of an appeal has the same effect as a decision which confirms the authority's decision, and
(b) references to a decision which confirms the authority's decision are to a decision which confirms it with or without variation.

Emergency prohibition orders

43 Emergency prohibition orders

(1) If –

(a) the local housing authority are satisfied that a category 1 hazard exists on any residential premises, and
(b) they are further satisfied that the hazard involves an imminent risk of serious harm to the health or safety of any of the occupiers of those or any other residential premises, and
(c) no management order is in force under Chapter 1 or 2 of Part 4 in relation to the premises mentioned in paragraph (a),

making an emergency prohibition order under this section in respect of the hazard is a course of action available to the authority in relation to the hazard for the purposes of section 5 (category 1 hazards: general duty to take enforcement action).

(2) An emergency prohibition order under this section is an order imposing, with immediate effect, such prohibition or prohibitions on the use of any premises as are specified in the order in accordance with subsection (3) and section 44.

(3) As regards the imposition of any such prohibition or prohibitions, the following provisions apply to an emergency prohibition order as they apply to a prohibition order under section 20 –

(a) subsections (3) to (5) of that section, and

(b) subsections (3) to (5) and (7) to (9) of section 22.

(4) Part 1 of Schedule 2 (service of copies of prohibition orders) applies in relation to an emergency prohibition order as it applies to a prohibition order, but any requirement to serve copies within a specified period of seven days is to be read as a reference to serve them on the day on which the emergency prohibition order is made (or, if that is not possible, as soon after that day as is possible).

(5) The following provisions also apply to an emergency prohibition order as they apply to a prohibition order (or to a prohibition order which has become operative, as the case may be) –

(a) section 25 (revocation and variation);
(b) sections 32 to 36 (enforcement);
(c) sections 37 to 39 (supplementary provisions); and
(d) Part 2 of Schedule 2 (notices relating to revocation or variation);
(e) Part 3 of that Schedule (appeals) so far as it relates to any decision to vary, or to refuse to revoke or vary, a prohibition order; and
(f) sections 584A and 584B of the Housing Act 1985 (c 68) (payment, and repayment, of compensation).

(6) For the purposes of the operation of any provision relating to prohibition orders as it applies in connection with emergency prohibition orders by virtue of this section or section 45, any reference in that provision to the specified premises is to be read as a reference to the premises specified, in accordance with section 44(2)(c), as the premises in relation to which prohibitions are imposed by the order.

44 Contents of emergency prohibition orders

(1) An emergency prohibition order under section 43 must comply with the following requirements of this section.

(2) The order must specify, in relation to the hazard (or each of the hazards) to which it relates –

(a) the nature of the hazard concerned and the residential premises on which it exists,
(b) the deficiency giving rise to the hazard,
(c) the premises in relation to which prohibitions are imposed by the order (see subsections (3) and (4) of section 22 as applied by section 43(3)), and
(d) any remedial action which the authority consider would, if taken in relation to the hazard, result in their revoking the order under section 25 (as applied by section 43(5)).

(3) The order must contain information about –

(a) the right to appeal under section 45 against the order, and
(b) the period within which an appeal may be made,

and specify the date on which the order is made.

Appeals

45 Appeals relating to emergency measures

(1) A person on whom a notice under section 41 has been served in connection with the taking of emergency remedial action under section 40 may appeal to a residential property tribunal against the decision of the local housing authority to take that action.

(2) A relevant person may appeal to a residential property tribunal against an emergency prohibition order.

(3) An appeal under subsection (1) or (2) must be made within the period of 28 days beginning with –

   (a) the date specified in the notice under section 41 as the date when the emergency remedial action was (or was to be) started, or
   (b) the date specified in the emergency prohibition order as the date on which the order was made,

as the case may be.

(4) A residential property tribunal may allow an appeal to be made to it after the end of that period if it is satisfied that there is a good reason for the failure to appeal before the end of that period (and for any delay since then in applying for permission to appeal out of time).

(5) An appeal under subsection (1) or (2) –

   (a) is to be by way of a re-hearing, but
   (b) may be determined having regard to matters of which the authority were unaware.

(6) The tribunal may –

   (a) in the case of an appeal under subsection (1), confirm, reverse or vary the decision of the authority;
   (b) in the case of an appeal under subsection (2), confirm or vary the emergency prohibition order or make an order revoking it as from a date specified in that order.

(7) Paragraph 16 of Schedule 2 applies for the purpose of identifying who is a relevant person for the purposes of subsection (2) in relation to an emergency prohibition order as it applies for the purpose of identifying who is a relevant person for the purposes of Part 3 of that Schedule in relation to a prohibition order.

Chapter 4
Demolition Orders and Slum Clearance Declarations

Demolition orders

46 Demolition orders

For section 265 of the Housing Act 1985 (c 68) substitute –

'265 Demolition orders

(1) If –

   (a) the local housing authority are satisfied that a category 1 hazard exists in a dwelling or HMO which is not a flat, and
   (b) this subsection is not disapplied by subsection (5),

making a demolition order in respect of the dwelling or HMO is a course of action available to the authority in relation to the hazard for the purposes of section 5 of the Housing Act 2004 (category 1 hazards: general duty to take enforcement action).

(2) If, in the case of any building containing one or more flats –

   (a) the local housing authority are satisfied that a category 1 hazard exists in one or more of the flats contained in the building or in any common parts of the building, and

(b) this subsection is not disapplied by subsection (5),

making a demolition order in respect of the building is a course of action available to the authority in relation to the hazard for the purposes of section 5 of the Housing Act 2004.

(3) The local housing authority may make a demolition order in respect of a dwelling or HMO which is not a flat if –

 (a) they are satisfied that a category 2 hazard exists in the dwelling or HMO,
 (b) this subsection is not disapplied by subsection (5), and
 (c) the circumstances of the case are circumstances specified or described in an order made by the Secretary of State.

(4) The local housing authority may make a demolition order in respect of any building containing one or more flats if –

 (a) they are satisfied that a category 2 hazard exists in one or more of the flats contained in the building or in any common parts of the building,
 (b) this subsection is not disapplied by subsection (5), and
 (c) the circumstances of the case are circumstances specified or described in an order made by the Secretary of State.

(5) None of subsections (1) to (4) applies if a management order under Chapter 1 or 2 of Part 4 is in force in relation to the premises concerned.

(6) This section also has effect subject to section 304(1) (no demolition order to be made in respect of listed building).

(7) In this section "HMO" means house in multiple occupation.

(8) An order made under subsection (3) or (4) –

 (a) may make different provision for different cases or descriptions of case (including different provision for different areas);
 (b) may contain such incidental, supplementary, consequential, transitory, transitional or saving provision as the Secretary of State considers appropriate; and
 (c) shall be made by statutory instrument which shall be subject to annulment in pursuance of a resolution of either House of Parliament.

(9) Sections 584A and 584B provide for the payment of compensation where demolition orders are made under this section, and for the repayment of such compensation in certain circumstances.'

Slum clearance declarations

47 Clearance areas

In section 289 of the Housing Act 1985 (c 68) (declaration of clearance area) for subsections (2) and (2A) substitute –

 '(2) If the local housing authority are satisfied, in relation to any area –

  (a) that each of the residential buildings in the area contains a category 1 hazard, and
  (b) that the other buildings (if any) in the area are dangerous or harmful to the health or safety of the inhabitants of the area,

 declaring the area to be a clearance area is a course of action available to the authority in relation to the hazard or hazards for the purposes of section 5 of the Housing Act 2004 (category 1 hazards: general duty to take enforcement action).

(2ZA) The local housing authority may declare an area to be a clearance area if they are satisfied that –

    (a) the residential buildings in the area are dangerous or harmful to the health or safety of the inhabitants of the area as a result of their bad arrangement or the narrowness or bad arrangement of the streets; and

    (b) that the other buildings (if any) in the area are dangerous or harmful to the health or safety of the inhabitants of the area.

(2ZB) The local housing authority may declare an area to be a clearance area if they are satisfied that –

    (a) that each of the residential buildings in the area contains a category 2 hazard,

    (b) that the other buildings (if any) in the area are dangerous or harmful to the health or safety of the inhabitants of the area, and

    (c) the circumstances of the case are circumstances specified or described in an order made by the Secretary of State.

Subsection (8) of section 265 applies in relation to an order under this subsection as it applies in relation to an order under subsection (3) or (4) of that section.

(2ZC) In this section "residential buildings" means buildings which are dwellings or houses in multiple occupation or contain one or more flats.

This is subject to subsection (2ZD).

(2ZD) For the purposes of subsection (2) or (2ZB) –

    (a) subsection (2ZC) applies as if "two or more flats" were substituted for "one or more flats"; and

    (b) a residential building containing two or more flats is only to be treated as containing a category 1 or 2 hazard if two or more of the flats within it contain such a hazard.

(2ZE) Subsections (2) to (2ZB) are subject to subsections (2B) to (4) and (5B).'

Appeals

48 Transfer of jurisdiction in respect of appeals relating to demolition orders etc

(1) Part 9 of the Housing Act 1985 (c 68) (slum clearance) is further amended as follows.

(2) In section 269 (right of appeal against demolition order etc) –

    (a) in subsection (1), for 'the county court' substitute 'a residential property tribunal';

    (b) in subsection (3), for 'court' substitute 'tribunal'; and

    (c) in subsection (6)(a) and (b), for 'Court of Appeal' substitute 'Lands Tribunal'.

(3) In section 272 (demolition orders) –

    (a) in subsection (2), for 'the court' in the first place it appears substitute 'a residential property tribunal', and in the second place it appears substitute 'such a tribunal';

    (b) in subsection (5), for the words from the beginning to 'and has' substitute 'A residential property tribunal has jurisdiction to hear and determine proceedings under subsection (1) (as well as those under subsection (2)), and a county court has'; and

    (c) in subsection (6), for 'the court' substitute 'a tribunal or court'.

(4) In section 317 (power of court to determine lease where premises demolished etc) –

    (a) in subsection (1), for 'the county court' substitute 'a residential property tribunal'; and

(b) in subsections (2) and (3), for 'court' substitute 'tribunal'.

(5) In section 318 (power of court to authorise execution of works on unfit premises or for improvement) –

(a) in the sidenote, for 'court' substitute 'tribunal';
(b) in subsection (1), for 'the court' in the first place it appears substitute 'a residential property tribunal', and in the second place it appears substitute 'the tribunal';
(c) in subsections (2) and (3), for 'court' substitute 'tribunal'; and
(d) omit subsection (4).

Chapter 5
General and Miscellaneous Provisions Relating to Enforcement Action

Recovery of expenses relating to enforcement action

49 Power to charge for certain enforcement action

(1) A local housing authority may make such reasonable charge as they consider appropriate as a means of recovering certain administrative and other expenses incurred by them in –

(a) serving an improvement notice under section 11 or 12;
(b) making a prohibition order under section 20 or 21;
(c) serving a hazard awareness notice under section 28 or 29;
(d) taking emergency remedial action under section 40;
(e) making an emergency prohibition order under section 43; or
(f) making a demolition order under section 265 of the Housing Act 1985 (c 68).

(2) The expenses are, in the case of the service of an improvement notice or a hazard awareness notice, the expenses incurred in –

(a) determining whether to serve the notice,
(b) identifying any action to be specified in the notice, and
(c) serving the notice.

(3) The expenses are, in the case of emergency remedial action under section 40, the expenses incurred in –

(a) determining whether to take such action, and
(b) serving the notice required by subsection (7) of that section.

(4) The expenses are, in the case of a prohibition order under section 20 or 21 of this Act, an emergency prohibition order under section 43 or a demolition order under section 265 of the Housing Act 1985, the expenses incurred in –

(a) determining whether to make the order, and
(b) serving copies of the order on persons as owners of premises.

(5) A local housing authority may make such reasonable charge as they consider appropriate as a means of recovering expenses incurred by them in –

(a) carrying out any review under section 17 or 26, or
(b) serving copies of the authority's decision on such a review.

(6) The amount of the charge may not exceed such amount as is specified by order of the appropriate national authority.

(7) Where a tribunal allows an appeal against the underlying notice or order mentioned in subsection (1), it may make such order as it considers appropriate reducing, quashing, or requiring the repayment of, any charge under this section made in respect of the notice or order.

50 Recovery of charge under section 49

(1) This section relates to the recovery by a local housing authority of a charge made by them under section 49.

(2) In the case of –

(a) an improvement notice under section 11 or 12, or
(b) a hazard awareness notice under section 28 or 29,

the charge may be recovered from the person on whom the notice is served.

(3) In the case of emergency remedial action under section 40, the charge may be recovered from the person served with the notice required by subsection (7) of that section.

(4) In the case of –

(a) a prohibition order under section 20 or 21,
(b) an emergency prohibition order under section 43, or
(c) a demolition order under section 265 of the Housing Act 1985 (c 68),

the charge may be recovered from any person on whom a copy of the order is served as an owner of the premises.

(5) A demand for payment of the charge must be served on the person from whom the authority seek to recover it.

(6) The demand becomes operative, if no appeal is brought against the underlying notice or order, at the end of the period of 21 days beginning with the date of service of the demand.

(7) If such an appeal is brought and a decision is given on the appeal which confirms the underlying notice or order, the demand becomes operative at the time when –

(a) the period within which an appeal to the Lands Tribunal may be brought expires without such an appeal having been brought, or
(b) a decision is given on such an appeal which confirms the notice or order.

(8) For the purposes of subsection (7) –

(a) the withdrawal of an appeal has the same effect as a decision which confirms the notice or order, and
(b) references to a decision which confirms the notice or order are to a decision which confirms it with or without variation.

(9) As from the time when the demand becomes operative, the sum recoverable by the authority is, until recovered, a charge on the premises concerned.

(10) The charge takes effect at that time as a legal charge which is a local land charge.

(11) For the purpose of enforcing the charge the authority have the same powers and remedies under the Law of Property Act 1925 (c 20) and otherwise as if they were mortgagees by deed having powers of sale and lease, of accepting surrenders of leases and of appointing a receiver.

(12) The power of appointing a receiver is exercisable at any time after the end of the period of one month beginning with the date on which the charge takes effect.

(13) The appropriate national authority may by regulations prescribe the form of, and the particulars to be contained in, a demand for payment of any charge under section 49.

Repeals

51 Repeal of power to improve existing enforcement procedures

Omit section 86 of the Housing Grants, Construction and Regeneration Act 1996 (c 53) (power to improve existing enforcement procedures in relation to unfitness for human habitation etc).

52 Repeal of provisions relating to demolition of obstructive buildings

Omit sections 283 to 288 of the Housing Act 1985 (c 68) (demolition of obstructive buildings).

53 Miscellaneous repeals etc in relation to fire hazards

(1) In the London Building Acts (Amendment) Act 1939 (c xcvii) –

(a) omit section 35(1)(c)(i) (protection against fire in certain old buildings let in flats or tenements);

(b) in section 36(1) (projecting shops in which persons are employed or sleep) omit 'or sleep'; and

(c) in section 37(1) (means of access to roofs), in paragraph (b) for the words from 'except' onwards substitute 'except to the extent that it is occupied for residential purposes;'.

(2) In the County of Merseyside Act 1980 (c x) omit section 48 (means of escape from fire) and section 49(1) and (2) (maintenance of means of escape from fire).

(3) In the Building Act 1984 (c 55) omit section 72(6)(a) (means of escape from fire in case of certain buildings let in flats or tenements).

(4) In the Leicestershire Act 1985 (c xvii) omit section 54(6)(a) (means of escape from fire in case of certain buildings used as flats or tenements).

Index

54 Index of defined expressions: Part 1

The following table shows where expressions used in this Part are defined or otherwise explained.

Expression	*Provision of this Act*
Appropriate national authority	Section 261(1)
Building containing one or more flats	Section 1(5)
Category 1 hazard	Section 2(1)
Category 2 hazard	Section 2(1)
Common parts	Section 1(5)
Compliance with improvement notice	Section 30(2)
District of local housing authority	Section 261(6)
Dwelling	Section 1(5), (6)
External common parts	Section 1(5)
Flat	Section 1(5) to (7)
Hazard	Section 2(1)
Hazard awareness notice	Section 28(2) or 29(2)

Expression	Provision of this Act
Health	Section 2(5)
HMO	Section 1(5), (6) (and see also section 1(8))
Improvement notice	Section 11(2) or 12(2)
Lease, lessee etc	Section 262(1) to (4)
Local housing authority	Section 261(2) to (5)
Occupier (and related expressions)	Section 262(6)
Owner	Section 262(7)
Person having control	Section 263(1) and (2)
Person managing	Section 263(3) and (4)
Prohibition order	Section 20(2) or 21(2)
Remedial action	Section 11(8)
Residential premises	Section 1(4)
Residential property tribunal	Section 229
Specified premises, in relation to an improvement notice	Section 13(5)
Specified premises, in relation to a prohibition order	Section 22(10)
Tenancy, tenant	Section 262(1) to (5)
Unoccupied HMO accommodation	Section 1(5) (and see also section 1(8)).

Part 2
Licensing of Houses in Multiple Occupation

Introductory

55 Licensing of HMOs to which this Part applies

(1) This Part provides for HMOs to be licensed by local housing authorities where –

    (a) they are HMOs to which this Part applies (see subsection (2)), and

    (b) they are required to be licensed under this Part (see section 61(1)).

(2) This Part applies to the following HMOs in the case of each local housing authority –

    (a) any HMO in the authority's district which falls within any prescribed description of HMO, and

    (b) if an area is for the time being designated by the authority under section 56 as subject to additional licensing, any HMO in that area which falls within any description of HMO specified in the designation.

(3) The appropriate national authority may by order prescribe descriptions of HMOs for the purposes of subsection (2)(a).

(4) The power conferred by subsection (3) may be exercised in such a way that this Part applies to all HMOs in the district of a local housing authority.

(5) Every local housing authority have the following general duties –

    (a) to make such arrangements as are necessary to secure the effective implementation in their district of the licensing regime provided for by this Part;

    (b) to ensure that all applications for licences and other issues falling to be determined by them under this Part are determined within a reasonable time; and

(c) to satisfy themselves, as soon as is reasonably practicable, that there are no Part 1 functions that ought to be exercised by them in relation to the premises in respect of which such applications are made.

(6) For the purposes of subsection (5)(c) –

(a) 'Part 1 function' means any duty under section 5 to take any course of action to which that section applies or any power to take any course of action to which section 7 applies; and
(b) the authority may take such steps as they consider appropriate (whether or not involving an inspection) to comply with their duty under subsection (5)(c) in relation to each of the premises in question, but they must in any event comply with it within the period of 5 years beginning with the date of the application for a licence.

Designation of additional licensing areas

56 Designation of areas subject to additional licensing

(1) A local housing authority may designate either –

(a) the area of their district, or
(b) an area in their district,

as subject to additional licensing in relation to a description of HMOs specified in the designation, if the requirements of this section are met.

(2) The authority must consider that a significant proportion of the HMOs of that description in the area are being managed sufficiently ineffectively as to give rise, or to be likely to give rise, to one or more particular problems either for those occupying the HMOs or for members of the public.

(3) Before making a designation the authority must –

(a) take reasonable steps to consult persons who are likely to be affected by the designation; and
(b) consider any representations made in accordance with the consultation and not withdrawn.

(4) The power to make a designation under this section may be exercised in such a way that this Part applies to all HMOs in the area in question.

(5) In forming an opinion as to the matter mentioned in subsection (2), the authority must have regard to any information regarding the extent to which any codes of practice approved under section 233 have been complied with by persons managing HMOs in the area in question.

(6) Section 57 applies for the purposes of this section.

57 Designations under section 56: further considerations

(1) This section applies to the power of a local housing authority to make designations under section 56.

(2) The authority must ensure that any exercise of the power is consistent with the authority's overall housing strategy.

(3) The authority must also seek to adopt a co-ordinated approach in connection with dealing with homelessness, empty properties and anti-social behaviour affecting the private rented sector, both –

(a) as regards combining licensing under this Part with other courses of action available to them, and
(b) as regards combining such licensing with measures taken by other persons.

(4) The authority must not make a particular designation under section 56 unless –

    (a) they have considered whether there are any other courses of action available to them (of whatever nature) that might provide an effective method of dealing with the problem or problems in question, and

    (b) they consider that making the designation will significantly assist them to deal with the problem or problems (whether or not they take any other course of action as well).

(5) In this Act 'anti-social behaviour' means conduct on the part of occupiers of, or visitors to, residential premises –

    (a) which causes or is likely to cause a nuisance or annoyance to persons residing, visiting or otherwise engaged in lawful activities in the vicinity of such premises, or

    (b) which involves or is likely to involve the use of such premises for illegal purposes.

58 Designation needs confirmation or general approval to be effective

(1) A designation of an area as subject to additional licensing cannot come into force unless –

    (a) it has been confirmed by the appropriate national authority; or

    (b) it falls within a description of designations in relation to which that authority has given a general approval in accordance with subsection (6).

(2) The appropriate national authority may either confirm, or refuse to confirm, a designation as it considers appropriate.

(3) If the appropriate national authority confirms a designation, the designation comes into force on the date specified for this purpose by that authority.

(4) That date must be no earlier than three months after the date on which the designation is confirmed.

(5) A general approval may be given in relation to a description of designations framed by reference to any matters or circumstances.

(6) Accordingly a general approval may (in particular) be given in relation to –

    (a) designations made by a specified local housing authority;

    (b) designations made by a local housing authority falling within a specified description of such authorities;

    (c) designations relating to HMOs of a specified description.

'Specified' means specified by the appropriate national authority in the approval.

(7)If, by virtue of a general approval, a designation does not need to be confirmed before it comes into force, the designation comes into force on the date specified for this purpose in the designation.

(8) That date must be no earlier than three months after the date on which the designation is made.

59 Notification requirements relating to designations

(1) This section applies to a designation –

    (a) when it is confirmed under section 58, or

    (b) (if it is not required to be so confirmed) when it is made by the local housing authority.

(2) As soon as the designation is confirmed or made, the authority must publish in the prescribed manner a notice stating –

(a) that the designation has been made,
(b) whether or not the designation was required to be confirmed and either that it has been confirmed or that a general approval under section 58 applied to it (giving details of the approval in question),
(c) the date on which the designation is to come into force, and
(d) any other information which may be prescribed.

(3) After publication of a notice under subsection (2), and for as long as the designation is in force, the local housing authority must make available to the public in accordance with any prescribed requirements –

(a) copies of the designation, and
(b) such information relating to the designation as is prescribed.

(4) In this section 'prescribed' means prescribed by regulations made by the appropriate national authority.

60 Duration, review and revocation of designations

(1) Unless previously revoked under subsection (4), a designation ceases to have effect at the time that is specified for this purpose in the designation.

(2) That time must be no later than five years after the date on which the designation comes into force.

(3) A local housing authority must from time to time review the operation of any designation made by them.

(4) If following a review they consider it appropriate to do so, the authority may revoke the designation.

(5) If they do revoke the designation, the designation ceases to have effect at the time that is specified by the authority for this purpose.

(6) On revoking a designation the authority must publish notice of the revocation in such manner as is prescribed by regulations made by the appropriate national authority.

HMOs required to be licensed

61 Requirement for HMOs to be licensed

(1) Every HMO to which this Part applies must be licensed under this Part unless –

(a) a temporary exemption notice is in force in relation to it under section 62, or
(b) an interim or final management order is in force in relation to it under Chapter 1 of Part 4.

(2) A licence under this Part is a licence authorising occupation of the house concerned by not more than a maximum number of households or persons specified in the licence.

(3) Sections 63 to 67 deal with applications for licences, the granting or refusal of licences and the imposition of licence conditions.

(4) The local housing authority must take all reasonable steps to secure that applications for licences are made to them in respect of HMOs in their area which are required to be licensed under this Part but are not.

(5) The appropriate national authority may by regulations provide for –

(a) any provision of this Part, or
(b) section 263 (in its operation for the purposes of any such provision),

to have effect in relation to a section 257 HMO with such modifications as are prescribed by the regulations.

A 'section 257 HMO' is an HMO which is a converted block of flats to which section 257 applies.

(6) In this Part (unless the context otherwise requires) –

(a) references to a licence are to a licence under this Part,
(b) references to a licence holder are to be read accordingly, and
(c) references to an HMO being (or not being) licensed under this Part are to its being (or not being) an HMO in respect of which a licence is in force under this Part.

62 Temporary exemption from licensing requirement

(1) This section applies where a person having control of or managing an HMO which is required to be licensed under this Part (see section 61(1)) but is not so licensed, notifies the local housing authority of his intention to take particular steps with a view to securing that the house is no longer required to be licensed.

(2) The authority may, if they think fit, serve on that person a notice under this section ('a temporary exemption notice') in respect of the house.

(3) If a temporary exemption notice is served under this section, the house is (in accordance with sections 61(1) and 85(1)) not required to be licensed either under this Part or under Part 3 during the period for which the notice is in force.

(4) A temporary exemption notice under this section is in force –

(a) for the period of 3 months beginning with the date on which it is served, or
(b) (in the case of a notice served by virtue of subsection (5)) for the period of 3 months after the date when the first notice ceases to be in force.

(5) If the authority –

(a) receive a further notification under subsection (1), and
(b) consider that there are exceptional circumstances that justify the service of a second temporary exemption notice in respect of the house that would take effect from the end of the period of 3 months applying to the first notice,

the authority may serve a second such notice on the person having control of or managing the house (but no further notice may be served by virtue of this subsection).

(6) If the authority decide not to serve a temporary exemption notice in response to a notification under subsection (1), they must without delay serve on the person concerned a notice informing him of –

(a) the decision,
(b) the reasons for it and the date on which it was made,
(c) the right to appeal against the decision under subsection (7), and
(d) the period within which an appeal may be made under that subsection.

(7) The person concerned may appeal to a residential property tribunal against the decision within the period of 28 days beginning with the date specified under subsection (6) as the date on which it was made.

(8) Such an appeal –

(a) is to be by way of a re-hearing, but

(b) may be determined having regard to matters of which the authority were unaware.

(9) The tribunal –

(a) may confirm or reverse the decision of the authority, and
(b) if it reverses the decision, must direct the authority to serve a temporary exemption notice that comes into force on such date as the tribunal directs.

Grant or refusal of licences

63 Applications for licences

(1) An application for a licence must be made to the local housing authority.

(2) The application must be made in accordance with such requirements as the authority may specify.

(3) The authority may, in particular, require the application to be accompanied by a fee fixed by the authority.

(4) The power of the authority to specify requirements under this section is subject to any regulations made under subsection (5).

(5) The appropriate national authority may by regulations make provision about the making of applications under this section.

(6) Such regulations may, in particular –

(a) specify the manner and form in which applications are to be made;
(b) require the applicant to give copies of the application, or information about it, to particular persons;
(c) specify the information which is to be supplied in connection with applications;
(d) specify the maximum fees which are to be charged (whether by specifying amounts or methods for calculating amounts);
(e) specify cases in which no fees are to be charged or fees are to be refunded.

(7) When fixing fees under this section, the local housing authority may (subject to any regulations made under subsection (5)) take into account –

(a) all costs incurred by the authority in carrying out their functions under this Part, and
(b) all costs incurred by them in carrying out their functions under Chapter 1 of Part 4 in relation to HMOs (so far as they are not recoverable under or by virtue of any provision of that Chapter).

64 Grant or refusal of licence

(1) Where an application in respect of an HMO is made to the local housing authority under section 63, the authority must either –

(a) grant a licence in accordance with subsection (2), or
(b) refuse to grant a licence.

(2) If the authority are satisfied as to the matters mentioned in subsection (3), they may grant a licence either –

(a) to the applicant, or
(b) to some other person, if both he and the applicant agree.

(3) The matters are –

(a) that the house is reasonably suitable for occupation by not more than the maximum number of households or persons mentioned in subsection (4) or that it can be made so suitable by the imposition of conditions under section 67;

(b) that the proposed licence holder –
  (i) is a fit and proper person to be the licence holder, and
  (ii) is, out of all the persons reasonably available to be the licence holder in respect of the house, the most appropriate person to be the licence holder;

(c) that the proposed manager of the house is either –
  (i) the person having control of the house, or
  (ii) a person who is an agent or employee of the person having control of the house;

(d) that the proposed manager of the house is a fit and proper person to be the manager of the house; and

(e) that the proposed management arrangements for the house are otherwise satisfactory.

(4) The maximum number of households or persons referred to in subsection (3)(a) is –

(a) the maximum number specified in the application, or
(b) some other maximum number decided by the authority.

(5) Sections 65 and 66 apply for the purposes of this section.

65 Tests as to suitability for multiple occupation

(1) The local housing authority cannot be satisfied for the purposes of section 64(3)(a) that the house is reasonably suitable for occupation by a particular maximum number of households or persons if they consider that it fails to meet prescribed standards for occupation by that number of households or persons.

(2) But the authority may decide that the house is not reasonably suitable for occupation by a particular maximum number of households or persons even if it does meet prescribed standards for occupation by that number of households or persons.

(3) In this section 'prescribed standards' means standards prescribed by regulations made by the appropriate national authority.

(4) The standards that may be so prescribed include –

(a) standards as to the number, type and quality of –
  (i) bathrooms, toilets, washbasins and showers,
  (ii) areas for food storage, preparation and cooking, and
  (iii) laundry facilities,

  which should be available in particular circumstances; and
(b) standards as to the number, type and quality of other facilities or equipment which should be available in particular circumstances.

66 Tests for fitness etc and satisfactory management arrangements

(1) In deciding for the purposes of section 64(3)(b) or (d) whether a person ('P') is a fit and proper person to be the licence holder or (as the case may be) the manager of the house, the local housing authority must have regard (among other things) to any evidence within subsection (2) or (3).

(2) Evidence is within this subsection if it shows that P has –

(a) committed any offence involving fraud or other dishonesty, or violence or drugs, or any offence listed in Schedule 3 to the Sexual Offences Act 2003 (c 42) (offences attracting notification requirements);

(b) practised unlawful discrimination on grounds of sex, colour, race, ethnic or national origins or disability in, or in connection with, the carrying on of any business;

(c) contravened any provision of the law relating to housing or of landlord and tenant law; or

(d) acted otherwise than in accordance with any applicable code of practice approved under section 233.

(3) Evidence is within this subsection if –

(a) it shows that any person associated or formerly associated with P (whether on a personal, work or other basis) has done any of the things set out in subsection (2)(a) to (d), and

(b) it appears to the authority that the evidence is relevant to the question whether P is a fit and proper person to be the licence holder or (as the case may be) the manager of the house.

(4) For the purposes of section 64(3)(b) the local housing authority must assume, unless the contrary is shown, that the person having control of the house is a more appropriate person to be the licence holder than a person not having control of it.

(5) In deciding for the purposes of section 64(3)(e) whether the proposed management arrangements for the house are otherwise satisfactory, the local housing authority must have regard (among other things) to the considerations mentioned in subsection (6).

(6) The considerations are –

(a) whether any person proposed to be involved in the management of the house has a sufficient level of competence to be so involved;

(b) whether any person proposed to be involved in the management of the house (other than the manager) is a fit and proper person to be so involved; and

(c) whether any proposed management structures and funding arrangements are suitable.

(7) Any reference in section 64(3)(c)(i) or (ii) or subsection (4) above to a person having control of the house, or to being a person of any other description, includes a reference to a person who is proposing to have control of the house, or (as the case may be) to be a person of that description, at the time when the licence would come into force.

67 Licence conditions

(1) A licence may include such conditions as the local housing authority consider appropriate for regulating all or any of the following –

(a) the management, use and occupation of the house concerned, and

(b) its condition and contents.

(2) Those conditions may, in particular, include (so far as appropriate in the circumstances) –

(a) conditions imposing restrictions or prohibitions on the use or occupation of particular parts of the house by persons occupying it;

(b) conditions requiring the taking of reasonable and practicable steps to prevent or reduce anti-social behaviour by persons occupying or visiting the house;

(c) conditions requiring facilities and equipment to be made available in the house for the purpose of meeting standards prescribed under section 65;

(d) conditions requiring such facilities and equipment to be kept in repair and proper working order;

(e) conditions requiring, in the case of any works needed in order for any such facilities or equipment to be made available or to meet any such standards, that the works are carried out within such period or periods as may be specified in, or determined under, the licence;

(f) conditions requiring the licence holder or the manager of the house to attend training courses in relation to any applicable code of practice approved under section 233.

(3) A licence must include the conditions required by Schedule 4.

(4) As regards the relationship between the authority's power to impose conditions under this section and functions exercisable by them under or for the purposes of Part 1 ('Part 1 functions') –

  (a) the authority must proceed on the basis that, in general, they should seek to identify, remove or reduce category 1 or category 2 hazards in the house by the exercise of Part 1 functions and not by means of licence conditions;
  (b) this does not, however, prevent the authority from imposing licence conditions relating to the installation or maintenance of facilities or equipment within subsection (2)(c) above, even if the same result could be achieved by the exercise of Part 1 functions;
  (c) the fact that licence conditions are imposed for a particular purpose that could be achieved by the exercise of Part 1 functions does not affect the way in which Part 1 functions can be subsequently exercised by the authority.

(5) A licence may not include conditions imposing restrictions or obligations on a particular person other than the licence holder unless that person has consented to the imposition of the restrictions or obligations.

(6) A licence may not include conditions requiring (or intended to secure) any alteration in the terms of any tenancy or licence under which any person occupies the house.

68 Licences: general requirements and duration

(1) A licence may not relate to more than one HMO.

(2) A licence may be granted before the time when it is required by virtue of this Part but, if so, the licence cannot come into force until that time.

(3) A licence –

  (a) comes into force at the time that is specified in or determined under the licence for this purpose, and
  (b) unless previously terminated by subsection (7) or revoked under section 70, continues in force for the period that is so specified or determined.

(4) That period must not end more than 5 years after –

  (a) the date on which the licence was granted, or
  (b) if the licence was granted as mentioned in subsection (2), the date when the licence comes into force.

(5) Subsection (3)(b) applies even if, at any time during that period, the HMO concerned subsequently ceases to be one to which this Part applies.

(6) A licence may not be transferred to another person.

(7) If the holder of the licence dies while the licence is in force, the licence ceases to be in force on his death.

(8) However, during the period of 3 months beginning with the date of the licence holder's death, the house is to be treated for the purposes of this Part and Part 3 as if on that date a temporary exemption notice had been served in respect of the house under section 62.

(9) If, at any time during that period ('the initial period'), the personal representatives of the licence holder request the local housing authority to do so, the authority may serve on them a notice which, during the period of 3 months after the date on which the initial period ends, has the same effect as a temporary exemption notice under section 62.

(10) Subsections (6) to (8) of section 62 apply (with any necessary modifications) in relation to a decision by the authority not to serve such a notice as they apply in relation to a decision not to serve a temporary exemption notice.

Variation and revocation of licences

69 Variation of licences

(1) The local housing authority may vary a licence –

(a) if they do so with the agreement of the licence holder, or
(b) if they consider that there has been a change of circumstances since the time when the licence was granted.

For this purpose 'change of circumstances' includes any discovery of new information.

(2) Subsection (3) applies where the authority –

(a) are considering whether to vary a licence under subsection (1)(b); and
(b) are considering –
(i) what number of households or persons is appropriate as the maximum number authorised to occupy the HMO to which the licence relates, or
(ii) the standards applicable to occupation by a particular number of households or persons.

(3) The authority must apply the same standards in relation to the circumstances existing at the time when they are considering whether to vary the licence as were applicable at the time when it was granted.

This is subject to subsection (4).

(4) If the standards –

(a) prescribed under section 65, and
(b) applicable at the time when the licence was granted,

have subsequently been revised or superseded by provisions of regulations under that section, the authority may apply the new standards.

(5) A variation made with the agreement of the licence holder takes effect at the time when it is made.

(6) Otherwise, a variation does not come into force until such time, if any, as is the operative time for the purposes of this subsection under paragraph 35 of Schedule 5 (time when period for appealing expires without an appeal being made or when decision to vary is confirmed on appeal).

(7) The power to vary a licence under this section is exercisable by the authority either –

(a) on an application made by the licence holder or a relevant person, or
(b) on the authority's own initiative.

(8) In subsection (7) 'relevant person' means any person (other than the licence holder) –

(a) who has an estate or interest in the HMO concerned (but is not a tenant under a lease with an unexpired term of 3 years or less), or
(b) who is a person managing or having control of the house (and does not fall within paragraph (a)), or
(c) on whom any restriction or obligation is imposed by the licence in accordance with section 67(5).

70 Revocation of licences

(1) The local housing authority may revoke a licence –

  (a) if they do so with the agreement of the licence holder;
  (b) in any of the cases mentioned in subsection (2) (circumstances relating to licence holder or other person);
  (c) in any of the cases mentioned in subsection (3) (circumstances relating to HMO concerned); or
  (d) in any other circumstances prescribed by regulations made by the appropriate national authority.

(2) The cases referred to in subsection (1)(b) are as follows –

  (a) where the authority consider that the licence holder or any other person has committed a serious breach of a condition of the licence or repeated breaches of such a condition;
  (b) where the authority no longer consider that the licence holder is a fit and proper person to be the licence holder; and
  (c) where the authority no longer consider that the management of the house is being carried on by persons who are in each case fit and proper persons to be involved in its management.

Section 66(1) applies in relation to paragraph (b) or (c) above as it applies in relation to section 64(3)(b) or (d).

(3) The cases referred to in subsection (1)(c) are as follows –

  (a) where the HMO to which the licence relates ceases to be an HMO to which this Part applies; and
  (b) where the authority consider at any time that, were the licence to expire at that time, they would, for a particular reason relating to the structure of the HMO, refuse to grant a new licence to the licence holder on similar terms in respect of it.

(4) Subsection (5) applies where the authority are considering whether to revoke a licence by virtue of subsection (3)(b) on the grounds that the HMO is not reasonably suitable for the number of households or persons specified in the licence as the maximum number authorised to occupy the house.

(5) The authority must apply the same standards in relation to the circumstances existing at the time when they are considering whether to revoke the licence as were applicable at the time when it was granted.

This is subject to subsection (6).

(6) If the standards –

  (a) prescribed under section 65, and
  (b) applicable at the time when the licence was granted,

have subsequently been revised or superseded by provisions of regulations under that section, the authority may apply the new standards.

(7) A revocation made with the agreement of the licence holder takes effect at the time when it is made.

(8) Otherwise, a revocation does not come into force until such time, if any, as is the operative time for the purposes of this subsection under paragraph 35 of Schedule 5 (time when period for appealing expires without an appeal being made or when decision to vary is confirmed on appeal).

(9) The power to revoke a licence under this section is exercisable by the authority either –

(a) on an application made by the licence holder or a relevant person, or

(b) on the authority's own initiative.

(10) In subsection (9) 'relevant person' means any person (other than the licence holder) –

(a) who has an estate or interest in the HMO concerned (but is not a tenant under a lease with an unexpired term of 3 years or less), or

(b) who is a person managing or having control of that house (and does not fall within paragraph (a)), or

(c) on whom any restriction or obligation is imposed by the licence in accordance with section 67(5).

Procedure and appeals

71 Procedural requirements and appeals against licence decisions

Schedule 5 (which deals with procedural requirements relating to the grant, refusal, variation or revocation of licences and with appeals against licence decisions) has effect for the purposes of this Part.

Enforcement

72 Offences in relation to licensing of HMOs

(1) A person commits an offence if he is a person having control of or managing an HMO which is required to be licensed under this Part (see section 61(1)) but is not so licensed.

(2) A person commits an offence if –

(a) he is a person having control of or managing an HMO which is licensed under this Part,

(b) he knowingly permits another person to occupy the house, and

(c) the other person's occupation results in the house being occupied by more households or persons than is authorised by the licence.

(3) A person commits an offence if –

(a) he is a licence holder or a person on whom restrictions or obligations under a licence are imposed in accordance with section 67(5), and

(b) he fails to comply with any condition of the licence.

(4) In proceedings against a person for an offence under subsection (1) it is a defence that, at the material time –

(a) a notification had been duly given in respect of the house under section 62(1), or

(b) an application for a licence had been duly made in respect of the house under section 63,

and that notification or application was still effective (see subsection (8)).

(5) In proceedings against a person for an offence under subsection (1), (2) or (3) it is a defence that he had a reasonable excuse –

(a) for having control of or managing the house in the circumstances mentioned in subsection (1), or

(b) for permitting the person to occupy the house, or

(c) for failing to comply with the condition,

as the case may be.

(6) A person who commits an offence under subsection (1) or (2) is liable on summary conviction to a fine not exceeding £20,000.

(7) A person who commits an offence under subsection (3) is liable on summary conviction to a fine not exceeding level 5 on the standard scale.

(8) For the purposes of subsection (4) a notification or application is 'effective' at a particular time if at that time it has not been withdrawn, and either –

(a) the authority have not decided whether to serve a temporary exemption notice, or (as the case may be) grant a licence, in pursuance of the notification or application, or
(b) if they have decided not to do so, one of the conditions set out in subsection (9) is met.

(9) The conditions are –

(a) that the period for appealing against the decision of the authority not to serve or grant such a notice or licence (or against any relevant decision of a residential property tribunal) has not expired, or
(b) that an appeal has been brought against the authority's decision (or against any relevant decision of such a tribunal) and the appeal has not been determined or withdrawn.

(10) In subsection (9) 'relevant decision' means a decision which is given on an appeal to the tribunal and confirms the authority's decision (with or without variation).

73 Other consequences of operating unlicensed HMOs: rent repayment orders

(1) For the purposes of this section an HMO is an 'unlicensed HMO' if –

(a) it is required to be licensed under this Part but is not so licensed, and
(b) neither of the conditions in subsection (2) is satisfied.

(2) The conditions are –

(a) that a notification has been duly given in respect of the HMO under section 62(1) and that notification is still effective (as defined by section 72(8));
(b) that an application for a licence has been duly made in respect of the HMO under section 63 and that application is still effective (as so defined).

(3) No rule of law relating to the validity or enforceability of contracts in circumstances involving illegality is to affect the validity or enforceability of –

(a) any provision requiring the payment of rent or the making of any other periodical payment in connection with any tenancy or licence of a part of an unlicensed HMO, or
(b) any other provision of such a tenancy or licence.

(4) But amounts paid in respect of rent or other periodical payments payable in connection with such a tenancy or licence may be recovered in accordance with subsection (5) and section 74.

(5) If –

(a) an application in respect of an HMO is made to a residential property tribunal by the local housing authority or an occupier of a part of the HMO, and
(b) the tribunal is satisfied as to the matters mentioned in subsection (6) or (8),

the tribunal may make an order (a 'rent repayment order') requiring the appropriate person to pay to the applicant such amount in respect of the housing benefit paid as mentioned in subsection (6)(b), or (as the case may be) the periodical payments paid as mentioned in subsection (8)(b), as is specified in the order (see section 74(2) to (8)).

(6) If the application is made by the local housing authority, the tribunal must be satisfied as to the following matters –

- (a) that, at any time within the period of 12 months ending with the date of the notice of intended proceedings required by subsection (7), the appropriate person has committed an offence under section 72(1) in relation to the HMO (whether or not he has been charged or convicted),
- (b) that housing benefit has been paid (to any person) in respect of periodical payments payable in connection with the occupation of a part or parts of the HMO during any period during which it appears to the tribunal that such an offence was being committed, and
- (c) that the requirements of subsection (7) have been complied with in relation to the application.

(7) Those requirements are as follows –

- (a) the authority must have served on the appropriate person a notice (a 'notice of intended proceedings') –
    - (i)   informing him that the authority are proposing to make an application under subsection (5),
    - (ii)   setting out the reasons why they propose to do so,
    - (iii) stating the amount that they will seek to recover under that subsection and how that amount is calculated, and
    - (iv) inviting him to make representations to them within a period specified in the notice of not less than 28 days;
- (b) that period must have expired; and
- (c) the authority must have considered any representations made to them within that period by the appropriate person.

(8) If the application is made by an occupier of a part of the HMO, the tribunal must be satisfied as to the following matters –

- (a) that the appropriate person has been convicted of an offence under section 72(1) in relation to the HMO, or has been required by a rent repayment order to make a payment in respect of housing benefit paid in connection with occupation of a part or parts of the HMO,
- (b) that the occupier paid, to a person having control of or managing the HMO, periodical payments in respect of occupation of part of the HMO during any period during which it appears to the tribunal that such an offence was being committed in relation to the HMO, and
- (c) that the application is made within the period of 12 months beginning with –
    - (i)   the date of the conviction or order, or
    - (ii)   if such a conviction was followed by such an order (or vice versa), the date of the later of them.

(9) Where a local housing authority serve a notice of intended proceedings on any person under this section, they must ensure –

- (a) that a copy of the notice is received by the department of the authority responsible for administering the housing benefit to which the proceedings would relate; and
- (b) that that department is subsequently kept informed of any matters relating to the proceedings that are likely to be of interest to it in connection with the administration of housing benefit.

(10) In this section –

'the appropriate person', in relation to any payment of housing benefit or periodical payment payable in connection with occupation of a part of an HMO, means the person who at the time of the payment was entitled to receive on his own account periodical payments payable in connection with such occupation;

'housing benefit' means housing benefit provided by virtue of a scheme under section 123 of the Social Security Contributions and Benefits Act 1992 (c 4);

'occupier', in relation to any periodical payment, means a person who was an occupier at the time of the payment, whether under a tenancy or licence or otherwise (and 'occupation' has a corresponding meaning);

'periodical payments' means periodical payments in respect of which housing benefit may be paid by virtue of regulation 10 of the Housing Benefit (General) Regulations 1987 (SI 1987/1971) or any corresponding provision replacing that regulation.

(11) For the purposes of this section an amount which –

(a) is not actually paid by an occupier but is used by him to discharge the whole or part of his liability in respect of a periodical payment (for example, by offsetting the amount against any such liability), and
(b) is not an amount of housing benefit,

is to be regarded as an amount paid by the occupier in respect of that periodical payment.

74 Further provisions about rent repayment orders

(1) This section applies in relation to rent repayment orders made by residential property tribunals under section 73(5).

(2) Where, on an application by the local housing authority, the tribunal is satisfied –

(a) that a person has been convicted of an offence under section 72(1) in relation to the HMO, and
(b) that housing benefit was paid (whether or not to the appropriate person) in respect of periodical payments payable in connection with occupation of a part or parts of the HMO during any period during which it appears to the tribunal that such an offence was being committed in relation to the HMO,

the tribunal must make a rent repayment order requiring the appropriate person to pay to the authority an amount equal to the total amount of housing benefit paid as mentioned in paragraph (b).

This is subject to subsections (3), (4) and (8).

(3) If the total of the amounts received by the appropriate person in respect of periodical payments payable as mentioned in paragraph (b) of subsection (2) ('the rent total') is less than the total amount of housing benefit paid as mentioned in that paragraph, the amount required to be paid by virtue of a rent repayment order made in accordance with that subsection is limited to the rent total.

(4) A rent repayment order made in accordance with subsection (2) may not require the payment of any amount which the tribunal is satisfied that, by reason of any exceptional circumstances, it would be unreasonable for that person to be required to pay.

(5) In a case where subsection (2) does not apply, the amount required to be paid by virtue of a rent repayment order under section 73(5) is to be such amount as the tribunal considers reasonable in the circumstances.

This is subject to subsections (6) to (8).

(6) In such a case the tribunal must, in particular, take into account the following matters –

(a) the total amount of relevant payments paid in connection with occupation of the HMO during any period during which it appears to the tribunal that an offence was being committed by the appropriate person in relation to the HMO under section 72(1);

(b) the extent to which that total amount –

    (i) consisted of, or derived from, payments of housing benefit, and

    (ii) was actually received by the appropriate person;

(c) whether the appropriate person has at any time been convicted of an offence under section 72(1) in relation to the HMO;

(d) the conduct and financial circumstances of the appropriate person; and

(e) where the application is made by an occupier, the conduct of the occupier.

(7) In subsection (6) 'relevant payments' means –

(a) in relation to an application by a local housing authority, payments of housing benefit or periodical payments payable by occupiers;

(b) in relation to an application by an occupier, periodical payments payable by the occupier, less any amount of housing benefit payable in respect of occupation of the part of the HMO occupied by him during the period in question.

(8) A rent repayment order may not require the payment of any amount which –

(a) (where the application is made by a local housing authority) is in respect of any time falling outside the period of 12 months mentioned in section 73(6)(a); or

(b) (where the application is made by an occupier) is in respect of any time falling outside the period of 12 months ending with the date of the occupier's application under section 73(5);

and the period to be taken into account under subsection (6)(a) above is restricted accordingly.

(9) Any amount payable to a local housing authority under a rent repayment order –

(a) does not, when recovered by the authority, constitute an amount of housing benefit recovered by them, and

(b) until recovered by them, is a legal charge on the HMO which is a local land charge.

(10) For the purpose of enforcing that charge the authority have the same powers and remedies under the Law of Property Act 1925 (c 20) and otherwise as if they were mortgagees by deed having powers of sale and lease, and of accepting surrenders of leases and of appointing a receiver.

(11) The power of appointing a receiver is exercisable at any time after the end of the period of one month beginning with the date on which the charge takes effect.

(12) If the authority subsequently grant a licence under this Part or Part 3 in respect of the HMO to the appropriate person or any person acting on his behalf, the conditions contained in the licence may include a condition requiring the licence holder –

(a) to pay to the authority any amount payable to them under the rent repayment order and not so far recovered by them; and

(b) to do so in such instalments as are specified in the licence.

(13) If the authority subsequently make a management order under Chapter 1 of Part 4 in respect of the HMO, the order may contain such provisions as the authority consider appropriate for the recovery of any amount payable to them under the rent repayment order and not so far recovered by them.

(14) Any amount payable to an occupier by virtue of a rent repayment order is recoverable by the occupier as a debt due to him from the appropriate person.

(15) The appropriate national authority may by regulations make such provision as it considers appropriate for supplementing the provisions of this section and section 73, and in particular –

(a) for securing that persons are not unfairly prejudiced by rent repayment orders (whether in cases where there have been over-payments of housing benefit or otherwise);

(b) for requiring or authorising amounts received by local housing authorities by virtue of rent repayment orders to be dealt with in such manner as is specified in the regulations.

(16) Section 73(10) and (11) apply for the purposes of this section as they apply for the purposes of section 73.

75 Other consequences of operating unlicensed HMOs: restriction on terminating tenancies

(1) No section 21 notice may be given in relation to a shorthold tenancy of a part of an unlicensed HMO so long as it remains such an HMO.

(2) In this section –

a 'section 21 notice' means a notice under section 21(1)(b) or (4)(a) of the Housing Act 1988 (c 50) (recovery of possession on termination of shorthold tenancy);

a 'shorthold tenancy' means an assured shorthold tenancy within the meaning of Chapter 2 of Part 1 of that Act;

'unlicensed HMO' has the same meaning as in section 73 of this Act.

Supplementary provisions

76 Transitional arrangements relating to introduction and termination of licensing

(1) Subsection (2) applies where –

(a) an order under section 55(3) which prescribes a particular description of HMOs comes into force; or

(b) a designation under section 56 comes into force in relation to HMOs of a particular description.

(2) This Part applies in relation to the occupation by persons or households of such HMOs on or after the coming into force of the order or designation even if their occupation began before, or in pursuance of a contract made before, it came into force.

This is subject to subsections (3) to (5).

(3) Subsection (4) applies where –

(a) an HMO which is licensed under this Part, or a part of such an HMO, is occupied by more households or persons than the number permitted by the licence; and

(b) the occupation of all or any of those households or persons began before, or in pursuance of a contract made before, the licence came into force.

(4) In proceedings against a person for an offence under section 72(2) it is a defence that at the material time he was taking all reasonable steps to try to reduce the number of households or persons occupying the house to the number permitted by the licence.

(5) Subsection (4) does not apply if the licence came into force immediately after a previous licence in respect of the same HMO unless the occupation in question began before, or in pursuance of a contract made before, the coming into force of the original licence.

(6) An order under section 270 may make provision as regards the licensing under this Part of HMOs –

(a) which are registered immediately before the appointed day under a scheme to which section 347 (schemes containing control provisions) or 348B (schemes containing special control provisions) of the Housing Act 1985 (c 68) applies, or

(b) in respect of which applications for registration under such a scheme are then pending.

(7) In subsection (6) 'the appointed day' means the day appointed for the coming into force of section 61.

77 Meaning of 'HMO'

In this Part –

(a) 'HMO' means a house in multiple occupation as defined by sections 254 to 259, and

(b) references to an HMO include (where the context permits) any yard, garden, outhouses and appurtenances belonging to, or usually enjoyed with, it (or any part of it).

78 Index of defined expressions: Part 2

The following table shows where expressions used in this Part are defined or otherwise explained.

Expression	*Provision of this Act*
Anti-social behaviour	Section 57(5)
Appropriate national authority	Section 261(1)
Category 1 hazard	Section 2(1)
Category 2 hazard	Section 2(1)
District of local housing authority	Section 261(6)
HMO	Section 77
HMO to which this Part applies	Section 55(2)
Licence and licence holder	Section 61(6)
Licence (to occupy premises)	Section 262(9)
Local housing authority	Section 261(2) to (5)
Modifications	Section 250(7)
Occupier (and related expressions)	Section 262(6)
Person having control	Section 263(1) and (2) (and see also section 66(7))
Person having estate or interest	Section 262(8)
Person managing	Section 263(3)
Person involved in management	Section 263(5)
Residential property tribunal	Section 229
Tenant	Section 262(1) to (5).

Part 3
Selective Licensing of Other Residential Accommodation

Introductory

79 Licensing of houses to which this Part applies

(1) This Part provides for houses to be licensed by local housing authorities where –

(a) they are houses to which this Part applies (see subsection (2)), and

(b) they are required to be licensed under this Part (see section 85(1)).

(2) This Part applies to a house if –

    (a) it is in an area that is for the time being designated under section 80 as subject to selective licensing, and

    (b) the whole of it is occupied either –

        (i) under a single tenancy or licence that is not an exempt tenancy or licence under subsection (3) or (4), or

        (ii) under two or more tenancies or licences in respect of different dwellings contained in it, none of which is an exempt tenancy or licence under subsection (3) or (4).

(3) A tenancy or licence is an exempt tenancy or licence if it is granted by a body which is registered as a social landlord under Part 1 of the Housing Act 1996 (c 52).

(4) In addition, the appropriate national authority may by order provide for a tenancy or licence to be an exempt tenancy or licence –

    (a) if it falls within any description of tenancy or licence specified in the order; or

    (b) in any other circumstances so specified.

(5) Every local housing authority have the following general duties –

    (a) to make such arrangements as are necessary to secure the effective implementation in their district of the licensing regime provided for by this Part; and

    (b) to ensure that all applications for licences and other issues falling to be determined by them under this Part are determined within a reasonable time.

Designation of selective licensing areas

80 Designation of selective licensing areas

(1) A local housing authority may designate either –

    (a) the area of their district, or

    (b) an area in their district,

as subject to selective licensing, if the requirements of subsections (2) and (9) are met.

(2) The authority must consider that –

    (a) the first or second set of general conditions mentioned in subsection (3) or (6), or

    (b) any conditions specified in an order under subsection (7) as an additional set of conditions,

are satisfied in relation to the area.

(3) The first set of general conditions are –

    (a) that the area is, or is likely to become, an area of low housing demand; and

    (b) that making a designation will, when combined with other measures taken in the area by the local housing authority, or by other persons together with the local housing authority, contribute to the improvement of the social or economic conditions in the area.

(4) In deciding whether an area is, or is likely to become, an area of low housing demand a local housing authority must take into account (among other matters) –

    (a) the value of residential premises in the area, in comparison to the value of similar premises in other areas which the authority consider to be comparable (whether in terms of types of housing, local amenities, availability of transport or otherwise);

    (b) the turnover of occupiers of residential premises;

    (c) the number of residential premises which are available to buy or rent and the length of time for which they remain unoccupied.

(5) The appropriate national authority may by order amend subsection (4) by adding new matters to those for the time being mentioned in that subsection.

(6) The second set of general conditions are –

    (a) that the area is experiencing a significant and persistent problem caused by anti-social behaviour;

    (b) that some or all of the private sector landlords who have let premises in the area (whether under leases or licences) are failing to take action to combat the problem that it would be appropriate for them to take; and

    (c) that making a designation will, when combined with other measures taken in the area by the local housing authority, or by other persons together with the local housing authority, lead to a reduction in, or the elimination of, the problem.

    'Private sector landlord' does not include a registered social landlord within the meaning of Part 1 of the Housing Act 1996 (c 52).

(7) The appropriate national authority may by order provide for any conditions specified in the order to apply as an additional set of conditions for the purposes of subsection (2).

(8) The conditions that may be specified include, in particular, conditions intended to permit a local housing authority to make a designation for the purpose of dealing with one or more specified problems affecting persons occupying Part 3 houses in the area.

    'Specified' means specified in an order under subsection (7).

(9) Before making a designation the local housing authority must –

    (a) take reasonable steps to consult persons who are likely to be affected by the designation; and

    (b) consider any representations made in accordance with the consultation and not withdrawn.

(10) Section 81 applies for the purposes of this section.

81 Designations under section 80: further considerations

(1) This section applies to the power of a local housing authority to make designations under section 80.

(2) The authority must ensure that any exercise of the power is consistent with the authority's overall housing strategy.

(3) The authority must also seek to adopt a co-ordinated approach in connection with dealing with homelessness, empty properties and anti-social behaviour, both –

    (a) as regards combining licensing under this Part with other courses of action available to them, and

    (b) as regards combining such licensing with measures taken by other persons.

(4) The authority must not make a particular designation under section 80 unless –

    (a) they have considered whether there are any other courses of action available to them (of whatever nature) that might provide an effective method of achieving the objective or objectives that the designation would be intended to achieve, and

    (b) they consider that making the designation will significantly assist them to achieve the objective or objectives (whether or not they take any other course of action as well).

82 Designation needs confirmation or general approval to be effective

(1) A designation of an area as subject to selective licensing cannot come into force unless –

- (a) it has been confirmed by the appropriate national authority; or
- (b) it falls within a description of designations in relation to which that authority has given a general approval in accordance with subsection (6).

(2) The appropriate national authority may either confirm, or refuse to confirm, a designation as it considers appropriate.

(3) If the appropriate national authority confirms a designation, the designation comes into force on a date specified for this purpose by that authority.

(4) That date must be no earlier than three months after the date on which the designation is confirmed.

(5) A general approval may be given in relation to a description of designations framed by reference to any matters or circumstances.

(6) Accordingly a general approval may (in particular) be given in relation to –

- (a) designations made by a specified local housing authority;
- (b) designations made by a local housing authority falling within a specified description of such authorities;
- (c) designations relating to Part 3 houses of a specified description.

'Specified' means specified by the appropriate national authority in the approval.

(7) If, by virtue of a general approval, a designation does not need to be confirmed before it comes into force, the designation comes into force on the date specified for this purpose in the designation.

(8) That date must be no earlier than three months after the date on which the designation is made.

(9) Where a designation comes into force, this Part applies in relation to the occupation by persons of houses in the area on or after the coming into force of the designation even if their occupation began before, or in pursuance of a contract made before, it came into force.

83 Notification requirements relating to designations

(1) This section applies to a designation –

- (a) when it is confirmed under section 82, or
- (b) (if it is not required to be so confirmed) when it is made by the local housing authority.

(2) As soon as the designation is confirmed or made, the authority must publish in the prescribed manner a notice stating –

- (a) that the designation has been made,
- (b) whether or not the designation was required to be confirmed and either that it has been confirmed or that a general approval under section 82 applied to it (giving details of the approval in question),
- (c) the date on which the designation is to come into force, and
- (d) any other information which may be prescribed.

(3) After publication of a notice under subsection (2), and for as long as the designation is in force, the local housing authority must make available to the public in accordance with any prescribed requirements –

- (a) copies of the designation, and

(b) such information relating to the designation as is prescribed.

(4) In this section 'prescribed' means prescribed by regulations made by the appropriate national authority.

84 Duration, review and revocation of designations

(1) Unless previously revoked under subsection (4), a designation ceases to have effect at the time that is specified for this purpose in the designation.

(2) That time must be no later than five years after the date on which the designation comes into force.

(3) A local housing authority must from time to time review the operation of any designation made by them.

(4) If following a review they consider it appropriate to do so, the authority may revoke the designation.

(5) If they do revoke the designation, the designation ceases to have effect on the date that is specified by the authority for this purpose.

(6) On revoking a designation, the authority must publish notice of the revocation in such manner as is prescribed by regulations made by the appropriate national authority.

Houses required to be licensed

85 Requirement for Part 3 houses to be licensed

(1) Every Part 3 house must be licensed under this Part unless –

(a) it is an HMO to which Part 2 applies (see section 55(2)), or
(b) a temporary exemption notice is in force in relation to it under section 86, or
(c) a management order is in force in relation to it under Chapter 1 or 2 of Part 4.

(2) A licence under this Part is a licence authorising occupation of the house concerned under one or more tenancies or licences within section 79(2)(b).

(3) Sections 87 to 90 deal with applications for licences, the granting or refusal of licences and the imposition of licence conditions.

(4) The local housing authority must take all reasonable steps to secure that applications for licences are made to them in respect of houses in their area which are required to be licensed under this Part but are not so licensed.

(5) In this Part, unless the context otherwise requires –

(a) references to a Part 3 house are to a house to which this Part applies (see section 79(2)),
(b) references to a licence are to a licence under this Part,
(c) references to a licence holder are to be read accordingly, and
(d) references to a house being (or not being) licensed under this Part are to its being (or not being) a house in respect of which a licence is in force under this Part.

86 Temporary exemption from licensing requirement

(1) This section applies where a person having control of or managing a Part 3 house which is required to be licensed under this Part (see section 85(1)) but is not so licensed, notifies the local housing authority of his intention to take particular steps with a view to securing that the house is no longer required to be licensed.

(2) The authority may, if they think fit, serve on that person a notice under this section ('a temporary exemption notice') in respect of the house.

(3) If a temporary exemption notice is served under this section, the house is (in accordance with section 85(1)) not required to be licensed under this Part during the period for which the notice is in force.

(4) A temporary exemption notice under this section is in force –

(a) for the period of 3 months beginning with the date on which it is served, or
(b) (in the case of a notice served by virtue of subsection (5)) for the period of 3 months after the date when the first notice ceases to be in force.

(5) If the authority –

(a) receive a further notification under subsection (1), and
(b) consider that there are exceptional circumstances that justify the service of a second temporary exemption notice in respect of the house that would take effect from the end of the period of 3 months applying to the first notice,

the authority may serve a second such notice on the person having control of or managing the house (but no further notice may be served by virtue of this subsection).

(6) If the authority decide not to serve a temporary exemption notice in response to a notification under subsection (1), they must without delay serve on the person concerned a notice informing him of –

(a) the decision,
(b) the reasons for it and the date on which it was made,
(c) the right to appeal against the decision under subsection (7), and
(d) the period within which an appeal may be made under that subsection.

(7) The person concerned may appeal to a residential property tribunal against the decision within the period of 28 days beginning with the date specified under subsection (6) as the date on which it was made.

(8) Such an appeal –

(a) is to be by way of a re-hearing, but
(b) may be determined having regard to matters of which the authority were unaware.

(9) The tribunal –

(a) may confirm or reverse the decision of the authority, and
(b) if it reverses the decision, must direct the authority to issue a temporary exemption notice with effect from such date as the tribunal directs.

Grant or refusal of licences

87 Applications for licences

(1) An application for a licence must be made to the local housing authority.

(2) The application must be made in accordance with such requirements as the authority may specify.

(3) The authority may, in particular, require the application to be accompanied by a fee fixed by the authority.

(4) The power of the authority to specify requirements under this section is subject to any regulations made under subsection (5).

(5) The appropriate national authority may by regulations make provision about the making of applications under this section.

(6) Such regulations may, in particular –

(a) specify the manner and form in which applications are to be made;
(b) require the applicant to give copies of the application, or information about it, to particular persons;
(c) specify the information which is to be supplied in connection with applications;
(d) specify the maximum fees which may be charged (whether by specifying amounts or methods for calculating amounts);
(e) specify cases in which no fees are to be charged or fees are to be refunded.

(7) When fixing fees under this section, the local housing authority may (subject to any regulations made under subsection (5)) take into account –

(a) all costs incurred by the authority in carrying out their functions under this Part, and
(b) all costs incurred by them in carrying out their functions under Chapter 1 of Part 4 in relation to Part 3 houses (so far as they are not recoverable under or by virtue of any provision of that Chapter).

88 Grant or refusal of licence

(1) Where an application in respect of a house is made to the local housing authority under section 87, the authority must either –

(a) grant a licence in accordance with subsection (2), or
(b) refuse to grant a licence.

(2) If the authority are satisfied as to the matters mentioned in subsection (3), they may grant a licence either –

(a) to the applicant, or
(b) to some other person, if both he and the applicant agree.

(3) The matters are –

(a) that the proposed licence holder –
   (i) is a fit and proper person to be the licence holder, and
   (ii) is, out of all the persons reasonably available to be the licence holder in respect of the house, the most appropriate person to be the licence holder;
(b) that the proposed manager of the house is either –
   (i) the person having control of the house, or
   (ii) a person who is an agent or employee of the person having control of the house;
(c) that the proposed manager of the house is a fit and proper person to be the manager of the house; and
(d) that the proposed management arrangements for the house are otherwise satisfactory.

(4) Section 89 applies for the purposes of this section.

89 Tests for fitness etc and satisfactory management arrangements

(1) In deciding for the purposes of section 88(3)(a) or (c) whether a person ('P') is a fit and proper person to be the licence holder or (as the case may be) the manager of the house, the local housing authority must have regard (among other things) to any evidence within subsection (2) or (3).

(2) Evidence is within this subsection if it shows that P has –

    (a) committed any offence involving fraud or other dishonesty, or violence or drugs, or any offence listed in Schedule 3 to the Sexual Offences Act 2003 (c 42) (offences attracting notification requirements);

    (b) practised unlawful discrimination on grounds of sex, colour, race, ethnic or national origins or disability in, or in connection with, the carrying on of any business; or

    (c) contravened any provision of the law relating to housing or of landlord and tenant law.

(3) Evidence is within this subsection if –

    (a) it shows that any person associated or formerly associated with P (whether on a personal, work or other basis) has done any of the things set out in subsection (2)(a) to (c), and

    (b) it appears to the authority that the evidence is relevant to the question whether P is a fit and proper person to be the licence holder or (as the case may be) the manager of the house.

(4) For the purposes of section 88(3)(a) the local housing authority must assume, unless the contrary is shown, that the person having control of the house is a more appropriate person to be the licence holder than a person not having control of it.

(5) In deciding for the purposes of section 88(3)(d) whether the proposed management arrangements for the house are otherwise satisfactory, the local housing authority must have regard (among other things) to the considerations mentioned in subsection (6).

(6) The considerations are –

    (a) whether any person proposed to be involved in the management of the house has a sufficient level of competence to be so involved;

    (b) whether any person proposed to be involved in the management of the house (other than the manager) is a fit and proper person to be so involved; and

    (c) whether any proposed management structures and funding arrangements are suitable.

(7) Any reference in section 88(3)(b)(i) or (ii) or subsection (4) above to a person having control of the house, or to being a person of any other description, includes a reference to a person who is proposing to have control of the house, or (as the case may be) to be a person of that description, at the time when the licence would come into force.

90 Licence conditions

(1) A licence may include such conditions as the local housing authority consider appropriate for regulating the management, use or occupation of the house concerned.

(2) Those conditions may, in particular, include (so far as appropriate in the circumstances) –

    (a) conditions imposing restrictions or prohibitions on the use or occupation of particular parts of the house by persons occupying it;

    (b) conditions requiring the taking of reasonable and practicable steps to prevent or reduce anti-social behaviour by persons occupying or visiting the house.

(3) A licence may also include –

    (a) conditions requiring facilities and equipment to be made available in the house for the purpose of meeting standards prescribed for the purposes of this section by regulations made by the appropriate national authority;

    (b) conditions requiring such facilities and equipment to be kept in repair and proper working order;

(c) conditions requiring, in the case of any works needed in order for any such facilities or equipment to be made available or to meet any such standards, that the works are carried out within such period or periods as may be specified in, or determined under, the licence.

(4) A licence must include the conditions required by Schedule 4.

(5) As regards the relationship between the authority's power to impose conditions under this section and functions exercisable by them under or for the purposes of Part 1 ('Part 1 functions') –

(a) the authority must proceed on the basis that, in general, they should seek to identify, remove or reduce category 1 or category 2 hazards in the house by the exercise of Part 1 functions and not by means of licence conditions;
(b) this does not, however, prevent the authority from imposing (in accordance with subsection (3)) licence conditions relating to the installation or maintenance of facilities or equipment within subsection (3)(a) above, even if the same result could be achieved by the exercise of Part 1 functions;
(c) the fact that licence conditions are imposed for a particular purpose that could be achieved by the exercise of Part 1 functions does not affect the way in which Part 1 functions can be subsequently exercised by the authority.

(6) A licence may not include conditions imposing restrictions or obligations on a particular person other than the licence holder unless that person has consented to the imposition of the restrictions or obligations.

(7) A licence may not include conditions requiring (or intended to secure) any alteration in the terms of any tenancy or licence under which any person occupies the house.

91 Licences: general requirements and duration

(1) A licence may not relate to more than one Part 3 house.

(2) A licence may be granted before the time when it is required by virtue of this Part but, if so, the licence cannot come into force until that time.

(3) A licence –

(a) comes into force at the time that is specified in or determined under the licence for this purpose, and
(b) unless previously terminated by subsection (7) or revoked under section 93, continues in force for the period that is so specified or determined.

(4) That period must not end more than 5 years after –

(a) the date on which the licence was granted, or
(b) if the licence was granted as mentioned in subsection (2), the date when the licence comes into force.

(5) Subsection (3)(b) applies even if, at any time during that period, the house concerned subsequently ceases to be a Part 3 house or becomes an HMO to which Part 2 applies (see section 55(2)).

(6) A licence may not be transferred to another person.

(7) If the holder of the licence dies while the licence is in force, the licence ceases to be in force on his death.

(8) However, during the period of 3 months beginning with the date of the licence holder's death, the house is to be treated for the purposes of this Part as if on that date a temporary exemption notice had been served in respect of the house under section 86.

(9) If, at any time during that period ('the initial period'), the personal representatives of the licence holder request the local housing authority to do so, the authority may serve on them a notice which, during the period of 3 months after the date on which the initial period ends, has the same effect as a temporary exemption notice under section 86.

(10) Subsections (6) to (8) of section 86 apply (with any necessary modifications) in relation to a decision by the authority not to serve such a notice as they apply in relation to a decision not to serve a temporary exemption notice.

Variation and revocation of licences

92 Variation of licences

(1) The local housing authority may vary a licence –

(a) if they do so with the agreement of the licence holder, or
(b) if they consider that there has been a change of circumstances since the time when the licence was granted.

For this purpose 'change of circumstances' includes any discovery of new information.

(2) A variation made with the agreement of the licence holder takes effect at the time when it is made.

(3) Otherwise, a variation does not come into force until such time, if any, as is the operative time for the purposes of this subsection under paragraph 35 of Schedule 5 (time when period for appealing expires without an appeal being made or when decision to vary is confirmed on appeal).

(4) The power to vary a licence under this section is exercisable by the authority either –

(a) on an application made by the licence holder or a relevant person, or
(b) on the authority's own initiative.

(5) In subsection (4) 'relevant person' means any person (other than the licence holder) –

(a) who has an estate or interest in the house concerned (but is not a tenant under a lease with an unexpired term of 3 years or less), or
(b) who is a person managing or having control of the house (and does not fall within paragraph (a)), or
(c) on whom any restriction or obligation is imposed by the licence in accordance with section 90(6).

93 Revocation of licences

(1) The local housing authority may revoke a licence –

(a) if they do so with the agreement of the licence holder,
(b) in any of the cases mentioned in subsection (2) (circumstances relating to licence holder or other person),
(c) in any of the cases mentioned in subsection (3) (circumstances relating to house concerned), or
(d) in any other circumstances prescribed by regulations made by the appropriate national authority.

(2) The cases referred to in subsection (1)(b) are as follows –

(a) where the authority consider that the licence holder or any other person has committed a serious breach of a condition of the licence or repeated breaches of such a condition;

(b) where the authority no longer consider that the licence holder is a fit and proper person to be the licence holder; and

(c) where the authority no longer consider that the management of the house is being carried on by persons who are in each case fit and proper persons to be involved in its management.

Section 89(1) applies in relation to paragraph (b) or (c) above as it applies in relation to section 88(3)(a) or (c).

(3) The cases referred to in subsection (1)(c) are as follows –

(a) where the house to which the licence relates ceases to be a Part 3 house;

(b) where a licence has been granted under Part 2 in respect of the house;

(c) where the authority consider at any time that, were the licence to expire at that time, they would, for a particular reason relating to the structure of the house, refuse to grant a new licence to the licence holder on similar terms in respect of it.

(4) A revocation made with the agreement of the licence holder takes effect at the time when it is made.

(5) Otherwise, a revocation does not come into force until such time, if any, as is the operative time for the purposes of this subsection under paragraph 35 of Schedule 5 (time when period for appealing expires without an appeal being made or when decision to vary is confirmed on appeal).

This is subject to subsection (6).

(6) A revocation made in a case within subsection (3)(b) cannot come into force before such time as would be the operative time for the purposes of subsection (5) under paragraph 35 of Schedule 5 on the assumption that paragraph 35 applied –

(a) to an appeal against the Part 2 licence under paragraph 31 of the Schedule as it applies to an appeal under paragraph 32 of the Schedule, and

(b) to the period for appealing against the Part 2 licence mentioned in paragraph 33(1) of the Schedule as it applies to the period mentioned in paragraph 33(2) of the Schedule.

(7) The power to revoke a licence under this section is exercisable by the authority either –

(a) on an application made by the licence holder or a relevant person, or

(b) on the authority's own initiative.

(8) In subsection (7) 'relevant person' means any person (other than the licence holder) –

(a) who has an estate or interest in the house concerned (but is not a tenant under a lease with an unexpired term of 3 years or less), or

(b) who is a person managing or having control of the house (and does not fall within paragraph (a)), or

(c) on whom any restriction or obligation is imposed by the licence in accordance with section 90(6).

Procedure and appeals

94 Procedural requirements and appeals against licence decisions

Schedule 5 (which deals with procedural requirements relating to the grant, refusal, variation or revocation of licences and with appeals against licence decisions) has effect for the purposes of this Part.

Enforcement

95 Offences in relation to licensing of houses under this Part

(1) A person commits an offence if he is a person having control of or managing a house which is required to be licensed under this Part (see section 85(1)) but is not so licensed.

(2) A person commits an offence if –

(a) he is a licence holder or a person on whom restrictions or obligations under a licence are imposed in accordance with section 90(6), and
(b) he fails to comply with any condition of the licence.

(3) In proceedings against a person for an offence under subsection (1) it is a defence that, at the material time –

(a) a notification had been duly given in respect of the house under section 62(1) or 86(1), or
(b) an application for a licence had been duly made in respect of the house under section 87,

and that notification or application was still effective (see subsection (7)).

(4) In proceedings against a person for an offence under subsection (1) or (2) it is a defence that he had a reasonable excuse –

(a) for having control of or managing the house in the circumstances mentioned in subsection (1), or
(b) for failing to comply with the condition,

as the case may be.

(5) A person who commits an offence under subsection (1) is liable on summary conviction to a fine not exceeding £20,000.

(6) A person who commits an offence under subsection (2) is liable on summary conviction to a fine not exceeding level 5 on the standard scale.

(7) For the purposes of subsection (3) a notification or application is 'effective' at a particular time if at that time it has not been withdrawn, and either –

(a) the authority have not decided whether to serve a temporary exemption notice, or (as the case may be) grant a licence, in pursuance of the notification or application, or
(b) if they have decided not to do so, one of the conditions set out in subsection (8) is met.

(8) The conditions are –

(a) that the period for appealing against the decision of the authority not to serve or grant such a notice or licence (or against any relevant decision of a residential property tribunal) has not expired, or
(b) that an appeal has been brought against the authority's decision (or against any relevant decision of such a tribunal) and the appeal has not been determined or withdrawn.

(9) In subsection (8) 'relevant decision' means a decision which is given on an appeal to the tribunal and confirms the authority's decision (with or without variation).

96 Other consequences of operating unlicensed houses: rent repayment orders

(1) For the purposes of this section a house is an 'unlicensed house' if –

(a) it is required to be licensed under this Part but is not so licensed, and
(b) neither of the conditions in subsection (2) is satisfied.

(2) The conditions are –

    (a) that a notification has been duly given in respect of the house under section 62(1) or 86(1) and that notification is still effective (as defined by section 95(7));

    (b) that an application for a licence has been duly made in respect of the house under section 87 and that application is still effective (as so defined).

(3) No rule of law relating to the validity or enforceability of contracts in circumstances involving illegality is to affect the validity or enforceability of –

    (a) any provision requiring the payment of rent or the making of any other periodical payment in connection with any tenancy or licence of the whole or a part of an unlicensed house, or

    (b) any other provision of such a tenancy or licence.

(4) But amounts paid in respect of rent or other periodical payments payable in connection with such a tenancy or licence may be recovered in accordance with subsection (5) and section 97.

(5) If –

    (a) an application in respect of a house is made to a residential property tribunal by the local housing authority or an occupier of the whole or part of the house, and

    (b) the tribunal is satisfied as to the matters mentioned in subsection (6) or (8),

the tribunal may make an order (a 'rent repayment order') requiring the appropriate person to pay to the applicant such amount in respect of the housing benefit paid as mentioned in subsection (6)(b), or (as the case may be) the periodical payments paid as mentioned in subsection (8)(b), as is specified in the order (see section 97(2) to (8)).

(6) If the application is made by the local housing authority, the tribunal must be satisfied as to the following matters –

    (a) that, at any time within the period of 12 months ending with the date of the notice of intended proceedings required by subsection (7), the appropriate person has committed an offence under section 95(1) in relation to the house (whether or not he has been charged or convicted),

    (b) that housing benefit has been paid (to any person) in respect of periodical payments payable in connection with the occupation of the whole or any part or parts of the house during any period during which it appears to the tribunal that such an offence was being committed, and

    (c) that the requirements of subsection (7) have been complied with in relation to the application.

(7) Those requirements are as follows –

    (a) the authority must have served on the appropriate person a notice (a 'notice of intended proceedings') –
        (i)   informing him that the authority are proposing to make an application under subsection (5),
        (ii) setting out the reasons why they propose to do so,
        (iii) stating the amount that they will seek to recover under that subsection and how that amount is calculated, and
        (iv) inviting him to make representations to them within a period specified in the notice of not less than 28 days;

    (b) that period must have expired; and

    (c) the authority must have considered any representations made to them within that period by the appropriate person.

(8) If the application is made by an occupier of the whole or part of the house, the tribunal must be satisfied as to the following matters –

(a) that the appropriate person has been convicted of an offence under section 95(1) in relation to the house, or has been required by a rent repayment order to make a payment in respect of housing benefit paid in connection with occupation of the whole or any part or parts of the house,

(b) that the occupier paid, to a person having control of or managing the house, periodical payments in respect of occupation of the whole or part of the house during any period during which it appears to the tribunal that such an offence was being committed in relation to the house, and

(c) that the application is made within the period of 12 months beginning with –
    (i) the date of the conviction or order, or
    (ii) if such a conviction was followed by such an order (or vice versa), the date of the later of them.

(9) Where a local housing authority serve a notice of intended proceedings on any person under this section, they must ensure –

(a) that a copy of the notice is received by the department of the authority responsible for administering the housing benefit to which the proceedings would relate; and

(b) that that department is subsequently kept informed of any matters relating to the proceedings that are likely to be of interest to it in connection with the administration of housing benefit.

(10) In this section –

'the appropriate person', in relation to any payment of housing benefit or periodical payment payable in connection with occupation of the whole or a part of a house, means the person who at the time of the payment was entitled to receive on his own account periodical payments payable in connection with such occupation;

'housing benefit' means housing benefit provided by virtue of a scheme under section 123 of the Social Security Contributions and Benefits Act 1992 (c 4);

'occupier', in relation to any periodical payment, means a person who was an occupier at the time of the payment, whether under a tenancy or licence (and 'occupation' has a corresponding meaning);

'periodical payments' means periodical payments in respect of which housing benefit may be paid by virtue of regulation 10 of the Housing Benefit (General) Regulations 1987 (SI 1987/1971) or any corresponding provision replacing that regulation.

(11) For the purposes of this section an amount which –

(a) is not actually paid by an occupier but is used by him to discharge the whole or part of his liability in respect of a periodical payment (for example, by offsetting the amount against any such liability), and

(b) is not an amount of housing benefit,

is to be regarded as an amount paid by the occupier in respect of that periodical payment.

97 Further provisions about rent repayment orders

(1) This section applies in relation to orders made by residential property tribunals under section 96(5).

(2) Where, on an application by the local housing authority, the tribunal is satisfied –

    (a) that a person has been convicted of an offence under section 95(1) in relation to the house, and

    (b) that housing benefit was paid (whether or not to the appropriate person) in respect of periodical payments payable in connection with occupation of the whole or any part or parts of the house during any period during which it appears to the tribunal that such an offence was being committed in relation to the house,

the tribunal must make a rent repayment order requiring the appropriate person to pay to the authority an amount equal to the total amount of housing benefit paid as mentioned in paragraph (b).

This is subject to subsections (3), (4) and (8).

(3) If the total of the amounts received by the appropriate person in respect of periodical payments payable as mentioned in paragraph (b) of subsection (2) ('the rent total') is less than the total amount of housing benefit paid as mentioned in that paragraph, the amount required to be paid by virtue of a rent repayment order made in accordance with that subsection is limited to the rent total.

(4) A rent repayment order made in accordance with subsection (2) may not require the payment of any amount which the tribunal is satisfied that, by reason of any exceptional circumstances, it would be unreasonable for that person to be required to pay.

(5) In a case where subsection (2) does not apply, the amount required to be paid by virtue of a rent repayment order under section 96(5) is to be such amount as the tribunal considers reasonable in the circumstances.

This is subject to subsections (6) to (8).

(6) In such a case the tribunal must, in particular, take into account the following matters –

    (a) the total amount of relevant payments paid in connection with occupation of the house during any period during which it appears to the tribunal that an offence was being committed by the appropriate person in relation to the house under section 95(1);

    (b) the extent to which that total amount –
        (i) consisted of, or derived from, payments of housing benefit, and
        (ii) was actually received by the appropriate person;

    (c) whether the appropriate person has at any time been convicted of an offence under section 95(1) in relation to the house;

    (d) the conduct and financial circumstances of the appropriate person; and

    (e) where the application is made by an occupier, the conduct of the occupier.

(7) In subsection (6) 'relevant payments' means –

    (a) in relation to an application by a local housing authority, payments of housing benefit or periodical payments payable by occupiers;

    (b) in relation to an application by an occupier, periodical payments payable by the occupier, less any amount of housing benefit payable in respect of occupation of the house, or (as the case may be) the part of it occupied by him, during the period in question.

(8) A rent repayment order may not require the payment of an amount which –

    (a) (where the application is made by a local housing authority) is in respect of any time falling outside the period of 12 months mentioned in section 96(6)(a); or

    (b) (where the application is made by an occupier) is in respect of any time falling outside the period of 12 months ending with the date of the occupier's application under section 96(5);

and the period to be taken into account under subsection (6)(a) above is restricted accordingly.

(9) Any amount payable to a local housing authority under a rent repayment order –

(a) does not, when recovered by the authority, constitute an amount of housing benefit recovered by them, and

(b) is, until recovered by them, a legal charge on the house which is a local land charge.

(10) For the purpose of enforcing that charge the authority have the same powers and remedies under the Law of Property Act 1925 (c 20) and otherwise as if they were mortgagees by deed having powers of sale and lease, and of accepting surrenders of leases and of appointing a receiver.

(11) The power of appointing a receiver is exercisable at any time after the end of the period of one month beginning with the date on which the charge takes effect.

(12) If the authority subsequently grant a licence under Part 2 or this Part in respect of the house to the appropriate person or any person acting on his behalf, the conditions contained in the licence may include a condition requiring the licence holder –

(a) to pay to the authority any amount payable to them under the rent repayment order and not so far recovered by them; and

(b) to do so in such instalments as are specified in the licence.

(13) If the authority subsequently make a management order under Chapter 1 of Part 4 in respect of the house, the order may contain such provisions as the authority consider appropriate for the recovery of any amount payable to them under the rent repayment order and not so far recovered by them.

(14) Any amount payable to an occupier by virtue of a rent repayment order is recoverable by the occupier as a debt due to him from the appropriate person.

(15) The appropriate national authority may by regulations make such provision as it considers appropriate for supplementing the provisions of this section and section 96, and in particular –

(a) for securing that persons are not unfairly prejudiced by rent repayment orders (whether in cases where there have been over-payments of housing benefit or otherwise);

(b) for requiring or authorising amounts received by local housing authorities by virtue of rent repayment orders to be dealt with in such manner as is specified in the regulations.

(16) Section 96(10) and (11) apply for the purposes of this section as they apply for the purposes of section 96.

98 Other consequences of operating unlicensed houses: restriction on terminating tenancies

(1) No section 21 notice may be given in relation to a shorthold tenancy of the whole or part of an unlicensed house so long as it remains such a house.

(2) In this section –

a 'section 21 notice' means a notice under section 21(1)(b) or (4)(a) of the Housing Act 1988 (c 50) (recovery of possession on termination of shorthold tenancy);

a 'shorthold tenancy' means an assured shorthold tenancy within the meaning of Chapter 2 of Part 1 of that Act;

'unlicensed house' has the same meaning as in section 96 of this Act.

Supplementary provisions

99 Meaning of 'house' etc

In this Part –

'dwelling' means a building or part of a building occupied or intended to be occupied as a separate dwelling;

'house' means a building or part of a building consisting of one or more dwellings;

and references to a house include (where the context permits) any yard, garden, outhouses and appurtenances belonging to, or usually enjoyed with, it (or any part of it).

100 Index of defined expressions: Part 3

The following table shows where expressions used in this Part are defined or otherwise explained.

Expression	Provision of this Act
Anti-social behaviour	Section 57(5)
Appropriate national authority	Section 261(1)
Category 1 hazard	Section 2(1)
Category 2 hazard	Section 2(1)
District of local housing authority	Section 261(6)
Dwelling	Section 99
House	Section 99
Licence and licence holder	Section 85(5)
Licence (to occupy premises)	Section 262(9)
Local housing authority	Section 261(2) to (5)
Occupier (and related expressions)	Section 262(6)
Part 3 house	Section 85(5), together with section 79(2)
Person having control	Section 263(1) and (2) (and see also section 89(7))
Person having estate or interest	Section 262(8)
Person managing	Section 263(3)
Person involved in management	Section 263(5)
Residential property tribunal	Section 229
Tenant	Section 262(1) to (5)

Part 4
Additional Control Provisions in Relation to Residential Accommodation

Chapter 1
Interim and Final Management Orders

Introductory

101 Interim and final management orders: introductory

(1) This Chapter deals with the making by a local housing authority of –

(a) an interim management order (see section 102), or

(b) a final management order (see section 113),

in respect of an HMO or a Part 3 house.

(2) Section 103 deals with the making of an interim management order in respect of a house to which that section applies.

(3) An interim management order is an order (expiring not more than 12 months after it is made) which is made for the purpose of securing that the following steps are taken in relation to the house –

(a) any immediate steps which the authority consider necessary to protect the health, safety or welfare of persons occupying the house, or persons occupying or having an estate or interest in any premises in the vicinity, and
(b) any other steps which the authority think appropriate with a view to the proper management of the house pending the grant of a licence under Part 2 or 3 in respect of the house or the making of a final management order in respect of it (or, if appropriate, the revocation of the interim management order).

(4) A final management order is an order (expiring not more than 5 years after it is made) which is made for the purpose of securing the proper management of the house on a long-term basis in accordance with a management scheme contained in the order.

(5) In this Chapter any reference to 'the house', in relation to an interim or final management order (other than an order under section 102(7)), is a reference to the HMO or Part 3 house to which the order relates.

(6) Subsection (5) has effect subject to sections 102(8) and 113(7) (exclusion of part occupied by resident landlord).

(7) In this Chapter 'third party', in relation to a house, means any person who has an estate or interest in the house (other than an immediate landlord and any person who is a tenant under a lease granted under section 107(3)(c) or 116(3)(c)).

Interim management orders: making and operation of orders

102 Making of interim management orders

(1) A local housing authority –

(a) are under a duty to make an interim management order in respect of a house in a case within subsection (2) or (3), and
(b) have power to make an interim management order in respect of a house in a case within subsection (4) or (7).

(2) The authority must make an interim management order in respect of a house if –

(a) it is an HMO or a Part 3 house which is required to be licensed under Part 2 or Part 3 (see section 61(1) or 85(1)) but is not so licensed, and
(b) they consider either –
(i) that there is no reasonable prospect of its being so licensed in the near future, or
(ii) that the health and safety condition is satisfied (see section 104).

(3) The authority must make an interim management order in respect of a house if –

(a) it is an HMO or a Part 3 house which is required to be licensed under Part 2 or Part 3 and is so licensed,
(b) they have revoked the licence concerned but the revocation is not yet in force, and
(c) they consider either –

(i)   that, on the revocation coming into force, there will be no reasonable prospect of the house being so licensed in the near future, or

(ii)   that, on the revocation coming into force, the health and safety condition will be satisfied (see section 104).

(4) The authority may make an interim management order in respect of a house if –

(a) it is an HMO other than one that is required to be licensed under Part 2, and

(b) on an application by the authority to a residential property tribunal, the tribunal by order authorises them to make such an order, either in the terms of a draft order submitted by them or in those terms as varied by the tribunal;

and the authority may make such an order despite any pending appeal against the order of the tribunal (but this is without prejudice to any order that may be made on the disposal of any such appeal).

(5) The tribunal may only authorise the authority to make an interim management order under subsection (4) if it considers that the health and safety condition is satisfied (see section 104).

(6) In determining whether to authorise the authority to make an interim management order in respect of an HMO under subsection (4), the tribunal must have regard to the extent to which any applicable code of practice approved under section 233 has been complied with in respect of the HMO in the past.

(7) The authority may make an interim management order in respect of a house if –

(a) it is a house to which section 103 (special interim management orders) applies, and

(b) on an application by the authority to a residential property tribunal, the tribunal by order authorises them to make such an order, either in the terms of a draft order submitted by them or in those terms as varied by the tribunal;

and the authority may make such an order despite any pending appeal against the order of the tribunal (but this is without prejudice to any order that may be made on the disposal of any such appeal).

Subsections (2) to (6) of section 103 apply in relation to the power of a residential property tribunal to authorise the making of an interim management order under this subsection.

(8) The authority may make an interim management order which is expressed not to apply to a part of the house that is occupied by a person who has an estate or interest in the whole of the house.

In relation to such an order, a reference in this Chapter to 'the house' does not include the part so excluded (unless the context requires otherwise, such as where the reference is to the house as an HMO or a Part 3 house).

(9) Nothing in this section requires or authorises the making of an interim management order in respect of a house if –

(a) an interim management order has been previously made in respect of it, and

(b) the authority have not exercised any relevant function in respect of the house at any time after the making of the interim management order.

(10) In subsection (9) 'relevant function' means the function of –

(a) granting a licence under Part 2 or 3,

(b) serving a temporary exemption notice under section 62 or section 86, or

(c) making a final management order under section 113.

103 Special interim management orders

(1) This section applies to a house if the whole of it is occupied either –

    (a) under a single tenancy or licence that is not an exempt tenancy or licence under section 79(3) or (4), or

    (b) under two or more tenancies or licences in respect of different dwellings contained in it, none of which is an exempt tenancy or licence under section 79(3) or (4).

(2) A residential property tribunal may only authorise the authority to make an interim management order in respect of such a house under section 102(7) if it considers that both of the following conditions are satisfied.

(3) The first condition is that the circumstances relating to the house fall within any category of circumstances prescribed for the purposes of this subsection by an order under subsection (5).

(4) The second condition is that the making of the order is necessary for the purpose of protecting the health, safety or welfare of persons occupying, visiting or otherwise engaging in lawful activities in the vicinity of the house.

(5) The appropriate national authority may by order –

    (a) prescribe categories of circumstances for the purposes of subsection (3),

    (b) provide for any of the provisions of this Act to apply in relation to houses to which this section applies, or interim or final management orders made in respect of them, with any modifications specified in the order.

(6) The categories prescribed by an order under subsection (5) are to reflect one or more of the following –

    (a) the first or second set of general conditions mentioned in subsection (3) or (6) of section 80, or

    (b) any additional set of conditions specified under subsection (7) of that section,

but (in each case) with such modifications as the appropriate national authority considers appropriate to adapt them to the circumstances of a single house.

(7) In this section 'house' has the same meaning as in Part 3 (see section 99).

(8) In this Chapter –

    (a) any reference to 'the house', in relation to an interim management order under section 102(7), is a reference to the house to which the order relates, and

    (b) any such reference includes (where the context permits) a reference to any yard, garden, outhouses and appurtenances belonging to, or usually enjoyed with, it (or any part of it).

104 The health and safety condition

(1) This section explains what 'the health and safety condition' is for the purposes of section 102.

(2) The health and safety condition is that the making of an interim management order is necessary for the purpose of protecting the health, safety or welfare of persons occupying the house, or persons occupying or having an estate or interest in any premises in the vicinity.

(3) A threat to evict persons occupying a house in order to avoid the house being required to be licensed under Part 2 may constitute a threat to the welfare of those persons for the purposes of subsection (2).

This does not affect the generality of that subsection.

(4) The health and safety condition is not to be regarded as satisfied for the purposes of section 102(2)(b)(ii) or (3)(c)(ii) where both of the conditions in subsections (5) and (6) are satisfied.

(5) The first condition is that the local housing authority either –

(a) (in a case within section 102(2)(b)(ii)) are required by section 5 (general duty to take enforcement action in respect of category 1 hazards) to take a course of action within subsection (2) of that section in relation to the house, or
(b) (in a case within section 102(3)(c)(ii)) consider that on the revocation coming into force they will be required to take such a course of action.

(6) The second condition is that the local housing authority consider that the health, safety or welfare of the persons in question would be adequately protected by taking that course of action.

105 Operation of interim management orders

(1) This section deals with the time when an interim management order comes into force or ceases to have effect.

(2) The order comes into force when it is made, unless it is made under section 102(3).

(3) If the order is made under section 102(3), it comes into force when the revocation of the licence comes into force.

(4) The order ceases to have effect at the end of the period of 12 months beginning with the date on which it is made, unless it ceases to have effect at some other time as mentioned below.

(5) If the order provides that it is to cease to have effect on a date falling before the end of that period, it accordingly ceases to have effect on that date.

(6) If the order is made under section 102(3) –

(a) it must include a provision for determining the date on which it will cease to have effect, and
(b) it accordingly ceases to have effect on the date so determined.

(7) That date must be no later than 12 months after the date on which the order comes into force.

(8) Subsections (9) and (10) apply where –

(a) a final management order ('the FMO') has been made under section 113 so as to replace the order ('the IMO'), but
(b) the FMO has not come into force because of an appeal to a residential property tribunal under paragraph 24 of Schedule 6 against the making of the FMO.

(9) If –

(a) the house would (but for the IMO being in force) be required to be licensed under Part 2 or 3 of this Act (see section 61(1) or 85(1)), and
(b) the date on which –
    (i) the FMO,
    (ii) any licence under Part 2 or 3, or
    (iii) another interim management order,

    comes into force in relation to the house (or part of it) following the disposal of the appeal is later than the date on which the IMO would cease to have effect apart from this subsection,

the IMO continues in force until that later date.

(10) If, on the application of the authority, the tribunal makes an order providing for the IMO to continue in force, pending the disposal of the appeal, until a date later than that on which the IMO would cease to have effect apart from this subsection, the IMO accordingly continues in force until that later date.

(11) This section has effect subject to sections 111 and 112 (variation or revocation of orders by authority) and to the power of revocation exercisable by a residential property tribunal on an appeal made under paragraph 24 or 28 of Schedule 6.

106 Local housing authority's duties once interim management order in force

(1) A local housing authority who have made an interim management order in respect of a house must comply with the following provisions as soon as practicable after the order has come into force.

(2) The authority must first take any immediate steps which they consider to be necessary for the purpose of protecting the health, safety or welfare of persons occupying the house, or persons occupying or having an estate or interest in any premises in the vicinity.

(3) The authority must also take such other steps as they consider appropriate with a view to the proper management of the house pending –

- (a) the grant of a licence or the making of a final management order in respect of the house as mentioned in subsection (4) or (5), or
- (b) the revocation of the interim management order as mentioned in subsection (5).

(4) If the house would (but for the order being in force) be required to be licensed under Part 2 or 3 of this Act (see section 61(1) or 85(1)), the authority must, after considering all the circumstances of the case, decide to take one of the following courses of action –

- (a) to grant a licence under that Part in respect of the house, or
- (b) to make a final management order in respect of it under section 113(1).

(5) If subsection (4) does not apply to the house, the authority must, after considering all the circumstances of the case, decide to take one of the following courses of action –

- (a) to make a final management order in respect of the house under section 113(3), or
- (b) to revoke the order under section 112 without taking any further action.

(6) In the following provisions, namely –

- (a) subsections (3) and (4), and
- (b) section 101(3)(b),

the reference to the grant of a licence under Part 2 or 3 in respect of the house includes a reference to serving a temporary exemption notice under section 62 or section 86 in respect of it (whether or not a notification is given under subsection (1) of that section).

(7) For the avoidance of doubt, the authority's duty under subsection (3) includes taking such steps as are necessary to ensure that, while the order is in force, reasonable provision is made for insurance of the house against destruction or damage by fire or other causes.

107 General effect of interim management orders

(1) This section applies while an interim management order is in force in relation to a house.

(2) The rights and powers conferred by subsection (3) are exercisable by the authority in performing their duties under section 106(1) to (3) in respect of the house.

(3) The authority –

 (a) have the right to possession of the house (subject to the rights of existing occupiers preserved by section 124(3));

 (b) have the right to do (and authorise a manager or other person to do) in relation to the house anything which a person having an estate or interest in the house would (but for the order) be entitled to do;

 (c) may create one or more of the following –

  (i) an interest in the house which, as far as possible, has all the incidents of a leasehold, or

  (ii) a right in the nature of a licence to occupy part of the house.

(4) But the authority may not under subsection (3)(c) create any interest or right in the nature of a lease or licence unless consent in writing has been given by the person who (but for the order) would have power to create the lease or licence in question.

(5) The authority –

 (a) do not under this section acquire any estate or interest in the house, and

 (b) accordingly are not entitled by virtue of this section to sell, lease, charge or make any other disposition of any such estate or interest;

but, where the immediate landlord of the house or part of it (within the meaning of section 109) is a lessee under a lease of the house or part, the authority is to be treated (subject to paragraph (a)) as if they were the lessee instead.

(6) Any enactment or rule of law relating to landlords and tenants or leases applies in relation to –

 (a) a lease in relation to which the authority are to be treated as the lessee under subsection (5), or

 (b) a lease to which the authority become a party under section 124(4),

as if the authority were the legal owner of the premises (but this is subject to section 124(7) to (9)).

(7) None of the following, namely –

 (a) the authority, or

 (b) any person authorised under subsection (3)(b),

is liable to any person having an estate or interest in the house for anything done or omitted to be done in the performance (or intended performance) of the authority's duties under section 106(1) to (3) unless the act or omission is due to the negligence of the authority or any such person.

(8) References in any enactment to housing accommodation provided or managed by a local housing authority do not include a house in relation to which an interim management order is in force.

(9) An interim management order which has come into force is a local land charge.

(10) The authority may apply to the Chief Land Registrar for the entry of an appropriate restriction in the register of title in respect of such an order.

(11) In this section 'enactment' includes an enactment comprised in subordinate legislation (within the meaning of the Interpretation Act 1978 (c 30)).

108 General effect of interim management orders: leases and licences granted by authority

(1) This section applies in relation to any interest or right created by the authority under section 107(3)(c).

(2) For the purposes of any enactment or rule of law –

    (a) any interest created by the authority under section 107(3)(c)(i) is to be treated as if it were a legal lease, and

    (b) any right created by the authority under section 107(3)(c)(ii) is to be treated as if it were a licence to occupy granted by the legal owner of the premises,

despite the fact that the authority have no legal estate in the premises (see section 107(5)(a)).

(3) Any enactment or rule of law relating to landlords and tenants or leases accordingly applies in relation to any interest created by the authority under section 107(3)(c)(i) as if the authority were the legal owner of the premises.

(4) References to leases and licences –

    (a) in this Chapter, and

    (b) in any other enactment,

accordingly include (where the context permits) interests and rights created by the authority under section 107(3)(c).

(5) The preceding provisions of this section have effect subject to –

    (a) section 124(7) to (9), and

    (b) any provision to the contrary contained in an order made by the appropriate national authority.

(6) In section 107(5)(b) the reference to leasing does not include the creation of interests under section 107(3)(c)(i).

(7) In this section –

    'enactment' has the meaning given by section 107(11);

    'legal lease' means a term of years absolute (within section 1(1)(b) of the Law of Property Act 1925 (c 20)).

109 General effect of interim management orders: immediate landlords, mortgagees etc

(1) This section applies in relation to –

    (a) immediate landlords, and

    (b) other persons with an estate or interest in the house,

while an interim management order is in force in relation to a house.

(2) A person who is an immediate landlord of the house or a part of it –

    (a) is not entitled to receive –

        (i) any rents or other payments from persons occupying the house or part which are payable to the local housing authority by virtue of section 124(4), or

        (ii) any rents or other payments from persons occupying the house or part which are payable to the authority by virtue of any leases or licences granted by them under section 107(3)(c);

    (b) may not exercise any rights or powers with respect to the management of the house or part; and

    (c) may not create any of the following –

        (i) any leasehold interest in the house or part (other than a lease of a reversion), or

(ii)   any licence or other right to occupy it.

(3) However (subject to subsection (2)(c)) nothing in section 107 or this section affects the ability of a person having an estate or interest in the house to make any disposition of that estate or interest.

(4) Nothing in section 107 or this section affects –

(a) the validity of any mortgage relating to the house or any rights or remedies available to the mortgagee under such a mortgage, or
(b) the validity of any lease of the house or part of it under which the immediate landlord is a lessee, or any superior lease, or (subject to section 107(5)) any rights or remedies available to the lessor under such a lease,

except to the extent that any of those rights or remedies would prevent the local housing authority from exercising their power under section 107(3)(c).

(5) In proceedings for the enforcement of any such rights or remedies the court may make such order as it thinks fit as regards the operation of the interim management order (including an order quashing it).

(6) For the purposes of this Chapter, as it applies in relation to an interim management order, a person is an 'immediate landlord' of the house or a part of it if –

(a) he is an owner or lessee of the house or part, and
(b) (but for the order) he would be entitled to receive the rents or other payments from persons occupying the house or part which are payable to the local housing authority by virtue of section 124(4).

110 Financial arrangements while order is in force

(1) This section applies to relevant expenditure of a local housing authority who have made an interim management order.

(2) 'Relevant expenditure' means expenditure reasonably incurred by the authority in connection with performing their duties under section 106(1) to (3) in respect of the house (including any premiums paid for insurance of the premises).

(3) Rent or other payments which the authority have collected or recovered, by virtue of this Chapter, from persons occupying the house may be used by the authority to meet –

(a) relevant expenditure, and
(b) any amounts of compensation payable to a third party by virtue of a decision of the authority under section 128.

(4) The authority must pay to such relevant landlord, or to such relevant landlords in such proportions, as they consider appropriate –

(a) any amount of rent or other payments collected or recovered as mentioned in subsection (3) that remains after deductions to meet relevant expenditure and any amounts of compensation payable as mentioned in that subsection, and
(b) (where appropriate) interest on that amount at a reasonable rate fixed by the authority,

and such payments are to be made at such intervals as the authority consider appropriate.

(5) The interim management order may provide for –

(a) the rate of interest which is to apply for the purposes of paragraph (b) of subsection (4); and

(b) the intervals at which payments are to be made under that subsection.

Paragraph 24(3) of Schedule 6 enables an appeal to be brought where the order does not provide for both of those matters.

(6) The authority must –

(a) keep full accounts of their income and expenditure in respect of the house; and
(b) afford to each relevant landlord, and to any other person who has an estate or interest in the house, all reasonable facilities for inspecting, taking copies of and verifying those accounts.

(7) A relevant landlord may apply to a residential property tribunal for an order –

(a) declaring that an amount shown in the accounts as expenditure of the authority does not constitute expenditure reasonably incurred by the authority as mentioned in subsection (2);
(b) requiring the authority to make such financial adjustments (in the accounts and otherwise) as are necessary to reflect the tribunal's declaration.

(8) In this section –

'expenditure' includes administrative costs;

'relevant landlord' means any person who is an immediate landlord of the house or part of it;

'rent or other payments' means rents or other payments payable under leases or licences or in respect of furniture within section 126(1).

Interim management orders: variation and revocation

111 Variation of interim management orders

(1) The local housing authority may vary an interim management order if they consider it appropriate to do so.

(2) A variation does not come into force until such time, if any, as is the operative time for the purposes of this subsection under paragraph 31 of Schedule 6 (time when period for appealing expires without an appeal being made or when decision to vary is confirmed on appeal).

(3) The power to vary an order under this section is exercisable by the authority either –

(a) on an application made by a relevant person, or
(b) on the authority's own initiative.

(4) In this section 'relevant person' means –

(a) any person who has an estate or interest in the house or part of it (but is not a tenant under a lease with an unexpired term of 3 years or less), or
(b) any other person who (but for the order) would be a person managing or having control of the house or part of it.

112 Revocation of interim management orders

(1) The local housing authority may revoke an interim management order in the following cases –

(a) if the order was made under section 102(2) or (3) and the house has ceased to be an HMO to which Part 2 applies or a Part 3 house (as the case may be);
(b) if the order was made under section 102(2) or (3) and a licence granted by them in respect of the house is due to come into force under Part 2 or Part 3 on the revocation of the order;

(c) if a final management order has been made by them in respect of the house so as to replace the order;

(d) if in any other circumstances the authority consider it appropriate to revoke the order.

(2) A revocation does not come into force until such time, if any, as is the operative time for the purposes of this subsection under paragraph 31 of Schedule 6 (time when period for appealing expires without an appeal being made or when decision to revoke is confirmed on appeal).

(3) The power to revoke an order under this section is exercisable by the authority either –

(a) on an application made by a relevant person, or

(b) on the authority's own initiative.

(4) In this section 'relevant person' means –

(a) any person who has an estate or interest in the house or part of it (but is not a tenant under a lease with an unexpired term of 3 years or less), or

(b) any other person who (but for the order) would be a person managing or having control of the house or part of it.

Final management orders: making and operation of orders

113 Making of final management orders

(1) A local housing authority who have made an interim management order in respect of a house under section 102 ('the IMO') –

(a) have a duty to make a final management order in respect of the house in a case within subsection (2), and

(b) have power to make such an order in a case within subsection (3).

(2) The authority must make a final management order so as to replace the IMO as from its expiry date if –

(a) on that date the house would be required to be licensed under Part 2 or 3 of this Act (see section 61(1) or 85(1)), and

(b) the authority consider that they are unable to grant a licence under Part 2 or 3 in respect of the house that would replace the IMO as from that date.

(3) The authority may make a final management order so as to replace the IMO as from its expiry date if –

(a) on that date the house will not be one that would be required to be licensed as mentioned in subsection (2)(a), and

(b) the authority consider that making the final management order is necessary for the purpose of protecting, on a long-term basis, the health, safety or welfare of persons occupying the house, or persons occupying or having an estate or interest in any premises in the vicinity.

(4) A local housing authority who have made a final management order in respect of a house under this section ('the existing order') –

(a) have a duty to make a final management order in respect of the house in a case within subsection (5), and

(b) have power to make such an order in a case within subsection (6).

(5) The authority must make a new final management order so as to replace the existing order as from its expiry date if –

(a) on that date the condition in subsection (2)(a) will be satisfied in relation to the house, and

(b) the authority consider that they are unable to grant a licence under Part 2 or 3 in respect of the house that would replace the existing order as from that date.

(6) The authority may make a new final management order so as to replace the existing order as from its expiry date if –

(a) on that date the condition in subsection (3)(a) will be satisfied in relation to the house, and
(b) the authority consider that making the new order is necessary for the purpose of protecting, on a long-term basis, the health, safety or welfare of persons within subsection (3)(b).

(7) The authority may make a final management order which is expressed not to apply to a part of the house that is occupied by a person who has an estate or interest in the whole of the house.

In relation to such an order, a reference in this Chapter to 'the house' does not include the part so excluded (unless the context requires otherwise, such as where the reference is to the house as an HMO or a Part 3 house).

(8) In this section 'expiry date', in relation to an interim or final management order, means –

(a) where the order is revoked, the date as from which it is revoked, and
(b) otherwise the date on which the order ceases to have effect under section 105 or 114;

and nothing in this section applies in relation to an interim or final management order which has been revoked on an appeal under Part 3 of Schedule 6.

114 Operation of final management orders

(1) This section deals with the time when a final management order comes into force or ceases to have effect.

(2) The order does not come into force until such time (if any) as is the operative time for the purposes of this subsection under paragraph 27 of Schedule 6 (time when period for appealing expires without an appeal being made or when order is confirmed on appeal).

(3) The order ceases to have effect at the end of the period of 5 years beginning with the date on which it comes into force, unless it ceases to have effect at some other time as mentioned below.

(4) If the order provides that it is to cease to have effect on a date falling before the end of that period, it accordingly ceases to have effect on that date.

(5) Subsections (6) and (7) apply where –

(a) a new final management order ('the new order') has been made so as to replace the order ('the existing order'), but
(b) the new order has not come into force because of an appeal to a residential property tribunal under paragraph 24 of Schedule 6 against the making of that order.

(6) If –

(a) the house would (but for the existing order being in force) be required to be licensed under Part 2 or 3 of this Act (see section 61(1) or 85(1)), and
(b) the date on which –
   (i) the new order, or
   (ii) any licence under Part 2 or 3, or
   (iii) a temporary exemption notice under section 62 or 86,

   comes into force in relation to the house (or part of it) following the disposal of the appeal is later than the date on which the existing order would cease to have effect apart from this subsection, the existing order continues in force until that later date.

(7) If, on the application of the authority, the tribunal makes an order providing for the existing order to continue in force, pending the disposal of the appeal, until a date later than that on which it would cease to have effect apart from this subsection, the existing order accordingly continues in force until that later date.

(8) This section has effect subject to sections 121 and 122 (variation or revocation of orders) and to the power of revocation exercisable by a residential property tribunal on an appeal made under paragraph 24 or 28 of Schedule 6.

115 Local housing authority's duties once final management order in force

(1) A local housing authority who have made a final management order in respect of a house must comply with the following provisions once the order has come into force.

(2) The local housing authority must take such steps as they consider appropriate with a view to the proper management of the house in accordance with the management scheme contained in the order (see section 119).

(3) The local housing authority must from time to time review –

   (a) the operation of the order and in particular the management scheme contained in it, and
   (b) whether keeping the order in force in relation to the house (with or without making any variations under section 121) is the best alternative available to them.

(4) If on a review the authority consider that any variations should be made under section 121, they must proceed to make those variations.

(5) If on a review the authority consider that either –

   (a) granting a licence under Part 2 or 3 in respect of the house, or
   (b) revoking the order under section 122 and taking no further action,

is the best alternative available to them, the authority must grant such a licence or revoke the order (as the case may be).

(6) For the avoidance of doubt, the authority's duty under subsection (2) includes taking such steps as are necessary to ensure that, while the order is in force, reasonable provision is made for insurance of the house against destruction or damage by fire or other causes.

116 General effect of final management orders

(1) This section applies while a final management order is in force in relation to a house.

(2) The rights and powers conferred by subsection (3) are exercisable by the authority in performing their duty under section 115(2) in respect of the house.

(3) The authority –

   (a) have the right to possession of the house (subject to the rights of existing and other occupiers preserved by section 124(3) and (6));
   (b) have the right to do (and authorise a manager or other person to do) in relation to the house anything which a person having an estate or interest in the house would (but for the order) be entitled to do;
   (c) may create one or more of the following –
     (i) an interest in the house which, as far as possible, has all the incidents of a leasehold, or

    (ii) a right in the nature of a licence to occupy part of the house.

(4) The powers of the authority under subsection (3)(c) are restricted as follows –

    (a) they may not create any interest or right in the nature of a lease or licence –
        (i)   which is for a fixed term expiring after the date on which the order is due to expire, or
        (ii) (subject to paragraph (b)) which is terminable by notice to quit, or an equivalent notice, of more than 4 weeks,

    unless consent in writing has been given by the person who would (but for the order) have power to create the lease or licence in question;
    (b) they may create an interest in the nature of an assured shorthold tenancy without any such consent so long as it is created before the beginning of the period of 6 months that ends with the date on which the order is due to expire.

(5) The authority –

    (a) do not under this section acquire any estate or interest in the house, and
    (b) accordingly are not entitled by virtue of this section to sell, lease, charge or make any other disposition of any such estate or interest;

but, where the immediate landlord of the house or part of it (within the meaning of section 118) is a lessee under a lease of the house or part, the authority is to be treated (subject to paragraph (a)) as if they were the lessee instead.

(6) Any enactment or rule of law relating to landlords and tenants or leases applies in relation to –

    (a) a lease in relation to which the authority are to be treated as the lessee under subsection (5), or
    (b) a lease to which the authority become a party under section 124(4),

as if the authority were the legal owner of the premises (but this is subject to section 124(7) to (9)).

(7) None of the following, namely –

    (a) the authority, or
    (b) any person authorised under subsection (3)(b),

is liable to any person having an estate or interest in the house for anything done or omitted to be done in the performance (or intended performance) of the authority's duty under section 115(2) unless the act or omission is due to the negligence of the authority or any such person.

(8) References in any enactment to housing accommodation provided or managed by a local housing authority do not include a house in relation to which a final management order is in force.

(9) A final management order which has come into force is a local land charge.

(10) The authority may apply to the Chief Land Registrar for the entry of an appropriate restriction in the register in respect of such an order.

(11) In this section 'enactment' includes an enactment comprised in subordinate legislation (within the meaning of the Interpretation Act 1978 (c 30)).

117 General effect of final management orders: leases and licences granted by authority

(1) This section applies in relation to any interest or right created by the authority under section 116(3)(c).

(2) For the purposes of any enactment or rule of law –

(a) any interest created by the authority under section 116(3)(c)(i) is to be treated as if it were a legal lease, and

(b) any right created by the authority under section 116(3)(c)(ii) is to be treated as if it were a licence to occupy granted by the legal owner of the premises,

despite the fact that the authority have no legal estate in the premises (see section 116(5)(a)).

(3) Any enactment or rule of law relating to landlords and tenants or leases accordingly applies in relation to any interest created by the authority under section 116(3)(c)(i) as if the authority were the legal owner of the premises.

(4) References to leases and licences –

(a) in this Chapter, and

(b) in any other enactment,

accordingly include (where the context permits) interests and rights created by the authority under section 116(3)(c).

(5) The preceding provisions of this section have effect subject to –

(a) section 124(7) to (9), and

(b) any provision to the contrary contained in an order made by the appropriate national authority.

(6) In section 116(5)(b) the reference to leasing does not include the creation of interests under section 116(3)(c)(i).

(7) In this section –

'enactment' has the meaning given by section 116(11);

'legal lease' means a term of years absolute (within section 1(1)(b) of the Law of Property Act 1925 (c 20)).

118 General effect of final management orders: immediate landlords, mortgagees etc

(1) This section applies in relation to –

(a) immediate landlords, and

(b) other persons with an estate or interest in the house,

while a final management order is in force in relation to a house.

(2) A person who is an immediate landlord of the house or a part of it –

(a) is not entitled to receive –

(i) any rents or other payments from persons occupying the house or part which are payable to the local housing authority by virtue of section 124(4), or

(ii) any rents or other payments from persons occupying the house or part which are payable to the authority by virtue of any leases or licences granted by them under section 107(3)(c) or 116(3)(c);

(b) may not exercise any rights or powers with respect to the management of the house or part; and

(c) may not create any of the following –

(i) any leasehold interest in the house or part (other than a lease of a reversion), or

(ii) any licence or other right to occupy it.

(3) However (subject to subsection (2)(c)) nothing in section 116 or this section affects the ability of a person having an estate or interest in the house to make any disposition of that estate or interest.

(4) Nothing in section 116 or this section affects –

(a) the validity of any mortgage relating to the house or any rights or remedies available to the mortgagee under such a mortgage, or

(b) the validity of any lease of the house or part of it under which the immediate landlord is a lessee, or any superior lease, or (subject to section 116(5)) any rights or remedies available to the lessor under such a lease,

except to the extent that any of those rights or remedies would prevent the local housing authority from exercising their power under section 116(3)(c).

(5) In proceedings for the enforcement of any such rights or remedies the court may make such order as it thinks fit as regards the operation of the final management order (including an order quashing it).

(6) For the purposes of this Chapter, as it applies in relation to a final management order, a person is an 'immediate landlord' of the house or a part of it if –

(a) he is an owner or lessee of the house or part, and

(b) (but for the order) he would be entitled to receive the rents or other payments from persons occupying the house or part which are payable to the authority by virtue of section 124(4).

119 Management schemes and accounts

(1) A final management order must contain a management scheme.

(2) A 'management scheme' is a scheme setting out how the local housing authority are to carry out their duty under section 115(2) as respects the management of the house.

(3) A management scheme is to be divided into two parts.

(4) Part 1 of the scheme is to contain a plan giving details of the way in which the authority propose to manage the house, which must (in particular) include –

(a) details of any works that the authority intend to carry out in connection with the house;

(b) an estimate of the capital and other expenditure to be incurred by the authority in respect of the house while the order is in force;

(c) the amount of rent or other payments that the authority will seek to obtain having regard to the condition or expected condition of the house at any time while the order is in force;

(d) the amount of any compensation that is payable to a third party by virtue of a decision of the authority under section 128 in respect of any interference in consequence of the final management order with the rights of that person;

(e) provision as to the payment of any such compensation;

(f) provision as to the payment by the authority to a relevant landlord, from time to time, of amounts of rent or other payments that remain after the deduction of –
   (i) relevant expenditure, and
   (ii) any amounts of compensation payable as mentioned in paragraph (d);

(g) provision as to the manner in which the authority are to pay to a relevant landlord, on the termination of the final management order, any amounts of rent or other payments that remain after the deduction of –
   (i) relevant expenditure, and
   (ii) any amounts of compensation payable as mentioned in paragraph (d);

(h) provision as to the manner in which the authority are to pay, on the termination of the final management order, any outstanding balance of compensation payable to a third party.

(5) Part 1 of the scheme may also state –

    (a) the authority's intentions as regards the use of rent or other payments to meet relevant expenditure;

    (b) the authority's intentions as regards the payment to a relevant landlord (where appropriate) of interest on amounts within subsection (4)(f) and (g);

    (c) that section 129(2) or (4) is not to apply in relation to an interim or (as the case may be) final management order that immediately preceded the final management order, and that instead the authority intend to use any balance or amount such as is mentioned in that subsection to meet –

        (i)   relevant expenditure incurred during the currency of the final management order, and

        (ii) any compensation that may become payable to a third party;

    (d) that section 129(3) or (5) is not to apply in relation to an interim or (as the case may be) final management order that immediately preceded the final management order ('the order'), and that instead the authority intend to use rent or other payments collected during the currency of the order to reimburse the authority in respect of any deficit or amount such as is mentioned in that subsection;

    (e) the authority's intentions as regards the recovery from a relevant landlord, with or without interest, of any amount of relevant expenditure that cannot be reimbursed out of the total amount of rent or other payments.

(6) Part 2 of the scheme is to describe in general terms how the authority intend to address the matters which caused them to make the final management order and may, for example, include –

    (a) descriptions of any steps that the authority intend to take to require persons occupying the house to comply with their obligations under any lease or licence or under the general law;

    (b) descriptions of any repairs that are needed to the property and an explanation as to why those repairs are necessary.

(7) The authority must –

    (a) keep full accounts of their income and expenditure in respect of the house; and

    (b) afford to each relevant landlord, and to any other person who has an estate or interest in the house, all reasonable facilities for inspecting, taking copies of and verifying those accounts.

(8) In this section –

    'relevant expenditure' means expenditure reasonably incurred by the authority in connection with performing their duties under section 115(2) in respect of the house (including any reasonable administrative costs and any premiums paid for insurance of the premises);

    'relevant landlord' means any person who is an immediate landlord of the house or part of it;

    'rent or other payments' means rent or other payments –

    (a) which are payable under leases or licences or in respect of furniture within section 126(1), and

    (b) which the authority have collected or recovered by virtue of this Chapter.

(9) In the provisions of this Chapter relating to varying, revoking or appealing against decisions relating to a final management order, any reference to such an order includes (where the context permits) a reference to the management scheme contained in it.

120 Enforcement of management scheme by relevant landlord

(1) An affected person may apply to a residential property tribunal for an order requiring the local housing authority to manage the whole or part of a house in accordance with the management scheme contained in a final management order made in respect of the house.

(2) On such an application the tribunal may, if it considers it appropriate to do so, make an order –

(a) requiring the local housing authority to manage the whole or part of the house in accordance with the management scheme, or
(b) revoking the final management order as from a date specified in the tribunal's order.

(3) An order under subsection (2) may –

(a) specify the steps which the authority are to take to manage the whole or part of the house in accordance with the management scheme,
(b) include provision varying the final management order,
(c) require the payment of money to an affected person by way of damages.

(4) In this section 'affected person' means –

(a) a relevant landlord (within the meaning of section 119), and
(b) any third party to whom compensation is payable by virtue of a decision of the authority under section 128.

Final management orders: variation and revocation

121 Variation of final management orders

(1) The local housing authority may vary a final management order if they consider it appropriate to do so.

(2) A variation does not come into force until such time, if any, as is the operative time for the purposes of this subsection under paragraph 31 of Schedule 6 (time when period for appealing expires without an appeal being made or when decision to vary is confirmed on appeal).

(3) The power to vary an order under this section is exercisable by the authority either –

(a) on an application made by a relevant person, or
(b) on the authority's own initiative.

(4) In this section 'relevant person' means –

(a) any person who has an estate or interest in the house or part of it (but is not a tenant under a lease with an unexpired term of 3 years or less), or
(b) any other person who (but for the order) would be a person managing or having control of the house or part of it.

122 Revocation of final management orders

(1) The local housing authority may revoke a final management order in the following cases –

(a) if the order was made under section 113(2) or (5) and the house has ceased to be an HMO to which Part 2 applies or a Part 3 house (as the case may be);
(b) if the order was made under section 113(2) or (5) and a licence granted by them in respect of the house is due to come into force under Part 2 or Part 3 as from the revocation of the order;
(c) if a further final management order has been made by them in respect of the house so as to replace the order;
(d) if in any other circumstances the authority consider it appropriate to revoke the order.

(2) A revocation does not come into force until such time, if any, as is the operative time for the purposes of this subsection under paragraph 31 of Schedule 6 (time when period for appealing expires without an appeal being made or when decision to vary is confirmed on appeal).

(3) The power to revoke an order under this section is exercisable by the authority either –

(a) on an application made by a relevant person, or
(b) on the authority's own initiative.

(4) In this section 'relevant person' means –

(a) any person who has an estate or interest in the house or part of it (but is not a tenant under a lease with an unexpired term of 3 years or less), or
(b) any other person who (but for the order) would be a person managing or having control of the house or part of it.

Interim and final management orders: procedure and appeals

123 Procedural requirements and appeals

Schedule 6 (which deals with procedural requirements relating to the making, variation or revocation of interim and final management orders and with appeals against decisions relating to such orders) has effect.

Interim and final management orders: other general provisions

124 Effect of management orders: occupiers

(1) This section applies to existing and new occupiers of a house in relation to which an interim or final management order is in force.

(2) In this section –

'existing occupier' means a person who, at the time when the order comes into force, either –

(a) (in the case of an HMO or a Part 3 house) is occupying part of the house and does not have an estate or interest in the whole of the house, or
(b) (in the case of a Part 3 house) is occupying the whole of the house,

but is not a new occupier within subsection (6);

'new occupier' means a person who, at a time when the order is in force, is occupying the whole or part of the house under a lease or licence granted under section 107(3)(c) or 116(3)(c).

(3) Sections 107 and 116 do not affect the rights or liabilities of an existing occupier under a lease or licence (whether in writing or not) under which he is occupying the whole or part of the house at the commencement date.

(4) Where the lessor or licensor under such a lease or licence –

(a) has an estate or interest in the house, and
(b) is not an existing occupier,

the lease or licence has effect while the order is in force as if the local housing authority were substituted in it for the lessor or licensor.

(5) Such a lease continues to have effect, as far as possible, as a lease despite the fact that the rights of the local housing authority, as substituted for the lessor, do not amount to an estate in law in the premises.

(6) Section 116 does not affect the rights or liabilities of a new occupier who, in the case of a final management order, is occupying the whole or part of the house at the time when the order comes into force.

(7) The provisions which exclude local authority lettings from the Rent Acts, namely –

    (a) sections 14 to 16 of the Rent Act 1977 (c 42), and

    (b) those sections as applied by Schedule 2 to the Rent (Agriculture) Act 1976 (c 80) and section 5(2) to (4) of that Act,

do not apply to a lease or agreement under which an existing or new occupier is occupying the whole or part of the house.

(8) Section 1(2) of, and paragraph 12 of Part 1 of Schedule 1 to, the Housing Act 1988 (c 50) (which exclude local authority lettings from Part 1 of that Act) do not apply to a lease or agreement under which an existing or new occupier is occupying the whole or part of the house.

(9) Nothing in this Chapter has the result that the authority are to be treated as the legal owner of any premises for the purposes of –

    (a) section 80 of the Housing Act 1985 (c 68) (the landlord condition for secure tenancies); or

    (b) section 124 of the Housing Act 1996 (c 52) (introductory tenancies).

(10) If, immediately before the coming into force of an interim or final management order, an existing occupier was occupying the whole or part of the house under –

    (a) a protected or statutory tenancy within the meaning of the Rent Act 1977 (c 42),

    (b) a protected or statutory tenancy within the meaning of the Rent (Agriculture) Act 1976 (c 80), or

    (c) an assured tenancy or assured agricultural occupancy within the meaning of Part 1 of the Housing Act 1988 (c 50),

nothing in this Chapter prevents the continuance of that tenancy or occupancy or affects the continued operation of any of those Acts in relation to the tenancy or occupancy after the coming into force of the order.

(11) In this section 'the commencement date' means the date on which the order came into force (or, if that order was preceded by one or more orders under this Chapter, the date when the first order came into force).

125 Effect of management orders: agreements and legal proceedings

(1) An agreement or instrument within subsection (2) has effect, while an interim or final management order is in force, as if any rights or liabilities of the immediate landlord under the agreement or instrument were instead rights or liabilities of the local housing authority.

(2) An agreement or instrument is within this subsection if –

    (a) it is effective on the commencement date,

    (b) one of the parties to it is a person who is the immediate landlord of the house or a part of the house ('the relevant premises'),

    (c) it relates to the house, whether in connection with –

        (i) any management activities with respect to the relevant premises, or

        (ii) the provision of any services or facilities for persons occupying those premises,

    or otherwise,

    (d) it is specified for the purposes of this subsection in the order or falls within a description of agreements or instruments so specified, and

    (e) the authority serve a notice in writing on all the parties to it stating that subsection (1) is to apply to it.

(3) An agreement or instrument is not within subsection (2) if –

(a) it is a lease within section 107(5) or 116(5), or

(b) it relates to any disposition by the immediate landlord which is not precluded by section 109(2) or 118(2), or

(c) it is within section 124(4).

(4) Proceedings in respect of any cause of action within subsection (5) may, while an interim or final management order is in force, be instituted or continued by or against the local housing authority instead of by or against the immediate landlord.

(5) A cause of action is within this subsection if –

(a) it is a cause of action (of any nature) which accrued to or against the immediate landlord of the house or a part of the house before the commencement date,

(b) it relates to the house as mentioned in subsection (2)(c),

(c) it is specified for the purposes of this subsection in the order or falls within a description of causes of action so specified, and

(d) the authority serve a notice in writing on all interested parties stating that subsection (4) is to apply to it.

(6) If, by virtue of this section, the authority become subject to any liability to pay damages in respect of anything done (or omitted to be done) before the commencement date by or on behalf of the immediate landlord of the house or a part of it, the immediate landlord is liable to reimburse to the authority an amount equal to the amount of the damages paid by them.

(7) In this section –

'agreement' includes arrangement;

'the commencement date' means the date on which the order comes into force (or, if that order was preceded by one or more orders under this Chapter, the date when the first order came into force);

'management activities' includes repair, maintenance, improvement and insurance.

126 Effect of management orders: furniture

(1) Subsection (2) applies where, on the date on which an interim or final management order comes into force, there is furniture in the house which a person occupying the house has the right to use in consideration of periodical payments to a person who is an immediate landlord of the house or a part of it (whether the payments are included in the rent payable by the occupier or not).

(2) The right to possession of the furniture against all persons other than the occupier vests in the local housing authority on that date and remains vested in the authority while the order is in force.

(3) The local housing authority may renounce the right to possession of the furniture conferred by subsection (2) if –

(a) an application in writing has been made to them for the purpose by the person owning the furniture, and

(b) they renounce the right by notice in writing served on that person not less than two weeks before the notice takes effect.

(4) If the authority's right to possession of furniture conferred by subsection (2) is a right exercisable against more than one person interested in the furniture, any of those persons may apply to a residential property tribunal for an adjustment of their respective rights and liabilities as regards the furniture.

(5) On such an application the tribunal may make an order for such an adjustment of rights and liabilities, either unconditionally or subject to such terms and conditions, as it considers appropriate.

(6) The terms and conditions may, in particular, include terms and conditions about the payment of money by a party to the proceedings to another party to the proceedings by way of compensation, damages or otherwise.

(7) In this section 'furniture' includes fittings and other articles.

127 Management orders: power to supply furniture

(1) The local housing authority may supply the house to which an interim or final management order relates with such furniture as they consider to be required.

(2) For the purposes of section 110 or a management scheme under section 119, any expenditure incurred by the authority under this section constitutes expenditure incurred by the authority in connection with performing their duty under section 106(3) or 115(2).

(3) In this section 'furniture' includes fittings and other articles.

128 Compensation payable to third parties

(1) If a third party requests them to do so at any time, the local housing authority must consider whether an amount by way of compensation should be paid to him in respect of any interference with his rights in consequence of an interim or final management order.

(2) The authority must notify the third party of their decision as soon as practicable.

(3) Where the local housing authority decide under subsection (1) that compensation ought to be paid to a third party in consequence of a final management order, they must vary the management scheme contained in the order so as to specify the amount of the compensation to be paid and to make provision as to its payment.

129 Termination of management orders: financial arrangements

(1) This section applies where an interim or final management order ceases to have effect for any reason.

(2) If, on the termination date for an interim management order, the total amount of rent or other payments collected or recovered as mentioned in section 110(3) exceeds the total amount of –

(a) the local housing authority's relevant expenditure, and
(b) any amounts of compensation payable to third parties by virtue of decisions of the authority under section 128,

the authority must, as soon as practicable after the termination date, pay the balance to such relevant landlord, or to such relevant landlords in such proportions, as they consider appropriate.

(3) If, on the termination date for an interim management order, the total amount of rent or other payments collected or recovered as mentioned in section 110(3) is less than the total amount of –

(a) the authority's relevant expenditure, and
(b) any amounts of compensation payable as mentioned in subsection (2)(b),

the difference is recoverable by the authority from such relevant landlord, or such relevant landlords in such proportions, as they consider appropriate.

(4) If, on the termination date for a final management order, any amount is payable to –

(a) a third party, or
(b) any relevant landlord in accordance with the management scheme under section 119,

that amount must be paid to that person by the local housing authority in the manner provided by the scheme.

(5) If, on the termination date for a final management order, any amount is payable to the local housing authority in accordance with the management scheme, that amount is recoverable by the local housing authority –

(a) from such relevant landlord, or
(b) from such relevant landlords in such proportions,

as is provided by the scheme.

(6) The provisions of any of subsections (2) to (5) do not, however, apply in relation to the order if –

(a) the order is followed by a final management order, and
(b) the management scheme contained in that final management order provides for that subsection not to apply in relation to the order (see section 119(5)(c) and (d)).

(7) Any sum recoverable by the authority under subsection (3) or (5) is, until recovered, a charge on the house.

(8) The charge takes effect on the termination date for the order as a legal charge which is a local land charge.

(9) For the purpose of enforcing the charge the authority have the same powers and remedies under the Law of Property Act 1925 (c 20) and otherwise as if they were mortgagees by deed having powers of sale and lease, of accepting surrenders of leases and of appointing a receiver.

(10) The power of appointing a receiver is exercisable at any time after the end of the period of one month beginning with the date on which the charge takes effect.

(11) If the order is to be followed by a licence granted under Part 2 or 3 in respect of the house, the conditions contained in the licence may include a condition requiring the licence holder –

(a) to repay to the authority any amount recoverable by them under subsection (3) or (5), and
(b) to do so in such instalments as are specified in the licence.

(12) In this section –

'relevant expenditure' has the same meaning as in section 110;

'relevant landlord' means a person who was the immediate landlord of the house or part of it immediately before the termination date or his successor in title for the time being;

'rent or other payments' means rents or other payments payable under leases or licences or in respect of furniture within section 126(1);

'the termination date' means the date on which the order ceases to have effect.

130 Termination of management orders: leases, agreements and proceedings

(1) This section applies where –

(a) an interim or final management order ceases to have effect for any reason, and
(b) the order is not immediately followed by a further order under this Chapter.

(2) As from the termination date –

(a) a lease or licence in which the local housing authority was substituted for another party by virtue of section 124(4) has effect with the substitution of the original party, or his successor in title, for the authority; and

(b) an agreement which (in accordance with section 108 or 117) has effect as a lease or licence granted by the authority under section 107 or 116 has effect with the substitution of the relevant landlord for the authority.

(3) If the relevant landlord is a lessee, nothing in a superior lease imposes liability on him or any superior lessee in respect of anything done before the termination date in pursuance of the terms of an agreement to which subsection (2)(b) applies.

(4) If the condition in subsection (5) is met, any other agreement entered into by the authority in the performance of their duties under section 106(1) to (3) or 115(2) in respect of the house has effect, as from the termination date, with the substitution of the relevant landlord for the authority.

(5) The condition is that the authority serve a notice on the other party or parties to the agreement stating that subsection (4) applies to the agreement.

(6) If the condition in subsection (7) is met –

(a) any rights or liabilities that were rights or liabilities of the authority immediately before the termination date by virtue of any provision of this Chapter or under any agreement to which subsection (4) applies are rights or liabilities of the relevant landlord instead, and

(b) any proceedings instituted or continued by or against the authority by virtue of any such provision or agreement may be continued by or against the relevant landlord instead,

as from the termination date.

(7) The condition is that the authority serve a notice on all interested parties stating that subsection (6) applies to the rights or liabilities or (as the case may be) the proceedings.

(8) If by virtue of this section a relevant landlord becomes subject to any liability to pay damages in respect of anything done (or omitted to be done) before the termination date by or on behalf of the authority, the authority are liable to reimburse to the relevant landlord an amount equal to the amount of the damages paid by him.

(9) Where two or more persons are relevant landlords in relation to different parts of the house, any reference in this section to 'the relevant landlord' is to be taken to refer to such one or more of them as is determined by agreement between them or (in default of agreement) by a residential property tribunal on an application made by any of them.

(10) This section applies to instruments as it applies to agreements.

(11) In this section –

'agreement' includes arrangement;

'relevant landlord' means a person who was the immediate landlord of the house immediately before the termination date or his successor in title for the time being;

'the termination date' means the date on which the order ceases to have effect.

131 Management orders: power of entry to carry out work

(1) The right mentioned in subsection (2) is exercisable by the local housing authority, or any person authorised in writing by them, at any time when an interim or final management order is in force.

(2) That right is the right at all reasonable times to enter any part of the house for the purpose of carrying out works, and is exercisable as against any person having an estate or interest in the house.

(3) Where part of a house is excluded from the provisions of an interim or final management order under section 102(8) or 113(7), the right conferred by subsection (1) is exercisable as respects that part so far as is reasonably required for the purpose of carrying out works in the part of the house which is subject to the order.

(4) If, after receiving reasonable notice of the intended action, any occupier of the whole or part of the house prevents any officer, employee, agent or contractor of the local housing authority from carrying out work in the house, a magistrates' court may order him to permit to be done on the premises anything which the authority consider to be necessary.

(5) A person who fails to comply with an order of the court under subsection (4) commits an offence.

(6) A person who commits an offence under subsection (5) is liable on summary conviction to a fine not exceeding level 5 on the standard scale.

Chapter 2
Interim and Final Empty Dwelling Management Orders

Introductory

132 Empty dwelling management orders: introductory

(1) This Chapter deals with the making by a local housing authority of –

   (a) an interim empty dwelling management order (an 'interim EDMO'), or
   (b) a final empty dwelling management order (a 'final EDMO'),

in respect of a dwelling.

(2) An interim EDMO is an order made to enable a local housing authority, with the consent of the relevant proprietor, to take steps for the purpose of securing that a dwelling becomes and continues to be occupied.

(3) A final EDMO is an order made, in succession to an interim EDMO or a previous final EDMO, for the purpose of securing that a dwelling is occupied.

(4) In this Chapter –

   (a) 'dwelling' means –
      (i) a building intended to be occupied as a separate dwelling, or
      (ii) a part of a building intended to be occupied as a separate dwelling which may be entered otherwise than through any non-residential accommodation in the building;
   (b) any reference to 'the dwelling', in relation to an interim EDMO or a final EDMO, is a reference to the dwelling to which the order relates;
   (c) 'relevant proprietor', in relation to a dwelling, means –
      (i) if the dwelling is let under one or more leases with an unexpired term of 7 years or more, the lessee under whichever of those leases has the shortest unexpired term; or
      (ii) in any other case, the person who has the freehold estate in the dwelling;
   (d) 'third party', in relation to a dwelling, means any person who has an estate or interest in the dwelling (other than the relevant proprietor and any person who is a tenant under a lease granted under paragraph 2(3)(c) or 10(3)(c) of Schedule 7); and

(e) any reference (however expressed) to rent or other payments in respect of occupation of a dwelling, includes any payments that the authority receive from persons in respect of unlawful occupation of the dwelling.

(5) In subsection (4)(c), the reference to an unexpired term of 7 years or more of a lease of a dwelling is –

(a) in relation to a dwelling in respect of which the local housing authority are considering making an interim EDMO, a reference to the unexpired term of the lease at the time the authority begin taking steps under section 133(3),

(b) in relation to a dwelling in respect of which an interim EDMO has been made, a reference to the unexpired term of the lease at the time the application for authorisation to make the interim EDMO was made under subsection (1) of that section, or

(c) in relation to a dwelling in respect of which a local housing authority are considering making or have made a final EDMO, a reference to the unexpired term of the lease at the time the application for authorisation to make the preceding interim EDMO was made under subsection (1) of that section.

'Preceding interim EDMO', in relation to a final EDMO, means the interim EDMO that immediately preceded the final EDMO or, where there has been a succession of final EDMOs, the interim EDMO that immediately preceded the first of them.

(6) Schedule 7 (which makes further provision regarding EDMOs) has effect.

Interim empty dwelling management orders

133 Making of interim EDMOs

(1) A local housing authority may make an interim EDMO in respect of a dwelling if –

(a) it is a dwelling to which this section applies, and

(b) on an application by the authority to a residential property tribunal, the tribunal by order authorises them under section 134 to make such an order, either in the terms of a draft order submitted by them or in those terms as varied by the tribunal.

(2) This section applies to a dwelling if –

(a) the dwelling is wholly unoccupied, and

(b) the relevant proprietor is not a public sector body.

'Wholly unoccupied' means that no part is occupied, whether lawfully or unlawfully.

(3) Before determining whether to make an application to a residential property tribunal for an authorisation under section 134, the authority must make reasonable efforts –

(a) to notify the relevant proprietor that they are considering making an interim EDMO in respect of the dwelling under this section, and

(b) to ascertain what steps (if any) he is taking, or is intending to take, to secure that the dwelling is occupied.

(4) In determining whether to make an application to a residential property tribunal for an authorisation under section 134, the authority must take into account the rights of the relevant proprietor of the dwelling and the interests of the wider community.

(5) The authority may make an interim EDMO in respect of the dwelling despite any pending appeal against the order of the tribunal (but this is without prejudice to any order that may be made on the disposal of any such appeal).

(6) An application to a residential property tribunal under this section for authorisation to make an interim EDMO in respect of a dwelling may include an application for an order under paragraph 22 of Schedule 7 determining a lease or licence of the dwelling.

(7) In this section 'public sector body' means a body mentioned in any of paragraphs (a) to (f) of paragraph 2(1) of Schedule 14.

(8) Part 1 of Schedule 6 applies in relation to the making of an interim EDMO in respect of a dwelling as it applies in relation to the making of an interim management order in respect of a house, subject to the following modifications –

(a) paragraph 7(2) does not apply;
(b) paragraph 7(4)(c) is to be read as referring instead to the date on which the order is to cease to have effect in accordance with paragraph 1(3) and (4) or 9(3) to (5) of Schedule 7;
(c) in paragraph 7(6) –
    (i) paragraph (a) is to be read as referring instead to Part 4 of Schedule 7; and
    (ii) paragraph (b) does not apply;
(d) paragraph 8(4) is to be read as defining 'relevant person' as any person who, to the knowledge of the local housing authority, is a person having an estate or interest in the dwelling (other than a person who is a tenant under a lease granted under paragraph 2(3)(c) of Schedule 7).

134 Authorisation to make interim EDMOs

(1) A residential property tribunal may authorise a local housing authority to make an interim EDMO in respect of a dwelling to which section 133 applies if the tribunal –

(a) is satisfied as to the matters mentioned in subsection (2), and
(b) is not satisfied that the case falls within one of the prescribed exceptions.

(2) The matters as to which the tribunal must be satisfied are –

(a) that the dwelling has been wholly unoccupied for at least 6 months or such longer period as may be prescribed,
(b) that there is no reasonable prospect that the dwelling will become occupied in the near future,
(c) that, if an interim order is made, there is a reasonable prospect that the dwelling will become occupied,
(d) that the authority have complied with section 133(3), and
(e) that any prescribed requirements have been complied with.

(3) In deciding whether to authorise a local housing authority to make an interim EDMO in respect of a dwelling, the tribunal must take into account –

(a) the interests of the community, and
(b) the effect that the order will have on the rights of the relevant proprietor and may have on the rights of third parties.

(4) On authorising a local housing authority to make an interim EDMO in respect of a dwelling, the tribunal may, if it thinks fit, make an order requiring the authority (if they make the EDMO) to pay to any third party specified in the order an amount of compensation in respect of any interference in consequence of the order with the rights of the third party.

(5) The appropriate national authority may by order –

(a) prescribe exceptions for the purposes of subsection (1)(b),
(b) prescribe a period of time for the purposes of subsection (2)(a), and

(c) prescribe requirements for the purposes of subsection (2)(e).

(6) An order under subsection (5)(a) may, in particular, include exceptions in relation to –

(a) dwellings that have been occupied solely or principally by the relevant proprietor who is at the material time temporarily resident elsewhere;
(b) dwellings that are holiday homes or that are otherwise occupied by the relevant proprietor or his guests on a temporary basis from time to time;
(c) dwellings undergoing repairs or renovation;
(d) dwellings in respect of which an application for planning permission or building control approval is outstanding;
(e) dwellings which are genuinely on the market for sale or letting;
(f) dwellings where the relevant proprietor has died not more than the prescribed number of months before the material time.

(7) In this section –

'building control approval' means approval for the carrying out of any works under building regulations;

'planning permission' has the meaning given by section 336(1) of the Town and Country Planning Act 1990 (c 8);

'prescribed' means prescribed by an order under subsection (5);

'wholly unoccupied' means that no part is occupied, whether lawfully or unlawfully.

135 Local housing authority's duties once interim EDMO in force

(1) A local housing authority who have made an interim EDMO in respect of a dwelling must comply with the following provisions as soon as practicable after the order has come into force (see paragraph 1 of Schedule 7).

(2) The authority must take such steps as they consider appropriate for the purpose of securing that the dwelling becomes and continues to be occupied.

(3) The authority must also take such other steps as they consider appropriate with a view to the proper management of the dwelling pending –

(a) the making of a final EDMO in respect of the dwelling under section 136, or
(b) the revocation of the interim EDMO.

(4) If the local housing authority conclude that there are no steps which they could appropriately take under the order for the purpose of securing that the dwelling becomes occupied, the authority must either –

(a) make a final EDMO in respect of the dwelling under section 136, or
(b) revoke the order under paragraph 7 of Schedule 7 without taking any further action.

(5) For the avoidance of doubt, the authority's duty under subsection (3) includes taking such steps as are necessary to ensure that, while the order is in force, reasonable provision is made for insurance of the dwelling against destruction or damage by fire or other causes.

Final empty dwelling management orders

136 Making of final EDMOs

(1) A local housing authority may make a final EDMO to replace an interim EDMO made under section 133 if –

(a) they consider that, unless a final EDMO is made in respect of the dwelling, the dwelling is likely to become or remain unoccupied;

(b) where the dwelling is unoccupied, they have taken all such steps as it was appropriate for them to take under the interim EDMO with a view to securing the occupation of the dwelling.

(2) A local housing authority may make a new final EDMO so as to replace a final EDMO made under this section if –

(a) they consider that unless a new final EDMO is made in respect of the dwelling, the dwelling is likely to become or remain unoccupied; and

(b) where the dwelling is unoccupied, they have taken all such steps as it was appropriate for them to take under the existing final EDMO with a view to securing the occupation of the dwelling.

(3) In deciding whether to make a final EDMO in respect of a dwelling, the authority must take into account –

(a) the interests of the community, and

(b) the effect that the order will have on the rights of the relevant proprietor and may have on the rights of third parties.

(4) Before making a final EDMO under this section, the authority must consider whether compensation should be paid by them to any third party in respect of any interference in consequence of the order with the rights of the third party.

(5) Part 1 of Schedule 6 applies in relation to the making of a final EDMO in respect of a dwelling as it applies in relation to the making of a final management order in respect of a house, subject to the following modifications –

(a) paragraph 7(2) does not apply;

(b) paragraph 7(4)(c) is to be read as referring instead to the date on which the order is to cease to have effect in accordance with paragraph 1(3) and (4) or 9(3) to (5) of Schedule 7;

(c) in paragraph 7(6) –

   (i) paragraph (a) is to be read as referring to Part 4 of Schedule 7, and

   (ii) paragraph (b) is to be read as referring instead to paragraph 27(2) of Schedule 7;

(d) paragraph 7(6) in addition is to be read as requiring the notice under paragraph 7(5) also to contain –

   (i) the decision of the authority as to whether to pay compensation to any third party,

   (ii) the amount of any such compensation to be paid, and

   (iii) information about the right of appeal against the decision under paragraph 34 of Schedule 7;

(e) paragraph 8(4) is to be read as defining 'relevant person' as any person who, to the knowledge of the local housing authority, is a person having an estate or interest in the dwelling (other than a person who is a tenant under a lease granted under paragraph 2(3)(c) or 10(3)(c) of Schedule 7).

137 Local housing authority's duties once final EDMO in force

(1) A local housing authority who have made a final EDMO in respect of a dwelling must comply with the following provisions once the order has come into force (see paragraph 9 of Schedule 7).

(2) The authority must take such steps as they consider appropriate for the purpose of securing that the dwelling is occupied.

(3) The authority must also take such other steps as they consider appropriate with a view to the proper management of the dwelling in accordance with the management scheme contained in the order (see paragraph 13 of Schedule 7).

(4) The authority must from time to time review –

(a) the operation of the order and in particular the management scheme contained in it,

(b) whether, if the dwelling is unoccupied, there are any steps which they could appropriately take under the order for the purpose of securing that the dwelling becomes occupied, and

(c) whether keeping the order in force in relation to the dwelling (with or without making any variations under paragraph 15 of Schedule 7) is necessary to secure that the dwelling becomes or remains occupied.

(5) If on a review the authority consider that any variations should be made under paragraph 15 of Schedule 7, they must proceed to make those variations.

(6) If the dwelling is unoccupied and on a review the authority conclude that either –

(a) there are no steps which they could appropriately take as mentioned in subsection (4)(b), or

(b) keeping the order in force is not necessary as mentioned in subsection (4)(c),

they must proceed to revoke the order.

(7) For the avoidance of doubt, the authority's duty under subsection (3) includes taking such steps as are necessary to ensure that, while the order is in force, reasonable provision is made for insurance of the dwelling against destruction or damage by fire or other causes.

Compensation

138 Compensation payable to third parties

(1) A third party may, while an interim EDMO is in force in respect of a dwelling, apply to a residential property tribunal for an order requiring the local housing authority to pay to him compensation in respect of any interference in consequence of the order with his rights in respect of the dwelling.

(2) On such an application, the tribunal may, if it thinks fit, make an order requiring the authority to pay to the third party an amount by way of compensation in respect of any such interference.

(3) If a third party requests them to do so at any time, the local housing authority must consider whether an amount by way of compensation should be paid to him in respect of any interference in consequence of a final EDMO with his rights.

(4) The authority must notify the third party of their decision as soon as practicable.

(5) Where the local housing authority decide under subsection (3) that compensation ought to be paid to a third party, they must vary the management scheme contained in the order so as to specify the amount of the compensation to be paid and to make provision as to its payment.

Chapter 3
Overcrowding Notices

139 Service of overcrowding notices

(1) This Chapter applies to any HMO –

(a) in relation to which no interim or final management order is in force; and

(b) which is not required to be licensed under Part 2.

(2) The local housing authority may serve an overcrowding notice on one or more relevant persons if, having regard to the rooms available, it considers that an excessive number of persons is being, or is likely to be, accommodated in the HMO concerned.

(3) The authority must, at least 7 days before serving an overcrowding notice –

(a) inform in writing every relevant person (whether or not the person on whom the authority is to serve the notice) of their intention to serve the notice; and
(b) ensure that, so far as is reasonably possible, every occupier of the HMO concerned is informed of the authority's intention.

(4) The authority must also give the persons informed under subsection (3) an opportunity of making representations about the proposal to serve an overcrowding notice.

(5) An overcrowding notice becomes operative, if no appeal is brought under section 143, at the end of the period of 21 days from the date of service of the notice.

(6) If no appeal is brought under section 143, an overcrowding notice is final and conclusive as to matters which could have been raised on such an appeal.

(7) A person who contravenes an overcrowding notice commits an offence and is liable on summary conviction to a fine not exceeding level 4 on the standard scale.

(8) In proceedings for an offence under subsection (7) it is a defence that the person had a reasonable excuse for contravening the notice.

(9) In this section 'relevant person' means a person who is, to the knowledge of the local housing authority –

(a) a person having an estate or interest in the HMO concerned, or
(b) a person managing or having control of it.

140 Contents of overcrowding notices

(1) An overcrowding notice must state in relation to each room in the HMO concerned –

(a) what the local housing authority consider to be the maximum number of persons by whom the room is suitable to be occupied as sleeping accommodation at any one time; or
(b) that the local housing authority consider that the room is unsuitable to be occupied as sleeping accommodation.

(2) An overcrowding notice may specify special maxima applicable where some or all of the persons occupying a room are under such age as may be specified in the notice.

(3) An overcrowding notice must contain –

(a) the requirement prescribed by section 141 (not to permit excessive number of persons to sleep in the house in multiple occupation); or
(b) the requirement prescribed by section 142 (not to admit new residents if number of persons is excessive).

(4) The local housing authority may at any time –

(a) withdraw an overcrowding notice which has been served on any person and which contains the requirement prescribed by section 142, and
(b) serve on him instead an overcrowding notice containing the requirement prescribed by section 141.

141 Requirement as to overcrowding generally

(1) The requirement prescribed by this section is that the person on whom the notice is served must refrain from –

(a) permitting a room to be occupied as sleeping accommodation otherwise than in accordance with the notice; or

(b) permitting persons to occupy the HMO as sleeping accommodation in such numbers that it is not possible to avoid persons of opposite sexes who are not living together as husband and wife sleeping in the same room.

(2) For the purposes of subsection (1)(b) –

(a) children under the age of 10 are to be disregarded; and

(b) it must be assumed that the persons occupying the HMO as sleeping accommodation sleep only in rooms for which a maximum is set by the notice and that the maximum set for each room is not exceeded.

142 Requirement as to new residents

(1) The requirement prescribed by this section is that the person on whom the notice is served must refrain from –

(a) permitting a room to be occupied by a new resident as sleeping accommodation otherwise than in accordance with the notice; or

(b) permitting a new resident to occupy any part of the HMO as sleeping accommodation if that is not possible without persons of opposite sexes who are not living together as husband and wife sleeping in the same room.

(2) In subsection (1) 'new resident' means a person who was not an occupier of the HMO immediately before the notice was served.

(3) For the purposes of subsection (1)(b) –

(a) children under the age of 10 are to be disregarded; and

(b) it must be assumed that the persons occupying any part of the HMO as sleeping accommodation sleep only in rooms for which a maximum is set by the notice and that the maximum set for each room is not exceeded.

143 Appeals against overcrowding notices

(1) A person aggrieved by an overcrowding notice may appeal to a residential property tribunal within the period of 21 days beginning with the date of service of the notice.

(2) Such an appeal –

(a) is to be by way of a re-hearing, but

(b) may be determined having regard to matters of which the authority were unaware.

(3) On an appeal the tribunal may by order confirm, quash or vary the notice.

(4) If an appeal is brought, the notice does not become operative until –

(a) a decision is given on the appeal which confirms the notice and the period within which an appeal to the Lands Tribunal may be brought expires without any such appeal having been brought; or

(b) if an appeal is brought to the Lands Tribunal, a decision is given on the appeal which confirms the notice.

(5) For the purposes of subsection (4) –

(a) the withdrawal of an appeal has the same effect as a decision which confirms the notice appealed against; and
(b) references to a decision which confirms the notice are to a decision which confirms it with or without variation.

(6) A residential property tribunal may allow an appeal to be made to it after the end of the period mentioned in subsection (1) if it is satisfied that there is good reason for the failure to appeal before the end of that period (and for any delay since then in applying for permission to appeal out of time).

144 Revocation and variation of overcrowding notices

(1) The local housing authority may at any time, on the application of a relevant person –

(a) revoke an overcrowding notice; or
(b) vary it so as to allow more people to be accommodated in the HMO concerned.

(2) The applicant may appeal to a residential property tribunal if the local housing authority –

(a) refuse an application under subsection (1); or
(b) do not notify the applicant of their decision within the period of 35 days beginning with the making of the application (or within such further period as the applicant may in writing allow).

(3) An appeal under subsection (2) must be made within –

(a) the period of 21 days beginning with the date when the applicant is notified by the authority of their decision to refuse the application, or
(b) the period of 21 days immediately following the end of the period (or further period) applying for the purposes of paragraph (b) of that subsection,

as the case may be.

(4) Section 143(2) applies to such an appeal as it applies to an appeal under that section.

(5) On an appeal the tribunal may revoke the notice or vary it in any manner in which it might have been varied by the local housing authority.

(6) A residential property tribunal may allow an appeal to be made to it after the end of the 21-day period mentioned in subsection (3)(a) or (b) if it is satisfied that there is good reason for the failure to appeal before the end of that period (and for any delay since then in applying for permission to appeal).

(7) In this section 'relevant person' means –

(a) any person who has an estate or interest in the HMO concerned, or
(b) any other person who is a person managing or having control of it.

Chapter 4
Supplementary Provisions

145 Supplementary provisions

(1) The appropriate national authority may by regulations make such provision as it considers appropriate for supplementing the provisions of Chapter 1 or 2 in relation to cases where a local housing authority are to be treated as the lessee under a lease under –

(a) section 107(5) or 116(5), or

(b) paragraph 2(6) or 10(6) of Schedule 7.

(2) Regulations under this section may, in particular, make provision –

(a) as respects rights and liabilities in such cases of –
  (i) the authority,
  (ii) the person who (apart from the relevant provision mentioned in subsection (1)) is the lessee under the lease, or
  (iii) other persons having an estate or interest in the premises demised under the lease;
(b) requiring the authority to give copies to the person mentioned in paragraph (a)(ii) of notices and other documents served on them in connection with the lease;
(c) for treating things done by or in relation to the authority as done by or in relation to that person, or vice versa.

146 Interpretation and modification of this Part

(1) In this Part –

'HMO' means a house in multiple occupation as defined by sections 254 to 259,

'Part 3 house' means a house to which Part 3 of this Act applies (see section 79(2)),

and any reference to an HMO or Part 3 house includes (where the context permits) a reference to any yard, garden, outhouses and appurtenances belonging to, or usually enjoyed with, it (or any part of it).

(2) For the purposes of this Part 'mortgage' includes a charge or lien, and 'mortgagee' is to be read accordingly.

(3) The appropriate national authority may by regulations provide for –

(a) any provision of this Part, or
(b) section 263 (in its operation for the purposes of any such provision),

to have effect in relation to a section 257 HMO with such modifications as are prescribed by the regulations.

(4) A 'section 257 HMO' is an HMO which is a converted block of flats to which section 257 applies.

147 Index of defined expressions: Part 4

The following table shows where expressions used in this Part are defined or otherwise explained.

Expression	*Provision of this Act*
Appropriate national authority	Section 261(1)
Dwelling	Section 132(4)(a) and (b)
Final EDMO	Section 132(1)(b)
Final management order	Section 101(4)
Health	Section 2(5)
HMO	Section 146(1)
The house	Section 101(5) or 103(8)
Immediate landlord	Section 109(6) or 118(6)
Interim EDMO	Section 132(1)(a)
Interim management order	Section 101(3)

Expression	*Provision of this Act*
Landlord	Section 262(3)
Lease, lessee, etc	Section 262(1) to (4)
Licence (to occupy premises)	Section 262(9)
Local housing authority	Section 261(2) to (5)
Modifications	Section 250(7)
Mortgage, mortgagee	Section 146(2)
Occupier (and related expressions)	Section 262(6)
Owner	Section 262(7)
Part 3 house	Section 146(1)
Person having control	Section 263(1) and (2)
Person having estate or interest	Section 262(8)
Person managing	Section 263(3)
Relevant proprietor	Section 132(4)(c) and (5)
Rent or other payments (in Chapter 2)	Section 132(4)(e)
Residential property tribunal	Section 229
Tenancy, tenant, etc	Section 262(1) to (5)
Third party (in Chapter 1)	Section 101(7)
Third party (in Chapter 2)	Section 132(4)(d).

Part 5
Home Information Packs

Preliminary

148 Meaning of 'residential property' and 'home information pack'

(1) In this Part –

'residential property' means premises in England and Wales consisting of a single dwelling-house, including any ancillary land; and

'dwelling-house' means a building or part of a building occupied or intended to be occupied as a separate dwelling (and includes one that is being or is to be constructed).

(2) References in this Part to a home information pack, in relation to a residential property, are to a collection of documents relating to the property or the terms on which it is or may become available for sale.

149 Meaning of 'on the market' and related expressions

(1) In this Part references to 'the market' are to the residential property market in England and Wales.

(2) A residential property is put on the market when the fact that it is or may become available for sale is, with the intention of marketing the property, first made public in England and Wales by or on behalf of the seller.

(3) A residential property which has been put on the market is to be regarded as remaining on the market until it is taken off the market or sold.

(4) A fact is made public when it is advertised or otherwise communicated (in whatever form and by whatever means) to the public or to a section of the public.

150 Acting as estate agent

(1) A person acts as estate agent for the seller of a residential property if he does anything, in the course of a business in England and Wales, in pursuance of marketing instructions from the seller.

(2) For this purpose –

'business in England and Wales' means a business carried on (in whole or in part) from a place in England and Wales; and

'marketing instructions' means instructions to carry out any activities with a view to –

(a) effecting the introduction to the seller of a person wishing to buy the property; or
(b) selling the property by auction or tender.

(3) It is immaterial for the purposes of this section whether or not a person describes himself as an estate agent.

Responsibility for marketing residential properties

151 Responsibility for marketing: general

(1) References in this Part to a responsible person, in relation to a residential property, are to any person who is for the time being responsible for marketing the property.

(2) Sections 152 and 153 identify for the purposes of this Part –

(a) the person or persons who are responsible for marketing a residential property which is on the market ('the property'); and
(b) when the responsibility of any such person arises and ceases.

(3) Only the seller or a person acting as estate agent for the seller may be responsible for marketing the property.

(4) A person may be responsible for marketing the property on more than one occasion.

152 Responsibility of person acting as estate agent

(1) A person acting as estate agent becomes responsible for marketing the property when action taken by him or on his behalf –

(a) puts the property on the market; or
(b) makes public the fact that the property is on the market.

(2) That responsibility ceases when the following conditions are satisfied, namely –

(a) his contract with the seller is terminated (whether by the withdrawal of his instructions or otherwise);
(b) he has ceased to take any action which makes public the fact that the property is on the market; and
(c) any such action being taken on his behalf has ceased.

(3) Any responsibility arising under this section also ceases when the property is taken off the market or sold.

153 Responsibility of the seller

(1) The seller becomes responsible for marketing the property when action taken by him or on his behalf –

(a) puts the property on the market; or

(b) makes public the fact that the property is on the market.

(2) That responsibility ceases when the following conditions are satisfied, namely –

(a) there is at least one person acting as his estate agent who is responsible for marketing the property;

(b) the seller has ceased to take any action which makes public the fact that the property is on the market; and

(c) any such action being taken on the seller's behalf has ceased.

(3) In this section the references to action taken on behalf of the seller exclude action taken by or on behalf of a person acting as his estate agent.

(4) Any responsibility arising under this section also ceases when the property is taken off the market or sold.

Duties of a responsible person where a property is on the market

154 Application of sections 155 to 158

(1) Where a residential property is on the market, a person responsible for marketing the property is subject to the duties relating to home information packs that are imposed by sections 155 to 158 until his responsibility ceases.

(2) Each of those duties is subject to any exception relating to that duty which is provided for in those sections.

(3) The duty under section 156(1) is also subject to any condition imposed under section 157.

155 Duty to have a home information pack

(1) It is the duty of a responsible person to have in his possession or under his control a home information pack for the property which complies with the requirements of any regulations under section 163.

(2) That duty does not apply where the responsible person is the seller at any time when –

(a) there is another person who is responsible for marketing the property under section 152; and

(b) the seller believes on reasonable grounds that the other responsible person has a home information pack for the property in his possession or under his control which complies with the requirements of any regulations under section 163.

156 Duty to provide copy of home information pack on request

(1) Where a potential buyer makes a request to a responsible person for a copy of the home information pack, or of a document (or part of a document) which is or ought to be included in that pack, it is the duty of the responsible person to comply with that request within the permitted period.

(2) The responsible person does not comply with that duty unless –

(a) he provides the potential buyer with a document which is –
  (i) a copy of the home information pack for the property as it stands at the time when the document is provided, or
  (ii) a copy of a document (or part of a document) which is included in that pack,

as the case may be; and

(b) that pack or document complies with the requirements of any regulations under section 163 at that time.

(3) In subsection (2) 'the home information pack' means the home information pack intended by the responsible person to be the one required by section 155.

(4) That duty does not apply if, before the end of the permitted period, the responsible person believes on reasonable grounds that the person making the request –

(a) is unlikely to have sufficient means to buy the property in question;
(b) is not genuinely interested in buying a property of a general description which applies to the property; or
(c) is not a person to whom the seller is likely to be prepared to sell the property.

Nothing in this subsection authorises the doing of anything which constitutes an unlawful act of discrimination.

(5) Subsection (4) does not apply if the responsible person knows or suspects that the person making the request is an officer of an enforcement authority.

(6) That duty does not apply where the responsible person is the seller if, when the request is made, the duty under section 155 does not (by virtue of subsection (2) of that section) apply to him.

(7) But where the duty under this section is excluded by subsection (6), it is the duty of the seller to take reasonable steps to inform the potential buyer that the request should be made to the other person.

(8) The responsible person may charge a sum not exceeding the reasonable cost of making and, if requested, sending a paper copy of the pack or document.

(9) The permitted period for the purposes of this section is (subject to section 157(5)) the period of 14 days beginning with the day on which the request is made.

(10) If the responsible person ceases to be responsible for marketing the property before the end of the permitted period (whether because the property has been taken off the market or sold or for any other reason), he ceases to be under any duty to comply with the request.

(11) A person does not comply with the duty under this section by providing a copy in electronic form unless the potential buyer consents to receiving it in that form.

Register of home condition reports

157 Section 156 (1) duty: imposition of conditions

(1) A potential buyer who has made a request to which section 156(1) applies may be required to comply with either or both of the following conditions before any copy is provided.

(2) The potential buyer may be required to pay a charge authorised by section 156(8).

(3) The potential buyer may be required to accept any terms specified in writing which –

(a) are proposed by the seller or in pursuance of his instructions; and
(b) relate to the use or disclosure of the copy (or any information contained in or derived from it).

(4) A condition is only effective if it is notified to the potential buyer before the end of the period of 14 days beginning with the day on which the request is made.

(5) Where the potential buyer has been so notified of either or both of the conditions authorised by this section, the permitted period for the purposes of section 156 is the period of 14 days beginning with –

(a) where one condition is involved, the day on which the potential buyer complies with it by –
  (i) making the payment demanded, or
  (ii) accepting the terms proposed (or such other terms as may be agreed between the seller and the potential buyer in substitution for those proposed),

as the case may be; or
(b) where both conditions are involved, the day (or the later of the days) on which the potential buyer complies with them by taking the action mentioned in paragraph (a)(i) and (ii).

158 Duty to ensure authenticity of documents in other situations

(1) Where a responsible person provides a potential buyer with, or allows a potential buyer to inspect, any document purporting to be –

(a) a copy of the home information pack for the property, or
(b) a copy of a document (or part of a document) included in that pack,

the responsible person is under a duty to ensure that the document is authentic.

(2) A document is not authentic for the purposes of subsection (1) unless, at the time when it is provided or inspected –

(a) it is a copy of the home information pack for the property or a document (or part of a document) included in that pack, as the case may be; and
(b) that pack or document complies with the requirements of any regulations under section 163.

(3) In subsection (2) 'the home information pack' means the pack intended by the responsible person to be the one required by section 155.

(4) The duty under this section does not apply to anything provided in pursuance of the duty under section 156.

Other duties of person acting as estate agent

159 Other duties of person acting as estate agent

(1) This section applies to a person acting as estate agent for the seller of a residential property where –

(a) the property is not on the market; or
(b) the property is on the market but the person so acting is not a person responsible for marketing the property.

(2) It is the duty of a person to whom this section applies to have in his possession or under his control, when any qualifying action is taken by him or on his behalf, a home information pack for the property which complies with the requirements of any regulations under section 163.

(3) In subsection (2) 'qualifying action' means action taken with the intention of marketing the property which –

(a) communicates to any person in England and Wales the fact that the property is or may become available for sale; but
(b) does not put the property on the market or make public the fact that the property is on the market.

(4) Where a person to whom this section applies provides a potential buyer with, or allows a potential buyer to inspect, any document purporting to be –

(a) a copy of the home information pack for the property; or
(b) a copy of a document (or part of a document) included in that pack;

it is his duty to ensure that it is an authentic copy.

(5) A document is not authentic for the purposes of subsection (4) unless, at the time when it is provided or inspected –

(a) it is a copy of the home information pack for the property or a document (or part of a document) included in that pack, as the case may be; and
(b) that pack or document complies with the requirements of any regulations under section 163.

(6) In subsection (5) 'the home information pack' means the home information pack intended by the person to whom this section applies to be the one required by subsection (2).

Exceptions from the duties

160 Residential properties not available with vacant possession

(1) The duties under sections 155 to 159 do not apply in relation to a residential property at any time when it is not available for sale with vacant possession.

(2) But for the purposes of this Part a residential property shall be presumed to be available with vacant possession, at any time when any of those duties would apply in relation to the property if it is so available, unless the contrary appears from the manner in which the property is being marketed at that time.

161 Power to provide for further exceptions

The Secretary of State may by regulations provide for other exceptions from any duty under sections 155 to 159 in such cases and circumstances, and to such extent, as may be specified in the regulations.

162 Suspension of duties under sections 155 to 159

(1) The Secretary of State may make an order suspending (or later reviving) the operation of any duty imposed by sections 155 to 159.

(2) An order under this section may provide for the suspension of a duty to take effect only for a period specified in the order.

(3) A duty which is (or is to any extent) revived after being suspended under this section is liable to be suspended again.

Contents of home information packs

163 Contents of home information packs

(1) The Secretary of State may make regulations prescribing –

(a) the documents which are required or authorised to be included in the home information pack for a residential property; and

 (b) particular information which is required or authorised to be included in, or which is to be excluded from, any such document.

(2) A document prescribed under subsection (1) must be one that the Secretary of State considers would disclose relevant information.

(3) Any particular information required or authorised to be included in a prescribed document must be information that the Secretary of State considers to be relevant information.

(4) In this section 'relevant information' means information about any matter connected with the property (or the sale of the property) that would be of interest to potential buyers.

(5) Without prejudice to the generality of subsection (4), the information which the Secretary of State may consider to be relevant information includes any information about –

 (a) the interest which is for sale and the terms on which it is proposed to sell it;
 (b) the title to the property;
 (c) anything relating to or affecting the property that is contained in –
  (i) a register required to be kept by or under any enactment (whenever passed); or
  (ii) records kept by a person who can reasonably be expected to give information derived from those records to the seller at his request (on payment, if required, of a reasonable charge);
 (d) the physical condition of the property (including any particular characteristics or features of the property);
 (e) the energy efficiency of the property;
 (f) any warranties or guarantees subsisting in relation to the property;
 (g) any taxes, service charges or other charges payable in relation to the property.

(6) The regulations may require or authorise the home information pack to include –

 (a) replies the seller proposes to give to prescribed pre-contract enquiries; and
 (b) documents or particular information indexing or otherwise explaining the contents of the pack.

(7) The regulations may require a prescribed document –

 (a) to be in such form as may be prescribed; and
 (b) to be prepared by a person of a prescribed description on such terms (if any) as may be prescribed.

(8) The terms mentioned in subsection (7)(b) may include terms which enable provisions of the contract under which the document is to be prepared to be enforced by –

 (a) a potential or actual buyer;
 (b) a mortgage lender; or
 (c) any other person involved in the sale of the property who is not a party to that contract.

(9) The regulations may –

 (a) provide for the time at which any document is to be included in or removed from the home information pack; and
 (b) make different provision for different areas, for different descriptions of properties or for other different circumstances (including the manner in which a residential property is marketed).

(10) In this section 'prescribed' means prescribed by regulations under this section.

164 Home condition reports

(1) Regulations under section 163 may make the provision mentioned in this section in relation to any description of document dealing with matters mentioned in section 163(5)(d) or (e) (reports on physical condition or energy efficiency) which is to be included in the home information pack.

(2) In this section 'home condition report' means a document of that description.

(3) The regulations may require a home condition report to be made by an individual who is a member of an approved certification scheme following an inspection carried out by him in accordance with the provisions of the scheme.

(4) The regulations shall, if the provision mentioned in subsection (3) is made, make provision for the approval by the Secretary of State of one or more suitable certification schemes (and for the withdrawal by him of any such approval).

(5) The regulations shall require the Secretary of State to be satisfied, before approving a certification scheme, that the scheme contains appropriate provision –

  (a) for ensuring that members of the scheme are fit and proper persons who are qualified (by their education, training and experience) to produce home condition reports;
  (b) for ensuring that members of the scheme have in force suitable indemnity insurance;
  (c) for facilitating the resolution of complaints against members of the scheme;
  (d) for requiring home condition reports made by members of the scheme to be entered on the register mentioned in section 165;
  (e) for the keeping of a public register of the members of the scheme; and
  (f) for such other purposes as may be specified in the regulations.

(6) Subsection (5)(d) only applies where provision for a register of home condition reports is made under section 165.

(7) The regulations may require or authorise an approved certification scheme to contain provision about any matter relating to the home condition reports with which the scheme is concerned (including the terms on which members of the scheme may undertake to produce a home condition report).

(8) Nothing in this section limits the power under section 163 to make provision about home condition reports in the regulations.

Register of home condition reports

165 Register of home condition reports

(1) Where the provision mentioned in section 164(3) is made in relation to an approved certification scheme, regulations under section 163 may make provision for and in connection with a register of the home condition reports made by members of the scheme.

(2) The regulations may provide for the register to be kept –

  (a) by (or on behalf of) the Secretary of State; or
  (b) by such other person as the regulations may specify.

(3) The regulations may require a person wishing to enter a home condition report onto the register to pay such fee as may be prescribed.

(4) No person may disclose –

  (a) the register or any document (or part of a document) contained in it; or
  (b) any information contained in, or derived from, the register,

except in accordance with any provision of the regulations which authorises or requires such a disclosure to be made.

(5) The provision which may be made under subsection (1) includes (without prejudice to the generality of that subsection) provision as to circumstances in which or purposes for which a person or a person of a prescribed description –

    (a) may (on payment of such fee, if any, as may be prescribed) –
        (i) inspect the register or any document (or part of a document) contained in it;
        (ii) take or be given copies of the register or any document (or part of a document) contained in it; or
        (iii) be given information contained in, or derived from, the register; or
    (b) may disclose anything obtained by virtue of provision made under paragraph (a).

(6) The purposes which may be so prescribed may be public purposes or purposes of private undertakings or other persons.

(7) A person who contravenes subsection (4) is guilty of an offence and liable on summary conviction to a fine not exceeding level 5 on the standard scale.

(8) Nothing in this section limits the power to make regulations under section 163.

Enforcement

166 Enforcement authorities

(1) Every local weights and measures authority is an enforcement authority for the purposes of this Part.

(2) It is the duty of each enforcement authority to enforce –

    (a) the duties under sections 155 to 159 and 167(4), and
    (b) any duty imposed under section 172(1),

in their area.

167 Power to require production of home information packs

(1) An authorised officer of an enforcement authority may require a person who appears to him to be or to have been subject to the duty under section 155 or 159(2), in relation to a residential property, to produce for inspection a copy of, or of any document included in, the home information pack for that property.

(2) The power conferred by subsection (1) includes power –

    (a) to require the production in a visible and legible documentary form of any document included in the home information pack in question which is held in electronic form; and
    (b) to take copies of any document produced for inspection.

(3) A requirement under this section may not be imposed more than six months after the last day on which the person concerned was subject to the duty under section 155 or 159(2) in relation to the property (as the case may be).

(4) Subject to subsection (5), it is the duty of a person subject to such a requirement to comply with it within the period of 7 days beginning with the day after that on which it is imposed.

(5) A person is not required to comply with such a requirement if he has a reasonable excuse for not complying with the requirement.

(6) In this section 'the home information pack' means –

(a) where a requirement under this section is imposed on a person at a time when he is subject to the duty under section 155 or 159(2), the home information pack intended by him to be the one he is required to have at that time; or

(b) in any other case, the home information pack intended by the person concerned, when he was last subject to the duty under section 155 or 159(2), to be the one he was required to have at that time.

168 Penalty charge notices

(1) An authorised officer of an enforcement authority may, if he believes that a person has committed a breach of –

(a) any duty under sections 155 to 159 and 167(4), or
(b) any duty imposed under section 172(1),

give a penalty charge notice to that person.

(2) A penalty charge notice may not be given after the end of the period of six months beginning with the day (or in the case of a continuing breach the last day) on which the breach of duty was committed.

(3) Schedule 8 (which makes further provision about penalty charge notices) has effect.

169 Offences relating to enforcement officers

(1) A person who obstructs an officer of an enforcement authority acting in pursuance of section 167 is guilty of an offence.

(2) A person who, not being an authorised officer of an enforcement authority, purports to act as such in pursuance of section 167 or 168 is guilty of an offence.

(3) A person guilty of an offence under this section is liable on summary conviction to a fine not exceeding level 5 on the standard scale.

170 Right of private action

(1) This section applies where a person ('the responsible person') has committed a breach of duty under section 156 by failing to comply with a request from a potential buyer of a residential property for a copy of a prescribed document.

(2) If the potential buyer commissions his own version of the prescribed document at a time when both of the conditions mentioned below are satisfied, he is entitled to recover from the responsible person any reasonable fee paid by him in order to obtain the document.

(3) The first condition is that –

(a) the property is on the market; or
(b) the potential buyer and the seller are attempting to reach an agreement for the sale of the property.

(4) The second condition is that the potential buyer has not been provided with an authentic copy of the prescribed document.

(5) A copy of a prescribed document is not authentic for the purposes of subsection (4) unless –

(a) it is a copy of a document included in the home information pack for the property as it stands at the time the copy is provided to the potential buyer; and

(b) the document so included complies with the requirements of any regulations under section 163 at that time.

(6) In subsection (5) 'the home information pack' means the home information pack intended by the responsible person to be the one required by section 155.

(7) In this section 'prescribed document' means a document (being one required to be included in the home information pack by regulations under section 163) which is prescribed by regulations made by the Secretary of State for the purposes of this section.

(8) It is immaterial for the purposes of this section that the request in question did not specify the prescribed document but was for a copy of the home information pack or a part of the pack which included (or ought to have included) that document.

Supplementary

171 Application of Part to sub-divided buildings

(1) This section applies where –

(a) two or more dwelling-houses in a sub-divided building are marketed for sale (with any ancillary land) as a single property; and
(b) any one or more of those dwelling-houses –
  (i) is not available for sale (with any ancillary land) as a separate residential property; but
  (ii) is available with vacant possession.

(2) This Part applies to the dwelling-houses mentioned in subsection (1)(a) (with any ancillary land) as if –

(a) they were a residential property, and
(b) section 160 were omitted.

(3) Subsection (2) does not affect the application of this Part to any of those dwelling-houses which is available for sale (with any ancillary land) as a separate residential property.

(4) In this section 'sub-divided building' means a building or part of a building originally constructed or adapted for use as a single dwelling which has been divided (on one or more occasions) into separate dwelling-houses.

172 Power to require estate agents to belong to a redress scheme

(1) The Secretary of State may by order require every estate agent to be a member of an approved redress scheme.

(2) Acting as estate agent for the seller of a residential property in contravention of such an order is a breach of duty under this Part.

(3) Before making such an order the Secretary of State must be satisfied that he has approved one or more redress schemes such that every estate agent who is (or will be) subject to the duty imposed by the order is eligible to join an approved redress scheme.

For this purpose 'estate agent' does not include a person who is (by virtue of a prohibition imposed by or under the Estate Agents Act 1979 (c 38)) unable lawfully to act as estate agent for the seller of a residential property.

(4) An order under this section may –

(a) exclude estate agents of a prescribed description from any duty imposed under subsection (1);

(b) limit any duty so imposed so that it applies only in relation to relevant complaints of a prescribed description.

(5) Nothing in this section is to be taken as preventing an approved redress scheme from providing –

(a) for membership to be open to persons who are not subject to any duty to belong to an approved redress scheme;
(b) for the investigation and determination of complaints, other than those in relation to which such a duty applies, made against members who have voluntarily accepted the jurisdiction of the scheme over such complaints;
(c) for the exclusion from investigation and determination under the scheme of any complaint in such cases or circumstances as may be specified in the scheme.

(6) In this section and sections 173 and 174 –

'approved redress scheme' means a redress scheme that is for the time being approved under section 173;

'estate agent' means a person who acts as estate agent for sellers of residential properties for which a home information pack is (or will be) required under this Part;

'redress scheme' means a scheme under which certain relevant complaints may be investigated and determined by an independent person (referred to in those sections as 'the ombudsman'); and

'relevant complaint' means a complaint against an estate agent which –

(a) is made by a person who at the material time is the seller or a potential buyer of a residential property; and
(b) relates to an act or omission affecting the complainant in the course of the estate agent's activities in relation to a home information pack that is (or will be) required for that property (including the giving of advice as to whether such a pack is required).

(7) For the purposes of the law relating to defamation, proceedings under an approved redress scheme in relation to the investigation and determination of a complaint which is subject to an order under this section are to be treated in the same way as proceedings before a court.

173 Approval of redress schemes

(1) If the Secretary of State considers that a redress scheme (including one made by him or in pursuance of arrangements made by him) is satisfactory for the purposes of section 172, he may approve it for those purposes.

(2) In determining whether a redress scheme is satisfactory the Secretary of State shall have regard to –

(a) the provisions of the scheme;
(b) the manner in which the scheme will be operated (so far as can be judged from the facts known to him); and
(c) the respective interests of members of the scheme and of sellers and potential buyers of residential properties.

(3) A redress scheme may not be approved unless it makes satisfactory provision about the following matters (among other things) –

(a) the matters about which complaints may be made (which may include non-compliance with the provisions of a code of practice or other document);

(b) the ombudsman's duties and powers in relation to the investigation and determination of complaints (which may include power to decide not to investigate or determine a complaint);

(c) the provision of information by the ombudsman to –

(i) persons exercising functions under other schemes providing a means of redress for consumers; and

(ii) the Secretary of State or any other person exercising regulatory functions in relation to the activities of estate agents.

(4) An application for approval of a redress scheme shall be made in such manner as the Secretary of State may determine, accompanied by such information as the Secretary of State may require.

(5) The person administering an approved redress scheme shall notify the Secretary of State of any change to the scheme as soon as practicable after the change is made.

174 Withdrawal of approval of redress schemes

(1) The Secretary of State may withdraw his approval of a redress scheme.

(2) But before withdrawing his approval, the Secretary of State shall serve on the person administering the scheme a notice stating –

(a) that he proposes to withdraw his approval;

(b) the grounds for the proposed withdrawal of approval; and

(c) that representations about the proposed withdrawal may be made within such period of not less than 14 days as is specified in the notice.

(3) The Secretary of State shall give notice of his decision on a proposal to withdraw approval, with his reasons, to the person administering the scheme.

(4) Withdrawal of approval has effect from such date as may be specified in that notice.

(5) The person administering the scheme shall give a copy of a notice under subsection (3) to every member of the scheme.

175 Office of Fair Trading

(1) An enforcement authority may notify the Office of Fair Trading of any breach of duty under this Part appearing to the authority to have been committed by a person acting as estate agent.

(2) An enforcement authority shall notify the Office of Fair Trading of –

(a) any penalty charge notice given by an officer of the authority under section 168;

(b) any notice given by the authority confirming or withdrawing a penalty charge notice; and

(c) the result of any appeal from the confirmation of a penalty charge notice.

(3) The Estate Agents Act 1979 (c 38) applies in relation to a person who has committed a breach of duty under this Part in the course of estate agency work (within the meaning of that Act) as it applies in relation to a person who has engaged in a practice such as is mentioned in section 3(1)(d) of that Act in the course of such work.

176 Grants

(1) The Secretary of State may make grants towards expenditure incurred by any person in connection with –

(a) the development of proposals for any provision to be made by regulations under section 163;

(b) the development of schemes which are intended to be certification schemes for the purposes of any provision made or expected to be made in regulations under section 163 by virtue of section 164; or

(c) the development of a register for the purposes of any provision made or expected to be made in regulations under section 163 by virtue of section 165.

(2) A grant under this section may be made on conditions, which may include (among other things) –

(a) conditions as to the purposes for which the grant or any part of it may be used; and

(b) conditions requiring the repayment of the grant or any part of it in such circumstances as may be specified in the conditions.

177 Interpretation of Part 5

(1) In this Part –

'ancillary land', in relation to a dwelling-house or a sub-divided building, means any land intended to be occupied and enjoyed together with that dwelling-house or building;

'long lease' means –

(a) a lease granted for a term certain exceeding 21 years, whether or not it is (or may become) terminable before the end of that term by notice given by the tenant or by re-entry or forfeiture; or

(b) a lease for a term fixed by law under a grant with a covenant or obligation for perpetual renewal, other than a lease by sub-demise from one which is not a long lease;

and for this purpose 'lease' does not include a mortgage term;

'potential buyer' means a person who claims that he is or may become interested in buying a residential property;

'sale', in relation to a residential property, means a disposal, or agreement to dispose, by way of sale of –

(a) the freehold interest;

(b) the interest under a long lease;

(c) an option to acquire the freehold interest or the interest under a long lease;

and 'seller' means a person contemplating disposing of such an interest (and related expressions shall be construed accordingly).

(2) Any reference in the definition of 'sale' to the disposal of an interest of a kind mentioned in that definition includes a reference to the creation of such an interest.

(3) A document which is not in electronic form is only to be regarded for the purposes of this Part as being under the control of a person while it is in the possession of another if he has the right to take immediate possession of the document on demand (and without payment).

(4) A document held in electronic form is only to be regarded for the purposes of this Part as being in a person's possession or under his control if he is readily able (using equipment available to him) –

(a) to view the document in a form that is visible and legible; and

(b) to produce copies of it in a visible and legible documentary form.

178 Index of defined expressions: Part 5

In this Part, the expressions listed in the left-hand column have the meaning given by, or are to be interpreted in accordance with, the provisions inserted in the right-hand column.

Expression	Provision of this Act
Acting as estate agent for the seller	Section 150
Ancillary land	Section 177(1)
Control of documents	Section 177(3) and (4)
Dwelling-house	Section 148(1)
Enforcement authority	Section 166
Home information pack	Section 148(2)
Long lease	Section 177(1)
Make public	Section 149(4)
Possession of electronic documents	Section 177(4)
Potential buyer	Section 177(1)
Putting on the market	Section 149(2)
Remaining on the market	Section 149(3)
Residential property	Section 148(1)
Responsible person	Section 151(1)
Sale (and related expressions)	Section 177(1)
Seller (and related expressions)	Section 177(1)
The market	Section 149(1).

Part 6
Other Provisions about Housing

Chapter 1
Secure Tenancies

Introductory tenancies

179 Extension of introductory tenancies

(1) Part 5 of the Housing Act 1996 (c 52) (conduct of tenants) is amended as follows.

(2) In section 125(2) (trial period for introductory tenancy to be one year) for 'subject as follows' substitute 'but this is subject to subsections (3) and (4) and to section 125A (extension of trial period by 6 months).'

(3) After section 125 insert –

'125A Extension of trial period by 6 months

(1) If both of the following conditions are met in relation to an introductory tenancy, the trial period is extended by 6 months.

(2) The first condition is that the landlord has served a notice of extension on the tenant at least 8 weeks before the original expiry date.

(3) The second condition is that either –

    (a) the tenant has not requested a review under section 125B in accordance with subsection (1) of that section, or

(b) if he has, the decision on the review was to confirm the landlord's decision to extend the trial period.

(4) A notice of extension is a notice –

(a) stating that the landlord has decided that the period for which the tenancy is to be an introductory tenancy should be extended by 6 months, and
(b) complying with subsection (5).

(5) A notice of extension must –

(a) set out the reasons for the landlord's decision, and
(b) inform the tenant of his right to request a review of the landlord's decision and of the time within which such a request must be made.

(6) In this section and section 125B "the original expiry date" means the last day of the period of one year that would apply as the trial period apart from this section.

125B Review of decision to extend trial period

(1) A request for review of the landlord's decision that the trial period for an introductory tenancy should be extended under section 125A must be made before the end of the period of 14 days beginning with the day on which the notice of extension is served.

(2) On a request being duly made to it, the landlord shall review its decision.

(3) The Secretary of State may make provision by regulations as to the procedure to be followed in connection with a review under this section.

Nothing in the following provisions affects the generality of this power.

(4) Provision may be made by regulations –

(a) requiring the decision on review to be made by a person of appropriate seniority who was not involved in the original decision, and
(b) as to the circumstances in which the person concerned is entitled to an oral hearing, and whether and by whom he may be represented at such a hearing.

(5) The landlord shall notify the tenant of the decision on the review.

If the decision is to confirm the original decision, the landlord shall also notify him of the reasons for the decision.

(6) The review shall be carried out and the tenant notified before the original expiry date.'

(4) The amendments made by this section do not apply in relation to any tenancy entered into before, or in pursuance of an agreement made before, the day on which this section comes into force.

Right to buy: when exercisable

180 Extension of qualifying period for right to buy

(1) In section 119(1) of the Housing Act 1985 (c 68) (qualifying period for right to buy) for 'two' substitute 'five'.

(2) In subsection (2)(a) of section 129 of that Act (discount) –

(a) for 'two' substitute 'five'; and

(b) for '32 per cent' substitute '35 per cent'.

(3) In subsection (2)(b) of that section –

(a) for 'two', where it appears for the second time, substitute 'five'; and
(b) for '44 per cent' substitute '50 per cent'.

(4) In subsection (2A)(b) of that section for 'two' substitute 'five'.

(5) The amendments made by this section do not apply in relation to a secure tenancy –

(a) if the tenancy was entered into before, or in pursuance of an agreement made before, the day on which this section comes into force, or
(b) if paragraph (a) does not apply but the tenant is a public sector tenant on that day and does not cease to be such a tenant at any time before serving a notice in respect of the tenancy under section 122 of that Act.

(6) In subsection (5) 'public sector tenant' has the same meaning as in Schedule 4 to that Act.

181 Exceptions to the right to buy: determination whether exception for dwelling-house suitable for elderly persons applies

(1) In Schedule 5 to the Housing Act 1985 (exceptions to the right to buy) paragraph 11 (single dwelling-house particularly suitable for elderly persons) is amended as follows.

(2) In sub-paragraph (4) (questions arising under paragraph 11 to be determined by the Secretary of State), for 'the Secretary of State' (in both places) substitute 'the appropriate tribunal or authority'.

(3) After sub-paragraph (5) insert –

'(5A) In this paragraph 'the appropriate tribunal or authority' means –

(a) in relation to England, a residential property tribunal; and
(b) in relation to Wales, the Secretary of State.

(5B) Section 231 of the Housing Act 2004 (appeals to Lands Tribunal) does not apply to any decision of a residential property tribunal under this paragraph.'

(4) Subsections (5) and (6) apply to any application under paragraph 11(4) in respect of a dwelling-house in England which –

(a) has been made to the Secretary of State before the day on which this section comes into force, and
(b) has not been determined by him before that day.

(5) If the application was made more than 28 days before that day, it is to be determined by the Secretary of State as if the amendments made by this section had not come into force.

(6) Otherwise –

(a) the application is to be determined by a residential property tribunal, and
(b) the Secretary of State must make all such arrangements as he considers necessary for the purpose of, or in connection with, enabling it to be so determined.

182 Exceptions to the right to buy: houses due to be demolished

(1) In Schedule 5 to the Housing Act 1985 (c 68) (exceptions to the right to buy) after paragraph 12 insert –

'Dwelling-house due to be demolished within 24 months

13

(1) The right to buy does not arise if a final demolition notice is in force in respect of the dwelling-house.

(2) A 'final demolition notice' is a notice –

    (a) stating that the landlord intends to demolish the dwelling-house or (as the case may be) the building containing it ('the relevant premises'),

    (b) setting out the reasons why the landlord intends to demolish the relevant premises,

    (c) specifying –

        (i) the date by which he intends to demolish those premises ('the proposed demolition date'), and

        (ii) the date when the notice will cease to be in force (unless extended under paragraph 15),

    (d) stating that one of conditions A to C in paragraph 14 is satisfied in relation to the notice (specifying the condition concerned), and

    (e) stating that the right to buy does not arise in respect of the dwelling-house while the notice is in force.

(3) If, at the time when the notice is served, there is an existing claim to exercise the right to buy in respect of the dwelling-house, the notice shall (instead of complying with sub-paragraph (2)(e)) state –

    (a) that that claim ceases to be effective on the notice coming into force, but

    (b) that section 138C confers a right to compensation in respect of certain expenditure,

and the notice shall also give details of that right to compensation and of how it may be exercised.

(4) The proposed demolition date must fall within the period of 24 months beginning with the date of service of the notice on the tenant.

(5) For the purposes of this paragraph a final demolition notice is in force in respect of the dwelling-house concerned during the period of 24 months mentioned in sub-paragraph (4), but this is subject to –

    (a) compliance with the conditions in sub-paragraphs (6) and (7) (in a case to which they apply), and

    (b) the provisions of paragraph 15(1) to (7).

(6) If –

    (a) the dwelling-house is contained in a building which contains one or more other dwelling-houses, and

    (b) the landlord intends to demolish the whole of the building,

the landlord must have served a final demolition notice on the occupier of each of the dwelling-houses contained in it (whether addressed to him by name or just as 'the occupier').

An accidental omission to serve a final demolition notice on one or more occupiers does not prevent the condition in this sub-paragraph from being satisfied.

(7) A notice stating that the landlord intends to demolish the relevant premises must have appeared –

(a) in a local or other newspaper circulating in the locality in which those premises are situated (other than one published by the landlord), and

(b) in any newspaper published by the landlord, and

(c) on the landlord's website (if he has one).

(8) The notice mentioned in sub-paragraph (7) must contain the following information –

(a) sufficient information to enable identification of the premises that the landlord intends to demolish;

(b) the reasons why the landlord intends to demolish those premises;

(c) the proposed demolition date;

(d) the date when any final demolition notice or notices relating to those premises will cease to be in force, unless extended or revoked under paragraph 15;

(e) that the right to buy will not arise in respect of those premises or (as the case may be) in respect of any dwelling-house contained in them;

(f) that there may be a right to compensation under section 138C in respect of certain expenditure incurred in respect of any existing claim.

(9) In this paragraph and paragraphs 14 and 15 any reference to the landlord, in the context of a reference to an intention or decision on his part to demolish or not to demolish any premises, or of a reference to the acquisition or transfer of any premises, includes a reference to a superior landlord.

14

(1) A final demolition notice may only be served for the purposes of paragraph 13 if one of conditions A to C is satisfied in relation to the notice.

(2) Condition A is that the proposed demolition of the dwelling-house does not form part of a scheme involving the demolition of other premises.

(3) Condition B is that –

(a) the proposed demolition of the dwelling-house does form part of a scheme involving the demolition of other premises, but

(b) none of those other premises needs to be acquired by the landlord in order for the landlord to be able to demolish them.

(4) Condition C is that –

(a) the proposed demolition of the dwelling-house does form part of a scheme involving the demolition of other premises, and

(b) one or more of those premises need to be acquired by the landlord in order for the landlord to be able to demolish them, but

(c) in each case arrangements for their acquisition are in place.

(5) For the purposes of sub-paragraph (4) arrangements for the acquisition of any premises are in place if –

(a) an agreement under which the landlord is entitled to acquire the premises is in force, or

(b) a notice to treat has been given in respect of the premises under section 5 of the Compulsory Purchase Act 1965, or

(c) a vesting declaration has been made in respect of the premises under section 4 of the Compulsory Purchase (Vesting Declarations) Act 1981.

(6) In this paragraph –

"premises" means premises of any description;

"scheme" includes arrangements of any description.

15

(1) The Secretary of State may, on an application by the landlord, give a direction extending or further extending the period during which a final demolition notice is in force in respect of a dwelling-house.

(2) A direction under sub-paragraph (1) may provide that any extension of that period is not to have effect unless the landlord complies with such requirements relating to the service of further notices as are specified in the direction.

(3) A direction under sub-paragraph (1) may only be given at a time when the demolition notice is in force (whether by virtue of paragraph 13 or this paragraph).

(4) If, while a final demolition notice is in force, the landlord decides not to demolish the dwelling-house in question, he must, as soon as is reasonably practicable, serve a notice ('a revocation notice') on the tenant which informs him –

(a) of the landlord's decision, and
(b) that the demolition notice is revoked as from the date of service of the revocation notice.

(5) If, while a final demolition notice is in force, it appears to the Secretary of State that the landlord has no intention of demolishing the dwelling-house in question, he may serve a notice ('a revocation notice') on the tenant which informs him –

(a) of the Secretary of State's conclusion, and
(b) that the demolition notice is revoked as from the date of service of the revocation notice.

Section 169 applies in relation to the Secretary of State's power under this sub-paragraph as it applies in relation to his powers under the provisions mentioned in subsection (1) of that section.

(6) But the Secretary of State may not serve a revocation notice unless he has previously served a notice on the landlord which informs him of the Secretary of State's intention to serve the revocation notice.

(7) Where a revocation notice is served under sub-paragraph (4) or (5), the demolition notice ceases to be in force as from the date of service of the revocation notice.

(8) Once a final demolition notice has (for any reason) ceased to be in force in respect of a dwelling-house without it being demolished, no further final demolition notice may be served in respect of it during the period of 5 years following the time when the notice ceases to be in force, unless –

(a) it is served with the consent of the Secretary of State, and
(b) it states that it is so served.

(9) The Secretary of State's consent under sub-paragraph (8) may be given subject to compliance with such conditions as he may specify.

16

(1) Any notice under paragraph 13 or 15 may be served on a person –

(a) by delivering it to him, by leaving it at his proper address or by sending it by post to him at that address, or

  (b) if the person is a body corporate, by serving it in accordance with paragraph (a) on the secretary of the body.

(2) For the purposes of this section and section 7 of the Interpretation Act 1978 (service of documents by post) the proper address of a person on whom a notice is to be served shall be –

  (a) in the case of a body corporate or its secretary, that of the registered or principal office of the body, and
  (b) in any other case, the last known address of that person.'

(2) The amendment made by this section does not apply in any case where the tenant's notice under section 122 of that Act (notice claiming to exercise right to buy) was served before the day on which this section comes into force.

183 Right to buy: claim suspended or terminated by demolition notice

(1) In section 138 of the Housing Act 1985 (c 68) (duty of landlord to convey freehold or grant lease), after the subsection (2D) inserted by section 193 of this Act, insert –

  '(2E) Subsection (1) also has effect subject to –

  (a) section 138A(2) (operation of subsection (1) suspended while initial demolition notice is in force), and
  (b) section 138B(2) (subsection (1) disapplied where final demolition notice is serv'

(2) After section 138 of that Act insert –

'138A Effect of initial demolition notice served before completion

(1) This section applies where –

  (a) an initial demolition notice is served on a secure tenant under Schedule 5A, and
  (b) the notice is served on the tenant before the landlord has made to him such a grant as is required by section 138(1) in respect of a claim by the tenant to exercise the right to buy.

(2) In such a case the landlord is not bound to comply with section 138(1), in connection with any such claim by the tenant, so long as the initial demolition notice remains in force under Schedule 5A.

(3) Section 138C provides a right to compensation in certain cases where this section applies.

138B Effect of final demolition notice served before completion

(1) This section applies where –

  (a) a secure tenant has claimed to exercise the right to buy, but
  (b) before the landlord has made to the tenant such a grant as is required by section 138(1) in respect of the claim, a final demolition notice is served on the tenant under paragraph 13 of Schedule 5.

(2) In such a case –

  (a) the tenant's claim ceases to be effective as from the time when the final demolition notice comes into force under that paragraph, and
  (b) section 138(1) accordingly does not apply to the landlord, in connection with the tenant's claim, at any time after the notice comes into force.

(3) Section 138C provides a right to compensation in certain cases where this section applies.

138C Compensation where demolition notice served

(1) This section applies where –

    (a) a secure tenant has claimed to exercise the right to buy,

    (b) before the landlord has made to the tenant such a grant as is required by section 138(1) in respect of the claim, either an initial demolition notice is served on the tenant under Schedule 5A or a final demolition notice is served on him under paragraph 13 of Schedule 5, and

    (c) the tenant's claim is established before that notice comes into force under Schedule 5A or paragraph 13 of Schedule 5 (as the case may be).

(2) If, within the period of three months beginning with the date when the notice comes into force ('the operative date'), the tenant serves on the landlord a written notice claiming an amount of compensation under subsection (3), the landlord shall pay that amount to the tenant.

(3) Compensation under this subsection is compensation in respect of expenditure reasonably incurred by the tenant before the operative date in respect of legal and other fees, and other professional costs and expenses, payable in connection with the exercise by him of the right to buy.

(4) A notice under subsection (2) must be accompanied by receipts or other documents showing that the tenant incurred the expenditure in question.'

(3) After Schedule 5 to the Act insert, as Schedule 5A, the Schedule set out in Schedule 9 to this Act.

(4) The amendments made by this section do not apply in any case where the tenant's notice under section 122 of the Act (notice claim to exercise right to buy) was served before the day on which this section comes into force.

184 Landlord's notice to complete

(1) Section 140 of the Housing Act 1985 (c 68) (landlord's first notice to complete) is amended as follows.

(2) In subsection (3) (notice not to be served earlier than twelve months after landlord's notice under section 125 or 146) for 'twelve' substitute 'three'.

(3) The amendment made by this section does not apply in any case where the tenant's notice under section 122 of that Act (notice claiming right to buy) was served before the day on which this section comes into force.

Right to buy: discounts

185 Repayment of discount: periods and amounts applicable

(1) Section 155 of the Housing Act 1985 (repayment of discount on early disposal) is amended in accordance with subsections (2) and (3).

(2) For subsections (2) and (3) substitute –

    '(2) In the case of a conveyance or grant in pursuance of the right to buy, the covenant shall be to pay the landlord such sum (if any) as the landlord may demand in accordance with section

155A on the occasion of the first relevant disposal (other than an exempted disposal) which takes place within the period of five years beginning with the conveyance or grant.

(3) In the case of a conveyance or grant in pursuance of the right to acquire on rent to mortgage terms, the covenant shall be to pay the landlord such sum (if any) as the landlord may demand in accordance with section 155B on the occasion of the first relevant disposal (other than an exempted disposal) which takes place within the period of five years beginning with the making of the initial payment.'

(3) In subsection (3A) (modifications where tenant has served operative notice of delay) for 'three years' substitute 'five years'.

(4) After section 155 insert –

'155A Amount of discount which may be demanded by landlord: right to buy

(1) For the purposes of the covenant mentioned in section 155(2), the landlord may demand such sum as he considers appropriate, up to and including the maximum amount specified in this section.

(2) The maximum amount which may be demanded by the landlord is a percentage of the price or premium paid for the first relevant disposal which is equal to the discount to which the secure tenant was entitled, where the discount is expressed as a percentage of the value which under section 127 was taken as the value of the dwelling-house at the relevant time.

(3) But for each complete year which has elapsed after the conveyance or grant and before the disposal the maximum amount which may be demanded by the landlord is reduced by one-fifth.

(4) This section is subject to section 155C

155B Amount of discount which may be demanded by landlord: right to acquire on rent to mortgage terms

(1) For the purposes of the covenant mentioned in section 155(3), the landlord may demand such sum as he considers appropriate, up to and including the maximum amount specified in this section.

(2) The maximum amount which may be demanded by the landlord is the discount (if any) to which the tenant was entitled on the making of –

    (a) the initial payment,
    (b) any interim payment made before the disposal, or
    (c) the final payment if so made,

reduced, in each case, by one-fifth for each complete year which has elapsed after the making of the initial payment and before the disposal.'

(5) The amendments made by this section do not apply in any case where the tenant's notice under section 122 of the Act (notice claiming to exercise right to buy) was served before the day on which this section comes into force.

(6) Subsection (7), however, applies in any such case if the first relevant disposal to which the covenant for repayment of discount applies takes place on or after the day on which this section comes into force.

(7) In the following provisions –

    (a) section 155(2) and (3) of the Housing Act 1985 (c 68) (as it has effect without the amendments made by this section), and

    (b) any covenant for repayment of discount,

any reference (however expressed) to a person being liable to pay an amount to the landlord on demand is to be read as a reference to his being liable to pay to the landlord so much of that amount (if any) as the landlord may demand.

(8) In subsections (6) and (7) 'covenant for repayment of discount' means the covenant contained in a conveyance or grant in accordance with section 155 of that Act.

186 Repayment of discount: increase attributable to home improvements to be disregarded

(1) After section 155B of the Housing Act 1985 (c 68) (inserted by section 185 of this Act) insert –

'155C Increase attributable to home improvements

(1) In calculating the maximum amount which may be demanded by the landlord under section 155A, such amount (if any) of the price or premium paid for the disposal which is attributable to improvements made to the dwelling-house –

    (a) by the person by whom the disposal is, or is to be, made, and

    (b) after the conveyance or grant and before the disposal,

shall be disregarded.

(2) The amount to be disregarded under this section shall be such amount as may be agreed between the parties or determined by the district valuer.

(3) The district valuer shall not be required by virtue of this section to make a determination for the purposes of this section unless –

    (a) it is reasonably practicable for him to do so; and

    (b) his reasonable costs in making the determination are paid by the person by whom the disposal is, or is to be, made.

(4) If the district valuer does not make a determination for the purposes of this section (and in default of an agreement), no amount is required to be disregarded under this section.'

(2) In section 181 of that Act (jurisdiction of county court) for 'and 158' substitute ', 155C and 158'.

187 Deferred resale agreements

(1) After section 163 of the Housing Act 1985 insert –

'163A Treatment of deferred resale agreements for purposes of section 155

(1) If a secure tenant or his successor in title enters into an agreement within subsection (3), any liability arising under the covenant required by section 155 shall be determined as if a relevant disposal which is not an exempted disposal had occurred at the appropriate time.

(2) In subsection (1) "the appropriate time" means –

(a) the time when the agreement is entered into, or

(b) if it was made before the beginning of the discount repayment period, immediately after the beginning of that period.

(3) An agreement is within this subsection if it is an agreement between the secure tenant or his successor in title and any other person –

(a) which is made (expressly or impliedly) in contemplation of, or in connection with, the tenant exercising, or having exercised, the right to buy,

(b) which is made before the end of the discount repayment period, and

(c) under which a relevant disposal (other than an exempted disposal) is or may be required to be made to any person after the end of that period.

(4) Such an agreement is within subsection (3) –

(a) whether or not the date on which the disposal is to take place is specified in the agreement, and

(b) whether or not any requirement to make the disposal is or may be made subject to the fulfilment of any condition.

(5) The Secretary of State may by order provide –

(a) for subsection (1) to apply to agreements of any description specified in the order in addition to those within subsection (3);

(b) for subsection (1) not to apply to agreements of any description so specified to which it would otherwise apply.

(6) An order under subsection (5) –

(a) may make different provision with respect to different cases or descriptions of case; and

(b) shall be made by statutory instrument which shall be subject to annulment in pursuance of a resolution of either House of Parliament.

(7) In this section –

"agreement" includes arrangement;

"the discount repayment period" means the period of three or five years that applies for the purposes of section 155(2) or (3) (depending on whether the tenant's notice under section 122 was given before or on or after the date of the coming into force of section 185 of the Housing Act 2004).'

(2) The amendment made by this section does not apply in relation to any agreement or arrangement made before the day on which this section comes into force.

Right to buy: landlord's right of first refusal

188 Right of first refusal for landlord etc

(1) After section 156 of the Housing Act 1985 (c 68) insert –

'156A Right of first refusal for landlord etc

(1) A conveyance of the freehold or grant of a lease in pursuance of this Part shall contain the following covenant, which shall be binding on the secure tenant and his successors in title.

This is subject to subsection (8).

(2) The covenant shall be to the effect that, until the end of the period of ten years beginning with the conveyance or grant, there will be no relevant disposal which is not an exempted disposal, unless the prescribed conditions have been satisfied in relation to that or a previous such disposal.

(3) In subsection (2) "the prescribed conditions" means such conditions as are prescribed by regulations under this section at the time when the conveyance or grant is made.

(4) The Secretary of State may by regulations prescribe such conditions as he considers appropriate for and in connection with conferring on –

(a) a landlord who has conveyed a freehold or granted a lease to a person ('the former tenant') in pursuance of this Part, or
(b) such other person as is determined in accordance with the regulations,

a right of first refusal to have a disposal within subsection (5) made to him for such consideration as is mentioned in section 158.

(5) The disposals within this subsection are –

(a) a reconveyance or conveyance of the dwelling-house; and
(b) a surrender or assignment of the lease.

(6) Regulations under this section may, in particular, make provision –

(a) for the former tenant to offer to make such a disposal to such person or persons as may be prescribed;
(b) for a prescribed recipient of such an offer to be able either to accept the offer or to nominate some other person as the person by whom the offer may be accepted;
(c) for the person who may be so nominated to be either a person of a prescribed description or a person whom the prescribed recipient considers, having regard to any prescribed matters, to be a more appropriate person to accept the offer;
(d) for a prescribed recipient making such a nomination to give a notification of the nomination to the person nominated, the former tenant and any other prescribed person;
(e) for authorising a nominated person to accept the offer and for determining which acceptance is to be effective where the offer is accepted by more than one person;
(f) for the period within which the offer may be accepted or within which any other prescribed step is to be, or may be, taken;
(g) for the circumstances in which the right of first refusal lapses (whether following the service of a notice to complete or otherwise) with the result that the former tenant is able to make a disposal on the open market;
(h) for the manner in which any offer, acceptance or notification is to be communicated.

(7) In subsection (6) any reference to the former tenant is a reference to the former tenant or his successor in title.

Nothing in that subsection affects the generality of subsection (4).

(8) In a case to which section 157(1) applies –

(a) the conveyance or grant may contain a covenant such as is mentioned in subsections (1) and (2) above instead of a covenant such as is mentioned in section 157(1), but
(b) it may do so only if the Secretary of State or, where the conveyance or grant is executed by a housing association within section 6A(3) or (4), the Relevant Authority consents.

(9) Consent may be given in relation to –

(a) a particular disposal, or

(b) disposals by a particular landlord or disposals by landlords generally,

and may, in any case, be given subject to conditions.

(10) Regulations under this section –

(a) may make different provision with respect to different cases or descriptions of case; and

(b) shall be made by statutory instrument which shall be subject to annulment in pursuance of a resolution of either House of Parliament.

(11) The limitation imposed by a covenant within subsection (2) (whether the covenant is imposed in pursuance of subsection (1) or (8)) is a local land charge.

(12) The Chief Land Registrar must enter in the register of title a restriction reflecting the limitation imposed by any such covenant.'

(2) In section 157 of that Act (restriction on disposal of dwelling-houses in National Parks etc) –

(a) in subsection (1), after 'the conveyance or grant may' insert '(subject to section 156A(8)';

(b) in subsection (2), omit ', subject to subsection (4),'; and

(c) omit subsections (4) and (5) (which provide for a landlord's right of first refusal).

(3) In section 158 of that Act (consideration for conveyance or surrender under section 157) –

(a) in the sidenote, for 'reconveyance or surrender under section 157' substitute 'disposal under section 156A';

(b) for subsection (1) substitute –

'(1) The consideration for such a disposal as is mentioned in section 156A(4) shall be such amount as may be agreed between the parties, or determined by the district valuer, as being the amount which is to be taken to be the value of the dwelling-house at the time when the offer is made (as determined in accordance with regulations under that section).';

(c) in subsection (2), for 'or surrendered' substitute ', conveyed, surrendered or assigned';

(d) in subsection (3), for 'the landlord accepts the offer,' substitute 'the offer is accepted in accordance with regulations under section 156A,'; and

(e) in subsection (4), for 'to reconvey or surrender' substitute ' (as determined in accordance with regulations under section 156A).'

(4) In section 162 of that Act (exempted disposals which end liability under covenants), after paragraph (a) insert –

'(aa) the covenant required by section 156A (right of first refusal for landlord etc) is not binding on the person to whom the disposal is made or any successor in title of his, and that covenant ceases to apply in relation to the property disposed of, and'.

(5) The amendments made by this section do not apply in relation to a conveyance of the freehold or grant of a lease in pursuance of Part 5 of that Act if the notice under section 122 of the Act (tenant's notice claiming to exercise right to buy) was served before the day on which this section comes into force.

(6) Accordingly, nothing in this section affects –

(a) the operation of a limitation contained in such a conveyance or grant in accordance with section 157(4) of that Act, or

(b) the operation, in relation to such a limitation, of section 157(6) (so far as it renders a disposal in breach of covenant void) or section 158 (consideration payable) of that Act.

Right to buy: information

189 Information to help tenants decide whether to exercise right to buy etc

(1) After section 121 of the Housing Act 1985 (c 68) insert –

'121A Information to help tenants decide whether to exercise right to buy etc

(1) Every body which lets dwelling-houses under secure tenancies shall prepare a document that contains information for its secure tenants about such matters as are specified in an order made by the Secretary of State.

(2) The matters that may be so specified are matters which the Secretary of State considers that it would be desirable for secure tenants to have information about when considering whether to exercise the right to buy or the right to acquire on rent to mortgage terms.

(3) The information contained in the document shall be restricted to information about the specified matters, and the information about those matters –

   (a) shall be such as the body concerned considers appropriate, but
   (b) shall be in a form which the body considers best suited to explaining those matters in simple terms.

(4) Once a body has prepared the document required by subsection (1), it shall revise it as often as it considers necessary in order to ensure that the information contained in it –

   (a) is kept up to date so far as is reasonably practicable, and
   (b) reflects any changes in the matters for the time being specified in an order under this section.

(5) An order under this section shall be made by statutory instrument which shall be subject to annulment in pursuance of a resolution of either House of Parliament.

121B Provision of information

(1) This section sets out when the document prepared by a body under section 121A is to be published or otherwise made available.

(2) The body shall –

   (a) publish the document (whether in its original or a revised form), and
   (b) supply copies of it to the body's secure tenants,

at such times as may be prescribed by, and otherwise in accordance with, an order made by the Secretary of State.

(3) The body shall make copies of the current version of the document available to be supplied, free of charge, to persons requesting them.

(4) The copies must be made available for that purpose –

   (a) at the body's principal offices, and
   (b) at such other places as it considers appropriate,

at reasonable hours.

(5) The body shall take such steps as it considers appropriate to bring to the attention of its secure tenants the fact that copies of the current version of the document can be obtained free

of charge from the places where, and at the times when, they are made available in accordance with subsection (4).

(6) In this section any reference to the current version of the document is to the version of the document that was last published by the body in accordance with subsection (2)(a).

(7) An order under this section shall be made by statutory instrument which shall be subject to annulment in pursuance of a resolution of either House of Parliament.'

(2) In section 104(1) of that Act (provision of information about tenancies), in paragraph (b) (information about Part 4 and Part 5), omit 'and Part V (the right to buy)'.

Right to buy: termination of rent to mortgage scheme

190 Termination of rent to mortgage scheme

(1) Before section 143 of the Housing Act 1985 (c 68) insert –

'142A Termination of the right to acquire on rent to mortgage terms

(1) As from the termination date, the right to acquire on rent to mortgage terms is not exercisable except in pursuance of a notice served under section 144 before that date.

(2) In this section 'the termination date' means the date falling 8 months after the date of the passing of the Housing Act 2004.'

(2) In section 143(1) of that Act after 'sections' insert '142A,'.

(3) In section 144(1) of that Act for 'A secure tenant' substitute 'Subject to section 142A, a secure tenant'.

Suspension of certain rights in connection with anti-social behaviour

191 Secure tenancies: withholding of consent to mutual exchange

(1) In Schedule 3 to the Housing Act 1985 (c 68) (grounds for withholding consent to assignment by way of exchange) after Ground 2 insert –

'Ground 2A

Either –

(a) a relevant order or suspended Ground 2 or 14 possession order is in force, or

(b) an application is pending before any court for a relevant order, a demotion order or a Ground 2 or 14 possession order to be made,

in respect of the tenant or the proposed assignee or a person who is residing with either of them.

A "relevant order" means –

an injunction under section 152 of the Housing Act 1996 (injunctions against anti-social behaviour);
an injunction to which a power of arrest is attached by virtue of section 153 of that Act (other injunctions against anti-social behaviour);
an injunction under section 153A, 153B or 153D of that Act (injunctions against anti-social behaviour on application of certain social landlords);

an anti-social behaviour order under section 1 of the Crime and Disorder Act 1998; or

an injunction to which a power of arrest is attached by virtue of section 91 of the Anti-social Behaviour Act 2003.

A "demotion order" means a demotion order under section 82A of this Act or section 6A of the Housing Act 1988.

A "Ground 2 or 14 possession order" means an order for possession under Ground 2 in Schedule 2 to this Act or Ground 14 in Schedule 2 to the Housing Act 1988.

Where the tenancy of the tenant or the proposed assignee is a joint tenancy, any reference to that person includes (where the context permits) a reference to any of the joint tenants.'

(2) The amendment made by this section applies in relation to applications for consent under section 92 of that Act (assignments by way of exchange) which are made on or after the day on which this section comes into force.

192 Right to buy: suspension by court order

(1) In section 121 of the Housing Act 1985 (circumstances in which right to buy cannot be exercised), after subsection (2) insert –

'(3) The right to buy cannot be exercised at any time during the suspension period under an order made under section 121A in respect of the secure tenancy.'

(2) After section 121 of that Act insert –

'121A Order suspending right to buy because of anti-social behaviour

(1) The court may, on the application of the landlord under a secure tenancy, make a suspension order in respect of the tenancy.

(2) A suspension order is an order providing that the right to buy may not be exercised in relation to the dwelling-house during such period as is specified in the order ("the suspension period").

(3) The court must not make a suspension order unless it is satisfied –

- (a) that the tenant, or a person residing in or visiting the dwelling-house, has engaged or threatened to engage in conduct to which section 153A or 153B of the Housing Act 1996 applies (anti-social behaviour or use of premises for unlawful purposes), and
- (b) that it is reasonable to make the order.

(4) When deciding whether it is reasonable to make the order, the court must consider, in particular –

- (a) whether it is desirable for the dwelling-house to be managed by the landlord during the suspension period; and
- (b) where the conduct mentioned in subsection (3)(a) consists of conduct by a person which is capable of causing nuisance or annoyance, the effect that the conduct (or the threat of it) has had on other persons, or would have if repeated.

(5) Where a suspension order is made –

- (a) any existing claim to exercise the right to buy in relation to the dwelling-house ceases to be effective as from the beginning of the suspension period, and

(b) section 138(1) shall not apply to the landlord, in connection with such a claim, at any time after the beginning of that period, but

(c) the order does not affect the computation of any period in accordance with Schedule 4.

(6) The court may, on the application of the landlord, make (on one or more occasions) a further order which extends the suspension period under the suspension order by such period as is specified in the further order.

(7) The court must not make such a further order unless it is satisfied –

(a) that, since the making of the suspension order (or the last order under subsection (6)), the tenant, or a person residing in or visiting the dwelling-house, has engaged or threatened to engage in conduct to which section 153A or 153B of the Housing Act 1996 applies, and

(b) that it is reasonable to make the further order.

(8) When deciding whether it is reasonable to make such a further order, the court must consider, in particular –

(a) whether it is desirable for the dwelling-house to be managed by the landlord during the further period of suspension; and

(b) where the conduct mentioned in subsection (7)(a) consists of conduct by a person which is capable of causing nuisance or annoyance, the effect that the conduct (or the threat of it) has had on other persons, or would have if repeated.

(9) In this section any reference to the tenant under a secure tenancy is, in relation to a joint tenancy, a reference to any of the joint tenants.'

(3) Regulations under –

(a) section 171C of that Act (modifications of Part 5 in relation to preserved right to buy), or

(b) section 17 of the Housing Act 1996 (c 52) (application of that Part in relation to right to acquire dwelling),

may make provision for continuing the effect of a suspension order where the secure tenancy in respect of which the order was made has been replaced by an assured tenancy.

193 Right to buy: suspension of landlord's obligation to complete

(1) In section 138 of the Housing Act 1985 (c 68) (duty of landlord to convey freehold or grant lease) after subsection (2) insert –

'(2A) Subsection (2B) applies if an application is pending before any court –

(a) for a demotion order or Ground 2 possession order to be made in respect of the tenant, or

(b) for a suspension order to be made in respect of the tenancy.

(2B) The landlord is not bound to comply with subsection (1) until such time (if any) as the application is determined without –

(a) a demotion order or an operative Ground 2 possession order being made in respect of the tenant, or

(b) a suspension order being made in respect of the tenancy,

or the application is withdrawn.

(2C) For the purposes of subsection (2A) and (2B) –

"demotion order" means a demotion order under section 82A;

"Ground 2 possession order" means an order for possession under Ground 2 in Schedule 2;

"operative Ground 2 possession order" means an order made under that Ground which requires possession of the dwelling-house to be given up on a date specified in the order;

"suspension order" means a suspension order under section 121A.

(2D) Subsection (1) has effect subject to section 121A(5) (disapplication of subsection (1) where suspension order is made).'

(2) The amendment made by this section does not apply in any case where the tenant's notice under section 122 of that Act (notice claiming to exercise right to buy) was served before the day on which this section comes into force.

194 Disclosure of information as to orders etc in respect of anti-social behaviour

(1) Any person may disclose relevant information to a landlord under a secure tenancy if the information is disclosed for the purpose of enabling the landlord –

(a) to decide whether either of the provisions of the Housing Act 1985 (c 68) mentioned in subsection (2) can be invoked in relation to the tenant under the tenancy; or
(b) to take any appropriate action in relation to the tenant in reliance on either of those provisions.

(2) The provisions are –

(a) Ground 2A in Schedule 3 (withholding of consent to mutual exchange where order in force or application pending in connection with anti-social behaviour), and
(b) section 138(2B) (landlord's obligation to complete suspended while application pending in connection with such behaviour).

(3) In this section –

(a) 'relevant information' means information relating to any order or application relevant for the purposes of either of the provisions mentioned in subsection (2), including (in particular) information identifying the person in respect of whom any such order or application has been made;
(b) 'secure tenancy' has the meaning given by section 79 of the Housing Act 1985; and
(c) any reference to the tenant under a secure tenancy is, in relation to a joint tenancy, a reference to any of the joint tenants.

(4) Regulations under –

(a) section 171C of the Housing Act 1985 (modifications of Part 5 in relation to preserved right to buy), or
(b) section 17 of the Housing Act 1996 (c 52) (application of that Part in relation to right to acquire dwelling),

may make provision corresponding to subsections (1) to (3) of this section so far as those subsections relate to section 138(2B) of the Housing Act 1985.

Chapter 2
Disposals Attracting Discounts other than under Right to Buy

Disposals by local authorities

195 Repayment of discount: periods and amounts applicable

(1) Section 35 of the Housing Act 1985 (repayment of discount on early disposal) is amended in accordance with subsections (2) and (3).

(2) In subsection (2) for the words from 'to pay to the authority' to the end of the subsection substitute 'to the following effect.'

(3) After subsection (2) insert –

'(3) The covenant shall be to pay to the authority such sum (if any) as the authority may demand in accordance with subsection (4) on the occasion of the first relevant disposal (other than an exempted disposal) which takes place within the period of five years beginning with the conveyance, grant or assignment.

(4) The authority may demand such sum as they consider appropriate, up to and including the maximum amount specified in this section.

(5) The maximum amount which may be demanded by the authority is a percentage of the price or premium paid for the first relevant disposal which is equal to the percentage discount given to the purchaser in respect of the disposal of the house under section 32.

(6) But for each complete year which has elapsed after the conveyance, grant or assignment and before the first relevant disposal the maximum amount which may be demanded by the landlord is reduced by one-fifth.

(7) Subsections (4) to (6) are subject to section 35A.'

(4) The amendments made by this section do not apply in any case where –

(a) the purchaser has accepted an offer for the disposal of the house from the authority, or
(b) the authority has accepted an offer for the disposal of the house from the purchaser,

before the day on which this section comes into force.

(5) Subsection (6), however, applies in any such case if the first relevant disposal by the purchaser to which the covenant for repayment of discount applies takes place on or after the day on which this section comes into force.

(6) In the following provisions –

(a) section 35(2) of the Housing Act 1985 (c 68) (as it has effect without the amendments made by this section), and
(b) any covenant for repayment of discount,

any reference (however expressed) to a person being liable to pay an amount to the authority on demand is to be read as a reference to his being liable to pay to the authority so much of that amount (if any) as the authority may demand.

(7) In subsections (5) and (6) 'covenant for repayment of discount' means the covenant contained in a conveyance, grant or assignment in accordance with section 35 of that Act.

196 Repayment of discount: increase attributable to home improvements to be disregarded

After section 35 of the Housing Act 1985 insert –

'35A Increase in value of house attributable to home improvements

(1) In calculating the maximum amount which may be demanded by the authority under section 35, such amount (if any) of the price or premium paid for the first relevant disposal which is attributable to improvements made to the house –

    (a) by the person by whom the disposal is, or is to be, made, and
    (b) after the conveyance, grant or assignment and before the disposal,

shall be disregarded.

(2) The amount to be disregarded under this section shall be such amount as may be agreed between the parties or determined by the district valuer.

(3) The district valuer shall not be required by virtue of this section to make a determination for the purposes of this section unless –

    (a) it is reasonably practicable for him to do so; and
    (b) his reasonable costs in making the determination are paid by the person by whom the disposal is, or is to be, made.

(4) If the district valuer does not make a determination for the purposes of this section (and in default of an agreement), no amount is required to be disregarded under this section.'

197 Local authority's right of first refusal

(1) After section 36 of the Housing Act 1985 (c 68) insert –

'36A Right of first refusal for local authority

(1) This section applies where, on a disposal of a house under section 32, a discount is given to the purchaser by the local authority in accordance with a consent given by the Secretary of State under subsection (2) of that section; but this section does not apply in any such case if the consent so provides.

(2) On the disposal the conveyance, grant or assignment shall contain the following covenant, which shall be binding on the purchaser and his successors in title.

(3) The covenant shall be to the effect that, until the end of the period of ten years beginning with the conveyance, grant or assignment, there will be no relevant disposal which is not an exempted disposal, unless the prescribed conditions have been satisfied in relation to that or a previous such disposal.

(4) In subsection (3) "the prescribed conditions" means such conditions as are prescribed by regulations under this section at the time when the conveyance, grant or assignment is made.

(5) The Secretary of State may by regulations prescribe such conditions as he considers appropriate for and in connection with conferring on –

    (a) a local authority which have made a disposal as mentioned in subsection (1), or
    (b) such other person as is determined in accordance with the regulations,

a right of first refusal to have a disposal within subsection (6) made to them or him for such consideration as is mentioned in section 36B.

(6) The disposals within this subsection are –

(a) a reconveyance or conveyance of the house; and

(b) a surrender or assignment of the lease.

(7) Regulations under this section may, in particular, make provision –

(a) for the purchaser to offer to make such a disposal to such person or persons as may be prescribed;

(b) for a prescribed recipient of such an offer to be able either to accept the offer or to nominate some other person as the person by whom the offer may be accepted;

(c) for the person who may be so nominated to be either a person of a prescribed description or a person whom the prescribed recipient considers, having regard to any prescribed matters, to be a more appropriate person to accept the offer;

(d) for a prescribed recipient making such a nomination to give a notification of the nomination to the person nominated, the purchaser and any other prescribed person;

(e) for authorising a nominated person to accept the offer and for determining which acceptance is to be effective where the offer is accepted by more than one person;

(f) for the period within which the offer may be accepted or within which any other prescribed step is to be, or may be, taken;

(g) for the circumstances in which the right of first refusal lapses (whether following the service of a notice to complete or otherwise) with the result that the purchaser is able to make a disposal on the open market;

(h) for the manner in which any offer, acceptance or notification is to be communicated.

(8) In subsection (7) any reference to the purchaser is a reference to the purchaser or his successor in title.

Nothing in that subsection affects the generality of subsection (5).

(9) Regulations under this section –

(a) may make different provision with respect to different cases or descriptions of case; and

(b) shall be made by statutory instrument which shall be subject to annulment in pursuance of a resolution of either House of Parliament.

(10) The limitation imposed by a covenant within subsection (3) is a local land charge.

(11) The Chief Land Registrar must enter in the register of title a restriction reflecting the limitation imposed by any such covenant.

36B Consideration payable for disposal under section 36A

(1) The consideration for a disposal made in respect of a right of first refusal as mentioned in section 36A(5) shall be such amount as may be agreed between the parties, or determined by the district valuer, as being the amount which is to be taken to be the value of the house at the time when the offer is made (as determined in accordance with regulations under that section).

(2) That value shall be taken to be the price which, at that time, the interest to be reconveyed, conveyed, surrendered or assigned would realise if sold on the open market by a willing vendor, on the assumption that any liability under the covenant required by section 35 (repayment of discount on early disposal) would be discharged by the vendor.

(3) If the offer is accepted in accordance with regulations under section 36A, no payment shall be required in pursuance of any such covenant as is mentioned in subsection (2), but the consideration shall be reduced, subject to subsection (4), by such amount (if any) as, on a disposal made at the time the offer was made, being a relevant disposal which is not an exempted disposal, would fall to be paid under that covenant.

(4) Where there is a charge on the house having priority over the charge to secure payment of the sum due under the covenant mentioned in subsection (2), the consideration shall not be reduced under subsection (3) below the amount necessary to discharge the outstanding sum secured by the first-mentioned charge at the date of the offer (as determined in accordance with regulations under section 36A).'

(2) In section 33(2) of the Housing Act 1985 (c 68) (covenants and conditions which may be imposed), after 'But' insert ', subject to sections 36A and 37,'.

(3) In section 37(1) of that Act (restriction on disposal of dwelling-houses in National Parks etc), after 'restriction on assignment)' insert 'or a covenant as mentioned in section 36A(3) (right of first refusal for local authority)'.

(4) In section 41 of that Act (exempted disposals which end liability under covenants), after paragraph (a) insert –

> '(aa) the covenant required by section 36A (right of first refusal for local authority) is not binding on the person to whom the disposal is made or any successor in title of his, and that covenant ceases to apply in relation to the property disposed of, and'.

(5) The amendments made by this section do not apply in relation to a disposal under section 32 of that Act if –

(a) the purchaser has accepted an offer for the disposal of the house from the authority, or
(b) the authority has accepted an offer for the disposal of the house from the purchaser,

before the day on which this section comes into force.

198 Deferred resale agreements

(1) After section 39 of the Housing Act 1985 insert –

'39A Treatment of deferred resale agreements for purposes of section 35

(1) If a purchaser or his successor in title enters into an agreement within subsection (3), any liability arising under the covenant required by section 35 shall be determined as if a relevant disposal which is not an exempted disposal had occurred at the appropriate time.

(2) In subsection (1) "the appropriate time" means –

(a) the time when the agreement is entered into, or
(b) if it was made before the beginning of the discount repayment period, immediately after the beginning of that period.

(3) An agreement is within this subsection if it is an agreement between the purchaser or his successor in title and any other person –

(a) which is made (expressly or impliedly) in contemplation of, or in connection with, a disposal to be made, or made, under section 32,
(b) which is made before the end of the discount repayment period, and

(c) under which a relevant disposal (other than an exempted disposal) is or may be required to be made to any person after the end of that period.

(4) Such an agreement is within subsection (3) –

(a) whether or not the date on which the relevant disposal is to take place is specified in the agreement, and

(b) whether or not any requirement to make that disposal is or may be made subject to the fulfilment of any condition.

(5) The Secretary of State may by order provide –

(a) for subsection (1) to apply to agreements of any description specified in the order in addition to those within subsection (3);

(b) for subsection (1) not to apply to agreements of any description so specified to which it would otherwise apply.

(6) An order under subsection (5) –

(a) may make different provision with respect to different cases or descriptions of case; and

(b) shall be made by statutory instrument which shall be subject to annulment in pursuance of a resolution of either House of Parliament.

(7) In this section –

"agreement" includes arrangement;

"the discount repayment period" means the period of 3 years that applies for the purposes of section 35(2) or the period of five years that applies for the purposes of section 35(3) (depending on whether an offer such as is mentioned in section 195(4) of the Housing Act 2004 was made before or on or after the coming into force of that section).'

(2) The amendment made by this section does not apply in relation to any agreement or arrangement made before the day on which this section comes into force.

Disposals by registered social landlords

199 Repayment of discount: periods and amounts payable

(1) For section 11 of the Housing Act 1996 (c 52) substitute –

'11 Covenant for repayment of discount on disposal

(1) Where on a disposal of a house by a registered social landlord, in accordance with a consent given by the Relevant Authority under section 9, a discount has been given to the purchaser, and the consent does not provide otherwise, the conveyance, grant or assignment shall contain a covenant binding on the purchaser and his successors in title to the following effect.

(2) The covenant shall be to pay to the landlord such sum (if any) as the landlord may demand in accordance with subsection (3) on the occasion of the first relevant disposal which is not an exempted disposal and which takes place within the period of five years beginning with the conveyance, grant or assignment.

(3) The landlord may demand such sum as he considers appropriate, up to and including the maximum amount specified in this section.

(4) The maximum amount which may be demanded by the landlord is a percentage of the price or premium paid for the first relevant disposal which is equal to the percentage discount given to the purchaser in respect of the disposal of the house by the landlord.

(5) But for each complete year which has elapsed after the conveyance, grant or assignment and before the first relevant disposal the maximum amount which may be demanded by the landlord is reduced by one-fifth.

(6) Subsections (3) to (5) are subject to section 11A.

11A Increase in value of house attributable to home improvements to be disregarded

(1) In calculating the maximum amount which may be demanded by the landlord under section 11, such amount (if any) of the price or premium paid for the first relevant disposal which is attributable to improvements made to the house –

    (a) by the person by whom the disposal is, or is to be, made, and
    (b) after the conveyance, grant or assignment and before the disposal,

shall be disregarded.

(2) The amount to be disregarded under this section shall be such amount as may be agreed between the parties or determined by the district valuer.

(3) The district valuer shall not be required by virtue of this section to make a determination for the purposes of this section unless –

    (a) it is reasonably practicable for him to do so; and
    (b) his reasonable costs in making the determination are paid by the person by whom the disposal is, or is to be, made.

(4) If the district valuer does not make a determination for the purposes of this section (and in default of an agreement), no amount is required to be disregarded under this section.

11B Liability to repay is a charge on the house

(1) The liability that may arise under the covenant required by section 11 is a charge on the house, taking effect as if it had been created by deed expressed to be by way of legal mortgage.

(2) Where there is a relevant disposal which is an exempted disposal by virtue of section 15(4)(d) or (e) (compulsory disposal or disposal of yard, garden, etc) –

    (a) the covenant required by section 11 is not binding on the person to whom the disposal is made or any successor in title of his, and
    (b) the covenant and the charge taking effect by virtue of this section cease to apply in relation to the property disposed of.'

(2) In section 12, for 'section 11' in each place where it occurs substitute 'section 11B'.

(3) The amendments made by this section do not apply in any case where –

    (a) the purchaser has accepted an offer for the disposal of the house from the landlord, or
    (b) the landlord has accepted an offer for the disposal of the house from the purchaser,

before the day on which this section comes into force.

(4) Subsection (5), however, applies in any such case if the first relevant disposal by the purchaser to which the covenant for repayment of discount applies takes place on or after the day on which this section comes into force.

(5) In the following provisions –

(a) section 11(2) of the Housing Act 1996 (c 52) (as it has effect without the amendments made by this section), and

(b) any covenant for repayment of discount,

any reference (however expressed) to a person being liable to pay an amount to the landlord on demand is to be read as a reference to his being liable to pay to the landlord so much of that amount (if any) as the landlord may demand.

(6) In subsections (4) and (5) 'covenant for repayment of discount' means the covenant contained in a conveyance, grant or assignment in accordance with section 11 of that Act.

200 Registered social landlord's right of first refusal

(1) After section 12 of the Housing Act 1996 insert –

'12A Right of first refusal for registered social landlord

(1) Where on a disposal of a house by a registered social landlord, in accordance with a consent given by the Relevant Authority under section 9, a discount has been given to the purchaser, and the consent does not provide otherwise, the conveyance, grant or assignment shall contain the following covenant, which shall be binding on the purchaser and his successors in title.

(2) The covenant shall be to the effect that, until the end of the period of ten years beginning with the conveyance, grant or assignment, there will be no relevant disposal which is not an exempted disposal, unless the prescribed conditions have been satisfied in relation to that or a previous such disposal.

(3) In subsection (2) "the prescribed conditions" means such conditions as are prescribed by regulations under this section at the time when the conveyance, grant or assignment is made.

(4) The Secretary of State may by regulations prescribe such conditions as he considers appropriate for and in connection with conferring on –

(a) a registered social landlord which has made a disposal as mentioned in subsection (1), or

(b) such other person as is determined in accordance with the regulations,

a right of first refusal to have a disposal within subsection (5) made to him for such consideration as is mentioned in section 12B.

(5) The disposals within this subsection are –

(a) a reconveyance or conveyance of the house; and

(b) a surrender or assignment of the lease.

(6) Regulations under this section may, in particular, make provision –

(a) for the purchaser to offer to make such a disposal to such person or persons as may be prescribed;

(b) for a prescribed recipient of such an offer to be able either to accept the offer or to nominate some other person as the person by whom the offer may be accepted;

(c) for the person who may be so nominated to be either a person of a prescribed description or a person whom the prescribed recipient considers, having regard to any prescribed matters, to be a more appropriate person to accept the offer;

(d) for a prescribed recipient making such a nomination to give a notification of the nomination to the person nominated, the purchaser and any other prescribed person;

(e) for authorising a nominated person to accept the offer and for determining which acceptance is to be effective where the offer is accepted by more than one person;

(f) for the period within which the offer may be accepted or within which any other prescribed step is to be, or may be, taken;

(g) for the circumstances in which the right of first refusal lapses (whether following the service of a notice to complete or otherwise) with the result that the purchaser is able to make a disposal on the open market;

(h) for the manner in which any offer, acceptance or notification is to be communicated.

(7) In subsection (6) any reference to the purchaser is a reference to the purchaser or his successor in title.

Nothing in that subsection affects the generality of subsection (4).

(8) Regulations under this section –

(a) may make different provision with respect to different cases or descriptions of case; and

(b) shall be made by statutory instrument which shall be subject to annulment in pursuance of a resolution of either House of Parliament.

(9) The limitation imposed by a covenant within subsection (2) is a local land charge.

(10) The Chief Land Registrar must enter in the register of title a restriction reflecting the limitation imposed by any such covenant.

(11) Where there is a relevant disposal which is an exempted disposal by virtue of section 15(4)(d) or (e) (compulsory disposal or disposal of yard, garden, &c) –

(a) the covenant required by this section is not binding on the person to whom the disposal is made or any successor in title of his, and

(b) the covenant ceases to apply in relation to the property disposed of.

12B Consideration payable for disposal under section 12A

(1) The consideration for a disposal made in respect of a right of first refusal as mentioned in section 12A(4) shall be such amount as may be agreed between the parties, or determined by the district valuer, as being the amount which is to be taken to be the value of the house at the time when the offer is made (as determined in accordance with regulations under that section).

(2) That value shall be taken to be the price which, at that time, the interest to be reconveyed, conveyed, surrendered or assigned would realise if sold on the open market by a willing vendor, on the assumption that any liability under the covenant required by section 11 (repayment of discount on early disposal) would be discharged by the vendor.

(3) If the offer is accepted in accordance with regulations under section 12A, no payment shall be required in pursuance of any such covenant as is mentioned in subsection (2), but the consideration shall be reduced, subject to subsection (4), by such amount (if any) as, on a disposal made at the time the offer was made, being a relevant disposal which is not an exempted disposal, would fall to be paid under that covenant.

(4) Where there is a charge on the house having priority over the charge to secure payment of the sum due under the covenant mentioned in subsection (2), the consideration shall not be reduced under subsection (3) below the amount necessary to discharge the outstanding sum secured by the first-mentioned charge at the date of the offer (as determined in accordance with regulations under section 12A).'

(2) In section 13(1) of the Housing Act 1996 (c 52) (restriction on disposal of houses in National Parks, &c), after 'restriction on assignment)' insert 'or a covenant as mentioned in section 12A(2) of this Act (right of first refusal for registered social landlord)'.

(3) The amendments made by this section do not apply in relation to a disposal under section 8 of that Act if –

(a) the purchaser has accepted an offer for the disposal of the house from the landlord, or
(b) the landlord has accepted an offer for the disposal of the house from the purchaser,

before the day on which this section comes into force.

201 Deferred resale agreements

(1) After section 15 of the Housing Act 1996 insert –

'15A Treatment of deferred resale agreements for purposes of section 11

(1) If a purchaser or his successor in title enters into an agreement within subsection (3), any liability arising under the covenant required by section 11 shall be determined as if a relevant disposal which is not an exempted disposal had occurred at the appropriate time.

(2) In subsection (1) "the appropriate time" means –

(a) the time when the agreement is entered into, or
(b) if it was made before the beginning of the discount repayment period, immediately after the beginning of that period.

(3) An agreement is within this subsection if it is an agreement between the purchaser or his successor in title and any other person –

(a) which is made (expressly or impliedly) in contemplation of, or in connection with, a disposal to be made, or made, by virtue of section 8,
(b) which is made before the end of the discount repayment period, and
(c) under which a relevant disposal which is not an exempted disposal is or may be required to be made to any person after the end of that period.

(4) Such an agreement is within subsection (3) –

(a) whether or not the date on which the relevant disposal is to take place is specified in the agreement, and
(b) whether or not any requirement to make that disposal is or may be made subject to the fulfilment of any condition.

(5) The Secretary of State may by order provide –

(a) for subsection (1) to apply to agreements of any description specified in the order in addition to those within subsection (3);
(b) for subsection (1) not to apply to agreements of any description so specified to which it would otherwise apply.

(6) An order under subsection (5) –

(a) may make different provision with respect to different cases or descriptions of case; and
(b) shall be made by statutory instrument which shall be subject to annulment in pursuance of a resolution of either House of Parliament.

(7) In this section –

"agreement" includes arrangement;

"the discount repayment period" means the period of three or five years that applies for the purposes of section 11(2) (depending on whether an offer such as is mentioned in section 199(3) of the Housing Act 2004 was made before or on or after the coming into force of that section).'

(2) The amendment made by this section does not apply in relation to any agreement or arrangement made before the day on which this section comes into force.

202 Right of assured tenant to acquire dwelling not affected by collective enfranchisement

(1) Section 16 of the Housing Act 1996 (c 52) (right of assured tenant of registered social landlord to acquire dwelling) is amended as follows.

(2) After subsection (3) insert –

'(3A) In subsection (3)(a) the reference to the freehold interest in the dwelling includes a reference to such an interest in the dwelling as is held by the landlord under a lease granted in pursuance of paragraph 3 of Schedule 9 to the Leasehold Reform, Housing and Urban Development Act 1993 (mandatory leaseback to former freeholder on collective enfranchisement).'

(3) The amendment made by subsection (2) applies in relation to the right conferred by section 16 as follows –

(a) it applies for the purposes of any exercise of that right on or after the day on which this section comes into force, and

(b) it so applies whether the lease granted in pursuance of paragraph 3 of Schedule 9 to the Leasehold Reform, Housing and Urban Development Act 1993 was granted on or after that day or before it.

Disposals by housing action trusts

203 Repayment of discount: periods and amounts payable

(1) Schedule 11 to the Housing Act 1988 (c 50) (provisions applicable to certain disposals of houses) is amended as follows.

(2) In paragraph 1(2) for the words from 'to pay to the housing action trust' to the end of the sub-paragraph substitute 'to the following effect.'

(3) After paragraph 1(2) insert –

'(3) The covenant shall be to pay to the housing action trust such sum (if any) as the trust may demand in accordance with sub-paragraph (4) on the occasion of the first relevant disposal (other than an exempted disposal) which takes place within the period of five years beginning with the conveyance, grant or assignment.

(4) The trust may demand such sum as it considers appropriate, up to and including the maximum amount specified in this paragraph.

(5) The maximum amount which may be demanded by the trust is a percentage of the price or premium paid for the first relevant disposal which is equal to the percentage discount given to the purchaser in respect of the disposal of the house under section 79.

(6) But for each complete year which has elapsed after the conveyance, grant or assignment and before the first relevant disposal the maximum amount which may be demanded by the trust is reduced by one-fifth.

(7) Sub-paragraphs (4) to (6) are subject to paragraph 1A.

Increase in value of house attributable to home improvements

1A

(1) In calculating the maximum amount which may be demanded by the housing action trust under paragraph 1, such amount (if any) of the price or premium paid for the first relevant disposal which is attributable to improvements made to the house –

    (a) by the person by whom the disposal is, or is to be, made, and
    (b) after the conveyance, grant or assignment and before the disposal,

shall be disregarded.

(2) The amount to be disregarded under this paragraph shall be such amount as may be agreed between the parties or determined by the district valuer.

(3) The district valuer shall not be required by virtue of this paragraph to make a determination for the purposes of this paragraph unless –

    (a) it is reasonably practicable for him to do so; and
    (b) his reasonable costs in making the determination are paid by the person by whom the disposal is, or is to be, made.

(4) If the district valuer does not make a determination for the purposes of this paragraph (and in default of an agreement), no amount is required to be disregarded under this paragraph.'

(4) The amendments made by this section do not apply in any case where –

    (a) the purchaser has accepted an offer for the disposal of the house from the housing action trust, or
    (b) the housing action trust has accepted an offer for the disposal of the house from the purchaser,

before the day on which this section comes into force.

(5) Subsection (6), however, applies in any such case if the first relevant disposal by the purchaser to which the covenant for repayment of discount applies takes place on or after the day on which this section comes into force.

(6) In the following provisions –

    (a) paragraph 1(2) of Schedule 11 to the Housing Act 1988 (c 50) (as it has effect without the amendments made by this section), and
    (b) any covenant for repayment of discount,

any reference (however expressed) to a person being liable to pay an amount to the housing action trust on demand is to be read as a reference to his being liable to pay to the trust so much of that amount (if any) as the trust may demand.

(7) In subsections (5) and (6) 'covenant for repayment of discount' means the covenant contained in a conveyance, grant or assignment in accordance with paragraph 1 of Schedule 11 to that Act.

204 Housing action trust's right of first refusal

(1) After paragraph 2 of Schedule 11 to the Housing Act 1988 insert –

'Right of first refusal for housing action trust

2A

(1) This paragraph applies where, on the disposal of a house under section 79 of this Act, a discount is given to the purchaser by the housing action trust in accordance with a consent given by the Secretary of State under subsection (1) of that section and that consent does not exclude the application of this paragraph.

(2) On the disposal, the conveyance, grant or assignment shall contain the following covenant, which shall be binding on the purchaser and his successors in title.

(3) The covenant shall be to the effect that, until the end of the period of ten years beginning with the conveyance, grant or assignment, there will be no relevant disposal which is not an exempted disposal, unless the prescribed conditions have been satisfied in relation to that or a previous such disposal.

(4) In sub-paragraph (3) "the prescribed conditions" means such conditions as are prescribed by regulations under this section at the time when the conveyance, grant or assignment is made.

(5) The Secretary of State may by regulations prescribe such conditions as he considers appropriate for and in connection with conferring on –

(a) a housing action trust which has made a disposal as mentioned in sub-paragraph (1), or
(b) such other person as is determined in accordance with the regulations,

a right of first refusal to have a disposal within sub-paragraph (6) made to him for such consideration as is mentioned in paragraph 2B.

(6) The disposals within this sub-paragraph are –

(a) a reconveyance or conveyance of the house; and
(b) a surrender or assignment of the lease.

(7) Regulations under this paragraph may, in particular, make provision –

(a) for the purchaser to offer to make such a disposal to such person or persons as may be prescribed;
(b) for a prescribed recipient of such an offer to be able either to accept the offer or to nominate some other person as the person by whom the offer may be accepted;
(c) for the person who may be so nominated to be either a person of a prescribed description or a person whom the prescribed recipient considers, having regard to any prescribed matters, to be a more appropriate person to accept the offer;
(d) for a prescribed recipient making such a nomination to give a notification of the nomination to the person nominated, the purchaser and any other prescribed person;
(e) for authorising a nominated person to accept the offer and for determining which acceptance is to be effective where the offer is accepted by more than one person;
(f) for the period within which the offer may be accepted or within which any other prescribed step is to be, or may be, taken;
(g) for the circumstances in which the right of first refusal lapses (whether following the service of a notice to complete or otherwise) with the result that the purchaser is able to make a disposal on the open market;
(h) for the manner in which any offer, acceptance or notification is to be communicated.

(8) In sub-paragraph (7) any reference to the purchaser is a reference to the purchaser or his successor in title.

Nothing in that sub-paragraph affects the generality of sub-paragraph (5).

(9) Regulations under this paragraph –

(a) may make different provision with respect to different cases or descriptions of case; and

(b) shall be made by statutory instrument which shall be subject to annulment in pursuance of a resolution of either House of Parliament.

(10) The limitation imposed by a covenant within sub-paragraph (3) is a local land charge.

(11) The Chief Land Registrar must enter in the register of title a restriction reflecting the limitation imposed by any such covenant.

Consideration payable for disposal under paragraph 2A

2B

(1) The consideration for a disposal made in respect of a right of first refusal as mentioned in paragraph 2A(5) shall be such amount as may be agreed between the parties, or determined by the district valuer, as being the amount which is to be taken to be the value of the house at the time when the offer is made (as determined in accordance with regulations under that paragraph).

(2) That value shall be taken to be the price which, at that time, the interest to be reconveyed, conveyed, surrendered or assigned would realise if sold on the open market by a willing vendor, on the assumption that any liability under the covenant required by paragraph 1 (repayment of discount on early disposal) would be discharged by the vendor.

(3) If the offer is accepted in accordance with regulations under paragraph 2A, no payment shall be required in pursuance of any such covenant as is mentioned in sub-paragraph (2), but the consideration shall be reduced, subject to sub-paragraph (4), by such amount (if any) as, on a disposal made at the time the offer was made, being a relevant disposal which is not an exempted disposal, would fall to be paid under that covenant.

(4) Where there is a charge on the house having priority over the charge to secure payment of the sum due under the covenant mentioned in sub-paragraph (2), the consideration shall not be reduced under sub-paragraph (3) below the amount necessary to discharge the outstanding sum secured by the first-mentioned charge at the date of the offer (as determined in accordance with regulations under paragraph 2A).'

(2) In paragraph 6 of Schedule 11 to that Act (exempted disposals ending obligation under covenants), at the end of paragraph (b) insert

'and

(c) the covenant required by paragraph 2A above is not binding on the person to whom the disposal is made or any successor in title of his; and

(d) that covenant ceases to apply in relation to the property disposed of.'

(3) The amendments made by this section do not apply in relation to a disposal under section 79 of that Act if –

(a) the purchaser has accepted an offer for the disposal of the house from the housing action trust, or

(b) the housing action trust has accepted an offer for the disposal of the house from the purchaser,

before the day on which this section comes into force.

205 Deferred resale agreements

(1) After paragraph 7 of Schedule 11 to the Housing Act 1988 (c 50) insert –

'Treatment of deferred resale agreements

8

(1) If a purchaser or his successor in title enters into an agreement within sub-paragraph (3), any liability arising under the covenant required by paragraph 1 shall be determined as if a relevant disposal which is not an exempted disposal had occurred at the appropriate time.

(2) In sub-paragraph (1) "the appropriate time" means –

    (a) the time when the agreement is entered into, or

    (b) if it was made before the beginning of the discount repayment period, immediately after the beginning of that period.

(3) An agreement is within this sub-paragraph if it is an agreement between the purchaser or his successor in title and any other person –

    (a) which is made (expressly or impliedly) in contemplation of, or in connection with, a disposal to be made, or made, under section 79,

    (b) which is made before the end of the discount repayment period, and

    (c) under which a relevant disposal (other than an exempted disposal) is or may be required to be made to any person after the end of that period.

(4) Such an agreement is within sub-paragraph (3) –

    (a) whether or not the date on which the relevant disposal is to take place is specified in the agreement, and

    (b) whether or not any requirement to make that disposal is or may be made subject to the fulfilment of any condition.

(5) The Secretary of State may by order provide –

    (a) for sub-paragraph (1) to apply to agreements of any description specified in the order in addition to those within sub-paragraph (3);

    (b) for sub-paragraph (1) not to apply to agreements of any description so specified to which it would otherwise apply.

(6) An order under sub-paragraph (5) –

    (a) may make different provision with respect to different cases or descriptions of case; and

    (b) shall be made by statutory instrument which shall be subject to annulment in pursuance of a resolution of either House of Parliament.

(7) In this paragraph –

    "agreement" includes arrangement;

    "the discount repayment period" means the period of 3 years that applies for the purposes of paragraph 1(2) or the period of five years that applies for the purposes of paragraph 1(3) (depending on whether an offer such as is mentioned in section 203(4) of the Housing Act 2004 was made before or on or after the coming into force of that section).'

(2) The amendment made by this section does not apply in relation to any agreement or arrangement made before the day on which this section comes into force.

Chapter 3
Mobile Homes

Site agreements

206 Particulars of site agreements to be given in advance

(1) For section 1 of the Mobile Homes Act 1983 (c 34) (particulars of agreements between site owners and occupiers of mobile homes) substitute –

'1 Particulars of agreements

(1) This Act applies to any agreement under which a person ("the occupier") is entitled –

(a) to station a mobile home on land forming part of a protected site; and
(b) to occupy the mobile home as his only or main residence.

(2) Before making an agreement to which this Act applies, the owner of the protected site ("the owner") shall give to the proposed occupier under the agreement a written statement which –

(a) specifies the names and addresses of the parties;
(b) includes particulars of the land on which the proposed occupier is to be entitled to station the mobile home that are sufficient to identify that land;
(c) sets out the express terms to be contained in the agreement;
(d) sets out the terms to be implied by section 2(1) below; and
(e) complies with such other requirements as may be prescribed by regulations made by the appropriate national authority.

(3) The written statement required by subsection (2) above must be given –

(a) not later than 28 days before the date on which any agreement for the sale of the mobile home to the proposed occupier is made, or
(b) (if no such agreement is made before the making of the agreement to which this Act applies) not later than 28 days before the date on which the agreement to which this Act applies is made.

(4) But if the proposed occupier consents in writing to that statement being given to him by a date ("the chosen date") which is less than 28 days before the date mentioned in subsection (3)(a) or (b) above, the statement must be given to him not later than the chosen date.

(5) If any express term –

(a) is contained in an agreement to which this Act applies, but
(b) was not set out in a written statement given to the proposed occupier in accordance with subsections (2) to (4) above,

the term is unenforceable by the owner or any person within section 3(1) below.

This is subject to any order made by the court under section 2(3) below.

(6) If the owner has failed to give the occupier a written statement in accordance with subsections (2) to (4) above, the occupier may, at any time after the making of the agreement, apply to the court for an order requiring the owner –

(a) to give him a written statement which complies with paragraphs (a) to (e) of subsection (2) (read with any modifications necessary to reflect the fact that the agreement has been made), and

(b) to do so not later than such date as is specified in the order.

(7) A statement required to be given to a person under this section may be either delivered to him personally or sent to him by post.

(8) Any reference in this section to the making of an agreement to which this Act applies includes a reference to any variation of an agreement by virtue of which the agreement becomes one to which this Act applies.

(9) Regulations under this section –

(a) shall be made by statutory instrument;
(b) if made by the Secretary of State, shall be subject to annulment in pursuance of a resolution of either House of Parliament; and
(c) may make different provision with respect to different cases or descriptions of case, including different provision for different areas.'

(2) Section 2 of that Act (terms of agreements) is amended as follows –

(a) in subsection (2), for 'within six months of the giving of the statement under section 1(2) above' substitute 'within the relevant period'; and
(b) for subsection (3) substitute –

'(3) The court may, on the application of either party made within the relevant period, make an order –

(a) varying or deleting any express term of the agreement;
(b) in the case of any express term to which section 1(6) above applies, provide for the term to have full effect or to have such effect subject to any variation specified in the order.

(3A) In subsections (2) and (3) above "the relevant period" means the period beginning with the date on which the agreement is made and ending –

(a) six months after that date, or
(b) where a written statement relating to the agreement is given to the occupier after that date (whether or not in compliance with an order under section 1(6) above), six months after the date on which the statement is given;

and section 1(8) above applies for the purposes of this subsection as it applies for the purposes of section 1.'

(3) In section 5(1) of that Act (interpretation) insert at the appropriate place –

'"the appropriate national authority" means –

(a) in relation to England, the Secretary of State, and
(b) in relation to Wales, the National Assembly for Wales;'.

(4) The amendments made by subsections (1) and (2) do not apply in relation to an agreement to which that Act applies where –

(a) the agreement, or
(b) (if it becomes one to which that Act applies as the result of any variation of it) the variation in question,

is made before the end of the period of 28 days beginning with the day on which those subsections come into force.

(5) The new section 1(9)(b) inserted by subsection (1) does not affect the continuing validity of any regulations made under section 1 of that Act before the passing of this Act.

207 Implied terms relating to termination of agreements or disposal of mobile homes

(1) Part 1 of Schedule 1 to the Mobile Homes Act 1983 (c 34) (terms implied in site agreements) is amended as follows.

(2) In paragraph 6 (termination by owner on ground of detrimental effect resulting from age and condition of mobile home) –

   (a) omit 'age and'; and
   (b) after sub-paragraph (2) insert –

   '(3) Sub-paragraphs (4) and (5) below apply if, on an application under sub-paragraph (1) above –

      (a) the court considers that, having regard to the present condition of the mobile home, paragraph (a) or (b) of that sub-paragraph applies to it, but
      (b) it also considers that it would be reasonably practicable for particular repairs to be carried out on the mobile home that would result in neither of those paragraphs applying to it, and
      (c) the occupier indicates that he intends to carry out those repairs.

   (4) In such a case the court may make an order adjourning proceedings on the application for such period specified in the order as the court considers reasonable to allow the repairs to be carried out.

   The repairs must be set out in the order.

   (5) If the court makes such an order, the application shall not be further proceeded with unless the court is satisfied that the specified period has expired without the repairs having been carried out.'

(3) In paragraph 8 (sale of mobile home to person approved by owner) –

   (a) after sub-paragraph (1) insert –

   '(1A) The occupier may serve on the owner a request for the owner to approve a person for the purposes of sub-paragraph (1) above.

   (1B) Where the owner receives such a request, he must, within the period of 28 days beginning with the date on which he received the request –

      (a) approve the person, unless it is reasonable for him not to do so, and
      (b) serve on the occupier notice of his decision whether or not to approve the person.

   (1C) A notice under sub-paragraph (1B) above must specify –

      (a) if the approval is given subject to conditions, the conditions, and
      (b) if the approval is withheld, the reasons for withholding it.

   (1D) The giving of approval subject to any condition that is not a reasonable condition does not satisfy the requirement in sub-paragraph (1B)(a) above.

   (1E) If the owner fails to notify the occupier as required by sub-paragraphs (1B) and (1C) above, the occupier may apply to the court for an order declaring that the person is approved for the purposes of sub-paragraph (1) above; and the court may make such an order if it thinks fit.

   (1F) It is for the owner –

(a) if he served a notice as mentioned in sub-paragraphs (1B) and (1C) and the question arises whether he served the notice within the required period of 28 days, to show that he did;

(b) if he gave his approval subject to any condition and the question arises whether the condition was a reasonable condition, to show that it was;

(c) if he did not give his approval and the question arises whether it was reasonable for him not to do so, to show that it was reasonable.

(1G) A request or notice under this paragraph –

(a) must be in writing, and

(b) may be served by post.';

(b) in sub-paragraph (2) for 'the Secretary of State' substitute 'the appropriate national authority'; and

(c) in sub-paragraph (3)(a) after 'which' insert ' (if made by the Secretary of State)'.

(4) After the existing provisions of paragraph 9 (gift of mobile home to person approved by owner), which become sub-paragraph (1), insert –

'(2) Sub-paragraphs (1A) to (1G) of paragraph 8 above shall apply in relation to the approval of a person for the purposes of sub-paragraph (1) above as they apply in relation to the approval of a person for the purposes of sub-paragraph (1) of that paragraph.'

(5) After Part 2 of Schedule 1 to the Mobile Homes Act 1983 (c 34) insert –

'Part 3
Supplementary Provisions

Duty to forward requests under paragraph 8 or 9 of Part 1

1

(1) This paragraph applies to –

(a) a request by the occupier for the owner to approve a person for the purposes of paragraph 8(1) of Part 1 (see paragraph 8(1A)), or

(b) a request by the occupier for the owner to approve a person for the purposes of paragraph 9(1) of Part 1 (see paragraph 8(1A) as applied by paragraph 9(2)).

(2) If a person ("the recipient") receives such a request and he –

(a) though not the owner, has an estate or interest in the protected site, and

(b) believes that another person is the owner (and that the other person has not received such a request),

the recipient owes a duty to the occupier to take such steps as are reasonable to secure that the other person receives the request within the period of 28 days beginning with the date on which the recipient receives it.

(3) In paragraph 8(1B) of Part 1 of this Schedule (as it applies to any request within sub-paragraph (1) above) any reference to the owner receiving such a request includes a reference to his receiving it in accordance with sub-paragraph (2) above.

Action for breach of duty under paragraph 1

2

(1) A claim that a person has broken the duty under paragraph 1(2) above may be made the subject of civil proceedings in like manner as any other claim in tort for breach of statutory duty.

(2) The right conferred by sub-paragraph (1) is in addition to any right to bring proceedings, in respect of a breach of any implied term having effect by virtue of paragraph 8 or 9 of Part 1 of this Schedule, against a person bound by that term.'

(6) The amendments made by this section apply in relation to an agreement to which the Mobile Homes Act 1983 applies that was made before the day on which this section comes into force ('the appointed day'), as well as in relation to one made on or after that day.

Any reference in this subsection to the making of an agreement to which that Act applies includes a reference to any variation of an agreement by virtue of which the agreement becomes one to which that Act applies.

(7) However –

(a) the amendments made by subsection (2) do not apply in relation to any application made before the appointed day for the purposes of paragraph 6 of Part 1 of Schedule 1 to that Act; and

(b) the amendments made by subsections (3)(a), (4) and (5) do not apply in relation to any request for approval made before the appointed day for the purposes of paragraph 8(1) or (as the case may be) 9(1) of that Part of that Schedule.

208 Power to amend terms implied in site agreements

(1) After section 2 of the Mobile Homes Act 1983 (c 34) insert –

'2A Power to amend implied terms

(1) The appropriate national authority may by order make such amendments of Part 1 or 2 of Schedule 1 to this Act as the authority considers appropriate.

(2) An order under this section –

(a) shall be made by statutory instrument;

(b) may make different provision with respect to different cases or descriptions of case, including different provision for different areas;

(c) may contain such incidental, supplementary, consequential, transitional or saving provisions as the authority making the order considers appropriate.

(3) Without prejudice to the generality of subsections (1) and (2), an order under this section may –

(a) make provision for or in connection with the determination by the court of such questions, or the making by the court of such orders, as are specified in the order;

(b) make such amendments of any provision of this Act as the authority making the order considers appropriate in consequence of any amendment made by the order in Part 1 or 2 of Schedule 1.

(4) The first order made under this section in relation to England or Wales respectively may provide for all or any of its provisions to apply in relation to agreements to which this Act

applies that were made at any time before the day on which the order comes into force (as well as in relation to such agreements made on or after that day).

(5) No order may be made by the appropriate national authority under this section unless the authority has consulted –

(a) such organisations as appear to it to be representative of interests substantially affected by the order; and

(b) such other persons as it considers appropriate.

(6) No order may be made by the Secretary of State under this section unless a draft of the order has been laid before, and approved by a resolution of, each House of Parliament.'

(2) For the purposes of subsection (5) of the section 2A inserted by this section, consultation undertaken before the date of the passing of this Act constitutes as effective compliance with that subsection as if undertaken on or after that date.

Protection from eviction etc

209 Protected sites to include sites for gypsies

(1) Section 1 of the Caravan Sites Act 1968 (c 52) (application of provisions for protection of residential occupiers of caravan sites) is amended as follows.

(2) In subsection (2) (under which 'protected site' includes certain local authority sites) for 'paragraph 11 of Schedule 1 to that Act (exemption of land occupied by local authorities) substitute 'paragraph 11 or 11A of Schedule 1 to that Act (exemption of gypsy and other local authority sites)'.

(3) The amendment made by subsection (2) above does not affect the operation of –

(a) section 2 of the Act (minimum length of notice) in relation to any notice given before the day on which this section comes into force, or

(b) section 3 of the Act (protection from eviction) in relation to any conduct occurring before that day, or

(c) section 4 of the Act (suspension of eviction orders) in relation to any proceedings begun before that day.

(4) In subsection (3)(b) the reference to section 3 of the Act is to that section whether as amended by section 210 of this Act or otherwise.

210 Extension of protection from harassment for occupiers of mobile homes

(1) Section 3 of the Caravan Sites Act 1968 (protection of occupiers against eviction and harassment) is amended as follows.

(2) In subsection (1) (offence where person, with the specified intent, does acts calculated to interfere with the peace or comfort of the occupier etc) for 'calculated to interfere' substitute 'likely to interfere'.

(3) After subsection (1) insert –

'(1A) Subject to the provisions of this section, the owner of a protected site or his agent shall be guilty of an offence under this section if, whether during the subsistence or after the expiration or determination of a residential contract –

(a) he does acts likely to interfere with the peace or comfort of the occupier or persons residing with him, or

(b) he persistently withdraws or withholds services or facilities reasonably required for the occupation of the caravan as a residence on the site, and (in either case) he knows, or has reasonable cause to believe, that that conduct is likely to cause the occupier to do any of the things mentioned in subsection (1)(c)(i) or (ii) of this section.

(1B) References in subsection (1A) of this section to the owner of a protected site include references to a person with an estate or interest in the site which is superior to that of the owner.'

(4) In subsection (3) (penalties for offences), for the words from 'be liable' onwards substitute

'be liable –

(a) on summary conviction, to a fine not exceeding the statutory maximum or to imprisonment for a term not exceeding 12 months, or to both;

(b) on conviction on indictment, to a fine or to imprisonment for a term not exceeding 2 years, or to both.'

(5) After subsection (4) insert –

'(4A) In proceedings for an offence under subsection (1A) of this section it shall be a defence to prove that the accused had reasonable grounds for doing the acts or withdrawing or withholding the services or facilities in question.'

(6) The amendments made by this section do not apply in relation to any conduct occurring before the day on which this section comes into force.

(7) In the case of an offence committed before section 154(1) of the Criminal Justice Act 2003 (c 44) comes into force, the amendment made by subsection (4) has effect as if for '12 months' there were substituted '6 months'.

211 Suspension of eviction orders

(1) In section 4(6) of the Caravan Sites Act 1968 (c 52) (provision for suspension of eviction orders) for the words from 'in the following cases' to the end of paragraph (b) substitute

'if –

(a) no site licence under Part 1 of that Act is in force in respect of the site, and

(b) paragraph 11 or 11A of Schedule 1 to the Caravan Sites and Control of Development Act 1960 (c 2) does not apply;'.

(2) The amendment made by subsection (1) does not apply in relation to proceedings begun before the day on which this section comes into force.

Chapter 4
Tenancy Deposit Schemes

212 Tenancy deposit schemes

(1) The appropriate national authority must make arrangements for securing that one or more tenancy deposit schemes are available for the purpose of safeguarding tenancy deposits paid in connection with shorthold tenancies.

(2) For the purposes of this Chapter a 'tenancy deposit scheme' is a scheme which –

(a) is made for the purpose of safeguarding tenancy deposits paid in connection with shorthold tenancies and facilitating the resolution of disputes arising in connection with such deposits, and

(b) complies with the requirements of Schedule 10.

(3) Arrangements under subsection (1) must be arrangements made with any body or person under which the body or person ('the scheme administrator') undertakes to establish and maintain a tenancy deposit scheme of a description specified in the arrangements.

(4) The appropriate national authority may –

(a) give financial assistance to the scheme administrator;
(b) make payments to the scheme administrator (otherwise than as financial assistance) in pursuance of arrangements under subsection (1).

(5) The appropriate national authority may, in such manner and on such terms as it thinks fit, guarantee the discharge of any financial obligation incurred by the scheme administrator in connection with arrangements under subsection (1).

(6) Arrangements under subsection (1) must require the scheme administrator to give the appropriate national authority, in such manner and at such times as it may specify, such information and facilities for obtaining information as it may specify.

(7) The appropriate national authority may make regulations conferring or imposing –

(a) on scheme administrators, or
(b) on scheme administrators of any description specified in the regulations,

such powers or duties in connection with arrangements under subsection (1) as are so specified.

(8) In this Chapter –

'authorised', in relation to a tenancy deposit scheme, means that the scheme is in force in accordance with arrangements under subsection (1);

'custodial scheme' and 'insurance scheme' have the meaning given by paragraph 1(2) and (3) of Schedule 10);

'money' means money in the form of cash or otherwise;

'shorthold tenancy' means an assured shorthold tenancy within the meaning of Chapter 2 of Part 1 of the Housing Act 1988 (c 50);

'tenancy deposit', in relation to a shorthold tenancy, means any money intended to be held (by the landlord or otherwise) as security for –

(a) the performance of any obligations of the tenant, or
(b) the discharge of any liability of his,

arising under or in connection with the tenancy.

(9) In this Chapter –

(a) references to a landlord or landlords in relation to any shorthold tenancy or tenancies include references to a person or persons acting on his or their behalf in relation to the tenancy or tenancies, and
(b) references to a tenancy deposit being held in accordance with a scheme include, in the case of a custodial scheme, references to an amount representing the deposit being held in accordance with the scheme.

213 Requirements relating to tenancy deposits

(1) Any tenancy deposit paid to a person in connection with a shorthold tenancy must, as from the time when it is received, be dealt with in accordance with an authorised scheme.

(2) No person may require the payment of a tenancy deposit in connection with a shorthold tenancy which is not to be subject to the requirement in subsection (1).

(3) Where a landlord receives a tenancy deposit in connection with a shorthold tenancy, the initial requirements of an authorised scheme must be complied with by the landlord in relation to the deposit within the period of 14 days beginning with the date on which it is received.

(4) For the purposes of this section 'the initial requirements' of an authorised scheme are such requirements imposed by the scheme as fall to be complied with by a landlord on receiving such a tenancy deposit.

(5) A landlord who has received such a tenancy deposit must give the tenant and any relevant person such information relating to –

(a) the authorised scheme applying to the deposit,
(b) compliance by the landlord with the initial requirements of the scheme in relation to the deposit, and
(c) the operation of provisions of this Chapter in relation to the deposit,

as may be prescribed.

(6) The information required by subsection (5) must be given to the tenant and any relevant person –

(a) in the prescribed form or in a form substantially to the same effect, and
(b) within the period of 14 days beginning with the date on which the deposit is received by the landlord.

(7) No person may, in connection with a shorthold tenancy, require a deposit which consists of property other than money.

(8) In subsection (7) 'deposit' means a transfer of property intended to be held (by the landlord or otherwise) as security for –

(a) the performance of any obligations of the tenant, or
(b) the discharge of any liability of his,

arising under or in connection with the tenancy.

(9) The provisions of this section apply despite any agreement to the contrary.

(10) In this section –

'prescribed' means prescribed by an order made by the appropriate national authority;

'property' means moveable property;

'relevant person' means any person who, in accordance with arrangements made with the tenant, paid the deposit on behalf of the tenant.

214 Proceedings relating to tenancy deposits

(1) Where a tenancy deposit has been paid in connection with a shorthold tenancy, the tenant or any relevant person (as defined by section 213(10)) may make an application to a county court on the grounds –

(a) that the initial requirements of an authorised scheme (see section 213(4)) have not, or section 213(6)(a) has not, been complied with in relation to the deposit; or

(b) that he has been notified by the landlord that a particular authorised scheme applies to the deposit but has been unable to obtain confirmation from the scheme administrator that the deposit is being held in accordance with the scheme.

(2) Subsections (3) and (4) apply if on such an application the court –

(a) is satisfied that those requirements have not, or section 213(6)(a) has not, been complied with in relation to the deposit, or
(b) is not satisfied that the deposit is being held in accordance with an authorised scheme,

as the case may be.

(3) The court must, as it thinks fit, either –

(a) order the person who appears to the court to be holding the deposit to repay it to the applicant, or
(b) order that person to pay the deposit into the designated account held by the scheme administrator under an authorised custodial scheme,

within the period of 14 days beginning with the date of the making of the order.

(4) The court must also order the landlord to pay to the applicant a sum of money equal to three times the amount of the deposit within the period of 14 days beginning with the date of the making of the order.

(5) Where any deposit given in connection with a shorthold tenancy could not be lawfully required as a result of section 213(7), the property in question is recoverable from the person holding it by the person by whom it was given as a deposit.

(6) In subsection (5) 'deposit' has the meaning given by section 213(8).

215 Sanctions for non-compliance

(1) If a tenancy deposit has been paid in connection with a shorthold tenancy, no section 21 notice may be given in relation to the tenancy at a time when –

(a) the deposit is not being held in accordance with an authorised scheme, or
(b) the initial requirements of such a scheme (see section 213(4)) have not been complied with in relation to the deposit.

(2) If section 213(6) is not complied with in relation to a deposit given in connection with a shorthold tenancy, no section 21 notice may be given in relation to the tenancy until such time as section 213(6)(a) is complied with.

(3) If any deposit given in connection with a shorthold tenancy could not be lawfully required as a result of section 213(7), no section 21 notice may be given in relation to the tenancy until such time as the property in question is returned to the person by whom it was given as a deposit.

(4) In subsection (3) 'deposit' has the meaning given by section 213(8).

(5) In this section a 'section 21 notice' means a notice under section 21(1)(b) or (4)(a) of the Housing Act 1988 (recovery of possession on termination of shorthold tenancy).

Chapter 5
Miscellaneous

Overcrowding

216 Overcrowding

(1) The appropriate national authority may by order make such provision as it considers appropriate for and in connection with –

(a) determining whether a dwelling is overcrowded for the purposes of Part 10 of the Housing Act 1985 (c 68) (overcrowding);

(b) introducing for the purposes of Chapter 3 of Part 4 of this Act a concept of overcrowding similar to that applying for the purposes of Part 10 (and accordingly removing the discretion of local housing authorities to decide particular issues arising under those sections);

(c) securing that overcrowding in premises to which Chapter 3 of Part 4 of this Act would otherwise apply, or any description of such premises, is regulated only by provisions of Part 10.

(2) An order under this section may, in particular, make provision for regulating the making by local housing authorities of determinations as to whether premises are overcrowded, including provision prescribing –

(a) factors that must be taken into account by such authorities when making such determinations;

(b) the procedure that is to be followed by them in connection with making such determinations.

(3) An order under this section may modify any enactment (including this Act).

(4) In this section –

(a) any reference to Part 10 of the Housing Act 1985 includes a reference to Part 10 as modified by an order under this section; and

(b) 'enactment' includes an enactment comprised in subordinate legislation (within the meaning of the Interpretation Act 1978 (c 30)).

Energy efficiency

217 Energy efficiency of residential accommodation: England

(1) The Secretary of State must take reasonable steps to ensure that by 2010 the general level of energy efficiency of residential accommodation in England has increased by at least 20 per cent compared with the general level of such energy efficiency in 2000.

(2) Nothing in this section affects the duties of the Secretary of State under section 2 of the Sustainable Energy Act 2003 (c 30) (energy efficiency aim in respect of residential accommodation in England).

(3) In this section 'residential accommodation' has the meaning given by section 1 of the Home Energy Conservation Act 1995 (c 10).

Registered social landlords

218 Amendments relating to registered social landlords

Schedule 11 (which makes amendments relating to registered social landlords) has effect.

219 Disclosure of information to registered social landlords for the purposes of section 1 of the Crime and Disorder Act 1998

In section 115(2) of the Crime and Disorder Act 1998 (c 37) after paragraph (d) insert –

'(da) a person registered under section 1 of the Housing Act 1996 as a social landlord;'.

Other provisions relating to social housing

220 Additional power to give grants for social housing

After section 27 of the Housing Act 1996 (c 52) insert –

'*Grants to bodies other than registered social landlords*

27A Grants to bodies other than registered social landlords

(1) The Relevant Authority may make grants under this section to persons other than registered social landlords.

(2) Grants under this section are grants for any of the following purposes –

(a) acquiring, or repairing and improving, or creating by the conversion of houses or other property, houses to be disposed of –
  (i)   under equity percentage arrangements, or
  (ii) on shared ownership terms;
(b) constructing houses to be disposed of –
  (i)   under equity percentage arrangements, or
  (ii) on shared ownership terms;
(c) providing loans to be secured by mortgages to assist persons to acquire houses for their own occupation;
(d) providing, constructing or improving houses to be kept available for letting;
(e) providing, constructing or improving houses for letting that are to be managed by such registered social landlords, and under arrangements containing such terms, as are approved by the Relevant Authority;
(f) such other purposes as may be specified in an order under subsection (3).

(3) The Secretary of State may by order make such provision in connection with the making of grants under this section as he considers appropriate.

(4) An order under subsection (3) may, in particular, make provision –

(a) defining "equity percentage arrangements" for the purposes of this section;
(b) specifying or describing the bodies from whom loans may be obtained by persons wishing to acquire houses for their own occupation;
(c) dealing with the priority of mortgages entered into by such persons;
(d) specifying purposes additional to those mentioned in subsection (2)(a) to (e).

(5) As regards grants made by the Housing Corporation, an order under subsection (3) may also require the imposition of conditions in connection with such grants, and for this purpose may –

(a) prescribe conditions that are to be so imposed;
(b) prescribe matters about which conditions are to be so imposed and any particular effects that such conditions are to achieve.

(6) The Relevant Authority shall specify in relation to grants under this section –

    (a) the procedure to be followed in relation to applications for grant,
    (b) the circumstances in which grant is or is not to be payable,
    (c) the method for calculating, and any limitations on, the amount of grant, and
    (d) the manner in which, and the time or times at which, grant is to be paid.

(7) If, by virtue of subsection (5), an order under subsection (3) requires conditions to be imposed by the Housing Corporation in connection with a grant to a person under this section, the Corporation in making the grant –

    (a) must provide that the grant is conditional on compliance by the person with such conditions as are required by the order; and
    (b) if it exercises its power to impose conditions under subsection (8), must not impose any that are inconsistent with the requirements of the order.

(8) In making a grant to a person under this section the Relevant Authority may provide that the grant is conditional on compliance by the person with such conditions as the Authority may specify.

(9) The conditions that may be so specified include conditions requiring the payment to the Relevant Authority in specified circumstances of a sum determined by the Authority (with or without interest).

(10) An order under subsection (3) shall be made by statutory instrument which shall be subject to annulment in pursuance of a resolution of either House of Parliament.

(11) In this section –

    "disposed of on shared ownership terms" has the meaning given by section 2(6);

    "letting" includes the grant of a licence to occupy.

27B Transfer of property funded by grants under section 27A

(1) Where –

    (a) any grant is paid or payable to any person under section 27A, and
    (b) at any time property to which the grant relates becomes vested in, or is leased for a term of years to, or reverts to, another person who is not a registered social landlord,

this Part shall have effect, in relation to times falling after that time, as if the grant, or such proportion of it as is determined or specified under subsection (4), had been paid or (as the case may be) were payable to that other person under section 27A.

(2) Where –

    (a) any amount is paid or payable to any person by way of grant under section 27A, and
    (b) at any time property to which the grant relates becomes vested in, or is leased for a term of years to, or reverts to, a registered social landlord,

this Part shall have effect, in relation to times falling after that time, as if the grant, or such proportion of it as is determined or specified under subsection (4), had been paid or (as the case may be) were payable to that other person under section 18.

(3) In such a case, the relevant section 18 conditions accordingly apply to that grant or proportion of it, in relation to times falling after that time, in place of those specified under section 27A(8).

"The relevant section 18 conditions" means such conditions specified under section 18(3) as would have applied at the time of the making of the grant if it had been made under section 18 to a registered social landlord.

(4) The proportion mentioned in subsection (1) or (2) is that which, in the circumstances of the particular case –

    (a) the Relevant Authority, acting in accordance with such principles as it may from time to time determine, may specify as being appropriate, or

    (b) the Relevant Authority may determine to be appropriate.'

221 Extension of right to acquire

After section 16 of the Housing Act 1996 (c 52) insert –

'16A Extension of section 16 to dwellings funded by grants under section 27A

(1) Section 16 applies in relation to a dwelling ("a funded dwelling") provided or acquired wholly or in part by means of a grant under section 27A (grants to bodies other than registered social landlords) with the following modifications.

(2) In section 16(1) the reference to a registered social landlord includes a reference to any person to whom a grant has been paid under section 27A.

(3) In section 16(2) and (4) any reference to section 18 includes a reference to section 27A.

(4) For the purposes of section 16 a funded dwelling is to be regarded as having remained within the social rented sector in relation to any relevant time if, since it was acquired or provided as mentioned in subsection (1) above, it was used –

    (a) by the recipient of the grant mentioned in that subsection, or

    (b) if section 27B applies in relation to the grant, by each person to whom the grant was, or is treated as having been, paid,

exclusively for the purposes for which the grant was made or any other purposes agreed to by the Relevant Authority.

(5) In subsection (4) "relevant time" means a time when the dwelling would not be treated as being within the social rented sector by virtue of section 16(3).'

222 Rights of pre-emption in connection with assured tenancies

(1) Section 5 of the Housing Act 1988 (c 50) (security of tenure for assured tenants) is amended as follows.

(2) After subsection (5) (certain obligations etc of tenant to be unenforceable) insert –

'(5A) Nothing in subsection (5) affects any right of pre-emption –

    (a) which is exercisable by the landlord under a tenancy in circumstances where the tenant indicates his intention to dispose of the whole of his interest under the tenancy, and

    (b) in pursuance of which the landlord would be required to pay, in respect of the acquisition of that interest, an amount representing its market value.

"Dispose" means dispose by assignment or surrender, and "acquisition" has a corresponding meaning.'

(3)   The amendment made by subsection (2) does not apply in relation to any right of pre-emption granted before the day on which this section comes into force.

223 Allocation of housing accommodation by local authorities

In section 167(2)(d) of the Housing Act 1996 (c 52) (people to whom preference is to be given in allocating housing accommodation) after 'medical or welfare grounds' insert '(including grounds relating to a disability)'.

Disabled facilities grant

224 Disabled facilities grant: caravans

(1) The Housing Grants, Construction and Regeneration Act 1996 (c 53) is amended as follows.

(2) In section 1(1)(c)(i) (grants in relation to qualifying park homes) for 'qualifying park homes' substitute 'caravans'.

(3) In section 19(1) (applications for grants) for paragraph (c) substitute –

'(c) that the applicant is an occupier (alone or jointly with others) of a qualifying houseboat or a caravan and, in the case of a caravan, that at the time the application was made the caravan was stationed on land within the authority's area.'

(4) In section 22A (certificates required in case of occupier's application) –

(a) for 'qualifying park home' in subsection (2)(b) and (3)(a) and (b) substitute 'caravan', and
(b) for 'pitch' in subsection (3)(a) substitute 'land'.

(5) In the following provisions for 'qualifying park home' substitute 'caravan' –

(a) section 23(1)(a)(i), (b)(i), (i) and (k) (purposes of grant);
(b) section 24(3)(b)(i) (approval of application);
(c) section 29(3) (restriction on grants for works already begun);
(d) section 41(1)(b) (change of circumstances).

(6) In section 57(2)(a) (power of authority to carry out works) –

(a) for 'qualifying park home', in each place where it occurs, substitute 'caravan', and
(b) for 'pitch' in sub-paragraph (i) substitute 'land'.

(7) In section 58 (minor definitions for the purposes of Chapter 1 of Part 1) –

(a) before the definition of 'common parts' insert –

'"caravan" –

(a) means a caravan within the meaning of Part 1 of the Caravan Sites and Control of Development Act 1960 (disregarding the amendment made by section 13(2) of the Caravan Sites Act 1968); and
(b) includes any yard, garden, outhouses and appurtenances belonging to it or usually enjoyed with it;' and

(b) for 'qualifying park home' in the definition of 'premises' substitute 'caravan', and
(c) omit the definition of 'qualifying park home'.

(8) In section 59 (index of defined expressions) –

(a) before the entry relating to 'certified date' insert –

'caravan   section 58'

and

(b) omit the entry relating to 'qualifying park home'.

(9) The amendments made by this section do not apply in relation to any application for a disabled facilities grant under the Housing Grants, Construction and Regeneration Act 1996 (c 53) that is made before the day on which this section comes into force.

Accommodation needs of gypsies and travellers

225 Duties of local housing authorities: accommodation needs of gypsies and travellers

(1) Every local housing authority must, when undertaking a review of housing needs in their district under section 8 of the Housing Act 1985 (c 68), carry out an assessment of the accommodation needs of gypsies and travellers residing in or resorting to their district.

(2) Subsection (3) applies where a local housing authority are required under section 87 of the Local Government Act 2003 (c 26) to prepare a strategy in respect of the meeting of such accommodation needs.

(3) The local authority who are that local housing authority must take the strategy into account in exercising their functions.

'Functions' includes functions exercisable otherwise than as a local housing authority.

(4) A local housing authority must have regard to any guidance issued under section 226 in –

(a) carrying out such an assessment as mentioned in subsection (1), and
(b) preparing any strategy that they are required to prepare as mentioned in subsection (2).

(5) In this section –

(a) 'gypsies and travellers' has the meaning given by regulations made by the appropriate national authority;
(b) 'accommodation needs' includes needs with respect to the provision of sites on which caravans can be stationed; and
(c) 'caravan' has the same meaning as in Part 1 of the Caravan Sites and Control of Development Act 1960.

226 Guidance in relation to section 225

(1) The appropriate national authority may issue guidance to local housing authorities regarding –

(a) the carrying out of assessments under section 225(1), and
(b) the preparation of any strategies that local housing authorities are required to prepare as mentioned in section 225(2).

(2) Before giving guidance under this section, or revising guidance already given, the Secretary of State must lay a draft of the proposed guidance or alterations before each House of Parliament.

(3) The Secretary of State must not give or revise the guidance before the end of the period of 40 days beginning with the day on which the draft is laid before each House of Parliament (or, if copies are laid before each House of Parliament on different days, the later of those days).

(4) The Secretary of State must not proceed with the proposed guidance or alterations if, within the period of 40 days mentioned in subsection (3), either House resolves that the guidance or alterations be withdrawn.

(5) Subsection (4) is without prejudice to the possibility of laying a further draft of the guidance or alterations before each House of Parliament.

(6) In calculating the period of 40 days mentioned in subsection (3), no account is to be taken of any time during which Parliament is dissolved or prorogued or during which both Houses are adjourned for more than four days.

Annual reports by local housing authorities

227 Removal of duty on local housing authorities to send annual reports to tenants etc

Omit section 167 of the Local Government and Housing Act 1989 (c 42) (duty of local housing authorities to send annual reports to tenants).

Social Housing Ombudsman for Wales

228 Social Housing Ombudsman for Wales

(1) After subsection (6) of section 51 of the Housing Act 1996 (c 52) (schemes for investigation of housing complaints) insert –

'(7) This section shall not apply in relation to social landlords in Wales (within the meaning given by section 51C).'

(2) After that section insert –

'51A Social Housing Ombudsman for Wales

(1) For the purpose of the investigation of complaints made about social landlords in Wales, there shall be an office of Social Housing Ombudsman for Wales or Ombwdsmon Tai Cymdeithasol Cymru.

(2) The person who is the Local Commissioner for Wales shall also be the Social Housing Ombudsman for Wales.

(3) If there is more than one person who is a Local Commissioner for Wales, the Commission for Local Administration in Wales shall designate one of them to be the Social Housing Ombudsman for Wales.

(4) If a person who is the Social Housing Ombudsman for Wales ceases to be a Local Commissioner for Wales, he shall cease to be the Social Housing Ombudsman for Wales.

(5) The power under section 23(6) of the Local Government Act 1974 to remove a Local Commissioner for Wales from office on grounds of incapacity or misbehaviour includes a power to remove him from that office on grounds of incapacity or misbehaviour which are exclusively or partly relevant to the office of Social Housing Ombudsman for Wales.

(6) "Local Commissioner for Wales" shall be construed in accordance with section 23 of the Local Government Act 1974.

(7) Schedule 2A (which contains further provision about the Social Housing Ombudsman for Wales) shall have effect.

51B Investigation of complaints

(1) The National Assembly for Wales may by regulations make provision about the investigation by the Social Housing Ombudsman for Wales of complaints made about social landlords in Wales.

(2) Regulations under subsection (1) may in particular make provision about –

    (a) the matters about which complaints may be made;

    (b) the grounds on which a matter may be excluded from investigation, including that the matter is the subject of court proceedings or was the subject of court proceedings where judgment on the merits was given;

    (c) the description of individual who may make a complaint;

    (d) a power of the Social Housing Ombudsman for Wales to investigate any complaint duly made (whether the complaint is subsequently withdrawn or not), and, where he investigates, the making of a determination;

    (e) a power of the Social Housing Ombudsman for Wales to propose alternative methods of resolving a dispute;

    (f) the powers of the Social Housing Ombudsman for Wales for the purposes of his investigations (including powers to consult and co-operate with other persons), and the procedure to be followed in the conduct of investigations;

    (g) the powers of the Social Housing Ombudsman for Wales on making a determination, which may include power –

        (i) to make recommendations as to action to be taken to remedy any injustice to the person aggrieved and to prevent any similar injustice being caused in the future,

        (ii) to make orders with regard to the payment of compensation or to order that a person is not to exercise, or require the performance of, certain rights or obligations, and

        (iii) to publish statements, or to make orders requiring the publication of statements, that a person has failed to comply with an order mentioned in sub-paragraph (ii);

    (h) the manner in which determinations are to be –

        (i) communicated to the complainant and the person against whom the complaint was made; and

        (ii) published (with or without excisions).

(3) Regulations under this section may contain such supplementary, incidental, consequential or transitional provisions and savings as the National Assembly for Wales considers appropriate.

(4) Regulations under this section may make different provision for different cases or descriptions of case.

(5) Regulations under this section shall be made by statutory instrument.

51C Meaning of "social landlord in Wales"

(1) "Social landlord in Wales" means –

    (a) a body which is registered as a social landlord in the register maintained by the National Assembly for Wales under section 1 of this Act;

    (b) a body which was at any time registered as a social landlord in that register (or in the register previously maintained under that section by the Secretary of State or Housing for Wales); and

(c) any other body which was at any time registered with Housing for Wales, the Secretary of State or the National Assembly for Wales and which owns or manages publicly-funded dwellings.

(2) In subsection (1)(c) a "publicly-funded" dwelling means a dwelling which was –

(a) provided by means of a grant under –
  (i)   section 18 of this Act (social housing grant); or
  (ii) section 50 of the Housing Act 1988, section 41 of the Housing Associations Act 1985, or section 29 or 29A of the Housing Act 1974 (housing association grant); or
(b) acquired on a disposal by a public sector landlord.

(3) The National Assembly for Wales may by order made by statutory instrument add to or amend the descriptions of landlords who are to be treated as social landlords in Wales.

(4) Before making any such order the National Assembly for Wales shall consult such persons as it considers appropriate.

(5) Any such order may contain such supplementary, incidental, consequential or transitional provisions and savings as the National Assembly for Wales considers appropriate.'

(3) After Schedule 2 to that Act there is inserted, as Schedule 2A, the Schedule set out in Schedule 12 to this Act.

(4) In Schedule 4 to the Local Government Act 1974 (c 7), in paragraph 1(3) (validity of acts despite disqualification for being appointed as, or for being, a Local Commissioner) after 'office' there is inserted 'or in the office of Social Housing Ombudsman for Wales'.

Part 7
Supplementary and Final Provisions

Residential property tribunals

229 Residential property tribunals

(1) Any jurisdiction conferred on a residential property tribunal by or under any enactment is exercisable by a rent assessment committee constituted in accordance with Schedule 10 to the Rent Act 1977 (c 42).

(2) When so constituted for exercising any such jurisdiction a rent assessment committee is known as a residential property tribunal.

(3) The appropriate national authority may by order make provision for and in connection with conferring on residential property tribunals, in relation to such matters as are specified in the order, such jurisdiction as is so specified.

(4) An order under subsection (3) may modify an enactment (including this Act).

(5) In this section 'enactment' includes an enactment comprised in subordinate legislation (within the meaning of the Interpretation Act 1978 (c 30)).

230 Powers and procedure of residential property tribunals

(1) A residential property tribunal exercising any jurisdiction by virtue of any enactment has, in addition to any specific powers exercisable by it in exercising that jurisdiction, the general power mentioned in subsection (2).

(2) The tribunal's general power is a power by order to give such directions as the tribunal considers necessary or desirable for securing the just, expeditious and economical disposal of the proceedings or any issue raised in or in connection with them.

(3) In deciding whether to give directions under its general power a tribunal must have regard to –

(a) the matters falling to be determined in the proceedings,
(b) any other circumstances appearing to the tribunal to be relevant, and
(c) the provisions of the enactment by virtue of which it is exercising jurisdiction and of any other enactment appearing to it to be relevant.

(4) A tribunal may give directions under its general power whether or not they were originally sought by a party to the proceedings.

(5) When exercising jurisdiction under this Act, the directions which may be given by a tribunal under its general power include (where appropriate) –

(a) directions requiring a licence to be granted under Part 2 or 3 of this Act;
(b) directions requiring any licence so granted to contain such terms as are specified in the directions;
(c) directions requiring any order made under Part 4 of this Act to contain such terms as are so specified;
(d) directions that any building or part of a building so specified is to be treated as if an HMO declaration had been served in respect of it on such date as is so specified (without there being any right to appeal against it under section 255(9));
(e) directions requiring the payment of money by one party to the proceedings to another by way of compensation, damages or otherwise.

(6) Nothing in any enactment conferring specific powers on a residential property tribunal is to be regarded as affecting the operation of the preceding provisions of this section.

(7) Schedule 13 (residential property tribunals: procedure) has effect.

(8) Section 229(5) applies also for the purposes of this section and Schedule 13.

231 Appeals from residential property tribunals

(1) A party to proceedings before a residential property tribunal may appeal to the Lands Tribunal from a decision of the residential property tribunal.

(2) But the appeal may only be made –

(a) with the permission of the residential property tribunal or the Lands Tribunal, and
(b) within the time specified by rules under section 3(6) of the Lands Tribunal Act 1949 (c 42).

(3) On the appeal –

(a) the Lands Tribunal may exercise any power which was available to the residential property tribunal, and
(b) a decision of the Lands Tribunal may be enforced in the same way as a decision of the residential property tribunal.

(4) Section 11(1) of the Tribunals and Inquiries Act 1992 (c 53) (appeals from certain tribunals to High Court) does not apply to any decision of a residential property tribunal.

(5) For the purposes of section 3(4) of the Lands Tribunal Act 1949 (which enables a person aggrieved by a decision of the Lands Tribunal to appeal to the Court of Appeal) a residential property tribunal is not to be regarded as an aggrieved person.

Register of licences and management orders

232 Register of licences and management orders

(1) Every local housing authority must establish and maintain a register of –

    (a) all licences granted by them under Part 2 or 3 which are in force;

    (b) all temporary exemption notices served by them under section 62 or section 86 which are in force; and

    (c) all management orders made by them under Chapter 1 or 2 of Part 4 which are in force.

(2) The register may, subject to any requirements that may be prescribed, be in such form as the authority consider appropriate.

(3) Each entry in the register is to contain such particulars as may be prescribed.

(4) The authority must ensure that the contents of the register are available at the authority's head office for inspection by members of the public at all reasonable times.

(5) If requested by a person to do so and subject to payment of such reasonable fee (if any) as the authority may determine, a local housing authority must supply the person with a copy (certified to be true) of the register or of an extract from it.

(6) A copy so certified is prima facie evidence of the matters mentioned in it.

(7) In this section 'prescribed' means prescribed by regulations made by the appropriate national authority.

Codes of practice and management regulations relating to HMOs etc

233 Approval of codes of practice with regard to the management of HMOs etc

(1) The appropriate national authority may by order –

    (a) approve a code of practice (whether prepared by that authority or another person) laying down standards of conduct and practice to be followed with regard to the management of houses in multiple occupation or of excepted accommodation;

    (b) approve a modification of such a code; or

    (c) withdraw the authority's approval of such a code or modification.

(2) Before approving a code of practice or a modification of a code of practice under this section the appropriate national authority must take reasonable steps to consult –

    (a) persons involved in the management of houses in multiple occupation or (as the case may be) excepted accommodation of the kind in question and persons occupying such houses or accommodation, or

    (b) persons whom the authority considers to represent the interests of those persons.

(3) The appropriate national authority may only approve a code of practice or a modification of a code if satisfied that –

    (a) the code or modification has been published (whether by the authority or by another person) in a manner that the authority considers appropriate for the purpose of bringing the code or modification to the attention of those likely to be affected by it; or

    (b) arrangements have been made for the code or modification to be so published.

(4) The appropriate national authority may approve a code of practice which makes different provision in relation to different cases or descriptions of case (including different provision for different areas).

(5) A failure to comply with a code of practice for the time being approved under this section does not of itself make a person liable to any civil or criminal proceedings.

(6) In this section 'excepted accommodation' means such description of living accommodation falling within any provision of Schedule 14 (buildings which are not HMOs for purposes of provisions other than Part 1) as is specified in an order under subsection (1).

234 Management regulations in respect of HMOs

(1) The appropriate national authority may by regulations make provision for the purpose of ensuring that, in respect of every house in multiple occupation of a description specified in the regulations –

    (a) there are in place satisfactory management arrangements; and
    (b) satisfactory standards of management are observed.

(2) The regulations may, in particular –

    (a) impose duties on the person managing a house in respect of the repair, maintenance, cleanliness and good order of the house and facilities and equipment in it;
    (b) impose duties on persons occupying a house for the purpose of ensuring that the person managing the house can effectively carry out any duty imposed on him by the regulations.

(3) A person commits an offence if he fails to comply with a regulation under this section.

(4) In proceedings against a person for an offence under subsection (3) it is a defence that he had a reasonable excuse for not complying with the regulation.

(5) A person who commits an offence under subsection (3) is liable on summary conviction to a fine not exceeding level 5 on the standard scale.

Information provisions

235 Power to require documents to be produced

(1) A person authorised in writing by a local housing authority may exercise the power conferred by subsection (2) in relation to documents reasonably required by the authority –

    (a) for any purpose connected with the exercise of any of the authority's functions under any of Parts 1 to 4 in relation to any premises, or
    (b) for the purpose of investigating whether any offence has been committed under any of those Parts in relation to any premises.

(2) A person so authorised may give a notice to a relevant person requiring him –

    (a) to produce any documents which –
        (i) are specified or described in the notice, or fall within a category of document which is specified or described in the notice, and
        (ii) are in his custody or under his control, and
    (b) to produce them at a time and place so specified and to a person so specified.

(3) The notice must include information about the possible consequences of not complying with the notice.

(4) The person to whom any document is produced in accordance with the notice may copy the document.

(5) No person may be required under this section to produce any document which he would be entitled to refuse to provide in proceedings in the High Court on grounds of legal professional privilege.

(6) In this section 'document' includes information recorded otherwise than in legible form, and in relation to information so recorded, any reference to the production of a document is a reference to the production of a copy of the information in legible form.

(7) In this section 'relevant person' means, in relation to any premises, a person within any of the following paragraphs –

(a) a person who is, or is proposed to be, the holder of a licence under Part 2 or 3 in respect of the premises, or a person on whom any obligation or restriction under such a licence is, or is proposed to be, imposed,

(b) a person who has an estate or interest in the premises,

(c) a person who is, or is proposing to be, managing or having control of the premises,

(d) a person who is, or is proposing to be, otherwise involved in the management of the premises,

(e) a person who occupies the premises.

236 Enforcement of powers to obtain information

(1) A person commits an offence if he fails to do anything required of him by a notice under section 235.

(2) In proceedings against a person for an offence under subsection (1) it is a defence that he had a reasonable excuse for failing to comply with the notice.

(3) A person who commits an offence under subsection (1) is liable on summary conviction to a fine not exceeding level 5 on the standard scale.

(4) A person commits an offence if he intentionally alters, suppresses or destroys any document which he has been required to produce by a notice under section 235.

(5) A person who commits an offence under subsection (4) is liable –

(a) on summary conviction, to a fine not exceeding the statutory maximum;

(b) on conviction on indictment, to a fine.

(6) In this section 'document' includes information recorded otherwise than in legible form, and in relation to information so recorded –

(a) the reference to the production of a document is a reference to the production of a copy of the information in legible form, and

(b) the reference to suppressing a document includes a reference to destroying the means of reproducing the information.

237 Use of information obtained for certain other statutory purposes

(1) A local housing authority may use any information to which this section applies –

(a) for any purpose connected with the exercise of any of the authority's functions under any of Parts 1 to 4 in relation to any premises, or

(b) for the purpose of investigating whether any offence has been committed under any of those Parts in relation to any premises.

(2) This section applies to any information which has been obtained by the authority in the exercise of functions under –

(a) section 134 of the Social Security Administration Act 1992 (c 5) (housing benefit), or

(b) Part 1 of the Local Government Finance Act 1992 (c 14) (council tax).

238 False or misleading information

(1) A person commits an offence if –

(a) he supplies any information to a local housing authority in connection with any of their functions under any of Parts 1 to 4 or this Part,

(b) the information is false or misleading, and

(c) he knows that it is false or misleading or is reckless as to whether it is false or misleading.

(2) A person commits an offence if –

(a) he supplies any information to another person which is false or misleading,

(b) he knows that it is false or misleading or is reckless as to whether it is false or misleading, and

(c) he knows that the information is to be used for the purpose of supplying information to a local housing authority in connection with any of their functions under any of Parts 1 to 4 or this Part.

(3) A person who commits an offence under subsection (1) or (2) is liable on summary conviction to a fine not exceeding level 5 on the standard scale.

(4) In this section 'false or misleading' means false or misleading in any material respect.

Enforcement

239 Powers of entry

(1) Subsection (3) applies where the local housing authority consider that a survey or examination of any premises is necessary and any of the following conditions is met –

(a) the authority consider that the survey or examination is necessary in order to carry out an inspection under section 4(1) or otherwise to determine whether any functions under any of Parts 1 to 4 or this Part should be exercised in relation to the premises;

(b) the premises are (within the meaning of Part 1) specified premises in relation to an improvement notice or prohibition order;

(c) a management order is in force under Chapter 1 or 2 of Part 4 in respect of the premises.

(2) Subsection (3) also applies where the proper officer of the local housing authority considers that a survey or examination of any premises is necessary in order to carry out an inspection under section 4(2).

(3) Where this subsection applies –

(a) a person authorised by the local housing authority (in a case within subsection (1)), or

(b) the proper officer (in a case within subsection (2)),

may enter the premises in question at any reasonable time for the purpose of carrying out a survey or examination of the premises.

(4) If –

(a) an interim or final management order is in force under Chapter 1 of Part 4 in respect of any premises consisting of part of a house ('the relevant premises'), and

(b) another part of the house is excluded from the order by virtue of section 102(8) or 113(7), the power of entry conferred by subsection (3) is exercisable in relation to any premises comprised in that other part so far as is necessary for the purpose of carrying out a survey or examination of the relevant premises.

(5) Before entering any premises in exercise of the power conferred by subsection (3), the authorised person or proper officer must have given at least 24 hours' notice of his intention to do so –

    (a) to the owner of the premises (if known), and
    (b) to the occupier (if any).

(6) Subsection (7) applies where the local housing authority consider that any premises need to be entered for the purpose of ascertaining whether an offence has been committed under section 72, 95 or 234(3).

(7) A person authorised by the local housing authority may enter the premises for that purpose –

    (a) at any reasonable time, but
    (b) without giving any prior notice as mentioned in subsection (5).

(8) A person exercising the power of entry conferred by subsection (3) or (7) may do such of the following as he thinks necessary for the purpose for which the power is being exercised –

    (a) take other persons with him;
    (b) take equipment or materials with him;
    (c) take measurements or photographs or make recordings;
    (d) leave recording equipment on the premises for later collection;
    (e) take samples of any articles or substances found on the premises.

(9) An authorisation for the purposes of this section –

    (a) must be in writing; and
    (b) must state the particular purpose or purposes for which the entry is authorised.

(10) A person authorised for the purposes of this section must, if required to do so, produce his authorisation for inspection by the owner or any occupier of the premises or anyone acting on his behalf.

(11) If the premises are unoccupied or the occupier is temporarily absent, a person exercising the power of entry conferred by subsection (3) or (7) must leave the premises as effectively secured against trespassers as he found them.

(12) In this section 'occupier', in relation to premises, means a person who occupies the premises, whether for residential or other purposes.

240 Warrant to authorise entry

(1) This section applies where a justice of the peace is satisfied, on a sworn information in writing, that admission to premises specified in the information is reasonably required for any of the purposes mentioned in subsection (2) by a person –

    (a) employed by, or
    (b) acting on the instructions of,

the local housing authority.

(2) The purposes are –

(a) surveying or examining premises in order to carry out an inspection under section 4(1) or (2) or otherwise to determine whether any functions under any of Parts 1 to 4 or this Part should be exercised in relation to the premises;

(b) surveying or examining premises –

    (i) which are (within the meaning of Part 1) specified premises in relation to an improvement notice or prohibition order, or

    (ii) in respect of which a management order is in force under Chapter 1 or 2 of Part 4;

(c) ascertaining whether an offence has been committed under section 72, 95 or 234(3).

(3) The justice may by warrant under his hand authorise the person mentioned in subsection (1) to enter on the premises for such of those purposes as may be specified in the warrant.

(4) But the justice must not grant the warrant unless he is satisfied –

(a) that admission to the premises has been sought in accordance with section 239(5) or (7) but has been refused;

(b) that the premises are unoccupied or that the occupier is temporarily absent and it might defeat the purpose of the entry to await his return; or

(c) that application for admission would defeat the purpose of the entry.

(5) The power of entry conferred by a warrant under this section includes power to enter by force (if necessary).

(6) Subsection (8) of section 239 applies to the person on whom that power is conferred as it applies to a person exercising the power of entry conferred by subsection (3) or (7) of that section.

(7) A warrant under this section must, if so required, be produced for inspection by the owner or any occupier of the premises or anyone acting on his behalf.

(8) If the premises are unoccupied or the occupier is temporarily absent, a person entering under the authority of a warrant under this section must leave the premises as effectively secured against trespassers as he found them.

(9) A warrant under this section continues in force until the purpose for which the entry is required is satisfied.

(10) In a case within section 239(4)(a) and (b), the powers conferred by this section are exercisable in relation to premises comprised in the excluded part of the house as well as in relation to the relevant premises.

(11) In this section 'occupier', in relation to premises, means a person who occupies the premises, whether for residential or other purposes.

241 Penalty for obstruction

(1) A person who obstructs a relevant person in the performance of anything which, by virtue of any of Parts 1 to 4 or this Part, that person is required or authorised to do commits an offence.

(2) In proceedings against a person for an offence under subsection (1) it is a defence that he had a reasonable excuse for obstructing the relevant person.

(3) A person who commits an offence under subsection (1) is liable on summary conviction to a fine not exceeding level 4 on the standard scale.

(4) In this section 'relevant person' means an officer of a local housing authority or any person authorised to enter premises by virtue of any of Parts 1 to 4 or section 239 or 240.

242 Additional notice requirements for protection of owners

(1) This section applies where an owner of premises gives a notice to the local housing authority for the purposes of this section informing them of his interest in the premises.

(2) The authority must give him notice of any action taken by them under any of Parts 1 to 4 or this Part in relation to the premises.

Authorisations

243 Authorisations for enforcement purposes etc

(1) This section applies to any authorisation given for the purposes of any of the following provisions –

  (a) section 131 (management orders: power of entry to carry out work),
  (b) section 235 (power to require documents to be produced),
  (c) section 239 (powers of entry),
  (d) paragraph 3(4) of Schedule 3 (improvement notices: power to enter to carry out work), and
  (e) paragraph 25 of Schedule 7 (EDMOs: power of entry to carry out work).

(2) Any such authorisation must be given by the appropriate officer of the local housing authority.

(3) For the purposes of this section a person is an 'appropriate officer' of a local housing authority, in relation to an authorisation given by the authority, if either –

  (a) he is a deputy chief officer of the authority (within the meaning of section 2 of the Local Government and Housing Act 1989 (c 42)), and
  (b) the duties of his post consist of or include duties relating to the exercise of the functions of the authority in connection with which the authorisation is given,

or he is an officer of the authority to whom such a deputy chief officer reports directly, or is directly accountable, as respects duties so relating.

Documents

244 Power to prescribe forms

(1) The appropriate national authority may by regulations prescribe the form of any notice, statement or other document which is required or authorised to be used under, or for the purposes of, this Act.

(2) The power conferred by this section is not exercisable where specific provision for prescribing the form of a document is made elsewhere in this Act.

245 Power to dispense with notices

(1) The appropriate national authority may dispense with the service of a notice which is required to be served by a local housing authority under this Act if satisfied that it is reasonable to do so.

(2) A dispensation may be given either before or after the time at which the notice is required to be served.

(3) A dispensation may be given either unconditionally or on such conditions (whether as to the service of other notices or otherwise) as the appropriate national authority considers appropriate.

(4) Before giving a dispensation under this section, the appropriate national authority shall, in particular, have regard to the need to ensure, so far as possible, that the interests of any person are not prejudiced by the dispensation.

246 Service of documents

(1) Subsection (2) applies where the local housing authority is, by virtue of any provision of Parts 1 to 4 or this Part, under a duty to serve a document on a person who, to the knowledge of the authority, is –

(a) a person having control of premises,
(b) a person managing premises, or
(c) a person having an estate or interest in premises,

or a person who (but for an interim or final management order under Chapter 1 of Part 4) would fall within paragraph (a) or (b).

(2) The local housing authority must take reasonable steps to identify the person or persons falling within the description in that provision.

(3) A person having an estate or interest in premises may for the purposes of any provision to which subsections (1) and (2) apply give notice to the local housing authority of his interest in the premises.

(4) The local housing authority must enter a notice under subsection (3) in its records.

(5) A document required or authorised by any of Parts 1 to 4 or this Part to be served on a person as –

(a) a person having control of premises,
(b) a person managing premises,
(c) a person having an estate or interest in premises, or
(d) a person who (but for an interim or final management order under Chapter 1 of Part 4) would fall within paragraph (a) or (b),

may, if it is not practicable after reasonable enquiry to ascertain the name or address of that person, be served in accordance with subsection (6).

(6) A person having such a connection with any premises as is mentioned in subsection (5)(a) to (d) is served in accordance with this subsection if –

(a) the document is addressed to him by describing his connection with the premises (naming them), and
(b) delivering the document to some person on the premises or, if there is no person on the premises to whom it can be delivered, by fixing it, or a copy of it, to some conspicuous part of the premises.

(7) Subsection (1)(c) or (5)(c) applies whether the provision requiring or authorising service of the document refers in terms to a person having an estate or interest in premises or instead refers to a class of person having such an estate or interest (such as owners, lessees or mortgagees).

(8) Where under any provision of Parts 1 to 4 or this Part a document is to be served on –

(a) the person having control of premises,
(b) the person managing premises, or
(c) the owner of premises,

and more than one person comes within the description in the provision, the document may be served on more than one of those persons.

(9) Section 233 of the Local Government Act 1972 (c 70) (service of notices by local authorities) applies in relation to the service of documents for any purposes of this Act by the authorities

mentioned in section 261(2)(d) and (e) of this Act as if they were local authorities within the meaning of section 233.

(10) In this section –

(a) references to a person managing premises include references to a person authorised to permit persons to occupy premises; and

(b) references to serving include references to similar expressions (such as giving or sending).

(11) In this section –

'document' includes anything in writing;

'premises' means premises however defined.

247 Licences and other documents in electronic form

(1) A local housing authority may, subject to subsection (3), issue a licence to a person under Part 2 or 3 by transmitting the text of the licence to him by electronic means, provided the text –

(a) is received by him in legible form, and

(b) is capable of being used for subsequent reference.

(2) A local housing authority may, subject to subsection (3), serve a relevant document on a person by transmitting the text of the document to him in the way mentioned in subsection (1).

(3) The recipient, or the person on whose behalf the recipient receives the document, must have indicated to the local housing authority the recipient's willingness to receive documents transmitted in the form and manner used.

(4) An indication for the purposes of subsection (3) –

(a) must be given to the local housing authority in such manner as they may require;

(b) may be a general indication or one that is limited to documents of a particular description;

(c) must state the address to be used and must be accompanied by such other information as the local housing authority require for the making of the transmission; and

(d) may be modified or withdrawn at any time by a notice given to the local housing authority in such manner as they may require.

(5) In this section any reference to serving includes a reference to similar expressions (such as giving or sending).

(6) In this section –

'document' includes anything in writing; and

'relevant document' means any document which a local housing authority are, by virtue of any provision of Parts 1 to 4 or this Part, under a duty to serve on any person.

248 Timing and location of things done electronically

(1) The Secretary of State may by regulations make provision specifying, for the purposes of any of Parts 1 to 4 or this Part, the manner of determining –

(a) the times at which things done under any of Parts 1 to 4 or this Part by means of electronic communications networks are done;

(b) the places at which things done under any of Parts 1 to 4 or this Part by means of such networks are done; and

(c) the places at which things transmitted by means of such networks are received.

(2) The Secretary of State may by regulations make provision about the manner of proving in any legal proceedings –

(a) that something done by means of an electronic communications network satisfies any requirements of any of Parts 1 to 4 or this Part for the doing of that thing; and
(b) the matters mentioned in subsection (1)(a) to (c).

(3) Regulations under this section may provide for such presumptions to apply (whether conclusive or not) as the Secretary of State considers appropriate.

(4) In this section 'electronic communications network' has the meaning given by section 32 of the Communications Act 2003 (c 21).

249 Proof of designations

(1) This subsection applies in respect of a copy of –

(a) a designation under section 56 (designation of an area as subject to additional licensing), or
(b) a designation under section 80 (designation of an area as subject to selective licensing),

which purports to be made by a local housing authority.

(2) A certificate endorsed on such a copy and purporting to be signed by the proper officer of the authority stating the matters set out in subsection (3) is prima facie evidence of the facts so stated without proof of the handwriting or official position of the person by whom it purports to be signed.

(3) Those matters are –

(a) that the designation was made by the authority,
(b) that the copy is a true copy of the designation, and
(c) that the designation did not require confirmation by the confirming authority, or that on a specified date the designation was confirmed by the confirming authority.

Other supplementary provisions

250 Orders and regulations

(1) Any power of the Secretary of State or the National Assembly for Wales to make an order or regulations under this Act is exercisable by statutory instrument.

(2) Any power of the Secretary of State or the National Assembly for Wales to make an order or regulations under this Act –

(a) may be exercised so as to make different provision for different cases or descriptions of case or different purposes or areas; and
(b) includes power to make such incidental, supplementary, consequential, transitory, transitional or saving provision as the Secretary of State or (as the case may be) the National Assembly for Wales considers appropriate.

(3) The Secretary of State must consult the National Assembly for Wales before making any regulations under Part 5 which relate to residential properties in Wales.

(4) Subject to subsections (5) and (6), any order or regulations made by the Secretary of State under this Act are to be subject to annulment in pursuance of a resolution of either House of Parliament.

(5) Subsection (4) does not apply to any order under section 270 or paragraph 3 of Schedule 10.

(6) Subsection (4) also does not apply to –

(a) any order under section 55(3) which makes the provision authorised by section 55(4),
(b) any order under section 80(5) or (7),
(c) any order under section 216 or 229(3),
(d) any order under section 265(2) which modifies any provision of an Act,
(e) any regulations under section 254(6),
(f) any regulations under paragraph 3 of Schedule 4 or orders under paragraph 11 of Schedule 10, or
(g) any regulations made by virtue of paragraph 11(3)(b) or 12(3)(b) of Schedule 13;

and no such order or regulations may be made by the Secretary of State (whether alone or with other provisions) unless a draft of the statutory instrument containing the order or regulations has been laid before, and approved by a resolution of, each House of Parliament.

(7) In this Act 'modify', in the context of a power to modify an enactment by order or regulations, includes repeal (and 'modifications' has a corresponding meaning).

251 Offences by bodies corporate

(1) Where an offence under this Act committed by a body corporate is proved to have been committed with the consent or connivance of, or to be attributable to any neglect on the part of –

(a) a director, manager, secretary or other similar officer of the body corporate, or
(b) a person purporting to act in such a capacity,

he as well as the body corporate commits the offence and is liable to be proceeded against and punished accordingly.

(2) Where the affairs of a body corporate are managed by its members, subsection (1) applies in relation to the acts and defaults of a member in connection with his functions of management as if he were a director of the body corporate.

252 Power to up-rate level of fines for certain offences

(1) Subsection (2) applies if the Secretary of State considers that there has been a change in the value of money since the relevant date.

(2) The Secretary of State may by order substitute for the sum or sums for the time being specified in any provision mentioned in subsection (3) such other sum or sums as he considers to be justified by the change.

(3) The provisions are –

(a) section 32(2)(b);
(b) section 35(6);
(c) section 72(6); and
(d) section 95(5).

(4) In subsection (1) 'the relevant date' means –

(a) the date of the passing of this Act; or
(b) where the sums specified in a provision mentioned in subsection (3) have been substituted by an order under subsection (2), the date of that order.

(5) Nothing in an order under subsection (2) affects the punishment for an offence committed before the order comes into force.

253 Local inquiries

The appropriate national authority may, for the purposes of the execution of any of the authority's functions under this Act, cause such local inquiries to be held as the authority considers appropriate.

Meaning of 'house in multiple occupation'

254 Meaning of 'house in multiple occupation'

(1) For the purposes of this Act a building or a part of a building is a 'house in multiple occupation' if –

  (a) it meets the conditions in subsection (2) ('the standard test');
  (b) it meets the conditions in subsection (3) ('the self-contained flat test');
  (c) it meets the conditions in subsection (4) ('the converted building test');
  (d) an HMO declaration is in force in respect of it under section 255; or
  (e) it is a converted block of flats to which section 257 applies.

(2) A building or a part of a building meets the standard test if –

  (a) it consists of one or more units of living accommodation not consisting of a self-contained flat or flats;
  (b) the living accommodation is occupied by persons who do not form a single household (see section 258);
  (c) the living accommodation is occupied by those persons as their only or main residence or they are to be treated as so occupying it (see section 259);
  (d) their occupation of the living accommodation constitutes the only use of that accommodation;
  (e) rents are payable or other consideration is to be provided in respect of at least one of those persons' occupation of the living accommodation; and
  (f) two or more of the households who occupy the living accommodation share one or more basic amenities or the living accommodation is lacking in one or more basic amenities.

(3) A part of a building meets the self-contained flat test if –

  (a) it consists of a self-contained flat; and
  (b) paragraphs (b) to (f) of subsection (2) apply (reading references to the living accommodation concerned as references to the flat).

(4) A building or a part of a building meets the converted building test if –

  (a) it is a converted building;
  (b) it contains one or more units of living accommodation that do not consist of a self-contained flat or flats (whether or not it also contains any such flat or flats);
  (c) the living accommodation is occupied by persons who do not form a single household (see section 258);
  (d) the living accommodation is occupied by those persons as their only or main residence or they are to be treated as so occupying it (see section 259);
  (e) their occupation of the living accommodation constitutes the only use of that accommodation; and
  (f) rents are payable or other consideration is to be provided in respect of at least one of those persons' occupation of the living accommodation.

(5) But for any purposes of this Act (other than those of Part 1) a building or part of a building within subsection (1) is not a house in multiple occupation if it is listed in Schedule 14.

(6) The appropriate national authority may by regulations –

  (a) make such amendments of this section and sections 255 to 259 as the authority considers appropriate with a view to securing that any building or part of a building of a description specified in the regulations is or is not to be a house in multiple occupation for any specified purposes of this Act;
  (b) provide for such amendments to have effect also for the purposes of definitions in other enactments that operate by reference to this Act;
  (c) make such consequential amendments of any provision of this Act, or any other enactment, as the authority considers appropriate.

(7) Regulations under subsection (6) may frame any description by reference to any matters or circumstances whatever.

(8) In this section –

  'basic amenities' means –

  (a) a toilet,
  (b) personal washing facilities, or
  (c) cooking facilities;

  'converted building' means a building or part of a building consisting of living accommodation in which one or more units of such accommodation have been created since the building or part was constructed;

  'enactment' includes an enactment comprised in subordinate legislation (within the meaning of the Interpretation Act 1978 (c 30);

  'self-contained flat' means a separate set of premises (whether or not on the same floor) –

  (a) which forms part of a building;
  (b) either the whole or a material part of which lies above or below some other part of the building; and
  (c) in which all three basic amenities are available for the exclusive use of its occupants.

255 HMO declarations

(1) If a local housing authority are satisfied that subsection (2) applies to a building or part of a building in their area, they may serve a notice under this section (an 'HMO declaration') declaring the building or part to be a house in multiple occupation.

(2) This subsection applies to a building or part of a building if the building or part meets any of the following tests (as it applies without the sole use condition) –

  (a) the standard test (see section 254(2)),
  (b) the self-contained flat test (see section 254(3)), or
  (c) the converted building test (see section 254(4)),

and the occupation, by persons who do not form a single household, of the living accommodation or flat referred to in the test in question constitutes a significant use of that accommodation or flat.

(3) In subsection (2) 'the sole use condition' means the condition contained in –

  (a) section 254(2)(d) (as it applies for the purposes of the standard test or the self-contained flat test), or
  (b) section 254(4)(e),

as the case may be.

(4) The notice must –

(a) state the date of the authority's decision to serve the notice,
(b) be served on each relevant person within the period of seven days beginning with the date of that decision,
(c) state the day on which it will come into force if no appeal is made under subsection (9) against the authority's decision, and
(d) set out the right to appeal against the decision under subsection (9) and the period within which an appeal may be made.

(5) The day stated in the notice under subsection (4)(c) must be not less than 28 days after the date of the authority's decision to serve the notice.

(6) If no appeal is made under subsection (9) before the end of that period of 28 days, the notice comes into force on the day stated in the notice.

(7) If such an appeal is made before the end of that period of 28 days, the notice does not come into force unless and until a decision is given on the appeal which confirms the notice and either –

(a) the period within which an appeal to the Lands Tribunal may be brought expires without such an appeal having been brought, or
(b) if an appeal to the Lands Tribunal is brought, a decision is given on the appeal which confirms the notice.

(8) For the purposes of subsection (7), the withdrawal of an appeal has the same effect as a decision which confirms the notice appealed against.

(9) Any relevant person may appeal to a residential property tribunal against a decision of the local housing authority to serve an HMO declaration.

The appeal must be made within the period of 28 days beginning with the date of the authority's decision.

(10) Such an appeal –

(a) is to be by way of a re-hearing, but
(b) may be determined having regard to matters of which the authority were unaware.

(11) The tribunal may –

(a) confirm or reverse the decision of the authority, and
(b) if it reverses the decision, revoke the HMO declaration.

(12) In this section and section 256 'relevant person', in relation to an HMO declaration, means any person who, to the knowledge of the local housing authority, is –

(a) a person having an estate or interest in the building or part of the building concerned (but is not a tenant under a lease with an unexpired term of 3 years of less), or
(b) a person managing or having control of that building or part (and not falling within paragraph (a)).

256 Revocation of HMO declarations

(1) A local housing authority may revoke an HMO declaration served under section 255 at any time if they consider that subsection (2) of that section no longer applies to the building or part of the building in respect of which the declaration was served.

(2) The power to revoke an HMO declaration is exercisable by the authority either –

(a) on an application made by a relevant person, or

(b) on the authority's own initiative.

(3) If, on an application by such a person, the authority decide not to revoke the HMO declaration, they must without delay serve on him a notice informing him of –

(a) the decision,
(b) the reasons for it and the date on which it was made,
(c) the right to appeal against it under subsection (4), and
(d) the period within which an appeal may be made under that subsection.

(4) A person who applies to a local housing authority for the revocation of an HMO declaration under subsection (1) may appeal to a residential property tribunal against a decision of the authority to refuse to revoke the notice.

The appeal must be made within the period of 28 days beginning with the date specified under subsection (3) as the date on which the decision was made.

(5) Such an appeal –

(a) is to be by way of a re-hearing, but
(b) may be determined having regard to matters of which the authority were unaware.

(6) The tribunal may –

(a) confirm or reverse the decision of the authority, and
(b) if it reverses the decision, revoke the HMO declaration.

257 HMOs: certain converted blocks of flats

(1) For the purposes of this section a 'converted block of flats' means a building or part of a building which –

(a) has been converted into, and
(b) consists of,

self-contained flats.

(2) This section applies to a converted block of flats if –

(a) building work undertaken in connection with the conversion did not comply with the appropriate building standards and still does not comply with them; and
(b) less than two-thirds of the self-contained flats are owner-occupied.

(3) In subsection (2) 'appropriate building standards' means –

(a) in the case of a converted block of flats –
    (i)   on which building work was completed before 1st June 1992 or which is dealt with by regulation 20 of the Building Regulations 1991 (SI 1991/2768), and
    (ii) which would not have been exempt under those Regulations,

    building standards equivalent to those imposed, in relation to a building or part of a building to which those Regulations applied, by those Regulations as they had effect on 1st June 1992; and
(b) in the case of any other converted block of flats, the requirements imposed at the time in relation to it by regulations under section 1 of the Building Act 1984 (c 55).

(4) For the purposes of subsection (2) a flat is 'owner-occupied' if it is occupied –

(a) by a person who has a lease of the flat which has been granted for a term of more than 21 years,

(b) by a person who has the freehold estate in the converted block of flats, or

(c) by a member of the household of a person within paragraph (a) or (b).

(5) The fact that this section applies to a converted block of flats (with the result that it is a house in multiple occupation under section 254(1)(e)), does not affect the status of any flat in the block as a house in multiple occupation.

(6) In this section 'self-contained flat' has the same meaning as in section 254.

258 HMOs: persons not forming a single household

(1) This section sets out when persons are to be regarded as not forming a single household for the purposes of section 254.

(2) Persons are to be regarded as not forming a single household unless –

(a) they are all members of the same family, or

(b) their circumstances are circumstances of a description specified for the purposes of this section in regulations made by the appropriate national authority.

(3) For the purposes of subsection (2)(a) a person is a member of the same family as another person if –

(a) those persons are married to each other or live together as husband and wife (or in an equivalent relationship in the case of persons of the same sex);

(b) one of them is a relative of the other; or

(c) one of them is, or is a relative of, one member of a couple and the other is a relative of the other member of the couple.

(4) For those purposes –

(a) a 'couple' means two persons who are married to each other or otherwise fall within subsection (3)(a);

(b) 'relative' means parent, grandparent, child, grandchild, brother, sister, uncle, aunt, nephew, niece or cousin;

(c) a relationship of the half-blood shall be treated as a relationship of the whole blood; and

(d) the stepchild of a person shall be treated as his child.

(5) Regulations under subsection (2)(b) may, in particular, secure that a group of persons are to be regarded as forming a single household only where (as the regulations may require) each member of the group has a prescribed relationship, or at least one of a number of prescribed relationships, to any one or more of the others.

(6) In subsection (5) 'prescribed relationship' means any relationship of a description specified in the regulations.

259 HMOs: persons treated as occupying premises as only or main residence

(1) This section sets out when persons are to be treated for the purposes of section 254 as occupying a building or part of a building as their only or main residence.

(2) A person is to be treated as so occupying a building or part of a building if it is occupied by the person –

(a) as the person's residence for the purpose of undertaking a full-time course of further or higher education;

(b) as a refuge, or

(c) in any other circumstances which are circumstances of a description specified for the purposes of this section in regulations made by the appropriate national authority.

(3) In subsection (2)(b) 'refuge' means a building or part of a building managed by a voluntary organisation and used wholly or mainly for the temporary accommodation of persons who have left their homes as a result of –

(a) physical violence or mental abuse, or

(b) threats of such violence or abuse,

from persons to whom they are or were married or with whom they are or were co-habiting.

260 HMOs: presumption that sole use condition or significant use condition is met

(1) Where a question arises in any proceedings as to whether either of the following is met in respect of a building or part of a building –

(a) the sole use condition, or

(b) the significant use condition,

it shall be presumed, for the purposes of the proceedings, that the condition is met unless the contrary is shown.

(2) In this section –

(a) 'the sole use condition' means the condition contained in –
  (i) section 254(2)(d) (as it applies for the purposes of the standard test or the self-contained flat test), or
  (ii) section 254(4)(e),

  as the case may be; and

(b) 'the significant use condition' means the condition contained in section 255(2) that the occupation of the living accommodation or flat referred to in that provision by persons who do not form a single household constitutes a significant use of that accommodation or flat.

Other general interpretation provisions

261 Meaning of 'appropriate national authority', 'local housing authority' etc

(1) In this Act 'the appropriate national authority' means –

(a) in relation to England, the Secretary of State; and

(b) in relation to Wales, the National Assembly for Wales.

(2) In this Act 'local housing authority' means, in relation to England –

(a) a unitary authority;

(b) a district council so far as it is not a unitary authority;

(c) a London borough council;

(d) the Common Council of the City of London (in its capacity as a local authority);

(e) the Sub-Treasurer of the Inner Temple or the Under-Treasurer of the Middle Temple (in his capacity as a local authority); and

(f) the Council of the Isles of Scilly.

(3) In subsection (2) 'unitary authority' means –

(a) the council of a county so far as it is the council for an area for which there are no district councils;

(b) the council of any district comprised in an area for which there is no county council.

(4) In this Act 'local housing authority' means, in relation to Wales, a county council or a county borough council.

(5) References in this Act to 'the local housing authority', in relation to land, are to the local housing authority in whose district the land is situated.

(6) References in this Act to the district of a local housing authority are to the area of the council concerned, that is to say –

(a) in the case of a unitary authority, the area or district;

(b) in the case of a district council so far as it is not a unitary authority, the district;

(c) in the case of an authority within subsection (2)(c) to (f), the London borough, the City of London, the Inner or Middle Temple or the Isles of Scilly (as the case may be); and

(d) in the case of a Welsh county council or a county borough council, the Welsh county or county borough.

(7) Section 618 of the Housing Act 1985 (c 68) (committees and members of Common Council of City of London) applies in relation to this Act as it applies in relation to that Act.

262 Meaning of 'lease', 'tenancy', 'occupier' and 'owner' etc

(1) In this Act 'lease' and 'tenancy' have the same meaning.

(2) Both expressions include –

(a) a sub-lease or sub-tenancy; and

(b) an agreement for a lease or tenancy (or sub-lease or sub-tenancy).

And see sections 108 and 117 and paragraphs 3 and 11 of Schedule 7 (which also extend the meaning of references to leases).

(3) The expressions 'lessor' and 'lessee' and 'landlord' and 'tenant' and references to letting, to the grant of a lease or to covenants or terms, are to be construed accordingly.

(4) In this Act 'lessee' includes a statutory tenant of the premises; and references to a lease or to a person to whom premises are let are to be construed accordingly.

(5) In this Act any reference to a person who is a tenant under a lease with an unexpired term of 3 years or less includes a statutory tenant as well as a tenant under a yearly or other periodic tenancy.

(6) In this Act 'occupier', in relation to premises, means a person who –

(a) occupies the premises as a residence, and

(b) (subject to the context) so occupies them whether as a tenant or other person having an estate or interest in the premises or as a licensee;

and related expressions are to be construed accordingly.

This subsection does not apply for the purposes of Part 5 and has effect subject to any other provision defining 'occupier' for any purposes of this Act.

(7) In this Act 'owner', in relation to premises –

(a) means a person (other than a mortgagee not in possession) who is for the time being entitled to dispose of the fee simple of the premises whether in possession or in reversion; and

(b) includes also a person holding or entitled to the rents and profits of the premises under a lease of which the unexpired term exceeds 3 years.

(8) In this Act 'person having an estate or interest', in relation to premises, includes a statutory tenant of the premises.

(9) In this Act 'licence', in the context of a licence to occupy premises –

(a) includes a licence which is not granted for a consideration, but
(b) excludes a licence granted as a temporary expedient to a person who entered the premises as a trespasser (whether or not, before the grant of the licence, another licence to occupy those or other premises had been granted to him);

and related expressions are to be construed accordingly.

And see sections 108 and 117 and paragraphs 3 and 11 of Schedule 7 (which also extend the meaning of references to licences).

263 Meaning of 'person having control' and 'person managing' etc

(1) In this Act 'person having control', in relation to premises, means (unless the context otherwise requires) the person who receives the rack-rent of the premises (whether on his own account or as agent or trustee of another person), or who would so receive it if the premises were let at a rack-rent.

(2) In subsection (1) 'rack-rent' means a rent which is not less than two-thirds of the full net annual value of the premises.

(3) In this Act 'person managing' means, in relation to premises, the person who, being an owner or lessee of the premises –

(a) receives (whether directly or through an agent or trustee) rents or other payments from –
    (i) in the case of a house in multiple occupation, persons who are in occupation as tenants or licensees of parts of the premises; and
    (ii) in the case of a house to which Part 3 applies (see section 79(2)), persons who are in occupation as tenants or licensees of parts of the premises, or of the whole of the premises; or
(b) would so receive those rents or other payments but for having entered into an arrangement (whether in pursuance of a court order or otherwise) with another person who is not an owner or lessee of the premises by virtue of which that other person receives the rents or other payments;

and includes, where those rents or other payments are received through another person as agent or trustee, that other person.

(4) In its application to Part 1, subsection (3) has effect with the omission of paragraph (a)(ii).

(5) References in this Act to any person involved in the management of a house in multiple occupation or a house to which Part 3 applies (see section 79(2)) include references to the person managing it.

264 Calculation of numbers of persons

(1) The appropriate national authority may prescribe rules with respect to the calculation of numbers of persons for the purposes of –

(a) any provision made by or under this Act which is specified in the rules, or
(b) any order or licence made or granted under this Act of any description which is so specified.

(2) The rules may provide –

(a) for persons under a particular age to be disregarded for the purposes of any such calculation;

(b) for persons under a particular age to be treated as constituting a fraction of a person for the purposes of any such calculation.

(3) The rules may be prescribed by order or regulations.

Final provisions

265 Minor and consequential amendments

(1) Schedule 15 (which contains minor and consequential amendments) has effect.

(2) The Secretary of State may by order make such supplementary, incidental or consequential provision as he considers appropriate –

(a) for the general purposes, or any particular purpose, of this Act; or

(b) in consequence of any provision made by or under this Act or for giving full effect to it.

(3) An order under subsection (2) may modify any enactment (including this Act).

'Enactment' includes an enactment comprised in subordinate legislation (within the meaning of the Interpretation Act 1978 (c 30)).

(4) The power conferred by subsection (2) is also exercisable by the National Assembly for Wales in relation to provision dealing with matters with respect to which functions are exercisable by the Assembly.

(5) Nothing in this Act affects the generality of the power conferred by this section.

266 Repeals

Schedule 16 (which contains repeals) has effect.

267 Devolution: Wales

In Schedule 1 to the National Assembly for Wales (Transfer of Functions) Order 1999 (SI 1999/672) references to the following Acts are to be treated as references to those Acts as amended by virtue of this Act –

(a) the Housing Act 1985 (c 68);

(b) the Housing Act 1988 (c 50);

(c) the Housing Act 1996 (c 52).

268 The Isles of Scilly

(1) This Secretary of State may by order provide that, in its application to the Isles of Scilly, this Act is have effect with such modifications as are specified in the order.

(2) Where a similar power is exercisable under another Act in relation to provisions of that Act which are amended by this Act, the power is exercisable in relation to those provisions as so amended.

269 Expenses

There shall be paid out of money provided by Parliament –

(a) any expenditure incurred by the Secretary of State by virtue of this Act;

(b) any increase attributable to this Act in the sums payable out of money so provided under any other enactment.

270 Short title, commencement and extent

(1) This Act may be cited as the Housing Act 2004.

(2) The following provisions come into force on the day on which this Act is passed –

    (a) sections 2, 9, 161 to 164, 176, 190, 208, 216, 233, 234, 244, 248, 250, 252, 264, 265(2) to (5), 267 to 269 and this section, and

    (b) any other provision of this Act so far as it confers any power to make an order or regulations which is exercisable by the Secretary of State or the National Assembly for Wales.

Subsections (3) to (7) have effect subject to paragraph (b).

(3) The following provisions come into force at the end of the period of two months beginning with the day on which this Act is passed –

    (a) sections 180, 182 to 189, 195 to 207, 209 to 211, 217, 218, 219, 222, 224, 245 to 247, 249, 251 and 253 to 263,

    (b) Schedule 9,

    (c) Schedule 11, except paragraphs 15 and 16, and

    (d) Schedule 14.

(4) The provisions listed in subsection (5) come into force –

    (a) where they are to come into force in relation only to Wales, on such day as the National Assembly for Wales may by order appoint, and

    (b) otherwise, on such day as the Secretary of State may by order appoint.

(5) The provisions referred to in subsection (4) are –

    (a) Part 1 (other than sections 2 and 9),

    (b) Parts 2 to 4,

    (c) sections 179, 181, 191 to 194, 212 to 215, 220, 221, 223, 225, 226, 227, 229 to 232, 235 to 243, 265(1) and 266,

    (d) Schedule 10,

    (e) paragraphs 15 and 16 of Schedule 11, and

    (f) Schedules 13, 15 and 16.

(6) Part 5 (other than sections 161 to 164 and 176) comes into force on such day as the Secretary of State may by order appoint.

(7) Section 228 and Schedule 12 come into force on such day as the National Assembly for Wales may by order appoint.

(8) Different days may be appointed for different purposes or different areas under subsection (4), (6) or (7).

(9) The Secretary of State may by order make such provision as he considers necessary or expedient for transitory, transitional or saving purposes in connection with the coming into force of any provision of this Act.

(10) The power conferred by subsection (9) is also exercisable by the National Assembly for Wales in relation to provision dealing with matters with respect to which functions are exercisable by the Assembly

(11) Subject to subsections (12) and (13), this Act extends to England and Wales only.

(12) Any amendment or repeal made by this Act has the same extent as the enactment to which it relates, except that any amendment or repeal in –

the Mobile Homes Act 1983 (c 34), or

the Crime and Disorder Act 1998 (c 37),

extends to England and Wales only.

(13) This section extends to the whole of the United Kingdom.

SCHEDULE 1
PROCEDURE AND APPEALS RELATING TO IMPROVEMENT NOTICES

Section 18

Part 1
Service of Improvement Notices

Service of improvement notices: premises licensed under Part 2 or 3

1 (1) This paragraph applies where the specified premises in the case of an improvement notice are –

   (a) a dwelling which is licensed under Part 3 of this Act, or
   (b) an HMO which is licensed under Part 2 or 3 of this Act.

(2) The local housing authority must serve the notice on the holder of the licence under that Part.

Service of improvement notices: premises which are neither licensed under Part 2 or 3 nor flats

2 (1) This paragraph applies where the specified premises in the case of an improvement notice are –

   (a) a dwelling which is not licensed under Part 3 of this Act, or
   (b) an HMO which is not licensed under Part 2 or 3 of this Act,

and which (in either case) is not a flat.

(2) The local housing authority must serve the notice –

   (a) (in the case of a dwelling) on the person having control of the dwelling;
   (b) (in the case of an HMO) either on the person having control of the HMO or on the person managing it.

Service of improvement notices: flats which are not licensed under Part 2 or 3

3 (1) This paragraph applies where any specified premises in the case of an improvement notice are –

   (a) a dwelling which is not licensed under Part 3 of this Act, or
   (b) an HMO which is not licensed under Part 2 or 3 of this Act,

and which (in either case) is a flat.

(2) In the case of dwelling which is a flat, the local housing authority must serve the notice on a person who –

   (a) is an owner of the flat, and
   (b) in the authority's opinion ought to take the action specified in the notice.

(3) In the case of an HMO which is a flat, the local housing authority must serve the notice either on a person who –

   (a) is an owner of the flat, and

(b) in the authority's opinion ought to take the action specified in the notice,

or on the person managing the flat.

Service of improvement notices: common parts

4 (1) This paragraph applies where any specified premises in the case of an improvement notice are –

(a) common parts of a building containing one or more flats; or
(b) any part of such a building which does not consist of residential premises.

(2) The local housing authority must serve the notice on a person who –

(a) is an owner of the specified premises concerned, and
(b) in the authority's opinion ought to take the action specified in the notice.

(3) For the purposes of this paragraph a person is an owner of any common parts of a building if he is an owner of the building or part of the building concerned, or (in the case of external common parts) of the particular premises in which the common parts are comprised.

Service of copies of improvement notices

5 (1) In addition to serving an improvement notice in accordance with any of paragraphs 1 to 4, the local housing authority must serve a copy of the notice on every other person who, to their knowledge –

(a) has a relevant interest in any specified premises, or
(b) is an occupier of any such premises.

(2) A 'relevant interest' means an interest as freeholder, mortgagee or lessee.

(3) For the purposes of this paragraph a person has a relevant interest in any common parts of a building if he has a relevant interest in the building or part of the building concerned, or (in the case of external common parts) in the particular premises in which the common parts are comprised.

(4) The copies required to be served under sub-paragraph (1) must be served within the period of seven days beginning with the day on which the notice is served.

Part 2
Service of Notices Relating to Revocation or Variation of Improvement Notices

Notice of revocation or variation

6 (1) This paragraph applies where the local housing authority decide to revoke or vary an improvement notice.

(2) The authority must serve –

(a) a notice under this paragraph, and
(b) copies of that notice,

on the persons on whom they would be required under Part 1 of this Schedule to serve an improvement notice and copies of it in respect of the specified premises.

(3) Sub-paragraph (4) applies if, in so doing, the authority serve a notice under this paragraph on a person who is not the person on whom the improvement notice was served ('the original recipient').

(4) The authority must serve a copy of the notice under this paragraph on the original recipient unless they consider that it would not be appropriate to do so.

(5) The documents required to be served under sub-paragraph (2) must be served within the period of seven days beginning with the day on which the decision is made.

7   A notice under paragraph 6 must set out –

   (a) the authority's decision to revoke or vary the improvement notice;
   (b) the reasons for the decision and the date on which it was made;
   (c) if the decision is to vary the notice –
       (i)   the right of appeal against the decision under Part 3 of this Schedule, and
       (ii)   the period within which an appeal may be made (see paragraph 14(2)).

Notice of refusal to revoke or vary notice

8   (1) This paragraph applies where the local housing authority refuse to revoke or vary an improvement notice.

(2) The authority must serve –

   (a) a notice under this paragraph, and
   (b) copies of that notice,

on the persons on whom they would be required to serve an improvement notice and copies of it under Part 1 of this Schedule.

(3) Sub-paragraph (4) applies if, in so doing, the authority serve a notice under this paragraph on a person who is not the person on whom the improvement notice was served ('the original recipient').

(4) The authority must serve a copy of the notice under this paragraph on the original recipient unless they consider that it would not be appropriate to do so.

(5) The documents required to be served under sub-paragraph (2) must be served within the period of seven days beginning with the day on which the decision is made.

9   A notice under paragraph 8 must set out –

   (a) the authority's decision not to revoke or vary the improvement notice;
   (b) the reasons for the decision and the date on which it was made;
   (c) the right of appeal against the decision under Part 3 of this Schedule; and
   (d) the period within which an appeal may be made (see paragraph 14(2)).

Part 3
Appeals Relating to Improvement Notices

Appeal against improvement notice

10 (1) The person on whom an improvement notice is served may appeal to a residential property tribunal against the notice.

(2) Paragraphs 11 and 12 set out two specific grounds on which an appeal may be made under this paragraph, but they do not affect the generality of sub-paragraph (1).

11 (1) An appeal may be made by a person under paragraph 10 on the ground that one or more other persons, as an owner or owners of the specified premises, ought to –

(a) take the action concerned, or

(b) pay the whole or part of the cost of taking that action.

(2) Where the grounds on which an appeal is made under paragraph 10 consist of or include the ground mentioned in sub-paragraph (1), the appellant must serve a copy of his notice of appeal on the other person or persons concerned.

12 (1) An appeal may be made by a person under paragraph 10 on the ground that one of the courses of action mentioned in sub-paragraph (2) is the best course of action in relation to the hazard in respect of which the notice was served.

(2) The courses of action are –

(a) making a prohibition order under section 20 or 21 of this Act;

(b) serving a hazard awareness notice under section 28 or 29 of this Act; and

(c) making a demolition order under section 265 of the Housing Act 1985 (c 68).

Appeal against decision relating to variation or revocation of improvement notice

13 (1) The relevant person may appeal to a residential property tribunal against –

(a) a decision by the local housing authority to vary an improvement notice, or

(b) a decision by the authority to refuse to revoke or vary an improvement notice.

(2) In sub-paragraph (1) 'the relevant person' means –

(a) in relation to a decision within paragraph (a) of that provision, the person on whom the notice was served;

(b) in relation to a decision within paragraph (b) of that provision, the person who applied for the revocation or variation.

Time limit for appeal

14 (1) Any appeal under paragraph 10 must be made within the period of 21 days beginning with the date on which the improvement notice was served in accordance with Part 1 of this Schedule.

(2) Any appeal under paragraph 13 must be made within the period of 28 days beginning with the date specified in the notice under paragraph 6 or 8 as the date on which the decision concerned was made.

(3) A residential property tribunal may allow an appeal to be made to it after the end of the period mentioned in sub-paragraph (1) or (2) if it is satisfied that there is a good reason for the failure to appeal before the end of that period (and for any delay since then in applying for permission to appeal out of time).

Powers of residential property tribunal on appeal under paragraph 10

15 (1) This paragraph applies to an appeal to a residential property tribunal under paragraph 10.

(2) The appeal –

(a) is to be by way of a re-hearing, but

(b) may be determined having regard to matters of which the authority were unaware.

(3) The tribunal may by order confirm, quash or vary the improvement notice.

(4) Paragraphs 16 and 17 make special provision in connection with the grounds of appeal set out in paragraphs 11 and 12.

16　(1) This paragraph applies where the grounds of appeal consist of or include that set out in paragraph 11.

(2) On the hearing of the appeal the tribunal may –

- (a) vary the improvement notice so as to require the action to be taken by any owner mentioned in the notice of appeal in accordance with paragraph 11; or
- (b) make such order as it considers appropriate with respect to the payment to be made by any such owner to the appellant or, where the action is taken by the local housing authority, to the authority.

(3) In the exercise of its powers under sub-paragraph (2), the tribunal must take into account, as between the appellant and any such owner –

- (a) their relative interests in the premises concerned (considering both the nature of the interests and the rights and obligations arising under or by virtue of them);
- (b) their relative responsibility for the state of the premises which gives rise to the need for the taking of the action concerned; and
- (c) the relative degree of benefit to be derived from the taking of the action concerned.

(4) Sub-paragraph (5) applies where, by virtue of the exercise of the tribunal's powers under sub-paragraph (2), a person other than the appellant is required to take the action specified in an improvement notice.

(5) So long as that other person remains an owner of the premises to which the notice relates, he is to be regarded for the purposes of this Part as the person on whom the notice was served (in place of any other person).

17　(1) This paragraph applies where the grounds of appeal consist of or include that set out in paragraph 12.

(2) When deciding whether one of the courses of action mentioned in paragraph 12(2) is the best course of action in relation to a particular hazard, the tribunal must have regard to any guidance given to the local housing authority under section 9.

(3) Sub-paragraph (4) applies where –

- (a) an appeal under paragraph 10 is allowed against an improvement notice in respect of a particular hazard; and
- (b) the reason, or one of the reasons, for allowing the appeal is that one of the courses of action mentioned in paragraph 12(2) is the best course of action in relation to that hazard.

(4) The tribunal must, if requested to do so by the appellant or the local housing authority, include in its decision a finding to that effect and identifying the course of action concerned.

Powers of residential property tribunal on appeal under paragraph 13

18　(1) This paragraph applies to an appeal to a residential property tribunal under paragraph 13.

(2) Paragraph 15(2) applies to such an appeal as it applies to an appeal under paragraph 10.

(3) The tribunal may by order confirm, reverse or vary the decision of the local housing authority.

(4) If the appeal is against a decision of the authority to refuse to revoke an improvement notice, the tribunal may make an order revoking the notice as from a date specified in the order.

'The operative time' for the purposes of section 15(5)

19 (1) This paragraph defines 'the operative time' for the purposes of section 15(5) (operation of improvement notices).

(2) If an appeal is made under paragraph 10 against an improvement notice which is not suspended, and a decision on the appeal is given which confirms the notice, 'the operative time' is as follows –

    (a) if the period within which an appeal to the Lands Tribunal may be brought expires without such an appeal having been brought, 'the operative time' is the end of that period;

    (b) if an appeal to the Lands Tribunal is brought, 'the operative time' is the time when a decision is given on the appeal which confirms the notice.

(3) If an appeal is made under paragraph 10 against an improvement notice which is suspended, and a decision is given on the appeal which confirms the notice, 'the operative time' is as follows –

    (a) the time that would be the operative time under sub-paragraph (2) if the notice were not suspended, or

    (b) if later, the time when the suspension ends.

(4) For the purposes of sub-paragraph (2) or (3) –

    (a) the withdrawal of an appeal has the same effect as a decision which confirms the notice, and

    (b) references to a decision which confirms the notice are to a decision which confirms it with or without variation.

'The operative time' for the purposes of section 16(7)

20 (1) This paragraph defines 'the operative time' for the purposes of section 16(7) (postponement of time when a variation of an improvement notice comes into force).

(2) If no appeal is made under paragraph 13 before the end of the period of 28 days mentioned in paragraph 14(2), 'the operative time' is the end of that period.

(3) If an appeal is made under paragraph 13 before the end of that period and a decision is given on the appeal which confirms the variation, 'the operative time' is as follows –

    (a) if the period within which an appeal to the Lands Tribunal may be brought expires without such an appeal having been brought, 'the operative time' is the end of that period;

    (b) if an appeal to the Lands Tribunal is brought, 'the operative time' is the time when a decision is given on the appeal which confirms the variation.

(4) For the purposes of sub-paragraph (3) –

    (a) the withdrawal of an appeal has the same effect as a decision which confirms the variation, and

    (b) references to a decision which confirms the variation are to a decision which confirms it with or without variation.

SCHEDULE 2
PROCEDURE AND APPEALS RELATING TO PROHIBITION ORDERS

Section 27

Part 1
Service of Copies of Prohibition Orders

Service on owners and occupiers of dwelling or HMO which is not a flat

1 (1) This paragraph applies to a prohibition order where the specified premises are a dwelling or HMO which is not a flat.

(2) The authority must serve copies of the order on every person who, to their knowledge, is –

    (a) an owner or occupier of the whole or part of the specified premises;
    (b) authorised to permit persons to occupy the whole or part of those premises; or
    (c) a mortgagee of the whole or part of those premises.

(3) The copies required to be served under sub-paragraph (2) must be served within the period of seven days beginning with the day on which the order is made.

(4) A copy of the order is to be regarded as having been served on every occupier in accordance with sub-paragraphs (2)(a) and (3) if a copy of the order is fixed to some conspicuous part of the specified premises within the period of seven days mentioned in sub-paragraph (3).

Service on owners and occupiers of building containing flats etc

2 (1) This paragraph applies to a prohibition order where the specified premises consist of or include the whole or any part of a building containing one or more flats or any common parts of such a building.

(2) The authority must serve copies of the order on every person who, to their knowledge, is –

    (a) an owner or occupier of the whole or part of the building;
    (b) authorised to permit persons to occupy the whole or part of the building; or
    (c) a mortgagee of the whole or part of the building.

(3) Where the specified premises consist of or include any external common parts of such a building, the authority must, in addition to complying with sub-paragraph (2), serve copies of the order on every person who, to their knowledge, is an owner or mortgagee of the premises in which the common parts are comprised.

(4) The copies required to be served under sub-paragraph (2) or (3) must be served within the period of seven days beginning with the day on which the order is made.

(5) A copy of the order is to be regarded as having been served on every occupier in accordance with sub-paragraphs (2)(a) and (4) if a copy of the order is fixed to some conspicuous part of the building within the period of seven days mentioned in sub-paragraph (4).

Part 2
Service of Notices Relating to Revocation or Variation of Prohibition Orders

Notice of revocation or variation

3 (1) This paragraph applies where the local housing authority decide to revoke or vary a prohibition order.

(2) The authority must serve a notice under this paragraph on each of the persons on whom they would be required under Part 1 of this Schedule to serve copies of a prohibition order in respect of the specified premises.

(3) The notices required to be served under sub-paragraph (2) must be served within the period of seven days beginning with the day on which the decision is made.

(4) Paragraph 1(4) applies in relation to the service of notices on occupiers in accordance with sub-paragraphs (2) and (3) as it applies in relation to the service on them of copies of a prohibition order in accordance with paragraph 1(2)(a) and (3).

4   A notice under paragraph 3 must set out –

   (a) the authority's decision to revoke or vary the order;
   (b) the reasons for the decision and the date on which it was made;
   (c) if the decision is to vary the order –
      (i)   the right of appeal against the decision under Part 3 of this Schedule; and
      (ii)   the period within which an appeal may be made (see paragraph 10(2)).

Notice of refusal to revoke or vary order

5   (1) This paragraph applies where the local housing authority refuse to revoke or vary a prohibition order.

(2) The authority must serve a notice under this paragraph on each of the persons on whom they would be required under Part 1 of this Schedule to serve copies of a prohibition order in respect of the specified premises.

(3) The notices required to be served under sub-paragraph (2) must be served within the period of seven days beginning with the day on which the decision is made.

(4) Paragraph 1(4) applies in relation to the service of notices on occupiers in accordance with sub-paragraphs (2) and (3) as it applies in relation to the service on them of copies of a prohibition order in accordance with paragraph 1(2)(a) and (3).

6   A notice under paragraph 5 must set out –

   (a) the authority's decision not to revoke or vary the notice;
   (b) the reasons for the decision and the date on which it was made;
   (c) the right of appeal against the decision under Part 3 of this Schedule; and
   (d) the period within which an appeal may be made (see paragraph 10(2)).

Part 3
Appeals Relating to Prohibition Orders

Appeal against prohibition order

7   (1) A relevant person may appeal to a residential property tribunal against a prohibition order.

(2) Paragraph 8 sets out a specific ground on which an appeal may be made under this paragraph, but it does not affect the generality of sub-paragraph (1).

8   (1) An appeal may be made by a person under paragraph 7 on the ground that one of the courses of action mentioned in sub-paragraph (2) is the best course of action in relation to the hazard in respect of which the order was made.

(2) The courses of action are –

   (a) serving an improvement notice under section 11 or 12 of this Act;

(b) serving a hazard awareness notice under section 28 or 29 of this Act;

(c) making a demolition order under section 265 of the Housing Act 1985 (c 68).

Appeal against decision relating to revocation or variation of prohibition order

9 A relevant person may appeal to a residential property tribunal against –

(a) a decision by the local housing authority to vary a prohibition order, or

(b) a decision by the authority to refuse to revoke or vary a prohibition order.

Time limit for appeal

10 (1) Any appeal under paragraph 7 must be made within the period of 28 days beginning with the date specified in the prohibition order as the date on which the order was made.

(2) Any appeal under paragraph 9 must be made within the period of 28 days beginning with the date specified in the notice under paragraph 3 or 5 as the date on which the decision concerned was made.

(3) A residential property tribunal may allow an appeal to be made to it after the end of the period mentioned in sub-paragraph (1) or (2) if it is satisfied that there is a good reason for the failure to appeal before the end of that period (and for any delay since then in applying for permission to appeal out of time).

Powers of residential property tribunal on appeal under paragraph 7

11 (1) This paragraph applies to an appeal to a residential property tribunal under paragraph 7.

(2) The appeal –

(a) is to be by way of a re-hearing, but

(b) may be determined having regard to matters of which the authority were unaware.

(3) The tribunal may by order confirm, quash or vary the prohibition order.

(4) Paragraph 12 makes special provision in connection with the ground of appeal set out in paragraph 8.

12 (1) This paragraph applies where the grounds of appeal consist of or include that set out in paragraph 8.

(2) When deciding whether one of the courses of action mentioned in paragraph 8(2) is the best course of action in relation to a particular hazard, the tribunal must have regard to any guidance given to the local housing authority under section 9.

(3) Sub-paragraph (4) applies where –

(a) an appeal under paragraph 7 is allowed against a prohibition order made in respect of a particular hazard; and

(b) the reason, or one of the reasons, for allowing the appeal is that one of the courses of action mentioned in paragraph 8(2) is the best course of action in relation to that hazard.

(4) The tribunal must, if requested to do so by the appellant or the local housing authority, include in its decision a finding to that effect and identifying the course of action concerned.

Powers of residential property tribunal on appeal under paragraph 9

13 (1) This paragraph applies to an appeal to a residential property tribunal under paragraph 9.

(2) Paragraph 11(2) applies to such an appeal as it applies to an appeal under paragraph 7.

(3) The tribunal may by order confirm, reverse or vary the decision of the local housing authority.

(4) If the appeal is against a decision of the authority to refuse to revoke a prohibition order, the tribunal may make an order revoking the prohibition order as from a date specified in its order.

'The operative time' for the purposes of section 24(5)

14 (1) This paragraph defines 'the operative time' for the purposes of section 24(5) (operation of prohibition orders).

(2) If an appeal is made under paragraph 7 against a prohibition order which is not suspended, and a decision on the appeal is given which confirms the order, 'the operative time' is as follows –

    (a) if the period within which an appeal to the Lands Tribunal may be brought expires without such an appeal having been brought, 'the operative time' is the end of that period;

    (b) if an appeal to the Lands Tribunal is brought, 'the operative time' is the time when a decision is given on the appeal which confirms the order.

(3) If an appeal is made under paragraph 7 against a prohibition order which is suspended, and a decision is given on the appeal which confirms the order, 'the operative time' is as follows –

    (a) the time that would be the operative time under sub-paragraph (2) if the order were not suspended, or

    (b) if later, the time when the suspension ends.

(4) For the purposes of sub-paragraph (2) or (3) –

    (a) the withdrawal of an appeal has the same effect as a decision which confirms the notice, and

    (b) references to a decision which confirms the order are to a decision which confirms it with or without variation.

'The operative time' for the purposes of section 25(7)

15 (1) This paragraph defines 'the operative time' for the purposes of section 25(7) (revocation or variation of prohibition orders).

(2) If no appeal is made under paragraph 9 before the end of the period of 28 days mentioned in paragraph 10(2), 'the operative time' is the end of that period.

(3) If an appeal is made under paragraph 10 within that period and a decision is given on the appeal which confirms the variation, 'the operative time' is as follows –

    (a) if the period within which an appeal to the Lands Tribunal may be brought expires without such an appeal having been brought, 'the operative time' is the end of that period;

    (b) if an appeal to the Lands Tribunal is brought, 'the operative time' is the time when a decision is given on the appeal which confirms the variation.

(4) For the purposes of sub-paragraph (3) –

    (a) the withdrawal of an appeal has the same effect as a decision which confirms the variation, and

    (b) references to a decision which confirms the variation are to a decision which confirms it with or without variation.

Meaning of 'relevant person'

16 (1) In this Part of this Schedule 'relevant person', in relation to a prohibition order, means a person who is –

    (a) an owner or occupier of the whole or part of the specified premises,

(b) authorised to permit persons to occupy the whole or part of those premises, or

(c) a mortgagee of the whole or part of those premises.

(2) If any specified premises are common parts of a building containing one or more flats, then in relation to those specified premises, 'relevant person' means every person who is an owner or mortgagee of the premises in which the common parts are comprised.

SCHEDULE 3
IMPROVEMENT NOTICES: ENFORCEMENT ACTION BY LOCAL HOUSING AUTHORITIES

Section 31

Part 1
Action Taken by Agreement

Power to take action by agreement

1 (1) The local housing authority may, by agreement with the person on whom an improvement notice has been served, take any action which that person is required to take in relation to any premises in pursuance of the notice.

(2) For that purpose the authority have all the rights which that person would have against any occupying tenant of, and any other person having an interest in, the premises (or any part of the premises).

(3) In this paragraph –

'improvement notice' means an improvement notice which has become operative under Chapter 2 of Part 1 of this Act;

'occupying tenant', in relation to any premises, means a person (other than an owner-occupier) who –

(a) occupies or is entitled to occupy the premises as a lessee;

(b) is a statutory tenant of the premises;

(c) occupies the premises under a restricted contract;

(d) is a protected occupier within the meaning of the Rent (Agriculture) Act 1976 (c 80); or

(e) is a licensee under an assured agricultural occupancy;

'owner-occupier', in relation to any premises, means the person who occupies or is entitled to occupy the premises as owner or lessee under a long tenancy (within the meaning of Part 1 of the Leasehold Reform Act 1967 (c 88)).

Expenses of taking action by agreement

2 Any action taken by the local housing authority under paragraph 1 is to be taken at the expense of the person on whom the notice is served.

Part 2
Power to Take Action without Agreement

Power to take action without agreement

3 (1) The local housing authority may themselves take the action required to be taken in relation to a hazard by an improvement notice if sub-paragraph (2) or (3) applies.

(2) This sub-paragraph applies if the notice is not complied with in relation to that hazard.

(3) This sub-paragraph applies if, before the end of the period which under section 30(2) is appropriate for completion of the action specified in the notice in relation to the hazard, they consider that reasonable progress is not being made towards compliance with the notice in relation to the hazard.

(4) Any person authorised in writing by the authority may enter any part of the specified premises for the purposes of the taking of any action which the authority are authorised to take under this paragraph.

(5) The right of entry conferred by sub-paragraph (4) may be exercised at any reasonable time.

(6) Any reference in this Part of this Schedule (of whatever nature) to a local housing authority entering any premises under this paragraph is a reference to their doing so in accordance with sub-paragraph (4).

(7) In this paragraph 'improvement notice' means an improvement notice which has become operative under Chapter 2 of Part 1 of this Act.

Notice requirements in relation to taking action without agreement

4 (1) The local housing authority must serve a notice under this paragraph before they enter any premises under paragraph 3 for the purpose of taking action in relation to a hazard.

(2) The notice must identify the improvement notice to which it relates and state –

    (a) the premises and hazard concerned;
    (b) that the authority intend to enter the premises;
    (c) the action which the authority intend to take on the premises; and
    (d) the power under which the authority intend to enter the premises and take the action.

(3) The notice must be served on the person on whom the improvement notice was served, and a copy of the notice must be served on any other person who is an occupier of the premises.

(4) The notice and any such copy must be served sufficiently in advance of the time when the authority intend to enter the premises as to give the recipients reasonable notice of the intended entry.

(5) A copy of the notice may also be served on any owner of the premises.

Obstruction of action taken without agreement

5 (1) If, at any relevant time –

    (a) the person on whom the notice under paragraph 4 was served is on the premises for the purpose of carrying out any works, or
    (b) any workman employed by that person, or by any contractor employed by that person, is on the premises for such a purpose,

that person is to be taken to have committed an offence under section 241(1).

(2) In proceedings for such an offence it is a defence that there was an urgent necessity to carry out the works in order to prevent danger to persons occupying the premises.

(3) In sub-paragraph (1) 'relevant time' means any time –

(a) after the end of the period of 7 days beginning with the date of service of the notice under paragraph 4, and
(b) when any workman or contractor employed by the local housing authority is taking action on the premises which has been mentioned in the notice in accordance with paragraph 4(2)(c).

Expenses in relation to taking action without agreement

6 (1) Part 3 of this Schedule applies with respect to the recovery by the local housing authority of expenses incurred by them in taking action under paragraph 3.

(2) Sub-paragraph (3) applies where, after a local housing authority have given notice under paragraph 4 of their intention to enter premises and take action, the action is in fact taken by the person on whom the improvement notice is served.

(3) Any administrative and other expenses incurred by the authority with a view to themselves taking the action are to be treated for the purposes of Part 3 of this Schedule as expenses incurred by them in taking action under paragraph 3.

Part 3
Recovery of Certain Expenses

Introductory

7 This Part of this Schedule applies for the purpose of enabling a local housing authority to recover expenses reasonably incurred by them in taking action under paragraph 3.

Recovery of expenses

8 (1) The expenses are recoverable by the local housing authority from the person on whom the improvement notice was served ('the relevant person').

(2) Where the relevant person receives the rent of the premises as agent or trustee for another person, the expenses are also recoverable by the local housing authority from the other person, or partly from him and partly from the relevant person.

(3) Sub-paragraph (4) applies where the relevant person proves in connection with a demand under paragraph 9 –

(a) that sub-paragraph (2) applies, and
(b) that he has not, and since the date of the service on him of the demand has not had, in his hands on behalf of the other person sufficient money to discharge the whole demand of the local housing authority.

(4) The liability of the relevant person is limited to the total amount of the money which he has, or has had, in his hands as mentioned in sub-paragraph (3)(b).

(5) Expenses are not recoverable under this paragraph so far as they are, by any direction given by a residential property tribunal on an appeal to the tribunal under paragraph 11, recoverable under an order of the tribunal.

Service of demand

9 (1) A demand for expenses recoverable under paragraph 8, together with interest in accordance with paragraph 10, must be served on each person from whom the local housing authority are seeking to recover them.

(2) If no appeal is brought, the demand becomes operative at the end of the period of 21 days beginning with the date of service of the demand.

(3) A demand which becomes operative under sub-paragraph (2) is final and conclusive as to matters which could have been raised on an appeal.

(4) Paragraph 11 deals with appeals against demands.

Interest

10 Expenses in respect of which a demand is served carry interest, at such reasonable rate as the local housing authority may determine, from the date of service until payment of all sums due under the demand.

Appeals

11 (1) A person on whom a demand for the recovery of expenses has been served may appeal to a residential property tribunal against the demand.

(2) An appeal must be made within the period of 21 days beginning with the date of service of the demand or copy of it under paragraph 9.

(3) A residential property tribunal may allow an appeal to be made to it after the end of the period mentioned in sub-paragraph (2) if it is satisfied that there is a good reason for the failure to appeal before the end of that period (and for any delay since then in applying for permission to appeal out of time).

(4) Where the demand relates to action taken by virtue of paragraph 3(3), an appeal may be brought on the ground that reasonable progress was being made towards compliance with the improvement notice when the local housing authority gave notice under paragraph 4 of their intention to enter and take the action.

This does not affect the generality of sub-paragraph (1).

(5) The tribunal may, on an appeal, make such order confirming, quashing or varying the demand as it considers appropriate.

(6) A demand against which an appeal is brought becomes operative as follows –

  (a) if a decision is given on the appeal which confirms the demand and the period within which an appeal to the Lands Tribunal may be brought expires without such an appeal having been brought, the demand becomes operative at end of that period;
  (b) if an appeal to the Lands Tribunal is brought and a decision is given on the appeal which confirms the demand, the demand becomes operative at the time of that decision.

(7) For the purposes of sub-paragraph (6) –

  (a) the withdrawal of an appeal has the same effect as a decision which confirms the demand, and
  (b) references to a decision which confirms the demand are to a decision which confirms it with or without variation.

(8) No question may be raised on appeal under this paragraph which might have been raised on an appeal against the improvement notice.

Expenses and interest recoverable from occupiers

12 (1) Where a demand becomes operative by virtue of paragraph 9(2) or 11(6), the local housing authority may serve a recovery notice on any person –

(a) who occupies the premises concerned, or part of those premises, as the tenant or licensee of the person on whom the demand was served under paragraph 9(1); and

(b) who, by virtue of his tenancy or licence, pays rent or any sum in the nature of rent to the person on whom the demand was served.

(2) A recovery notice is a notice –

(a) stating the amount of expenses recoverable by the local housing authority; and

(b) requiring all future payments by the tenant or licensee of rent or sums in the nature of rent (whether already accrued due or not) to be made direct to the authority until the expenses recoverable by the authority, together with any accrued interest on them, have been duly paid.

(3) In the case of a demand which was served on any person as agent or trustee for another person ('the principal'), sub-paragraph (1) has effect as if the references in paragraphs (a) and (b) to the person on whom the demand was served were references to that person or the principal.

(4) The effect of a recovery notice, once served under sub-paragraph (1), is to transfer to the local housing authority the right to recover, receive and give a discharge for the rent or sums in the nature of rent.

(5) This is subject to any direction to the contrary contained in a further notice served by the local housing authority on the tenant or licensee.

(6) In addition, the right to recover, receive and give a discharge for any rent or sums in the nature of rent is postponed to any right in respect of that rent or those sums which may at any time be vested in a superior landlord by virtue of a notice under section 6 of the Law of Distress Amendment Act 1908 (c 53).

Expenses and interest to be a charge on the premises

13 (1) Until recovered, the expenses recoverable by the local housing authority, together with any accrued interest on them, are a charge on the premises to which the improvement notice related.

(2) The charge takes effect when the demand for the expenses and interest becomes operative by virtue of paragraph 9(2) or 11(6).

(3) For the purpose of enforcing the charge, the local housing authority have the same powers and remedies, under the Law of Property Act 1925 (c 20) and otherwise, as if they were mortgagees by deed having powers of sale and lease, of accepting surrenders of leases and of appointing a receiver.

(4) The power of appointing a receiver is exercisable at any time after the end of one month beginning with the date when the charge takes effect.

Recovery of expenses and interest from other persons profiting from taking of action

14 (1) Sub-paragraph (2) applies if, on an application to a residential property tribunal, the local housing authority satisfy the tribunal that –

(a) the expenses and interest have not been and are unlikely to be recovered; and

(b) a person is profiting by the taking of the action under paragraph 3 in respect of which the expenses were incurred in that he is obtaining rents or other payments which would not have been obtainable if the number of persons living in the premises was limited to that appropriate for the premises in their state before the action was taken.

(2) The tribunal may, if satisfied that the person concerned has had proper notice of the application, order him to make such payments to the local housing authority as the tribunal considers to be just.

SCHEDULE 4
LICENCES UNDER PARTS 2 AND 3: MANDATORY CONDITIONS

Sections 67 and 90

Conditions to be included in licences under Part 2 or 3

1 (1) A licence under Part 2 or 3 must include the following conditions.

(2) Conditions requiring the licence holder, if gas is supplied to the house, to produce to the local housing authority annually for their inspection a gas safety certificate obtained in respect of the house within the last 12 months.

(3) Conditions requiring the licence holder –

(a) to keep electrical appliances and furniture made available by him in the house in a safe condition;

(b) to supply the authority, on demand, with a declaration by him as to the safety of such appliances and furniture.

(4) Conditions requiring the licence holder –

(a) to ensure that smoke alarms are installed in the house and to keep them in proper working order;

(b) to supply the authority, on demand, with a declaration by him as to the condition and positioning of such alarms.

(5) Conditions requiring the licence holder to supply to the occupiers of the house a written statement of the terms on which they occupy it.

Additional conditions to be included in licences under Part 3

2 A licence under Part 3 must include conditions requiring the licence holder to demand references from persons who wish to occupy the house.

Power to prescribe conditions

3 The appropriate national authority may by regulations amend this Schedule so as to alter (by the addition or removal of conditions) the conditions which must be included –

(a) in a licence under Part 2 or 3, or

(b) only in a licence under one of those Parts.

Interpretation

4   In this Schedule 'the house' means the HMO or Part 3 house in respect of which the licence is granted.

SCHEDULE 5
LICENCES UNDER PARTS 2 AND 3: PROCEDURE AND APPEALS

Sections 71 and 94

Part 1
Procedure Relating to Grant or Refusal of Licences

Requirements before grant of licence

1   Before granting a licence, the local housing authority must –

   (a) serve a notice under this paragraph, together with a copy of the proposed licence, on the applicant for the licence and each relevant person, and

   (b) consider any representations made in accordance with the notice and not withdrawn.

2   The notice under paragraph 1 must state that the authority are proposing to grant the licence and set out –

   (a) the reasons for granting the licence,

   (b) the main terms of the licence, and

   (c) the end of the consultation period.

3   (1) This paragraph applies if, having considered representations made in accordance with a notice under paragraph 1 or this paragraph, the local housing authority propose to grant a licence with modifications.

(2) Before granting the licence the authority must –

   (a) serve a notice under this paragraph on the applicant for the licence and each relevant person, and

   (b) consider any representations made in accordance with the notice and not withdrawn.

4   The notice under paragraph 3 must set out –

   (a) the proposed modifications,

   (b) the reasons for them, and

   (c) the end of the consultation period.

Requirements before refusal to grant licence

5   Before refusing to grant a licence, the local housing authority must –

   (a) serve a notice under this paragraph on the applicant for the licence and each relevant person, and

   (b) consider any representations made in accordance with the notice and not withdrawn.

6   The notice under paragraph 5 must state that the local housing authority are proposing to refuse to grant the licence and set out –

   (a) the reasons for refusing to grant the licence, and

(b) the end of the consultation period.

Requirements following grant or refusal of licence

7   (1) This paragraph applies where the local housing authority decide to grant a licence.

(2) The local housing authority must serve on the applicant for the licence (and, if different, the licence holder) and each relevant person –

(a) a copy of the licence, and
(b) a notice setting out –
   (i) the reasons for deciding to grant the licence and the date on which the decision was made,
   (ii) the right of appeal against the decision under Part 3 of this Schedule, and
   (iii) the period within which an appeal may be made (see paragraph 33(1)).

(3) The documents required to be served under sub-paragraph (2) must be served within the period of seven days beginning with the day on which the decision is made.

8   (1) This paragraph applies where the local housing authority refuse to grant a licence.

(2) The local housing authority must serve on the applicant for the licence and each relevant person a notice setting out –

(a) the authority's decision not to grant the licence,
(b) the reasons for the decision and the date on which it was made,
(c) the right of appeal against the decision under Part 3 of this Schedule, and
(d) the period within which an appeal may be made (see paragraph 33(1)).

(3) The notices required to be served under sub-paragraph (2) must be served within the period of seven days beginning with the day on which the decision is made.

Exceptions from requirements in relation to grant or refusal of licences

9   The requirements of paragraph 3 (and those of paragraph 1) do not apply if the local housing authority –

(a) have already served a notice under paragraph 1 but not paragraph 3 in relation to the proposed licence, and
(b) consider that the modifications which are now being proposed are not material in any respect.

10   The requirements of paragraph 3 (and those of paragraph 1) do not apply if the local housing authority –

(a) have already served notices under paragraphs 1 and 3 in relation to the matter concerned, and
(b) consider that the further modifications which are now being proposed do not differ in any material respect from the modifications in relation to which a notice was last served under paragraph 3.

11   Paragraphs 5, 6 and 8 do not apply to a refusal to grant a licence on particular terms if the local housing authority are proposing to grant the licence on different terms.

Meaning of 'the end of the consultation period'

12   (1) In this Part of this Schedule 'the end of the consultation period' means the last day for making representations in respect of the matter in question.

(2) The end of the consultation period must be –

(a) in the case of a notice under paragraph 1 or 5, a day which is at least 14 days after the date of service of the notice; and
(b) in the case of a notice under paragraph 3, a day which is at least 7 days after the date of service of the notice.

(3) In sub-paragraph (2) 'the date of service' of a notice means, in a case where more than one notice is served, the date on which the last of the notices is served.

Meaning of 'licence' and 'relevant person'

13 (1) In this Part of this Schedule 'licence' means a licence under Part 2 or 3 of this Act.

(2) In this Part of this Schedule 'relevant person', in relation to a licence under Part 2 or 3 of this Act, means any person (other than a person excluded by sub-paragraph (3)) –

(a) who, to the knowledge of the local housing authority concerned, is –
    (i) a person having an estate or interest in the HMO or Part 3 house in question, or
    (ii) a person managing or having control of that HMO or Part 3 house (and not falling within sub-paragraph (i)), or
(b) on whom any restriction or obligation is or is to be imposed by the licence in accordance with section 67(5) or 90(6).

(3) The persons excluded by this sub-paragraph are –

(a) the applicant for the licence and (if different) the licence holder, and
(b) any tenant under a lease with an unexpired term of 3 years or less.

Part 2
Procedure Relating to Variation or Revocation of Licences

Variation of licences

14 Before varying a licence, the local housing authority must –

(a) serve a notice under this paragraph on the licence holder and each relevant person, and
(b) consider any representations made in accordance with the notice and not withdrawn.

15 The notice under paragraph 14 must state that the local housing authority are proposing to make the variation and set out –

(a) the effect of the variation,
(b) the reasons for the variation, and
(c) the end of the consultation period.

16 (1) This paragraph applies where the local housing authority decide to vary a licence.

(2) The local housing authority must serve on the licence holder and each relevant person –

(a) a copy of the authority's decision to vary the licence, and
(b) a notice setting out –
    (i)   the reasons for the decision and the date on which it was made,
    (ii) the right of appeal against the decision under Part 3 of this Schedule, and
    (iii) the period within which an appeal may be made (see paragraph 33(2)).

(3) The documents required to be served under sub-paragraph (2) must be served within the period of seven days beginning with the day on which the decision is made.

Exceptions from requirements of paragraph 14

17 The requirements of paragraph 14 do not apply if –

(a) the local housing authority consider that the variation is not material, or
(b) the variation is agreed by the licence holder and the local housing authority consider that it would not be appropriate to comply with the requirements of that paragraph.

18 The requirements of paragraph 14 do not apply if the local housing authority –

(a) have already served a notice under that paragraph in relation to a proposed variation, and
(b) consider that the variation which is now being proposed is not materially different from the previous proposed variation.

Refusal to vary a licence

19 Before refusing to vary a licence, the local housing authority must –

(a) serve a notice under this paragraph on the licence holder and each relevant person, and
(b) consider any representations made in accordance with the notice and not withdrawn.

20 The notice under paragraph 19 must state that the authority are proposing to refuse to vary the licence and set out –

(a) the reasons for refusing to vary the licence, and
(b) the end of the consultation period.

21 (1) This paragraph applies where the local housing authority refuse to vary a licence.

(2) The authority must serve on the licence holder and each relevant person a notice setting out –

(a) the authority's decision not to vary the licence,
(b) the reasons for the decision and the date on which it was made,
(c) the right of appeal against the decision under Part 3 of this Schedule, and
(d) the period within which an appeal may be made (see paragraph 33(2)).

(3) The documents required to be served under sub-paragraph (2) must be served within the period of seven days beginning with the day on which the decision is made.

Revocation of licences

22 Before revoking a licence, the local housing authority must –

(a) serve a notice on the licence holder under this paragraph and each relevant person, and
(b) consider any representations made in accordance with the notice and not withdrawn.

23 The notice under paragraph 22 must state that the authority are proposing to revoke the licence and set out –

(a) the reasons for the revocation, and
(b) the end of the consultation period.

24 (1) This paragraph applies where the local housing authority decide to revoke a licence.

(2) The authority must serve on the licence holder and each relevant person –

(a) a copy of the authority's decision to revoke the licence, and
(b) a notice setting out –
    (i) the reasons for the decision and the date on which it was made,

(ii) the right of appeal against the decision under Part 3 of this Schedule, and
(iii) the period within which an appeal may be made (see paragraph 33(2)).

(3) The documents required to be served under sub-paragraph (2) must be served within the period of seven days beginning with the day on which the decision is made.

Exception from requirements of paragraph 22

25   The requirements of paragraph 22 do not apply if the revocation is agreed by the licence holder and the local housing authority consider that it would not be appropriate to comply with the requirements of that paragraph.

Refusal to revoke a licence

26   Before refusing to revoke a licence, the local housing authority must –

(a) serve a notice under this paragraph on the licence holder and each relevant person, and
(b) consider any representations made in accordance with the notice and not withdrawn.

27   The notice under paragraph 26 must state that the authority are proposing to refuse to revoke the licence and set out –

(a) the reasons for refusing to revoke the licence, and
(b) the end of the consultation period.

28   (1) This paragraph applies where the local housing authority refuse to revoke a licence.

(2) The authority must serve on the licence holder and each relevant person a notice setting out –

(a) the authority's decision not to revoke the licence,
(b) the reasons for the decision and the date on which it was made,
(c) the right of appeal against the decision under Part 3 of this Schedule, and
(d) the period within which an appeal may be made (see paragraph 33(2)).

(3) The notices required to be served under sub-paragraph (2) must be served within the period of seven days beginning with the day on which the decision is made.

Meaning of 'the end of the consultation period'

29   (1) In this Part of this Schedule 'the end of the consultation period' means the last day on which representations may be made in respect of the matter in question.

(2) That date must be at least 14 days after the date of service of the notice in question.

(3) In sub-paragraph (2) 'the date of service' of a notice means, in a case where more than one notice is served, the date on which the last of the notices is served.

Meaning of 'licence' and 'relevant person'

30   (1) In this Part of this Schedule 'licence' means a licence under Part 2 or 3 of this Act.

(2) In this Part of this Schedule 'relevant person', in relation to a licence under Part 2 or 3 of this Act, means any person (other than a person excluded by sub-paragraph (3)) –

(a) who, to the knowledge of the local housing authority concerned, is –
(i) a person having an estate or interest in the HMO or Part 3 house in question, or
(ii) a person managing or having control of that HMO or Part 3 house (and not falling within sub-paragraph (i)), or

(b) on whom any restriction or obligation is or is to be imposed by the licence in accordance with section 67(5) or 90(6).

(3) The persons excluded by this sub-paragraph are –

(a) the licence holder, and
(b) any tenant under a lease with an unexpired term of 3 years or less.

Part 3
Appeals against Licence Decisions

Right to appeal against refusal or grant of licence

31 (1) The applicant or any relevant person may appeal to a residential property tribunal against a decision by the local housing authority on an application for a licence –

(a) to refuse to grant the licence, or
(b) to grant the licence.

(2) An appeal under sub-paragraph (1)(b) may, in particular, relate to any of the terms of the licence.

Right to appeal against decision or refusal to vary or revoke licence

32 (1) The licence holder or any relevant person may appeal to a residential property tribunal against a decision by the local housing authority –

(a) to vary or revoke a licence, or
(b) to refuse to vary or revoke a licence.

(2) But this does not apply to the licence holder in a case where the decision to vary or revoke the licence was made with his agreement.

Time limits for appeals

33 (1) Any appeal under paragraph 31 against a decision to grant, or (as the case may be) to refuse to grant, a licence must be made within the period of 28 days beginning with the date specified in the notice under paragraph 7 or 8 as the date on which the decision was made.

(2) Any appeal under paragraph 32 against a decision to vary or revoke, or (as the case may be) to refuse to vary or revoke, a licence must be made within the period of 28 days beginning with the date specified in the notice under paragraph 16, 21, 24 or 28 as the date on which the decision was made.

(3) A residential property tribunal may allow an appeal to be made to it after the end of the period mentioned in sub-paragraph (1) or (2) if it is satisfied that there is a good reason for the failure to appeal before the end of that period (and for any delay since then in applying for permission to appeal out of time).

Powers of residential property tribunal hearing appeal

34 (1) This paragraph applies to appeals to a residential property tribunal under paragraph 31 or 32.

(2) An appeal –

   (a) is to be by way of a re-hearing, but

   (b) may be determined having regard to matters of which the authority were unaware.

(3) The tribunal may confirm, reverse or vary the decision of the local housing authority.

(4) On an appeal under paragraph 31 the tribunal may direct the authority to grant a licence to the applicant for the licence on such terms as the tribunal may direct.

'The operative time' for the purposes of section 69(6), 70(8), 92(3) or 93(5)

35   (1) This paragraph defines 'the operative time' for the purposes of –

   (a) section 69(6) or 70(8) (variation or revocation of licence under Part 2 of this Act), or

   (b) section 92(3) or 93(5) (variation or revocation of licence under Part 3 of this Act).

(2) If the period of 28 days mentioned in paragraph 33(2) has expired without an appeal having been made under paragraph 32, 'the operative time' is the end of that period.

(3) If an appeal is made under paragraph 32 within that period and a decision is given on the appeal which confirms the variation or revocation, 'the operative time' is as follows –

   (a) if the period within which an appeal to the Lands Tribunal may be brought expires without such an appeal having been brought, 'the operative time' is the end of that period;

   (b) if an appeal to the Lands Tribunal is brought, 'the operative time' is the time when a decision is given on the appeal which confirms the variation or revocation.

(4) For the purposes of sub-paragraph (3) –

   (a) the withdrawal of an appeal has the same effect as a decision confirming the variation or revocation appealed against; and

   (b) references to a decision which confirms a variation are to a decision which confirms it with or without variation.

Meaning of 'licence' and 'relevant person'

36   (1) In this Part of this Schedule 'licence' means a licence under Part 2 or 3 of this Act.

(2) In this Part of this Schedule 'relevant person', in relation to a licence under Part 2 or 3 of this Act, means any person (other than a person excluded by sub-paragraph (3)) –

   (a) who is –

      (i)   a person having an estate or interest in the HMO or Part 3 house concerned, or

      (ii) a person managing or having control of that HMO or Part 3 house (and not falling within sub-paragraph (i)), or

   (b) on whom any restriction or obligation is or is to be imposed by the licence in accordance with section 67(5) or 90(6).

(3) The persons excluded by this sub-paragraph are –

   (a) the applicant for the licence and (if different) the licence holder, and

   (b) any tenant under a lease with an unexpired term of 3 years or less.

SCHEDULE 6
Management Orders: Procedure and Appeals

Section 123

Part 1

Procedure Relating to Making of Management Orders

Requirements before making final management order

1   Before making a final management order, the local housing authority must –

   (a) serve a copy of the proposed order, together with a notice under this paragraph, on each relevant person; and

   (b) consider any representations made in accordance with the notice and not withdrawn.

2   The notice under paragraph 1 must state that the authority are proposing to make a final management order and set out –

   (a) the reasons for making the order;

   (b) the main terms of the proposed order (including those of the management scheme to be contained in it); and

   (c) the end of the consultation period.

3   (1) This paragraph applies if, having considered representations made in accordance with a notice under paragraph 1 or this paragraph, the local housing authority propose to make a final management order with modifications.

(2) Before making the order, the authority must –

   (a) serve a notice under this paragraph on each relevant person; and

   (b) consider any representations made in accordance with the notice and not withdrawn.

4   The notice under paragraph 3 must set out –

   (a) the proposed modifications;

   (b) the reasons for them; and

   (c) the end of the consultation period.

Exceptions from requirements relating to making of final management order

5   The requirements of paragraph 3 (and those of paragraph 1) do not apply if the local housing authority –

   (a) have already served notice under paragraph 1 but not paragraph 3 in relation to the proposed final management order; and

   (b) consider that the modifications which are now being proposed are not material in any respect.

6   The requirements of paragraph 3 (and those of paragraph 1) do not apply if the local housing authority –

   (a) have already served notices under paragraphs 1 and 3 in relation to the matter concerned; and

   (b) consider that the further modifications which are now being proposed do not differ in any material respect from the modifications in relation to which a notice was last served under paragraph 3.

Requirements following making of interim or final management order

7 (1) This paragraph applies where the local housing authority make an interim management order or a final management order.

(2) As soon as practicable after the order is made, the authority must serve on the occupiers of the house –

    (a) a copy of the order, and
    (b) a notice under this sub-paragraph.

(3) Those documents are to be regarded as having been served on the occupiers if they are fixed to a conspicuous part of the house.

(4) The notice under sub-paragraph (2) must set out –

    (a) the reasons for making the order and the date on which it was made,
    (b) the general effect of the order, and
    (c) the date on which the order is to cease to have effect in accordance with section 105(4) and (5) or 114(3) and (4) (or, if applicable, how the date mentioned in section 105(6) is to be determined),

and (if it is a final management order) give a general description of the way in which the house is to be managed by the authority in accordance with the management scheme contained in the order.

(5) The authority must also serve a copy of the order, together with a notice under this sub-paragraph, on each relevant person.

(6) The notice under sub-paragraph (5) must comply with sub-paragraph (4) and also contain information about –

    (a) the right of appeal against the order under Part 3 of this Schedule, and
    (b) the period within which any such appeal may be made (see paragraph 25(2)).

(7) The documents required to be served on each relevant person under sub-paragraph (5) must be served within the period of seven days beginning with the day on which the order is made.

Meaning of 'the end of the consultation period' and 'relevant person'

8 (1) In this Part of this Schedule 'the end of the consultation period' means the last day for making representations in respect of the matter in question.

(2) The end of the consultation period must be –

    (a) in the case of a notice under paragraph 1, a day which is at least 14 days after the date of service of the notice; and
    (b) in the case of a notice under paragraph 3, a day which is at least 7 days after the date of service of the notice.

(3) In sub-paragraph (2) 'the date of service' of a notice means, in a case where more than one notice is served, the date on which the last of the notices is served.

(4) In this Part of this Schedule 'relevant person' means any person who, to the knowledge of the local housing authority, is –

    (a) a person having an estate or interest in the house or part of it (but who is not a tenant under a lease with an unexpired term of 3 years or less), or
    (b) any other person who (but for the order) would be a person managing or having control of the house or part of it.

Part 2
Procedure Relating to Variation or Revocation of Management Orders

Variation of management orders

9 Before varying an interim or final management order, the local housing authority must –

(a) serve a notice under this paragraph on each relevant person, and
(b) consider any representations made in accordance with the notice and not withdrawn.

10 The notice under paragraph 9 must state that the authority are proposing to make the variation and specify –

(a) the effect of the variation,
(b) the reasons for the variation, and
(c) the end of the consultation period.

11 (1) This paragraph applies where the local housing authority decide to vary an interim or final management order.

(2) The local housing authority must serve on each relevant person –

(a) a copy of the authority's decision to vary the order, and
(b) a notice setting out –
    (i) the reasons for the decision and the date on which it was made,
    (ii) the right of appeal against the decision under Part 3 of this Schedule, and
    (iii) the period within which an appeal may be made (see paragraph 29(2)).

(3) The documents required to be served on each relevant person under sub-paragraph (2) must be served within the period of seven days beginning with the day on which the decision is made.

Exceptions from requirements of paragraph 9

12 The requirements of paragraph 9 do not apply if the local housing authority consider that the variation is not material.

13 The requirements of paragraph9 do not apply if the local housing authority –

(a) have already served a notice under that paragraph in relation to a proposed variation; and
(b) consider that the variation which is now being proposed is not materially different from the previous proposed variation.

Refusal to vary interim or final management order

14 Before refusing to vary an interim or final management order, the local housing authority must –

(a) serve a notice under this paragraph on each relevant person, and
(b) consider any representations made in accordance with the notice and not withdrawn.

15 The notice under paragraph 14 must state that the authority are proposing to refuse to make the variation and set out –

(a) the reasons for refusing to make the variation, and
(b) the end of the consultation period.

16 (1) This paragraph applies where the local housing authority refuse to vary an interim or final management order.

(2) The authority must serve on each relevant person a notice setting out –

(a) the authority's decision not to vary the order;
(b) the reasons for the decision and the date on which it was made;
(c) the right of appeal against the decision under Part 3 of this Schedule; and
(d) the period within which an appeal may be made (see paragraph 29(2)).

(3) The notices required to be served on each relevant person under sub-paragraph (2) must be served within the period of seven days beginning with the day on which the decision is made.

Revocation of management orders

17 Before revoking an interim or final management order, the local housing authority must –

(a) serve a notice under this paragraph on each relevant person, and
(b) consider any representations made in accordance with the notice and not withdrawn.

18 The notice under paragraph 17 must state that the authority are proposing to revoke the order and specify –

(a) the reasons for the revocation, and
(b) the end of the consultation period.

19 (1) This paragraph applies where the local housing authority decide to revoke an interim or final management order.

(2) The authority must serve on each relevant person –

(a) a copy of the authority's decision to revoke the order; and
(b) a notice setting out –
　(i)　the reasons for the decision and the date on which it was made;
　(ii)　the right of appeal against the decision under Part 3 of this Schedule; and
　(iii)　the period within which an appeal may be made (see paragraph 29(2)).

(3) The documents required to be served on each relevant person under sub-paragraph (2) must be served within the period of seven days beginning with the day on which the decision is made.

Refusal to revoke management order

20 Before refusing to revoke an interim or final management order, the local housing authority must –

(a) serve a notice under this paragraph on each relevant person; and
(b) consider any representations made in accordance with the notice and not withdrawn.

21 The notice under paragraph 20 must state that the authority are proposing to refuse to revoke the order and set out –

(a) the reasons for refusing to revoke the order, and
(b) the end of the consultation period.

22 (1) This paragraph applies where the local housing authority refuse to revoke an interim or final management order.

(2) The authority must serve on each relevant person a notice setting out –

(a) the authority's decision not to revoke the order;
(b) the reasons for the decision and the date on which it was made;

(c) the right of appeal against the decision under Part 3 of this Schedule; and

(d) the period within which an appeal may be made (see paragraph 29(2)).

(3) The notices required to be served on each relevant person under sub-paragraph (2) must be served within the period of seven days beginning with the day on which the decision is made.

Meaning of 'the end of the consultation period' and 'relevant person'

23 (1) In this Part of this Schedule 'the end of the consultation period' means the last day for making representations in respect of the matter in question.

(2) The end of the consultation period must be a day which is at least 14 days after the date of service of the notice.

(3) In sub-paragraph (2) 'the date of service' of a notice means, in a case where more than one notice is served, the date on which the last of the notices is served.

(4) In this Part of this Schedule 'relevant person' means any person who, to the knowledge of the local housing authority, is –

(a) a person having an estate or interest in the house or part of it (but who is not a tenant under a lease with an unexpired term of 3 years or less), or

(b) any other person who (but for the order) would be a person managing or having control of the house or part of it.

Part 3
Appeals Against Decisions Relating to Management Orders

Right to appeal against making of order etc

24 (1) A relevant person may appeal to a residential property tribunal against –

(a) a decision of the local housing authority to make an interim or final management order, or

(b) the terms of such an order (including, if it is a final management order, those of the management scheme contained in it).

(2) Except to the extent that an appeal may be made in accordance with sub-paragraphs (3) and (4), sub-paragraph (1) does not apply to an interim management order made under section 102(4) or (7) or in accordance with a direction given under paragraph 26(5).

(3) An appeal may be made under sub-paragraph (1)(b) on the grounds that the terms of an interim management order do not provide for one or both of the matters mentioned in section 110(5)(a) and (b) (which relate to payments of surplus rent etc).

(4) Where an appeal is made under sub-paragraph (1)(b) only on those grounds –

(a) the appeal may be brought at any time while the order is in force (with the result that nothing in sub-paragraph (5) or paragraph 25 applies in relation to the appeal); and

(b) the powers of the residential property tribunal under paragraph 26 are limited to determining whether the order should be varied by the tribunal so as to include a term providing for the matter or matters in question, and (if so) what provision should be made by the term.

(5) If no appeal is brought against an interim or final management order under this paragraph within the time allowed by paragraph 25 for making such an appeal, the order is final and conclusive as to the matters which could have been raised on appeal.

Time limits for appeals under paragraph 24

25   (1) This paragraph applies in relation to an appeal under paragraph 24 in respect of an interim or final management order.

(2) Any such appeal must be made within the period of 28 days beginning with the date specified in the notice under paragraph 7(5) as the date on which the order was made.

(3) A residential property tribunal may allow an appeal to be made to it after the end of the period mentioned in sub-paragraph (2) if it is satisfied that there is a good reason for the failure to appeal before the end of that period (and for any delay since then in applying for permission to appeal out of time).

Powers of residential property tribunal on appeal under paragraph 24

26   (1) This paragraph applies to an appeal to a residential property tribunal under paragraph 24 in respect of an interim or final management order.

(2) The appeal –

   (a) is to be by way of a re-hearing, but
   (b) may be determined having regard to matters of which the authority were unaware.

(3) The tribunal may confirm or vary the order or revoke it –

   (a) (in the case of an interim management order) as from a date specified in the tribunal's order, or
   (b) (in the case of a final management order) as from the date of the tribunal's order.

(4) If –

   (a) the tribunal revokes an interim or final management order,
   (b) it appears to the tribunal that, on the revocation of the order, the house will be required to be licensed under Part 2 or 3 of this Act, and
   (c) the tribunal does not give a direction under sub-paragraph (5) or (6),

the tribunal must direct the local housing authority to grant such a licence to such person and on such terms as the tribunal may direct.

(5) If the tribunal revokes a final management order, the tribunal may direct the local housing authority to make an interim management order in respect of the house or part of it on such terms as the tribunal may direct.

This applies despite section 102(9).

(6) If the tribunal revokes a final management order, the tribunal may direct the local housing authority to serve a temporary exemption notice under section 62 or 86 in respect of the house that comes into force on such date as the tribunal directs.

(7) The revocation of an interim management order by the tribunal does not affect the validity of anything previously done in pursuance of the order.

'The operative time' for the purposes of section 114(2)

27   (1) This paragraph defines 'the operative time' for the purposes of section 114(2).

(2) If no appeal is made under paragraph 24 before the end of the period of 28 days mentioned in paragraph 25(2), 'the operative time' is the end of that period.

(3) If an appeal is made under paragraph 24 before the end of that period, and a decision is given on the appeal which confirms the order, 'the operative time' is as follows –

(a) if the period within which an appeal to the Lands Tribunal may be brought expires without such an appeal having been brought, 'the operative time' is the end of that period;
(b) if an appeal to the Lands Tribunal is brought, 'the operative time' is the time when a decision is given on the appeal which confirms the order.

(4) For the purposes of sub-paragraph (3) –

(a) the withdrawal of an appeal has the same effect as a decision which confirms the order, and
(b) references to a decision which confirms the order are to a decision which confirms it with or without variation.

Right to appeal against decision or refusal to vary or revoke interim management order

28 A relevant person may appeal to a residential property tribunal against –

(a) a decision of a local housing authority to vary or revoke an interim or final management order, or
(b) a refusal of a local housing authority to vary or revoke an interim or final management order.

Time limits for appeals under paragraph 28

29 (1) This paragraph applies in relation to an appeal under paragraph 28 against a decision to vary or revoke, or (as the case may be) to refuse to vary or revoke, an interim or final management order.

(2) Any such appeal must be made before the end of the period of 28 days beginning with the date specified in the notice under paragraph 11, 16, 19 or 22 as the date on which the decision concerned was made.

(3) A residential property tribunal may allow an appeal to be made to it after the end of the period mentioned in sub-paragraph (2) if it is satisfied that there is a good reason for the failure to appeal before the end of that period (and for any delay since then in applying for permission to appeal out of time).

Powers of residential property tribunal on appeal under paragraph 28

30 (1) This paragraph applies to an appeal to a residential property tribunal under paragraph 28 against a decision to vary or revoke, or (as the case may be) to refuse to vary or revoke, an interim or final management order.

(2) Paragraph 26(2) applies to such an appeal as it applies to an appeal under paragraph 24.

(3) The tribunal may confirm, reverse or vary the decision of the local housing authority.

(4) If the appeal is against a decision of the authority to refuse to revoke the order, the tribunal may make an order revoking the order as from a date specified in its order.

'The operative time' for the purposes of section 111(2), 112(2), 121(2) or 122(2)

31 (1) This paragraph defines 'the operative time' for the purposes of –

(a) section 111(2) or 112(2) (variation or revocation of interim management order), or
(b) section 121(2) or 122(2) (variation or revocation of final management order).

(2) If no appeal is made under paragraph 28 before the end of the period of 28 days mentioned in paragraph 29(2), 'the operative time' is the end of that period.

(3) If an appeal is made under paragraph 28 within that period, and a decision is given on the appeal which confirms the variation or revocation, 'the operative time' is as follows –

(a) if the period within which an appeal to the Lands Tribunal may be brought expires without such an appeal having been brought, 'the operative time' is the end of that period;

(b) if an appeal to the Lands Tribunal is brought, 'the operative time' is the time when a decision is given on the appeal which confirms the variation or revocation.

(4) For the purposes of sub-paragraph (3) –

(a) the withdrawal of an appeal has the same effect as a decision which confirms the variation or revocation appealed against; and

(b) references to a decision which confirms a variation are to a decision which confirms it with or without variation.

Right to appeal against decision in respect of compensation payable to third parties

32   (1) This paragraph applies where a local housing authority have made a decision under section 128 as to whether compensation should be paid to a third party in respect of any interference with his rights in consequence of an interim or final management order.

(2) The third party may appeal to a residential property tribunal against –

(a) a decision by the authority not to pay compensation to him, or

(b) a decision of the authority so far as relating to the amount of compensation that should be paid.

Time limits for appeals under paragraph 32

33   (1) This paragraph applies in relation to an appeal under paragraph 32 against a decision of a local housing authority not to pay compensation to a third party or as to the amount of compensation to be paid.

(2) Any such appeal must be made within the period of 28 days beginning with the date the authority notifies the third party under section 128(2).

(3) A residential property tribunal may allow an appeal to be made to it after the end of the period mentioned in sub-paragraph (2) if it is satisfied that there is good reason for the failure to appeal before the end of that period (and for any delay since then in applying for permission to appeal out of time).

Powers of residential property tribunal on appeal under paragraph 32

34   (1) This paragraph applies in relation to an appeal under paragraph 32 against a decision of a local housing authority not to pay compensation to a third party or as to the amount of compensation to be paid.

(2) The appeal –

(a) is to be by way of re-hearing, but

(b) may be determined having regard to matters of which the authority were unaware.

(3) The tribunal may confirm, reverse or vary the decision of the local housing authority.

(4) Where the tribunal reverses or varies a decision of the authority in respect of a final management order, it must make an order varying the management scheme contained in the final management order accordingly.

Meaning of 'relevant person'

35 In this Part of this Schedule 'relevant person' means –

(a) any person who has an estate or interest in the house or part of it (but is not a tenant under a lease with an unexpired term of 3 years or less), or

(b) any other person who (but for the order) would be a person managing or having control of the house or part of it.

SCHEDULE 7
FURTHER PROVISIONS REGARDING EMPTY DWELLING MANAGEMENT ORDERS

Section 132

Part 1
Interim EDMOs

Operation of interim EDMOs

1 (1) This paragraph deals with the time when an interim EDMO comes into force or ceases to have effect.

(2) The order comes into force when it is made.

(3) The order ceases to have effect at the end of the period of 12 months beginning with the date on which it is made, unless it ceases to have effect at some other time as mentioned below.

(4) If the order provides that it is to cease to have effect on a date falling before the end of that period, it accordingly ceases to have effect on that date.

(5) Sub-paragraphs (6) and (7) apply where –

(a) a final EDMO ('the final EDMO') has been made under section 136 so as to replace the order ('the interim EDMO'), but

(b) the final EDMO has not come into force because of an appeal to a residential property tribunal under paragraph 26 against the making of the final EDMO.

(6) If the date on which the final EDMO comes into force in relation to the dwelling following the disposal of the appeal is later than the date on which the interim EDMO would cease to have effect apart from this sub-paragraph, the interim EDMO continues in force until that later date.

(7) If, on the application of the authority, the tribunal makes an order providing for the interim EDMO to continue in force, pending the disposal of the appeal, until a date later than that on which the interim EDMO would cease to have effect apart from this sub-paragraph, the interim EDMO accordingly continues in force until that later date.

(8) This paragraph has effect subject to paragraphs 6 and 7 (variation or revocation of orders by authority) and to the power of revocation exercisable by a residential property tribunal on an appeal made under paragraph 30.

General effect of interim EDMOs

2 (1) This paragraph applies while an interim EDMO is in force in relation to a dwelling.

(2) The rights and powers conferred by sub-paragraph (3) are exercisable by the authority in performing their duties under section 135(1) to (3) in respect of the dwelling.

(3) The authority –

- (a) have the right to possession of the dwelling (subject to the rights of existing occupiers preserved by paragraph 18(3));
- (b) have the right to do (and authorise a manager or other person to do) in relation to the dwelling anything which the relevant proprietor of the dwelling would (but for the order) be entitled to do;
- (c) may create one or more of the following –
    - (i) an interest in the dwelling which, as far as possible, has all the incidents of a leasehold, or
    - (ii) a right in the nature of a licence to occupy part of the dwelling;
- (d) may apply to a residential property tribunal for an order under paragraph 22 determining a lease or licence of the dwelling.

(4) But the authority may not under sub-paragraph (3)(c) create any interest or right in the nature of a lease or licence unless –

- (a) consent in writing has been given by the relevant proprietor of the dwelling, and
- (b) where the relevant proprietor is a lessee under a lease of the dwelling, the interest or right is created for a term that is less than the term of that lease.

(5) The authority –

- (a) do not under this paragraph acquire any estate or interest in the dwelling, and
- (b) accordingly are not entitled by virtue of this paragraph to sell, lease, charge or make any other disposition of any such estate or interest.

(6) But, where the relevant proprietor of the dwelling is a lessee under a lease of the dwelling, the authority are to be treated (subject to sub-paragraph (5)(a)) as if they were the lessee instead.

(7) Any enactment or rule of law relating to landlords and tenants or leases applies in relation to –

- (a) a lease in relation to which the authority are to be treated as the lessee under sub-paragraph (6), or
- (b) a lease to which the authority become a party under paragraph 4(2),

as if the authority were the legal owner of the premises (but this is subject to paragraph 4(4) to (6)).

(8) None of the following, namely –

- (a) the authority, or
- (b) any person authorised under sub-paragraph (3)(b),

is liable to any person having an estate or interest in the dwelling for anything done or omitted to be done in the performance (or intended performance) of the authority's duties under section 135(1) to (3) unless the act or omission is due to negligence of the authority or any such person.

(9) An interim EDMO which has come into force is a local land charge.

(10) The authority may apply to the Chief Land Registrar for the entry of an appropriate restriction in the register of title in respect of such an order.

(11) In this paragraph 'enactment' includes an enactment comprised in subordinate legislation (within the meaning of the Interpretation Act 1978 (c 30)).

General effect of interim EDMOs: leases and licences granted by authority

3 (1) This paragraph applies in relation to any interest or right created by the authority under paragraph 2(3)(c).

(2) For the purposes of any enactment or rule of law –

(a) any interest created by the authority under paragraph 2(3)(c)(i) is to be treated as if it were a legal lease, and

(b) any right created by the authority under paragraph 2(3)(c)(ii) is to be treated as if it were a licence to occupy granted by the legal owner of the dwelling,

despite the fact that the authority have no legal estate in the dwelling (see paragraph 2(5)(a)).

(3) Any enactment or rule of law relating to landlords and tenants or leases accordingly applies in relation to any interest created by the authority under paragraph 2(3)(c)(i) as if the authority were the legal owner of the dwelling.

(4) References to leases and licences –

(a) in this Chapter, and

(b) in any other enactment,

accordingly include (where the context permits) interests and rights created by the authority under paragraph 2(3)(c).

(5) The preceding provisions of this paragraph have effect subject to –

(a) paragraph 4(4) to (6), and

(b) any provision to the contrary contained in an order made by the appropriate national authority.

(6) In paragraph 2(5)(b) the reference to leasing does not include the creation of interests under paragraph 2(3)(c)(i).

(7) In this paragraph –

'enactment' has the meaning given by paragraph 2(11);

'legal lease' means a term of years absolute (within section 1(1)(b) of the Law of Property Act 1925 (c 20)).

General effect of interim EDMOs: relevant proprietor, mortgagees etc

4 (1) This paragraph applies in relation to –

(a) the relevant proprietor, and

(b) other persons with an estate or interest in the dwelling,

while an interim EDMO is in force in relation to a dwelling.

(2) Where the relevant proprietor is a lessor or licensor under a lease or licence of the dwelling, the lease or licence has effect while the order is in force as if the local housing authority were substituted in it for the lessor or licensor.

(3) Such a lease continues to have effect, as far as possible, as a lease despite the fact that the rights of the local housing authority, as substituted for the lessor, do not amount to an estate in law in the dwelling.

(4) The provisions mentioned in sub-paragraph (5) do not apply to a lease or licence within sub-paragraph (2).

(5) The provisions are –

(a) the provisions which exclude local authority lettings from the Rent Acts, namely –
    (i) sections 14 to 16 of the Rent Act 1977 (c 42), and
    (ii) those sections as applied by Schedule 2 to the Rent (Agriculture) Act 1976 (c 80) and section 5(2) to (4) of that Act; and
(b) section 1(2) of, and paragraph 12 of Part 1 of Schedule 1 to, the Housing Act 1988 (c 50) (which exclude local authority lettings from Part 1 of that Act).

(6) Nothing in this Chapter has the result that the authority are to be treated as the legal owner of any premises for the purposes of –

(a) section 80 of the Housing Act 1985 (c 68) (the landlord condition for secure tenancies); or
(b) section 124 of the Housing Act 1996 (c 52) (introductory tenancies).

(7) The relevant proprietor of the dwelling –

(a) is not entitled to receive any rents or other payments made in respect of occupation of the dwelling;
(b) may not exercise any rights or powers with respect to the management of the dwelling; and
(c) may not create any of the following –
    (i) any leasehold interest in the dwelling or a part of it (other than a lease of a reversion), or
    (ii) any licence or other right to occupy it.

(8) However (subject to sub-paragraph (7)(c)) nothing in paragraph 2 or this paragraph affects the ability of a person having an estate or interest in the dwelling to make any disposition of that estate or interest.

(9) Nothing in paragraph 2 or this paragraph affects –

(a) the validity of any mortgage relating to the dwelling or any rights or remedies available to the mortgagee under such a mortgage, or
(b) the validity of any lease of the dwelling under which the relevant proprietor is a lessee, or any superior lease, or (subject to paragraph 2(6)) any rights or remedies available to the lessor under such a lease,

except to the extent that any of those rights or remedies would prevent the local housing authority from exercising their power under paragraph 2(3)(c).

(10) In proceedings for the enforcement of any such rights or remedies the court may make such order as it thinks fit as regards the operation of the interim EDMO (including an order quashing it).

Financial arrangements while order is in force

5 (1) This paragraph applies to relevant expenditure of a local housing authority who have made an interim EDMO.

(2) 'Relevant expenditure' means –

(a) expenditure incurred by the authority with the consent of the relevant proprietor, or
(b) any other expenditure reasonably incurred by the authority,

in connection with performing their duties under section 135(1) to (3) in respect of the dwelling (including any premiums paid for insurance of the premises).

(3) Rent or other payments which the authority have collected or recovered, by virtue of this Chapter, from persons occupying or having the right to occupy the dwelling may be used by the authority to meet –

(a) relevant expenditure, and
(b) any amounts of compensation payable to a third party by virtue of an order under section 134(4) or 138(2) or to a dispossessed landlord or tenant by virtue of an order under paragraph 22(5).

(4) The authority must pay to the relevant proprietor –

(a) any amount of rent or other payments collected or recovered as mentioned in sub-paragraph (3) that remains after deductions to meet relevant expenditure and any amounts of compensation payable as mentioned in that sub-paragraph, and
(b) (where appropriate) interest on that amount at a reasonable rate fixed by the authority,

and such payments are to be made at such intervals as the authority consider appropriate.

(5) The interim EDMO may provide for –

(a) the rate of interest which is to apply for the purposes of paragraph (b) of sub-paragraph (4); and
(b) the intervals at which payments are to be made under that sub-paragraph.

Paragraph 26(1)(c) enables an appeal to be brought where the order does not provide for both of those matters.

(6) The authority must –

(a) keep full accounts of their income and expenditure in respect of the dwelling; and
(b) afford to the relevant proprietor, and to any other person who has an estate or interest in the dwelling, all reasonable facilities for inspecting, taking copies of and verifying those accounts.

(7) The relevant proprietor may apply to a residential property tribunal for an order –

(a) declaring that an amount shown in the accounts as expenditure of the authority does not constitute relevant expenditure (see sub-paragraph (2));
(b) requiring the authority to make such financial adjustments (in the accounts and otherwise) as are necessary to reflect the tribunal's declaration.

(8) In this paragraph –

'dispossessed landlord or tenant' means a person who was a lessor, lessee, licensor or licensee under a lease or licence determined by an order under paragraph 22;

'expenditure' includes administrative costs.

Variation or revocation of interim EDMOs

6 (1) The local housing authority may vary an interim EDMO if they consider it appropriate to do so.

(2) A variation does not come into force until such time, if any, as is the operative time for the purposes of this sub-paragraph under paragraph 33 (time when period for appealing expires without an appeal being made or when decision to vary is confirmed on appeal).

(3) The power to vary an order under this paragraph is exercisable by the authority either –

(a) on an application made by a relevant person, or
(b) on the authority's own initiative.

(4) In this paragraph 'relevant person' means any person who has an estate or interest in the dwelling (other than a person who is a tenant under a lease granted under paragraph 2(3)(c)).

7   (1) The local housing authority may revoke an interim EDMO in the following cases –

(a) where the authority conclude that there are no steps which they could appropriately take for the purpose of securing that the dwelling is occupied (see section 135(4));
(b) where the authority are satisfied that –
  (i)   the dwelling will either become or continue to be occupied, despite the order being revoked, or
  (ii) that the dwelling is to be sold;
(c) where a final EDMO has been made by the authority in respect of the dwelling so as to replace the order;
(d) where the authority conclude that it would be appropriate to revoke the order in order to prevent or stop interference with the rights of a third party in consequence of the order; and
(e) where in any other circumstances the authority consider it appropriate to revoke the order.

(2) But, in a case where the dwelling is occupied, the local housing authority may not revoke an interim EDMO under sub-paragraph (1)(b), (d) or (e) unless the relevant proprietor consents.

(3) A revocation does not come into force until such time, if any, as is the operative time for the purposes of this sub-paragraph under paragraph 33 (time when period for appealing expires without an appeal being made or when decision to revoke is confirmed on appeal).

(4) The power to revoke an order under this paragraph is exercisable by the authority either –

(a) on an application made by a relevant person, or
(b) on the authority's own initiative.

(5) Where a relevant person applies to the authority for the revocation of an order under this paragraph, the authority may refuse to revoke the order unless the relevant proprietor (or some other person) agrees to pay to the authority any deficit such as is mentioned in paragraph 23(4).

(6) In this paragraph 'relevant person' means any person who has an estate or interest in the dwelling (other than a person who is a tenant under a lease granted under paragraph 2(3)(c)).

8   (1) Part 2 of Schedule 6 applies in relation to the variation or revocation of an interim EDMO as it applies in relation to the variation or revocation of an interim management order.

(2) But Part 2 of that Schedule so applies as if –

(a) references to the right of appeal under Part 3 of the Schedule and to paragraph 29(2) were to the right of appeal under Part 4 of this Schedule and to paragraph 31(2) of this Schedule, and
(b) paragraph 23(4) defined 'relevant person' as any person who, to the knowledge of the local housing authority, is a person having an estate or interest in the dwelling (other than a person who is a tenant under a lease granted under paragraph 2(3)(c) of this Schedule).

Part 2
Final EDMOs

Operation of final EDMOs

9 (1) This paragraph deals with the time when a final EDMO comes into force or ceases to have effect.

(2) The order does not come into force until such time (if any) as is the operative time for the purposes of this sub-paragraph under paragraph 29 (time when period for appealing expires without an appeal being made or when order is confirmed on appeal).

(3) The order ceases to have effect at the end of the period of 7 years beginning with the date on which it comes into force, unless it ceases to have effect at some other time as mentioned below.

(4) If the order provides that it is to cease to have effect on a date falling before the end of that period, it accordingly ceases to have effect on that date.

(5) If –

   (a) the order provides that it is to cease to have effect on a date falling after the end of that period, and
   (b) the relevant proprietor of the dwelling has consented to that provision,

the order accordingly ceases to have effect on that date.

(6) Sub-paragraphs (7) and (8) apply where –

   (a) a new final EDMO ('the new order') has been made so as to replace the order ('the existing order'), but
   (b) the new order has not come into force because of an appeal to a residential property tribunal under paragraph 26 against the making of that order.

(7) If the date on which the new order comes into force in relation to the dwelling following the disposal of the appeal is later than the date on which the existing order would cease to have effect apart from this sub-paragraph, the existing order continues in force until that later date.

(8) If, on the application of the authority, the tribunal makes an order providing for the existing order to continue in force, pending the disposal of the appeal, until a date later than that on which it would cease to have effect apart from this sub-paragraph, the existing order accordingly continues in force until that later date.

(9) This paragraph has effect subject to paragraphs 15 and 16 (variation or revocation of orders) and to the power of revocation exercisable by a residential property tribunal on an appeal made under paragraph 26 or 30.

General effect of final EDMOs

10 (1) This paragraph applies while a final EDMO is in force in relation to a dwelling.

(2) The rights and powers conferred by sub-paragraph (3) are exercisable by the authority in performing their duties under section 137(1) to (3) in respect of the dwelling.

(3) The authority –

   (a) have the right to possession of the dwelling (subject to the rights of existing and other occupiers preserved by paragraph 18(3) and (4));

(b) have the right to do (and authorise a manager or other person to do) in relation to the dwelling anything which the relevant proprietor of the dwelling would (but for the order) be entitled to do;

(c) may create one or more of the following –

    (i) an interest in the dwelling which, as far as possible, has all the incidents of a leasehold, or

    (ii) a right in the nature of a licence to occupy part of the dwelling;

(d) may apply to a residential property tribunal for an order under paragraph 22 determining a lease or licence of the dwelling.

(4) The powers of the authority under sub-paragraph (3)(c) are restricted as follows –

(a) they may not create any interest or right in the nature of a lease or licence –

    (i) which is for a fixed term expiring after the date on which the order is due to expire, or

    (ii) (subject to paragraph (b)) which is terminable by notice to quit, or an equivalent notice, of more than 4 weeks,

unless consent in writing has been given by the relevant proprietor;

(b) they may create an interest in the nature of an assured shorthold tenancy without any such consent so long as it is created before the beginning of the period of 6 months that ends with the date on which the order is due to expire.

(5) The authority –

(a) do not under this paragraph acquire any estate or interest in the dwelling, and

(b) accordingly are not entitled by virtue of this paragraph to sell, lease, charge or make any other disposition of any such estate or interest.

(6) But, where the relevant proprietor of the dwelling is a lessee under a lease of the dwelling, the authority are to be treated (subject to sub-paragraph (5)(a)) as if they were the lessee instead.

(7) Any enactment or rule of law relating to landlords and tenants or leases applies in relation to –

(a) a lease in relation to which the authority are to be treated as the lessee under sub-paragraph (6), or

(b) a lease to which the authority become a party under paragraph 12(2),

as if the authority were the legal owner of the premises (but this is subject to paragraph 12(4) to (6)).

(8) None of the following, namely –

(a) the authority, or

(b) any person authorised under sub-paragraph (3)(b),

is liable to any person having an estate or interest in the dwelling for anything done or omitted to be done in the performance (or intended performance) of the authority's duties under section 137(1) to (3) unless the act or omission is due to negligence of the authority or any such person.

(9) A final EDMO which has come into force is a local land charge.

(10) The authority may apply to the Chief Land Registrar for the entry of an appropriate restriction in the register in respect of such an order.

(11) In this paragraph 'enactment' includes an enactment comprised in subordinate legislation (within the meaning of the Interpretation Act 1978 (c 30)).

General effect of final EDMOs: leases and licences granted by authority

11 (1) This paragraph applies in relation to any interest or right created by the authority under paragraph 10(3)(c).

(2) For the purposes of any enactment or rule of law –

(a) any interest created by the authority under paragraph 10(3)(c)(i) is to be treated as if it were a legal lease, and

(b) any right created by the authority under paragraph 10(3)(c)(ii) is to be treated as if it were a licence to occupy granted by the legal owner of the dwelling,

despite the fact that the authority have no legal estate in the dwelling (see paragraph 10(5)(a)).

(3) Any enactment or rule of law relating to landlords and tenants or leases accordingly applies in relation to any interest created by the authority under paragraph 10(3)(c)(i) as if the authority were the legal owner of the dwelling.

(4) References to leases and licences –

(a) in this Chapter, and

(b) in any other enactment,

accordingly include (where the context permits) interests and rights created by the authority under paragraph 10(3)(c).

(5) The preceding provisions of this paragraph have effect subject to –

(a) paragraph 12(4) to (6), and

(b) any provision to the contrary contained in an order made by the appropriate national authority.

(6) In paragraph 10(5)(b) the reference to leasing does not include the creation of interests under paragraph 10(3)(c)(i).

(7) In this paragraph –

'enactment' has the meaning given by paragraph 10(11);

'legal lease' means a term of years absolute (within section 1(1)(b) of the Law of Property Act 1925 (c 20)).

General effect of final EDMOs: relevant proprietor, mortgagees etc

12 (1) This paragraph applies in relation to –

(a) the relevant proprietor, and

(b) other persons with an estate or interest in the dwelling,

while a final EDMO is in force in relation to a dwelling.

(2) Where the relevant proprietor is a lessor or licensor under a lease or licence of the dwelling, the lease or licence has effect while the order is in force as if the local housing authority were substituted in it for the lessor or licensor.

(3) Such a lease continues to have effect, as far as possible, as a lease despite the fact that the rights of the local housing authority, as substituted for the lessor, do not amount to an estate in law in the dwelling.

(4) The provisions mentioned in sub-paragraph (5) do not apply to a lease or licence within sub-paragraph (2).

(5) The provisions are –

(a) the provisions which exclude local authority lettings from the Rent Acts, namely –

    (i)   sections 14 to 16 of the Rent Act 1977 (c 42), and

    (ii)   those sections as applied by Schedule 2 to the Rent (Agriculture) Act 1976 (c 80) and section 5(2) to (4) of that Act; and

(b) section 1(2) of, and paragraph 12 of Part 1 of Schedule 1 to, the Housing Act 1988 (c 50) (which exclude local authority lettings from Part 1 of that Act).

(6) Nothing in this Chapter has the result that the authority are to be treated as the legal owner of any premises for the purposes of –

(a) section 80 of the Housing Act 1985 (c 68) (the landlord condition for secure tenancies); or

(b) section 124 of the Housing Act 1996 (c 52) (introductory tenancies).

(7) The relevant proprietor of the dwelling –

(a) is not entitled to receive any rents or other payments made in respect of occupation of the dwelling;

(b) may not exercise any rights or powers with respect to the management of the dwelling; and

(c) may not create any of the following –

    (i)   any leasehold interest in the dwelling or a part of it (other than a lease of a reversion), or

    (ii)   any licence or other right to occupy it.

(8) However (subject to sub-paragraph (7)(c)) nothing in paragraph 10 or this paragraph affects the ability of a person having an estate or interest in the dwelling to make any disposition of that estate or interest.

(9) Nothing in paragraph 10 or this paragraph affects –

(a) the validity of any mortgage relating to the dwelling or any rights or remedies available to the mortgagee under such a mortgage, or

(b) the validity of any lease of the dwelling under which the relevant proprietor is a lessee, or any superior lease, or (subject to paragraph 10(6)) any rights or remedies available to the lessor under such a lease;

except to the extent that any of those rights or remedies would prevent the local housing authority from exercising their power under paragraph 10(3)(c).

(10) In proceedings for the enforcement of any such rights or remedies the court may make such order as it thinks fit as regards the operation of the final EDMO (including an order quashing it).

Management scheme and accounts

13   (1) A final EDMO must contain a management scheme.

(2) A 'management scheme' is a scheme setting out how the local housing authority are to carry out their duties under section 137(1) to (3) as respects the dwelling.

(3) The scheme is to contain a plan giving details of the way in which the authority propose to manage the dwelling, which must (in particular) include –

(a) details of any works that the authority intend to carry out in connection with the dwelling;

(b) an estimate of the capital and other expenditure to be incurred by the authority in respect of the dwelling while the order is in force;

(c) the amount of rent which, in the opinion of the authority, the dwelling might reasonably be expected to fetch on the open market at the time the management scheme is made;

(d) the amount of rent or other payments that the authority will seek to obtain;

(e) the amount of any compensation that is payable to a third party by virtue of a decision of the authority under section 136(4) or 138(3) in respect of any interference in consequence of the final EDMO with the rights of that person;

(f) provision as to the payment of any such compensation and of any compensation payable to a dispossessed landlord or tenant by virtue of an order under paragraph 22(5);

(g) where the amount of rent payable to the authority in respect of the dwelling for a period is less than the amount of rent mentioned in paragraph (c) in respect of a period of the same length, provision as to the following –
  (i) the deduction from the difference of relevant expenditure and any amounts of compensation payable to a third party or dispossessed landlord or tenant;
  (ii) the payment of any remaining amount to the relevant proprietor;
  (iii) the deduction from time to time of any remaining amount from any amount that the authority are entitled to recover from the proprietor under paragraph 23(5) or (6);

(h) provision as to the payment by the authority to the relevant proprietor from time to time of amounts of rent or other payments that remain after the deduction of –
  (i) relevant expenditure, and
  (ii) any amount of compensation payable to a third party or dispossessed landlord or tenant;

(i) provision as to the manner in which the authority are to pay to the relevant proprietor, on the termination of the final EDMO, the balance of any amounts of rent or other payments that remain after the deduction of relevant expenditure and any amounts of compensation payable to a third party or dispossessed landlord or tenant;

(j) provision as to the manner in which the authority are to pay, on the termination of the final EDMO, any outstanding amount of compensation payable to a third party or dispossessed landlord or tenant.

(4) The scheme may also state –

(a) the authority's intentions as regards the use of rent or other payments to meet relevant expenditure;

(b) the authority's intentions as regards the payment to the relevant proprietor (where appropriate) of interest on amounts within sub-paragraph (3)(h) and (i);

(c) that paragraph 23(2) or, where the relevant proprietor consents, paragraph 23(3)(c) is not to apply in relation to an interim EDMO or (as the case may be) final EDMO that immediately preceded the final EDMO, and that instead the authority intend to use any balance such as is mentioned in that sub-paragraph to meet –
  (i) relevant expenditure incurred during the currency of that final EDMO, and
  (ii) any compensation that may become payable to a third party or a dispossessed landlord or tenant;

(d) that paragraph 23(4) to (6) are not to apply in relation to an interim EDMO or, where the relevant proprietor consents, a final EDMO that immediately preceded the final EDMO, and that instead the authority intend to use rent or other payments collected during the currency of that final EDMO to reimburse the authority in respect of any deficit such as is mentioned in paragraph 23(4);

(e) the authority's intentions as regards the recovery from the relevant proprietor, with or without interest, of any amount of relevant expenditure incurred under a previous interim EDMO or final EDMO that the authority are entitled to recover from the proprietor under paragraph 23(5) or (6).

(5) The authority must –

(a) keep full accounts of their income and expenditure in respect of the dwelling; and

(b) afford to the relevant proprietor, and to any other person who has an estate or interest in the dwelling, all reasonable facilities for inspecting, taking copies of and verifying those accounts.

(6) In this paragraph –

'dispossessed landlord or tenant' means a person who was a lessor, lessee, licensor or licensee under a lease or licence determined by an order under paragraph 22;

'relevant expenditure' means –

(a) expenditure incurred by the authority with the consent of the relevant proprietor, or
(b) any other expenditure reasonably incurred by the authority, in connection with performing their duties under section 135(1) to (3) or 137(1) to (3) in respect of the dwelling (including any reasonable administrative costs and any premiums paid for insurance of the premises);

'rent or other payments' means rent or other payments collected or recovered, by virtue of this Chapter, from persons occupying or having the right to occupy the dwelling.

(7) In any provision of this Chapter relating to varying, revoking or appealing against decisions relating to a final EDMO, any reference to such an order includes (where the context permits) a reference to the management scheme contained in it.

Application to residential property tribunal in respect of breach of management scheme

14 (1) An affected person may apply to a residential property tribunal for an order requiring the local housing authority to manage a dwelling in accordance with the management scheme contained in a final EDMO made in respect of the dwelling.

(2) On such an application the tribunal may, if it considers it appropriate to do so, make an order –

(a) requiring the authority to manage the dwelling in accordance with the management scheme, or
(b) revoking the final EDMO as from a date specified in the tribunal's order.

(3) An order under sub-paragraph (2) may –

(a) set out the steps which the authority are to take to manage the dwelling in accordance with the management scheme,
(b) include provision varying the final EDMO, and
(c) require the payment of money to an affected person by way of damages.

(4) In this paragraph 'affected person' means –

(a) the relevant proprietor, and
(b) any third party to whom compensation is payable by virtue of an order under section 134(4) or 138(2) or a decision of the authority under section 136(4) or 138(3) or who was a lessor, lessee, licensor or licensee under a lease or licence determined by an order of the residential property tribunal under paragraph 22 and to whom compensation is payable by virtue of an order under sub-paragraph (5) of that paragraph.

Variation or revocation of final EDMOs

15 (1) The local housing authority may vary a final EDMO if they consider it appropriate to do so.

(2) A variation does not come into force until such time, if any, as is the operative time for the purposes of this sub-paragraph under paragraph 33 (time when period for appealing expires without an appeal being made or when decision to vary is confirmed on appeal).

(3) The power to vary an order under this paragraph is exercisable by the authority either –

(a) on an application made by a relevant person, or

(b) on the authority's own initiative.

(4) In this paragraph 'relevant person' means any person who has an estate or interest in the dwelling (other than a person who is a tenant under a lease granted under paragraph 2(3)(c) or 10(3)(c)).

16 (1) The local housing authority may revoke a final EDMO in the following cases –

(a) where the authority conclude that there are no steps which they could appropriately take as mentioned in section 137(4)(b) or that keeping the order in force is not necessary as mentioned in section 137(4)(c);

(b) where the authority are satisfied that –
   (i) the dwelling will either become or continue to be occupied, despite the order being revoked, or
   (ii) that the dwelling is to be sold;

(c) where a further final EDMO has been made by the authority in respect of the dwelling so as to replace the order;

(d) where the authority conclude that it would be appropriate to revoke the order in order to prevent or stop interference with the rights of a third party in consequence of the order; and

(e) where in any other circumstances the authority consider it appropriate to revoke the order.

(2) But, in a case where the dwelling is occupied, the local housing authority may not revoke a final EDMO under sub-paragraph (1)(b), (d) or (e) unless the relevant proprietor consents.

(3) A revocation does not come into force until such time, if any, as is the operative time for the purposes of this sub-paragraph under paragraph 33 (time when period for appealing expires without an appeal being made or when decision to revoke is confirmed on appeal).

(4) The power to revoke an order under this paragraph is exercisable by the authority either –

(a) on an application made by a relevant person, or
(b) on the authority's own initiative.

(5) Where a relevant person applies to the authority for the revocation of an order under this paragraph, the authority may refuse to revoke the order unless the relevant proprietor (or some other person) agrees to pay to the authority any deficit such as is mentioned in paragraph 23(4).

(6) In this paragraph 'relevant person' means any person who has an estate or interest in the dwelling (other than a person who is a tenant under a lease granted under paragraph 2(3)(c) or 10(3)(c)).

17 (1) Part 2 of Schedule 6 applies in relation to the variation or revocation of a final EDMO as it applies in relation to the variation or revocation of a final management order.

(2) But Part 2 of that Schedule so applies as if –

(a) references to the right of appeal under Part 3 of the Schedule and to paragraph 29(2) were to the right of appeal under Part 4 of this Schedule and to paragraph 31(2) of this Schedule, and

(b) paragraph 23(4) defined 'relevant person' as any person who, to the knowledge of the local housing authority, is a person having an estate or interest in the dwelling (other than a person who is a tenant under a lease granted under paragraph 2(3)(c) or 10(3)(c) of this Schedule).

Part 3
Interim and Final EDMOs: General Provisions (other than Provisions Relating to Appeals)

Effect of EDMOs: persons occupying or having a right to occupy the dwelling

18   (1) This paragraph applies to existing and new occupiers of a dwelling in relation to which an interim EDMO or final EDMO is in force.

(2) In this paragraph –

> 'existing occupier' means a person other than the relevant proprietor who, at the time when the order comes into force –

> (a) has the right to occupy the dwelling, but
> (b) is not a new occupier within sub-paragraph (4);

> 'new occupier' means a person who, at a time when the order is in force, is occupying the dwelling under a lease or licence granted under paragraph 2(3)(c) or 10(3)(c).

(3) Paragraphs 2 and 10 do not affect the rights or liabilities of an existing occupier under a lease or licence (whether in writing or not) under which he has the right to occupy the dwelling at the commencement date.

(4) Paragraph 10 does not affect the rights and liabilities of a new occupier who, in the case of a final EDMO, is occupying the dwelling at the time when the order comes into force.

(5) The provisions mentioned in sub-paragraph (6) do not apply to a lease or agreement under which a new occupier has the right to occupy or is occupying the dwelling.

(6) The provisions are –

> (a) the provisions which exclude local authority lettings from the Rent Acts, namely –
> > (i)   sections 14 to 16 of the Rent Act 1977 (c 42), and
> > (ii) those sections as applied by Schedule 2 to the Rent (Agriculture) Act 1976 (c 80) and section 5(2) to (4) of that Act; and
> (b) section 1(2) of, and paragraph 12 of Part 1 of Schedule 1 to, the Housing Act 1988 (c 50) (which exclude local authority lettings from Part 1 of that Act).

(7) If, immediately before the coming into force of an interim EDMO or final EDMO, an existing occupier had the right to occupy the dwelling under –

> (a) a protected or statutory tenancy within the meaning of the Rent Act 1977,
> (b) a protected or statutory tenancy within the meaning of the Rent (Agriculture) Act 1976, or
> (c) an assured tenancy or assured agricultural occupancy within the meaning of Part 1 of the Housing Act 1988,

nothing in this Chapter (except an order under paragraph 22 determining a lease or licence) prevents the continuance of that tenancy or occupancy or affects the continued operation of any of those Acts in relation to the tenancy or occupancy after the coming into force of the order.

(8) In this paragraph 'the commencement date' means the date on which the order came into force (or, if that order was preceded by one or more orders under this Chapter, the date when the first order came into force).

Effect of EDMOs: agreements and legal proceedings

19 (1) An agreement or instrument within sub-paragraph (2) has effect, while an interim EDMO or final EDMO is in force, as if any rights or liabilities of the relevant proprietor under the agreement or instrument were instead rights or liabilities of the local housing authority.

(2) An agreement or instrument is within this sub-paragraph if –

- (a) it is effective on the commencement date,
- (b) one of the parties to it is the relevant proprietor of the dwelling,
- (c) it relates to the dwelling, whether in connection with any management activities with respect to it, or otherwise,
- (d) it is specified for the purposes of this sub-paragraph in the order or falls within a description of agreements or instruments so specified, and
- (e) the authority serve a notice in writing on all the parties to it stating that sub-paragraph (1) is to apply to it.

(3) An agreement or instrument is not within sub-paragraph (2) if –

- (a) it is a lease or licence within paragraph 2(6) or 10(6), or
- (b) it relates to any disposition by the relevant proprietor which is not precluded by paragraph 4(7) or 12(7).

(4) Proceedings in respect of any cause of action within sub-paragraph (5) may, while an interim EDMO or final EDMO is in force, be instituted or continued by or against the local housing authority instead of by or against the relevant proprietor.

(5) A cause of action is within this sub-paragraph if –

- (a) it is a cause of action (of any nature) which accrued to or against the relevant proprietor of the dwelling before the commencement date,
- (b) it relates to the dwelling as mentioned in sub-paragraph (2)(c),
- (c) it is specified for the purposes of this sub-paragraph in the order or falls within a description of causes of action so specified, and
- (d) the authority serve a notice in writing on all interested parties stating that sub-paragraph (4) is to apply to it.

(6) If, by virtue of this paragraph, the authority become subject to any liability to pay damages in respect of anything done (or omitted to be done) before the commencement date by or on behalf of the relevant proprietor of the dwelling, the relevant proprietor is liable to reimburse to the authority an amount equal to the amount of damages paid by them.

(7) In this paragraph –

'agreement' includes arrangement;

'the commencement date' means the date on which the order comes into force (or, if that order was preceded by one or more orders under this Chapter, the date when the first order came into force);

'management activities' includes repair, maintenance, improvement and insurance.

Effect of EDMOs: furniture

20 (1) Sub-paragraph (2) applies where, on the date on which an interim EDMO or final EDMO comes into force, there is furniture owned by the relevant proprietor in the dwelling.

(2) Subject to sub-paragraphs (3) and (4), the right to possession of the furniture against all persons vests in the local housing authority on that date and remains vested in the authority while the order is in force.

(3) The right of the local housing authority under sub-paragraph (2) to possession of the furniture is subject to the rights of any person who, on the date on which the interim EDMO or final EDMO comes into force, has the right to possession of the dwelling.

(4) Where –

(a) the local housing authority have the right to possession of the furniture under sub-paragraph (2), and
(b) they have not granted a right to possession of the furniture to any other person,

they must, on a request by the relevant proprietor, give up possession of the furniture to him.

(5) The local housing authority may renounce the right to possession of the furniture conferred by sub-paragraph (2) by serving notice on the relevant proprietor not less than two weeks before the renunciation is to have effect.

(6) Where the local housing authority renounce the right to possession of the furniture under sub-paragraph (5), they must make appropriate arrangements for storage of the furniture at their own cost.

(7) In this paragraph 'furniture' includes fittings and other articles.

EDMOs: power to supply furniture

21   (1) The local housing authority may supply the dwelling to which an interim EDMO or final EDMO relates with such furniture as they consider to be required.

(2) For the purposes of paragraph 5 or paragraph 13, any expenditure incurred by the authority under this paragraph constitutes expenditure incurred by the authority in connection with performing their duties under section 135(1) to (3) or 137(1) to (3).

(3) In this paragraph 'furniture' includes fittings and other articles.

Power of a residential property tribunal to determine certain leases and licences

22   (1) A residential property tribunal may make an order determining a lease or licence to which this paragraph applies if –

(a) the case falls within sub-paragraph (3) or (4), and
(b) the tribunal are satisfied that the dwelling is not being occupied and that the local housing authority need to have the right to possession of the dwelling in order to secure that the dwelling becomes occupied.

(2) This paragraph applies to the following leases and licences of a dwelling –

(a) a lease of the dwelling in respect of which the relevant proprietor is the lessor,
(b) a sub-lease of any such lease, and
(c) a licence of the dwelling.

(3) A case falls within this sub-paragraph if –

(a) an interim or final EDMO is in force in respect of the dwelling, and
(b) the local housing authority have applied under paragraph 2(3)(d) or 10(3)(d) for an order determining the lease or licence.

(4) A case falls within this sub-paragraph if –

(a) the local housing authority have applied to the residential property tribunal under section 133 for an order authorising them to make an interim EDMO in respect of the dwelling and an order determining the lease or licence, and

(b) the residential property tribunal has decided to authorise the authority to make an interim EDMO in respect of the dwelling.

(5) An order under this paragraph may include provision requiring the local housing authority to pay such amount or amounts to one or more of the lessor, lessee, licensor or licensee by way of compensation in respect of the determination of the lease or licence as the tribunal determines.

(6) Where –

(a) a final EDMO is in force in respect of a dwelling, and

(b) the tribunal makes an order requiring the local housing authority to pay an amount of compensation to a lessor, lessee, licensor or licensee in respect of the determination of a lease or licence of the dwelling,

the tribunal must make an order varying the management scheme contained in the final EDMO so as to make provision as to the payment of that compensation.

Termination of EDMOs: financial arrangements

23 (1) This paragraph applies where an interim EDMO or final EDMO ceases to have effect for any reason.

(2) If, on the termination date for an interim EDMO, the total amount of rent or other payments collected or recovered as mentioned in paragraph 5(3) exceeds the total amount of –

(a) the authority's relevant expenditure, and

(b) any amounts of compensation payable to third parties by virtue of orders under section 134(4) or 138(2) or decisions of the authority under section 136(4) or 138(3),

the authority must, as soon as possible after the termination date, pay the balance to the relevant proprietor.

(3) If, on the termination date for a final EDMO, any balance is payable to –

(a) a third party,

(b) a dispossessed landlord or tenant, or

(c) the relevant proprietor,

in accordance with the management scheme under paragraph 13, that amount must be paid to that person by the local housing authority in the manner provided by the scheme.

(4) Sub-paragraphs (5) and (6) apply where, on the termination date for an interim EDMO or final EDMO, the total amount of rent or other payments collected or recovered as mentioned in paragraph 5(3) is less than the total amount of the authority's relevant expenditure together with any such amounts of compensation as are mentioned in sub-paragraph (2)(b) above.

(5) The authority may recover from the relevant proprietor –

(a) the amount of any relevant expenditure (not exceeding the deficit mentioned in sub-paragraph (4)) which he has agreed in writing to pay either as a condition of revocation of the order or otherwise, and

(b) where the relevant proprietor is a tenant under a lease in respect of the dwelling, the amount of any outstanding service charges payable under the lease.

(6) In the case of an interim EDMO ceasing to have effect, the authority may recover the deficit mentioned in sub-paragraph (4) from the relevant proprietor if, in their opinion, he unreasonably refused to consent to the creation of an interest or right as mentioned in paragraph 2(3)(c) while the order was in force.

(7) The provisions of any of sub-paragraphs (2) to (6) do not, however, apply in relation to the order if –

(a) the order is followed by a final EDMO, and
(b) the management scheme contained in that final EDMO provides for those sub-paragraphs not to apply in relation to the order (see paragraph 13(4)(c) and (d)).

(8) Any sum recoverable by the authority under sub-paragraph (5) or (6) is, until recovered, a charge on the dwelling.

(9) The charge takes effect on the termination date for the order as a legal charge which is a local land charge.

(10) For the purpose of enforcing the charge the authority have the same powers and remedies under the Law of Property Act 1925 (c 20) and otherwise as if they were mortgagees by deed having powers of sale and lease, of accepting surrenders of leases and of appointing a receiver.

(11) The power of appointing a receiver is exercisable at any time after the end of the period of one month beginning with the date on which the charge takes effect.

(12) In this paragraph –

'dispossessed landlord or tenant' means a person who was a lessor, lessee, licensor or licensee under a lease or licence determined by an order under paragraph 22;

'relevant expenditure' has the same meaning as in paragraph 5 (in relation to an interim EDMO) or paragraph 13 (in relation to a final EDMO);

'service charge' has the meaning given by section 18 of the Landlord and Tenant Act 1985 (c 70);

'the termination date' means the date on which the order ceases to have effect.

Termination of EDMOs: leases, agreements and proceedings

24   (1) This paragraph applies where –

(a) an interim EDMO or final EDMO ceases to have effect for any reason, and
(b) the order is not immediately followed by a further order under this Chapter.

(2) As from the termination date, an agreement which (in accordance with paragraph 3 or 11) has effect as a lease or licence granted by the authority under paragraph 2 or 10 has effect with the substitution of the relevant proprietor for the authority.

(3) If the relevant proprietor is a lessee, nothing in a superior lease imposes liability on him or any superior lessee in respect of anything done before the termination date in pursuance of the terms of an agreement to which sub-paragraph (2) applies.

(4) If the condition in sub-paragraph (5) is met, any other agreement entered into by the authority in the performance of their duties under section 135(1) to (3) or 137(1) to (3) in respect of the dwelling has effect, as from the termination date, with the substitution of the relevant proprietor for the authority.

(5) The condition is that the authority serve a notice on the other party or parties to the agreement stating that sub-paragraph (4) applies to the agreement.

(6) If the condition in sub-paragraph (7) is met –

(a) any rights or liabilities that were rights or liabilities of the authority immediately before the termination date by virtue of any provision of this Chapter, or under any agreement to which sub-paragraph (4) applies, are rights or liabilities of the relevant proprietor instead, and

(b) any proceedings instituted or continued by or against the authority by virtue of any such provision or agreement may be continued by or against the relevant proprietor instead,

as from the termination date.

(7) The condition is that the authority serve a notice on all interested parties stating that sub-paragraph (6) applies to the rights or liabilities or (as the case may be) the proceedings.

(8) If by virtue of this paragraph a relevant proprietor becomes subject to any liability to pay damages in respect of anything done (or omitted to be done) before the termination date by or on behalf of the authority, the authority are liable to reimburse to the relevant proprietor an amount equal to the amount of the damages paid by him.

(9) This paragraph applies to instruments as it applies to agreements.

(10) In this paragraph –

'agreement' includes arrangement;

'the termination date' means the date on which the order ceases to have effect.

EDMOs: power of entry to carry out work

25 (1) The right mentioned in sub-paragraph (2) is exercisable by the local housing authority, or any person authorised in writing by them, at any time when an interim EDMO or final EDMO is in force.

(2) That right is the right at all reasonable times to enter any part of the dwelling for the purpose of carrying out works, and is exercisable as against any person having an estate or interest in the dwelling.

(3) If, after receiving reasonable notice of the intended action, any occupier of the dwelling prevents any officer, employee, agent or contractor of the local housing authority from carrying out work in the dwelling, a magistrates' court may order him to permit to be done on the premises anything which the authority consider to be necessary.

(4) A person who fails to comply with an order of the court under sub-paragraph (3) commits an offence.

(5) A person who commits an offence under sub-paragraph (4) is liable on summary conviction to a fine not exceeding level 5 on the standard scale.

Part 4

Appeals

Appeals: decisions relating to EDMOs

26 (1) A relevant person may appeal to a residential property tribunal against –

(a) a decision of the local housing authority to make a final EDMO,

(b) the terms of a final EDMO (including the terms of the management scheme contained in it), or

(c) the terms of an interim EDMO on the grounds that they do not provide for one or both of the matters mentioned in paragraph 5(5)(a) and (b) (which relate to payments of surplus rent etc).

(2) Where an appeal is made under sub-paragraph (1)(c) –

(a) the appeal may be brought at any time while the order is in force (with the result that nothing in sub-paragraph (3) or paragraph 27 applies in relation to the appeal); and

(b) the powers of the residential property tribunal under paragraph 28 are limited to determining whether the order should be varied by the tribunal so as to include a term providing for the matter or matters in question, and (if so) what provision should be made by the term.

(3) If no appeal is brought under this paragraph in respect of a final EDMO within the time allowed by paragraph 27 for making such an appeal, the order is final and conclusive as to the matters which could have been raised on appeal.

Appeals: time limits for appeals under paragraph 26

27   (1) This paragraph applies in relation to an appeal under paragraph 26 in respect of a final EDMO.

(2) Any such appeal must be made within the period of 28 days beginning with the date specified in the notice under paragraph 7(5) of Schedule 6 (as applied by section 136(5)) as the date on which the order was made.

(3) A residential property tribunal may allow an appeal to be made to it after the end of the period mentioned in sub-paragraph (2) if it is satisfied that there is a good reason for the failure to appeal before the end of that period (and for any delay since then in applying for permission to appeal out of time).

Appeals: powers of residential property tribunal on appeal under paragraph 26

28   (1) This paragraph applies to an appeal to a residential property tribunal under paragraph 26 in respect of an interim EDMO or a final EDMO.

(2) The appeal –

(a) is to be by way of a re-hearing, but

(b) may be determined having regard to matters of which the authority were unaware.

(3) The tribunal may –

(a) in the case of an interim EDMO, vary the order as mentioned in paragraph 26(2)(b), or

(b) in the case of a final EDMO, confirm or vary the order or revoke it as from the date of the tribunal's order.

'The operative time' for the purposes of paragraph 9(2)

29   (1) This paragraph defines 'the operative time' for the purposes of paragraph 9(2).

(2) If no appeal is made under paragraph 26 before the end of the period of 28 days mentioned in paragraph 27(2), 'the operative time' is the end of that period.

(3) If an appeal is made under paragraph 26 before the end of that period, and a decision is given on the appeal which confirms the order, 'the operative time' is as follows –

(a) if the period within which an appeal to the Lands Tribunal may be brought expires without such an appeal having been brought, 'the operative time' is the end of that period;

(b) if an appeal to the Lands Tribunal is brought, 'the operative time' is the time when a decision is given on the appeal which confirms the order.

(4) For the purposes of sub-paragraph (3) –

(a) the withdrawal of an appeal has the same effect as a decision which confirms the order, and
(b) references to a decision which confirms the order are to a decision which confirms it with or without variation.

Right to appeal against decision or refusal to vary or revoke EDMO

30 A relevant person may appeal to a residential property tribunal against –

(a) a decision of a local housing authority to vary or revoke an interim EDMO or a final EDMO, or
(b) a refusal of a local housing authority to vary or revoke an interim EDMO or a final EDMO.

Time limits for appeals under paragraph 30

31 (1) This paragraph applies in relation to an appeal under paragraph 30 against a decision to vary or revoke, or (as the case may be) to refuse to vary or revoke, an interim EDMO or a final EDMO.

(2) Any such appeal must be made before the end of the period of 28 days beginning with the date specified in the notice under paragraph 11, 16, 19 or 22 of Schedule 6 (as applied by paragraph 8 or 17 of this Schedule (as the case may be)) as the date on which the decision concerned was made.

(3) A residential property tribunal may allow an appeal to be made to it after the end of the period mentioned in sub-paragraph (2) if it is satisfied that there is a good reason for the failure to appeal before the end of that period (and for any delay since then in applying for permission to appeal out of time).

Powers of residential property tribunal on appeal under paragraph 30

32 (1) This paragraph applies to an appeal to a residential property tribunal under paragraph 30 against a decision to vary or revoke, or (as the case may be) to refuse to vary or revoke, an interim EDMO or final EDMO.

(2) The appeal –

(a) is to be by way of a re-hearing, but
(b) may be determined having regard to matters of which the authority were unaware.

(3) The tribunal may confirm, reverse or vary the decision of the local housing authority.

(4) If the appeal is against a decision of the authority to refuse to revoke the order, the tribunal may make an order revoking the order as from a date specified in its order.

'The operative time' for the purposes of paragraphs 6, 7, 15 and 16

33 (1) This paragraph defines 'the operative time' for the purposes of –

(a) paragraph 6(2) or 7(3) (variation or revocation of interim EDMO), or
(b) paragraph 15(2) or 16(3) (variation or revocation of final EDMO).

(2) If no appeal is made under paragraph 30 before the end of the period of 28 days mentioned in paragraph 31(2), 'the operative time' is the end of that period.

(3) If an appeal is made under paragraph 30 before the end of that period, and a decision is given on the appeal which confirms the variation or revocation, 'the operative time' is as follows –

  (a) if the period within which an appeal to the Lands Tribunal may be brought expires without such an appeal having been brought, 'the operative time' is the end of that period;
  (b) if an appeal to the Lands Tribunal is brought, 'the operative time' is the time when a decision is given on the appeal which confirms the variation or revocation.

(4) For the purposes of sub-paragraph (3) –

  (a) the withdrawal of an appeal has the same effect as a decision which confirms the variation or revocation appealed against; and
  (b) references to a decision which confirms a variation are to a decision which confirms it with or without variation.

Right to appeal against decision in respect of compensation payable to third parties

34 (1) This paragraph applies where a local housing authority have made a decision under section 136(4) or 138(3) as to whether compensation should be paid to a third party in respect of any interference with his rights in consequence of a final EDMO.

(2) The third party may appeal to a residential property tribunal against –

  (a) a decision by the authority not to pay compensation to him, or
  (b) a decision of the authority so far as relating to the amount of compensation that should be paid.

Time limits for appeals under paragraph 34

35 (1) This paragraph applies in relation to an appeal under paragraph 34 against a decision of a local housing authority not to pay compensation to a third party or as to the amount of compensation to be paid.

(2) Any such appeal must be made –

  (a) where the decision is made before the final EDMO is made, within the period of 28 days beginning with the date specified in the notice under paragraph 7(5) of Schedule 6 (as applied by section 136(5)) as the date on which the order was made, or
  (b) in any other case, within the period of 28 days beginning with the date the authority notifies the third party under section 138(4).

(3) A residential property tribunal may allow an appeal to be made to it after the end of the period mentioned in sub-paragraph (2) if it is satisfied that there is good reason for the failure to appeal before the end of that period (and for any delay since then in applying for permission to appeal out of time).

Powers of residential property tribunal on appeal under paragraph 34

36 (1) This paragraph applies in relation to an appeal under paragraph 34 against a decision of a local housing authority not to pay compensation to a third party or as to the amount of compensation to be paid.

(2) The appeal –

  (a) is to be by way of re-hearing, but
  (b) may be determined having regard to matters of which the authority were unaware.

(3) The tribunal may confirm, reverse or vary the decision of the local housing authority.

(4) Where the tribunal reverses or varies the decision of the authority, it must make an order varying the management scheme contained in the final EDMO accordingly.

Meaning of 'relevant person' for the purposes of this Part

37 In this Part of this Schedule 'relevant person' means any person who has an estate or interest in the dwelling (other than a person who is a tenant under a lease granted under paragraph 2(3)(c) or 10(3)(c)).

SCHEDULE 8
Penalty Charge Notices under Section 168

Section 168

1 A penalty charge notice given to a person under section 168 by an officer of an enforcement authority must –

(a) state the officer's belief that that person has committed a breach of duty;
(b) give such particulars of the circumstances as may be necessary to give reasonable notice of the breach of duty;
(c) require that person, within a period specified in the notice –
  (i) to pay a penalty charge specified in the notice; or
  (ii) to give notice to the enforcement authority that he wishes the authority to review the notice;
(d) state the effect of paragraph 8;
(e) specify the person to whom and the address at which the penalty charge may be paid and the method or methods by which payment may be made; and
(f) specify the person to whom and the address at which a notice requesting a review may be sent (and to which any representations relating to the review may be addressed).

2 The penalty charge specified in the notice shall be of such amount (not exceeding £500) as may be prescribed for the time being by regulations made by the Secretary of State.

3 (1) The period specified under paragraph 1(c) must not be less than 28 days beginning with the day after that on which the penalty charge notice was given.

(2) The enforcement authority may extend the period for complying with the requirement mentioned in paragraph 1(c) in any particular case if they consider it appropriate to do so.

4 The enforcement authority may, if they consider that the penalty charge notice ought not to have been given, give the recipient a notice withdrawing the penalty charge notice.

5 (1) If, within the period specified under paragraph 1(c) (or that period as extended under paragraph 3(2)), the recipient of the penalty charge notice gives notice to the enforcement authority requesting a review, the authority shall –

(a) consider any representations made by the recipient and all other circumstances of the case;
(b) decide whether to confirm or withdraw the notice; and
(c) give notice of their decision to the recipient.

(2) A notice under sub-paragraph (1)(c) confirming the penalty charge notice must also state the effect of paragraphs 6(1) to (3) and 8(1) and (3).

(3) If the authority are not satisfied –

(a) that the recipient committed the breach of duty specified in the notice;

(b) that the notice was given within the time allowed by section 168(2) and complies with the other requirements imposed by or under this Schedule; and

(c) that in the circumstances of the case it was appropriate for a penalty charge notice to be given to the recipient,

they shall withdraw the penalty charge notice.

6 (1) If after a review the penalty charge notice is confirmed by the enforcement authority, the recipient may, within the period of 28 days beginning with the day after that on which the notice under paragraph 5(1)(c) is given, appeal to the county court against the penalty charge notice.

(2) The county court may extend the period for appealing against the notice.

(3) Such an appeal must be on one (or more) of the following grounds –

(a) that the recipient did not commit the breach of duty specified in the penalty charge notice;

(b) that the notice was not given within the time allowed by section 168(2) or does not comply with any other requirement imposed by or under this Schedule; or

(c) that in the circumstances of the case it was inappropriate for the notice to be given to the recipient.

(4) An appeal against a penalty charge notice shall be by way of a rehearing; and the court shall either uphold the notice or quash it.

7 If the penalty charge notice is withdrawn or quashed, the authority shall repay any amount previously paid as a penalty charge in pursuance of the notice.

8 (1) The amount of the penalty charge is recoverable from the recipient of the penalty charge notice as a debt owed to the authority unless –

(a) the notice has been withdrawn or quashed, or

(b) the charge has been paid.

(2) Proceedings for the recovery of the penalty charge may not be commenced before the end of the period mentioned in paragraph 5(1).

(3) And if within that period the recipient of the penalty charge notice gives notice to the authority that he wishes the authority to review the penalty charge notice, such proceedings may not be commenced –

(a) before the end of the period mentioned in paragraph 6(1), and

(b) where the recipient appeals against the penalty charge notice, before the end of the period of 28 days beginning with the day on which the appeal is withdrawn or determined.

9 In proceedings for the recovery of the penalty charge, a certificate which –

(a) purports to be signed by or on behalf of the person having responsibility for the financial affairs of the enforcement authority; and

(b) states that payment of the penalty charge was or was not received by a date specified in the certificate;

is evidence of the facts stated.

10 (1) A penalty charge notice and any other notice mentioned in this Schedule may be given by post.

(2) Any such notice may be given –

(a) in the case of a body corporate, to the secretary or clerk of that body; and

(b) in the case of a partnership, to any partner or to a person having control or management of the partnership business.

11 The Secretary of State may by regulations make provision supplementary or incidental to the preceding provisions of this Part, including in particular provision prescribing –

(a) the form of penalty charge notices or any other notice mentioned in this Schedule;

(b) circumstances in which penalty charge notices may not be given;

(c) the method or methods by which penalty charges may be paid.

SCHEDULE 9
New Schedule 5A to the Housing Act 1985: Initial Demolition Notices

Section 183

'SCHEDULE 5A
Initial Demolition Notices

Section 138A

Initial demolition notices

1 (1) For the purposes of this Schedule an "initial demolition notice" is a notice served on a secure tenant –

(a) stating that the landlord intends to demolish the dwelling-house or (as the case may be) the building containing it ("the relevant premises"),

(b) setting out the reasons why the landlord intends to demolish the relevant premises,

(c) specifying the period within which he intends to demolish those premises, and

(d) stating that, while the notice remains in force, he will not be under any obligation to make such a grant as is mentioned in section 138(1) in respect of any claim made by the tenant to exercise the right to buy in respect of the dwelling-house.

(2) An initial demolition notice must also state –

(a) that the notice does not prevent –

   (i) the making by the tenant of any such claim, or

   (ii) the taking of steps under this Part in connection with any such claim up to the point where section 138(1) would otherwise operate in relation to the claim, or

   (iii) the operation of that provision in most circumstances where the notice ceases to be in force, but

(b) that, if the landlord subsequently serves a final demolition notice in respect of the dwelling-house, the right to buy will not arise in respect of it while that notice is in force and any existing claim will cease to be effective.

(3) If, at the time when an initial demolition notice is served, there is an existing claim to exercise the right to buy in respect of the dwelling-house, the notice shall –

(a) state that section 138C confers a right to compensation in respect of certain expenditure, and

(b) give details of that right to compensation and of how it may be exercised.

(4) The period specified in accordance with sub-paragraph (1)(c) must not –

(a) allow the landlord more than what is, in the circumstances, a reasonable period to carry out the proposed demolition of the relevant premises (whether on their own or as part of a scheme involving the demolition of other premises); or

(b) in any case expire more than five years after the date of service of the notice on the tenant.

Period of validity of initial demolition notice

2 (1) For the purposes of this Schedule an initial demolition notice –

(a) comes into force in respect of the dwelling-house concerned on the date of service of the notice on the tenant, and

(b) ceases to be so in force at the end of the period specified in accordance with paragraph 1(1)(c),

but this is subject to compliance with the conditions mentioned in sub-paragraph (2) (in a case to which they apply) and to paragraph 3.

(2) The conditions in sub-paragraphs (6) and (7) of paragraph 13 of Schedule 5 (publicity for final demolition notices) shall apply in relation to an initial demolition notice as they apply in relation to a final demolition notice.

(3) The notice mentioned in paragraph 13(7) (as it applies in accordance with sub-paragraph (2) above) must contain the following information –

(a) sufficient information to enable identification of the premises that the landlord intends to demolish,

(b) the reasons why the landlord intends to demolish those premises,

(c) the period within which the landlord intends to demolish those premises,

(d) the date when any initial demolition notice or notices relating to those premises will cease to be in force, unless revoked or otherwise terminated under or by virtue of paragraph 3 below,

(e) that, during the period of validity of any such notice or notices, the landlord will not be under any obligation to make such a grant as is mentioned in section 138(1) in respect of any claim to exercise the right to buy in respect of any dwelling-house contained in those premises,

(f) that there may be a right to compensation under section 138C in respect of certain expenditure incurred in respect of any existing claim.

Revocation or termination of initial demolition notices

3 (1) Paragraph 15(4) to (7) of Schedule 5 (revocation notices) shall apply in relation to an initial demolition notice as they apply in relation to a final demolition notice.

(2) If a compulsory purchase order has been made for the purpose of enabling the landlord to demolish the dwelling-house in respect of which he has served an initial demolition notice (whether or not it would enable him to demolish any other premises as well) and –

(a) a relevant decision within sub-paragraph (3)(a) becomes effective while the notice is in force, or

(b) a relevant decision within sub-paragraph (3)(b) becomes final while the notice is in force,

the notice ceases to be in force as from the date when the decision becomes effective or final.

(3) A "relevant decision" is –

(a) a decision under Part 2 of the Acquisition of Land Act 1981 to confirm the order with modifications, or not to confirm the whole or part of the order, or

(b) a decision of the High Court to quash the whole or part of the order under section 24 of that Act,

where the effect of the decision is that the landlord will not be able, by virtue of that order, to carry out the demolition of the dwelling-house.

(4) A relevant decision within sub-paragraph (3)(a) becomes effective –

(a) at the end of the period of 16 weeks beginning with the date of the decision, if no application for judicial review is made in respect of the decision within that period, or

(b) if such an application is so made, at the time when –

   (i) a decision on the application which upholds the relevant decision becomes final, or

   (ii) the application is abandoned or otherwise ceases to have effect.

(5) A relevant decision within sub-paragraph (3)(b), or a decision within sub-paragraph (4)(b), becomes final –

(a) if not appealed against, at the end of the period for bringing an appeal, or

(b) if appealed against, at the time when the appeal (or any further appeal) is disposed of.

(6) An appeal is disposed of –

(a) if it is determined and the period for bringing any further appeal has ended, or

(b) if it is abandoned or otherwise ceases to have effect.

(7) Where an initial demolition notice ceases to be in force under sub-paragraph (2), the landlord must, as soon as is reasonably practicable, serve a notice on the tenant which informs him –

(a) that the notice has ceased to be in force as from the date in question, and

(b) of the reason why it has ceased to be in force.

(8) If, while an initial demolition notice is in force in respect of a dwelling-house, a final demolition notice comes into force under paragraph 13 of Schedule 5 in respect of that dwelling-house, the initial demolition notice ceases to be in force as from the date when the final demolition notice comes into force.

(9) In such a case the final demolition notice must state that it is replacing the initial demolition notice.

Restriction on serving further demolition notices

4 (1) This paragraph applies where an initial demolition notice ("the relevant notice") has (for any reason) ceased to be in force in respect of a dwelling-house without it being demolished.

(2) No further initial demolition notice may be served in respect of the dwelling-house during the period of 5 years following the time when the relevant notice ceases to be in force, unless –

(a) it is served with the consent of the Secretary of State, and

(b) it states that it is so served.

(3) Subject to sub-paragraph (4), no final demolition notice may be served in respect of the dwelling-house during the period of 5 years following the time when the relevant notice ceases to be in force, unless –

(a) it is served with the consent of the Secretary of State, and

(b) it states that it is so served.

(4) Sub-paragraph (3) does not apply to a final demolition notice which is served at a time when an initial demolition notice served in accordance with sub-paragraph (2) is in force.

(5) The Secretary of State's consent under sub-paragraph (2) or (3) may be given subject to compliance with such conditions as he may specify.

Service of notices

5   Paragraph 16 of Schedule 13 (service of notices) applies in relation to notices under this Schedule as it applies in relation to notices under paragraph 13 or 15 of that Schedule.

Interpretation

6   (1) In this Schedule any reference to the landlord, in the context of a reference to the demolition or intended demolition of any premises, includes a reference to a superior landlord.

(2) In this Schedule –

"final demolition notice" means a final demolition notice served under paragraph 13 of Schedule 5;

"premises" means premises of any description;

"scheme" includes arrangements of any description.'

SCHEDULE 10
PROVISIONS RELATING TO TENANCY DEPOSIT SCHEMES

Section 212

Schemes to be custodial schemes or insurance schemes

1   (1) A tenancy deposit scheme must be either –

(a) a custodial scheme, or

(b) an insurance scheme.

(2) A 'custodial scheme' is a scheme under which –

(a) tenancy deposits in connection with shorthold tenancies are paid to the landlords under the tenancies,

(b) amounts representing the deposits are then paid by the landlords into a designated account held by the scheme administrator, and

(c) those amounts are kept by the scheme administrator in that account until such time as, in accordance with the scheme, they fall to be paid (wholly or in part) to the landlords or tenants under the tenancies.

(3) An 'insurance scheme' is a scheme under which –

(a) tenancy deposits in connection with shorthold tenancies are paid to the landlords under the tenancies,

(b) such deposits are retained by the landlords on the basis that, at the end of the tenancies –

(i) such amounts in respect of the deposits as are agreed between the tenants and the landlords will be repaid to the tenants, and

(ii) such amounts as the tenants request to be repaid to them and which are not so repaid will, in accordance with directions given by the scheme administrator, be paid into a designated account held by the scheme administrator,

(c) amounts paid into that account are kept by the scheme administrator in the account until such time as, in accordance with the scheme, they fall to be paid (wholly or in part) to the landlords or tenants under the tenancies,

(d) landlords undertake to reimburse the scheme administrator, in accordance with directions given by him, in respect of any amounts in respect of the deposits paid to the tenants by the scheme administrator (other than amounts paid to the tenants as mentioned in paragraph (c)), and

(e) insurance is maintained by the scheme administrator in respect of failures by landlords to comply with such directions.

Provisions applying to custodial and insurance schemes

2 (1) A custodial scheme must conform with the following provisions –

paragraphs 3 and 4, and

paragraphs 9 and 10.

(2) An insurance scheme must conform with the following provisions –

paragraphs 5 to 8, and

paragraphs 9 and 10.

Custodial schemes: general

3 (1) This paragraph applies to a custodial scheme.

(2) The scheme must provide for any landlord who receives a tenancy deposit in connection with a shorthold tenancy to pay an amount equal to the deposit into a designated account held by the scheme administrator.

(3) The designated account must not contain anything other than amounts paid into it as mentioned in sub-paragraph (2) and any interest accruing on such amounts.

(4) Subject to sub-paragraph (5), the scheme administrator may retain any interest accruing on such amounts.

(5) The relevant arrangements under section 212(1) may provide for any amount paid in accordance with paragraph 4 to be paid with interest –

(a) in respect of the period during which the relevant amount has remained in the designated account, and

(b) at such rate as the appropriate national authority may specify by order.

(6) With the exception of any interest retained in accordance with sub-paragraph (4), nothing contained in the designated account may be used to fund the administration of the scheme.

(7) In this paragraph 'the relevant amount', in relation to a tenancy deposit, means the amount paid into the designated account in respect of the deposit.

Custodial schemes: termination of tenancies

4 (1) A custodial scheme must make provision –

(a) for enabling the tenant and the landlord under a shorthold tenancy in connection with which a tenancy deposit is held in accordance with the scheme to apply, at any time after the tenancy has ended, for the whole or part of the relevant amount to be paid to him, and

(b) for such an application to be dealt with by the scheme administrator in accordance with the following provisions of this paragraph.

(2) Sub-paragraph (3) applies where the tenant and the landlord notify the scheme administrator that they have agreed that the relevant amount should be paid –

(a) wholly to one of them, or

(b) partly to the one and partly to the other.

(3) If, having received such a notification, the scheme administrator is satisfied that the tenant and the landlord have so agreed, the scheme administrator must arrange for the relevant amount to be paid, in accordance with the agreement, within the period of 10 days beginning with the date on which the notification is received by the scheme administrator.

(4) Sub-paragraph (5) applies where the tenant or the landlord notifies the scheme administrator that –

(a) a court has decided that the relevant amount is payable either wholly to one of them or partly to the one and partly to the other, and

(b) that decision has become final.

(5) If, having received such a notification, the scheme administrator is satisfied as to the matters mentioned in sub-paragraph (4)(a) and (b), the scheme administrator must arrange for the relevant amount to be paid, in accordance with the decision, within the period of 10 days beginning with the date on which the notification is received by the scheme administrator.

(6) For the purposes of this Schedule a decision becomes final –

(a) if not appealed against, at the end of the period for bringing an appeal, or

(b) if appealed against, at the time when the appeal (or any further appeal) is disposed of.

(7) An appeal is disposed of –

(a) if it is determined and the period for bringing any further appeal has ended, or

(b) if it is abandoned or otherwise ceases to have effect.

(8) In this paragraph 'the relevant amount' has the meaning given by paragraph 3(7).

Insurance schemes: general

5 (1) This paragraph applies to an insurance scheme.

(2) The scheme must provide that any landlord by whom a tenancy deposit is retained under the scheme must give the scheme administrator an undertaking that, if the scheme administrator directs the landlord to pay him any amount in respect of the deposit in accordance with paragraph 6(3) or (7), the landlord will comply with such a direction.

(3) The scheme must require the scheme administrator to effect, and maintain in force, adequate insurance in respect of failures by landlords by whom tenancy deposits are retained under the scheme to comply with such directions as are mentioned in sub-paragraph (2).

(4) If the scheme provides for landlords participating in the scheme to be members of the scheme, the scheme may provide for a landlord's membership to be terminated by the scheme administrator in the event of any such failure on the part of the landlord.

(5) The scheme may provide for landlords participating in the scheme to pay to the scheme administrator –

(a) fees in respect of the administration of the scheme, and
(b) contributions in respect of the cost of the insurance referred to in sub-paragraph (3).

Insurance schemes: termination of tenancies

6 (1) An insurance scheme must make provision in accordance with this paragraph and paragraphs 7 and 8 in relation to the respective obligations of the landlord and the scheme administrator where –

(a) a tenancy deposit has been retained by the landlord under the scheme, and
(b) the tenancy has ended.

(2) Sub-paragraphs (3) to (9) apply where the tenant notifies the scheme administrator that –

(a) the tenant has requested the landlord to repay to him the whole or any part of the deposit, and
(b) the amount in question ('the outstanding amount') has not been repaid to him within the period of 10 days beginning with the date on which the request was made.

(3) On receiving a notification in accordance with sub-paragraph (2), the scheme administrator must direct the landlord –

(a) to pay an amount equal to the outstanding amount into a designated account held by the scheme administrator, and
(b) to do so within the period of 10 days beginning with the date on which the direction is received by the landlord.

(4) The following sub-paragraphs apply where the tenant or the landlord notifies the scheme administrator –

(a) that a court has decided that the outstanding amount is payable either wholly to one of them or partly to the one and partly to the other and the decision has become final (see paragraph 4(6) and (7)), or
(b) that the tenant and landlord have agreed that such an amount is to be paid either wholly to one of them or partly to the one and partly to the other.

(5) If the scheme administrator is satisfied as to the matters mentioned in sub-paragraph (4)(a) or (b) (as the case may be), he must –

(a) pay to the tenant any amount due to him in accordance with the decision or agreement (and, to the extent possible, pay that amount out of any amount held by him by virtue of sub-paragraph (3)), and
(b) comply with sub-paragraph (6) or (7), as the case may be.

(6) Where any amount held by the scheme administrator by virtue of sub-paragraph (3) is more than any amount due to the tenant in accordance with the decision or agreement, the scheme administrator must pay the balance to the landlord.

(7) Where any amount so held by the scheme administrator is less than any amount so due to the tenant, the scheme administrator must direct the landlord to pay him the difference within the period of 10 days beginning with the date on which the direction is received by the landlord.

(8) The scheme administrator must pay any amounts required to be paid to the tenant or the landlord as mentioned in sub-paragraph (5)(a) or (6) within 10 days beginning with the date on which the notification is received by the scheme administrator.

(9) The landlord must comply with any direction given in accordance with sub-paragraph (3) or (7).

7 (1) The designated account held by the scheme administrator must not contain anything other than amounts paid into it as mentioned in paragraph 6(3) and any interest accruing on such amounts.

(2) Subject to sub-paragraph (3), the scheme administrator may retain any interest accruing on such amounts.

(3) The relevant arrangements under section 212(1) may provide for any amount paid in accordance with paragraph 6(5)(a) or (6) to be paid with interest –

(a) in respect of the period during which the relevant amount has remained in the designated account, and
(b) at such rate as the appropriate national authority may specify for the purposes of paragraph 3(5)(b).

(4) With the exception of any interest retained in accordance with sub-paragraph (2), nothing contained in the designated account may be used to fund the administration of the scheme.

(5) In this paragraph 'the relevant amount', in relation to a tenancy deposit, means the amount, in respect of the deposit, paid into the designated account by virtue of a direction given in accordance with paragraph 6(3).

8 (1) The scheme must make provision for preventing double recovery by a tenant in respect of the whole or part of the deposit, and may in that connection make provision –

(a) for excluding or modifying any requirement imposed by the scheme in accordance with paragraph 6 or 7, and
(b) for requiring the repayment of amounts paid to the tenant by the scheme administrator.

(2) In this paragraph 'double recovery', in relation to an amount of a tenancy deposit, means recovering that amount both from the scheme administrator and from the landlord.

Notifications to tenants

9 (1) Every custodial scheme or insurance scheme must provide for the scheme administrator to respond as soon as is practicable to any request within sub-paragraph (2) made by the tenant under a shorthold tenancy.

(2) A request is within this sub-paragraph if it is a request by the tenant to receive confirmation that a deposit paid in connection with the tenancy is being held in accordance with the scheme.

Dispute resolution procedures

10 (1) Every custodial scheme or insurance scheme must provide for facilities to be available for enabling disputes relating to tenancy deposits subject to the scheme to be resolved without recourse to litigation.

(2) The scheme must not, however, make the use of such facilities compulsory in the event of such a dispute.

Power to amend

11   The appropriate national authority may by order make such amendments of this Schedule as it considers appropriate.

Interpretation

12   In this Schedule references to tenants under shorthold tenancies include references to persons who, in accordance with arrangements made with such tenants, have paid tenancy deposits on behalf of the tenants.

SCHEDULE 11
REGISTERED SOCIAL LANDLORDS

Section 18
Section 218

Housing Associations Act 1985 (c 69)

1   In section 87 of the Housing Associations Act 1985 (financial assistance with respect to formation, management, etc of certain housing associations) omit –

(a) in subsection (3), the words from ', acting' onwards, and
(b) subsection (6).

Housing Act 1988 (c 50)

2   The Housing Act 1988 is amended as follows.

3   In section 50(2) (housing association grants) omit the words from ', acting' onwards.

4   In section 52(2) (recovery etc of grants) omit the words from ', acting' to 'determine,'.

5   Omit section 55 (surplus rental income).

6   In section 59(1A) (interpretation) for '55' substitute '54'.

Housing Act 1996 (c 52)

7   The Housing Act 1996 is amended as follows.

8   In section 18(2) (social housing grants) omit the words from ', acting' to 'determine,'.

9   In section 20(3) (purchase grant where right to acquire exercised) omit the words from ', acting' to 'determine,'.

10   In section 21(3) (purchase grant in respect of other disposals) omit the words from ', acting' to 'determine,'.

11   In section 28 (grants under sections 50 to 55 of the Housing Act 1988), in the sidenote and in subsection (6), for '55' substitute '54'.

12   (1) In section 31(2) (offence of intentionally altering etc document required to be produced under section 30), for paragraph (b) substitute –

'(b) on conviction on indictment, to imprisonment for a term not exceeding two years or to a fine, or both.'

(2) The amendment made by sub-paragraph (1) does not apply in relation to any offence committed before the day on which that sub-paragraph comes into force.

13 (1) Section 36 (issue of guidance by the Relevant Authority) is amended as follows.

(2) In subsection (2) (particular matters with respect to which guidance may be issued under the section) for 'this section' substitute 'subsection (1)'.

(3) After subsection (2) insert –

'(2A) The Relevant Authority may also issue guidance with respect to –

(a) the governance of bodies that are registered social landlords;
(b) the effective management of such bodies;
(c) establishing and maintaining the financial viability of such bodies.'

(4) In subsection (7) (guidance relevant to whether there has been mismanagement) after 'there has been' insert 'misconduct or'.

14 In paragraph 1(2) of Schedule 1 (payments by way of gift, dividend or bonus) after paragraph (b) insert –

'(c) the payment of a sum, in accordance with the constitution or rules of the body, to a registered social landlord which is a subsidiary or associate of the body.'

15 (1) Paragraph 15 of Schedule 1 (transfer of net assets on dissolution or winding up) is amended as follows.

(2) In sub-paragraph (1)(b), after '1985' insert ' (including such a company which is also a registered charity)'.

(3) At the end of sub-paragraph (4) insert –

'And in such a case any registered social landlord specified in a direction under sub-paragraph (2) must be one to which paragraphs (a) and (b) above apply.'

16 After paragraph 15 insert –

'Transfer of net assets on termination of charity not within paragraph 15(1)

15A (1) The Secretary of State may by regulations provide for any provisions of paragraph 15(2) to (6) to apply in relation to a registered social landlord within sub-paragraph (2) –

(a) in such circumstances, and
(b) with such modifications,

as may be specified in the regulations.

(2) A registered social landlord is within this sub-paragraph if –

(a) it is a registered charity, and
(b) it does not fall within sub-paragraph (1) of paragraph 15.

(3) Regulations under this paragraph may in particular provide that any provision of the regulations requiring the transfer of any property of the charity is to have effect notwithstanding –

(a) anything in the terms of its trusts, or
(b) any resolution, order or other thing done for the purposes of, or in connection with, the termination of the charity in any manner specified in the regulations.

(4) Any regulations under this paragraph shall be made by statutory instrument which shall be subject to annulment in pursuance of a resolution of either House of Parliament.'

17 (1) Paragraph 16 of Schedule 1 (general requirements as to accounts and audit) is amended as follows.

(2) Omit sub-paragraph (4) (auditor's report to state whether accounts comply with paragraph 16).

(3) For sub-paragraph (5) substitute –

'(5) Every registered social landlord shall furnish to the Relevant Authority –

(a) a copy of its accounts, and
(b) (subject to sub-paragraph (7)) a copy of the auditor's report in respect of them,

within six months of the end of the period to which they relate.

(6) The auditor's report shall state, in addition to any other matters which it is required to state, whether in the auditor's opinion the accounts comply with the requirements laid down under this paragraph.

(7) The provisions of sub-paragraphs (5)(b) and (6) do not apply where, by virtue of any enactment –

(a) any accounts of a registered social landlord are not required to be audited, and
(b) instead a report is required to be prepared in respect of them by a person appointed for the purpose ("the reporting accountant"),

and sub-paragraph (8) shall apply in place of those provisions.

(8) In such a case –

(a) the registered social landlord shall furnish to the Relevant Authority a copy of the reporting accountant's report in respect of the accounts within six months of the end of the period to which they relate; and
(b) that report shall state, in addition to any other matters which it is required to state, whether in the reporting accountant's opinion the accounts comply with the requirements laid down under this paragraph.'

18 After paragraph 16 of Schedule 1 insert –

'Companies exempt from audit requirements: accountant's report

16A (1) This paragraph applies to registered social landlords which are companies registered under the Companies Act 1985 ("RSL companies").

(2) In section 249A of the Companies Act 1985 (exemptions from audit) –

(a) subsection (2) shall apply in relation to an RSL company which meets the total exemption conditions in respect of a financial year (whether it is a charity or not), and
(b) that subsection shall apply in relation to such a company in the same way as it applies in relation to an RSL company which is a charity and meets the report conditions in relation to a financial year; and
(c) subsection (1) accordingly does not have effect in relation to an RSL company.

(3) In section 249C of that Act (report required for the purposes of section 249A(2)), subsection (3) shall apply in relation to an RSL company within sub-paragraph (2)(a) above as if the reference to satisfying the requirements of section 249A(4) were a reference to meeting the total exemption conditions.

(4) The Relevant Authority may, in respect of any relevant financial year of an RSL company, give a direction to the company requiring it –

(a) to appoint a qualified auditor to audit its accounts and balance sheet for that year, and
(b) to furnish to the Relevant Authority a copy of the auditor's report by such date as is specified in the direction.

(5) For the purposes of sub-paragraph (4), a financial year of an RSL company is a "relevant financial year" if –

(a) it precedes that in which the direction is given, and
(b) the company met either the total exemption conditions or the report conditions in respect of that year, and
(c) its accounts and balance sheet for that year were not audited in accordance with Part 7 of the Companies Act 1985.

(6) In this paragraph –

(a) "financial year" has the meaning given by section 223 of the Companies Act 1985;
(b) "qualified auditor" means a person who is eligible for appointment as auditor of the company under Part 2 of the Companies Act 1989;
(c) any reference to a company meeting the report conditions is to be read in accordance with section 249A(4) of the Companies Act 1985; and
(d) any reference to a company meeting the total exemption conditions is to be read in accordance with section 249A(3) or section 249A(3) and (3A) of that Act, depending on whether it is a charity.'

19 For paragraph 17 of Schedule 1 (appointment of auditors by industrial and provident societies), together with the heading preceding it, substitute –

'Industrial and provident societies exempt from audit requirements: accountant's report

17 (1) This paragraph applies to registered social landlords which are industrial and provident societies.

(2) Section 9A of the Friendly and Industrial and Provident Societies Act 1968 (duty to obtain accountant's reports where section 4 applied) shall have effect, in its application to such a landlord, with the omission of subsection (1)(b) (accountant's report required only where turnover exceeds a specified sum).

(3) The Relevant Authority may, in respect of any relevant year of account of such a landlord, give a direction to the landlord requiring it –

(a) to appoint a qualified auditor to audit its accounts and balance sheet for that year, and
(b) to furnish to the Relevant Authority a copy of the auditor's report by such date as is specified in the direction.

(4) For the purposes of sub-paragraph (3), a year of account of a landlord is a "relevant year of account" if –

(a) it precedes that in which the direction is given, and
(b) at the end of it there is in force in relation to it a disapplication under section 4A(1) of the Friendly and Industrial and Provident Societies Act 1968.

(5) In this paragraph –

"qualified auditor" means a person who is a qualified auditor for the purposes of the Friendly and Industrial and Provident Societies Act 1968;

"year of account" has the meaning given by section 21(1) of that Act.'

20 (1) Paragraph 18 of Schedule 1 (accounting and audit requirements for charities) is amended as follows.

(2) In the cross-heading preceding the paragraph, after 'and audit' insert 'or reporting'.

(3) In sub-paragraph (1) (application of provisions to registered social landlord which is a registered charity) omit the words from ' (which impose' onwards.

(4) For sub-paragraph (4) substitute –

'(4) The charity must appoint a qualified auditor ("the auditor") to audit the accounts prepared in accordance with sub-paragraph (3) in respect of each period of account in which –

(a) the charity's gross income (within the meaning of the Charities Act 1993) arising in connection with its housing activities, or
(b) its total expenditure arising in connection with those activities,

exceeds the sum for the time being specified in section 43(1) of the Charities Act 1993 (audit required for charities where gross income or total income exceeds the specified sum).

(4A) Where sub-paragraph (4) does not apply in respect of a period of account, the charity must appoint a qualified auditor ('the reporting accountant') to make such a report as is mentioned in paragraph 18A(1) in respect of the period of account.

(4B) In sub-paragraphs (4) and (4A) 'qualified auditor' means a person who is eligible for appointment as auditor of the charity under Part 2 of the Companies Act 1989 or who would be so eligible if the charity were a company registered under the Companies Act 1985.'

21 After paragraph 18 of Schedule 1 insert –

'Charities exempt from audit requirements: accountant's report

18A (1) The report referred to in paragraph 18(4A) is a report –

(a) relating to the charity's accounts prepared in accordance with paragraph 18(3) in respect of the period of account in question, and
(b) complying with sub-paragraphs (2) and (3) below.

(2) The report must state whether, in the opinion of the reporting accountant –

(a) the revenue account or accounts and the balance sheet are in agreement with the books of account kept by the charity under paragraph 18(2),
(b) on the basis of the information contained in those books of account, the revenue account or accounts and the balance sheet comply with the requirements of the Charities Act 1993, and
(c) on the basis of the information contained in those books of account, paragraph 18(4A) applied to the charity in respect of the period of account in question.

(3) The report must also state the name of the reporting accountant and be signed by him.

(4) Paragraph 18(7) applies to the reporting accountant and his functions under this paragraph as it applies to an auditor and his functions under paragraph 18.

(5) The Relevant Authority may, in respect of a relevant period of account of a charity, give a direction to the charity requiring it –

(a) to appoint a qualified auditor to audit its accounts for that period, and

(b) to furnish to the Relevant Authority a copy of the auditor's report by such date as is specified in the direction;

and paragraph 18(5) to (7) apply to an auditor so appointed as they apply to an auditor appointed under paragraph 18.

(6) For the purposes of sub-paragraph (5), a period of account of a charity is a relevant period of account if –

(a) it precedes that in which the direction is given; and

(b) paragraph 18(4A) applied in relation to it.

(7) In this paragraph "period of account" and "qualified auditor" have the same meaning as in paragraph 18(4A).'

22 (1) Paragraph 19 of Schedule 1 (responsibility for securing compliance with accounting requirements) is amended as follows.

(2) In sub-paragraph (2) –

(a) in paragraph (c), after 'and audit' insert 'or reporting';

(b) omit paragraph (d) (but not the 'or' at the end); and

(c) for 'level 3' substitute 'level 5'.

(3) The amendment made by sub-paragraph (2)(c) does not apply in relation to any offence committed before the day on which that sub-paragraph comes into force.

(4) After sub-paragraph (4) insert –

'(5) Where any of paragraphs (a) to (e) of sub-paragraph (2) applies in respect of any default on the part of a registered social landlord, the High Court may, on the application of the Relevant Authority, make such order as the court thinks fit for requiring the default to be made good.

Any such order may provide that all the costs or expenses of and incidental to the application shall be borne by the registered social landlord or by any of its officers who are responsible for the default.'

23 After paragraph 19 of Schedule 1 insert –

'Disclosure of information by auditors etc to the Relevant Authority

19A (1) A person who is, or has been, an auditor of a registered social landlord does not contravene any duty to which he is subject merely because he gives to the Relevant Authority –

(a) information on a matter of which he became aware in his capacity as auditor of the registered social landlord, or

(b) his opinion on such a matter,

if he is acting in good faith and he reasonably believes that the information or opinion is relevant to any functions of the Relevant Authority.

(2) Sub-paragraph (1) applies whether or not the person is responding to a request from the Relevant Authority.

(3) This paragraph applies to a person who is, or has been, a reporting accountant as it applies to a person who is, or has been, an auditor.

(4) A "reporting accountant" means a person appointed as mentioned in paragraph 16(7)(b).'

24 (1) Paragraph 20 of Schedule 1 (inquiry into affairs of registered social landlord) is amended as follows.

(2) After sub-paragraph (4) insert –

'(4A) The person or persons conducting the inquiry may determine the procedure to be followed in connection with the inquiry.'

(3) At the end of sub-paragraph (7) add ', and the Relevant Authority may arrange for the whole or part of an interim or final report to be published in such manner as it considers appropriate.'

(4) After sub-paragraph (7) insert –

'(8) A local authority may, if they think fit, contribute to the expenses of the Relevant Authority in connection with any inquiry under this paragraph.'

25 After paragraph 20 of Schedule 1 insert –

'Evidence

20A (1) For the purposes of an inquiry the person or persons conducting it may serve a notice on an appropriate person directing him to attend at a specified time and place and do either or both of the following, namely –

(a) give evidence;
(b) produce any specified documents, or documents of a specified description, which are in his custody or under his control and relate to any matter relevant to the inquiry.

(2) The person or persons conducting such an inquiry –

(a) may take evidence on oath and for that purpose administer oaths, or
(b) instead of administering an oath, require the person examined to make and subscribe a declaration of the truth of the matters about which he is examined.

(3) In this paragraph –

"appropriate person" means a person listed in section 30(2);

"document" has the same meaning as in section 30;

"inquiry" means an inquiry under paragraph 20.

(4) A person may not be required under this paragraph to disclose anything that, by virtue of section 30(4), he could not be required to disclose under section 30.

(5) Section 31 (enforcement of notice to provide information, &c) applies in relation to a notice given under this paragraph by the person or persons conducting an inquiry as it applies in relation to a notice given under section 30 by the Relevant Authority, but subject to sub-paragraph (6).

(6) A person guilty of an offence under section 31(1) as it applies in accordance with sub-paragraph (5) is liable –

(a) on summary conviction, to a fine not exceeding the statutory maximum;
(b) on conviction on indictment, to imprisonment for a term not exceeding two years or to a fine, or both.

(7) Any person who, in purported compliance with a notice given under this paragraph by the person or persons conducting an inquiry, knowingly or recklessly provides any information which is false or misleading in a material particular commits an offence and is liable to the penalties mentioned in sub-paragraph (6).

(8) Proceedings for an offence under sub-paragraph (7) may be brought only by or with the consent of the Relevant Authority or the Director of Public Prosecutions.'

26 (1) Paragraph 21 of Schedule 1 (power of appointed person to obtain information) is amended as follows.

(2) At the end of sub-paragraph (3) (application of section 31 to notice under paragraph 20) add ', but subject to sub-paragraph (4).'

(3) After sub-paragraph (3) add –

'(4) A person guilty of an offence under section 31(1) as it applies in accordance with sub-paragraph (3) is liable –

(a) on summary conviction, to a fine not exceeding the statutory maximum;
(b) on conviction on indictment, to imprisonment for a term not exceeding two years or to a fine, or both.

(5) Any person who, in purported compliance with a notice given under this paragraph by an appointed person, knowingly or recklessly provides any information which is false or misleading in a material particular commits an offence and is liable to the penalties mentioned in sub-paragraph (4).

(6) Proceedings for an offence under sub-paragraph (5) may be brought only by or with the consent of the Relevant Authority or the Director of Public Prosecutions.'

(5) The amendments made by this paragraph do not apply in relation to any offence committed or other thing done before the day on which this paragraph comes into force.

SCHEDULE 12
New Schedule 2A to the Housing Act 1996

Section 228(3)

'SCHEDULE 2A
Further Provision about the Social Housing Ombudsman for Wales

Section 51A(7)

Status

1 The Social Housing Ombudsman for Wales ("the Ombudsman") shall be a corporation sole.

Remuneration, etc

2 The National Assembly for Wales may pay to or in respect of the Ombudsman such amounts, by way of remuneration, pensions, allowances or gratuities or by way of provision for any such benefits, as it considers appropriate.

3 If a person ceases to be the Ombudsman and it appears to the National Assembly for Wales that there are special circumstances which make it right that the person should receive compensation, the National Assembly for Wales may pay to that person a sum of such amount as it considers appropriate.

Staff and advisers

4 (1) The Ombudsman may appoint such staff as he considers necessary for assisting him in the exercise of his functions.

(2) The Ombudsman shall include among his staff such persons having a command of the Welsh language as he considers are needed to enable him to investigate complaints in Welsh.

(3) To assist him in the exercise of his functions, the Ombudsman may obtain advice from any person who, in his opinion, is qualified to give it.

(4) The Ombudsman may pay to any person from whom he obtains advice under sub-paragraph (3) such fees or allowances as he may determine.

Delegation of functions

5 (1) Any function of the Ombudsman may be exercised by –

(a) a member of his staff, or
(b) a member of the staff of the Commission for Local Administration in Wales,

if authorised by the Ombudsman for that purpose.

(2) The Ombudsman may, with the approval of the National Assembly for Wales, make arrangements with persons under which they, or members of their staff, may perform functions of the Ombudsman.

(3) References in any provision made by or under an enactment to a member of staff of the Ombudsman include any person exercising any function of his by virtue of sub-paragraph (1)(b).

Reports and determinations

6 (1) The Ombudsman –

(a) shall annually prepare and lay before the National Assembly for Wales a general report on the performance of his functions; and
(b) may from time to time prepare and lay before the National Assembly for Wales such other reports with respect to his functions as he thinks fit.

(2) The National Assembly for Wales shall, and the Ombudsman may, publish reports laid before the National Assembly for Wales under sub-paragraph (1).

7 The Ombudsman may, subject to any provision made by regulations under section 51B, publish his determination on any complaint.

8 (1) The Ombudsman may include in any report or determination published under paragraph 6 or 7 statements, communications, reports, papers or other documentary evidence obtained in the exercise of his functions.

(2) In publishing any report or determination, the Ombudsman shall have regard to the need for excluding so far as practicable –

(a) any matter which relates to the private affairs of an individual, where publication would seriously and prejudicially affect the interests of that individual, and

(b) any matter which relates specifically to a social landlord in Wales, where publication would seriously and prejudicially affect its interests,

unless inclusion of the matter concerned is necessary for the purposes of the report or determination.

Expenses

9 (1) The expenses of the Ombudsman shall, so far as they cannot be met out of income received by him, be met by the National Assembly for Wales.

(2) Those expenses include any sums payable by the Ombudsman in consequence of a breach, in the course of the performance of any of his functions, of any contractual or other duty (whether that breach occurs by reason of his act or omission or that of a member of his staff or any other person assisting him in the exercise of his functions).

Absolute privilege for communications etc

10 For the purposes of the law of defamation, absolute privilege attaches to –

(a) any communication between the Ombudsman and any person by or against whom a complaint is made to him;

(b) any determination by the Ombudsman; and

(c) the publication by him of any report or such a determination under paragraph 6, 7 or 8.

Disclosure of information

11 (1) Information obtained by the Ombudsman in the course of or for the purposes of an investigation of a complaint must not be disclosed except –

(a) for the purposes of the investigation, of any determination made in respect of the complaint or of the publication of a determination under paragraph 7;

(b) as provided in paragraph 12 or 17 or any regulations under section 51B;

(c) for the purposes of any proceedings for an offence of perjury alleged to have been committed in the course of an investigation of a complaint by the Ombudsman; or

(d) for the purposes of an inquiry with a view to the taking of any proceedings as mentioned in paragraph (c).

(2) The Ombudsman shall not be called upon to give evidence in any proceedings (other than proceedings within sub-paragraph (1)(c)) of matters coming to his knowledge in the course of an investigation of a complaint.

(3) Information obtained from the Information Commissioner by virtue of section 76 of the Freedom of Information Act 2000 shall be treated for the purposes of sub-paragraph (1) as obtained for the purposes of an investigation and, in relation to such information, the reference in paragraph (a) of that sub-paragraph to the investigation shall have effect as a reference to any investigation.

12 The Ombudsman may disclose to the Information Commissioner any information obtained by, or furnished to, the Ombudsman by virtue of or for the purposes of section 51A or 51B if the information appears to him to relate to –

(a) a matter in respect of which the Information Commissioner could exercise any power conferred by –

    (i) Part V of the Data Protection Act 1998 (enforcement),

    (ii) section 48 of the Freedom of Information Act 2000 (practice recommendations), or

    (iii) Part IV of that Act (enforcement), or

  (b) the commission of an offence under –

    (i) any provision of the Data Protection Act 1998 other than paragraph 12 of Schedule 9 (obstruction of execution of warrant), or

    (ii) section 77 of the Freedom of Information Act 2000 (offence of altering etc records with intent to prevent disclosure).

Accounts and audit

13 (1) The Ombudsman shall keep proper accounting records.

(2) The Ombudsman shall, for each financial year, prepare accounts in accordance with directions given to him by the Treasury.

(3) The directions which the Treasury may give under sub-paragraph (2) include, in particular, directions as to –

  (a) the information to be contained in the accounts and the manner in which it is to be presented,

  (b) the methods and principles in accordance with which the accounts are to be prepared, and

  (c) the additional information (if any) that is to accompany the accounts.

(4) In this paragraph and in paragraph 14, "financial year" means the twelve months ending with 31st March.

14 (1) The accounts prepared by the Ombudsman for any financial year shall be submitted by him to the Auditor General for Wales no later than the 30th November of the following year.

(2) The Auditor General for Wales shall –

  (a) examine and certify any accounts submitted to him under this paragraph, and

  (b) no later than four months after the accounts are submitted to him, lay before the National Assembly for Wales a copy of them as certified by him together with his report on them.

(3) In examining any accounts submitted to him under this paragraph, the Auditor General for Wales shall, in particular, satisfy himself that the expenditure to which the accounts relate has been incurred lawfully and in accordance with the authority which governs it.

Accounting officer

15 (1) The accounting officer for the Office of the Ombudsman shall be the Ombudsman.

(2) But where –

  (a) the Ombudsman is incapable of discharging his responsibilities as accounting officer, or

  (b) the office of the Ombudsman is vacant (and there is no acting Ombudsman),

the Treasury may designate a member of the Ombudsman's staff to be the accounting officer for so long as paragraph (a) or (b) applies.

(3) The accounting officer for the Office of the Ombudsman shall have, in relation to –

(a) the accounts of the Ombudsman, and
(b) the finances of the Office of the Ombudsman,

the responsibilities which are from time to time specified by the Treasury.

(4) In this paragraph references to responsibilities include in particular –

(a) responsibilities in relation to the signing of accounts,
(b) responsibilities for the propriety and regularity of the finances of the Office of the Ombudsman, and
(c) responsibilities for the economy, efficiency and effectiveness with which the resources of the Office of the Ombudsman are used.

(5) The responsibilities which may be specified under this paragraph include responsibilities owed to –

(a) the National Assembly for Wales, the executive committee or the Audit Committee, or
(b) the House of Commons or its Committee of Public Accounts.

(6) If requested to do so by the House of Commons Committee of Public Accounts, the Audit Committee may –

(a) on behalf of the Committee of Public Accounts take evidence from the accounting officer for the Office of the Ombudsman, and
(b) report to the Committee of Public Accounts and transmit to that Committee any evidence so taken.

(7) In this paragraph and paragraphs 16 and 17, "the Office of the Ombudsman" means the Ombudsman and the members of his staff.

(8) Section 13 of the National Audit Act 1983 (interpretation of references to the Committee of Public Accounts) applies for the purposes of this paragraph as for those of that Act.

Examinations into use of resources

16 (1) The Auditor General for Wales may carry out examinations into the economy, efficiency and effectiveness with which the Ombudsman has used the resources of the Office of the Ombudsman in discharging his functions.

(2) Sub-paragraph (1) shall not be construed as entitling the Auditor General for Wales to question the merits of the policy objectives of the Ombudsman.

(3) In determining how to exercise his functions under this paragraph, the Auditor General for Wales shall take into account the views of the Audit Committee as to the examinations which he should carry out under this paragraph.

(4) The Auditor General for Wales may lay before the National Assembly for Wales a report of the results of any examination carried out by him under this paragraph.

(5) Section 7 of the National Audit Act 1983 (economy, efficiency and effectiveness examinations by Comptroller and Auditor General) applies to the Ombudsman.

(6) The Auditor General for Wales and the Comptroller and Auditor General may co-operate with, and give assistance to, each other in connection with the carrying out of examinations in respect of the Ombudsman under this paragraph or section 7 of the National Audit Act 1983.

17 (1) For the purpose of enabling him to carry out examinations into, and report to Parliament on, the finances of the Office of the Ombudsman, the Comptroller and Auditor General –

(a) shall have a right of access at all reasonable times to all such documents in the custody or under the control of the Ombudsman, or of the Auditor General for Wales, as he may reasonably require for that purpose, and

(b) shall be entitled to require from any person holding or accountable for any of those documents any assistance, information or explanation which he reasonably thinks necessary for that purpose.

(2) The Comptroller and Auditor General shall –

(a) consult the Auditor General for Wales, and

(b) take into account any relevant work done or being done by the Auditor General for Wales,

before he acts in reliance on sub-paragraph (1) or carries out an examination in respect of the Ombudsman under section 7 of the National Audit Act 1983 (economy etc examinations).'

SCHEDULE 13
RESIDENTIAL PROPERTY TRIBUNALS: PROCEDURE

Section 230

Procedure regulations

1 (1) The appropriate national authority may make regulations about the procedure of residential property tribunals.

(2) Nothing in the following provisions of this Schedule affects the generality of sub-paragraph (1).

(3) In those provisions –

'procedure regulations' means regulations under this paragraph;

'tribunal' means a residential property tribunal.

Appeals

2 (1) Procedure regulations may include provision, in relation to applications to tribunals –

(a) about the form of such applications and the particulars to be contained in them,

(b) requiring the service of notices of such applications, and

(c) in the case of applications under section 102(4) or (7) or 133(1), requiring the service of copies of the draft orders submitted with the applications.

(2) Procedure regulations may include provision, in relation to appeals to tribunals –

(a) about the form of notices of appeal and the particulars to be contained in them, and

(b) requiring the service of copies of such notices.

(3) Procedure regulations may include provision dispensing with the service of the notices or copies mentioned in sub-paragraph (1)(b) or (2)(b) in such cases of urgency as are specified in the regulations.

Transfers

3 (1) This paragraph applies where, in any proceedings before a court, there falls for determination a question which a tribunal would have jurisdiction to determine on an application or appeal to the tribunal.

(2) The court –

    (a) may by order transfer to the tribunal so much of the proceedings as relate to the determination of that question, and

    (b) may then dispose of all or any remaining proceedings, or adjourn the disposal of all or any remaining proceedings pending the determination of that question by the tribunal, as it thinks fit.

(3) When the tribunal has determined the question, the court may give effect to the determination in an order of the court.

(4) Rules of court may prescribe the procedure to be followed in a court in connection with or in consequence of a transfer under this paragraph.

(5) Procedure regulations may prescribe the procedure to be followed in a tribunal consequent on a transfer under this paragraph.

(6) Nothing in this Act affects any power of a court to make an order that could be made by a tribunal (such as an order quashing a licence granted or order made by a local housing authority) in a case where –

    (a) the court has not made a transfer under this paragraph, and

    (b) the order is made by the court in connection with disposing of any proceedings before it.

Parties etc

4 (1) Procedure regulations may include provision enabling persons to be joined as parties to the proceedings.

(2) Procedure regulations may include provision enabling persons who are not parties to proceedings before a tribunal to make oral or written representations to the tribunal.

Information

5 (1) Procedure regulations may include –

    (a) provision relating to the supply of information and documents by a party to the proceedings, and

    (b) in particular any provision authorised by the following provisions of this paragraph.

(2) The regulations may include provision for requiring, or empowering the tribunal to require, a party to proceedings before a tribunal –

    (a) to supply to the tribunal information or documents specified, or of a description specified, in the regulations or in an order made by the tribunal;

    (b) to supply to any other party copies of any information or documents supplied to the tribunal;

    (c) to supply any such information, documents or copies by such time as is specified in or determined in accordance with the regulations or order.

(3) The regulations may also include provision –

    (a) for granting a party to the proceedings such disclosure or inspection of documents, or such right to further information, as might be granted by a county court;

    (b) for requiring persons to attend to give evidence and produce documents;

    (c) for authorising the administration of oaths to witnesses.

(4) The regulations may include provision empowering a tribunal to dismiss, or allow, the whole or part of an appeal or application in a case where a party to the proceedings has failed to comply with –

(a) a requirement imposed by regulations made by virtue of this paragraph, or
(b) an order of the tribunal made by virtue of any such regulations.

Pre-trial reviews etc

6 (1) Procedure regulations may include provision for the holding of a pre-trial review (on the application of a party to the proceedings or on the tribunal's own initiative).

(2) Procedure regulations may provide for functions of a tribunal in relation to, or at, a pre-trial review to be exercised by a single qualified member of the panel.

(3) Procedure regulations may provide for other functions as to preliminary or incidental matters to be exercised by a single qualified member of the panel.

(4) For the purposes of this paragraph –

(a) a person is a qualified member of the panel if he was appointed to it by the Lord Chancellor; and
(b) 'the panel' means the panel provided for in Schedule 10 to the Rent Act 1977 (c 42).

Interim orders

7 Procedure regulations may include provision empowering tribunals to make orders, on an interim basis –

(a) suspending, in whole or in part, the effect of any decision, notice, order or licence which is the subject matter of proceedings before them;
(b) granting any remedy which they would have had power to grant in their final decisions.

Additional relief

8 (1) Procedure regulations may include provision as to –

(a) any additional relief which tribunals may grant in respect of proceedings before them; and
(b) the grounds on which such relief may be granted.

(2) In this paragraph 'additional relief' means relief additional to any relief specifically authorised by any provision of Parts 1 to 4 of this Act.

Dismissal

9 Procedure regulations may include provision empowering tribunals to dismiss applications, appeals or transferred proceedings, in whole or in part, on the ground that they are –

(a) frivolous or vexatious, or
(b) otherwise an abuse of process.

Determination without hearing

10 (1) Procedure regulations may include provision for the determination of applications, appeals or transferred proceedings without an oral hearing.

(2) Procedure regulations may include provision enabling a single qualified member of the panel to decide whether an oral hearing is appropriate in a particular case.

(3) Procedure regulations may provide for a single qualified member of the panel to make determinations without an oral hearing.

(4) For the purposes of this paragraph –

    (a) a person is a qualified member of the panel if he was appointed to it by the Lord Chancellor; and

    (b) 'the panel' means the panel provided for in Schedule 10 to the Rent Act 1977 (c 42).

Fees

11 (1) Procedure regulations may include provision requiring the payment of fees in respect of applications, appeals or transfers of proceedings to, or oral hearings by, tribunals.

(2) The fees payable shall be such as are specified in or determined in accordance with procedure regulations.

(3) But the fee (or, where fees are payable in respect of both an application, appeal or transfer and an oral hearing, the aggregate of the fees) payable by a person in respect of any proceedings must not exceed –

    (a) £500, or

    (b) such other amount as may be specified in procedure regulations.

(4) Procedure regulations may empower a tribunal to require a party to proceedings before it to reimburse another party to the proceedings the whole or any part of any fees paid by him.

(5) Procedure regulations may provide for the reduction or waiver of fees by reference to the financial resources of the party by whom they are to be paid or met.

(6) If they do so they may apply, subject to such modifications as may be specified in the regulations, any other statutory means-testing regime as it has effect from time to time.

Costs

12 (1) A tribunal may determine that a party to proceedings before it is to pay the costs incurred by another party in connection with the proceedings in any circumstances falling within sub-paragraph (2).

(2) The circumstances are where –

    (a) he has failed to comply with an order made by the tribunal;

    (b) in accordance with regulations made by virtue of paragraph 5(4), the tribunal dismisses, or allows, the whole or part of an application or appeal by reason of his failure to comply with a requirement imposed by regulations made by virtue of paragraph 5;

    (c) in accordance with regulations made by virtue of paragraph 9, the tribunal dismisses the whole or part of an application or appeal made by him to the tribunal; or

    (d) he has, in the opinion of the tribunal, acted frivolously, vexatiously, abusively, disruptively or otherwise unreasonably in connection with the proceedings.

(3) The amount which a party to proceedings may be ordered to pay in the proceedings by a determination under this paragraph must not exceed –

    (a) £500, or

    (b) such other amount as may be specified in procedure regulations.

(4) A person may not be required to pay costs incurred by another person in connection with proceedings before a tribunal, except –

(a) by a determination under this paragraph, or

(b) in accordance with provision made by any enactment other than this paragraph.

Enforcement

13 Procedure regulations may provide for decisions of tribunals to be enforceable, with the permission of a county court, in the same way as orders of such a court.

SCHEDULE 14
BUILDINGS WHICH ARE NOT HMOS FOR PURPOSES OF THIS ACT (EXCLUDING PART 1)

Section 254

Introduction: buildings (or parts) which are not HMOs for purposes of this Act (excluding Part 1)

1 (1) The following paragraphs list buildings which are not houses in multiple occupation for any purposes of this Act other than those of Part 1.

(2) In this Schedule 'building' includes a part of a building.

Buildings controlled or managed by public sector bodies etc

2 (1) A building where the person managing or having control of it is –

(a) a local housing authority,

(b) a body which is registered as a social landlord under Part 1 of the Housing Act 1996 (c 52),

(c) a police authority established under section 3 of the Police Act 1996 (c 16),

(d) the Metropolitan Police Authority established under section 5B of that Act,

(e) a fire and rescue authority, or

(f) a health service body within the meaning of section 4 of the National Health Service and Community Care Act 1990 (c 19).

(2) In sub-paragraph (1)(e) 'fire and rescue authority' means a fire and rescue authority under the Fire and Rescue Services Act 2004 (c 21).

Buildings regulated otherwise than under this Act

3 Any building whose occupation is regulated otherwise than by or under this Act and which is of a description specified for the purposes of this paragraph in regulations made by the appropriate national authority.

Buildings occupied by students

4 (1) Any building –

(a) which is occupied solely or principally by persons who occupy it for the purpose of undertaking a full-time course of further or higher education at a specified educational establishment or at an educational establishment of a specified description, and

(b) where the person managing or having control of it is the educational establishment in question or a specified person or a person of a specified description.

(2) In sub-paragraph (1) 'specified' means specified for the purposes of this paragraph in regulations made by the appropriate national authority.

(3) Sub-paragraph (4) applies in connection with any decision by the appropriate national authority as to whether to make, or revoke, any regulations specifying –

    (a) a particular educational establishment, or
    (b) a particular description of educational establishments.

(4) The appropriate national authority may have regard to the extent to which, in its opinion –

    (a) the management by or on behalf of the establishment in question of any building or buildings occupied for connected educational purposes is in conformity with any code of practice for the time being approved under section 233 which appears to the authority to be relevant, or
    (b) the management of such buildings by or on behalf of establishments of the description in question is in general in conformity with any such code of practice,

as the case may be.

(5) In sub-paragraph (4) 'occupied for connected educational purposes', in relation to a building managed by or on behalf of an educational establishment, means occupied solely or principally by persons who occupy it for the purpose of undertaking a full-time course of further or higher education at the establishment.

Buildings occupied by religious communities

5   (1) Any building which is occupied principally for the purposes of a religious community whose principal occupation is prayer, contemplation, education or the relief of suffering.

(2) This paragraph does not apply in the case of a converted block of flats to which section 257 applies.

Buildings occupied by owners

6   (1) Any building which is occupied only by persons within the following paragraphs –

    (a) one or more persons who have, whether in the whole or any part of it, either the freehold estate or a leasehold interest granted for a term of more than 21 years;
    (b) any member of the household of such a person or persons;
    (c) no more than such number of other persons as is specified for the purposes of this paragraph in regulations made by the appropriate national authority.

(2) This paragraph does not apply in the case of a converted block of flats to which section 257 applies, except for the purpose of determining the status of any flat in the block.

Buildings occupied by two persons

7   Any building which is occupied only by two persons who form two households.

SCHEDULE 15
Minor and Consequential Amendments

Section 265(1)

Parliamentary Commissioner Act 1967 (c 13)

1 (1) Section 11A of the Parliamentary Commissioner Act 1967 (consultation between Parliamentary Commissioner and Welsh Administration Ombudsman or Health Service Commissioners) is amended as follows.

(2) In the sidenote for 'Welsh Administration Ombudsman or Health Service Commissioners' substitute 'other Commissioners or Ombudsmen'.

(3) In subsection (1) –

(a) after 'Ombudsman' insert ', of the Social Housing Ombudsman for Wales'; and
(b) in paragraph (b) for 'or' substitute ', under regulations under section 51B of the Housing Act 1996 or under'.

(4) In subsection (2) after 'Ombudsman' insert ', the Social Housing Ombudsman for Wales'.

Land Compensation Act 1973 (c 26)

2 The Land Compensation Act 1973 has effect subject to the following amendments.

3 (1) Section 29 (right to home loss payment where person displaced from dwelling) is amended as follows.

(2) In subsection (1) –

(a) for paragraph (b) substitute –

'(b) the making of a housing order in respect of the dwelling;'; and

(b) in paragraph (ii) for the words from 'the order' onwards substitute 'the housing order;'.

(3) In subsection (3A) for the words from 'the acceptance' onwards substitute 'the carrying out of any improvement to the dwelling unless he is permanently displaced from it in consequence of the carrying out of that improvement.'

(4) For subsection (7) substitute –

'(7) In this section "a housing order" means –

(a) a prohibition order under section 20 or 21 of the Housing Act 2004, or
(b) a demolition order under section 265 of the Housing Act 1985.'

4 (1) Section 33D (loss payments: exclusions) is amended as follows.

(2) In subsection (4) for paragraphs (b) and (c) substitute –

'(b) notice under section 11 of the Housing Act 2004 (improvement notice relating to category 1 hazard);
(c) notice under section 12 of that Act (improvement notice relating to category 2 hazard);'.

(3) For subsection (5) substitute –

'(5) These are the orders –

(a) an order under section 20 of the Housing Act 2004 (prohibition order relating to category 1 hazard);

(b) an order under section 21 of that Act (prohibition order relating to category 2 hazard);

(c) an order under section 43 of that Act (emergency prohibition orders);

(d) an order under section 265 of the Housing Act 1985 (demolition order relating to category 1 or 2 hazard).'

5   (1) Section 37 (disturbance payments for persons with compensatable interests) is amended as follows.

(2) In subsection (1) –

(a) for paragraph (b) substitute –

'(b) the making of a housing order in respect of a house or building on the land;'; and

(b) in paragraph (ii) for the words from 'the order' onwards substitute 'the housing order;'.

(3) In subsection (2)(c) for 'closing' substitute 'prohibition'.

(4) In subsection (3) for the words from 'any such order' onwards substitute 'a housing order within paragraph (b) of that subsection unless he was in lawful possession as aforesaid at the time when the order was made.'

(5) In subsection (3A) for the words from 'the acceptance' onwards substitute 'the carrying out of any improvement to a house or building unless he is permanently displaced in consequence of the carrying out of that improvement.'

(6) In subsection (9) omit 'or undertaking'.

6   (1) Section 39 (duty to rehouse residential occupiers) is amended as follows.

(2) In subsection (1) for paragraph (b) substitute –

'(b) the making of a housing order in respect of a house or building on the land;'.

(3) In subsection (6) for the words from 'any such order' onwards substitute 'a housing order within paragraph (b) of that subsection unless he was residing in the accommodation in question at the time when the order was made.'

(4) In subsection (6A) for the words from 'the acceptance' onwards substitute 'the carrying out of any improvement to a house or building unless he is permanently displaced from the residential accommodation in question in consequence of the carrying out of that improvement.'

(5) In subsection (9) omit 'or undertaking'.

Local Government Act 1974 (c 7)

7   (1) Section 33 of the Local Government Act 1974 (consultation between the Local Commissioner, other commissioners and the Welsh Administration Ombudsman) is amended as follows.

(2) In the sidenote for 'the Parliamentary Commissioner and the Health Service Commissioners' substitute 'and other Commissioners and Ombudsmen'.

(3) In subsection (1) –

(a) after paragraph (a) insert –

'(aza) by the Social Housing Ombudsman for Wales, in accordance with regulations under section 51B of the Housing Act 1996,';

(b) omit 'the' after 'appropriate Commissioner or'; and

(c) after 'the Act of 1967' insert ', under the Housing Act 1996'.

(4) In subsection (2) –

(a) after 'Parliamentary Commissioner' insert ', the Social Housing Ombudsman for Wales'; and

(b) omit 'the' after 'that Commissioner or'.

(5) In subsection (5) after '1967' insert ', in paragraph 13(1) of Schedule 2A to the Housing Act 1996'.

Greater London Council (General Powers) Act 1981 (c xvii)

8 In section 9(1) of the Greater London Council (General Powers) Act 1981 –

(a) for the words from 'a registration scheme' to 'section 354 of that Act,' substitute 'a licence under Part 2 of the Housing Act 2004'; and

(b) for '358' substitute '134'.

Mobile Homes Act 1983 (c 34)

9 In section 2 of the Mobile Homes Act 1983 (terms of agreements) after subsection (4) insert –

'(5) The supplementary provisions in Part 3 of Schedule 1 to this Act have effect for the purposes of paragraphs 8 and 9 of Part 1 of that Schedule. '

Housing Act 1985 (c 68)

10 The Housing Act 1985 has effect subject to the following amendments.

11 In section 8(2) (periodical review of housing needs) for 'section 605' substitute 'section 3 of the Housing Act 2004'.

12 For section 252(c) (definition of 'house in multiple occupation' for purposes of Part 8) substitute –

'(c) "house in multiple occupation" means a house in multiple occupation as defined by sections 254 to 259 of the Housing Act 2004, as they have effect for the purposes of Part 1 of that Act (that is, without the exclusions contained in Schedule 14 to that Act), but does not include any part of such a house which is occupied as a separate dwelling by persons who form a single household.'

13 For section 268 (service of notice of demolition and closing orders) substitute –

'268 Service of copies of demolition order

(1) A local housing authority who have made a demolition order must serve a copy of the order on every person who, to their knowledge, is –

(a) an owner or occupier of the whole or part of the premises to which the order relates,

(b) authorised to permit persons to occupy the whole or part of those premises, or

(c) a mortgagee of the whole or part of the premises.

(2) The copies required to be served under subsection (1) shall be served within the period of seven days beginning with the day on which the order is made.

(3) A copy of the order is to be regarded as having been served on every occupier in accordance with subsections (1) and (2) if a copy of the order is fixed to some conspicuous part of the premises within the period of seven days mentioned in subsection (2).

(4) A demolition order against which no appeal is brought under section 269 becomes operative at the end of the period of 28 days beginning with the day on which the order is made and is final and conclusive as to matters which could be raised on an appeal.

(5) Section 246 of the Housing Act 2004 (service of notices) –

   (a) applies in relation to copies required to be served under this section (instead of section 617 below), and
   (b) so applies as it applies in relation to documents required to be served under any provision of Parts 1 to 4 of that Act.'

14   In section 269(1) (right of appeal against demolition or closing order) for the words from 'demolition or closing order' to 'the order,' substitute 'demolition order may, within the period of 28 days beginning with the day on which the order is made,'.

15   After section 269 insert –

'269A Appeals suggesting certain other courses of action

(1) One ground of appeal under section 269 in relation to a demolition order made under section 265 is that a course of action mentioned in subsection (2) is the best course of action in relation to the hazard concerned.

(2) The courses of action are –

   (a) serving an improvement notice under section 11 or 12 of the Housing Act 2004;
   (b) making a prohibition order under section 20 or 21 of that Act;
   (c) serving a hazard awareness notice under section 28 or 29 of that Act; or
   (d) declaring the area in which the premises concerned are situated to be a clearance area in accordance with section 289 of this Act.

(3) Subsection (4) applies where –

   (a) a residential property tribunal is hearing an appeal under section 269 in relation to a demolition order made under section 265; and
   (b) the grounds on which the appeal is brought are or include the ground that a course of action mentioned in subsection (2) is the best course of action in relation to each hazard concerned.

(4) The tribunal shall have regard to any guidance given to the local housing authority under section 9 of the Housing Act 2004.

(5) Subsection (6) applies where –

   (a) an appeal under section 269 is allowed against a demolition order made under section 265; and
   (b) the reason or one of the reasons for allowing the appeal is that a course of action mentioned in subsection (2) is the best course of action in relation to the hazard concerned.

(6) The tribunal shall, if requested to do so by the appellant or the local housing authority, include in its decision a finding to that effect and identifying the course of action concerned.

(7) Subsection (1) of this section is without prejudice to the generality of section 269.'

16   In section 274 (demolition orders: power to permit reconstruction of condemned house) for subsections (2) to (5) substitute –

   '(2) If the authority are satisfied that the result of the works will be –

(a) in the case of a demolition order made under section 265(1) or (2), that the hazard concerned ceases to be a category 1 hazard, or

(b) in the case of a demolition order made under section 265(3) or (4), that a prescribed state of affairs exists,

they may, in order that the person submitting the proposals may have an opportunity of carrying out the works, extend for such period as they may specify the time within which the owner of the premises is required under section 271 to demolish them.

(3) In subsection (2) "prescribed state of affairs" means such state of affairs as may be specified or described in an order made by the Secretary of State.

(4) An order under subsection (3) –

(a) may make different provision for different cases or descriptions of case (including different provision for different areas);

(b) may contain such incidental, supplementary, consequential, transitory, transitional or saving provision as the Secretary of State considers appropriate; and

(c) shall be made by statutory instrument which shall be subject to annulment in pursuance of a resolution of either House of Parliament.

(5) That time may be further extended by the authority, once or more often as the case may require, if –

(a) the works have begun and appear to the authority to be making satisfactory progress, or

(b) though they have not begun, the authority think there has been no unreasonable delay.

(6) Where the authority determine to extend, or further extend, the time within which the owner of any premises is required under section 271 to demolish them, notice of the determination shall be served by the authority on every person having an interest in the premises or part of the premises, whether as freeholder, mortgagee or otherwise.

(7) If the works are completed to the satisfaction of the authority they shall revoke the demolition order (but without prejudice to any subsequent proceedings under this Part or Part 1 of the Housing Act 2004).'

17 After section 274 insert –

'274A Effect of certain enforcement action under the Housing Act 2004

A demolition order which has been made in respect of any premises shall cease to have effect if a management order under Chapter 1 or 2 of Part 4 of the Housing Act 2004 comes into force in relation to the premises.'

18 For section 275 (demolition orders: substitution of closing orders) substitute –

'275 Demolition orders: substitution of prohibition order to permit use otherwise than for human habitation

(1) If –

(a) an owner of any premises in respect of which a demolition order has become operative, or

(b) any other person who has an interest in the premises,

submits proposals to the local housing authority for the use of the premises for a purpose other than human habitation, the authority may, if they think fit, determine the demolition order and make a prohibition order under section 20 or 21 of the Housing Act 2004 in respect of the hazard concerned.

(2) The authority shall serve notice that the demolition order has been determined, and a copy of the prohibition order, on every person on whom they are required by Part 1 of Schedule 2 to the Housing Act 2004 to serve a copy of the prohibition order.'

19   (1) Section 289 (declaration of clearance area) is amended as follows.

(2) In subsection (2F)(b) for 'are unfit for human habitation' substitute 'contain category 1 or category 2 hazards'.

(3) In subsection (3) –

  (a) in sub-paragraph (i), for the words from 'unfit' to 'health' substitute 'dangerous or harmful to health or safety'; and
  (b) in sub-paragraph (ii), for 'injurious to health' substitute 'harmful to health or safety'.

20   For section 300 (purchase of houses liable to be demolished or closed) substitute –

'300 Purchase of houses liable to be demolished or to be subject to a prohibition order

(1) Where –

  (a) the local housing authority would be required under section 5 of the Housing Act 2004 to make a demolition order under section 265(1) or (2) of this Act in respect of a dwelling, a house in multiple occupation or a building containing one or more flats, and
  (b) it appears to them that the dwelling, house in multiple occupation or, as the case may be, building is or can be rendered capable of providing accommodation of a standard which is adequate for the time being,

they may purchase it instead.

(2) Where –

  (a) the local housing authority would be required under section 5 of the Housing Act 2004 to make a relevant prohibition order in respect of a dwelling, a house in multiple occupation or a building containing one or more flats, and
  (b) it appears to them that the dwelling, house in multiple occupation or, as the case may be, building is or can be rendered capable of providing accommodation of a standard which is adequate for the time being,

they may purchase it instead.

(3) In subsection (2) "relevant prohibition order" means a prohibition order under section 20 of the Housing Act 2004 which imposes in relation to the whole of the dwelling, house in multiple occupation or building a prohibition on its use for all purposes other than any purpose approved by the authority.

(4) Where an authority have determined to purchase any premises under subsection (1) –

  (a) they shall serve a notice of their determination on the persons on whom they would have been required by section 268(1) to serve a copy of a demolition order, and
  (b) sections 268(4) and 269(1), (2), (3) and (6) (operative date and right of appeal) apply to such a notice as they apply to a demolition order.

(5) Where an authority have determined to purchase any premises under subsection (2) –

(a) they shall serve a notice of their determination on the persons on whom they would have been required by Part 1 of Schedule 2 to the Housing Act 2004 (service of prohibition orders) to serve a copy of the relevant prohibition order; and

(b) section 24 of that Act and Parts 1 and 3 of that Schedule (operative date, right of appeal etc) apply to such a notice as they apply to a prohibition order which is not suspended or to appeals against such an order (as the case may be).

(6) At any time after the notice has become operative the authority may purchase the dwelling, house in multiple occupation or building by agreement or be authorised by the Secretary of State to purchase it compulsorily.

(7) This section does not apply where section 304(1) applies (listed building or building protected pending listing).'

21 For section 304 (closing orders in relation to listed buildings) substitute –

'304 Demolition order not to be made in respect of listed building

(1) A local housing authority shall not make a demolition order under section 265 (power to make a demolition order) in respect of a listed building.

(2) Where a dwelling, house in multiple occupation or building in respect of which a demolition order has been made becomes a listed building, the local housing authority shall determine the order (whether or not it has become operative).

(3) The local housing authority shall serve notice that the demolition order has been determined on every person on whom they would be required by section 268 to serve a copy of a new demolition order in relation to the premises.

(4) The Secretary of State may give notice in respect of a dwelling, house in multiple occupation or building to the local housing authority stating that its architectural or historic interest is sufficient to render it inexpedient that it should be demolished pending determination of the question whether it should be a listed building; and the provisions of this section apply to a dwelling, house in multiple occupation or building in respect of which such a notice is in force as they apply to a listed building.'

22 In section 307(1) (saving for rights arising from breach of covenant etc) for the words from 'relating to' to 'prejudices' substitute 'relating to the demolition or purchase of unfit premises prejudices'.

23 In section 308(3) (approval of owner's proposals for re-development) –

(a) after 'Part' insert 'or Chapter 2 of Part 1 of the Housing Act 2004'; and
(b) for ', closing or purchase of unfit premises' substitute 'or purchase of premises or the prohibition of uses of premises'.

24 Omit section 310 (certificate of fitness for human habitation resulting from owner's improvements or alterations).

25 In section 318(1)(a) (power of court to authorise execution of works on unfit premises or for improvement) –

(a) for 'dwelling-houses' substitute 'dwellings'; and
(b) for 'injurious to health or unfit for human habitation' substitute 'harmful to health or safety'.

26 For section 322 substitute –

'322 Minor definitions

(1) In this Part the following expressions have the same meaning as in Part 1 of the Housing Act 2004 (see sections 1(5) to (7) and 2(1) of that Act) –

"building containing one or more flats",

"category 1 hazard",

"category 2 hazard",

"common parts", in relation to a building containing one or more flats,

"dwelling",

"flat",

"hazard".

(2) In this Part –

"health" includes mental health;

"house in multiple occupation" means a house in multiple occupation as defined by sections 254 to 259 of the Housing Act 2004, as they have effect for the purposes of Part 1 of that Act (that is, without the exclusions contained in Schedule 14 to that Act);

"owner", in relation to premises –

(a) means a person (other than a mortgagee not in possession) who is for the time being entitled to dispose of the fee simple in premises, whether in possession or reversion, and

(b) includes also a person holding or entitled to the rents and profits of the premises under a lease of which the unexpired term exceeds three years;

"premises" in relation to a demolition order, means the dwelling, house in multiple occupation or building in respect of which the order is made.

(3) This Part applies to unoccupied HMO accommodation (as defined by section 1(5) of the Housing Act 2004) as it applies to a house in multiple occupation, and references to a house in multiple occupation in this Part are to be read accordingly.'

27   In section 323 (index of defined expressions: Part 9) insert at the appropriate places –

'building containing one or more flats	section 322'
'category 1 hazard	section 322'
'category 2 hazard	section 322'
'common parts	section 322'
'dwelling	section 322'
'hazard	section 322'
'health	section 322'
'residential property tribunal	section 229 of the Housing Act 2004'.

28   In section 439 (requirements as to fitness of premises before advancing money for certain purposes), omit subsections (1) and (2).

29 In section 582 (compulsory purchase orders: restriction on recovery of possession of houses in multiple occupation) for subsection (8) substitute –

'(8) In this section "house in multiple occupation" has the meaning given by sections 254 to 259 of the Housing Act 2004 for the purposes of that Act (other than Part 1).'

30 For section 584A (compensation payable in case of closing and demolition orders) substitute –

'584 A Compensation payable in case of prohibition and demolition orders

(1) Subject to subsection (3), where a relevant prohibition order becomes operative in respect of any premises or a demolition order under section 265 is made in respect of any premises, the local housing authority shall pay to every owner of the premises an amount determined in accordance with subsection (2).

(2) The amount referred to in subsection (1) is the diminution in the compulsory purchase value of the owner's interest in the premises as a result of the coming into operation of the relevant prohibition order or, as the case may be, the making of the demolition order; and that amount –

(a) shall be determined as at the date of the coming into operation or making of the order in question; and
(b) shall be determined (in default of agreement) as if it were compensation payable in respect of the compulsory purchase of the interest in question and shall be dealt with accordingly.

(3) In any case where –

(a) a relevant prohibition order has been made in respect of any premises, and
(b) that order is revoked and a demolition order is made in its place,

the amount payable to the owner under subsection (1) in connection with the demolition order shall be reduced by the amount (if any) paid to the owner or a previous owner under that subsection in connection with the relevant prohibition order.

(4) For the purposes of this section –

"compulsory purchase value", in relation to an owner's interest in premises, means the compensation which would be payable in respect of the compulsory purchase of that interest if it fell to be assessed in accordance with the Land Compensation Act 1961;

"premises", in relation to a demolition order, has the meaning given by section 322;

"premises", in relation to a prohibition order, means premises which are specified premises in relation to the order within the meaning of Part 1 of the Housing Act 2004;

"relevant prohibition order" means a prohibition order under section 20 or 21 of the Housing Act 2004 which imposes in relation to the whole of any premises a prohibition on their use for all purposes other than any purpose approved by the authority.'

31 For section 584B (repayment on revocation of demolition or closing order) substitute –

'584B Repayment on revocation of demolition or prohibition order

(1) Where a payment in respect of any premises has been made by a local housing authority under section 584A(1) in connection with a demolition order or relevant prohibition order and –

- (a) the demolition order is revoked under section 274 (revocation of demolition order to permit reconstruction of premises), or
- (b) the relevant prohibition order is revoked under section 25(1) or (2) of the Housing Act 2004,

then, if at that time the person to whom the payment was made has the same interest in the premises as he had at the time the payment was made, he shall on demand repay to the authority the amount of the payment.

(2) In any case where –

- (a) a payment in respect of any premises has been made by a local housing authority under section 584A(1) in connection with a relevant prohibition order, and
- (b) by virtue of section 25(3) of the Housing Act 2004, the order is revoked as respects part of the premises and not varied, and
- (c) the person to whom the payment was made (in this section referred to as "the recipient") had at the time the payment was made, an owner's interest in the part of the premises concerned (whether or not he had such an interest in the rest of the premises),

then, if at the time of the revocation of the relevant prohibition order the recipient has the same interest in the premises as he had at the time the payment was made, he shall on demand pay to the authority an amount determined in accordance with subsections (4), (5) and (6).

(3) In any case where –

- (a) a payment in respect of any premises has been made by a local housing authority under section 584A(1) in connection with a relevant prohibition order, and
- (b) by virtue of section 25(4) of the Housing Act 2004, the order is varied,

then, if at the time of the variation of the order the recipient has the same interest in the premises as he had at the time the payment was made, he shall on demand pay to the authority an amount determined in accordance with subsections (4), (5) and (6).

(4) The amount referred to in subsection (2) or (3) is whichever is the less of –

- (a) the amount by which the value of the interest of the recipient in the premises increases as a result of the revocation or variation of the relevant prohibition order; and
- (b) the amount paid to the recipient under section 584A(1) in respect of his interest in the premises;

and the amount referred to in paragraph (a) shall be determined as at the date of the revocation or variation of the relevant prohibition order.

(5) For the purpose of assessing the amount referred to in subsection (4)(a), the rules set out in section 5 of the Land Compensation Act 1961 shall, so far as applicable and subject to any necessary modifications, have effect as they have effect for the purpose of assessing compensation for the compulsory acquisition of an interest in land.

(6) Any dispute as to the amount referred to in subsection (4)(a) shall be referred to and determined by the Lands Tribunal; and section 2 and subsections (1)(a) and (4) to (6) of

section 4 of the Land Compensation Act 1961 shall, subject to any necessary modifications, apply for the purposes of this section as they apply for the purposes of that Act.

(7) In this section "premises" and "relevant prohibition order" have the same meaning as in section 584A.'

Landlord and Tenant Act 1985 (c 70)

32 (1) Section 20C of the Landlord and Tenant Act 1985 (limitation of service charges: costs of proceedings) is amended as follows.

(2) In subsection (1) after 'a court' insert ', residential property tribunal'.

(3) In subsection (2) after paragraph (a) insert –

'(aa) in the case of proceedings before a residential property tribunal, to a leasehold valuation tribunal;'.

Housing Act 1988 (c 50)

33 In paragraph 47 of Schedule 17 to the Housing Act 1988 (amendments of Part 9 of Housing Act 1985) for 'sections 264(5), 270(3), 276 and 286(3)' substitute 'section 270(3)'.

Local Government and Housing Act 1989 (c 42)

34 In section 100 of the Local Government and Housing Act 1989 (interpretation of Part 7) for the definition of 'house in multiple occupation' substitute –

'"house in multiple occupation" means a house in multiple occupation as defined by sections 254 to 259 of the Housing Act 2004, as they have effect for the purposes of Part 1 of that Act (that is, without the exclusions contained in Schedule 14 to that Act), but does not include any part of such a house which is occupied as a separate dwelling by persons who form a single household;'.

35 In section 195(2) of that Act (short title, commencement and extent) for '167' substitute '168'.

Water Industry Act 1991 (c 56)

36 For paragraph 2(2) of Schedule 4A to the Water Industry Act 1991 (premises that are not to be disconnected for non-payment of charges) substitute –

'(2) In this paragraph "house in multiple occupation" means a house in multiple occupation as defined by sections 254 to 259 of the Housing Act 2004, as they have effect for the purposes of Part 1 of that Act (that is, without the exclusions contained in Schedule 14 to that Act).'

Health Service Commissioners Act 1993 (c 46)

37 (1) Section 18 of the Health Service Commissioners Act 1993 (consultation during investigations) is amended as follows.

(2) In subsection (1) –

(a) omit 'or' at the end of paragraph (c);
(b) at the end of paragraph (d) insert

'or

(e) by the Social Housing Ombudsman for Wales under regulations under section 51B of
the Housing Act 1996,';

(c) omit 'the' after 'appropriate Commissioner or'; and

(d) omit 'the' after 'that Commissioner or'.

(3) In subsection (2) omit 'the Welsh Administration'.

Home Energy Conservation Act 1995 (c 10)

38   For paragraph (aa)(i) of the definition of 'residential accommodation' in section 1(1) of the
Home Energy Conservation Act 1995 (interpretation) substitute –

'(i) in England and Wales, a house in multiple occupation as defined by sections 254 to
259 of the Housing Act 2004, as they have effect for the purposes of Part 1 of that Act
(that is, without the exclusions contained in Schedule 14 to that Act),'.

Gas Act 1995 (c 45)

39   In paragraph 2 of Schedule 4 to the Gas Act 1995 (statutory undertakers), in sub-paragraph
(1)(xxxvi) for 'sections 283(2) and' substitute 'section'.

Housing Act 1996 (c 52)

40   The Housing Act 1996 has effect subject to the following amendments.

41   In section 52(1) (general provisions as to orders) after '17,' insert '27A,'.

42   In section 54 (determinations requiring approval), at the end of paragraph (b) insert

'or

(c) any determination under section 27B (transfer of property funded by grants under
section 27A),'.

43   In section 210 (homelessness: suitability of accommodation) –

(a) for 'Parts IX, X and XI' substitute 'Parts 9 and 10'; and

(b) for '; overcrowding; houses in multiple occupation)' substitute 'and overcrowding) and
Parts 1 to 4 of the Housing Act 2004'.

Housing Grants, Construction and Regeneration Act 1996 (c 53)

44   In section 24 of the Housing Grants, Construction and Regeneration Act 1996 (considerations of fitness before approving applications for certain grants), omit subsection (4).

Government of Wales Act 1998 (c 38)

45   (1) Paragraph 27 of Schedule 9 to the Government of Wales Act 1998 (consultation by
Welsh Administration Ombudsman with other Ombudsmen) is amended as follows.

(2) In sub-paragraph (1) –

(a) omit 'or' at the end of paragraph (b);

(b) at the end of paragraph (c) insert

'or

(d) by the Social Housing Ombudsman for Wales under regulations under section 51B of the Housing Act 1996,';

(c) after 'appropriate Commissioner' insert 'or Ombudsman'; and

(d) after 'that Commissioner' insert 'or Ombudsman'.

(3) In sub-paragraph (2) after 'Commissioner' insert 'or Ombudsman'.

Freedom of Information Act 2000 (c 36)

46 In the table in section 76(1) of the Freedom of Information Act 2000, after the entry relating to the Welsh Administration Ombudsman, insert –

| 'The Social Housing Ombudsman for Wales | Part 1, Chapter 5 of the Housing Act 1996 (c 52).' |

Local Government Act 2003 (c 26)

47 In section 87 of the Local Government Act 2003 (housing strategies and statements) for subsection (4) substitute –

'(4) In this section –

'housing' includes accommodation needs for gypsies and travellers within the meaning of section 225 of the Housing Act 2004;

'local housing authority' has the same meaning as in the Housing Act 1985 (c 68).'

SCHEDULE 16
REPEALS

Section 266

Short title and chapter	Extent of repeal
London Building Acts (Amendment) Act 1939 (c xcvii)	Section 35(1)(c)(i). In section 36(1), the words 'or sleep'.
Friendly and Industrial and Provident Societies Act 1968 (c 55)	Section 4A(3)(b).
Land Compensation Act 1973 (c 26)	In section 37(9), the words 'or undertaking'. In section 39(9), the words 'or undertaking'.
Local Government Act 1974 (c 7)	In section 33, in subsection (1) the 'the' after 'appropriate Commissioner or', and in subsection (2) the 'the' after 'that Commissioner or'.
County of Merseyside Act 1980 (c x)	Section 48. Section 49(1) and (2). In section 132(2), the words 'In section 48 (Means of escape from fire), subsection (5);'. Section 139(3).
Civil Aviation Act 1982 (c 16)	In Schedule 2, in the entry relating to the Housing Act 1985 in paragraph 4, '283,'.
Mobile Homes Act 1983 (c 34)	In Part 1 of Schedule 1, in paragraph 6(1), the words 'age and'.
Building Act 1984 (c 55)	Section 72(6)(a).

Short title and chapter	Extent of repeal
Housing Act 1985 (c 68)	In section 104(1)(b), the words 'and Part V (the right to buy)'.
	In section 157, in subsection (2) the words ', subject to subsection (4),', and subsections (4) and (5).
	Sections 189 to 208.
	Section 264.
	In section 267, in the sidenote the words 'and closing orders', and subsections (2) and (3).
	Section 269(2A) and (3A).
	Sections 276 to 279.
	Sections 283 to 288.
	Section 289(5A).
	In section 305, subsection (5) and, in subsection (8), the words from 'and' to the end of the subsection.
	Section 310.
	In section 311, in subsection (1) the words 'or section 310 (owner's improvements or alterations)' and in subsection (3) the words 'or 310, as the case may be'.
	In section 316(1), the words ', or obstructive building order'.
	In section 317, in the sidenote the words 'or closed', and in subsection (1) the words 'or closing'.
	Section 318(4).
	In section 319(1)(b), the words 'or closing' and ', or an obstructive building order,'.
	In section 323, the entries relating to 'closing order', 'fit (or unfit) for human habitation', 'house', 'obstructive building', 'obstructive building order' and 'unfit (or fit) for human habitation'.
	Sections 345 to 400.
	Section 439(1) and (2).
	Sections 604 to 606.
	In section 623(1), the words 'and 'flat', except in the expression 'flat in multiple occupation',' and the definitions of 'house in multiple occupation' and 'flat in multiple occupation'.
	In section 624, the entries relating to 'flat', 'flat in multiple occupation' and 'house in multiple occupation'.
	Schedule 10.
	Schedule 13.
Housing Associations Act 1985 (c 69)	In section 87, in subsection (3) the words from ', acting' onwards, and subsection (6).
Housing (Consequential Provisions) Act 1985 (c 71)	In Schedule 2, paragraph 24(2)(d).
Leicestershire Act 1985 (c xvii)	Section 54(6)(a).
Airports Act 1986 (c 31)	In Schedule 2, in the entry relating to the Housing Act 1985 in paragraph 1(1), '283,'.
Housing Act 1988 (c 50)	In section 50(2), the words from ', acting' onwards.
	In section 52(2), the words from ', acting' to 'determine,'.
	Section 55.
	In section 57(a), 'or 55'.
	Section 130.
	Schedule 15.
Electricity Act 1989 (c 29)	In Schedule 16, paragraph 1(1)(xl).

Short title and chapter	Extent of repeal
Local Government and Housing Act 1989 (c 42)	In section 165(1), paragraphs (a) and (c). Section 167. In Schedule 9, paragraphs 1 to 14, 16, 17(2) and (4), 20(2) and (3), 21 to 23, 25(1), 29, 32, 33(1), 36, 42, 43(b), 44 to 71, 75, 83, 84 and 86.
Health Service Commissioners Act 1993 (c 46)	In section 18, in subsection (1), the 'or' at the end of paragraph (c), the 'the' after 'appropriate Commissioner or' and the 'the' after 'that Commissioner or', and in subsection (2) the words 'the Welsh Administration'.
Housing Act 1996 (c 52)	In section 18(2), the words from ', acting' to 'determine,'. In section 20(3), the words from ', acting' to 'determine,'. In section 21(3), the words from ', acting' to 'determine,'. Sections 65 to 79. In Schedule 1, paragraph 16(4), in paragraph 18(1) the words from ' (which impose' onwards, and in paragraph 19(2) paragraph (d) (but not the 'or' at the end).
Housing Grants, Construction and Regeneration Act 1996 (c 53)	Section 24(4). In section 58, the definition of 'qualifying park home'. In section 59, the entries relating to 'fit for human habitation' and 'qualifying park home'. Sections 81 to 91. Section 97. In Schedule 1, paragraph 10.
Government of Wales Act 1998 (c 38)	In Schedule 9, in paragraph 27(1) the 'or' at the end of paragraph (b).
Transport Act 2000 (c 38)	In Schedule 5, in paragraph 1(2)(o), '283,'.

Appendix 2

HOUSING HEALTH AND SAFETY RATING SYSTEM GUIDANCE (VERSION 2) – SELECTED EXTRACTS

November 2004
Safe & Healthy Housing Research Unit, Warwick Law School
Office of the Deputy Prime Minister: London

CHAPTER 3

Overview of Rating Hazards

3.01   The HHSRS uses judgments made by the surveyor,[1] based on an inspection of the whole dwelling, to generate a numerical score. The information observed during the inspection (or survey) should be properly and accurately recorded as this will provide evidence to justify and support the judgments which form the basis of the numerical Hazard Score.

3.02   The Rating System assessment procedure requires, for each hazard, two judgments from the surveyor. These are an assessment of:
(a)   the likelihood, over the next twelve months, of an occurrence that could result in harm to a member of the vulnerable age group; and
(b)   the range of potential outcomes from such an occurrence.

3.03   This approach is more logical than merely attempting to judge the severity of the hazard on a linear scale.[2] It ensures that the severity of a threat which is very likely to occur but will result in a minor outcome can be compared with one which is highly unlikely to occur but if it did would have a major outcome. It also allows differentiation between similar hazards where the likelihood may be the same, but the outcome very different (see Box 1).

---

1   The term 'surveyor' used in this Guidance includes environmental health practitioner or other local authority officer.
2   See *Housing Health and Safety Rating System: Report on Development* (July 2000) DETR, London, in particular chapter 5.

BOX 1

Similar Hazards, with Differing Outcomes

Example –

There is a window with a low internal sill (about 250mm above the floor) and with a loose, easy to open catch to the large side hung opening light. A small child could climb onto the sill and open the window relatively easily, and, once there could fall out through the open window. The likelihood of this occurring over the next twelve months is judged to be around 1 in 180.

If that window is in the bedroom of a flat on the ground floor, with grass immediately below, the outcome would be relatively minor – 99% Class IV (bruising) and perhaps 1% Class III (a strain or sprain). This would give a Hazard Score of 7 (Band J).

However, if that same window is in the bedroom of a flat on the 2nd floor, with a paved area immediately below, the outcome would be major – 10% Class I (paralysis or even death), 80% Class II (serious fractures) and 10% Class III (a strain or sprain). In this case, with the same likelihood of 1 in 180, the Hazard Score would be 1,016 (Band C).

Although in both cases the likelihood is the same, the Hazard Score reflects the dramatically different outcome.

3.04 Using these two judgments, the HHSRS Formula is used to generate the numerical Hazard Score for each of the hazards. The Formula and the use of numbers to represent the surveyor's judgments provides the means to compare very different hazards. It is this approach which enables hazards which have a slow and insidious effect to be compared with ones where the effect is relatively instantaneous; and enable hazards which may result in physical injury to be compared with ones which could cause illnesses or affect mental health.

The HHSRS Formula

3.05 Three sets of figures are used to generate a Hazard Score, these are:

(a) a weighting for each Class of Harm[1] reflecting the degree of incapacity to the victim resulting from the occurrence;

(b) the likelihood of an occurrence involving a member of a vulnerable age group, expressed as a ratio; and

(c) the spread of possible harms resulting from an occurrence, expressed by percentage for each of the four Classes of Harm.

3.06 The first of these, the weighting given to each Class of Harms, remains fixed and is shown in Table 1.[2] This built-in fixed weighting means that, given the same likelihood, those hazards which cannot result in death (eg risks from poor ergonomics) will not produce a Score as high as those which may cause death (eg risks from carbon monoxide).

---

1   See paras 2.09–2.11 above, for the interpretation of these terms, and Annex C for Examples for each Class.

2   The Classes of harm and the weightings are based on those proposed in *A Risk Assessment Procedure for Health and Safety in Buildings* (2000) CRC, London.

Table 1 *Weighting for the Classes of Harm*

Class of Harm	Weighting
I Extreme	10,000
II Severe	1,000
III Serious	300
IV Moderate	10

3.07   The other two sets of figures represent the informed professional judgments made by the surveyor of the likelihood and of the potential spread of harms.

3.08   The Hazard Score is calculated as the sum of the products of the weightings for each Class of Harm which could result from the particular hazard, multiplied by the likelihood of an occurrence, and multiplied by the set of percentages showing the spread of Harms. (See Figure 1.)

Figure 1   *The HHSRS Formula*

	Class of Harm Weighting		Likelihood		Spread of Harm (%)	
I	10,000	$\times$	$\dfrac{1}{L}$	$\times$	O1	= S1
II	1,000	$\times$	$\dfrac{1}{L}$	$\times$	O2	= S2
III	300	$\times$	$\dfrac{1}{L}$	$\times$	O3	= S3
IV	10	$\times$	$\dfrac{1}{L}$	$\times$	O4	= S4
					Hazard Score	= (S1 + S2 + S3 + S4)

Where –
L = the Likelihood of an occurrence
O = the Outcome expressed as a percentage for each Class of Harm
S = the row product for each Class of Harm.

3.09   General advice and guidance on assessing the likelihood and outcomes is given in the following paragraphs. More specific guidance on assessments for each individual hazards is given in the Hazard Profiles.

Judging the Likelihood

3.10   The surveyor judges the likelihood of an occurrence over the next twelve months which could result in harm to a member of a vulnerable age group. For the HHSRS, the judgment is limited to the likelihood of an occurrence resulting in outcomes which would or should require some medical attention – a visit to a doctor or a hospital. This is because the Rating System deals only with those hazards which could cause significant harm outcomes (and so carry a significant Class of Harm weighting). It is only these outcomes for which there is recorded data to inform the judgment.[1]

3.11   The judgment of the likelihood made by the surveyor involves taking account of the conditions (deficiencies) identified during the survey, in particular whether those conditions will increase or reduce the average likelihood of an occurrence.

3.12   Thus, the surveyor should assess the likelihood having regard to:

(a)   the average likelihood given for the particular type and age of dwelling;

(b)   the dwelling characteristics and conditions identified during the survey, which are the responsibility of the landlord, and which:

    i.   may increase the likelihood of an occurrence; and

    ii.   those which may reduce the likelihood of such an occurrence.

(See Box 2.)

BOX 2

Judging the Likelihood

Example –

For *falls on stairs*, the surveyor determines the likelihood of a fall occurring over the following twelve months which could result in a Class I to IV Harm to a member of the vulnerable age group. This involves taking account of such matters as the going, the presence or absence of handrails, the state of repair of the treads, variations in tread or riser dimensions, and the available lighting.

For *dampness and mould growth etc*, the surveyor determines the likelihood of the dampness causing Class I to IV Harm to a member of the vulnerable age group over the next twelve month period, taking into account the extent and degree of the dampness and its location in the dwelling.

3.13   To inform the surveyor's judgment, national average likelihoods of an occurrence involving a person in the vulnerable age group are given in the Hazard Profiles (see Annex D).[2] Where data is available, these are given for different age groups and types of dwellings. These averages represent the likelihood for the typical condition that could be expected in a dwelling of that particular age and type. Also provided in the Hazard profiles is guidance on dwelling characteristics which may affect the likelihood of an occurrence.[3]

---

1   It is this data which has been used to calculate the statistical evidence for each Hazard.
2   Note that these are <u>national</u> averages, which may differ from local averages.
3   Also available to inform the surveyor's judgment are the *Worked Examples and Statistical Evidence to Support the Housing Health and Safety Rating System: Volume II – Summary of Results.*

3.14 Assessing likelihood is not determining or predicting that there definitely *will* be an occurrence. Even where it is judged that there is a very high likelihood, such as a 1 in 10 probability, it is accepting that the likelihood of no occurrence is nine times greater than that of an occurrence.

3.15 The surveyor is not expected to give an exact likelihood ratio, but to select one of the standard HHSRS likelihood ranges – eg, the range of 1 in 24 to 1 in 42; or the range of 1 in 420 to 1 in 750. For each of the standard ranges a representative scale point is used in the Hazard Rating Formula to calculate the Hazard Score. See Box 3 for the standard HHSRS ranges of likelihoods, and the Representative Scale Points of those ranges that is used in the Hazard Rating Formula.[1]

BOX 3

HHSRS Standard Range of Likelihoods –

			Representative Scale Point
Less likely than			
		1 in 4,200	1 in 5,600
1 in 4,200	to	1 in 2,400	3,200
2,400	to	1,300	1,800
1,300	to	750	1,000
750	to	420	560
420	to	240	320
240	to	130	180
130	to	75	100
75	to	42	56
42	to	24	32
24	to	13	18
13	to	7.5	10
7.5	to	4	5.6
4	to	2.5	3.2
2.5	to	1.5	1.8
More likely than		1 in 1.5	1 in 1.0

The surveyor judges the range for the likelihood. The HHSRS Hazard Formula uses scale points to represent that range.

3.16 Some hazards may be present in several locations. However, the surveyor judges the likelihood range for the dwelling as a whole. Falls on the level, for example, will include reviewing the condition of all the floors within the dwelling and all the paths and yards associated with the dwelling. Damp and mould growth will involve reviewing the extent and severity of the dampness and any mould growth in all rooms within the dwelling. For these, the surveyor should assess the collective likelihood of an occurrence at the dwelling as a whole. This should take into account all the factors associated with the use of each location and how that may affect the exposure to that particular hazard at the dwelling as a whole. (See Box 4.)

---

1   An explanation of the calculation of the standard ranges and the Representation Scale Points is given in paras 2.24–2.27.

BOX 4

Assessing the Likelihood for Falls associated with stairs

Example –

There are three sets of steps and stairs to a house:

1. At the front gate there are two steps. These are of rough concrete and have high risers. There is a crude loose handrail to one side.
2. At the front door there are four steps of smooth concrete. The bottom step is higher than the others. There is a steel tube handrail to one side.
3. The internal stairs have two winders at the top. The stairs are fairly steep, but not more than the average for this type of dwelling (a 1930s, detached house) and there is a handrail to one side.

The main stairs are assessed as giving the same likelihood of a major fall as the average for inter-war houses (ie around 1 in 230). However, the state and condition of the steps at the gate and to the front door – particularly dangerous in icy weather and at night – is judged to substantially increase the overall probability that, in the next twelve months, an elderly person (60 years or more) will have a fall that could result in some injury. While the occupants may use the rear door (with only a single low step), they cannot avoid using the steps close to the front gate. In this case, the likelihood of a member of the vulnerable age group falling in the next twelve months is judged to be in the range of 1 in 24 to 1 in 13 – a Representative Scale Point of 1 in 18.

Judging the Spread of Harm outcomes

3.17 After judging the likelihood of an occurrence, the surveyor makes the second judgment, that of the possible harm outcomes for the vulnerable age group which could result from such an occurrence. This is done by assessing the range of outcomes, normally by starting with Class I, then Class II and so on, giving the highest percentage to the most probable outcome.

3.18 National average spreads of harm outcomes for each hazard are given in the Hazard Profiles (see Annex D).[1] Where data is available, these are given for different age groups and types of dwellings. As with the average likelihoods, these represent the harm outcomes for the typical condition that could be expected in a dwelling of that particular age and type. Also given in the Hazard Profiles is guidance on dwelling characteristics that may affect the outcomes.

3.19 The spread of outcomes should be assessed having regard to:

(a) the average spread of harm outcomes given for the particular type and age of dwelling;
(b) the dwelling characteristics and conditions identified during the survey which are the responsibility of the landlord, and which:
    i   may increase the severity of those outcomes; and
    ii   those which may mitigate the severity of those outcomes.

---

1   These are *national* averages which may differ from local averages.

3.20   As for likelihood, the surveyor is not expected to give an exact spread of outcomes, but select one of the standard HHSRS outcome ranges. For each of the standard ranges there is a representative scale point which is used in the Hazard Rating Formula. See Box 5 for the standard HHSRS ranges of outcomes and for the Representative Scale Points used in the Formula to generate the Hazard Score.[1]

BOX 5

HHSRS Standard Range of Class of Harm Outcomes –

			Representative Scale Point
Below		0.05%	0.00%
0.05%	to	0.15%	0.10%
0.15%	to	0.3%	0.22%
0.3%	to	0.7%	0.46%
0.7%	to	1.5%	1.00%
1.5%	to	3.0%	2.20%
3.0%	to	7.0%	4.60%
7.0%	to	15.0%	10.0%
15.0%	to	26.0%	21.5%
26.0%	to	38.0%	31.6%
Above		38.0%	46.4%

3.21   As the spread of outcomes is given as percentages, the total must, obviously, equal 100. For example, using the Paper Scoring Form (see Annex B), the surveyor should select the representative scale points for three of the Classes of Harm, and the fourth Class should be 100 minus the sum of the other three Classes. (This calculation is made automatically by the HHSRS scoring programs.)

3.22   For those hazards which may be present in several locations, the surveyor should take account of the state, condition and other factors related to each location and how that might affect the likelihood of an occurrence and so increase or lessen the overall possible severity of the range of harm outcomes. (See Box 6.)

---

1   An explanation of the calculation of the standard ranges and the Representation Scale Points is given in paras 2.24–2.27.

BOX 6

Assessing the Outcomes for Falls associated with stairs

Example –

Using the same example as above, a house with three sets of steps and stairs –

1. At the front gate there are two steps. These are of rough concrete and have high risers. There is a crude loose handrail to one side.
2. At the front door there are four steps of smooth concrete. The bottom step is higher than the others. There is a steel tube handrail to one side.
3. The internal stairs have two winders at the top. The stairs are fairly steep, but not more than the average for this type of dwelling (a 1930s, detached house) and there is a handrail to one side.

There is nothing to suggest that the outcomes from a fall on the internal stairs will be anything other than average (ie 2.1%, 7.4%, 20.5% and 70.0% for Classes I, II, III, and IV respectively). However, the state and condition of the steps to the front door steps and those near the front gate, are such that it is judged that the Class I outcome to a person aged 60 years or more from a fall at either of these locations will be increased, particularly if that fall was in cold weather or at night. The Representative Scale Points of the outcomes are judged to be 4.6%, 10.00%, 21.5% and 63.8% respectively.

Generating a Hazard Score

3.23   Using the same falls associated with stairs example as given in Box 6 above, the Likelihood of 1 in 18 and the Outcomes of 4.5%, 10.0%, 21.5% and 63.8% for Classes of Harm I to IV respectively are used by the HHSRS Formula to generate a Hazard Score of 3,505 (See Box 7).

BOX 7

Generating a Hazard Score

	Class of Harm Weighting		Likelihood		Spread of Harm (%)	
I	10,000	$\times$	$\dfrac{1}{18}$	$\times$	4.6	= 2,556
II	1,000	$\times$	$\dfrac{1}{18}$	$\times$	10.0	= 556
III	300	$\times$	$\dfrac{1}{18}$	$\times$	21.5	= 358
IV	10	$\times$	$\dfrac{1}{18}$	$\times$	63.8	= 35
					Hazard Score	**= 3,505**

3.24 Average Hazard Scores for each hazard are given in the Hazard Profiles (see Annex D), and, where data is available, for different age groups and types of dwellings. These have been calculated using the Hazard Rating Formula and the average likelihoods and outcomes.

The Hazard Bands

3.25 The numerical Hazard Score can appear too specific. It can also falsely imply that the score is a precise statement of the risk, rather than a representation of the surveyor's judgment.

3.26 Hazard Bands have been devised to avoid emphasis being placed on what may appear to be a precise numerical Hazard Score. These also provide a simple means for handling the potentially wide range of Scores – from under 0.2 to 1,000,000.[1] There are ten Hazard Bands (see Box 8), with Band J being the safest, and Band A being the most dangerous.

BOX 8

HHSRS Bands –

Band	Hazard Score Range
A	5,000 or more
B	2,000 to 4,999
C	1,000 to 1,999
D	500 to 999
E	200 to 499
F	100 to 199
G	50 to 99
H	20 to 49
I	10 to 19
J	9 or less

3.27 The Hazard Band is the first factor to be taken into account in determining the appropriate enforcement action – for guidance on which, see the Enforcement Guidance.

CHAPTER 4

The Assessment of Conditions Using the HHSRS

4.01 Once the survey has been completed, the surveyor[2] makes the assessment. This involves:

(a)　determining whether there are any deficiencies present by assessing whether each dwelling element and the dwelling as a whole meets the relevant Ideal;

1　A 1 in 5,600 likelihood with 100% Class IV outcome, and a 1 in 1 likelihood of 100% Class I outcome respectively.

2　The term 'surveyor' used in this Guidance includes environmental health practitioner or other local authority officer.

(b)   determining whether any deficiencies contribute to one or more hazards, and if so, which hazards; and
(c)   for each hazard which is obviously worse than average for that type and age of property, the surveyor assesses:
    i)   the likelihood of an occurrence over the next twelve months; and
    ii)   the probable spread of harms which could result from such an occurrence.

The Survey Procedure

4.02   A survey is, of course, a means of gathering information on which to base decisions. As those decisions could result in enforcement action, the survey should be thorough and comprehensive. The observations and findings from the survey should be accurately recorded and stored for future reference, particularly as they may be needed to substantiate the judgments made and justify decisions taken which may affect someone's home and someone's property.

4.03   For the purposes of assessment using the Rating System, the survey should be detailed enough to gather all the necessary information on the state and condition of a dwelling, and particularly on any deficiencies. As with all surveys, a simple logical approach should be adopted to ensure all internal and external parts of the dwelling are inspected. For local authority officers, such surveys generally will be restricted to visual and surface inspection, without any destructive investigations and limited by furniture and furnishings.

Assessing the Condition

Linking Deficiencies and Hazards

4.04   The first stage in assessing the condition of a dwelling is a review of the deficiencies identified during the survey.

4.05   As defined above (paras 2.02–2–03) for the purposes of the HHSRS, a deficiency is a failure of an element to meet the Ideal, whether that failure is inherent, such as a result of the original construction or manufacture, or a result of deterioration or of disrepair and a lack of maintenance. While a deficiency may have implications in building and aesthetic terms, for the purposes of the HHSRS its prime importance is whether the effect from that deficiency has the potential to cause harm – ie when the deficiency results in a hazard (see paras 2.12–2.13).

4.06   A single deficiency may contribute, to differing degrees, to more than one hazard. For example, the single deficiency of disrepair to a ceiling could, dependent upon the nature and extent of that disrepair, lead to the following hazards:

- excessive cold (through increased heat loss);
- fire (by allowing fire and smoke to spread to other parts of the dwelling);
- lead (from old paint);
- infections from other sources (by providing means of access and harbourage for pests); and
- noise (because of an increase in noise penetration between rooms).

The contribution a single deficiency makes to each hazard will vary, perhaps from the relatively insignificant to the substantial.

4.07   Similarly, several deficiencies may contribute to the same hazard. Disrepair to a ceiling, an ill-fitting door, and the lack of a smoke detector may all contribute to the hazard of fire, as each could lead to smoke and flames spreading to other parts of the dwelling without means of detection and warning.

4.08   Finally, there may be similar deficiencies in various locations throughout the dwelling which all contribute to the same hazard. There may be, for example, dampness affecting walls to several rooms and areas within the dwelling. It is the cumulative contribution of those deficiencies to the hazard of damp and mould growth which should be assessed. Similarly, there may be deficiencies to steps to the entrance path to the dwelling, deficiencies to the main stairs within the dwelling and deficiencies to the rear door steps. It is the cumulative contribution of these deficiencies to the hazard of falls associated with stairs/steps which is assessed.

4.09   Guidance on the matters to be taken into account in assessing the potential contribution to a hazard by a deficiency is given in the Causes and the *Preventive Measures* and the *Ideal* sections of the Hazard Profiles in Annex D. However over time research may be published that will overtake the evidence used in the profiles.

Note –
It is imperative that users of the Rating System keep up to date with published research and other relevant information which can be used to supplement that given in the Hazard Profiles (Annex D) and which may influence their judgment as to likelihood and/or spread of harms.

Identifying Hazards

4.10   Identifying and assessing hazards involves an understanding of the basic physiological and psychological requirements for human life, and of the functions of a dwelling as a whole and of each individual dwelling element.

4.11   As a minimum, a dwelling should be capable of satisfying the basic and fundamental needs for the everyday life of a household. It should provide shelter, space and facilities for the occupants. And, it should be suitable for the spectrum of households and individuals who could normally be expected to occupy a dwelling of that size and type.

4.12   As well as satisfying the general principle behind the Rating System (see paras 1.12–1.18), the dwelling should not contain any deficiencies and consequential hazards which interfere with the household establishing a home or which might endanger the occupants and any visitors.

4.13   Determining whether a deficiency contributes to one or more hazards also requires an understanding on the part of the surveyor of the function(s) of each element and facility, and competence in assessing how the deficiency interferes with a function so as to create a hazard. (See Box 9 for some examples of the functions of individual elements.)

BOX 9

Functions and Requirements of Elements – Some Examples[1]

Doors – External doors provide for access into and out of the dwelling or building, and also complete the weather protection, privacy and security provided by the external structure. They should be close-fitting when closed, provided with appropriate door furniture so as to be capable of being readily opened and closed and secured against unauthorised entry.

Internal doors allow for access between different parts of the dwelling. When closed, they complete the separation provided by the internal walls, and provide for privacy by separating a room (such as a bathroom, a wc compartment and a bedroom) from other parts of the dwelling. As well as being able to be readily opened and closed, internal doors should satisfy similar functions to the internal walls, such as sound insulation and limiting the spread of fire.

Walls – In traditionally built dwellings, the external walls will provide for support for floors and the roof. They also give weather protection, thermal and sound insulation and limit the spread of fire.

Internal walls divide the dwelling into separate rooms and areas, enabling different activities to be carried out. They also provide for privacy for individual members of a household allowing personal and domestic activities to be carried out in proper conditions and in private. Internal walls may provide support for other elements and should give thermal and sound insulation and should limit the spread of fire. The surfaces of internal walls should be capable of being decorated and easily maintained in a clean condition; this is especially so in such areas as kitchens and bathrooms where hygiene is of particular importance.

Paths, Yards etc – External paths, yards, and steps should be laid so as to be even and self-draining. This includes paths giving access from public or shared areas, and those giving access to amenity spaces.

Rainwater Goods – Eavesgutters are intended to collect rain water draining off roofs and carry it safely to rain water fall pipes which in turn should carry it safely to a drainage inlet or soakaway.

Kitchens – These are primarily food preparation areas. All surfaces and fittings and fixtures, such as sinks, worktops and food stores, should be designed, fitted and maintained so that they and the kitchen area can be readily cleansed and maintained in an hygienic condition. All surfaces and fittings in bathrooms and wc compartments should also be designed, fitted and maintained to facilitate cleaning and the maintenance of hygiene.

Thermal Efficiency – The dwelling should be provided with adequate thermal insulation and a suitable and effective means of space heating so that the dwelling space can be economically maintained at reasonable temperatures.

---

1   Additional information on features of elements contributing to, or mitigating against, each individual Hazard category is given in Annex D.

Assessing Hazards

4.14 Using details of the deficiencies identified which contribute to hazards, the surveyor should score each hazard which is obviously worse than the average for that age and type of dwelling. To assist in this process it may be useful to list each of the deficiencies contributing to a hazard, then review them during the rating process for that hazard. This process can be repeated for each hazard obviously worse than average.

> **Note –**
> For enforcement purposes it should not be necessary to review and assess every potential hazard. Average Hazard Scores are provided in the Profiles for all dwellings, and where data is available for ranges of age and type of dwellings.

4.15 To fully assess some hazards, destructive investigations may be necessary, but the surveyor may not be in a position to carry these out. In other cases, such as for Excess Cold, Noise, and Radon, further investigations and measurements may be needed to verify the existence and seriousness of the hazard. For these, a preliminary assessment should be made, with the proviso that verification by measurement or further investigation will be necessary.

4.16 First, after reviewing the deficiencies identified during the survey which contribute to a hazard, the surveyor should assess the likelihood of a member of the vulnerable age group suffering a potentially harmful occurrence in the next twelve months. Second, the surveyor should judge the possible harm outcomes that could result from such an occurrence. (These two stages are described in paras 3.10–3.16 and paras 3.17–3.22 above respectively.)

4.17 The Representative Scale Points are used to reflect the surveyors judgments and a single numerical Hazard Score is generated by the HHSRS Formula for that hazard.

4.18 This scoring procedure should be repeated for all hazards that are considered to be worse than average – ie where the Hazard Scores are likely to be significantly above the average for the housing stock.

4.19 Finally, the Hazard Band for all the significant hazards should be recorded. These form the first factor in the enforcement decision-making process. Guidance on that process is given in the Enforcement Guidance.

Options for Calculating the Hazard Scores

4.20 Three options for calculating and recording the Likelihood and Outcome judgments and for calculating the Hazard Score have been developed. These are:

- a paper scoring form;
- scoring programs for handheld computers (PDAs); and
- a scoring program for desk top PCs.

4.21 All three options have a similar appearance for recording Likelihood and Outcome judgments. However, the scoring programs use the Hazard Formula and the prescribed calculation method to generate the Hazard Score and Band as the Likelihood and Outcomes are entered. The scoring programs for handheld computers has the advantage that it can be used on site. Both programs save the data, which can be reviewed when printed from a desk top PC, or exported into other software.[1]

4.22   Having assessed the likelihood, the surveyor should enter his or her decision into the Likelihood Scoring grid in the electronic program or the paper scoring form. (Figure 3 shows the grid layout for the paper scoring form. A similar grid is displayed on the scoring screens for the survey programs.)

Figure 3   *Likelihood Scoring Grid*

LIKELIHOOD

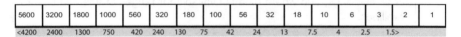

5600	3200	1800	1000	560	320	180	100	56	32	18	10	6	3	2	1
<4200	2400	1300	750	420	240	130	75	42	24	13	7.5	4	2.5	1.5>	

4.23   For the scoring programs, having chosen the hazard to be scored, a screen appears with the appropriate average likelihood for the particular age and type of property marked as a green line. Selecting the assessed likelihood range displays the Representative Scale Point which will be used in the HHSRS Formula.

4.24   For the paper scoring form, it is recommended to mark the average likelihood for the particular age and type of property with a vertical line (as indicated in the relevant Hazard Profile) and then the assessed likelihood range for the surveyed dwelling circled. The given Representative Scale Point (shown within the blocks of the grid) should be used in the HHSRS Formula when calculating the Hazard Score and Band.

4.25   Having assessed the spread of harm outcomes, the surveyor should enter his or her decision into the Outcomes Scoring grid in the electronic program or the paper scoring form. (Figure 4 shows the grid layout for the paper scoring form. A similar grid is displayed on the scoring screens for the survey programs.)

Figure 4   *Classes of Harm Outcomes Grid*

OUTCOMES

	<0.05	0.15	0.3	0.7	1.5	3	7	15	26	38>			
Class I	0	0.1	0.2	0.5	1.0	2.2	4.6	10.0	21.5	31.6	46.4		**Class IV**	
Class II	0	0.1	0.2	0.5	1.0	2.2	4.6	10.0	21.5	31.6	46.4		100-(I+II+III)	
Class III	0	0.1	0.2	0.5	1.0	2.2	4.6	10.0	21.5	31.6	46.4			
	<0.05	0.15	0.3	0.7	1.5	3	7	15	26	38>			

4.26   As for the Likelihood scale, having chosen the hazard to be scored, the scoring programs will display a screen with the appropriate average spread of outcomes for the particular age and type of property marked by a green line. For each Class of Harm, selecting the assessed percentage range displays the Representative Scale Point, which will be used in the HHSRS Formula.

4.27   For the paper scoring form, the average spread of harms for the particular age and type of property can be marked for each of the Classes of Harm (obtained from the

---

1   For getting started and using the HHSRS Scoring software see the Handbook.

relevant Hazard Profile) and then the percentage range as assessed for each Class for the surveyed dwelling can be circled. It is important to remember that the spread of outcomes is a percentage and that the total therefore must equal 100. The given Representative Scale Points (shown in the block of the grids) should be used in the HHSRS Formula.

4.28   As the likelihood and outcomes are entered into the scoring programs (both those for hand-held computers and PCs), the hazard score is generated automatically. In each case, the program shows the Hazard Band for the score. Where the score generated is within the top or bottom 10th of the band, the programs will show a '+' or '–' sign, indicating whether the score is close to the Band above or below respectively (see Box 10). This indicator alerts the surveyor, who may then wish to review the assessment so as to be confident of the resulting Score and Band.

BOX 10

Hazard +/– Sub-Bands

Sub Band	Hazard Score
A–	5,000 – 5,400
B+	4,600 – 5,000
B–	2,000 – 2,200
C+	1,800 – 2,000
C–	1,000 – 1,070
D+	930 – 1,000
D–	500 – 540
E+	460 – 500
E–	200 – 220
F+	180 – 200
F–	100 – 107
G+	93 – 100
G–	50 – 54
H+	46 – 50
H–	20 – 22
I+	18 – 20
I–	10 – 11
J+	9 – 10

Supplemental Stage for Crowding

4.29   For all Hazards, the Hazard Score and Band are based on the assessment of the dwelling without taking account of the current occupants (if any). This means that the Scores and Bands relate to the dwelling and so does not vary with a change of occupancy.

Note –
The current occupants are taken into account as one of the other factors in the enforcement decision-making process.

4.30   For the assessment of Crowding, which can only occur in an occupied dwelling, a supplemental stage may be necessary to determine whether the dwelling is crowded, and if so, the severity of the Hazard and whether enforcement action should be considered.

4.31   For example, disregarding the current occupants, a two storey pre-1920 house may be assessed as average, having adequate space for sleeping, living and recreation for up to four persons (irrespective of age). This gives a Hazard Score of 22 (Band H-). However if this dwelling is currently occupied by five persons – two parents and their three children, then there is mis-match between the household and the dwelling. In this case the likelihood of a harmful occurrence should be re-assessed taking account of the current occupation. For Crowding only, it is this adjusted Hazard Score and Band which form the first factor in the enforcement decision-making process.

Scoring Hazards Schematic

Survey the dwelling
Carry out a full survey of the dwelling
to identify all deficiencies, particularly
those which could contribute to any of
the 29 Hazards.

For each Hazard to be scored

Relevant Deficiencies
Review deficiencies identified which
could contribute to Hazard.

Score the Hazard
Assess for this dwelling:

a) the likelihood range; and
b) the outcome range for each Class
of Harm.

Taking into account national averages
for particular type and age of dwelling.

Hazard Score and Band Generated

**Determine Appropriate Enforcement
Action**
The Hazard Band is one of the factors
to take into account in determining the
appropriate enforcement action.
On this see the Enforcement
Guidance.

CHAPTER 5

Flats and Other Dwellings in Multi-Occupied Buildings

Supplemental Guidance

5.01   This additional guidance is for the use and application of the HHSRS for enforcement purposes in the case of dwellings in multi-occupied buildings. These are dwellings within a larger building, whether purpose-built or created by conversion, which are:

(a)   self-contained;

(b)   non-self-contained, where not all rooms are behind one entrance door to the dwelling, but where no facilities or rooms are shared;

(c)   non-self-contained, where some rooms are shared (for example dining or living rooms), but where no facilities are shared; and/or

(d)   non-self-contained, and where one or more of the following facilities are shared in common with other units within the building, that is:

   i   sanitary accommodation;

   ii   personal washing facilities;

   iii   food storage facilities;

   iv   food preparation facilities; and/or

   v   food cooking facilities.

> **Note –**
> Separate additional guidance is given below for premises where sleeping accommodation is provided in dormitories.

5.02   The HHSRS has been devised and designed so that it can be applied to any form of dwelling (see paras 2.04–2.06). This means that any form of dwelling can be assessed, whether it is self-contained or not, and whether it is contained within a larger building or not. To achieve, this, it is only necessary to survey and assess the dwelling and those parts and areas (whether shared or not) which are associated with that unit.

5.03   Assessments using the Rating System, therefore, include:

(a)   those rooms and areas of the dwelling which are in exclusive occupation (ie not shared in common with others);

(b)   any rooms or areas (whether internal or external) which are shared with others;

(c)   the means of access to the dwelling; and

(d)   the building associated with the dwelling.

The assessment does not include any public areas not associated with the building.

Judging Likelihood and Outcomes

5.04   For those rooms and areas which are not shared with others, the assessment is as described above (see paras 4.14–4.19).

5.05   For all rooms and areas shared with others, the assessment should take into account any increase in the likelihood and/or outcomes which could result from the sharing and the degree of that sharing (ie the number of other dwellings sharing the rooms and areas). For example, does that sharing increase the risk of infection, or is it likely to cause stress to an occupant of the dwelling being rated? Guidance on the potential effect of sharing in the individual Hazard Profiles in Annex D. Where data is available, statistical averages are given in the Hazard Profiles for multi-occupied buildings, and these should be used to inform the judgments.

5.06 For the means of access and the building containing the dwelling, the assessment should be related to the potential hazards in those parts and the effect they could have on a potential occupier from the relevant age group in the dwelling being rated.

5.07 Where more than one dwelling in a multi-occupied building is being surveyed and rated, then the assessment of the shared rooms and areas, means of access, and the building should be reviewed in relation to the subsequent dwelling(s). There should be no need to re-survey those parts.

Dormitory Style Accommodation

5.08 For residential premises providing dormitory style sleeping accommodation, it is the whole of the premises which is assessed, taking account of the potential effect the sharing may have on the potential users from the vulnerable age groups. For such accommodation there are no national averages available for the individual hazards, and the assessment must rely on professional judgment.

ANNEX D

Profiles of potential health and safety hazards in dwellings

Introduction

There are 29 hazards. These are arranged in four main groups reflecting the basic health requirements. The four groups are sub-divided according to the nature of the hazards.

HAZARD GROUPS AND SUB-GROUPS

A   Physiological Requirements
     including – Hygrothermal conditions and Pollutants (non-microbial)

B   Psychological Requirements
     including – Space, Security, Light, and Noise

C   Protection against Infection
     including – Hygiene, Sanitation, and Water supply

D   Protection against Accidents
     including – Falls, Electric shock, Burns and Scalds, and Building related Collisions

---

The profiles provide a summary of information to assist in the assessment of hazards. It is assumed that practitioners using the HHSRS for enforcement purposes will have a broad understanding of the relationship between housing and health, and will have read widely around the relevant subject area. Practitioners are also expected to keep up to date with developments, including any changes to the standards relevant to the 'Ideal', and any new research findings.

Each hazard is profiled under the following headings:

- *Description of the hazard* – This defines the hazard, specifying what is included and what is excluded.

- *Potential for harm* – This sets out how the hazard can affect health, outlining typical illnesses or injuries which may result from exposure to the hazard. The prevalence of the hazard, and typical numbers of people affected nationally each year, are identified.

  The national statistical averages[1] for the likelihood and spread of harms are given in a table, together with the average hazard scores. For all hazards these are the national averages for a specified age group of the population living in all dwellings of a stated age and type.[2]

The statistical averages have been calculated for the age range of the population most vulnerable to that particular hazard. This age group is identified, and it is this vulnerable age group that is to be considered when assessing the hazard. For some hazards no age group is more vulnerable than others, and for these the statistics relate to the total population of England.

The averages are given for up to eight different ages and types of dwellings, and for all dwellings. Generally, the average likelihood is statistically significant for each of the eight dwelling ages and types, being based on a large sample of the vulnerable population in such dwellings. However, where the likelihood is low the sample of occurrences is sometimes too small to provide an accurate spread of harms. In these cases, the average outcomes are given for all flats or, where samples are particularly small, for all dwellings.[3] The strength of the evidence for the statistical averages is indicated, together with any note of where there might be over or under estimation in the national averages given.

- *Causes:* – This section discusses potential sources of the hazard. Where multi-occupation could have an impact on the causes and possible severity of the hazard this is also identified.

  It also discusses the contribution to a hazard which could be attributed to dwelling features and to human behaviour. This should assist in assessing whether the deficiencies identified could mean that the likelihood or spread of harms deviates from the averages for the particular age and type of dwelling.

- *Preventive measures and the Ideal:* – This gives an indication of measures and the optimum standard intended to avoid or minimise the hazard – that is, the optimum current at the time of preparation of this Guidance, January 2004. This is usually based on British Standards or relevant UK Building Regulation Approved Documents. Where there is no appropriate UK guidance, reference is made to international standards.

- *Relevant matters affecting likelihood and harm outcome:* – A check-list of dwelling features which may affect the likelihood and the severity of the outcome is given. In many cases the same features can affect both the likelihood and the severity of the outcome. Where different dwelling features affect the likelihood and spread of harm outcomes, the lists are given separately.

- *Hazard assessment:* – Where appropriate, this gives advice to supplement the relevant matters. Any differences in the assessment relevant to multi-occupied buildings are identified.

---

1   For most hazards these are the averages for England in the years 1997 to 1999 given in *Statistical Evidence to Support the Housing Health and Safety Rating System – Volume II Summary of Results*, May 2003, ODPM, London. Note that these are *national* averages, and may differ from the local averages.
2   This differs from the bases of the averages given in Version 1. In that case the averages varied for each hazard, while for this Version 2 the base is the same for all hazards.
3   For further details see *Statistical Evidence to Support the Housing Health and Safety Rating System – Volume III Technical Appendix*, October 2003, ODPM, London.

THE HAZARD PROFILES

A PHYSIOLOGICAL REQUIREMENTS
Hygrothermal Conditions
1   Damp and mould growth
2   Excess cold
3   Excess heat
Pollutants (non-microbial)
4   Asbestos (and MMF)
5   Biocides
6   Carbon Monoxide and fuel combustion products
7   Lead
8   Radiation
9   Uncombusted fuel gas
10   Volatile Organic Compounds

B PSYCHOLOGICAL REQUIREMENTS
Space, Security, Light and Noise
11   Crowding and space
12   Entry by intruders
13   Lighting
14   Noise

C PROTECTION AGAINST INFECTION
Hygiene, Sanitation and Water Supply
15   Domestic hygiene, Pests and Refuse
16   Food safety
17   Personal hygiene, Sanitation and Drainage
18   Water supply for Domestic Purpose

D PROTECTION AGAINST ACCIDENTS
Falls
19   Falls associated with baths etc
20   Falls on the level
21   Falls associated with stairs and steps
22   Falls between levels
Electric Shocks, Fires, Burns and Scalds
23   Electrical hazards
24   Fire
25   Hot surfaces and materials
Collisions, Cuts and Strains
26   Collision and entrapment
27   Explosions
28   Ergonomics
29   Structural collapse and failing elements
13   Lighting
14   Noise

C PROTECTION AGAINST INFECTION
Hygiene, Sanitation and Water Supply
15   Domestic hygiene, Pests and Refuse
16   Food safety
17   Personal hygiene, Sanitation and Drainage
18   Water supply for Domestic Purpose

D PROTECTION AGAINST ACCIDENTS
Falls
19   Falls associated with baths etc
20   Falls on the level
21   Falls associated with stairs and steps
22   Falls between levels
Electric Shocks, Fires, Burns and Scalds
23   Electrical hazards
24   Fire
25   Hot surfaces and materials
Collisions, Cuts and Strains
26   Collision and entrapment
27   Explosions
28   Ergonomics
29   Structural collapse and failing elements

Index